MIDDLE EAST CONFLICTS FROM ANCIENT EGYPT TO THE 21ST CENTURY

MIDDLE EAST CONFLICTS FROM ANCIENT EGYPT TO THE 21ST CENTURY

An Encyclopedia and Document Collection

VOLUME 4: DOCUMENTS

Priscilla Roberts
Documents Editor

An Imprint of ABC-CLIO, LLC
Santa Barbara, California • Denver, Colorado

Copyright © 2019 by ABC-CLIO, LLC

All rights reserved. No part of this publication may be reproduced, stored in a retrieval system, or transmitted, in any form or by any means, electronic, mechanical, photocopying, recording, or otherwise, except for the inclusion of brief quotations in a review, without prior permission in writing from the publisher.

Every reasonable effort has been made to trace the owners of copyright materials in this book, but in some instances this has proven impossible. The editors and publishers will be glad to receive information leading to more complete acknowledgments in subsequent printings of the book and in the meantime extend their apologies for any omissions.

Library of Congress Cataloging-in-Publication Data

Names: Tucker, Spencer, 1937– editor.
Title: Middle East conflicts from Ancient Egypt to the 21st century : an encyclopedia and document collection / Spencer C. Tucker, Editor.
Description: Santa Barbara, CA : ABC-CLIO, [2019] | Includes bibliographical references and index. |
Identifiers: LCCN 2019020655 (print) | LCCN 2019021604 (ebook) | ISBN 9781440853531 (ebook) | ISBN 9781440853524 (set : alk. paper) | ISBN 9781440853548 (volume 1 : alk. paper) | ISBN 9781440853555 (volume 2 : alk. paper) | ISBN 9781440853562 (volume 3 : alk. paper) | ISBN 9781440853579 (volume 4 : alk. paper)
Subjects: LCSH: Middle East—History, Military. | Arab countries—History, Military. | Middle East—History, Military—Encyclopedias. | Arab countries—History, Military—Encyclopedias.
Classification: LCC DS63.15 (ebook) | LCC DS63.15 .M53 2019 (print) | DDC 355.020956/03—dc23
LC record available at https://lccn.loc.gov/2019020655

ISBN: 978-1-4408-5352-4 (set)
    978-1-4408-5354-8 (vol. 1)
    978-1-4408-5355-5 (vol. 2)
    978-1-4408-5356-2 (vol. 3)
    978-1-4408-5357-9 (vol. 4)
    978-1-4408-5353-1 (ebook)

23 22 21 20 19   1 2 3 4 5

This book is also available as an eBook.

ABC-CLIO
An Imprint of ABC-CLIO, LLC

ABC-CLIO, LLC
147 Castilian Drive
Santa Barbara, California 93117
www.abc-clio.com

This book is printed on acid-free paper ∞
Manufactured in the United States of America

To Laurent Boetsch:
Gentleman scholar, linguist, university president,
leader in international education, and esteemed friend.

About the Editors

Spencer C. Tucker, PhD, has been senior fellow in military history at ABC-CLIO since 2003. He is the author or editor of 66 books and encyclopedias, many of which have won prestigious awards. Tucker's last academic position before his retirement from teaching was the John Biggs Chair in Military History at the Virginia Military Institute. He has been a Fulbright scholar, a visiting research associate at the Smithsonian Institution, and, as a U.S. Army captain, an intelligence analyst in the Pentagon. His recently published works include *World War I: The Definitive Encyclopedia and Document Collection, Wars That Changed History: 50 of the World's Greatest Conflicts,* and *Enduring Controversies in Military History: Critical Analyses and Context,* all published by ABC-CLIO.

Priscilla Roberts, PhD, is an associate professor of business at the City University of Macau and codirector of the university's Asia-Pacific Business Research Centre. With Spencer C. Tucker and others, she has coedited and contributed the documents volumes to 11 ABC-CLIO encyclopedias on the Korean War, World War I, World War II, the Cold War, the Arab-Israeli conflict, and Middle East wars. Roberts is the editor of *Cuban Missile Crisis: The Essential Reference Guide, World War II: The Essential Reference Guide, Voices of World War II: Contemporary Accounts of Daily Life, Arab-Israeli Conflict: The Essential Reference Guide, Arab-Israeli Conflict: A Documentary and Reference Guide,* and *The Cold War: Interpreting Conflict through Primary Documents.* In addition, she is the author of numerous other books and articles in international history. Roberts spent 2003 at George Washington University as a Fulbright scholar and has received numerous other academic awards for research in the United States, Great Britain, Australia, Canada, Hong Kong, and Macao. She earned her PhD at King's College, Cambridge, England, and specializes in 20th-century diplomatic and international history.

Contents

Volume 1: A–F
List of Entries   ix
List of Maps   xxiii
Preface   xxv
Introduction   xxvii
General Maps   xxxv
Entries   1

Volume II: G–N
List of Entries   ix
List of Maps   xxiii
General Maps   xxv
Entries   441

Volume III: O–Z
List of Entries   ix
List of Maps   xxiii
General Maps   xxv
Entries   901
Chronology   1383
Glossary   1389
Selective Bibliography   1391
Editors and Contributors   1397

Volume IV: Documents
List of Documents   ix
Documents   1405
Index   1775

List of Documents

1. Sargon of Akkad (r. ca. 2340–2284 BCE): The Nippur Inscription
2. A Chronicle Concerning Sargon and Naram-Sin, Kings of Agade, and Other Early Babylonian and Assyrian Rulers
3. Code of Hammurabi, Preamble and Epilogue (ca. 1754 BCE)
4. Josephus Flavius Quotes Manetho on the Hyksos (ca. 1650–1550 BCE)
5. Thutmose III, The Annals (ca. 1438 BCE): The Battle of Megiddo
6. Biography of Amenemhab (ca. 1440 BCE)
7. King Burnaburias of Kassite Babylon Writes to Pharaoh Akhenaten (1352–1347 BCE)
8. Thucydides (ca. 400–423 BCE) on the Trojan War (ca. 1260–1180 BCE)
9. King Nebuchadnezzar I of Babylon (r. ca. 1125–1104 BCE): Inscription (ca. 1100 BCE)
10. Tiglath-Pileser III of Assyria (r. 744–727 BCE): Tablet Inscription (ca. 727 BCE)
11. Nebuchadnezzar II of Babylon: The East India House Inscription (ca. 565 BCE)
12. The Cylinder of Cyrus II the Great (ca. 538 BCE)
13. Darius the Great (r. ca. 522–486 BCE): The Large Inscription from Behistun
14. Artemisia of Caria (r. 484–460 BCE), as Described by Polyaenus, in *Stratagems in War* (ca. 163 CE)
15. Xenophon Describes the Battle of Aegospotami (405 BCE)
16. Arrian (ca. 101–200 CE) on the Character of Alexander the Great (r. 336–323 BCE)
17. Appian of Alexandria Describes Seleucus I Nicator (ca. 358–281 BCE)
18. Inscription of Antiochus I Soter, King of Babylon (r. 281–261 BCE)
19. Temple of Philae, Egypt, Inscription Commemorating the Suppression of a Rebellion Against Pharaoh Ptolemy V Epiphanes (186 BCE)
20. King Antiochus IV Epiphanes Sacks Jerusalem (167 BCE)
21. Flavius Josephus Describes the Maccabeean Revolt (167–160 BCE)
22. Appian Describes the Last Days of King Mithridates VI Eupator Dionysius of Pontus (63 BCE)
23. Julius Caesar Wins the Battle of the Nile and Takes Alexandria, Egypt (January 47 BCE)
24. The Battle of Actium (September 2, 31 BCE): Plutarch's *Life of Antony*
25. The Siege of Jerusalem (70 CE)
26. The Siege of Masada (April 15, 73 CE)
27. Emperor Titus (r. 79–81), as Viewed by Cassius Dio
28. Emperor Hadrian (r. 117–138), Described by Cassius Dio
29. The Bar Kochba Revolt (132–135 CE)

x List of Documents

30. The Karnamik-I-Ardashir, or the Records of Ardashir (ca. 180–242 CE)
31. The Persian Capture of the Roman Emperor Valerian (r. 253–260): Accounts by John Zonaras and Zosimus
32. Queen Zenobia of Palmyra
33. Shapur II the Great and Emperor Constantius: Correspondence (358 CE)
34. Belisarius Wins the Battle of Dara (530)
35. The Nika Revolt, Constantinople (January 532)
36. The Battle of al-Badr (March 13, 624)
37. The Battle of Nineveh (December 12, 627)
38. The Conquest of Mecca (630)
39. Abu Bakr Launches the Ridda Wars (632)
40. The Battle of Ajnadain (July/August 634)
41. Al-Baladhuri: The Battle of the Yarmuk (August 20, 636)
42. The Battle of al-Qādisiyyah (November 16–19, 636)
43. Emperor Heraclius Concludes Peace with Persia (628) and Contemplates the Muslim Threat (ca. 636–638)
44. The Battle of Akroinon (May 740)
45. Harun al-Rashid at War with the Byzantine Empire (803–806)
46. The Siege of Baghdad (August 812–September 813)
47. The Zanj Slave Revolts: An Account of the Zanj Leader's Advance on al-Basra with His Army (October 22–24, 869)
48. Urban II: Speech at the Council of Clermont (November 27, 1095), Recounted by Fulcher of Chartres
49. The Siege of Antioch (1197–1198): Count Stephen of Blois to His Wife Adèle (March 29, 1098)
50. The Fall of Jerusalem (July 1099)
51. Joscelin I of Courtenay on His Deathbed (1131)
52. Manuel I Komnenos (r. 1143–1180)
53. Conrad III: Letters to the Abbot of Corvey on the Germans' Crusade (1148)
54. Account of Conflict between the Muslims and the Georgians (1162–1163)
55. King Amalric of Jerusalem: Letters to King Louis VII of France (1163–1165)
56. The Leper King: Baldwin IV of Jerusalem (r. 1174–1185)
57. Guy of Lusignan, King of Jerusalem (r. 1186–1192)
58. King Richard I the Lionheart of England (September 3, 1189)
59. The Siege and Capture of Acre (July 1191)
60. Assassins Kill Marquis Conrad of Montferrat (April 28, 1192)
61. Henry VI of Germany and the Byzantine Empire (1196–1197)
62. Emperor Alexios V Doukas Mourtzouphlos (r. January–April 1204)
63. The Crusader Siege and Capture of Constantinople (April 8–13, 1204)
64. Baldwin I of Constantinople (r. 1204–1206): A Byzantine View
65. Emperor Frederick II to Henry III of England (March 17, 1229)
66. Gerold of Lausanne, Latin Patriarch of Jerusalem, to All the Faithful (1229)
67. Richard, Earl of Cornwall and Count of Poitou, to Baldwin of Reviers, Earl of Devon, the Abbot of Beaulieu, and Robert, Clerk (July 1241)
68. The Battle of Köse Dağ (June 26, 1243)
69. The Battle of La Forbie (October 17–18, 1244): Robert, Patriarch of Jerusalem and Papal Legate, and Other Prelates in the Holy Land to the Prelates of France and England (November 25, 1244)
70. Jamal ad-Din ibn Wasil (ca. 1282) on the Battle of Fariskur (April 8, 1250)
71. The Siege and Capture of Baghdad (January–February 1258)
72. Baybars (r. 1260–1277)
73. The End of the Latin Empire of Constantinople: The Taking of Constantinople (July 25, 1261)
74. Hulegu, Ilkhan of Persia, to Louis IX of France (April 10, 1262)
75. Abu l-Fida' on the Fall of Acre (June 12, 1291)
76. Osman I (r. ca. 1299–1326), as Described by Nikolaos Sekoundinos
77. The Crusade of Smyrna (1344)
78. Philippe de Mézières on the Fall of Alexandria (October 10, 1365)
79. Murad I and the Battle of Kosovo (June 15, 1389)
80. Bayezid I (r. 1389–1403)
81. The Crusade of Nikopolis (September 25, 1396)
82. The Battle of Ankara (July 20, 1402)
83. A Muslim View of the Death of Tamerlane (1405)
84. The Battle of Khirokitia (July 7, 1426)
85. The Fall of Constantinople (1453): A Muslim Account
86. Sultan Mehmed II (r. 1450–1481), as Described by Nikolaos Sekoundinos (January 24, 1454)
87. The Fall of Trebizond (August 1461)
88. Brother Jacopo dalla Castellana: The Loss of Negroponte (June–July 1470)

List of Documents

89. Giovan Maria Angiolello: The Battle of Otlukbeli (August 11, 1473)
90. The Poetry of Shah Ismail I of Persia: Mathnavi No. 3 (ca. 1500–1510)
91. Letters between Ottoman Sultan Selim I and Shah Ismail I of Persia (1514)
92. The Battle of Chaldiran (August 23, 1514)
93. The Ottoman Conquest of Egypt (1516–1517)
94. Ottoman Sultan Selim I (r. 1512–1520): Poem on His Conquests
95. The Ottoman Capture of Rhodes (1522)
96. Hayreddin Barbarossa and the Battle of Preveza, September 28, 1538
97. Kâtib Çelebi, Precious Gifts from the Expeditions in the Seas: The Ottoman Conquest of Cyprus (1570–1571)
98. Sebastian Veniero Describes the Battle of Lepanto (October 7, 1571)
99. The Battle of Sarab (September 10, 1618)
100. The Ottomans Fail to Capture Baghdad from Persia: Letter of a Senior Ottoman Officer to Moṣlī Čelebī (1626)
101. Grand Vizier Köprülü Mehmed Pasha (ca. 1583–1661)
102. Evliyá Efendí Describes the Austro-Ottoman Wars (1660–1664)
103. Ottoman Sultan Mahmud IV's Declaration of War on Emperor Leopold I, Signed at Adrianople (February 20, 1683)
104. Napoleon Bonaparte: Proclamations to His Troops and to the People of Egypt (June–July 1798)
105. The Battle of the Pyramids (July 21, 1798): Napoleon Bonaparte, Letter to the Directory in Paris (July 24, 1798)
106. Sir Edward Berry: Report on the Battle of the Nile (August 1, 1798)
107. Admiral Horatio Nelson to Lord Minto (August 29, 1798)
108. Napoleon Bonaparte Besieges Acre (March 18–May 18, 1799)
109. The Treaty of Gulistan (October 2, 1813)
110. "Fall of Turkey—Treaty of Adrianople," *The Spectator* (October 17, 1829)
111. British Foreign Minister Palmerston to Viscount Beauvale, British Ambassador in Vienna (June 28, 1839)
112. The Rescript of Gülhane, Gülhane Hatt-ı Hümayunu (November 3, 1839)
113. Prince Pyotr Gortschakoff: General Order after the Fall of Sebastopol (August 30, 1855)
114. The Bombardment of Alexandria: Report from the *London Weekly Times* (July 16, 1882)
115. The Earl of Cromer (Evelyn Baring) on the British Takeover of Egypt (1882)
116. Sir Frederick Stephenson to William Stephenson (October 13, 1886)
117. Theodor Herzl, *The Jewish State* (1896)
118. The Young Turks: Proclamation for the Ottoman Empire (1908)
119. The Adana Massacres (April 1909)
120. Ottoman Abrogation of the Capitulations (September 9, 1914)
121. The Ottoman Empire Declares War on the Allies: Proclamation by Sultan Mehmed (October 29, 1914)
122. The Ottoman Empire: Official Rejection of Treaties of Dependency (October 29, 1914)
123. General Nikolai Yudenich: Diary Entries on the Early Caucasus Campaign (November 1914–January 1915)
124. The British Fleet Fails to Force the Dardanelles (March 18, 1915)
125. The Gallipoli Campaign: Ellis Ashmead-Bartlett to British Prime Minister Herbert Henry Asquith (September 8, 1915)
126. Sir Henry McMahon, British High Commissioner in Cairo, to Husain Ibn Ali, the Sharif of Mecca (October 24, 1915)
127. The Sykes-Picot Agreement: Sir Edward Grey to Paul Cambon (May 15–16, 1916)
128. Lord Bryce Reports on the Armenian Massacres (June 1916)
129. Proclamation Published in Mecca by Sharif Hussein (June 27, 1916)
130. Personal Notes of T. E. Lawrence on the Sharifial Family (October 27, 1916)
131. Copy of Letter from Mustapha Kemal to Enver Pasha (September 30, 1917)
132. The Balfour Declaration: Arthur Balfour to Lord Rothschild (November 2, 1917)
133. Sir Edmund Allenby on the Fall of Jerusalem (December 9, 1917)
134. General Liman von Sanders to Major General von Seekt (December 13, 1917): Condition of the Turkish Army Today
135. Emir Faisal: Memorandum to the Supreme Council at the Paris Peace Conference (January 1, 1919)

136. A Report on Mesopotamia by T. E. Lawrence, *The Sunday Times* (August 22, 1920)
137. Mustafa Kemal Ataturk Assails the Treaty of Sèvres (June–October 1921)
138. Ze'ev (Vladimir) Jabotinsky: "The Iron Wall: We and the Arabs" (November 4, 1923)
139. Shah Reza Pahlavi and the Roosevelt Administration (August–October 1938)
140. The Arab Revolt in Palestine: Bernard Montgomery to Sir Ronald "Bill" Adam (December 4, 1938)
141. Haj Amin al-Husseini: Summons to a Jihad against Britain (May 10, 1941)
142. General Bernard Montgomery: Message to the Troops Following El Alamein (November 11, 1942)
143. The Declaration of the Establishment of the State of Israel (May 14, 1948)
144. Arab League Statement (May 15, 1948)
145. United Nations Press Release: General Lundstrom Gives an Eyewitness Account of Bernadotte's Death (September 18, 1948)
146. Sir John Bagot Glubb on Arab Refugees (1950–1951)
147. Loy Henderson, U.S. Ambassador to Iran: Despatch to the U.S. Department of State Regarding the Coup in Iran (August 23, 1953)
148. The Baghdad Pact (February 24, 1955)
149. Moshe Dayan: Eulogy for Roi Rotberg (April 29, 1956)
150. King Faisal II of Iraq: Speech during Luncheon at the Guildhall, London (July 17, 1956)
151. Egyptian Law Nationalizing the Suez Canal Company (July 26, 1956) and Gamal Abdel Nasser, Speech on Nationalization of Suez Canal Company, Alexandria, Egypt (July 26, 1956)
152. The Eisenhower Doctrine (January 5, 1957)
153. Golda Meir: Statement to the Knesset (October 23, 1973)
154. President Jimmy Carter: The Carter Doctrine, State of the Union Address (January 23, 1980)
155. President Ronald Reagan: Address to the Nation on Events in Lebanon and Grenada (October 27, 1983)
156. The Program of Hezbollah (February 16, 1986)
157. Communiqué of the Intifada (January 8, 1988)
158. President Ronald Reagan: Letter to Thomas P. O'Neill, Speaker of the House of Representatives and President Pro Tempore of the Senate, on the Destruction of an Iranian Jetliner by the U.S. Navy over the Persian Gulf (July 4, 1988)
159. Defining the Hamas Movement: The Hamas Charter (1988)
160. Jad al-Haqq, Sheikh al-Azhar: "Fatwa against the Iraqi Invasion of Kuwait" (1990)
161. Amnesty International: Report on Kuwait (December 19, 1990)
162. Iraqi President Saddam Hussein: "The Mother of All Battles" Speech (January 20, 1991)
163. Yitzkah Rabin's Last Speech: Peace Rally, Kings of Israel Square, Tel Aviv (November 4, 1995)
164. Sheikh Omar Abdel-Rahman: Messages to His Followers (1995–1999)
165. President Bill Clinton: Televised Address to the Nation on Operation DESERT FOX (December 16, 1998)
166. The War on Terror: President George W. Bush, Address to a Joint Session of Congress and the American People on the U.S. Response to the September 11 Terrorist Attacks (September 20, 2001)
167. Osama bin Laden: "Letter to the American People" (November 2002)
168. Mustafa Setmariam Nasar (Abu Mus'ab As-Suri): *The Global Islamic Resistance Call* (2004)
169. Lieutenant General Anthony Jones and Major General George R. Fay: Executive Summary of Report, Investigation of Intelligence Activities at Abu Ghraib (August 23, 2004)
170. Ariel Sharon: Speech at the United Nations Assembly (September 15, 2005)
171. White House Fact Sheet: "The New Way Forward in Iraq" (January 10, 2007)
172. General David H. Petraeus: Report to Congress on the Situation in Iraq (September 10–11, 2007)
173. Israeli Prime Minister Benjamin Netanyahu: Speech to the United States Congress (March 2, 2015)
174. Yemeni Civilians' Report: "We Lived Days in Hell: Civilian Perspectives on the Conflict in Yemen" (January 10, 2017)
175. Sheikh Abdul-Mahdi Al-Karbalai: The Friday Prayer Sermon from the Imam Al-Hussein Shrine (December 15, 2017)
176. Egypt's Muslim Brotherhood Condemns the Frantic Crackdown against Journalists and Activists (May 30, 2018)

Documents

1. Sargon of Akkad (r. ca. 2340–2284 BCE): The Nippur Inscription

Introduction

Few original sources relating to the reign of Sargon of Akkad, conqueror of the city-states of Sumeria, have survived. Among the most important is a tablet dating back to the Old Babylonian period, discovered at Nippur during the 1890s. This tablet contained a copy of the inscriptions written on the pedestal of a statue erected by Sargon himself in the temple of Enlil, his patron deity, that gave triumphant descriptions of his battles, campaigns, and conquests. He began his career as cup-bearer to King Ur-Zababa of Kish, who was overthrown by Luzalzagesi, the king of Uruk or Erech. Sargon in his turn defeated Luzalzagesi in battle, publicly exhibiting him in a neck-stock in Enlil, Akkad's capital. Although the record is fragmentary, Sargon was clearly an energetic and successful military leader who forcibly imposed his rule over much of the surrounding region, destroying the walled defenses of those cities he conquered. He may have sent his armies as far afield as India, Egypt, and Ethiopia.

Document

Sargon, the king of Akkad, the *mashkim* of Inanna, the king of Kish, the *guda*-priest of An, the king of the Land, the great *ensi* (governor) of Enlil, laid waste the city Erech, destroyed its wall; fought with the men of Erech, conquered them; fought with Lugalzaggesi, the king of Erech, took him prisoner (and) brought him in a neck-stock to the gate of Enlil.

Sargon, the king of Akkad, fought with the men of Ur, conquered them, laid waste their city, (and) destroyed its walls; laid waste E-Ninmar, destroyed its walls, laid waste its territory from Lagash to the sea, washed his weapons in the sea; fought with the men of Umma, conquered them, laid waste their city, (and) destroyed its walls.

To Sargon, the king of the Land, Enlil gave no rival; (indeed) Enlil gave him the entire territory from the sea above to the sea below. Akkadians (literally, "sons of Akkad") held the *ensi*-ships (everywhere) from the lower sea and above; the men of Mari (and) the men of Elam served Sargon, the king of the Land (as their master).

Sargon, the king of the Land, restored Kish (and) gave that city to them (the men of Kish) as a dwelling place.

Whoever destroys this inscription—may Utu tear out his foundation (from under him); may he bereave him of his seed.

Sargon, the king of Kish, triumphed in thirty-four battles (over the cities) up to the edge of the sea (and) destroyed their walls. He made the ships from Meluhha, the ships from Magan, (and) the ships from Dilmun tie up alongside the quay of Agade.

Sargon, the king, prostrated himself before Dagan (and) made supplication to him; (and) he (Dagan) gave him the upper land, (namely) Mari, Yarmuti, (and) Ibla, up to the Cedar Forest (and) up to the Silver Mountain.

Sargon, the king, to whom Enlil permitted no rival—5,400 warriors ate bread daily before him.

Whoever destroys this inscription—may An destroy his name; may Enlil exterminate his seed; may Inanna. . . .

Source: Samuel Noah Kramer, *The Sumerians: Their History, Culture, and Character* (Chicago: University of Chicago Press, 1963), 324. © University of Chicago Press. Reprinted with permission.

2. A Chronicle Concerning Sargon and Naram-Sin, Kings of Agade, and Other Early Babylonian and Assyrian Rulers

Introduction

A clay tablet excavated in the late 19th century and preserved in the British Museum, written sometime after Sargon's reign, provided a summary of the achievements of Sargon of Akkad and his immediate successors, including his grandson, Naram-Sin (r. ca. 2254–2218 BCE). It was slightly less grandiloquent and triumphalist in tone than the surviving inscription that Sargon himself approved for inclusion on his own statue. His career and attainments were to serve as a model for later Mesopotamian rulers, including those of Assyria and Babylon. Historians have even suggested that he was the first ruler to invent the concept of empire, in terms of domination of a multiethnic state. Naram-Sin is the first king known to have arrogated to himself godlike status. This did not prevent the disintegration of the Akkadian Empire, which fell apart during either his long reign or that of his son, Shah Kali-Sharri, conquered by the Gutians.

Document

Sargon, king of Agade, through the royal gift of Ishtar was exalted, and he possessed no foe or rival. His glory over the world he poured out. The Sea in the East he crossed, and in the eleventh year the Country of the West in its full extent his hand subdued.

He united them under one control; he set up his images in the West; their booty he brought over at (his) word. The sons of his palace for five *kasbu* (around) he settled, and over the hosts of the world he reigned supreme.

Against Kaṣalla he marched, and he turned Kaṣalla into mounds and heaps of ruins; he destroyed (the land and left not) enough for a bird to rest thereon.

Afterwards in his old age all the lands revolted against him, and they besieged him in Agade; and Sargon went forth to battle and defeated them; he accomplished their overthrow, and their widespreading host he destroyed.

Afterwards he attacked the land of Subartu in his might, and they submitted to his arms, and Sargon settled that revolt, and defeated them; he accomplished their overthrow, and their widespreading host he destroyed, and he brought their possessions into Agade.

The soil from the trenches of Babylon he removed, and the boundaries of Agade he made like those of Babylon.

But because of the evil which he had committed the great lord Marduk was angry, and he destroyed his people by famine. From the rising of the Sun unto the setting of the Sun they opposed him and gave [him] no rest.

Narâm-Sin, the [grand]son of Sargon, [marched] against the city of Apirak, and he constructed mines (against it), and Rish-Ad[ad], the king of Apirak, and the governor of Apirak his hand sub[dued]. He marched against Magan, and Mannu-dannu, the king of Magan, [his hand subdued].

Source: L. W. King, ed., *Chronicles Concerning the Early Babylonian Kings, Including Records of the Early History of the Kassites and the Country of the Sea*, Vol. 2, *Texts and Translations* (London: Luzac, 1907), 3–10.

3. Code of Hammurabi, Preamble and Epilogue (ca. 1754 BCE)

Introduction

King Hammurabi of Babylon (r. ca. 1810–1750 BCE) is remembered primarily for his extensive code of laws, promulgated around 1754 BCE, toward the end of his 60-year reign. Hammurabi was also, however, a warrior king who waged war against several smaller neighboring kingdoms during his later years, subduing and conquering them. The body of his legal code, issued around 6 years before Hammurabi's death, was devoted to enumerating detailed provisions related to the often severe punishments and penalties for wrongdoers who offended against the laws of Babylon. The preamble and epilogue, however, described Hammurabi's military successes as well as the benefits that his rule had brought to his subjects. These were ascribed not just to Hammurabi's own abilities but also to the special favor with which the gods looked upon him, supposedly a reward for the reverence he showed toward these deities. His successors were also threatened with curses should they alter his legal code. These were features that would for many centuries characterize subsequent royal proclamations.

Document

When Anu the Sublime, King of the Anunaki, and Bel, the lord of Heaven and earth, who decreed the fate of the land, assigned to Marduk, the over-ruling son of Ea, God of righteousness, dominion over earthly man, and made him great among the Igigi, they called Babylon by his illustrious name, made it great on earth, and founded an everlasting kingdom in it, whose foundations are laid so solidly as those of heaven and earth; then Anu and Bel called by name me, Hammurabi, the exalted prince, who feared God, to bring about the rule of righteousness in the land, to destroy the wicked and the evil-doers; so that the strong should not harm the weak; so that I should rule over the black-headed people like Shamash, and enlighten the land, to further the well-being of mankind.

Hammurabi, the prince, called of Bel am I, making riches and increase, enriching Nippur and Dur-ilu beyond compare, sublime patron of E-kur; who reestablished Eridu and purified the worship of E-apsu; who conquered the four quarters of the world, made great the name of Babylon, rejoiced the heart of Marduk, his lord who daily pays his devotions in Saggil; the royal scion whom Sin made; who enriched Ur; the humble, the reverent, who brings wealth to Gish-shir-gal; the white king, heard of Shamash, the mighty, who again laid the foundations of Sippara; who clothed the gravestones of Malkat with green; who made E-babbar great, which is like the heavens, the warrior who guarded Larsa and renewed E-babbar, with Shamash as his helper; the lord who granted new life to Uruk, who brought plenteous water to its inhabitants, raised the head of E-anna, and perfected the beauty of Anu and Nana; shield of the land, who reunited the scattered inhabitants of Isin; who richly endowed E-gal-mach; the protecting king of the city, brother of the god Zamama; who firmly founded the farms of Kish, crowned E-me-te-ursag with glory, redoubled the great holy treasures of Nana, managed the temple of Harsag-kalama; the grave of the enemy, whose help brought about the victory; who increased the power of Cuthah; made all glorious in E-shidlam, the black steer, who gored the enemy; beloved of the god Nebo, who rejoiced the inhabitants of Borsippa, the Sublime; who is indefatigable for E-zida; the divine king of the city; the White, Wise; who broadened the fields of Dilbat, who heaped up the harvests for Urash; the Mighty, the lord to whom come scepter and crown, with which he clothes himself; the Elect of Ma-ma; who fixed the temple bounds of Kesh, who made rich the holy feasts of Nin-tu; the provident, solicitous, who provided food and drink for Lagash and Girsu, who provided large sacrificial offerings for the temple of Ningirsu; who captured the enemy, the Elect of the oracle who fulfilled the prediction of Hallab, who rejoiced the heart of Anunit; the pure prince, whose prayer is accepted by Adad; who satisfied the heart of Adad, the warrior, in Karkar, who restored the vessels for worship in E-ud-gal-gal; the king who granted life to the city of Adab; the guide of E-mach;

the princely king of the city, the irresistible warrior, who granted life to the inhabitants of Mashkanshabri, and brought abundance to the temple of Shidlam; the White, Potent, who penetrated the secret cave of the bandits, saved the inhabitants of Malka from misfortune, and fixed their home fast in wealth; who established pure sacrificial gifts for Ea and Dam-gal-nun-na, who made his kingdom everlastingly great; the princely king of the city, who subjected the districts on the Ud-kib-nun-na Canal to the sway of Dagon, his Creator; who spared the inhabitants of Mera and Tutul; the sublime prince, who makes the face of Ninni shine; who presents holy meals to the divinity of Nin-a-zu, who cared for its inhabitants in their need, provided a portion for them in Babylon in peace; the shepherd of the oppressed and of the slaves; whose deeds find favor before Anunit, who provided for Anunit in the temple of Dumash in the suburb of Agade; who recognizes the right, who rules by law; who gave back to the city of Ashur its protecting god; who let the name of Ishtar of Nineveh remain in E-mish-mish; the Sublime, who humbles himself before the great gods; successor of Sumula-il; the mighty son of Sin-muballit; the royal scion of Eternity; the mighty monarch, the sun of Babylon, whose rays shed light over the land of Sumer and Akkad; the king, obeyed by the four quarters of the world; Beloved of Ninni, am I.

When Marduk sent me to rule over men, to give the protection of right to the land, I did right and righteousness in . . . , and brought about the well-being of the oppressed. . . .

THE EPILOGUE

Laws of justice which Hammurabi, the wise king, established. A righteous law, and pious statute did he teach the land. Hammurabi, the protecting king am I. I have not withdrawn myself from the men, whom Bel gave to me, the rule over whom Marduk gave to me, I was not negligent, but I made them a peaceful abiding-place. I expounded all great difficulties, I made the light shine upon them. With the mighty weapons which Zamama and Ishtar entrusted to me, with the keen vision with which Ea endowed me, with the wisdom that Marduk gave me, I have uprooted the enemy above and below (in north and south), subdued the earth, brought prosperity to the land, guaranteed security to the inhabitants in their homes; a disturber was not permitted. The great gods have called me, I am the salvation-bearing shepherd, whose staff is straight, the good shadow that is spread over my city; on my breast I cherish the inhabitants of the land of Sumer and Akkad; in my shelter I have let them repose in peace; in my deep wisdom have I enclosed them. That the strong might not injure the weak, in order to protect the widows and orphans, I have in Babylon the city where Anu and Bel raise high their head, in E-Sagil, the Temple, whose foundations stand firm as heaven and earth, in order to bespeak justice in the land, to settle all disputes, and heal all injuries, set up these my precious words, written upon my memorial stone, before the image of me, as king of righteousness.

The king who ruleth among the kings of the cities am I. My words are well considered; there is no wisdom like unto mine. By the command of Shamash, the great judge of heaven and earth, let righteousness go forth in the land: by the order of Marduk, my lord, let no destruction befall my monument. In E-Sagil, which I love, let my name be ever repeated; let the oppressed, who has a case at law, come and stand before this my image as king of righteousness; let him read the inscription, and understand my precious words: the inscription will explain his case to him; he will find out what is just, and his heart will be glad, so that he will say:

"Hammurabi is a ruler, who is as a father to his subjects, who holds the words of Marduk in reverence, who has achieved conquest for Marduk over the north and south, who rejoices the heart of Marduk, his lord, who has bestowed benefits for ever and ever on his subjects, and has established order in the land."

When he reads the record, let him pray with full heart to Marduk, my lord, and Zarpanit, my lady; and then shall the protecting deities and the gods, who frequent E-Sagil, graciously grant the desires daily presented before Marduk, my lord, and Zarpanit, my lady.

In future time, through all coming generations, let the king, who may be in the land, observe the words of righteousness which I have written on my monument; let him not alter the law of the land which I have given, the edicts which I have enacted; my monument let him not mar. If such a ruler have wisdom, and be able to keep his land in order, he shall observe the words which I have written in this inscription; the rule, statute, and law of the land which I have given; the decisions which I have made will this inscription show him; let him rule his subjects accordingly, speak justice to them, give right decisions, root out the miscreants and criminals from this land, and grant prosperity to his subjects.

Hammurabi, the king of righteousness, on whom Shamash has conferred right (or law) am I. My words are well considered; my deeds are not equaled; to bring low those that were high; to humble the proud, to expel insolence. If a succeeding ruler considers my words, which I have written in this my inscription, if he do not annul my law, nor corrupt my words, nor change my monument, then may Shamash lengthen that king's reign, as he has that of me, the king of righteousness, that he may reign in righteousness over his subjects. If this ruler do not esteem my words, which I have written in my inscription, if he despise my curses, and fear not the curse of God, if he destroy the law which I have given, corrupt my words, change my monument, efface my name, write his name there, or on account of the curses commission another so to do, that man, whether king or ruler, patesi, or commoner, no matter what he be, may the great God (Anu), the Father of the gods, who has ordered my rule, withdraw from him the glory of royalty, break his scepter, curse his destiny. May Bel, the lord, who fixeth destiny, whose command can not be altered, who has made my kingdom great, order a rebellion which his hand can not control; may he let the wind of the overthrow of his habitation blow, may he ordain the years of his rule in groaning, years of scarcity, years of famine, darkness without light, death with seeing eyes be fated to him; may he (Bel) order with his potent mouth the destruction of his city, the dispersion of his subjects, the cutting off of his rule, the removal of his name and memory from the land. May Belit, the great Mother, whose command is potent in E-Kur (the Babylonian Olympus), the Mistress, who harkens graciously to my petitions, in the seat of judgment and decision (where Bel fixes destiny), turn his affairs evil before Bel, and put the devastation of his land, the destruction of his subjects, the pouring out of his life like water into the mouth of King Bel. May Ea, the great ruler, whose fated decrees come to pass, the thinker of the gods, the omniscient, who maketh long the days of my life, withdraw understanding and wisdom from him, lead him to forgetfulness, shut up his rivers at their sources, and not allow corn or sustenance for man to grow in his land. May Shamash, the great Judge of heaven and earth, who supporteth all means of livelihood, Lord of life-courage, shatter his dominion, annul his law, destroy his way, make vain the march of his troops, send him in his visions forecasts of the uprooting of the foundations of his throne and of the destruction of his land. May the condemnation of Shamash overtake him forthwith; may he be deprived of water above among the living, and his spirit below in the earth. May Sin (the Moon-god), the Lord of Heaven, the divine father, whose crescent gives light among the gods, take away the crown and regal throne from him; may he put upon him heavy guilt, great decay, that nothing may be lower than he. May he destine him as fated, days, months and years of dominion filled with sighing and tears, increase of the burden of dominion, a life that is like unto death. May Adad, the lord of fruitfulness, ruler of heaven and earth, my helper, withhold from him rain from heaven, and the flood of water from the springs, destroying his land by famine and want; may he rage mightily over his city, and make his land into flood-hills (heaps of ruined cities). May Zamama, the great warrior, the first-born son of E-Kur, who goeth at my right hand, shatter his weapons on the field of battle, turn day into night for him, and let his foe triumph over him. May Ishtar, the goddess of fighting and war, who unfetters my weapons, my gracious protecting spirit, who loveth my dominion, curse his kingdom in her angry heart; in her great wrath, change his grace into evil, and shatter his weapons on the place of fighting and war. May she create disorder and sedition for him, strike down his warriors, that the earth may drink their blood, and throw down the piles of corpses of his warriors on the field; may she not grant him a life of mercy, deliver him into the hands of his enemies, and imprison him in the land of his enemies. May Nergal, the mighty among the gods, whose contest is irresistible, who grants me victory, in his great might burn up his subjects like a slender reedstalk, cut off his limbs with his mighty weapons, and shatter him like an earthen image. May Nin-tu, the sublime mistress of the lands, the fruitful mother, deny him a son, vouchsafe him no name, give him no successor among men. May Nin-karak, the daughter of Anu, who adjudges grace to me, cause to come upon his members in E-kur high fever, severe wounds, that can not be healed, whose nature the physician does not understand, which he can not treat with dressing, which, like the bite of death, can not be removed, until they have sapped away his life.

May he lament the loss of his life-power, and may the great gods of heaven and earth, the Anunaki, altogether inflict a curse and evil upon the confines of the temple, the walls of this E-barra (the Sun temple of Sippara), upon his dominion, his land, his warriors, his subjects, and his troops. May Bel curse him with the potent curses of his mouth that can not be altered, and may they come upon him forthwith.

Source: "The Code of Hammurabi," The Avalon Project, http://avalon.law.yale.edu/ancient/hamframe.asp; C. F. Horne, *The Sacred Books and Early Literature of the East; with an Historical Survey and Descriptions*, Vol. 1, *Babylonia and Assyria* (New York: Parke, Austin, and Lipscomb, 1917), 114–116, 141–145.

4. Josephus Flavius Quotes Manetho on the Hyksos (ca. 1650–1550 BCE)

Introduction

Very little that is definite is known about the Hyksos, the outsiders who invaded Egypt and took over much of the country for around a century, beginning in 1650 BCE, until their eventual overthrow and expulsion by a coalition of native Egyptian rulers. The Jewish historian Josephus Flavius, writing at the end of the first century CE, drew on and quoted from the *Aegyptiaca* of Manetho, an Egyptian priestly scribe who apparently wrote an account of them in the late third or early fourth centuries BCE. It is possible, however, that the *Aegyptiaca* was in reality written during the reign of Emperor Augustus, early in the first century BCE, by the Greek historian Ptolemy of Mendes, who took Manetho's identity in an effort to add authority to his own writing. Josephus wished to identify the Hyksos with the Jews or Israelites who, according to the Bible, settled in Egypt for several generations before departing to settle in present-day Palestine or Israel. Historians find this conjecture unconvincing, but there is still considerable uncertainty as to the precise antecedents of the Hyksos, whose Egyptian name meant "rulers from the foreign countries." However inaccurate the account by Manetho—as quoted by Josephus—may be, it is almost the only extant information on the Hyksos.

Document

I will begin with Egyptian documents. These I cannot indeed set before you in their ancient form; but in Manetho we have a native Egyptian who was manifestly imbued with Greek culture. He wrote in Greek the history of his nation, translated, as he himself tells us, from sacred tablets; and on many points of Egyptian history he convicts [the historian] Herodotus of having erred through ignorance. In the second book of his *History of Egypt*, this writer Manetho speaks of us as follows. I shall quote his own words, just as if I had brought forward the man himself as a witness:

"Tutimaeus. In his reign, for what cause I know not, a blast of God smote us; and unexpectedly, from the regions of the East, invaders of obscure race marched in confidence of victory against our land. By main force they easily seized it without striking a blow; and having overpowered the rulers of the land, they then burned our cities ruthlessly, razed to the ground the temples of the gods, and treated all the natives with a cruel hostility, massacring some and leading into slavery the wives and children of others. Finally, they appointed as king one of their number whose name was Salitis. He had his seat at Memphis, levying tribute from Upper and Lower Egypt, and always leaving garrisons behind in the most advantageous positions. Above all, he fortified the district to the east, foreseeing that the Assyrians, as they grew stronger, would one day covet and attack his kingdom.

"In the Saïte [Sethroïte] nome he found a city very favourably situated on the east of the Bubastite branch of the Nile, and called Auaris after an ancient religious tradition. This place he rebuilt and fortified with massive walls, planting there a garrison of as many as 240,000 heavy-armed men to guard his frontier. Here he would come in summer-time, partly to serve out rations and pay his troops, partly to train them carefully in manoeuvres and so strike terror into foreign tribes. After reigning for 19 years, Salitis died; and a second king, named Bnôn, succeeded and reigned for 44 years. Next to him came Apachnan, who ruled for 36 years and 7 months; then Apôphis for 61, and Iannas for 50 years and 1 month; then finally Assis for 49 years and 2 months. These six kings, their first rulers, were ever more and more eager to extirpate the Egyptian stock. Their race as a whole was called Hyksôs, that is 'king-shepherds': for hyk in the sacred language means 'king', and sôs in common speech is 'shepherd' or 'shepherds'; hence the compound word 'Hyksôs'. Some say that they were Arabs."

In another copy the expression hyk, it is said, does not mean "kings": on the contrary, the compound refers to "captive-shepherds." In Egyptian hyk, in fact, and hak when aspirated expressly denote "captives". This explanation seems to me the more convincing and more in keeping with ancient history.

These kings whom I have enumerated above, and their descendants, ruling over the so-called Shepherds, dominated Egypt, according to Manetho, for 511 years. Thereafter, he says, there came a revolt of the kings of the Thebaïd and the rest of Egypt against the Shepherds, and a fierce and prolonged war broke out between them. By a king whose name was Misphragmuthôsis, the Shepherds, he says, were defeated, driven out of all the rest of Egypt, and confined in a region measuring within its circumference 10,000 arûrae, by name Auaris. According to Manetho, the Shepherds enclosed this whole area with a high, strong wall, in order to safeguard all their possessions and spoils. Thummôsis, the son of Misphragmuthôsis (he continues), attempted by siege to force them to surrender, blockading the fortress with an army of 480,000 men. Finally, giving up the siege in despair, he concluded a treaty by which they should all depart from Egypt and go unmolested where they pleased. On these terms the Shepherds, with their possessions and households complete, no fewer than 240,000 persons, left Egypt and journeyed over the desert into Syria.

Source: *Manetho*, translated by W. G. Waddell, Loeb Classical Library Volume 350 (Cambridge, MA: Harvard University Press, 1940), 77–89. Loeb Classical Library © is a registered trademark of the President and Fellows of Harvard College.

5. Thutmose III, The Annals (ca. 1438 BCE): The Battle of Megiddo

Introduction

Thutmose III (r. 1479–1425 BCE) became sole pharaoh of Egypt on the death of his stepmother Hatshepsut around 1458 BCE. At that time, Egypt was facing a rebellion against its rule by 300 cities in the Levant, led by Megiddo and Kadesh. The young king, now in sole control, launched the first of many military campaigns intended to suppress rebellion and extend Egyptian territory. His armies marched into Palestine, where they eventually defeated the rebel forces and took the city of Megiddo, winning massive booty and imposing a heavy tribute upon the rebels. This was only the beginning of numerous military campaigns that Thutmose III waged on a nearly annual basis over the next two decades. The victory at Megiddo opened the way for Thutmose III's eventual defeat and capture of Kadesh and the extension of Egyptian territory into present-day northern Syria. Around 1438 BCE a lengthy account of his military campaigns, known as the Annals of Thutmose, was inscribed on the walls of the Temple of Amon at Karnak.

Document

Year 22, fourth month of the second season (eighth month), on the twenty-fifth day [His Majesty was in] Tharu on the first victorious expedition to [extend] the boundaries of Egypt with might. . . .

Now, (at) that period [the Asiatics had fallen into] disagreement, each man [fighting] against [his neighbor]. Now, it happened that the tribes, the people who were there in the city of Sharuhen; behold, from Yeraza to the marshes of the earth, (they) had begun to revolt against His Majesty.

Year 23, first (month) of the third season (ninth month), on the fourth day, the day of the feast of the king's coronation, (he arrived) at the city, the possession of the ruler, Gaza.

[Year 23] first month of the third season (ninth month), on the fifth day; departure from this place in might, in power, and in triumph, to overthrow that wretched foe, to extend the boundaries of Egypt, according as his father, Amon-Re, had commanded that he seize.

Year 23, first month of the third season (ninth month), on the sixteenth day, (he arrived) at the city of Yehem.

5. Thutmose III, The Annals: The Battle of Megiddo

[His Majesty] ordered a consultation with his valiant troops, saying as follows: "That wretched enemy, [the chief] of Kadesh has come and entered into Megiddo; he [is there] at this moment. He has gathered to himself the chiefs of [all] the countries [which are] on the water of Egypt, and as far as Naharin, consisting of [the countries] of the Kharu, the Kode, their horses, their troops, thus he speaks, 'I have arisen to [fight against His Majesty] in Megiddo.' Tell ye me . . . ."

They spoke in the presence of His Majesty, "How is it, that [we] should go upon this road, which threatens to be narrow? While they [come] and say that the enemy is there waiting, [hold]ing the way against a multitude. Will not horse come behind [horse and man behind] man likewise? Shall our [advance-guard] be fighting while our [rear guard] is yet standing yonder in Aruna not having fought? There are yet two (other) roads: one road, behold, it [will] . . . us, for it comes forth at Taanach, the other, behold, it will [bring us upon] the way north of Zefti, so that we shall come out to the north of Megiddo. Let our victorious lord proceed upon [the road] he desires; (but) cause us not to go by a difficult road."

Then . . . [messengers] concerning [this] design which they had uttered, in view of what had been said [by] the majesty of the Court, L. P. H. [Life! Prosperity! Health!]: "I [swear], as Re loves me, as my father Amon, favors me, as my [nostrils] are rejuvenated with satisfying life, My Majesty will proceed upon this road of Aruna. Let him who will among you, go upon those roads ye have mentioned, and let him who will among you, come in the following of My Majesty. Shall they think among those enemies whom Re detests: 'Does His Majesty proceed upon another road? He begins to be fearful of us,' so will they think."

They spoke before His Majesty: "May thy father Amon, lord of Thebes, presider over Karnak, [grant thee life]. Behold, we are the following of Thy Majesty in every place, whither [Thy Majesty] proceedeth; as the servant is behind his master."

[Then His Majesty] commanded the entire army [to march upon] that road which threatened to be [narrow. His Majesty] swore, saying: "None shall go forth [in the way] before My Majesty, in. . . ." He went forth at the head of his army himself, showing [the way] by his (own) footsteps; horse behind [horse, His Majesty] being at the head of his army.

Year 23, first month of the third season (ninth month), on the nineteenth day, the watch in [safety] in the royal tent was at the city of Aruna. My Majesty proceeded northward under (the protection of my) father, Amon-Re, lord of Thebes, [who went] before me, while Harakhte [strengthened my arms] . . . (my) father, Amon-Re, lord of Thebes, victorious of the sword . . . over My Majesty.

[The enemy] went forth in numerous battle array. The southern wing was in Taa[nach], the northern wing was on the ground south of. . . . His Majesty cried out to them before they fell; behold, that wretched foe . . . of [the city of] Aruna.

Now, the rear of the victorious army of His Majesty was at the city of Aruna, the front was going forth to the valley of . . . , they filled the opening of this valley. Then [they] said in the presence of His Majesty, L. P. H.: "Behold, His Majesty goeth forth with his victorious army, and it has filled the hollow of the valley; let our victorious lord hearken to us this time and let our lord protect for us the rear of his army and his people. Let the rear of the army come forth to us behind; then shall they (also) fight against these barbarians; then we shall not (need to) take thought for the rear of our army." His Majesty halted outside and waited there, protecting the rear of his victorious army.

Behold, when the front had reached the exit upon this road, the shadow had turned, and when His Majesty arrived at the south of Megiddo on the bank of the brook of Kina, the seventh hour was turning (measured) by the sun.

Then was set up the camp of His Majesty, and command was given to the whole army, saying: "Equip yourselves! Prepare your weapons! for we shall advance to fight with that wretched foe in the morning." Therefore the king rested in the royal tent, the [affairs] of the chiefs were arranged, and the provisions of the attendants. The watch of the army went about, saying, "Steady of heart! Steady of heart! Watchful! Watchful! Watch for life at the tent of the king." One came to say to His Majesty, "The land is well, and the infantry of the South and North likewise."

Year 23, first (month) of the third season (ninth month), on the twenty-first day, the day of the feast of the new moon, behold, command was given to the entire army to move.... His Majesty went forth in a chariot of electrum, arrayed in his weapons of war, like Horus, the Smiter, lord of power; like Montu of Thebes, while his father, Amon, strengthened his arms. The southern wing of this army of His Majesty was on a hill south of the [brook of] Kina, the northern wing was at the northwest of Megiddo, while His Majesty was in their center, with Amon as the protection of his members, ... the valor of his limbs. Then His Majesty prevailed against them at the head of his army, and when they saw His Majesty prevailing against them they fled headlong to Megiddo in fear, abandoning their horses and their chariots of gold and silver. The people hauled them (up), pulling (them) by their clothing, into this city; the people of this city having closed (it) against them [and lowered] clothing to pull them up into this city. Now, if only the army of His Majesty had not given their heart to plundering the things of the enemy, they would have captured Megiddo at this moment, when the wretched foe of Kadesh and the wretched foe of this city were hauled up in haste to bring them into this city. The fear of His Majesty had entered [their hearts], their arms were powerless, his serpent diadem was [victorious] among them.

Then were captured their horses, their chariots of gold and silver were made spoil; their champions lay stretched out like fishes on the ground. The victorious army of His Majesty went around counting their portions. Behold, there was captured the tent of that wretched foe [in] which was [his] son.... The whole army made jubilee, giving praise to Amon for the victory which he had granted to his son on [this day, giving praise] to His Majesty, exalting his victories. They brought up the booty which they had taken, consisting of hands, of living prisoners, of horses, chariots of gold and silver, of....

[Then spake His Majesty on hearing] the words of his army, saying: "Had ye captured [this city] afterward, behold, I would have given ... Re this day; because every chief of every country that has revolted is within it; and because it is the capture of a thousand cities, this capture of Megiddo. Capture ye [mightily, mightily], ..."

[His Majesty commanded] the officers of the troops to go ..., [assigning to] each his place. They measured this city, [surrounding it] with an inclosure, walled about with green timber of all their pleasant trees. His Majesty himself was upon the fortification east of this city, [inspect]ing....

It was [wa]lled about with a thick wall ... with its thick wall. Its name was made: "Menkeperre (Thutmose III)-is-the-Surrounder-of-the-Asiatics." People were stationed to watch over the tent of His Majesty; to whom it was said: "Steady of heart! Watch...." His Majesty [commanded, saying: "Let not on]e among them [come forth] outside, beyond this wall, except to come out in order to [knock] at the door of their fortifications."

Now, all that His Majesty did to this city, to that wretched foe and his wretched army, was recorded on (each) day by its (the day's) name, under the title of: ... Then it was recorded upon a roll of leather in the temple of Amon this day.

Behold, the chiefs of this country came to render their portions, to do obeisance to the fame of His Majesty, to crave breath for their nostrils, because of the greatness of his power, because of the might of the fame of His Majesty ... the country ... came to his fame, bearing their gifts, consisting of silver, gold, lapis lazuli, malachite; bringing clean grain, wine, large cattle, and small cattle—for the army of His Majesty. Each of the Kode among them bore the tribute southward. Behold, His Majesty appointed the chiefs anew for....

... 340 living prisoners; 83 hands; 2,041 mares; 191 foals; 6 stallions; ... young ... ; a chariot, wrought with gold, (its) pole of gold, belonging to that foe; a beautiful chariot, wrought with gold, belonging to the chief of [Megiddo]; ... 892 chariot[s] of his wretched army; total, 924 (chariots); a beautiful [suit] of bronze armor, belonging to that foe; a beautiful [suit] of bronze armor, belonging to the chief of Megiddo; ..., 200 suits of armor, belonging to his wretched army; 502 bows; 7 poles of wood, wrought with silver, belonging to the tent of that foe. Behold, the army of [His Majesty] took ..., 297 ..., 1,929 large cattle, 2,000 small cattle, 20,500 white small cattle.

List of that which was afterward taken by the King, of the household goods of that foe who was in [the city of] Yenoam, in Nuges, and in Herenkeru, together with all the goods of those cities which submitted themselves, which were brought to [His

Majesty: 474].... : 38 lords of theirs, 87 children of that foe and of the chiefs who were with him, 5 lords of theirs, 1,796 male and female slaves with their children, non-combatants, who surrendered because of famine with that foe, 103 men; total, 2,503. Besides flat dishes of costly stone and gold, various vessels, . . . , a large (two-handled) vase of the work of Kharu, . . . vases, flat dishes, . . .-dishes, various drinking-vessels, 3 large kettles, [8]7 knives, amounting to 784 deben. Gold in rings found in the hands of the artificers, and silver in many rings, 966 deben and 1 kidet. A silver statue in beaten work . . . the head of gold, the staff with human faces; 6 chairs of that foe, of ivory, ebony and carob wood, wrought with gold; 6 footstools belonging to them; 6 large tables of ivory and carob wood, a staff of carob wood, wrought with gold and all costly stones in the fashion of a scepter, belonging to that foe, all of it wrought with gold; a statue of that foe, of ebony wrought with gold, the head of which [was inlaid] with lapis lazuli . . . ; vessels of bronze, much clothing of that foe.

Behold, the cultivable land was divided into fields, which the inspectors of the royal house, L.P.H., calculated, in order to reap their harvest. Statement of the harvest which was brought to His Majesty from the fields of Megiddo: 208,200 (+ x) fourfold heket of grain, besides that which was cut as forage by the army of His Majesty....

His Majesty commanded to cause that the victories which his father [Amon] had given him should be recorded upon the stone wall in the temple which His Majesty made answer [for his father Amon, setting forth each expedition] by its name, together with the plunder which His Majesty brought therefrom. It was done according to [all the command which his father, Re, gave to him.]

Source: James Henry Breasted, *Ancient Records of Egypt: Historical Documents*, Vol. 2, *The Eighteenth Dynasty* (Chicago: University of Chicago Press, 1906), 179–189, 193.

6. Biography of Amenemhab (ca. 1440 BCE)

Introduction

Relatively few testimonies from nonroyal personages of the ancient Near East have survived. Amenemhab was a senior military general under first Pharaoh Thutmose III and then his son and successor Amenhotep II (r. 1427–1401 BCE), who made Amenemhab deputy commander of the Egyptian Army. Amenemhab fought in many of Thutmose III's campaigns and narrated an account of his career and experiences, which was inscribed on the wall of his tomb in the necropolis of Thebes in Egypt. Amenemhab, whose wife was nurse to the royal family, emphasized his closeness to Thutmose III, describing himself as "Attendant of his lord on his expeditions in the countries of the south and north, not separated from the Lord of the Two Lands on the battlefield in the hour of repelling millions of men." Amenemhab seems to have taken part in most of the campaigns of Thutmose III's final decade, including several battles in Negeb, Naharin, and Tikhsi; the siege of the city of Senzar; two sieges of the ever rebellious city of Kadesh 12 years apart; and an elephant hunt. Some of these events were not recorded in the Annals of Thutmose III, an indication that almost certainly a great deal of military information about the ancient Near East is irretrievably lost to posterity. It is also clear that Amenemhab felt deep personal loyalty and devotion to Thutmose III, which may help to explain the king's success as a military leader.

Document

The officer, Amenemhab; he says:

I was the very faithful one of the sovereign, L.P.H. [Life! Prosperity! Health!], the wise-hearted of the King of Upper Egypt, the excellent-hearted of the King of Lower Egypt. I followed my lord on his expeditions in the northern and the southern country. He desired that I should be the companion of his feet, while he was upon the battlefield of his victories, while his valor fortified the heart.

I fought hand to hand in the land of Negeb. I brought off three men, Asiatics, as living prisoners.

When His Majesty came to Naharin I brought off three men from the fight there; I set them before His Majesty as living prisoners.

Again I fought hand to hand (on) that expedition in the land of 'The-Height-of-Wan' on the West of Aleppo. I brought off 13 Asiatics as living prisoners, 13 men; 70 living asses; 13 bronze spears; the bronze was wrought with gold. . . .

Again I fought (on) that expedition in the land of Carchemish. I brought off . . . as living prisoners. I crossed over the water of Naharin, while they were in my hand, to . . . ; I set them before my lord. He rewarded me with a great reward; list thereof: . . . .

I beheld the royal victories of the King Menkheperre (Thutmose III), given life, in the country of Senzar, when he made a [great] s[laughter among] them. I fought hand to hand before the king, I brought off a hand there. He gave to me the gold of honor; list thereof: . . . two silver rings.

Again I beheld his bravery, while I was among his followers. [He] captured [the city of] Kadesh; I was not absent from the place where he was; I brought off two men, lords, as [living prisoners; I set them] before the king, the Lord of the Two Lands, Thutmose (III), living forever. He gave to me gold because of bravery, before the whole people . . . ; list thereof: of the finest gold: a lion; 2 necklaces, 2 flies, 4 arm rings.

I saw my lord in . . . in all his forms in the country of the ends of [the earth]. . . . Then I was raised to be the . . . of the army, like. . . .

Again I beheld his victory in the country of Tikhsi the wretched, in the city of Mero. I fought hand to hand therein before the king. I brought off Asiatics, 3 men, as living prisoners. Then my lord gave to me the gold of honor; list thereof: 2 golden necklaces, 4 arm rings, 2 flies, a lion, a female slave, and a male slave.

Again [I beheld] another excellent deed which the Lord of the Two Lands did in Niy. He hunted 120 elephants, for the sake of their tusks and. . . . I engaged the largest which was among them, which fought against His Majesty; I cut off his hand [trunk] while he was alive [before] His Majesty, while I stood in the water between two rocks. Then my lord rewarded me with gold; [he] gave . . . and 3 changes of clothing.

The prince of Kadesh sent forth a mare before [the army]; in order to [distract the horses], she entered among the army. I pursued after her on foot, with my sword, and I ripped open her belly; I cut off her tail, I set it before the king; while there was thanksgiving to god for it! He gave (me) joy, it filled my body, (with) rejoicing, he endued my limbs.

His Majesty sent forth every valiant man of his army, in order to pierce the wall for the first time, which Kadesh had made. I was the one who pierced it, being the first of all the valiant; no other before me did (it). I went forth, I brought off 2 men, lords, as living prisoners. Again my lord rewarded me because of it, with every good thing for satisfying the heart, of the king's presence.

I made this capture while [I] was an officer of the navy. . . . I was the commander of [his vessel]. . . . I was the chief of his associates on the voyage . . . at his beautiful Feast of Opet, when all the land was in acclamation.

Lo, the king completed his lifetime of many years, splendid in valor, in [migh]t, and in triumph; from year 1 to year 54, third month of the second season, the last day (of the month) under [the majesty of] King Menkheperre (Thutmose III), triumphant. He mounted to heaven, [he] joined the sun; the divine limbs mingling with him who begat him.

When the morning brightened, the sun arose, and the heavens shone, King Okhepreure, Son of Re, Amenhotep (II), given life, was established upon the throne of his father, he assumed the royal titular. He . . . all, he mingled with . . . in . . . the Red Land; he cut off the heads of their chiefs. Diademed as Horus, son of Isis, [he] took . . . the Kenemetyew, every land, Bowed down because of his fame; with their tribute upon their backs, [that he might grant] to them the breath of life.

His Majesty noticed me rowing won[derfully] with him in [his] vessel: 'Khammat' was its name. I was rowing [with] both hands at his beautiful feast of Luxor, likewise to the splendors.... I was brought to the midst of the palace, one caused that I should stand before [the king, O]khepru[re] (Amenhotep II),.... I bowed down immediately before His Majesty; he said to me, "I know thy character; I was abiding in the nest, while thou wert in the following of my father. I commission thee with office that thou shalt be deputy of the army as I have said, watch thou the élite troops of the King." The deputy, Mahu, executed (all) that his lord said.

Source: James Henry Breasted, *Ancient Records of Egypt: Historical Documents*, Vol. 2, *The Eighteenth Dynasty* (Chicago: University of Chicago Press, 1906), 230–234, 319.

7. King Burnaburias of Kassite Babylon Writes to Pharaoh Akhenaten (1352–1347 BCE)

Introduction

Rather little in the way of documents has survived from the Kassite kingdom based in Babylon. A cache of tablets of royal correspondence from El Amarna in Egypt, palace of the unconventional Egyptian pharaoh Akhenaten (Amenhotep IV) (r. 1352–1336 BCE), does, however, include three letters from King Burnaburias of Babylon (r. 1375–1347 BCE) to Akhenaten. Burnaburias seemed particularly eager that the Egyptians should send him munificent amounts of gold to fund expenses of some kind and that these funds and other valuables should reach him securely. He sought punishment for officials who had apparently plundered treasures sent to him while in transit. Burnaburias was also concerned that the Assyrians, who were vassals of his own, should not transfer their allegiance to the Egyptians. He claimed that he himself and his father, King Kurigalzu, had been scrupulous in not seeking to extend their influence over the Canaanites, recognizing that they were vassals of the Egyptians, and that he clearly expected Akhenaten to respect these lines of demarcation. The letters give insight into the state of constant competition for power and jostling for dominance that characterized relationships among the kingdoms of the Near East.

Documents

To Napkhururia [Akhenaten or Amenhotep IV Nefer-khepru-re], Great King, king of Egypt, thus speaks Burnaburiash, Great King, king of Karaduniash [Babylon], your brother.

I and my house, my horses and my chariots, my notables and my land, we are well. May well-being reign over my brother and his house, his horses and his cars, his notables and his land.

From the day on which the envoy of my brother arrived before me, my body has not been well, and his envoy has never eaten or drunk before me. See, if you question your envoy, he cannot tell you that my body is not well, and.... And as my body is not well and my brother....

I vented my anger with my brother with the following words: Should my brother not know that I am ill? Why has he not supported my head? Why has he not worried and sent his messengers?

The envoy of my brother has spoken thus: The way is not short, so that your brother can find out and send you greetings. The passage is long to your brother. Who can inform him, so that he sends a greeting to you quickly?

He next spoke thus: Question your messenger if the passage is not long....

As I asked my messenger, and he said that the way was long, no longer make I my brother the object of my anger.

As one has said that in the land of my brother there is everything, and that my brother lacks nothing, of everything there is also in my land, and I lack nothing. For a long time we have had good relations between us kings, and we exchange greetings. These relations between us must remain.... Only, four mines [about 4 pounds] of beautiful lapis lazuli have I sent to my brother as a gift, and also five teams of horses. When the times are good, I will send with my future messengers many beautiful gifts, and anything that my brother wishes, he can write....

I have started an undertaking, and for this reason I write to my brother. My brother should send me much gold, that I need for my work. But the gold that my brother sends me, do not leave it to some official. Let the eyes of my brother inspect it, and let my brother seal it and send it! Because as far as the previous gold is concerned, which my brother did not inspect personally, but which was sealed and sent by an official of my brother, of the 40 mines [about 40 pounds] which I put in the furnace, there was barely anything of value left.

And with regard to Salmu, my envoy, twice has his caravan been plundered. Once it was plundered by Biriazama, and his other caravan by Pamahu, a governor of a land that belongs to you. And this matter, my brother, you must put right! When my envoy appears before my brother, then let also appear Salmu. His ... has to be returned to him, and the damages have to be made good.

[To] Napkhuhru-ri[ya] [Akhenaten] the king of Egypt my brother [it is spoken] thus:

Burra-buryas the king of Kara[dunyas] thy brother—unto myself (is) peace; unto thee, thy country, thy house, thy wives, thy children, thy officers, thy horses (and) thy chariots may there ever be peace!

I and my brother with one another have conferred amicably, and this is what we have said as follows: as our fathers with one another, we also have friendly dealings. Again my ministers who came with Akhi-dhabu into the country of Kinakhkhi trusted to destiny, from Akhi-dhabu to visit my brother they passed; in the city of Kikhinnatuni of the country of Kinakhkhi Sum-Adda the son of Balumme (and) Sutatna the son of Saratum of the city of Akku, when they had sent their men, slew my ministers and carried off their treasures which they [were taking] for [a present to the king of Egypt].

I have sent to you [therefore] a complainant [who] may speak to thee [thus]:

Kinakhkhi (is) thy country and the king [is thy servant ?]. In thy country I have been injured; do thou punish [the offender]. The silver which they carried off [was] a present [for thee], and the men who (are) my servants they have slain. Slay them and requite the blood (of my messengers); but if thou doest not put these men to death, (the inhabitants) of the high-road that belongs to me will turn and verily will slay thy ambassadors, and a breach will be made in the agreement (to respect the persons) of ambassadors, and this man [Burna-buryas] will be estranged from thee.

One of my men Sum-Adda, having cut off his feet, detained him with him; and as for another man, Sutatna of Akku, having made him stand on (his) head, he stood upon his face.

As for these men ... one has spoken thus: I have seen indeed ... [what] thou askest that indeed thou knowest. [By way of a pre]sent, 1 maneh of alabaster I have despatched to thee. [By] my ambassadors a costly gift I have [sent to thee]. [On account of the re]port which my brother has heard my ambassadors do not detain; the costly present let them offer [to thee].

To Naphkhururia [Akhenaten], king of Egypt, thus speaks Burnaburiash, king of Karduniash [Babylon], your brother: I am well. May the well-being reign over you, your house, your women, your children, your land, your great ones, your horses, your chariots.

When my father and your father had dealings in good friendship, they sent each other beautiful presents, and nothing they refused. Now, my brother has sent me only two mines [2 pounds] of gold. But this is a very small amount: send, then, as much as your father did! And if you have little (gold), send half of what your father sent! Why have you sent me only two mines of gold? My work in the houses of the Gods is abundant, and now I have begun an undertaking: Send much gold! And you, whatever do you need from my land, write and it will be sent to you.

At the time of Kurigalzu, my father, the Kinahi [Canaanites] went to him in the following terms: the borders of the country . . . we want to pass to the other side, and join you.

My father gave them the following answer: Forget the idea of dealing with me! I will not declare myself against my brother, the king of Egypt, nor will I treat with someone else! Should I not rather plunder you? He is my ally.

My father committed no acts against your father.

Now (with respect to this): The Assyrians, vassals of mine, I have not sent to you, as they claim. Why have they been received in your land? If I am dear to you, do not let them conclude any business. May they return here with empty hands! As a gift, I send you three mines [3 pounds] of beautiful lapis lazuli and five teams of horses for five wooden chariots.

Source: A. H. Sayce, *Records of the Past: Being English Translations of the Ancient Monuments of Egypt and Western Asia,* 2nd series, Vol. 3 (London: Samuel Bagster, 1890), http://www.reshafim.org.il/ad/egypt/amarnaletters.htm.

8. Thucydides (ca. 400–423 BCE) on the Trojan War (ca. 1260–1180 BCE)

Introduction

The Greeks themselves showed considerable skepticism as to the accuracy of the popular accounts of the Trojan War that were available to them. Writing in the early fifth century BCE after being exiled from his native city, the Athenian historian and general Thucydides began his *History of the Peloponnesian War* with a discussion of the causes and scale of the fabled Greek war against Troy. While not doubting that the conflict had taken place, he had no faith in the mythological version that placed great emphasis on the role of gods, goddesses, and minor deities. Nor did he believe that the Greek armies that attacked Troy had been anywhere near as formidable a force as the poet Homer represented them.

Other evidence seems to confirm the existence of Troy around the relevant period. Surviving fragmentary correspondence from the mid-14th to 13th centuries BCE between a Hittite (Hatti) king, probably Hattusili III, and the king of Ahhiyawa, which has been identified with Mycenae, refers to the kingdom of Wilusa, which seems to be located in Anatolia, where the ruins of a city with a history reflecting that of Troy would eventually be discovered in the 19th century. The Hittite monarch also mentioned past tensions between the Hatti or Hittites and Ahhiyawa over Wilusa, which had subsequently been resolved largely because the Hatti had conceded that they were in the wrong and yielded to Ahhiyawan wishes.

Document

[J]udging from the evidence which I am able to trust after most careful enquiry, I should imagine that former ages were not great either in their wars or in anything else. . . .

Thus the several Hellenic tribes (and I mean by the term Hellenes those who, while forming separate communities, had a common language, and were afterwards called by a common name), owing to their weakness and isolation, were never united in any great enterprise before the Trojan War. And they only made the expedition against Troy after they had gained considerable experience of the sea.

Minos [king of Crete] is the first to whom tradition ascribes the possession of a navy. He made himself master of a great part of what is now termed the Hellenic sea; he conquered the Cyclades, and was the first coloniser of most of them, expelling the Carians and appointing his own sons to govern in them. Lastly, it was he who, from a natural desire to protect his growing revenues, sought, as far as he was able, to clear the sea of pirates. . . .

After Minos had established his navy, communication by sea became more general. For, he having expelled the marauders when he colonised the greater part of the islands, the dwellers on the sea-coast began to grow richer and to live in a more settled manner; and some of them, finding their wealth increase beyond their expectations, surrounded their towns with walls. The love of gain made the weaker willing to serve the stronger, and the command of wealth enabled the more powerful to subjugate the lesser cities. This was the state of society which was beginning to prevail at the time of the Trojan War.

I am inclined to think that Agamemnon succeeded in collecting the expedition, not because the suitors of Helen had bound themselves by oath to Tyndareus, but because he was the most powerful king of his time. Those Peloponnesians who possess the most accurate traditions say that originally Pelops gained his power by the great wealth which he brought with him from Asia into a poor country, whereby he was enabled, although a stranger, to give his name to the Peloponnesus; and that still greater fortune attended his descendants after the death of Eurystheus, king of Mycenae, who was slain in Attica by the Heraclidae. For Atreus the son of Pelops was the maternal uncle of Eurystheus, who, when he went on the expedition, naturally committed to his charge the kingdom of Mycenae. Now Atreus had been banished by his father on account of the murder of Chrysippus. But Eurystheus never returned; and the Mycenaeans, dreading the Heraclidae, were ready to welcome Atreus, who was considered a powerful man and had ingratiated himself with the multitude. So he succeeded to the throne of Mycenae and the other dominions of Eurystheus. Thus the house of Pelops prevailed over that of Perseus.

And it was, as I believe, because Agamemnon inherited this power and also because he was the greatest naval potentate of his time that he was able to assemble the expedition; and the other princes followed him, not from good-will, but from fear. Of the chiefs who came to Troy, he, if the witness of Homer be accepted, brought the greatest number of ships himself, besides supplying the Arcadians with them. In the *Handing down of the Sceptre* he is described as "The king of many islands, and of all Argos." But, living on the mainland, he could not have ruled over any except the adjacent islands (which would not be 'many') unless he had possessed a considerable navy. From this expedition we must form our conjectures about the character of still earlier times.

When it is said that Mycenae was but a small place, or that any other city which existed in those days is inconsiderable in our own, this argument will hardly prove that the expedition was not as great as the poets relate and as is commonly imagined. Suppose the city of Sparta to be deserted, and nothing left but the temples and the ground-plan, distant ages would be very unwilling to believe that the power of the Lacedaemonians was at all equal to their fame. And yet they own two-fifths of the Peloponnesus, and are acknowledged leaders of the whole, as well as of numerous allies in the rest of Hellas. But their city is not built continuously, and has no splendid temples or other edifices; it rather resembles a group of villages like the ancient towns of Hellas, and would therefore make a poor show. Whereas, if the same fate befell the Athenians, the ruins of Athens would strike the eye, and we should infer their power to have been twice as great as it really is. We ought not then to be unduly sceptical. The greatness of cities should be estimated by their real power and not by appearances. And we may fairly suppose the Trojan expedition to have been greater than any which preceded it, although according to Homer, if we may once more appeal to his testimony, not equal to those of our own day. He was a poet, and may therefore be expected to exaggerate; yet, even upon his showing, the expedition was comparatively small. For it numbered, as he tells us, twelve hundred ships, those of the Boeotians carrying one hundred and twenty men each, those of Philoctetes fifty; and by these numbers he may be presumed to indicate the largest and the smallest ships; else why in the catalogue is nothing said about the size of any others? That the crews were all fighting men as well as rowers he clearly implies when speaking of the ships of Philoctetes; for he tells us that all the oarsmen were likewise archers. And it is not to be supposed that many who were not sailors would accompany the expedition, except the kings and principal officers; for the troops had to cross the sea, bringing with them the materials of war, in vessels without decks, built after the old piratical fashion. Now if we take a mean between the crews, the invading forces will appear not to have been very numerous when we remember that they were drawn from the whole of Hellas.

The cause of the inferiority was not so much the want of men as the want of money; the invading army was limited, by the difficulty of obtaining supplies, to such a number as might be expected to live on the country in which they were to fight. After their arrival at Troy, when they had won a battle (as they clearly did, for otherwise they could not have fortified their camp), even then they appear not to have used the whole of their force, but to have been driven by want of provisions to the cultivation of the Chersonese and to pillage. And in consequence of this dispersion of their forces, the Trojans were enabled to hold out against them during the whole ten years, being always a match for those who remained on the spot. Whereas if the besieging army had brought abundant supplies, and, instead of betaking themselves to agriculture or pillage, had carried on the war persistently with all their forces, they would easily have been masters of the field and have taken the city; since, even divided as they were, and with only a part of their army available at any one time, they held their ground. Or, again, they might have regularly invested Troy, and the place would have been captured in less time and with less trouble. Poverty was the real reason why the achievements of former ages were insignificant, and why the Trojan War, the most celebrated of them all, when brought to the test of facts, falls short of its fame and of the prevailing traditions to which the poets have given authority.

Source: Thucydides, *History of the Peloponnesian War*, translated by Benjamin Jowett (Oxford, UK: Clarendon, 1881), Book 1, chaps. 2–4, 8–11.

9. King Nebuchadnezzar I of Babylon (r. ca. 1125–1104 BCE): Inscription (ca. 1100 BCE)

Introduction

Nebuchadnezzar (Nebuchadrezzar) I of Babylon, the fourth king of the second dynasty of Isin and fourth dynasty of the early Babylonian Empire, was determined to destroy the power of the neighboring kingdom of Elam, which had inflicted a series of humiliating defeats on Babylon. For much of his reign of 22 years, Nebuchadnezzar apparently conducted campaigns against Elam. He did so in alliance with the Kassite chieftain Ritti-Marduk. This inscription describes how Nebuchadnezzar waged battle against Elam, a war in the course of which he captured and reportedly sacked the Elamite capital city of Susa and retrieved a statue of the god Marduk previously seized from the temple of Esagila in Babylon by the Elamites. Nebuchadnezzar also reinstated Babylonian rule over former vassals in the territories he invaded. Elamite power never recovered from this defeat, and the country disintegrated into petty competing states. Nebuchadnezzar was less successful, however, in checking the rise of Assyrian power.

Document

At the time that Nebuchadrezzar, the lofty and majestic prince, King of Babylon, pre-eminent among kings, the warlike patesi, the governor of Babylon, the sun of his country, who makes his people to prosper, who preserves boundaries and establishes land-marks (?), the just king, who pronounced righteous judgment, the warlike hero, whose resources are devoted to battle, the bearer of the mighty bow, who fears no battle, who overthrew the mighty land of the Lullubi with his weapons, the conqueror of the west-land, the plunderer of the Kassites, who sets up kings, the prince beloved of Marduk—the king of the gods, Marduk, commissioned him, and he advanced his weapons to avenge Akkad. From Der, the city of Anu, he spread slaughter for thirty double-miles. In the month of Tammuz he set out upon a campaign; the * * * burned like fire, and the sand (?) of the road scorched like a flame; there was no water for * * * and the supply of drinking water was cut off; the splendid mighty steeds stood still, and the nerve of the brave heroes failed. The majestic king advances, the gods urging him on, Nebuchadrezzar marches forward, who has no rival, who does not fear the difficult country * * * Ritti-Marduk, the head of the house of Karziyabku, his charioteer, did not remain (?) at the right hand of the king, his lord, but pushed forward his chariot. The mighty king hastened and came to the bank of the Ula. Then the kings took their stand round about to make battle, fire flashed forth in their midst, the face of the sun was darkened by the dust, the hurricane broke loose, the storm raged. In the storm of their battle, the charioteer does not see the man by his side. Ritti-Marduk, the head of the house of Karziyabku, his charioteer, did not remain (?) at the right hand of the king, his lord, but pushed forward his chariot. He did not fear battle, but proceeded against the enemy of his lord * * * . By the command of the gods, Ishtar and Ramman, the lords of battle, he spread disaster broadcast, and overthrew the country of the King of Elam, and the King Nebuchadrezzar remained the victor, seizing Elam and carrying away its possessions. As soon as he had turned back to Akkad, victorious and joyful of heart, Nebuchadrezzar, the king, his lord, gave direction to Ritti-Marduk, the head of the house of Karziyabku, whom the king, his lord, had put to the test among the enemies and hostile warriors, concerning the cities of the house of Karziyabku, a district of Namar, as much as there was of it, which under former kings had been independent, but through enemies had illegally come under the dominion of Namar; and the king rendered a decision, and the cities (received) their freedom as in former times: within the entire dominion of Namar, the servants of the king, as well as the governor of Namar (and) the commandant, are not to enter a city; the master of the horses is to bring neither stallions nor mares into the cities; revenue of oxen or sheep for the king or the governor of Namar is not to be taken; a * * * or an homer of balsam is not to be given to the tax-gatherer; the master of the riding-horses is not to enter the cities; nor is he to take therefrom mares for the riding-horses; nor is any one to cut down the hedges of the parks or date-palm groves; along the wall of Bit-Shamash or Shanbasha no one is to build a bridge or make a road; neither are the soldiers of Nippur or Babylon, nor any of the soldiers of the king, as many as reside in the cities of the house of Karziyabku, to cause the arrest of any one either in city or in field.

From the entire domain of Namar, Nebuchadrezzar, the king of the world, freed the cities of Ritti-Marduk, the son of Karziyabku, the territory belonging to Namar, as much as there was of it, for all time, and he appointed the soldiers, who dwelt in these cities, for the special support of the governor of Namar and the commandant.

At the declaration of freedom of these cities there were present Nazi-Marduk, the son of Karkume, the kalu of Akkad; Arad-Nana, the son of Mudammiq-Ramman, the secretary of state; Marduk-kuduri-uçur, the minister of Bel; Tubia-enna, an officer; Muqqut-gish-ge, the son of Çapri, the keeper of the palace-gate; Shamash-nadin-shum, the son of Att-iluma, the governor of Ishin; Bau-shum-iddin, the son of Hunna, the governor of Babylon; Balatsu-Gula, the son of Arad-Ea, the prefect; Marduk-kin-apli, the son of Himile, the keeper of the treasure (?); Arad-Gula, the son of Kalbi, the governor of Ushti; Tab-ashab-Marduk, the son of Esaggilzir, the governor of Halman; Bel-nadin-shum, the son of Habban, the governor of Namar; and Nabu-kuduri-uçur, the commandant of Namar.

The scribe who wrote this tablet was Bel-tabni-bullit, the seer.

Whenever in after time, be it by the sons of Habban, or any one else who is placed in the governorship of Namar, be it the mayors of Namar, small or great, as many as there are of them, of the cities of the house of Karziyabku, which the king has freed from the dominion of Namar, there is one who does not reverence the king or his gods and turns and establishes a dominion, and obliterates the name of the god and the king, as it stands written, and writes in another (name), or employs a fool, a deaf man, a blind man, or a knave to destroy this tablet with a stone, or to burn it in the fire, or to cast it into the river, or to hide it in a field where it can not be found:

May the great gods, as many as are mentioned in heaven and earth, curse that man with fury; may god and king cover him deep with disgrace!

May Ninib, the king of heaven and earth, and Gula, the mistress of E-sharra, destroy his boundaries and blot out his seed!

May Ramman, the chief one in heaven and earth, the lord of canals and rains, fill his rivers with obstructions, bring upon him hunger and want, and bind upon him distress, frailty, and mischief!

May frailty fasten its grip (?) upon the inhabitants of his city!

May Shumalia, the mistress of the snow-capped mountains, who dwells upon the summits and traverses the peaks; may Ramman, Nergal, and Nana, the gods of Namar; may Shir, Shubu, the son of the temple of Der, Sin, and the Lady of Akkad, the gods of the house of Habban—may these great gods in the anger of their heart meditate against him!

May another acquire the house which he has built!

With a dagger in his neck and a * * * in his eyes, may he cast himself upon his face before his captor, and may he, unmindful of his pleading, cut off his life!

In the overturning of his house may his hands roll in mire!

As long as he lives may he drag sorrow after him, and as long as heaven and earth stand may his seed be blotted out!

Source: Robert Francis Harper, ed., *Assyrian and Babylonian Literature: Selected Translations* (New York: D. Appleton, 1901), 8–11.

10. Tiglath-Pileser III of Assyria (r. 744–727 BCE): Tablet Inscription (ca. 727 BCE)

Introduction

The Assyrian ruler Tiglath-Pileser III, like other Middle Eastern monarchs, left behind him monuments and tablets describing his accomplishments. He spent most of his 17 years as king campaigning against his neighbors and building palaces and temples, which were financed and embellished by the spoils of his conquests. The inscriptions proclaiming his triumphs glorified the brutality with which he waged war, sacking and devastating cities, annexing the lands of other rulers, enslaving and deporting the inhabitants, and on occasion impaling defeated enemies. Tiglath-Pileser III seemed to take positive delight in leaving a trail of ruin and destruction in his wake. One defeated ruler was impaled outside his own city. After enslaving and sometimes killing his opponents and their families, Tiglath-Pileser III usually appointed his own eunuchs as provincial governors, possibly because they would have no progeny who might in future represent a threat to his own authority.

Document

Palace of Tiglath-piles[er (III), great king, mighty king, king of the world, king of Assyria, king of Babylon, king of] Sumer and Akkad, king of the four quarters (of the world); valiant man who, with the help of (the god) Aššur, his lord, [smashed like pots] all [who were unsubmissive to him], swept over (them) like [the] Deluge, and considered (them) as (mere) ghosts; the king who [marched about] at the command of the gods Aššur, Šamaš, and Marduk, the great gods, [and] exercised authority over lands fr[om the Bi]tter Sea of Bīt-Yakīn, as far as Mount Bikni in the east, up to the Sea of the Setting Sun, as far as Egypt, [from] the horizon to the zenith, and exercised kingship over them.

From the beginning of my reign until my seventeenth *palû*, I captured, defeated, (and) plundered the (tribes) Itu'u, [Rubu]'u, Hamarānu, LuHu'atu, Hatallu, Rubbû, Rapiqu, Hīrānu, Rabi-ilu, Nasiru, Gulusu, Nabātu, Rahiqu, Ka[piru], Rummulutu, Adilê, Gibrê, Ubudu, Gurumu, Hudadu, Hindiru (Hindaru), Damunu, Dunanu, Nilqu, Radê, Dai[. . .]nu, Ubulu, Karma'u, Amlatu, Ru'u'a, Qabi'u, Li'ta'u, Marusu, Amatu, Hagarānu, (and those living in) the cities Dūr-Kurigalzu (and) Adin[ni], the fortresses of Sarragitu, Labbanat, (and) Kār-bēl-mātāti, all of the Arameans on the banks of the Tigris, Euphrates, and Surap[pu] Rivers, as far as the Uqnû River, which is by the shore of the Lower Sea. I annexed to Assyria the Arameans, as many as there were, and I placed a eunuch of mine as provincial governor over them.

I built a city on top of a *tell* (lit. "a heaped-up ruin mound") called umut (and) named it Kār-Aššur. I brought the people of (foreign) lands conquered by me therein.

In Sippar, Nippur, Babylon, Borsippa, Cutha, Kish, Dilbat, and Uruk, cult centers without rival, I offered pure sacrifices to the deities Bēl (Marduk), Zarpanītu, Nabû, Tašmētu, Nergal, (and) Laṣ, the great gods, my lords, and they loved my priestly services.

I exercised authority over the extensive land of Karduniaš (Babylonia) to its full extent and exercised kingship over it.

I overwhelmed the (tribe) Puqudu like a (cast) net, defeated them, (and) carried off much booty from them. I annexed to Assyria that (tribe) Puqudu, the city Lahīru of Idibirīna, (and) the cities Hilimmu (and) Pillatu, which are on the border of the land Elam (and) I placed (them) under the authority of a eunuch of mine, the provincial governor of the city Arrapha. I deported (the people of) the land Labdudu, as many as there were, and settled (them) in Assyria.

I ensnared Chaldea in its entirety as with a bird-snare. As for Nabû-ušabši of (the land Bīt)-Šilāni (lit. "son of Šilāni"), I defeated him on the outskirts of the city Sarrabānu, his city. Moreover, I impaled him before the gate of his city, while making (the people of) his land watch. By means of earthworks [and] battering rams, I captured the city Sarrabānu. I carried off 55,000 people, together with their possessions, his booty, his property, his goods, his wife, his sons, his daughters, and his gods. I de[stroyed, devastated, (and) bu]rned [with fire] that city, together with cities in its environs, and turned (them) into mounds of ruins (lit. "mounds and ruins").

I captured the cities of Tarbasu (and) Yaballu. I car[ried off] 30,000 people, together with their possessions, their [pro]perty, their goods, and their gods. I destroyed [t]hose [cities], together with cities in their environs, (making them) like *tells* after the Deluge.

Zaqiru of (the land Bīt)-Ša'alli (lit. "son of Ša'alli") neglected the loyalty oath (sworn by) the great gods and [conspir]ed with [my enemies]. I personally captured him, together with his nobles, placed them in iron fetters, and took (them) to Assyria. The people of the land Bīt-Ša'alli became frightened and they made the city Dūr-[Bali āya], their royal [city], their fortress. By means of artificial mounds and siege machines, I conquered that city and utterly demolished (it). I carried off 40,500 people, together with their possessions, th[eir] booty, their [property], their goods, (as well as) his (Zaqiru's) wife, his sons, his daughters, and his gods.

I conquered the city Amlilatu. I carried off (its) people, together with their possessions, its booty, its property, (and) its goods. I swept over the land Bīt-Ša'alli in its entirety like the Deluge and devastated its settlements. I annexed those lands to Assyria.

I confined Mukīn-zēri of (the land Bīt)-Amukāni (lit. "son of Amukāni") to Sapê (Šapīya), his royal city. I inflicted a heavy defeat upon him before his city gates. I cut down the orchards (and) musukkannu-trees that were near his (city) wall; I did not leave a single one (standing). I killed date-palms throughout his land by ripping off their (text: "its") fruit and filling the meadows (with them).

I destroyed, devastated, (and) burned with fire all of his cities. Like tells after the Deluge, I destroyed the lands Bīt-Šilāni, Bīt-Amukāni, and Bīt-Ša'alli in their entirety, (and) turned (them) into mounds of ruins (lit. "mounds and ruins").

I received the payment of Balāssu of (the land Bīt)-Dakkūri (lit. "son of Dakkūri") (and) Nādinu of (the city) Larak: silver, gold, (and) precious stones. (As for) Marduk-apla-iddina (II) (Merodach-baladan) of (the land Bīt)-Yakīn (lit. "son of Yakīn"), a king of the Sea(land) who had not come before any of the kings, my ancestors, and who had not kissed their feet, fear of the brilliance of (the god) Aššur, my lord, overwhelmed him and he came to the city Sapīya (Šapīya), before me, and kissed my feet. I received as his payment natural, unrefined gold in great quantity, jewelry made of gold, a gold necklace, pearls (lit. "precious stones, produce of the sea"), beams of ebony, ellūtu-wood, *ašqulālu*-plant(s), *amīlānu*-plant(s), multi-colored garments, all types of aromatics, oxen, and sheep and goats.

As with a bird-snare, I ensnared the lands Namri, Bīt-Sangibūti, Bīt-amban, Sumurzu, (Bīt)-Barrūa, Bīt-Zualzaš, (and) Bīt-Matti, the city Niqqu of the land Tupliaš, the lands Bīt-Taranzāya, Parsua, Bīt-Zatti, Bīt-Abdadāni, Bīt-Kapsi, Bīt-Sangi, (and) Bīt-Urzakki, the cities Bīt-Ištar (and) Zakruti, the lands Gizinikissi (and) Niššāya, the cities Sibur (and) Urimzan, the lands Ra'usan, Uparia, Bustus, Ariarma—the *land of roosters*—Sa[k]sukni, Araquttu, Karzibra, Gukinnana, (and) Bīt-Sagbat, Mount Silhazu, [which] they call the fortress of the Babylonian(s), Mount Rūa, as far as the salt desert of the lands Ušqaqāna (and) Šikrakki—(the land) of gold—(and) the districts of the mighty Medes to their full extent.

I inflicted a heavy [de]feat upon them. I carried off 60,500 people, together with their possessions, their horses, their mules, their Bactrian camels, their oxen, (and) their sheep and goats, without number. I destroyed, devastated, (and) burned with fire their [cit]ies. I turned (them) into mounds of ruins (lit. "mounds and ruins").

I annexed to Assyria the lands Namri, Bīt-Sangibūti, Bīt-amban, Sumurzu, Bīt-Barrūa, Bīt-Zualzaš, (and) [Bīt]-Matti, the city Niqqu of the land Tupliaš, the lands Bīt-Taranzāya, Parsua, Bīt-Zatti, Bīt-Abdadāni, Bīt-Kapsi, Bīt-Sangi, (and) Bīt-Urzakki, (and) the cities Bīt-Ištar (and) Zakruti, (cities) of the mighty Medes.

I rebuilt the cities inside them (those lands), set up the weapon of (the god) Aššur, my lord, therein, (and) brought the people of (foreign) lands conquered by me therein. I placed [. . .] eunuchs of mine as provincial governors over them.

I erected my royal image in the land Tikrakki, in the cities Bīt-Ištar (and) Sibur, in the land Ariarma—the *land of roosters*—(and) at [Mount S]ilhazu, which they call the fortress of the Babylonian(s).

[I received] the payme[nt of the Med]es, the people of the land Ellipu, and the city rulers of all of the mountain regions, as far as Mount Bikni—[. . .], horses, mules, Bactrian camels, oxen, and sheep and goats, without num[ber].

[Iranzu of the land Mann]ea [heard about] the glorious valor of (the god) Aššur, my lord, that I [had accomplished again and again] throughout all of the mountain regions [and the brilliance] of (the god) Aššur, my lord, overwhelmed him. He came to the city Dūr-Tiglath-pileser ("Fort Tiglath-pileser"), which [. . . , be]fore me, (and) kiss[ed my feet. I *received* . . . hor]ses, mules, oxen, and sheep and goats, military equipment, [. . .].

[I sent a eu]nuch of mine, Aššur-dainanni, against the mighty Medes in the ea[st. He took 5,000 horses, people, oxen, and sheep and goats, without number].

I captured the lands [Ullu]ba (and) HabHu in their (text: "its") entirety (and) I annexed (them) to Assyria. [(. . .) I built a city in the land Ulluba (and) I named it Aššur-iqīša]. Inside (it), I founded [a palace for] my royal [resid]ence. I set up the weapon of (the god) Aššur, my lord, therein, (and) [settled the] people of (foreign) la[nds conquered by me therein. . . .].

[(As for) Sarduri of the land U]rartu, Sulumal of the land Melid, Tarhula[ra of the land Gurgum, . . .] Kuštašpi of the land Kummuhu, [they (Sarduri and allies) . . .] to capture and plunder [Assyrian territory. . . . Be]tween the lands Kištan and Halpi, districts of the land K[ummuhu, I (utterly) defeated them and. . . . With the blood of] their [warr]iors [I dyed] the Sinzi River as red as dyed wool. [. . .] I took their [entire ca]mp away from them. In the midst of [that] bat[tle, I . . .] . . . , (their) royal beds [. . .]

[Lacuna]

I se[t the rest of her (Samsi's) possessions (and) her tents, her people's safeguard *within* her camp], on fire. [Samsi became startled by my mighty weapons and] she [brought camels, she-camels, with their young, to As]syria, before me. I placed [a representative (of mine) ov]er her [and . . . 10,000 soldiers . . .].

The people of the cities [Mas]'a, Tema, Saba, Hayappa, Badanu, (and) [Hatte, (and) the (tribes) Idiba'ilu, . . . , who are on the border of the west]ern [lands], whom none (of my predecessors) had known about, and whose country is remote, [heard about] the fame of my majesty (and) [my heroic deeds, and (thus) they beseeched my lordship]. As one, [they brought] befo[re me gold, sil]ver, camels, she-camels, (and) all types of aromatics as their payment [and they kissed my feet]. I appointed [Id]ibi'ilu as the "gatekeeper" facing Egypt.

In all of the (foreign) lands that . . . [. . . I received the paymen]t of Kuštašpi of the land Kummuhu, Urik(ki) of the land Que, Sibitti-bi'il of the city [Byblos, Hiram of the land Tyre, Pisīris of the city Carchemish, Ēnī]-il of the land Hamath, Panammû of the city Sam'al, Tarhulara of the city Gurgum, Sulu[mal of the land Melid, Dadīlu of the city Kaska, U]assurme of the land Tabal, Ušhitti of the city Tuna, Urballâ of the city Tuhana, Tuham[mi of the city Ištunda, Urimmi of the city ubišna, Ma]ttan-bi'il (Mattan-Ba'al) of the city Arvad, Sanīpu of the land Bīt-Ammon, Salāmānu of the land Moab, . . . [. . . of . . . , . . . of . . . , Mi]tinti of the land Ashkelon, Jehoahaz of the land Judah, Qauš-malaka of the land Edom, Mu . . . [. . . of . . . , , . . . of . . . , (and) Ha]nūnu of the city Gaza: gold, silver, tin, iron, lead, multi-colored garments, linen garments, the garments of their lands, red-purple wool, [..., all kinds of] costly articles, produce of the sea (and) dry land, commodities of their lands, royal treasures, horses (and) mules broken to the yo[ke, ...].

[U]assurme of the land Tabal acted as if he were the equal of Assyria and he did not come before me. [I sent] a eunuch of mine, the chief [eunuch, to the land Tabal. ...]. I placed [Hu]llî, a commoner (lit. "son of a nobody") on his royal throne. [I received] 10 talents of gold, 1,000 talents of silver, 2,000 horses, (and) [... mules as his audience gift].

I sent a eunuch of mine, the chief eunuch, to the city Tyre. [I received] from Metenna of the city Tyre 150 talents of gold (and) [2,000 talents of silver as his audience gift].

With the keen understanding (and) broad knowledge that the sage of the gods, the prince, the god Nudimmud (Ea), granted to me, I built in Kalhu a cedar palace, [... for my lordly residence] and a *bīt-ilāni*, a replica of a palace of the land atti (Syria-Palestine), for my pleasure. I made the dimensions of its site [... large cubits in length (and) sixty large cubits in width] larger than the former palaces of my ancestors [by (re)claiming] (land) from the Tigris River (by filling it in). [...] ... [...].

I cleverly made plans with (the help of) all of the skilled craftsmen and ... [...] ... [...]. Like the base of a mountain, I piled up heavy limestone (blocks to a depth of) twenty large cubits in the raging waters and I [... stopped its] flooding. I put up their terraces, secured their foundations, and raised high their summits. (To a height of) one half nindanu (and) two-thirds of a cubit, [I] constructed rooms of [...] and I made their gates face north.

[I decor]ated (lit. "I established") (them) with ivory, ebony, boxwood, *musukkannu-wood*, c[eda]r, *šur*[mēnu]-wood, [*burāšu-juniper,* and] juniper—(which was) tribute from the kings of the land Hatti (Syria-Palestine) (and) from Aramean and Chaldean rulers whom I sub[dued (and) ...] with the power of my heroism—(and) I filled (them) with splendor.

(To a height of) five and one half nindanu (and) four cubits, from the depth of the water to (their) copings, I designed their structure and I made their workmanship more resp[len]dent than the palaces of (foreign) lands.

I roofed them with long beams of cedar, which are as sweet to smell as the scent of ašūru-wood, a product of Mount Am[anus], Mount Lebanon, (and) Mount Ammanāna, thus I demonstrated appropriate care (for their roofing). In order to splendidly provide appropriate decorations for the locks [...] ..., I fashioned stones of the stonecutter's craft and (thus) made (its) gate(s) befitting (a royal palace).

I fastened bands of shiny silver (*zahalû*) and [*ešmarû*-silver] on double doors of cedar (and) *šurmēnu*-wood, which bestow (great) pleasure on those who enter them (and) whose fragrance wafts into the heart, and I hung (them) wherever there were gates.

I set up in (its) entrances (statues of) lions, *šēdu*, (and) lamassu, whose features are very skillfully wrought (and) which are clothed with splendor, and I erected (them there) as objects of wonder (for the people). I laid threshold slabs of gypsum (and) parūtu-alabaster at their feet (lit. "beneath them") and (thus) I brightened the(ir) exit(s).

Moreover, I placed stone images, guardians of the great gods, creatures of the apsû (i.e., fish-men), around (the palace's) supporting wall, thus I endowed (them) with a terrifying quality.

To put the finishing touch on them (the palatial halls), I arranged knobbed pegs of gold, silver, and bronze around them, and (thus) I made their appearance bright.

For my royal abode, I set up therein a glittering chamber inlaid with precious stones. I named them "(The) Palatial Halls of Joy Which Bear Abundance, Which Bless the King, (and) Which Make Their Builder Long-[Liv]ed."

I na[m]ed their gates "Gates of Justice Which Give the Correct Judgment for the Rulers of the Four Quarters (of the World), Which O[ff]er the Yield of the Mountains and the Seas, (and) Which Admit the Produce of Mankind Before the King Their Lord."

Source: Website Royal Inscriptions of the Neo-Assyrian Period Project, http://oracc.museum.upenn.edu/rinap/corpus/.

11. Nebuchadnezzar II of Babylon: The East India House Inscription (ca. 565 BCE)

Introduction

In this inscription, the Babylonian emperor Nebuchadnezzar (Nebuchadrezzar) II (r. 605–562 BCE) described at length his rebuilding of Babylon, his capital city. The king stressed his devotion to the god Marduk, whom he believed had brought him victory in battle against the Assyrians and others, and also his veneration of a range of other gods and goddesses whom he likewise considered patrons. A considerable amount of the booty and additional manpower that accrued to Nebuchadnezzar in the course of his lengthy military campaigns was ultimately lavished on the shrines and temples of these divinities as well as on beautifying Babylon, the king's beloved capital city and main residence. The Jews whom he deported from Palestine were among those forced to labor on these projects. During Nebuchadnezzar's lengthy reign the political and military dominance of Assyria over the surrounding region was finally broken, never to be restored.

Document

Nebuchadrezzar, King of Babylon, the exalted prince, the favourite of Marduk, the lofty patesi, the beloved of Nabu, the arbiter, the possessor of wisdom, who seeks out the path of their divinity, who reverences their lordship; the untiring governor, who ponders daily concerning the maintenance of Esagila and Ezida, and is continually anxious for the shrines of Babylon and Borsippa; the wise, the pious, the maintainer of Esagila and Ezida, the chief son of Nabopolassar, King of Babylon, am I.

From the time that the lord my god, Marduk, had created me and had formed my embryo in the womb, at the time I was born, at the time I was created, I sought out the shrines of the god, the path of the god I followed. As for Marduk, the great lord, the god of my creator, his clever deeds I held in great esteem. As for Nabu, his true son, the beloved of my royalty, the lofty path of his divinity I steadfastly followed; with all my faithful heart I loved the worship of their divinity, I reverenced their lordship.

At the time that Marduk, the great lord, lifted up my royal head and entrusted me with the rule of all people; and Nabu, the ruler of the host of heaven and earth, gave into my hands a righteous scepter for the governing of the people; then, as for me, I stood in awe of them and sought out their divinity, for the renown of their famous name I reverenced both god and goddess. To Marduk my lord I made supplication; I read his prayers, and the word of my heart reached up to him. To him I spoke:

> O eternal prince! Lord of all being!
> To the king whom thou lovest, and
> Whose name thou hast proclaimed
> As was pleasing to thee,
> Do thou lead aright his name,
> Guide him in a straight path.
> I am the prince, thy favourite,
> The creature of thy hand;
> Thou hast created me, and
> With dominion over all people
> Thou hast intrusted me.
> According to thy favour, O lord,
> Which thou dost bestow on

All people,
Cause me to love thy exalted lordship,
And create in my heart
The worship of thy divinity,
And grant whatever is pleasing to thee,
Because thou hast fashioned my life.

He, the pre-eminent, the honoured, the leader of the gods, the Prince Marduk, heard my supplication and received my prayer. He made his exalted lordship favourable to me, the fear of his divinity he established in my heart, he incited my heart to do his service. I reverenced his lordship. Under his exalted protection, far-off lands, distant mountains, from the Upper Sea to the Lower Sea, steep trails, unopened paths, where motion was impeded, where there was no foothold, difficult roads, journeys without water, I traversed, and the unruly I overthrew; I bound as captives my enemies; the land I set in order and the people I made to prosper; both bad and good among the people I took under my care (?); silver, gold, costly precious stones, bronze, palm-wood, cedar-wood, all kinds of precious things, a rich abundance, the product of the mountains, the wealth of the seas, a heavy gift, a splendid present, to my city Babylon I brought into his presence, and I undertook restorations in Esagila, the palace of his lordship.

E-kua, the shrine of the lord of the gods, Marduk, I made to glisten like the sun; its walls (?), with massive gold like imtu-stone, with ugnu-stone and alabaster (?)—the abode of the house—I decorated. The gate Hili-shud, the gate of splendour, and the gate of Ezida and Esagila I made as brilliant as the sun. The brilliant abode, the seat of the arbiters of fate, which is the place of congregation, the shrine of the Fates, where, on Zagmuku, the beginning of the year, on the eighth and the eleventh day, the king, the god of heaven and earth, the lord of heaven, takes up his residence, where the gods of heaven and earth reverently pay obedience and stand bowed down before him; a fate of a far-distant day, as the fate of my life, they determine therein: that shrine, the shrine of royalty, the shrine of lordly power, belonging to the leader of the gods, the Prince Marduk, which a former king had constructed with silver, I decorated with shining gold and brilliant ornaments. The vessels of the Temple of Esagila, with massive gold, Ma-kua (the ship of peace) with bright metals and precious stones I adorned like the stars of the heavens. The temples of Babylon I rebuilt and restored. As for E-temen-an-ki (house of the foundation of heaven and earth) with burned brick and bright ugnu-stone I raised on high its turrets. To the rebuilding of Esagila my heart incited me; I held it constantly in mind. I selected the best of my cedar trees, which I had brought from Mount Lebanon, the snow-capped forest, for the roofing of E-kua, the shrine of his lordship, and I decorated with brilliant gold the inner sides of the mighty cedar trunks, used in the roofing of E-kua. I adorned the under side of the roof of cedar with gold and precious stones. Concerning the rebuilding of Esagila I prayed every morning to the king of the god, the lord of lords.

Borsippa, the city of his abode, I beautified. Ezida, the eternal house, in the midst thereof I built. With silver, gold, precious stones, bronze, palm-wood, and cedar-wood I completed its construction. The cedar-wood of the roof of the shrines of Nabu I decorated with gold. The cedar-wood of the roof of the gate of Nana I decorated with shining silver. The wild-bulls and the doors of the gate of the shrine, the lintels, the bars, the bolt (?), and the lock I adorned with bright metal; and the cedar-wood of the roof, its eaves (?), I adorned with silver. The path to the shrine and the way to the temple were inclosed with esh-maru-metal; the rooms of the shrines in its midst were silver-work; the wild-bulls and the doors of the gates I made to shine brightly with za-ha-li-e metal. I adorned the temple with ornaments, I filled it with splendour for the astonished gaze (of all people). The shrines of Borsippa I rebuilt and restored. As for E-ur-VII-an-ki (the house of the seven spheres of heaven and earth) with burned brick and bright ugnu-stone I raised on high its turrets. The ship (ark) of the river Gan-ul, the conveyance of his highness, the ship of the procession of Zagmuku—a festival of Babylon—its hull and its inner compartments I decorated with rows of marble and (precious) stones.

E-sigisshe-sigisshe, the exalted festival-place of the lord of the gods Marduk, the promoter of merriment and rejoicing among the Igigi and the Anunnaki, I constructed mountain-high with bitumen and burned brick on the walls of Babylon. E-mah, the Temple of the Lady of the Mountain, in the heart of Babylon, for the lofty goddess, the mother who bore me, I built in Babylon.

11. Nebuchadnezzar II of Babylon: The East India House Inscription

For Nabu, the exalted messenger, with bitumen and burned brick I constructed in Babylon. For Sin, who looks with favour upon my forces, E-gish-shir-gal, I built in Babylon. For Shamash, the exalted judge * * * E-di-tar-kalama, his temple, I built very high with bitumen and burned brick in Babylon. For Ramman, who establishes abundance in my land, E-nam-hi, his temple, I built in Babylon. For Gula, who spares and protects my life, E-sa-be and E-har-sag-el-la, her temples, I built artistically with bitumen and burned brick in Babylon. For Nin-lil-an-na (the lady of heaven), the lady who loves me, E-dur(?)-garza, her temple, I built very high at the side of the wall of Babylon. For Tur-e, who breaks in pieces the weapons of my enemies, his temple I built in Borsippa. For Gula, the lady who makes me of good cheer, E-gula, E-ti-la, and E-zi-ba-ti-la, her three shrines, I built in Borsippa. For Sin, who burdens himself with my welfare, E-dim-an-na, his temple, I built with brilliancy on the wall round about Ezida.

Imgur-Bel and Nimitti-Bel, the large walls of Babylon which Nabopolassar, King of Babylon, the father, my begetter, had made, but had not completed their construction—their moat he had dug, and by means of two strong walls with bitumen and burned brick he had strengthened their banks; a wall along the Arahtu canal he had made, and with the dike of burned brick on the other side of the Euphrates he had joined it, but had not completed the rest. From Du-azag-ki-nam-tar-tar-re-e-ne, the shrine of Fates, as far as A-ibur-shabu(m), the street of Babylon, in front of the Gate of the Lady, I constructed a way with brick and tur-mi-na-tur-da stone as a procession street for the great lord Marduk. As for me, his first-born son, the beloved of his heart, Imgur-Bel and Nimitti-Bel, the great walls of Babylon, I completed. The sides of the wall of its moat, two strong walls, with bitumen and burned brick I built, and to the wall which my father had strengthened I joined it, and I surrounded the city for its protection with a wall of burned brick toward the east, and I constructed a wall about Babylon. A-ibur-shabu(m), the street of Babylon, I filled in with a high terrace as a procession street for the great lord Marduk, and partly with brick and tur-mi-na-tur-da stone, partly with brick and stone from the mountain, A-ibur-shabu, from Bab-Ella (the shining gate) as far as Nana-sakipat-tebisha, I macadamized for a procession street of his divinity; I joined it to what my father had built, and I constructed the boulevard Nana-sakipat-tebisha.

The entrances of the city gates on both sides of Imgur-Bel and Nimitti-Bel, on account of the filling in of the street of Babylon, had become too low, and I tore down these gates and at the water's edge I firmly laid their foundation with bitumen and burned brick, and with burned brick and brilliant ugnu-stone, out of which the wild-bulls and the serpents are constructed, skilfully I built them. I laid in rows mighty cedar trees for their roof. I set in place in their gates the cedar doors, with a sheathing of copper, the thresholds and the hinges, made of bronze. I stationed at their thresholds strong wild-bulls of bronze and serpents standing erect. I filled with splendour these city gates for the astonished gaze (of all people). That the shaft of battle might not reach Imgur-Bel, the wall of Babylon—what no former king had done—for four thousand land cubits on the sides of Babylon, afar off, to make approach impossible, I surrounded Babylon with a large wall toward the east. I dug its moat and strengthened its bank with bitumen and burned brick, and built a strong wall on its bank mountain-high. Its wide city gates I put in position, and the doors of cedar, with a sheathing of copper, I set in place. That a terrible enemy might not push forward to the sides of Babylon, I surrounded the land with large bodies of water, like the volume of the sea; and that the plying (of ships) as on the raging sea or the briny gulf might not bring about a breach in their banks, I threw up against them a levee of mud, and surrounded them with a wall of burned brick. I skilfully strengthened the watch-tower, and made the city Babylon a fortification. Tabi-suburshu, the wall of Borsippa, I built anew; I dug its moat, and strengthened its bank with bitumen and burned brick.

Nebuchadrezzar, King of Babylon, whom Marduk, the great lord, called to look after the welfare of his city Babylon, am I. Esagila and Ezida I made as brilliant as the sun. The shrines of the great gods I made to shine like the day. In former times, in the days of old, down to the reign of Nabopolassar, King of Babylon, the father, my begetter, the numerous kings, my predecessors, whose names the god had called to sovereignty, in their well-beloved cities which they loved, had built palaces, taken up their residences, collected their possessions therein, gathered together their property, and on the festival of Zag-muku, the procession of the lord of the gods, Marduk, had entered Babylon. From the time that Marduk created me to sovereignty, and Nabu, his eternal son, gave me rule over his subjects, like my precious soul I loved their shining presence. With the exception of Babylon and Borsippa I did not adorn a single city. In Babylon, my well-beloved city, which I love, the palace, a house for the astonished gaze of the people, a meeting-place for the land, a brilliant chamber, a royal residence, in Babylon, which is in

Babylonia, from Imgur-Bel as far as Libil-hegalla, the eastern canal, from the bank of the Euphrates as far as A-ibur-shabu—which Nabopolassar, King of Babylon, the father, my begetter, with brick had constructed, and wherein he had taken up his residence—on account of the waters of a flood its foundation had become weak, and on account of the terracing of the street of Babylon, the gates of this palace had become too low. Its wall, made of brick, I tore down, and I sought out its platform foundation, and the bottom of the water I reached. Its foundation at the water's edge I firmly laid, and with bitumen and burned brick I raised it mountain-high. I laid in rows mighty cedar trees for its roof. I set in place in its gates the cedar doors, with a sheathing of copper, the thresholds and the hinges, made of bronze. I gathered together therein silver, gold, precious stones, all kinds of precious and valuable things, possessions, property, the insignia of my exalted position. I collected within it the results of my splendid bravery, a royal treasure. Because my heart did not love the abode of my royalty in another city, in no human habitation did I build a residence for my lordship. Property, the insignia of royalty, I did not establish anywhere else. In Babylon a chamber for my dwelling-place, as befits royalty, was not to be found. Because the fear of Marduk, my lord, was in my heart, in Babylon, his treasure city, in order to enlarge my royal residence, his street I did not change, his shrine I did not impair, his canal I did not dam up, his chamber I kept constantly (?) in mind.

That the shaft of battle might not reach Imgur-Bel, the wall of Babylon, at a distance of four hundred and ninety land cubits on the sides of Nimitti-Bel, the outer wall of Babylon, for the protection of the two large walls, with bitumen and burned brick I built a wall mountain-high, and between them I built a structure of burned brick, and I built very high in its tower a large chamber with bitumen and burned brick for my royal dwelling-place, and joined it to my father's palace, and in a prosperous month, on a favourable day, I firmly laid its foundation in the bowels of the earth, and I raised high its turrets like a mountain. On the fifteenth day I brought to completion its construction, and I beautified the dwelling of my lordship. Mighty cedar trees from the snow-capped mountains, ashuhu trees with broad trunks, and cypress trees, (with) costly stones, I laid in rows for its roofing. Doors of palm-wood, of cedar, and of cypress, of ushu and ivory, inlaid with silver and gold, and with a sheathing of copper, the thresholds and hinges, made of bronze, I set in place in its gates. I surrounded its turrets with a cornice of ugnu-stone and threw around it mountain-high a strong wall with bitumen and burned brick. On the sides of the wall of Babylon I built a large wall out of large blocks of stone, such as are found on the lofty mountains, and like a mountain I raised on high its battlements. I built that house for the astonished gaze (of all people) and for the spectacle of the whole world I filled it with splendor. All kinds of abundance, the fear of the brilliancy of my royalty, were round about its sides, and that the wicked and the perverse might not enter it, and that I might keep afar off from the sides of the wall of Babylon the battle shaft of the terrible enemy, I fortified the city Babylon mountain-high. To Marduk, my lord, I made supplication, I lifted up my hands:

> O Marduk, lord, leader of the gods,
> Powerful prince,
> Thou hast created me, and
> With sovereignty over all men
> Thou hast intrusted me.
> Like my precious soul
> I love thy exalted presence.
> With the exception of thy city Babylon
> In no human habitation
> Have I adorned a city.
> As I love
> The fear of thy divinity,
> As I follow in the path of thy lordship,
> Look with favour upon the lifting up of my hands,
> Give ear to my prayers.
> Truly I am the king, the restorer,
> Who makes cheerful thy heart,
> The clever governor,

The restorer of all thy cities.
By thy command,
O merciful Marduk,
The temple which I have built,
May it endure for all time, and
May I be satisfied with its splendour!
In its midst
May I attain an old age,
May I be sated with offspring!
Of the kings of the four quarters of the world,
Of all mankind,
Their heavy tribute
May I receive therein!
From the horizon of the heaven to the zenith,
Toward the east,
May I have no enemies,
May I possess no foes,
May my descendants live therein
Forever, and
Rule over the Black-headed races!

Source: Robert Francis Harper, ed., *Assyrian and Babylonian Literature: Selected Translations* (New York: Appleton, 1901), 134–143.

12. The Cylinder of Cyrus II the Great (ca. 538 BCE)

Introduction

Babylon's ascendancy in the sixth century BCE was short-lived and soon fell victim to the rising power of the Persian Achaemenid Empire. Claiming that Nabonidus, who in 556 BCE seized power in Babylon through a coup, had neglected the worship of Marduk in favor of the moon god, in 539 BCE Cyrus the Great of Persia marched against Babylonian territories, defeating the main Babylonian army at the Battle of Opis. Thanks to the unpopularity of Nabonidus, Cyrus claimed—though other accounts suggest that a siege was necessary or that Babylon was taken by surprise—that the population welcomed him into the city. At Cyrus's behest an account of his bloodless conquest was written on a cylinder, which was buried in the foundations of Babylon as an attestation of the purported new era. Cyrus presented his takeover of Babylon as a restoration of legitimate rule and promised to give "proper attention to the needs of Babylon and its cities."

Document

* * * his troops (?)

* * * quarters (of the world).

* * * a weakling was appointed to the government of his land

* * * a similar one he appointed over them,

like Esagila he made * * * to Ur and the rest of the cities,

a command unbefitting them * * * daily he planned and, in enmity, he allowed the regular offering to cease; he appointed * * * he established within the city. As for the worship of Marduk, king of the gods, who destroyed (?) * * *

he showed hostility toward his city daily * * * his (people), he brought all of them to ruin through servitude without rest.

The lord of the gods became furious with anger at their complaints, and [abandoned] their territory. The gods, who dwelt among them, left their abodes,

in anger that he had brought (strange deities) into Babylon. Marduk in * * * turned (?) to all the habitations whose sites had been ruined,

and the people of Sumer and Akkad, who resembled corpses * * * he granted mercy. He searched through all lands, he saw him,

and he sought the righteous prince, after his own heart, whom he took by the hand. Cyrus, King of An-shan, he called by name; to sovereignty over the whole world he appointed him.

The country of Qutu, all the Umman-manda, he made submissive to him. As for the Black-headed People, whom he (Marduk) caused his (Cyrus') hands to conquer,

in justice and right he cared for them. Marduk, the great lord, guardian of his people, looked with joy on his pious works and upright heart;

he commanded him to go to his city Babylon, and he caused him to take the road to Babylon, going by his side as a friend and companion.

His numerous troops, the number of which, like the waters of a river, can not be known, in full armour, marched at his side.

Without skirmish or battle he permitted him to enter Babylon. He spared his city Babylon in (its) calamity. Nobonidus, the king, who did not reverence him, he delivered into his hand.

All the people of Babylon, all Sumer and Akkad, nobles and governors, prostrated themselves before him, kissed his feet, rejoiced at his sovereignty, showed happiness in their faces.

The lord, who by his power brings the dead to life, who with (his) care and protection benefits all men—they gladly did him homage, they heeded his command.

I am Cyrus, king of the world, the great king, the powerful king, King of Babylon, King of Sumer and Akkad, king of the four quarters (of the world),

son of Cambyses, the great king, King of Anshan; grandson of Cyrus, the great king, King of Anshan; great-grandson of Tiespis, the great king, King of Anshan,

of ancient seed-royal, whose reign Bel and Nabu love, whose sovereignty they regard necessary to their happiness. When I made my gracious entrance into Babylon,

with joy and rejoicing I took up my lordly residence in the royal palace. Marduk, the great lord, [granted] me favour among the Babylonians, and I gave daily care to his worship.

I gave proper attention to the needs of Babylon and its cities. The Babylonians * * * as much as they desired * * * the servitude, which was not honourable, was removed (?) from them.

I quieted their sighing (and) soothed their sorrow. Marduk, the great lord, rejoiced over my [pious] deeds, and he graciously blessed me, Cyrus, the king who worships him, and Cambyses, my own son, and all my troops,

while we, in his presence, and with sincerity, gladly lauded his exalted [divinity]. All the kings dwelling in royal halls,

of all the quarters (of the world), from the Upper to the Lower Sea, dwelling * * * all the kings of the west country, who dwell in tents,

brought me their heavy taxes, and in Babylon kissed my feet. From * * * as far as Asshur and Shushan,

Agane, Eshnunak, Zamban, Meturnu, Durilu as far as the border of the land of Quti, the cities on the other side of the Tigris, whose sites were of ancient foundation—

the gods, who dwelt in them, I restored to their places, and I gave them a habitation for all time. I collected all their people and restored (them) to their dwelling-places

and the gods of Sumer and Akkad, whom Nabonidus, to the anger of the lord of the gods, had brought into Babylon, by the command of Marduk, the great lord, peacefully

in their own shrines I made them dwell, in habitations giving joy to their hearts. May all the gods whom I brought into their own cities,

daily before Bel and Nabu pray that I may have a long life, may they speak a gracious word for me, and may they say to Marduk, my lord: "Cyrus, the king who worships thee, and Cambyses his son

* * * their * * *." I permitted all the lands to dwell in quiet.

[Remainder of inscription too badly mutilated to translate.]

Source: Robert Francis Harper, ed., *Assyrian and Babylonian Literature: Selected Translations* (New York: Appleton, 1901), 171–174.

13. Darius the Great (r. ca. 522–486 BCE): The Large Inscription from Behistun

Introduction

The Persian emperor Darius I the Great came from a relatively minor branch of the Achaemenid royal family. He had to fight his way to power, emerging the victor in a civil war within Persia and then in one year (521 BCE) brutally suppressing no fewer than 19 rebellions against his rule. Several of the rebel leaders, particularly those who claimed to be the descendants of legitimate monarchs whom earlier Persian rulers had conquered, were captured and then crucified.

Darius had a lengthy account of these events carved on the limestone cliffs of Behistun in Kermanshah Province in present-day Iran overlooking the main highway connecting Babylon, the Babylonian capital, to Ecbatana, the capital of Media. Written in Old Persian, Elamite, and Babylonian cuneiform scripts, the text covered an area 15 meters high and 25 meters wide inscribed 100 meters above the ground. It was illustrated with bas-reliefs depicting the victorious Darius and his prostrate and conquered enemies. Both the sculpture and the words were designed to emphasize Darius's legitimacy as emperor and the harsh and deliberate terror that those who rebelled against his rule could expect. The inscription, part of a larger complex containing Parthian temples and bas-reliefs and a massive statue of Hercules, was declared a UNESCO World Heritage site in 2006.

Document

[I am Darius, the great king, king of kings, king of countries,] the Achaemenian, king of all men, a Persian, the King of Persia.

Thus speaks Darius the king: My father is Hystaspes, the father of Hystaspes [is Arsamnes, the father of Arsamnes is] Ariaramnes, the father of Ariaramnes is Shishpish (Tëispes), the father of Shishpish is Achaemenes.

Thus speaks Darius the king: For this reason [we are called Achaemenians, from of old] we [have been rested,] from of old (?) (members) of our family have been kings.

Thus speaks Darius the king: Eight members of my family preceding me have ruled as kings; [I am the ninth; in two lines we are nine kings.]

[Thus] speaks [Darius the king:] Under the protection of Ahura-mazda I am king; Ahura-mazda gave me the sovereignty.

Thus speaks Darius the king: These [are the countries which came to me; by the will of Ahura-mazda] I became their king: Persia, Elam, Babylonia, Assyria, Arabia, Miçir (Egypt), the islands in the gulf, Sparda, Ionia, [Media, Armenia, Cappadocia, Parthia, Drangiana,] Aremu (Aria), Humarizmu (Chorasia), Bactria, Sogdiana, Paruparaësana, Nammiri, Satagu, [Arachosia, Maka—in all twenty-three countries.]

[Thus speaks Darius the king:] These are the countries which obey me, under the protection of Ahura-mazda; they became subject to me, [they brought me] tribute, they did that [which I commanded them by night or day.]

Thus speaks Darius the king: The prudent man within these lands [I have richly rewarded; the hostile I have severely punished;] under the protection of Ahura-mazda I have established my ordinances as laws in the midst of these countries; [they have done as they were commanded] by me.

Thus speaks [Darius the king:] Ahura-mazda gave me my sovereignty, Ahura-mazda was my strong support until [I attained] this sovereignty; [by the will of Ahura-mazda this kingdom] is subject to me.

Thus speaks Darius the king: This is what I have done under the protection of Ahura-mazda since I have become king. [One of our family, Cambyses by name, the son of Cyrus] was king here before (me). The brother of this Cambyses was Bardiya (Smerdis); (they had) one father and one mother. [Now, Cambyses slew this Bardiya; when] Cambyses slew Bardiya, it was not [known] to the people that Bardiya had been slain. Later Cambyses [went] to Egypt; [when Cambyses] had gone [to] Egypt, then the people became hostile in heart, and treachery became rife in the provinces, in Persia, and in Media, [and also in the other provinces.]

[Thus speaks Darius the king: There was a certain man, a Magian, Gaumata by name, who raised a rebellion] from Pishihumadu, where is a mountain, Arakatri by name; from this place, on the fourteenth day of the month of Adar, he [raised a rebellion; he deceived the people (saying), "I am Bardiya, the son of Cyrus, the brother of] Cambyses"; afterward the whole people became hostile to Cambyses and went over to him—Persia and Media [as well as the other provinces; he seized the sovereignty. It was the ninth day of the month of Garmapada when] he seized [the sovereignty]. Thereafter Cambyses committed suicide.

Thus speaks Darius the king: [This sovereignty, which Gaumata the Magian had wrenched from Cambyses,] this (sovereignty) had belonged to our family from of old; afterward this Gaumata the Magian [wrenched] the sovereignty from [Cambyses—both Persia and Media, as well as the other provinces; he acted in accord with his own will,] he became king.

Thus speaks Darius the king: There was no one, [neither Persian nor Median, nor any of our family who] could take the sovereignty away from this Gaumata the Magian. The people feared him greatly; [he would kill many who had known the former Bardiya; for this reason he would kill the people, "that"] they may not discover (?) that I am not Bardiya, the son of Cyrus." No one ventured to say anything against [Gaumata the Magian until I came.] Afterward I prayed to Ahura-mazda; Ahura-mazda was my strong support; under the protection of Ahura-mazda [on the tenth day of the month Bagayadish, I with a few men slew] this [Gaumata] the Magian and the men (of note) who were with him. In the city Sihiubati, in a district Nisa by name which is in Media, [I slew him; I took the sovereignty away from him. By the will of Ahura-mazda I became king.] Ahura-mazda gave me the sovereignty.

Thus speaks Darius the king: The sovereignty which [had been taken] away [from our family I restored again;] I established [it in its original place,] I exercised it. [I restored] the temples of the gods which this Gaumata the Magian had destroyed, (and I) [restored sustenance for the people, the flocks, and the habitation of houses (?), which] this Gaumata the Magian had taken away from them; I restored the people to their place, Persia, Media, [and the other provinces. As (it was) formerly, I replaced what had been taken away]; under the protection of Ahura-mazda, I did this. I exercised care until I [reinstated] our house in its place; as (it was) formerly, when this Gaumata the Magian had not removed our house, [I exercised care (to make it)] under the protection of Ahura-mazda.

[Thus speaks] Darius [the king: This is what I did after I had become king.]

Thus speaks Darius the king: After I had gone and slain Gaumata the Magian, there was a man [Atrina (Ashina) by name, the son of Upadarma, who] rose up [in Susa] and spoke as follows: "I am the King of Elam"; thereupon the Elamites became hostile to me [and went over to that Atrina; he became king in Susa. And a man, a Babylonian,] Nidintu-Bel by name, the son of Aniri, rose up in Babylon, deceiving the people as follows: "I am [Nebuchadrezzar, the son of Nabonidus"; thereupon the entire Babylonian people] went over [to that Nidintu-Bel;] Babylon revolted, he seized the sovereignty of Babylon.

Thus speaks Darius the king: [Thereupon I sent to Susa, that Atrina was brought bound to me] and I slew him.

Thus speaks Darius the king: Afterward I marched to Babylon against [that Nidintu-Bel who called himself Nebuchadrezzar. The host] of Nidintu-Bel had taken up a position on ships (?) and occupied (?) the banks (?) of the Tigris. [Thereupon I divided my army into two parts (?); I placed the one on camels, the other I supplied with horses.] Ahura-mazda was my strong support, under the protection of Ahura-mazda we crossed the Tigris. I smote [the army of Nidintu-Bel;] on the twenty-sixth of Kislev we fought the battle.

[Thus] speaks [Darius the king:] Thereupon I marched to Babylon; before Babylon was reached there was a city by the name of Zazanu on the banks of the Euphrates; [hither that Nidintu-Bel who said, "I am Nebuchadrezzar," [had come forth against me with his host to offer battle]; thereupon we joined battle; Ahura-mazda was my strong support, under the protection of Ahura-mazda (I smote) the host of Nidintu-Bel; [the enemy was driven into the water, the water bore him away. On the second] day [of the month of Anamaka] we fought the battle.

Thus speaks Darius the king: Thereupon this Nidintu-Bel, accompanied by a few soldiers upon (horses) [went to Babylon. Afterward] I (too) went [to Babylon;] under the protection of Ahura-mazda I took Babylon and seized Nidintu-Bel; then I [slew this Nidintu-Bel] in Babylon.

[Thus speaks] Darius [the king: While] I was [in Babylon], these are the provinces which revolted against me: Persia, Elam, Media, Assyria, [Egypt, Parthia, Margiana,] Satagu, Nammiri.

[Thus speaks Darius the king: There was a man], Martiya by name, the son of Shinshahrish; he lived in the city Kugunaka in Persia; he rose up in Elam [and he spoke to the people as follows: "I am] Imanisi, King [of Elam."]

[Thus speaks Darius the king: At that time I was in friendly relations with Elam; the Elamites feared me; they seized] that Martiya, who was chief over them, and of their own accord they slew him.

[Thus speaks] Darius the king: [A man,] Parumartish (Fravartish) [by name, a Median, rose up in Media; he spoke to the people] as follows: "I am Hashatriti, of the seed of Umaku-Ishtar"; thereupon the people of Media, as many as there were in the palace, [rebelled] against me [and went over to the Fravartish; he became king in] Media.

[Thus speaks Darius the king: The Persian and Median army which was with me was small;] thereupon I sent the army to Media; (my) servant, Umidarna (Vidarna) by name, a Persian, [I placed at its head. I spoke to him as follows: "Go smite that Median army which does not call itself mine." Thereupon] Umidarna marched to Media with the army. As he approached a city, Maru by name, which is in Media, [he joined battle with the Medes. (He) who was chief among the Medes did not maintain (his position). Ahura-mazda bore me aid;] under the protection of Ahura-mazda my army smote these rebels. On the twenty-seventh day of the month of Tebet they engaged in battle; [there is a place, Kampada by name,] which is in Media; here they waited for me until I came to Media.

[Thus speaks Darius the king: There was an Armenian, Dadarshish by name, a servant of mine; I sent him to Armenia; I spoke to him as follows: "Go,] smite the rebellious army which does not obey me"; [thereupon Dadarshish went forth. When he arrived in Armenia the rebels assembled themselves, and marched against Dadarshish] to give battle. Thereupon Dadarshish joined battle with them in a city called Zuzu in Armenia. [Ahura-mazda bore me aid; by the will of Ahura-mazda my army utterly smote that rebellious army. On the eighth day of the month of Thuravurahara the battle was fought.]

[Thus speaks Darius the king: A second time] the rebels assembled themselves and marched against Dadarshish to give battle. Thereupon they joined battle [at a stronghold by the name of Tigra in Armenia. Ahura-mazda bore me aid; by the will of Ahura-mazda my army utterly smote that rebellious army. On the eighteenth day of the month of Thuravahara the] battle [was fought.] They killed five hundred and forty-six of them, and took five hundred and twenty alive. Later, for a third time, the rebels [assembled themselves and marched against Dadarshish to give battle; at a stronghold by the name of Uh-yama in Armenia, they joined battle. Ahura-mazda bore me aid;] under the protection of Ahura-mazda my army smote the rebels. On the ninth day of the month Tishrit they fought the battle. [After this Dadarshish waited in(active?) for me until I came to Media.]

Thus speaks Darius the king: My servant, Umisi (Vaumisa) by name, a Persian, (I sent) to Armenia. [I spoke to him as follows: "Go, smite the army which is rebellious and does not call itself mine." Thereupon Vaumisa went, and when he came to Armenia] the rebels assembled themselves and marched against Umisi to give battle; afterward they engaged in battle [in a place by the name of Izitush in Assyria. Ahura-mazda bore me aid; by the will of Ahura-mazda my army utterly smote that rebellious army. On the fifteenth day of the month of Anamaka the battle was fought.] They killed two thousand and twenty-four of them. For a second time, the rebels assembled and marched against Umisi to give battle; [at a place Autiyara by name, in Armenia, they fought the battle. Ahura-mazda bore me aid; by the will of Ahura-mazda my army] smote the rebels. On the thirtieth day of the month of Aru they engaged in battle. They killed two thousand and forty-five of them, and took twenty-five hundred and fifty-nine alive. [After this Vaumisa waited in Armenia for me until I came to Media.]

[Thus speaks Darius the king: Thereupon I went away from Babylon and (proceeded)] toward Media. As I approached Media (there was) a city, Kundur by name, in Media; thither [marched that Fravartish, who called himself king in Media, against me to give battle. Thereupon we fought a battle.] Ahura-mazda was my strong support; under the protection of Ahura-mazda, [I smote] the army of Parumartish. [On the twenty-sixth day of the month of Adukani we fought the battle.]

[Thus speaks Darius the king: Thereafter that Fravartish] departed [thence with] a few horsemen and came to a district by the name of Raga in Media. Thereupon [I sent] an army [against them. Fravartish was seized and brought to me. I cut off his nose (and) ears, and I cut out his tongue, and I put out his eyes. At court he was kept in chains;] all the people saw him. Later I crucified him in Ecbatana; [and the men who were his most prominent supporters I impaled in prison in Ecbatana.]

[Thus speaks Darius the king: A man, Citrantakhma by name, a Sagartian, rebelled against me,] and spoke to the people as follows: "I am a king of the seed of Umaku-Ishtar." Thereupon I (sent forth) a Median army; [Takh-maspada, my servant, I made their chief. I spoke to them as follows: "Go, smite the army which has rebelled and does not call itself mine." Thereupon Takhmaspada departed with the army and] he engaged [in battle] with Citrantakhma. Ahura-mazda was my strong support; under the protection of Ahura-mazda, [my army utterly smote the rebellious army, and they seized Citrantakhma and brought him to me. Then I cut off his nose and ears and put out his eyes. He was kept in chains at my court;] all the people saw him. Afterward I crucified him in Arbela. The totality of the slain and the living * * *

[Thus speaks Darius the king: This is what was done by me in Media.]

[Thus speaks Darius the king: Parthia and Hyrcania rebelled, and declared themselves (supporters) of] Parumartish * * * Hystaspes my father lived in Parthia, and the people forsook him [in a body?]. Thereupon Hystaspes marched away with the army which (remained) true. At a place by the name of Vispauvatish, in Parthia, they fought the battle]. Ahura-mazda was my strong support; under the protection of Ahura-mazda, Hystaspes smote these rebels. On the twenty-second day [of the month of Viyakhna the battle was fought.]

[Thus speaks Darius the king: Thereupon I sent a Persian army from Raga to Hystaspes;] when the army had come to Hystaspes, Hystaspes (took) that army [and marched forth. At a place by the name of Patigrabana, in Parthia, he fought a battle with the rebels. Ahura-mazda bore me aid; by the will of Ahura-mazda, Hystaspes utterly smote that rebellious army. On the first day of the month Garmapada] they fought the battle. They killed sixty-five hundred and seventy of them, and took forty-one hundred and ninety-two alive.

[Thus speaks Darius the king: Thereupon the land became mine. This is what was done by me in Parthia.]

Thus speaks Darius the king: A province, Margu (Margiana) by name, rebelled against me. [They made] a man by the name of Parada (Frada) [a Margianian, their chief. Thereupon I sent my servant, a Persian, by the name of Dadarshish, satrap in Bactria, against that one. I spoke to him as follows: "Go, smite the army which does not call itself mine."] Thereupon Dadarshish marched forth with the army; they fought a battle with the Margians. [Ahura-mazda bore me aid; by the will of Ahura-mazda my army utterly smote that rebellious army. On the twenty-third day of the month of Atriyadiya the battle was fought.] [They killed] forty-two hundred and three of them, and took sixty-five hundred and seventy-two alive.

Thus [speaks] Darius the king: [Thereupon the land became mine. This is what was done by me in Bactria.]

[Thus speaks Darius the king: There was a man, Vahyazdata]; he dwelt [in a place by the name of Tarava, in a region] by the name of [Yautiya,] in Persia. He rose up in Persia and spoke to the people [as follows: "I am Bardiya, the son of Cyrus." Thereupon the Persian people who were in the palace broke allegiance (?); they rebelled against me and went over to that Vahyazdata; he became king in Persia.]

Thus speaks Darius the king: Thereupon I [sent forth] the Persian army [which was with me; I made a Persian, named Artavardiya, a servant of mine, their chief. The rest] of the Persian army marched with me to Media. Then Artavardiya [marched] with the army [to Persia. As he came to Persia there was a city by the name of Rakha in Persia; hither this Vahyazdata, who called himself Bardiya, had come with an army against Artavardiya to offer battle. Thereupon] they fought the battle. Ahura-mazda was my strong support; under the protection of Ahura-mazda [my army utterly smote that army of that Vahyazdata. On the twelfth day of the month of Thuravahara the battle was fought.]

[Thus speaks Darius the king: Thereupon] this Vahyazdata departed with a few horsemen for [Paishiyauvada. Thither he marched again with an army against Vahyazdata to offer battle. At a mountain, Paraga by name, they engaged in battle.] Ahura-mazda was my strong support; under the protection of Ahura-mazda my army smote the army of Vahyazdata. [On the sixth day of the month of Garmapada the battle was fought; and they seized that Vahyazdata and took the men who were his chief supporters.]

Thus speaks Darius the king: Thereafter I crucified this Vahyazdata and all the men who were with him; [in a city, Uvadaicaya by name, in] Persia, I did this. . . .

Thus speaks Darius the king: That which I [did came to pass solely through the grace of Ahura-mazda. Since I have been king I have fought nineteen battles; by the will of Ahura-mazda I smote them.]

Source: Robert Francis Harper, ed., *Assyrian and Babylonian Literature: Selected Translations* (New York: Appleton, 1901), 174–187.

14. Artemisia of Caria (r. 484–460 BCE), as Described by Polyaenus, in *Stratagems in War* (ca. 163 CE)

Introduction

The redoubtable Artemisia of Caria, an ally of Persian king Xerxes at the Battle of Salamis, won the respect of her male colleagues for the determination and resourcefulness she showed when fighting. She had no hesitation in hoisting false colors to fend off enemy attack. On more than one occasion, she turned on another vessel on her own side in order to make enemy ships believe that she was one of their allies. Her resilience won her the respect of the second-century CE Macedonian author and rhetorician Polyaenus. He listed her among no fewer than 46 accomplished women who displayed both courage and intelligence in tackling and confounding their enemies and turning the tables on them.

Document

Artemisia, in the naval battle at Salamis, found that the Persians were defeated, and she herself was near to falling into the hands of the Greeks. She ordered the Persian colours to be taken down, and the master of the ship to bear down upon, and attack a Persian vessel, that was passing by her. The Greeks, seeing this, supposed her to be one of their allies; they drew off and left her alone, directing their forces against other parts of the Persian fleet. Artemisia in the meantime sheered off, and escaped safely to Caria.

Artemisia, the daughter of Lygdamis, sank a ship of the Calyndian allies, which was commanded by Damasithymus. In acknowledgement of her gallantry, the king sent her a complete suit of Greek armour; and he presented the captain of the ship with a distaff and spindle.

Artemisia always chose a long ship, and carried on board with her Greek, as well as barbarian, colours. When she chased a Greek ship, she hoisted the barbarian colours; but when she was chased by a Greek ship, she hoisted the Greek colours; so that the enemy might mistake her for a Greek, and give up the pursuit. Artemisia planted soldiers in ambush near Latmus; and herself, with a numerous train of women, eunuchs and musicians, celebrated a sacrifice at the grove of the Mother of the Gods, which was about seven stades distant from the city. When the inhabitants of Latmus came out to see the magnificent procession, the soldiers entered the city and took possession of it. Thus did Artemisia, by flutes and cymbals, possess herself of what she had in vain endeavoured to obtain by force of arms.

Artemisia, queen of Caria, fought as an ally of Xerxes against the Greeks. At the famous battle of Salamis, the king acknowledged her to have excelled herself above all the officers in the fleet. And even in the heat of the action, observing the manner in which she distinguished herself, he exclaimed: "O Zeus, surely you have formed women out of man's materials, and men out of woman's."

Source: Polyaenus, *Stratagems of War*, translated by R. Shepherd (London: George Nicol, 1793), Book 8, chap. 53, http://www.attalus.org/translate/polyaenus8B.html#53.1.

15. Xenophon Describes the Battle of Aegospotami (405 BCE)

Introduction

The Athenian historian and professional soldier Xenophon took on the task of continuing Thucydides's *History of the Peloponnesian War*. Exiled to Sparta, Xenophon had particularly good access to eyewitness Spartan recollections and other sources on the course of the war and subsequent events. Ultimately, Xenophon carried his history up to 359 BCE. He gave a graphic description of the Battle of Aegospotami, the naval engagement that ensured Athenian defeat and Spartan domination over Greece for the next 30 years. Lysander, the Spartan admiral, deliberately refused to do battle with the Athenian fleet for several days, eventually taking their ships by surprise.

Document

Now Lysander, leaving Rhodes, and coasting along Ionia, made his way to the Hellespont, having an eye to the passage of vessels through the Straits, and, in a more hostile sense, on the cities which had revolted from Sparta. The Athenians also set sail from Chios, but stood out to open sea, since the seaboard of Asia was hostile to them. Lysander was again on the move; leaving Abydos, he passed up channel to Lampsacus, which town was allied with Athens; the men of Abydos and the rest of the troops advancing by land, under the command of the Lacedaemonian Thorax.

They then attacked and took by storm the town, which was wealthy, and with its stores of wine and wheat and other commodities was pillaged by the soldiery. All free-born persons, however, were without exception released by Lysander.

And now the Athenian fleet, following close on his heels, came to moorings at Elaeus, in the Chersonesus, one hundred and eighty sail in all. It was not until they had reached this place, and were getting their early meal, that the news of what had happened at Lampsacus reached them.

Then they instantly set sail again to Sestos, and, having halted long enough merely to take in stores, sailed on further to Aegospotami, a point facing Lampsacus, where the Hellespont is not quite two miles broad. Here they took their evening meal.

The night following, or rather early next morning, with the first streak of dawn, Lysander gave the signal for the men to take their breakfasts and get on board their vessels; and so, having got all ready for a naval engagement, with his ports closed and movable bulwarks attached, he issued the order that no one was to stir from his post or put out to sea.

As the sun rose the Athenians drew up their vessels facing the harbour, in line of battle ready for action; but Lysander declining to come out to meet them, as the day advanced they retired again to Aegospotami.

Then Lysander ordered the swiftest of his ships to follow the Athenians, and as soon as the crews had disembarked, to watch what they did, sail back, and report to him. Until these look-outs returned he would permit no disembarkation from his ships. This performance he repeated for four successive days, and each day the Athenians put out to sea and challenged an engagement.

But now Alcibiades, from one of his fortresses, could espy the position of his fellow-countrymen, moored on an open beach beyond reach of any city, and forced to send for supplies to Sestos, which was nearly two miles distant, while their enemies were safely lodged in a harbour, with a city adjoining, and everything within reach. The situation did not please him, and he advised them to shift their anchorage to Sestos, where they would have the advantage of a harbour and a city. "Once there," he concluded, "you can engage the enemy whenever it suits you."

But the generals, and more particularly Tydeus and Menander, bade him go about his business. "We are generals now—not you," they said; and so he went away.

And now for five days in succession the Athenians had sailed out to offer battle, and for the fifth time retired, followed by the same swift sailors of the enemy. But this time Lysander's orders to the vessels so sent in pursuit were, that as soon as they saw the enemy's crew fairly disembarked and dispersed along the shores of the Chersonesus (a practice, it should be mentioned, which had grown upon them from day to day owing to the distance at which eatables had to be purchased, and out of sheer contempt, no doubt, of Lysander, who refused to accept battle), they were to begin their return voyage, and when in mid-channel to hoist a shield. The orders were punctually carried out, and Lysander at once signalled to his whole squadron to put across with all speed, while Thorax, with the land forces, was to march parallel with the fleet along the coast. Aware of the enemy's fleet, which he could see bearing down upon him, Conon had only time to signal to the crews to join their ships and rally to the rescue with all their might. But the men were scattered far and wide, and some of the vessels had only two out of their three banks of rowers, some only a single one, while others again were completely empty. Conon's own ship, with seven others in attendance on him and the "Paralus," put out to sea, a little cluster of nine vessels, with their full complement of men; but every one of the remaining one hundred and seventy-one vessels were captured by Lysander on the beach. As to the men themselves, the large majority of them were easily made prisoners on shore, a few only escaping to the small fortresses of the neighbourhood.

Meanwhile Conon and his nine vessels made good their escape. For himself, knowing that the fortune of Athens was ruined, he put into Abarnis, the promontory of Lampsacus, and there picked up the great sails of Lysander's ships, and then with eight ships set sail himself to seek refuge with Evagoras in Cyprus, while the "Paralus" started for Athens with tidings of what had taken place.

Source: Xenophon, *Hellenica,* translated by H. G. Dakyns (London: Macmillan, 1897), Book 2, chap. 1.

16. Arrian (ca. 101–200 CE) on the Character of Alexander the Great (r. 336–323 BCE)

Introduction

The Greek historian Arrian, writing in the second century CE, produced a lengthy account of the life of Alexander the Great based on primary sources from contemporary associates of the Macedonian king. At the end of this document Arrian offered a reasonably balanced assessment of the character of Alexander, who died unexpectedly before reaching the age of 33. According to Arrian, Alexander was one of the few great kings and heroes known to history who on occasion showed remorse for cruel acts. Given Alexander's achievements, Arrian thought it not unreasonable that he should seek to ascribe divine parentage to himself; indeed, he thought it quite likely that supernatural intervention had played a role in mandating the existence of Alexander. The person and career of Alexander undoubtedly caught the imagination of both his contemporaries and later generations to a degree unsurpassed by almost any other historical figure. Arrian's final words make it clear that he himself was not exempt from the fascination that the figure and accomplishments of the young Macedonian king exerted over posterity. His accomplishments, especially his destruction of the Persian Empire, undoubtedly reshaped the long-term future of the Middle East.

Document

Character of Alexander

Alexander died in the hundred and fourteenth Olympiad, in the archonship of Hegesias at Athens. According to the statement of Aristobulus, he lived thirty-two years, and had reached the eighth month of his thirty-third year. He had reigned twelve years and these eight months. He was very handsome in person, and much devoted to exertion, very active in mind, very heroic in courage, very tenacious of honour, exceedingly fond of incurring danger, and strictly observant of his duty to the gods. In regard to the pleasures of the body, he had perfect self-control; and of those of the mind, praise was the only one of which he was insatiable. He was very clever in recognising what was necessary to be done, even when it was still a matter unnoticed by others; and very successful in conjecturing from the observation of facts what was likely to occur. In marshalling, arming, and ruling an army, he was exceedingly skilful; and very renowned for rousing the courage of his soldiers, filling them with hopes of success, and dispelling their fear in the midst of danger by his own freedom from fear. Therefore even what he had to do in secret he did with the greatest boldness. He was also very clever in getting the start of his enemies, and snatching from them their advantages by secretly forestalling them, before any one even feared what was about to happen. He was likewise very steadfast in keeping the agreements and settlements which he made, as well as very secure from being entrapped by deceivers. Finally, he was very sparing in the expenditure of money for the gratification of his own pleasures; but he was exceedingly bountiful in spending it for the benefit of his associates.

Apology for Alexander's Errors

That Alexander should have committed errors in his conduct from quickness of temper or from wrath, and that he should have been induced to comport himself like the Persian monarchs to an immoderate degree, I do not think remarkable if we fairly consider both his youth and his uninterrupted career of good fortune; likewise that kings have no associates in pleasure who aim at their best interests, but that they will always have associates urging them to do wrong. However, I am certain that Alexander was the only one of the ancient kings who, from nobility of character, repented of the errors which he had committed. The majority of men, even if they have become conscious that they have committed an error, make the mistake of thinking that they can conceal their sin by defending their error as if it had been a just action. But it seems to me that the only cure for sin is for the sinner to confess it, and to be visibly repentant in regard to it. Thus the suffering will not appear altogether intolerable to those who have undergone unpleasant treatment, if the person who inflicted it confesses that he has acted dishonourably; and this good hope for the future is left to the man himself, that he will never again commit a similar sin, if he is seen to be vexed at his former errors. I do not think that even his tracing his origin to a god was a great error on Alexander's part, if it was not perhaps merely a device to induce his subjects to show him reverence. Nor does he seem to me to have been a less renowned king than Minos, Aeacus, or Rhadamanthus, to whom no insolence is attributed by the men of old, because they traced their origin to Zeus. Nor does he seem at all inferior to Theseus or Ion, the former being the reputed son of Poseidon, and the latter of Apollo. His adoption of the Persian mode of dressing also seems to me to have been a political device in regard to the foreigners, that the king might not appear altogether an alien to them; and in regard to the Macedonians, to show them that he had a refuge from their rashness of temper and insolence. For this reason I think, he mixed the Persian royal guards, who carried golden apples at the end of their spears, among the ranks of the Macedonians, and the Persian peers with the Macedonian body-guards. Aristobulus also asserts that Alexander used to have long drinking parties, not for the purpose of enjoying the wine, as he was not a great wine-drinker, but in order to exhibit his sociality and friendly feeling to his Companions.

Eulogy of Alexander

Whoever therefore reproaches Alexander as a bad man, let him do so; but let him first not only bring before his mind all his actions deserving reproach, but also gather into one view all his deeds of every kind. Then, indeed, let him reflect who he is himself, and what kind of fortune he has experienced; and then consider who that man was whom he reproaches as bad, and to what a height of human success he attained, becoming without any dispute king of both continents, and reaching every place by his fame; while he himself who reproaches him is of smaller account, spending his labour on petty objects, which, however, he does not succeed in effecting, petty as they are. For my own part, I think there was at that time no race of men, no city, nor even a single individual to whom Alexander's name and fame had not penetrated. For this reason it seems to me that a hero totally unlike any other human being could not have been born without the agency of the deity. And this is said to have been revealed after Alexander's death by the oracular responses, by the visions which presented themselves to various people, and by the dreams which were seen by different individuals. It is also shown by the honour paid to him by men up to the present time, and by the recollection which is still held of him as more than human. Even at the present time, after so long an interval, other oracular responses in his honour have been received by the nation of the Macedonians. In relating the history of Alexander's achievements, there are some things which I have been compelled to censure; but I am not ashamed to admire Alexander himself. Those actions I have branded as bad, both from a regard to my own veracity, and at the same time for the benefit of mankind. For this reason I think that I undertook the task of writing this history not without the divine inspiration.

Source: Arrian, *The Anabasis of Alexander*, translated by E. J. Chinnock (London: Hodder and Stoughton, 1884), Book 7, chaps. 29–31.

17. Appian of Alexandria Describes Seleucus I Nicator (ca. 358–281 BCE)

Introduction

Seleucus I Nicator, who founded the Seleucid Empire based in Babylon, was one of the Diadochi (successors), companions of Alexander the Great who divided up his conquests among them. The road to power for him was less than straightforward, as Alexander's effective heirs quickly began fighting among themselves. Seleucus, together with Ptolemy I of Egypt, ultimately emerged as one of the two great winners in this contest. After the deaths of Alexander's half brother and two young sons, they each took the title of king as opposed to the allegiance as satraps of Macedonia that they had originally professed. The Greek historian Appian of Alexandria, writing in the second century CE, gave an insightful description of the career of Seleucus, focusing particularly on the skill with which he expanded his original territorial domains, amassing the largest holdings of any of Alexander's successors.

Document

It will not be amiss to tell how the Macedonians, who ruled Syria before the Romans, acquired the same country. After the Persians, Alexander became the sovereign of Syria as well as of all other peoples whom he found. He died leaving one son very small and another yet unborn. The Macedonians, who were loyal to the race of Philip, chose Ardiæus, the brother of Alexander, as king during the minority of Alexander's sons, although he was considered to be hardly of sound mind, and they changed his name from Ardiæus to Philip. They also kept careful guard over the wife, who was enceinte. Meanwhile Alexander's friends continued in charge of the conquered nations, divided into satrapies, which Perdiccas parcelled among them by the authority of King Philip. Not long afterward, when the true kings died, these satraps became kings. The first satrap of Syria was Laomedon of Mitylene, who derived his authority from Perdiccas and from Antipater, who succeeded the latter as prime minister. To this Laomedon, Ptolemy, the satrap of Egypt, came with a fleet and offered him a large sum of money if he would hand over Syria to him, because it was well situated for defending Egypt and for attacking Cyprus. When Laomedon refused Ptolemy seized him. Laomedon bribed his guards and escaped to Alcetas in Caria. Thus Ptolemy ruled Syria for a while, left a garrison there, and returned to Egypt.

Antigonus was satrap of Phrygia, Lycia, and Pamphylia. Having been left as overseer of all Asia when Antipater went to Europe, he besieged Eumenes, the satrap of Cappadocia, who had been publicly declared an enemy of the Macedonians. The latter fled and brought Media under his power, but Antigonus afterward captured and killed him. When he returned he was received magnificently by Seleucus, the satrap of Babylon. One day Seleucus punished one of the governors without consulting Antigonus, who was present, and the latter became angry and demanded an accounting of his money and possessions. As Seleucus was inferior to Antigonus in power he fled to Ptolemy in Egypt. Thereupon Antigonus removed Blitor, the governor of Mesopotamia, from office, because he allowed Seleucus to escape, and took upon himself the government of Babylon, Mesopotamia, and all the countries from Media to the Hellespont, Antipater having died in the meantime. The other satraps at once became envious of his possession of so large a share of the territory; for which reason chiefly, and at the instance of Seleucus, Ptolemy, Lysimachus, the satrap of Thrace, and Cassander, the son of Antipater and leader of the Macedonians after his father's death, entered into a league with each other. They sent a joint embassy to Antigonus and demanded that he should share with them and with the other Macedonians who had lost their satrapies, his newly acquired lands and money. Antigonus treated their demand with scorn, and they jointly made war against him. Antigonus prepared to meet them. He drove out all of Ptolemy's garrisons in Syria and stripped him of all the possessions that he still retained in Phoenicia and Cœle-Syria.

Then he marched beyond the Cilician gates, leaving his son Demetrius, who was about twenty-two years of age, at Gaza with an army to meet Ptolemy, who was coming from Egypt, but the latter defeated the young man badly in a battle near Gaza and compelled him to fly to his father. Ptolemy immediately sent Seleucus to Babylon to resume the government and gave him 1000 foot-soldiers and 300 horse for the purpose. With this small force Seleucus took Babylon, the inhabitants receiving him with enthusiasm, and within a short time he augmented his power greatly. Nevertheless Antigonus warded off the attack of Ptolemy and gained a splendid naval victory over him near Cyprus, in which his son Demetrius was the commander. On account of this very notable exploit the army began to call both Antigonus and Demetrius kings, as their own kings (Ardiæus, the son of Philip and Olympias, and the two sons of Alexander) were now dead. Ptolemy's army also saluted him as king lest by inferiority of rank he should be deemed less lofty than the victors in the late battle. Thus for these men similar consequences followed contrary events. All the others followed suit, and all the satraps became kings.

In this way Seleucus became king of Babylonia. He also acquired the kingdom of Media, slaying with his own hand in battle Nicator whom Antigonus had left as satrap of that country. He afterward waged many wars with Macedonians and barbarians. The two principal ones were with Macedonians, the second with Lysimachus, king of Thrace, the first with Antigonus at Ipsus in Phrygia, where Antigonus commanded in person and fought in person although he was above eighty years of age. Antigonus was killed in battle, and then all the kings who had been in league with Seleucus against him divided his territory among themselves. At this division all Syria from the Euphrates to the sea, also inland Phrygia, fell to the lot of Seleucus. Always lying in wait for the neighboring nations, strong in arms and persuasive in council, he acquired Mesopotamia, Armenia, the so-called Seleucid Cappadocia, the Persians, Parthians, Bactrians, Arabs, Tapyri, Sogdiani, Arachotes, Hyrcanians, and other adjacent peoples that had been subdued by Alexander, as far as the river Indus, so that the boundaries of his empire were the most extensive in Asia after that of Alexander. The whole region from Phrygia to the Indus was subject to Seleucus. He crossed the Indus and waged war with Androcottus, king of the Indians, who dwelt on the banks of that stream, until they came to an understanding with each other and contracted a marriage relationship. Some of these exploits were performed before the death of Antigonus and some afterward.

It is said that while he was still serving under Alexander and following him in the war against the Persians he consulted the Didymæan oracle to inquire about his return to Macedonia and that he received for answer:—

"Do not hurry back to Europe; Asia will be much better for you." . . .

Such are the prophecies I have heard of concerning Seleucus. Directly after the death of Alexander he became the leader of the Companion cavalry, which Hephæstion, and afterwards Perdiccas, commanded during the life of Alexander. After commanding the horse he became satrap of Babylon, and after satrap, king. As he was very successful in war he acquired the surname of Nicator. At least that seems more probable than that he received it from the killing of Nicator. He was of such a large and powerful frame that once when a wild bull was brought for sacrifice to Alexander and broke loose from his ropes, Seleucus held him alone, with nothing but his hands, for which reason his statues are ornamented with horns. He built cities throughout the entire length of his dominions and named sixteen of them Antioch after his father, five Laodicea after his mother, nine after himself, and four after his wives, that is, three Apamea and one Stratonicea. Of these the two most renowned at the present time are the two Seleucias, one on the sea and the other on the river Tigris, Laodicea in Phœnicia, Antioch under Mount Lebanon, and Apamea in Syria. To others he gave names from Greece or Macedonia, or from his own exploits, or in honor of Alexander; whence it comes to pass that in Syria and among the barbarous regions of upper Asia many of the towns bear Greek and Macedonian names, such as Berrhœa, Edessa, Perinthus, Maronea, Callipolis, Achaia, Pella, Orophus, Amphipolis, Arethusa, Astacus, Tegea, Chalcis, Larissa, Heræa, and Apollonia; in Parthia also Sotera, Calliope, Charis, Hecatompylos, Achaia; in India Alexandropolis; in Scythia Alexandreschata. From the victories of Seleucus come the names of Nicephorium in Mesopotamia and of Nicopolis in Armenia very near Cappadocia.

Source: Appian, *The Syrian Wars*, trans. and ed. Horace White (Cambridge, MA: Harvard University Press, 1913), chap. 9, paras. 52–57.

18. Inscription of Antiochus I Soter, King of Babylon (r. 281–261 BCE)

Introduction

Antiochus I Soter of Babylon faced many problems during his reign as he sought to defend the empire his father had gained following the death of Alexander the Great against internal revolts and external threats. A forceful ruler and military commander, Antiochus nonetheless failed to attain his ambitions to wrest Coele-Syria and Phoenicia from Ptolemaic Egypt and to eliminate

Eumenes of Pergamum. This inscription, probably commissioned sometime in Antiochus's final decade, has a slightly plaintive quality, as he begs the gods, in exchange for the temples he has built in their honor, to grant him extensive conquests, "victory over his foes," and a lengthy and prosperous reign not just for himself but also for his son.

Document

Antiochus, the great king, the powerful king, king of the world, King of Babylon, king of lands, patron of Esagila and Ezida, chief son of Seleucus, king of the Macedonians, King of Babylon, am I.

When my heart incited me to rebuild Esagila and Ezida, and I made bricks for Esagila and Ezida in the land of the Hittites with my white hands with oil * * * and to lay the foundation of Esagila and Ezida I * * * In the month Adar, on the twentieth day, in the forty-third year, I laid the foundations of Ezida, the eternal temple, the Temple of Nabu in Borsippa.

O Nabu, exalted son, powerful leader of the gods, who for exaltation was born (established), the first-born son of Marduk, offspring of Erua, the queen, who controls birth, look with favour, and by thy exalted command, which can not be altered, the overthrow of the country of my enemy, the victory of my power, suzerainty over my foes, a kingdom of righteousness, a reign (full) of rejoicing, years of good cheer, abundance of offspring, as a present to the kingdom of Antiochus, and of Seleucus, the king, his son [do thou grant] for all time!

O Nabu, son of Esaglia, first-born of Marduk, of highest rank, offspring of Erua, the queen, when thou enterest with joy and rejoicing into Ezida, the eternal temple, the temple of thy divinity, the dwelling which cheers thy heart, at thy righteous command, which can not be hindered, may my days be long!

   May my years be many!
   May my throne be (firmly) established!
   May my reign become old!

With thy exalted scepter, that holds fast the circuit of heaven and earth, at thy bright mouth (illustrious command) may they establish my good fortune!

The lands from the rising of the sun to the setting of the sun, may my hands conquer!

May I force tribute from them, and for the completion of Esagila and Ezida may I bring (it)!

O Nabu, chief son, when thou enterest into Ezida, the eternal temple, good fortune for Antiochus, king of lands, Seleucus, the king, his son, Stratonice, his consort, the queen—may their good fortune be (firmly) established at thy command!

Source: Robert Francis Harper, ed., *Assyrian and Babylonian Literature: Selected Translations* (New York: D. Appleton, 1901), 194–195.

19. Temple of Philae, Egypt, Inscription Commemorating the Suppression of a Rebellion Against Pharaoh Ptolemy V Epiphanes (186 BCE)

Introduction

The reign of Ptolemy V Epiphanes of Egypt saw major internal rebellions against his rule that were finally suppressed in 186 BCE. An inscription in the Temple of Philae celebrated the eventual end of these revolts and the execution of the leader, Ankhwennefer, together with many of his associates. While Ptolemy V (r. 210–180 BCE), who became king in 205 BCE at age five, eventually succeeded in maintaining domestic control of his country, he lost most of his external possessions in Asia Minor to Antiochus III the Great of Syria and Philip V of Macedon. The priests, whose wealthy temples had been targets of the rebels within Egypt, clearly welcomed the royal victory at home.

Document

... which is the 9th day of the Egyptian month (?) Mesore, [in year 19] of the king, the young one, who has appeared as king in place [of his father, lord of the diadems] whose might is great, who has established Egypt and improved it, whose heart is kind [towards the gods, who ... his enemies while he improves the life of his people, the lord of the years of] jubilee, [in the likeness] of Ptah, the exalted one, the king in the likeness [of Ra], the King of Upper and Lower Egypt, the son of the two Gods Father-loving {*Philopator*}, beloved of Ptah, to whom Ra has given [the victory], the living image of Amon, the Son of Ra, Ptolemy—may he live for ever, the God Epiphanes, [the son of] Ptolemy [and Arsinoë], the Gods Father-loving {*Philopator*}. When the priest of Alexander, the Saviour Gods {*Soter*}, [the Gods Brotherly] {*Philadelphus*}, the Gods Beneficient {*Euergetes*}, [the Gods Father-loving {*Philopator*} and the Gods Manifest {*Epiphanes*} was ...;] the athlophoros [of Berenice Euergetes] was ... daughter of Ptolemy; the kanephoros [of Arsinoë Philadelphus was Demetria, the daughter of] Philinus; and the priestess of Arsinoë Philadelphus was Eirene, the daughter of Ptolemy.

On this day, a decree *made by* the superintendents of the temples, the prophets, the keepers of the secrets, the priests who enter the sacred place and adorn the gods with garments *and the scribes* of the gods' words, and the personnel of the House of Life, and the others priests from the shrines of Upper and Lower Egypt, who are in Alexandria, they being gathered at the sanctuary of Isis and of the two Gods Brotherly {*Philadelphus*}, the two Gods Beneficient {*Euergetes*}, the two Gods Father-loving {*Philopator*}, and the two Gods Manifest {*Epiphanes*}, the Lords of Bright-eye {*Egypt*}, after it was reported to his majesty by the confidant of his majesty, the beloved of the king, the commander-in-chief of the cavalry, Aristonicus, son of Aristonicus, about Eumenos, who is among the top favourites of his majesty, saying, "He {*Eumenos*} has campaigned in South-land {*Upper Egypt*}, in the district of Dominion {*Thebes*}, against the rebel, the enemy of the gods, Ankhwennefer. Now the son of the enemy *leader* is dead, together with the band of Nubians who had joined him; he {*Eumenos*} has slaughtered them and seized that insurgent alive," *then* they {*the priests*} said:

Whereas the King of Upper and Lower Egypt, the Son of Ra, Ptolemy—may he live for ever, beloved of Ptah, the son of the King of Upper and Lower Egypt and the ruler, the Lady of the Two Lands *of Egypt,* Arsinoë, the two Gods Father-loving {*Philopator*}—and his wife, the ruler, the Lady of the Two Lands *of Egypt,* Cleopatra, the two Gods Manifest {*Epiphanes*}, have been doing every good thing in the 'Riverbanks of Horus' {*Egypt*} and what is on them and those who are in charge of their excellent offices in their entirety, their hearts being well disposed towards the gods, * * *

{*The next section enumerates the ways in which the royal couple had favoured the temples and priests of the Egyptian gods, financially and otherwise.*}

In return for these *good deeds,* which [the King of Upper and Lower Egypt, the Son of Ra,] Ptolemy—may he live for ever, beloved of Ptah, the God Manifest {*Epiphanes*} has done, all the gods and goddesses have granted to him *the following success.*

The rebel against the gods, {*Ankhwennefer*}, he who had made war in Egypt, gathering insolent people from all districts on account of their crimes, they did terrible things to the governors of the nomes, they desecrated (?) the temples, they damaged (?) the divine statues, they molested (?) the priests and suppressed (?) the offerings on the altars and in the shrines. They sacked (?) the towns and their population, women and children included, committing all kinds of crimes in the time of anarchy. They stole the taxes of the nomes, they damaged the irrigation works.

The king of Upper and Lower Egypt Ptolemy, loved by Ptah, has given many orders and showed considerable care for protecting the temples. He stationed Greek troops and soldiers of people who had come to Egypt, who obeyed his orders, being joined with him and being like people born with him. They did not allow the rebels, who had instigated war against him and against his father, to approach (?). His Majesty caused that great quantities of silver and gold came to the land to bring troops to Egypt, money from the taxes of the nomes, in order to protect the temples of Egypt against the impious men who violated them.

On the 3rd of Mesore it was announced to his Majesty: Ankhwennefer has been captured alive in the battle against him in year 19, on the 24th day of Epeiph. His son was killed, the commander of the army of impious men, together with the leaders of the Nubians who fought on his side. He was brought to the place where the king was. He was punished by death for the crimes, which he had committed, and so were the other criminals, those who had rebelled in the sedition, which they had made. * * *

{*The next section instructs that statues of the king as 'Lord of Victory' should be erected in all sanctuaries in the land; and the day of the presentation of the report of the victory, as well as the day of the victory over the rebels, was to be celebrated in temples every year.*}

And when [the statue of the king is brought out in procession,] then also the statue of the queen shall be brought forth and paraded with him on these days. And furthermore the statue of the Lady of the Two Lands *of Egypt* shall be placed at the side of the royal statue on these days, every year and every half a year. And on the night before *the festivals,* all ritual ceremonies (?) shall be held, making music in the way prescribed in the temples of *both parts of Egypt.*

This decree shall be inscribed on [a stele of hard stone], [in hieroglyphs, in demotic script and] in the Greek language, and it shall be placed in the court of the common people in the sanctuary of each temple, in the temples of the first, second and third rank, [by the side of the statue of the king], giving life like Ra for ever.

Source: "Second Philae Decree," Attalus, http://www.attalus.org/docs/other/inscr_18.html.

20. King Antiochus IV Epiphanes Sacks Jerusalem (167 BCE)

Introduction

The Jews deeply resented the sack of Jerusalem by King Antiochus IV Epiphanes of Babylon and his subsequent imposition on them of an alien religion. In the First Book of Maccabees an unknown Jewish author left a vivid account of the traumatic impact of these actions, which eventually sparked a full-scale Jewish rebellion. This narrative was originally written in Hebrew, but only a Greek translation survives. This was far from the first occasion on which the Jewish kingdom in Palestine and its people had fallen victim to overweening predatory empires; both Assyria and Babylon conquered the Jews, sacking the country and exiling many of the able-bodied among its population to forced labor on grandiose building projects elsewhere in the Assyrian and Babylonian domains. Unlike most of the largely unknown victims of the wars in the region, however, the Jews recorded their sufferings in several books of the Old Testament. These testimonies offer a sharp contrast to the boastful proclamations glorifying their conquests issued by the great military rulers of the region.

Document

And after Antiochus had ravaged Egypt in the hundred and forty-third year [of the kingdom of the Greeks], he returned and went up against Israel.

And he went up to Jerusalem with a great multitude.

And he proudly entered into the sanctuary, and took away the golden altar, and the candlestick of light, and all the vessels thereof, and the table of proposition, and the pouring vessels, and the vials, and the little mortars of gold, and the veil, and the crowns, and the golden ornament that was before the temple: and he broke them all in pieces.

And he took the silver and gold, and the precious vessels: and he took the hidden treasures which he found: and when he had taken all away he departed into his own country.

20. King Antiochus IV Epiphanes Sacks Jerusalem

And he made a great slaughter of men, and spoke very proudly.

And there was great mourning in Israel, and in every place where they were.

And the princes, and the ancients mourned, and the virgins and the young men were made feeble, and the beauty of the women was changed.

Every bridegroom took up lamentation: and the bride that sat in the marriage bed, mourned:

And the land was moved for the inhabitants thereof, and all the house of Jacob was covered with confusion.

And after two full years the king sent the chief collector of his tributes to the cities of Judea, and he came to Jerusalem with a great multitude.

And he spoke to them peaceable words in deceit: and they believed him.

And he fell upon the city suddenly, and struck it with a great slaughter, and destroyed much people in Israel.

And he took the spoils of the city, and burnt it with fire, and threw down the houses thereof, and the walls thereof round about:

And they took the women captive, and the children, and the cattle they possessed.

And they built the city of David with a great and strong wall, and with strong towers, and made it a fortress for them:

And they placed there a sinful nation, wicked men, and they fortified themselves therein: and they stored up armour, and victuals, and gathered together the spoils of Jerusalem;

And laid them up there: and they became a great snare.

And this was a place to lie in wait against the sanctuary, and an evil devil in Israel.

And they shed innocent blood round about the sanctuary, and defiled the holy place.

And the inhabitants of Jerusalem fled away by reason of them, and the city was made the habitation to strangers, and she became a stranger to her own seed, and her children forsook her.

Her sanctuary was desolate like a wilderness, her festival days were turned into mourning, her sabbaths into reproach, her honours were brought to nothing.

Her dishonour was increased according to her glory, and her excellency was turned into mourning.

And king Antiochus wrote to all his kingdom, that all the people should be one: and every one should leave his own law.

And all nations consented according to the word of king Antiochus.

And many of Israel consented to his service, and they sacrificed to idols, and profaned the sabbath.

And the king sent letters by the hands of messengers to Jerusalem, and to all the cities of Judea: that they should follow the law of the nations of the earth,

And should forbid holocausts and sacrifices, and atonements to be made in the temple of God.

And should prohibit the sabbath, and the festival days, to be celebrated.

And he commanded the holy places to be profaned, and the holy people of Israel.

And he commanded altars to be built, and temples, and idols, and swine's flesh to be immolated, and unclean beasts.

And that they should leave their children uncircumcised, and let their souls be defiled with all uncleannesses, and abominations, to the end that they should forget the law, and should change all the justifications of God.

And that whosoever would not do according to the word of king Antiochus should be put to death.

According to all these words he wrote to his whole kingdom: and he appointed rulers over the people that should force them to do these things.

And they commanded the cities of Judea to sacrifice.

Then many of the people were gathered to them that had forsaken the law of the Lord: and they committed evils in the land:

And they drove away the people of Israel into lurking holes, and into the secret places of fugitives.

On the fifteenth day of the month Casleu, in the hundred and forty-fifth year, king Antiochus set up the abominable idol of desolation upon the altar of God, and they built altars throughout all the cities of Judea round about:

And they burnt incense, and sacrificed at the doors of the houses, and in the streets.

And they cut in pieces, and burnt with fire the books of the law of God:

And every one with whom the books of the testament of the Lord were found, and whosoever observed the law of the Lord, they put to death, according to the edict of the king.

Thus by their power did they deal with the people of Israel, that were found in the cities month after month.

And on the five and twentieth day of the month they sacrificed upon the altar of the idol that was over against the altar of God.

Now the women that circumcised their children were slain according to the commandment of king Antiochus.

And they hanged the children about their necks in all their houses: and those that had circumcised them, they put to death.

And many of the people of Israel determined with themselves, that they would not eat unclean things: and they chose rather to die than to be defiled with unclean meats.

And they would not break the holy law of God and they were put to death:

And there was very great wrath upon the people.

Source: "The First Book of the Machabees (Douay Version)," Chapter 1, verses 21–67, in *Books of the Maccabees* (Scotts Valley, CA: CreateSpace, 2014), 100–103.

21. Flavius Josephus Describes the Maccabeean Revolt (167–160 BCE)

Introduction

The first-century CE Jewish scholar and historian Flavius Josephus, who chronicled the various Jewish uprisings against Roman rule, preceded these with a brief narrative account of the Maccabeean Revolt against the Seleucids in the second century BCE. Josephus, who was of aristocratic and priestly Jewish descent, fought against the Romans in the First Jewish-Roman War of 67 CE. Josephus, one of two survivors of a mass suicide pact at the siege of the city of Yodfat, surrendered to the forces commanded by the Roman general Flavius Vespasian, who later became emperor of Rome, an ascent that Josephus apparently predicted. The fulfillment of this prophecy led Vespasian to free the captive former rebel, whom he had originally enslaved. Josephus subsequently became a Roman citizen and a client of the Flavian family and was close to Vespasian's elder son, Emperor Titus. The Romans found him to be a useful source of information on Jewish history and politics, which he interpreted to them both in person and in his writings.

Document

At the same time that Antiochus, who was called Epiphanes, had a quarrel with the sixth Ptolemy about his right to the whole country of Syria, a great sedition fell among the men of power in Judea, and they had a contention about obtaining the government; while each of those that were of dignity could not endure to be subject to their equals. However, Onias, one of the high priests, got the better, and cast the sons of Tobias out of the city; who fled to Antiochus, and besought him to make use of them for his leaders, and to make an expedition into Judea. The king being thereto disposed beforehand, complied with them, and came upon the Jews with a great army, and took their city by force, and slew a great multitude of those that favored Ptolemy, and sent out his soldiers to plunder them without mercy. He also spoiled the temple, and put a stop to the constant practice of offering a daily sacrifice of expiation for three years and six months. But Onias, the high priest, fled to Ptolemy, and received a place from him in the Nomus of Heliopolis, where he built a city resembling Jerusalem, and a temple that was like its temple concerning which we shall speak more in its proper place hereafter.

Now Antiochus was not satisfied either with his unexpected taking the city, or with its pillage, or with the great slaughter he had made there; but being overcome with his violent passions, and remembering what he had suffered during the siege, he compelled the Jews to dissolve the laws of their country, and to keep their infants uncircumcised, and to sacrifice swine's flesh upon the altar; against which they all opposed themselves, and the most approved among them were put to death. Bacchides also, who was sent to keep the fortresses, having these wicked commands, joined to his own natural barbarity, indulged all sorts of the extremest wickedness, and tormented the worthiest of the inhabitants, man by man, and threatened their city every day with open destruction, till at length he provoked the poor sufferers by the extremity of his wicked doings to avenge themselves.

Accordingly Matthias, the son of Asamoneus, one of the priests who lived in a village called Modin, armed himself, together with his own family, which had five sons of his in it, and slew Bacchides with daggers; and thereupon, out of the fear of the many garrisons [of the enemy], he fled to the mountains; and so many of the people followed him, that he was encouraged to come down from the mountains, and to give battle to Antiochus's generals, when he beat them, and drove them out of Judea. So he came to the government by this his success, and became the prince of his own people by their own free consent, and then died, leaving the government to Judas, his eldest son.

Now Judas, supposing that Antiochus would not lie still, gathered an army out of his own countrymen, and was the first that made a league of friendship with the Romans, and drove Epiphanes out of the country when he had made a second expedition into it, and this by giving him a great defeat there; and when he was warmed by this great success, he made an assault upon the garrison that was in the city, for it had not been cut off hitherto; so he ejected them out of the upper city, and drove the soldiers into the lower, which part of the city was called the Citadel. He then got the temple under his power, and cleansed the whole place, and walled it round about, and made new vessels for sacred ministrations, and brought them into the temple, because the former vessels had been profaned. He also built another altar, and began to offer the sacrifices; and when the city had already received its sacred constitution again, Antiochus died; whose son Antiochus succeeded him in the kingdom, and in his hatred to the Jews also.

So this Antiochus got together fifty thousand footmen, and five thousand horsemen, and fourscore elephants, and marched through Judea into the mountainous parts. He then took Bethsura, which was a small city; but at a place called Bethzacharis, where the passage was narrow, Judas met him with his army. However, before the forces joined battle, Judas's brother Eleazar, seeing the very highest of the elephants adorned with a large tower, and with military trappings of gold to guard him, and supposing that Antiochus himself was upon him, he ran a great way before his own army, and cutting his way through the enemy's troops, he got up to the elephant; yet could he not reach him who seemed to be the king, by reason of his being so high; but still he ran his weapon into the belly of the beast, and brought him down upon himself, and was crushed to death, having done no more than attempted great things, and showed that he preferred glory before life. Now he that governed the elephant was but a private man; and had he proved to be Antiochus, Eleazar had performed nothing more by this bold stroke than that it might appear he chose to die, when he had the bare hope of thereby doing a glorious action; nay, this disappointment proved an omen to his brother [Judas] how the entire battle would end. It is true that the Jews fought it out bravely for a long time, but the king's forces, being superior in number, and having fortune on their side, obtained the victory. And when a great many of his men were slain, Judas took the rest with him, and fled to the toparchy of Gophna. So Antiochus went to Jerusalem, and staid there but a few days, for he wanted provisions, and so he went his way. He left indeed a garrison behind him, such as he thought sufficient to keep the place, but drew the rest of his army off, to take their winter-quarters in Syria.

Now, after the king was departed, Judas was not idle; for as many of his own nation came to him, so did he gather those that had escaped out of the battle together, and gave battle again to Antiochus's generals at a village called Adasa; and being too hard for his enemies in the battle, and killing a great number of them, he was at last himself slain also. Nor was it many days afterward that his brother John had a plot laid against him by Antiochus's party, and was slain by them.

When Jonathan, who was Judas's brother, succeeded him, he behaved himself with great circumspection in other respects, with relation to his own people; and he corroborated his authority by preserving his friendship with the Romans. He also made a league with Antiochus the son. Yet was not all this sufficient for his security; for the tyrant Trypho, who was guardian to Antiochus's son, laid a plot against him; and besides that, endeavored to take off his friends, and caught Jonathan by a wile, as he was going to Ptolemais to Antiochus, with a few persons in his company, and put him in bonds, and then made an expedition against the Jews; but when he was afterward driven away by Simon, who was Jonathan's brother, and was enraged at his defeat, he put Jonathan to death.

However, Simon managed the public affairs after a courageous manner, and took Gazara, and Joppa, and Jamnia, which were cities in his neighborhood. He also got the garrison under, and demolished the citadel. He was afterward an auxiliary to Antiochus, against Trypho, whom he besieged in Dora, before he went on his expedition against the Medes; yet could not he make the king ashamed of his ambition, though he had assisted him in killing Trypho; for it was not long ere Antiochus sent Cendebeus his general with an army to lay waste Judea, and to subdue Simon; yet he, though he was now in years, conducted the war as if he were a much younger man. He also sent his sons with a band of strong men against Antiochus, while he took part of the army himself with him, and fell upon him from another quarter. He also laid a great many men in ambush in many places of the mountains, and was superior in all his attacks upon them; and when he had been conqueror after so glorious a manner, he was made high priest, and also freed the Jews from the dominion of the Macedonians, after one hundred and seventy years of the empire [of Seleucus].

Source: Flavius Josephus, "The History of the Jews," Book 1, chaps. 31–50, in *The Works of Flavius Josephus,* translated by William Whiston and John E. Beardsley (Cambridge, MA: Harvard University Press, 1895).

22. Appian Describes the Last Days of King Mithridates VI Eupator Dionysius of Pontus (63 BCE)

Introduction

The Greek historian Appian of Alexandria, writing in the second century CE, left a compelling description of Mithridates VI of Pontus in northern Anatolia who waged lengthy wars resisting Roman dominion in the first century BCE. Claiming descent from

Persian king Cyrus the Great as well as Alexander the Great, Mithridates displayed enormous persistence and determination in his efforts to exercise control over the Black Sea, for more than a quarter century mounting and orchestrating repeated revolts against Roman rule. After his final defeat in 63 BCE, he contemplated allying with the Gauls in present-day France to invade Italy and take the war to the Romans' home. Instead, betrayed by his favorite son, Pharnaces, Mithridates committed suicide in 63 BCE. Even his enemies respected him, according him a lavish funeral. The grudging admiration he won from his opponents is demonstrated in Appian's account of the final days of Mithridates, which he followed with a posthumous assessment of the dead king.

Document

Although bereft of so many children and castles and of his whole kingdom, and in no way fit for war, and although he could not expect any aid from the Scythians, still no inferior position, none corresponding to his present misfortunes, even then found a place in [Mithridates'] mind. He proposed to turn his course to the Gauls, whose friendship he had cultivated a long time for this purpose, and with them to invade Italy, hoping that many of the Italians themselves would join him on account of their hatred of the Romans; for he had heard that such had been Hannibal's policy after the Romans had waged war against him in Spain, and that he had become in this way an object of the greatest terror to them. He knew that almost all of Italy had lately revolted from the Romans by reason of their hatred and had waged war against them for a very long time, and had sustained Spartacus, the gladiator, against them, although he was a man of no repute. Filled with these ideas he was for hastening to the Gauls, but his soldiers, though the very bold enterprise might be attractive, were deterred chiefly by its magnitude, and by the long distance of the expedition in foreign territory, against men whom they could not overcome even in their own country. They thought also that Mithridates, in utter despair, wanted to end his life in a valiant and kingly way rather than in idleness. So they tolerated him and remained silent, for there was nothing mean or contemptible about him even in his misfortunes.

While affairs were in this plight Pharnaces, the son whom he was most fond of and whom he had often designated as his successor, either alarmed about the expedition and the kingdom (for he still had hopes of pardon from the Romans, but reckoned that he should lose everything completely if his father should invade Italy), or spurred by other motives, formed a conspiracy against his father. His fellow-conspirators were captured and put to the torture, but Menophanes persuaded the king that it would not be seemly, just as he was starting on his expedition, to put to death the son who had been until then the dearest to him. People were liable to such turns, he said, in time of war, and when they came to an end things quieted down again. In this way Mithridates was persuaded to pardon his son, but the latter, still fearing his father's anger, and knowing that the army shrank from the expedition, went by night to the leading Roman deserters who were encamped very near the king, and by representing to them in its true light, and as they well knew it, the danger of their advancing against Italy, and by making them many promises if they would refuse to go, induced them to desert from his father. After Pharnaces had persuaded them he sent emissaries the same night to other camps near by and won them over. Early in the morning the first deserters raised a shout, and those next to them repeated it, and so on. Even the naval force joined in the cry, not all of them having been advised beforehand perhaps, but eager for a change, despising failure, and always ready to attach themselves to a new hope. Others, who were ignorant of the conspiracy, thought that all had been corrupted, and that if they remained alone they would be scorned by the majority, and so from fear and necessity rather than inclination joined in the shouting. Mithridates, being awakened by the noise, sent messengers out to inquire what the shouters wanted. The latter made no concealment, but said, "We want your son to be king; we want a young man instead of an old one who is ruled by eunuchs, the slayer of so many of his sons, his generals, and his friends."

When Mithridates heard this he went out to reason with them. A part of his own guard then ran to join the deserters, but the latter refused to admit them unless they would do some irreparable deed as a proof of their fidelity, pointing at the same time to Mithridates. So they hastened to kill his horse, for he himself had fled, and at the same time saluted Pharnaces as king, as though the rebels were already victorious, and one of them brought a broad papyrus leaf from a temple and crowned him with it in place of a diadem. The king saw these things from a high portico, and he sent messenger after messenger to Pharnaces asking permission to fly in safety. When none of his messengers returned, fearing lest he should be delivered up to the Romans, he praised the body-guards and friends who had been faithful to him and sent them to the new king, but the army killed some of them under a misapprehension as they were approaching. Mithridates then took out some poison that he always carried next to his sword, and mixed it. . . . Seeing a certain Bituitus there, an officer of the Gauls, he said to him,

"I have profited much from your right arm against my enemies. I shall profit from it most of all if you will kill me, and save from the danger of being led in a Roman triumph one who has been an autocrat so many years, and the ruler of so great a kingdom, but who is now unable to die by poison because, like a fool, he has fortified himself against the poison of others. Although I have kept watch and ward against all the poisons that one takes with his food, I have not provided against that domestic poison, always the most dangerous to kings, the treachery of army, children, and friends." Bituitus, thus appealed to, rendered the king the service that he desired.

So died Mithridates, who was the sixteenth in descent from Darius, the son of Hystaspes, king of the Persians, and the eighth from that Mithridates who left the Macedonians and acquired the kingdom of Pontus. He lived sixty-eight or sixty-nine years, and of these he reigned fifty-seven, for the kingdom came to him when he was an orphan. He subdued the neighboring barbarians and many of the Scythians, and waged a formidable war against the Romans for forty years, during which he frequently conquered Bithynia and Cappadocia, besides making incursions into the Roman province of Asia and into Phrygia, Paphlagonia, Galatia, and Macedonia. He invaded Greece, where he performed many remarkable exploits, and ruled the sea from Cilicia to the Adriatic until Sulla confined him again to his paternal kingdom after destroying 160,000 of his soldiers. Notwithstanding these great losses he renewed the war without difficulty. He fought with the greatest generals of his time. He was vanquished by Sulla, Lucullus, and Pompey, although several times he got the better of them also. Lucius Cassius, Quintus Oppius, and Manius Aquilius he took prisoners and carried them around with him. The last he killed because he was the cause of the war. The others he surrendered to Sulla. He defeated Fimbria, Murena, the consul Cotta, Fabius, and Triarius. He was always high-spirited and indomitable even in misfortunes. Until finally overthrown he left no avenue of attack against the Romans untried. He made alliances with the Samnites and the Gauls, and he sent legates to Sertorius in Spain. He was often wounded by enemies and by conspirators, but he never desisted from anything on that account, even when he was an old man. None of the conspiracies ever escaped his detection, not even the last one, but he voluntarily overlooked it and perished in consequence of it—so ungrateful is the wickedness that has been once pardoned. He was bloodthirsty and cruel to all—the slayer of his mother, his brother, three sons, and three daughters. He had a large frame, as his armor, which he sent to Nemea and to Delphi, shows, and was so strong that he rode horseback and hurled the javelin to the last, and could ride 1000 stades in one day, changing horses at intervals. He used to drive a chariot with sixteen horses at once. He cultivated Greek learning, and thus became acquainted with the religious cult of Greece, and was fond of music. He was abstemious and patient of labor for the most part, and yielded only to pleasures with women.

Such was the end of Mithridates, who bore the surnames of Eupator and Dionysus. When the Romans heard of his death they held a festival because they were delivered from a troublesome enemy. Pharnaces sent his father's corpse to Pompey at Sinope in a trireme, together with the persons who captured Manius, and many hostages, both Greek and barbarian, and asked that he should be allowed to rule either his paternal kingdom, or Bosporus alone, which his brother, Machares, had received from Mithridates. Pompey provided for the expenses of the funeral of Mithridates and directed his servants to give his remains a royal interment, and to place them in the tombs of the kings in Sinope, because he admired his great achievements and considered him the first of the kings of his time.

Source: Appian, *The Mithridatic Wars*, ed. Horace White (Cambridge, MA: Harvard University Press, 1913), chap 16, paras. 109–113.

23. Julius Caesar Wins the Battle of the Nile and Takes Alexandria, Egypt (January 47 BCE)

Introduction

Roman general Julius Caesar, who had already conquered Gaul, came to Egypt in 48 BCE in pursuit of his Roman rival, Gnaeus Pompeius Magnus. By the time Caesar arrived Pompey was dead, murdered by King Ptolemy XIII in an effort to ingratiate himself with Caesar. Caesar remained in Alexandria, where he quickly became embroiled in an ongoing civil war that pitted

Ptolemy and Arsinoe, one of his sisters, against another sister, Cleopatra. Caesar and 4,000 men remained in Alexandria, where he appeared to favor Cleopatra over her rival siblings, which led Ptolemy to besiege him. Captured and then released by Caesar, Ptolemy promptly turned his efforts to raising an army capable of defeating Caesar, who himself received reinforcements led by a close friend, Mithridates of Pergamum. This excerpt from Caesar's official report on his campaign to Rome, written on his behalf by an associate, describes the ensuing battle between the two. Ptolemy reportedly drowned, and Arsinoe was exiled. Caesar placed their sister on the throne as Cleopatra VII, together with yet another younger brother, who became Ptolemy XIV. The report does not mention that Caesar stayed on in Alexandria to enjoy a love affair with the much younger and attractive new queen of Egypt.

Document

About the same time Mithridates of Pergamus, a man of illustrious descent, distinguished for his bravery and knowledge of the art of war, and who held a very high place in the friendship and confidence of Caesar, having been sent in the beginning of the Alexandrian war, to raise succors in Syria and Cilicia, arrived by land at the head of a great body of troops, which his diligence, and the affection of these two provinces, had enabled him to draw together in a very short time. He conducted them first to Pelusium, where Egypt joins Syria. Achillas, who was perfectly well acquainted with its importance, had seized and put a strong garrison into it. For Egypt is considered as defended on all sides by strong barriers; on the side of the sea by the Pharos, and on the side of Syria by Pelusium, which are accounted the two keys of that kingdom. He attacked it so briskly with a large body of troops, fresh men continually succeeding in the place of those that were fatigued, and urged the assault with so much firmness and perseverance, that he carried it the same day on which he attacked it, and placed a garrison in it. Thence he pursued his march to Alexandria, reducing all the provinces through which he passed, and conciliating them to Caesar, by that authority which always accompanies the conqueror.

Not far from Alexandria lies Delta, the most celebrated province of Egypt, which derives its name from the Greek letter so called. For the Nile, dividing into two channels, which gradually diverge as they approach the sea, into which they at last discharge themselves, at a considerable distance from one another, leaves an intermediate space in form of a triangle. The king [Ptolemy] understanding that Mithridates was approaching this place, and knowing he must pass the river, sent a large body of troops against him, sufficient, as he thought, if not to overwhelm and crush him, at least to stop his march, for though he earnestly desired to see him defeated, yet he thought it a great point gained, to hinder his junction with Caesar. The troops that first passed the river, and came up with Mithridates, attacked him immediately, hastening to snatch the honor of victory from the troops that were marching to their aid. Mithridates at first confined himself to the defense of his camp, which he had with great prudence fortified according to the custom of the Romans: but observing that they advanced insolently and without caution, he sallied upon them from all parts, and put a great number of them to the sword; insomuch that, but for their knowledge of the ground, and the neighborhood of the vessels in which they had passed the river, they must have been all destroyed. But recovering by degrees from their terror, and joining the troops that followed them, they again prepared to attack Mithridates.

A messenger was sent by Mithridates to Caesar, to inform him of what had happened. The king learned from his followers that the action had taken place. Thus, much about the same time, Ptolemy set out to crush Mithridates, and Caesar to relieve him. The king made use of the more expeditious conveyance of the Nile, where he had a large fleet in readiness. Caesar declined the navigation of the river, that he might not be obliged to engage the enemy's fleet; and coasting along the African shore, found means to join the victorious troops of Mithridates, before Ptolemy could attack him. The king had encamped in a place fortified by nature, being an eminence surrounded on all sides by a plain. Three of its sides were secured by various defenses. One was washed by the river Nile, the other was steep and inaccessible, and the third was defended by a morass.

Between Ptolemy's camp and Caesar's route lay a narrow river with very steep banks, which discharged itself into the Nile. This river was about seven miles from the king's camp; who, understanding that Caesar was directing his march that way, sent all his cavalry, with a choice body of light-armed foot, to prevent Caesar from crossing, and maintain an unequal fight from the banks, where courage had no opportunity to exert itself, and cowardice ran no hazard. Our men, both horse and foot, were extremely mortified, that the Alexandrians should so long maintain their ground against them. Wherefore, some of the German cavalry, dispersing in quest of a ford, found means to swim the river where the banks were lowest; and the legionaries at the same time cutting down several large trees, that reached from one bank to another, and constructing suddenly a mound, by their help got to the other side. The enemy were so much in dread of their attack, that they betook themselves to flight; but in vain: for very few returned to the king, almost all being cut to pieces in the pursuit.

Caesar, upon this success, judging that his sudden approach must strike great terror into the Alexandrians, advanced toward their camp with his victorious army. But finding it well intrenched, strongly fortified by nature, and the ramparts covered with armed soldiers, he did not think proper that his troops, who were very much fatigued both by their march and the late battle, should attack it; and therefore encamped at a small distance from the enemy. Next day he attacked a fort, in a village not far off, which the king had fortified and joined to his camp by a line of communication, with a view to keep possession of the village. He attacked it with his whole army, and took it by storm; not because it would have been difficult to carry it with a few forces; but with the design of falling immediately upon the enemy's camp, during the alarm which the loss of this fort must give them. Accordingly, the Romans, in continuing the pursuit of those that fled from the fort, arrived at last before the Alexandrian camp, and commenced a most furious action at a distance. There were two approaches by which it might be attacked; one by the plain, of which we have spoken before, the other by a narrow pass, between their camp and the Nile. The first, which was much the easiest, was defended by a numerous body of their best troops; and the access on the side of the Nile gave the enemy great advantage in distressing and wounding our men; for they were exposed to a double shower of darts: in front from the rampart, behind from the river; where the enemy had stationed a great number of ships, furnished with archers and slingers, that kept up a continual discharge.

Caesar, observing that his troops fought with the utmost ardor, and yet made no great progress, on account of the disadvantage of the ground; and perceiving they had left the highest part of their camp unguarded, because, it being sufficiently fortified by nature, they had all crowded to the other attacks, partly to have a share in the action, partly to be spectators of the issue; he ordered some cohorts to wheel round the camp, and gain that ascent: appointing Carfulenus to command them, a man distinguished for bravery and acquaintance with the service. When they had reached the place, as there were but very few to defend it, our men attacked them so briskly that the Alexandrians, terrified by the cries they heard behind them, and seeing themselves attacked both in front and rear, fled in the utmost consternation on all sides. Our men, animated by the confusion of the enemy, entered the camp in several places at the same time, and running down from the higher ground, put a great number of them to the sword. The Alexandrians, endeavoring to escape, threw themselves in crowds over the rampart in the quarter next the river. The foremost tumbling into the ditch, where they were crushed to death, furnished an easy passage for those that followed. It is ascertained that the king escaped from the camp, and was received on board a ship; but by the crowd that followed him, the ship in which he fled was overloaded and sunk.

After this speedy and successful action, Caesar, in consequence of so great a victory, marched the nearest way by land to Alexandria with his cavalry, and entered triumphant into that part of the town which was possessed by the enemy's guards. He was not mistaken in thinking that the Alexandrians, upon hearing of the issue of the battle, would give over all thoughts of war. Accordingly, as soon as he arrived, he reaped the just fruit of his valor and magnanimity. For all the multitude of the inhabitants, throwing down their arms, abandoning their works, and assuming the habit of suppliants, preceded by all those sacred symbols of religion with which they were wont to mollify their offended kings, met Caesar on his arrival and surrendered. Caesar, accepting their submission, and encouraging them, advanced through the enemy's works into his own quarter of the town, where he was received with the universal congratulations of his party, who were no less overjoyed at his arrival and presence, than at the happy issue of the war.

Caesar, having thus made himself master of Alexandria and Egypt, lodged the government in the hands of those to whom Ptolemy had bequeathed it by will, conjuring the Roman people not to permit any change. For the eldest of Ptolemy's two sons being dead, Caesar settled the kingdom upon the youngest, in conjunction with Cleopatra, the elder of the two sisters, who had always continued under his protection and guardianship. The younger, Arsinoe, in whose name Ganymed, as we have seen, tyrannically reigned for some time he thought proper to banish the kingdom, that she might not raise any new disturbance, through the agency of seditious men, before the king's authority should be firmly established. Taking the sixth veteran legion with him into Syria, he left the rest in Egypt to support the authority of the king and queen, neither of whom stood well in the affections of their subjects, on account of their attachment to Caesar, nor could be supposed to have given any fixed foundation to their power, in an administration of only a few days' continuance. It was also for the honor and interest of the republic that if they continued faithful our forces should protect them; but if ungrateful that they should be restrained by the same power. Having thus settled the kingdom, he marched by land into Syria.

Source: Aulus Hirtius, *Caesar's Commentaries,* translated by W. A. McDevitte and W. S. Bohn (New York: Harper, 1869), chaps. 26–33.

24. The Battle of Actium (September 2, 31 BCE): Plutarch's *Life of Antony*

Introduction

The Battle of Actium was the final major engagement of the Roman Civil War that had been in sporadic progress since at least 49 BCE, when Gnaeus Pompeius Magnus and Julius Caesar had competed for supreme power in Rome. Following Caesar's political murder in 44BCE, his supporters, led by his close friend Mark Antony and his nephew and adopted son Octavianus Caesar, pursued and defeated his assassins. The two then became rivals of each other. The initial arrangement whereby Antony governed the eastern part of the Roman Empire and Octavianus the western part became increasingly precarious, especially after Antony married but then repudiated Octavia, the sister of Octavianus, leaving her to return to Queen Cleopatra VII of Egypt, with whom he had begun an affair around 42 BCE. In 32 BCE, after Antony claimed that Octavianus had exceeded the authority allotted to him, open hostilities broke out between the two and their respective allies, resulting in the naval Battle of Actium.

This was the decisive battle of the final wars of the Roman Republic. Antony's fleet and that of Cleopatra fought against the predominantly smaller but more maneuverable ships of Octavianus. Subsequent historians blamed Cleopatra's cowardice and bad advice for the defeat but were undoubtedly prejudiced against her, so their accounts—written under a government for which this battle was a crucial founding event—may not be entirely reliable. A strategic retreat by Cleopatra's forces prompted panic in Antony's fleet, which then fled the scene, leaving many of his land forces no option but to surrender or desert. With much of his army lost, Antony effectively became a fugitive. Octavianus subsequently followed his opponents to Egypt, besieging them in Alexandria. Once he had defeated them, with both Antony and Cleopatra committing suicide, his authority within Rome's dominions was unchallenged, and he controlled the Mediterranean. Awarded the title of "Princeps" (first citizen) and later acclaimed as "Augustus," he was effectively Rome's first emperor. Ruling a further four decades, until 14 CE, Augustus had the time to consolidate his authority and reduce Rome's former republican institutions to mere ceremonial window dressing.

Document

When the forces came together for the war, Antony had no fewer than five hundred fighting ships, among which were many vessels of eight and ten banks of oars, arrayed in pompous and festal fashion; he also had one hundred thousand infantry soldiers and twelve thousand horsemen. Of subject kings who fought with him, there were Bocchus the king of Libya, Tarcondemus the king of Upper Cilicia, Archelaüs of Cappadocia, Philadelphus of Paphlagonia, Mithridates of Commagene, and Sadalas of Thrace. These were with him, while from Pontus Polemon sent an army, and Malchus from Arabia, and Herod the Jew, besides Amyntas the king of Lycaonia and Galatia; the king of the Medes also sent an auxiliary force. Caesar had two hundred and fifty ships of war, eighty thousand infantry, and about as many horsemen as his enemies. Antony's authority extended over the country from the Euphrates and Armenia to the Ionian sea and Illyria; Caesar's over the country reaching from Illyria to the Western Ocean and from the ocean back to the Tuscan and Sicilian seas. Of Libya, the part extending opposite to Italy, Gaul, and Iberia as far as the pillars of Hercules, belonged to Caesar; the part extending from Cyrene as far as Armenia, to Antony.

But to such an extent, now, was Antony an appendage of the woman that although he was far superior on land, he wished the decision to rest with his navy, to please Cleopatra, and that too when he saw that for lack of crews his trierarchs were haling together out of long-suffering Greece wayfarers, mule-drivers, harvesters, and ephebi, and that even then their ships were not fully manned, but most of them were deficient and sailed wretchedly. Caesar's fleet, on the other hand, was perfectly equipped, and consisted of ships which had not been built for a display of height or mass, but were easily steered, swift, and fully manned. This fleet Caesar kept assembled at Tarentum and Brundisium, and he sent to Antony a demand to waste no time, but to come with his forces; Caesar himself would furnish his armament with unobstructed roadsteads and harbours, and would withdraw with his land forces a day's journey for a horseman from the sea-shore, until Antony should have safely landed and fixed his camp. This boastful language Antony matched by challenging Caesar to single combat, although he was an older man than Caesar; and if Caesar declined this, Antony demanded that they should fight out the issue at Pharsalus, as Caesar and Pompey had once done. But while Antony was lying at anchor off Actium, where now Nicopolis stands, Caesar got the start of him by crossing the Ionian sea and occupying a place in Epirus called Toruné (that is, ladle); and when Antony and his friends were disturbed by this, since their infantry forces were belated, Cleopatra, jesting, said: "What is there dreadful in Caesar's sitting at a ladle?"

But Antony, when the enemy sailed against him at daybreak, was afraid lest they should capture his ships while they had no fighting crews, and therefore armed the rowers and drew them up on the decks so as to make a show; then he grouped his ships at the mouth of the gulf near Actium, their ranks of oars on either side lifted and poised as for the stroke, and their prows towards the enemy, as if they were fully manned and prepared to fight. Caesar, thus outwitted and deceived, withdrew. Antony was also thought to have shown great skill in enclosing the potable water within certain barriers and thus depriving the enemy of it, since the places round about afforded little, and that of bad quality. . . .

There were also defections among the kings, and Amyntas and Deiotarus went over to Caesar. Besides, since his navy was unlucky in everything and always too late to be of assistance, Antony was again compelled to turn his attention to his land forces. Canidius also, the commander of the land forces, changed his mind in presence of the danger, and advised Antony to send Cleopatra away, to withdraw into Thrace or Macedonia, and there to decide the issue by a land battle. For Dicomes the king of the Getae promised to come to their aid with a large force; and it would be no disgrace, Canidius urged, for them to give up the sea to Caesar, who had practised himself there in the Sicilian war; but it would be a strange thing for Antony, who was most experienced in land conflicts, not to avail himself of the strength and equipment of his numerous legionary soldiers, but to distribute his forces among ships and so fritter them away.

However, Cleopatra prevailed with her opinion that the war should be decided by the ships, although she was already contemplating flight, and was disposing her own forces, not where they would be helpful in winning the victory, but where they could most easily get away if the cause was lost. . . .

When it had been decided to deliver a sea battle, Antony burned all the Egyptian ships except sixty; but the largest and best, from those having three to those having ten banks of oars, he manned, putting on board twenty thousand heavy-armed soldiers and two thousand archers. . . .

During that day, then, and the three following days the sea was tossed up by a strong wind and prevented the battle; but on the fifth, the weather becoming fine and the sea calm, they came to an engagement. Antony had the right wing, with Publicola, Coelius the left, and in the centre were Marcus Octavius and Marcus Insteius. Caesar posted Agrippa on the left, and reserved the right wing for himself. Of the land forces, that of Antony was commanded by Canidius, that of Caesar by Taurus, who drew them up along the sea and remained quiet. As for the leaders themselves, Antony visited all his ships in a row-boat, exhorting the soldiers, owing to the weight of their ships, to fight without changing their position, as if they were on land; he also ordered the masters of the ships to receive the attacks of the enemy as if their ships were lying quietly at anchor, and to maintain their position at the mouth of the gulf, which was narrow and difficult. Caesar, we are told, who had left his tent while it was still dark and was going round to visit his ships, was met by a man driving an ass. Caesar asked the man his name, and he, recognizing Caesar, replied: "My name is Prosper, and my ass's name is Victor." Therefore, when Caesar afterwards decided the place with the beaks of ships, he set up bronze figures of an ass and a man. After surveying the rest of his line of battle, he was carried in a small boat to his right wing, and there was astonished to see the enemy lying motionless in the narrows; indeed, their ships had the appearance

24. The Battle of Actium: Plutarch's *Life of Antony*

of riding at anchor. For a long time he was convinced that this was really the case, and kept his own ships at a distance of about eight furlongs from the enemy. But it was now the sixth hour, and since a wind was rising from the sea, the soldiers of Antony became impatient at the delay, and, relying on the height and size of their own ships as making them unassailable, they put their left wing in motion. When Caesar saw this he was delighted, and ordered his right wing to row backwards, wishing to draw the enemy still farther out from the gulf and the narrows, and then to surround them with his own agile vessels and come to close quarters with ships which, owing to their great size and the smallness of their crews, were slow and ineffective.

Though the struggle was beginning to be at close range, the ships did not ram or crush one another at all, since Antony's, owing to their weight, had no impetus, which chiefly gives effect to the blows of the beaks, while Caesar's not only avoided dashing front to front against rough and hard bronze armour, but did not even venture to ram the enemy's ships in the side. For their beaks would easily have been broken off by impact against vessels constructed of huge square timbers fastened together with iron. The struggle was therefore like a land battle; or, to speak more truly, like the storming of a walled town. For three or four of Caesar's vessels were engaged at the same time about one of Antony's, and the crews fought with wicker shields and spears and punting-poles and fiery missiles; the soldiers of Antony also shot with catapults from wooden towers.

And now, as Agrippa was extending the left wing with a view to encircling the enemy, Publicola was forced to advance against him, and so was separated from the centre. The centre falling into confusion and engaging with Arruntius, although the sea-fight was still undecided and equally favourable to both sides, suddenly the sixty ships of Cleopatra were seen hoisting their sails for flight and making off through the midst of the combatants; for they had been posted in the rear of the large vessels, and threw them into confusion as they plunged through. The enemy looked on with amazement, seeing that they took advantage of the wind and made for Peloponnesus. Here, indeed, Antony made it clear to all the world that he was swayed neither by the sentiments of a commander nor of a brave man, nor even by his own, but, as someone in pleasantry said that the soul of the lover dwells in another's body, he was dragged along by the woman as if he had become incorporate with her and must go where she did. For no sooner did he see her ship sailing off than he forgot everything else, betrayed and ran away from those who were fighting and dying in his cause, got into a five-oared galley, where Alexas the Syrian and Scellius were his only companions, and hastened after the woman who had already ruined him and would make his ruin still more complete.

Cleopatra recognized him and raised a signal on her ship; so Antony came up and was taken on board, but he neither saw nor was seen by her. Instead, he went forward alone to the prow and sat down by himself in silence, holding his head in both hands.... He spent three days by himself at the prow, either because he was angry with Cleopatra, or ashamed to see her, and then put in at Taenarum. Here the women in Cleopatra's company at first brought them into a parley, and then persuaded them to eat and sleep together.

Presently not a few of their heavy transport ships and some of their friends began to gather about them after the defeat, bringing word that the fleet was destroyed, but that, in their opinion, the land forces still held together....

This, then, was the situation of Antony. But at Actium his fleet held out for a long time against Caesar, and only after it had been most severely damaged by the high sea which rose against it did it reluctantly, and at the tenth hour, give up the struggle. There were not more than five thousand dead, but three hundred ships were captured, as Caesar himself has written. Only a few were aware that Antony had fled, and to those who heard of it the story was at first an incredible one, that he had gone off and left nineteen legions of undefeated men-at-arms and twelve thousand horsemen, as if he had not many times experienced both kinds of fortune and were not exercised by the reverses of countless wars and fightings. His soldiers, too, had a great longing for him, and expected that he would presently make his appearance from some quarter or other; and they displayed so much fidelity and bravery that even after his flight had become evident they held together for seven days, paying no heed to the messages which Caesar sent them. But at last, after Canidius their general had run away by night and forsaken the camp, being now destitute of all things and betrayed by their commanders, they went over to the conqueror.

Source: Plutarch, "The Life of Antony," chaps. 61–68, in Plutarch, *The Parallel Lives* (Cambridge, MA: Harvard University Press, 1920).

25. The Siege of Jerusalem (70 CE)

Introduction

In 69 CE General Titus Flavius Vespasianus, who commanded the Roman forces that were in the process of suppressing the Jewish rebellion in Judaea that erupted in 67 CE, became emperor. He delegated to his elder son Titus, who had previously served under his command, the task of completing the subjugation of Judaea. The culmination of this campaign came when Titus besieged, took, and sacked the City of Jerusalem, the secular and religious capital of the Jews. Many of the inhabitants died of famine, and others were killed by the Roman troops, who subsequently demolished much of the city. The abandonment in 67 CE of an earlier Roman siege of the city had resulted in a wholesale Roman defeat at the Battle of Beth Horon, an event that had emboldened cities throughout the province of Judaea to rebel. Although some dedicated Jewish insurgents still continued last-ditch resistance, the capture and destruction of Jerusalem by Roman forces carried, as this account by the Jewish-born historian Flavius Josephus suggests, great symbolic resonance among the entire Jewish community.

Document

How Cæsar raised banks round about the upper city [i.e. Mount Sion]: and when they were compleated, gave orders that the machines should be brought. He then possessed himself of the whole city.

Now when [Titus] Cæsar perceived that the upper city was so steep, that it could not possibly be taken without raising banks against it, he distributed the several parts of that work among his army; and this on the twentieth day of the month Lous [Ab] [A.D. 70]. Now the carriage of the materials was a difficult task: since all the trees, as I have already told you, that were about the city, within the distance of a hundred furlongs, had their branches cut off already, in order to make the former banks. The works that belonged to the four legions were erected on the west side of the city; over against the royal palace. But the whole body of the auxiliary troops, with the rest of the multitude that were with them, [erected their banks] at the Xystus: whence they reached to the bridge, and that tower of Simon, which he had built, as a citadel for himself, against John, when they were at war one with another....

4. And now were the banks finished on the seventh day of the month Gorpieus [Elul] [A.D. 70], in eighteen days' time: when the Romans brought their machines against the wall. But for the seditious, some of them, as despairing of saving the city, retired from the wall to the citadel. Others of them went down into the subterranean vaults: though still a great many of them defended themselves against those that brought the engines for the battery. Yet did the Romans overcome them, by their number, and by their strength: and, what was the principal thing of all, by going cheerfully about their work, while the Jews were quite dejected, and become weak. Now as soon as a part of the wall was battered down, and certain of the towers yielded to the impression of the battering rams, those that opposed themselves fled away; and such a terror fell upon the tyrants, as was much greater than the occasion required. For before the enemy got over the breach they were quite stunned, and were immediately for flying away. And now one might see these men, who had hitherto been so insolent and arrogant in their wicked practices, to be cast down, and to tremble: insomuch that it would pity one's heart to observe the change that was made in those vile persons. Accordingly they ran with great violence upon the Roman wall that encompassed them, in order to force away those that guarded it, and to break through it, and get away. But when they saw that those who had formerly been faithful to them had gone away (as indeed they were fled whithersoever the great distress they were in persuaded them to flee;) as also when those that came running before the rest told them, that the western wall was intirely overthrown, while others said the Romans were gotten in, and others that they were near, and looking out for them which were only the dictates of their fear, which imposed upon their sight: they fell upon their face, and greatly lamented their own mad conduct; and their nerves were so terribly loosed, that they could not fly away. And here one may chiefly reflect on the power of God exercised upon these wicked wretches, and on the good fortune of the Romans. For these tyrants did now wholly deprive themselves of the security they had in their own power, and came down from those very towers of their own accord, wherein they could have never been taken by force, nor, indeed, any other way than by famine. And thus did the Romans, when they had taken such great pains about weaker walls, get by good fortune what they could never have gotten by their engines. For three of these towers were too strong for all mechanical engines whatsoever. Concerning which we have treated above.

5. So they now left these towers of themselves, or rather they were ejected out of them by God himself, and fled immediately to that valley which was under Siloam. Where they again recovered themselves out of the dread they were in for a while, and ran violently against that part of the Roman wall which lay on that side. But as their courage was too much depressed to make their attacks with sufficient force, and their power was now broken with fear and affliction, they were repulsed by the guards, and dispersing themselves at distances from each other, went down into the subterranean caverns. So the Romans being now become masters of the walls, they both placed their ensigns upon the towers, and made joyful acclamations for the victory they had gained: as having found the end of this war, much lighter than its beginning. For when they had gotten upon the last wall, without any bloodshed, they could hardly believe what they found to be true; but seeing no body to oppose them, they stood in doubt what such an unusual solitude could mean. But when they went in numbers into the lanes of the city, with their swords drawn, they slew those whom they overtook without mercy, and set fire to the houses whither the Jews were fled, and burnt every soul in them, and laid waste a great many of the rest: and when they were come to the houses to plunder them, they found in them intire families of dead men, and the upper rooms full of dead corpses: that is of such as died by the famine. They then stood in an horror at this sight: and went out, without touching any thing. But although they had this commiseration for such as were destroyed in that manner, yet had they not the same for those that were still alive, but they ran every one through whom they met with, and obstructed the very lanes with their dead bodies, and made the whole city run down with blood, to such a degree indeed, that the fire of many of the houses was quenched with these men's blood. And truly so it happened, that though the slayers left off at the evening, yet did the fire greatly prevail in the night. And as all was burning, came that eighth day of the month Gorpieus [Elul] upon Jerusalem, a city that had been liable to so many miseries during this siege, that had it always enjoyed as much happiness from its first foundation, it would certainly have been the envy of the world. Nor did it on any other account so much deserve these sore misfortunes, as by producing such a generation of men as were the occasions of this its overthrow.

Source: Josephus, "The Wars of the Jews," Book 6, chap. 19, in Flavius Josephus, *The Works of Flavius Josephus*, translated by William Whiston (London: George Routledge, 1906).

26. The Siege of Masada (April 15, 73 CE)

Introduction

After the siege and destruction of the city of Jerusalem, the surviving zealots among the Jews took refuge in the inaccessible and forbidding fortress of Masada, harrying the surrounding countryside. In 72 CE, Emperor Vespasian dispatched an army of 8,000 men to Palestine to mop up the surviving Jewish resistance. With the help of slave labor, they built a massive ramp up to the fort. The historian Flavius Josephus, himself a former Jewish rebel and sole survivor of a group suicide, who had attached himself to Vespasian and his family earlier in the revolt, described how as the Romans were on the brink of taking the citadel the Jewish leader Eleazar exhorted his 967 followers to commit mass suicide, which they all did. Josephus claimed to have received this account of the end of the siege from two Roman soldiers who took part in the operation. Josephus was therefore not an eyewitness to the events he described. While details of his account have been questioned and the full story may have been less simple, there was probably a substantial core of truth to his narrative.

Document

For now it was that the Roman general came, and led his army against Eleazar and those Sicarii who held the fortress Masada together with him; and for the whole country adjoining, he presently gained it, and put garrisons into the most proper places of it; he also built a wall quite round the entire fortress, that none of the besieged might easily escape; he also set his men to guard the several parts of it; he also pitched his camp in such an agreeable place as he had chosen for the siege, and at which place the rock belonging to the fortress did make the nearest approach to the neighboring mountain, which yet was a place of difficulty for getting plenty of provisions; for it was not only food that was to be brought from a great distance [to the army], and this with a great deal of pain to those Jews who were appointed for that purpose, but water was also to be brought to the camp, because the place afforded no fountain that was near it. When therefore Silva had ordered these affairs beforehand, he fell to besieging the place; which siege was likely to stand in need of a great deal of skill and pains, by reason of the strength of the fortress. . . .

However, neither did Eleazar once think of flying away; nor would he permit any one else to do so. But when he saw their wall burned down by the fire; and could devise no other way of escaping, or room for their farther courage; and setting before their eyes what the Romans would do to them, their children, and their wives, if they got them into their power; he consulted about having them all slain. . . .

How the people that were in the fortress were prevailed on by the words of Eleazar, two women and five children only excepted; and all submitted to be killed by one another.

Now as Eleazar was proceeding on in his exhortation, they all cut him off short, and made haste to do the work, as full of an unconquerable ardor of mind, and moved with a demoniacal fury. So they went their ways, as one still endeavouring to be before another; and as thinking that this eagerness would be a demonstration of their courage, and good conduct; if they could avoid appearing in the last class. So great was the zeal they were in to slay their wives, and children, and themselves also. Nor indeed, when they came to the work itself, did their courage fail them, as one might imagine it would have done: but they then held fast the same resolution, without wavering, which they had upon the hearing of Eleazar's speech, while yet every one of them still retained the natural passion of love to themselves, and their families: because the reasoning they went upon appeared to them to be very just, even with regard to those that were dearest to them. For the husbands tenderly embraced their wives, and took their children into their arms, and gave the longest parting kisses to them, with tears in their eyes. Yet at the same time did they compleat what they had resolved on; as if they had been executed by the hands of strangers. And they had nothing else for their comfort, but the necessity they were in of doing this execution, to avoid that prospect they had of the miseries they were to suffer from their enemies. Nor was there at length any one of these men found that scrupled to act their part in this terrible execution: but every one of them dispatched his dearest relations. Miserable men indeed were they! whose distress forced them to slay their own wives, and children, with their own hands, as the lightest of those evils that were before them. So they being not able to bear the grief they were under for what they had done any longer; and esteeming it an injury to those they had slain to live even the shortest space of time after them, they presently laid all they had upon an heap, and set fire to it. They then chose ten men by lot, out of them; to slay all the rest. Every one of whom laid himself down by his wife, and children, on the ground, and threw his arms about them, and they offered their necks to the stroke of those who by lot executed that melancholy office. And when these ten had, without fear, slain them all, they made the same rule for casting lots for themselves; that he whose lot it was should first kill the other nine; and after all should kill himself. Accordingly all these had courage sufficient to be no way behind one another in doing or suffering. So, for a conclusion, the nine offered their necks to the executioner; and he who was the last of all took a view of all the other bodies; lest perchance some or other among so many that were slain should want his assistance to be quite dispatched: and when he perceived that they were all slain, he set fire to the palace, and with the great force of his hand ran his sword entirely through himself, and fell down dead near to his own relations. So these people died with this intention, that they would not leave so much as one soul among them all alive to be subject to the Romans. Yet was there an ancient woman, and another who was of kin to Eleazar, and superior to most women in prudence and learning, with five children: who had concealed themselves in caverns underground; and had carried water thither for their drink; and were hidden there when the rest were intent upon the slaughter of one another. Those others were nine hundred and sixty in number: the women, and children being withal included in that computation. This calamitous slaughter was made on the fifteenth day of the month Xanthicus [Nisan] [A.D. 73].

Now for the Romans, they expected that they should be fought in the morning: when accordingly they put on their armour, and laid bridges of planks upon their ladders from their banks, to make an assault upon the fortress. Which they did. But saw nobody as an enemy, but a terrible solitude on every side, with a fire within the place, as well as a perfect silence. So they were at a loss to guess at what had happened. At length they made a shout, as if it had been at a blow given by the battering ram, to try whether they could bring any one out that was within. The women heard this noise, and came out of their underground cavern; and informed the Romans what had been done, as it was done: and the second of them clearly described all both what was said, and what was done; and the manner of it. Yet did they not easily give their attention to such a desperate undertaking, and did not believe it could be as they said. They also attempted to put the fire out, and quickly cutting themselves a way through it, they came within the palace, and so met with the multitude of the slain: but could take no pleasure in the fact, though it were done to their enemies. Nor could they do other than wonder at the courage of their resolution, and the immoveable contempt of death which so great a number of them had shewn, when they went through with such an action as that was.

Source: Josephus, "The Wars of the Jews," Book 7, chaps. 8–9, in Flavius Josephus, *The Works of Flavius Josephus*, translated by William Whiston (London: George Routledge, 1906).

27. Emperor Titus (r. 79–81), as Viewed by Cassius Dio

Introduction

Emperor Titus became Roman monarch in his own right following the death of his father, Vespasian. Both emperors were military men, professional soldiers with a lengthy record of campaigns in Asia and Europe. Titus was best known for his suppression of the Jewish revolt of 70–73, which had won him a triumph in Rome. He had a lengthy love affair with Queen Berenice of Judaea, from the pro-Roman Herodian ruling family, but the two never formally married. Titus, a pragmatist, may have feared an unfavorable popular reception in Rome to such an alliance. Although he had worked very close with his father, effectively sharing power with the older man, Titus's reign as sole emperor lasted a mere two years before he succumbed to an infection at the age of 41. The historian Cassius Dio left a somewhat skeptical assessment of his record during this time, suggesting that had Titus remained longer in office, he might have become more authoritarian. It is equally possible that he would have given Rome greater stability than was the case under his younger brother, the erratic and tyrannical Emperor Domitian, who succeeded Titus and was rumored to have poisoned him.

Document

Titus after becoming ruler committed no act of murder or of amatory passion, but showed himself upright, though plotted against, and self-controlled, though Berenice came to Rome again. This may have been because he had really undergone a change; indeed, for men to wield power as assistants to another is a very different thing from exercising independent authority themselves. In the former case, they are heedless of the good name of the sovereignty and in their greed misuse the authority it gives them, thus doing many things that make their power the object of envy and slander; but actual monarchs, knowing that everything depends upon them, have an eye to good repute also. It was this realization, doubtless, that caused Titus to say to someone whose society he had previously affected: "It is not the same thing to request a favour of another as to decide a case yourself, nor the same to ask something of another as it is to give it to someone yourself." Again, his satisfactory record may also have been due to the fact that he survived his accession but a very short time (short, that is, for a ruler), for he was thus given no opportunity for wrongdoing. For he lived after this only two years, two months and twenty days—in addition to the thirty-nine years, five months and twenty-five days he had already lived at that time. In this respect, indeed, he is regarded as having equalled the long reign of Augustus, since it is maintained that Augustus would never have been loved had he lived a shorter time, nor Titus had he lived longer. For Augustus, though at the outset he showed himself rather harsh because of the wars and the factional strife, was later able, in the course of time, to achieve a brilliant reputation for his kindly deeds; Titus, on the other hand, ruled with mildness and died at the height of his glory, whereas, if he had lived a long time, it might have been shown that he owes his present fame more to good fortune than to merit.

Be that as it may, Titus during his reign put no senator to death, nor, indeed, was anyone else slain by him during his rule. Cases based on the charge of maiestas he would never entertain himself nor allow others to entertain; for he declared: "It is impossible for me to be insulted or abused in any way. For I do naught that deserves censure, and I care not for what is reported falsely. As for the emperors who are dead and gone, they will avenge themselves in case anyone does them a wrong, if in very truth they are demigods and possess any power." He also instituted various other measures designed to render men's lives more secure and free from trouble. Thus, he issued an edict confirming all gifts that had been bestowed upon any persons by the former emperors, thus saving them the trouble of petitioning him individually about the matter. He also banished the informers from the City.

In money matters he was frugal and made no unnecessary expenditures, yet he did not punish anyone for following a different course.

Source: "Cassius Dio: Roman History, Epitome of Book LXVI," University of Chicago, http://penelope.uchicago.edu/Thayer/E/Roman/Texts/Cassius_Dio/66*.html.

28. Emperor Hadrian (r. 117–138), as Described by Cassius Dio

Introduction

The Greek historian Cassius Dio, writing in the late second and early third centuries, described Emperor Hadrian, who succeeded the childless Emperor Trajan on the latter's death in 117. Hadrian, a nephew by marriage to Trajan and an excellent soldier who was around 40 when he ascended the throne, was an energetic emperor who made upgrading his military forces a top priority. He consolidated the Roman Empire within defensible boundaries and sought to instil a sense of unity among its disparate peoples. An enthusiast for Hellenic Greek culture, Hadrian constructed numerous temples and sought to encourage learning and the arts. He spent most of his reign traveling around his extensive dominions on inspection tours.

Document

Hadrian had not been adopted by [the Emperor] Trajan; he was merely a compatriot and former ward of his, was of near kin to him and had married his niece,—in short, he was a companion of his, sharing his daily life, and had been assigned to Syria for the Parthian War. . . .

In a certain letter that Hadrian wrote, in which were many high-minded sentiments, he swore that he would neither do anything contrary to the public interest nor put to death any senator, and he invoked destruction upon himself if he should violate these promises in any wise. . . .

Hadrian was a pleasant man to meet and he possessed a certain charm.

As regards birth Hadrian was the son of a man of senatorial rank, an ex-praetor, Hadrianus Afer by name. By nature he was fond of literary study in both the Greek and Latin languages, and has left behind a variety of prose writings as well as compositions in verse. For his ambition was insatiable, and hence he practised all conceivable pursuits, even the most trivial; for example, he modelled and painted, and declared that there was nothing pertaining to peace or war, to imperial or private life, of which he was not cognizant. All this, of course, did people no harm; but his jealousy of all who excelled in any respect was most terrible and caused the downfall of many, besides utterly destroying several. For, inasmuch as he wished to surpass everybody in everything, he hated those who attained eminence in any direction. . . .

Other traits for which people found fault with him were his great strictness, his curiosity and his meddlesomeness. Yet he balanced and atoned for these defects by his careful oversight, his prudence, his munificence and his skill; furthermore, he did not stir up any war, and he terminated those already in progress; and he deprived no one of money unjustly, while upon many—communities and private citizens, senators and knights—he bestowed large sums. Indeed, he did not even wait to be asked, but acted in absolutely every case according to the individual needs. He subjected the legions to the strictest discipline, so that, though strong, they were neither insubordinate nor insolent; and he aided the allied and subject cities most munificently. He had seen many of them,—more, in fact, than any other emperor,—and he assisted practically all of them, giving to some a water supply, to others harbours, food, public works, money and various honours, differing the different cities. . . .

Hadrian travelled through one province after another, visiting the various regions and cities and inspecting all the garrisons and forts. Some of these he removed to more desirable places, some he abolished, and he also established some new ones. He personally viewed and investigated absolutely everything, not merely the usual appurtenances of camps, such as weapons, engines, trenches, ramparts and palisades, but also the private affairs of every one, both of the men serving in the ranks and of the officers themselves,—their lives, their quarters and their habits,—and he reformed and corrected in many cases practices and arrangements for living that had become too luxurious. He drilled the men for every kind of battle, honouring some and reproving others, and he taught them all what should be done. And in order that they should be benefited by observing him, he everywhere led a rigorous life and either walked or rode on horseback on all occasions, never once at this period setting foot in either a chariot or a four-wheeled vehicle. He covered his head neither in hot weather nor in cold, but alike amid German snows and under scorching Egyptian suns he went about with his head bare. In fine, both by his example and by his precepts he so trained and disciplined the whole military force throughout the entire empire that even to-day the methods then introduced by him are the soldiers' law of campaigning. This best explains why he lived for the most part at peace with foreign nations; for as they saw his state of preparation and were themselves not only free from aggression but received money besides, they made no uprising. So excellently, indeed, had his soldiery been trained that the cavalry of the Batavians, as they were called, swam the Ister with their arms. Seeing all this, the barbarians stood in terror of the Romans, they employed Hadrian as an arbitrator of their differences. . . .

Source: "Cassius Dio: Roman History, Epitome of Book LXIX," University of Chicago, http://penelope.uchicago.edu/Thayer/E/Roman/Texts/Cassius_Dio/69*.html.

29. The Bar Kochba Revolt (132–135 CE)

Introduction

The Jews of the Roman province of Judaea and the broader Roman Empire were perpetually restive. Even after the suppression of the Jewish revolt of 67–73 CE, further revolts occurred. At the time he became emperor in 117, Hadrian was in the process of suppressing the Jewish Kitos Rebellion (Rebellion of the Diaspora), a Jewish uprising that began in 115 and involved the Jewish population in the provinces of Cyrenaica, Egypt, Mesopotamia, Syria, Cyprus, and Judaea. Other discontented groups joined them. Hadrian ended the war by abandoning many of Rome's less defensible territories and concentrating on consolidation of what remained within sustainable boundaries. Toward the end of his reign in 132 CE, he nonetheless faced another major Jewish rebellion within Judaea itself, the Bar Kochba Revolt, which represented the most serious military challenge of his reign. Over the following three years, as the historian Cassius Dio described, Roman generals suppressed the rebels with great brutality, laying waste to the province.

Document

At Jerusalem [the Emperor Hadrian] founded a city in place of the one which had been razed to the ground, naming it Aelia Capitolina, and on the site of the temple of the god he raised a new temple to Jupiter. This brought on a war of no slight importance nor of brief duration, for the Jews deemed it intolerable that foreign races should be settled in their city and foreign religious rites planted there. So long, indeed, as Hadrian was close by in Egypt and again in Syria, they remained quiet, save in so far as they purposely made of poor quality such weapons as they were called upon to furnish, in order that the Romans might reject them and they themselves might thus have the use of them; but when he went farther away, they openly revolted. To be sure, they did not dare try conclusions with the Romans in the open field, but they occupied the advantageous positions in the country and strengthened them with mines and walls, in order that they might have places of refuge whenever they should be hard pressed, and might meet together unobserved under ground; and they pierced these subterranean passages from above at intervals to let in air and light.

At first the Romans took no account of them. Soon, however, all Judaea had been stirred up, and the Jews everywhere were showing signs of disturbance, were gathering together, and giving evidence of great hostility to the Romans, partly by secret and partly by overt acts; many outside nations, too, were joining them through eagerness for gain, and the whole earth, one might almost say, was being stirred up over the matter. Then, indeed, Hadrian sent against them his best generals. First of these was Julius Severus, who was dispatched from Britain, where he was governor, against the Jews. Severus did not venture to attack his opponents in the open at any one point, in view of their numbers and their desperation, but by intercepting small groups, thanks to the number of his soldiers and his under-officers, and by depriving them of food and shutting them up, he was able, rather slowly, to be sure, but with comparatively little danger, to crush, exhaust and exterminate them. Very few of them in fact survived. Fifty of their most important outposts and nine hundred and eighty-five of their most famous villages were razed to the ground. Five hundred and eighty thousand men were slain in the various raids and battles, and the number of those that perished by famine, disease and fire was past finding out. Thus nearly the whole of Judaea was made desolate, a result of which the people had had forewarning before the war. For the tomb of Solomon, which the Jews regard as an object of veneration, fell to pieces of itself and collapsed, and many wolves and hyenas rushed howling into their cities. Many Romans, moreover, perished in this war. . . .

This, then, was the end of the war with the Jews.

Source: "Cassius Dio: Roman History, Epitome of Book LXIX," University of Chicago, http://penelope.uchicago.edu/Thayer/E/Roman/Texts/Cassius _Dio/69*.html.

30. The Karnamik-I-Ardashir, or the Records of Ardashir (ca. 180–242 CE)

Introduction

Mythology proliferated around the life and reign of Ardashir, the great king of Persia (180–242 CE), who overthrew the Parthian Arsacid dynasty in 224 and founded the Sassanid dynasty, which would wage war first with Rome and then Byzantium for the next four centuries. The new rulers of Persia were Zoroastrians, who worshipped Ahuramazda, a god of fire and light. The Records of Ardashir, probably composed or at least written down some time in the sixth century CE, are the earliest Persian account of the rise of Ardashir, apparently a local Persian governor of Pars, a tributary of Parthian king Artabanus V. Ardashir won control of Pars, possibly by disposing of his father and brother, and gradually extended his power over surrounding minor lords and governors. Eventually around 223 he mounted an outright rebellion against Artabanus V, claiming that he did so in the name of Ahuramazda and associating himself with the famous former Achmaenid dynasty of Persia, including such rulers as Cyrus the Great and Darius the Great. In April 224 at the Battle of Hormozgdan, Ardashir and Artabanus confronted each other directly, and Artabanus was killed in battle. His death marked the end of the Arsacid dynasty and the beginning of four centuries of rule by the Sassanids.

Document

Chapter I

In the records of Ardashir, Founder of the Sassanian Kingdom, son of Papak, it is written as follows: That after the death of Alexander [the Great], inhabitant of Arum, there were in the territory of Iran two hundred and forty princes. Spahan, Pars, and the borderlands that were nearest to them, were in the hands of Artabanus [last of the Parthian kings], the chief king. Papak was the frontier governor of Pars, and was one of the commissioners appointed by Artabanus. The seat of Artabanus was in Stakhra. And Papak had no son to preserve his name. And Sasan was a shepherd employed by Papak, who always remained with the horses and cattle belonging to the latter, and he was descended from the line of King Darab [Darayavaush or Darius III], son of Darae.

During the evil reign of Alexander, the descendants of Darab privately lived in distant lands, wandering with Kurdish shepherds. Papak did not know that Sasan was descended from the family of Darab, son of Darae. One night Papak saw in a dream as though the sun was shining from the head of Sasan and giving light to the whole world. Another night he dreamt that Sasan was seated on a richly adorned white elephant, and that all those that stood around him in the kingdom made obeisance to him, praised, and blessed him. The next third night he, accordingly, saw as if the sacred fires Frobag, Gushasp, and Burzin-Mitro were burning in the house of Sasan and giving light to the whole world. He wondered at it, and directly invited to his presence the sages and interpreters of dreams, and narrated to them the visions he had seen in his dreams during those three nights.

The interpreters of dreams spoke thus: "The person that was seen in that dream, he or somebody from among the sons of that man will succeed to the sovereignty of this world, because the sun and the richly adorned white elephant that you observed represented vigor and the triumph of opulence; the sacred fire of Frobag, the religious intelligence of the great men among the Mobads; and the sacred fire Gushasp, warriors and military chieftains; and the sacred fire Burzin-Mitro, the farmers and agriculturists of the world: and thus this sovereignty will fall to that man or the descendants of that man."

On hearing these words, Papak dispatched somebody to call Sasan to his presence, and questioned him as follows: "From what race and family art thou? Out of thy fore-fathers and ancestors was there anybody who had exercised sovereignty or chieftainship before?" Sasan solicited from Papak his support and protection in these words: "Do me no hurt or harm." Papak accepted the request, and Sasan declared before Papak his own secret as it stood. On hearing his reply Papak was delighted, and so he ordered Sasan thus: "Elevate thy body by taking a bath."

Meanwhile Papak directed his servants that a suit of clothes fit to be worn by a king should be brought and given to Sasan, and Sasan wore the royal garments accordingly. Papak further directed in the case of Sasan that he should be nourished with invigorating, fresh and proper food for several days. Later on he gave him his daughter in marriage, and according to the law of nature she, in a short time, was pregnant by Sasan, and from her Ardashir was born. When Papak observed the youthful body and cleverness of Ardashir, he interpreted it thus: "The dream which I beheld was true." He regarded Ardashir as his own son, and brought him up as a dear child.

When Ardashir reached the age which was the time for higher instruction he became so proficient in literary knowledge, riding, and other arts that he was renowned throughout Pars. When Ardashir attained the age of fifteen years information reached Artabanus that Papak had a son proficient and accomplished in learning and riding. He wrote a letter to Papak to this effect: "We have heard that you have a son, who is accomplished and very proficient in learning and riding; our desire has been that you should send him to our court, and he shall be near us, so that he will associate with our sons and princes, and we might order for him position and reward according to the learning which he possesses."

As Artabanus was powerful and very absolute, it was improper on the part of Papak to do anything contrary to or to evade his command. Immediately therefore he sent Ardashir well-equipped with ten servants and a superb present of many marvelous, magnificent, and suitable things for the acceptance of Artabanus. When Artabanus saw Ardashir he was glad, expressed to him his affectionate regard, and ordered that he should every day accompany his sons and princes to the chase and the polo-ground.

Ardashir acted accordingly.

By the help of Providence he became more victorious and warlike than all, on the polo and the riding-ground, at Chatrang and Vine-Artakhshir, and in several other arts. One day Artabanus went a-hunting with his chevaliers and Ardashir. An elk which happened to be running in the desert was then pursued by Ardashir and the eldest son of Artabanus. And Ardashir, on reaching close to the elk, struck him with an arrow in such a manner that the arrow pierced through the belly as far as its feathers, passed through the other side, and the animal died instantly. When Artabanus and the chevaliers approached them, they expressed wonder at such a dart and asked: "Who struck that arrow?" Ardashir replied: "I did it." The son of Artabanus said: "No, because I did it."

Ardashir became angry and spoke thus to the son of Artabanus: "It is not possible to appropriate the art and heroism of another through tyranny, unpleasantness, falsehood, and injustice. This is an excellent forest, and the wild asses here are many. Let us try here a second time, and bring into display our goodness or evil nature and dexterity." Artabanus thereby felt offended and thereafter did not allow Ardashir to ride on horseback.

He sent the latter to his stables of horses and cattle, and ordered him as follows: "Take care of those animals so that you do not go in the day or night from before those horses and cattle a-hunting, to the playground or the college of learning." Ardashir understood that Artabanus spoke in this manner from envy and grudge, and directly wrote a letter to Papak, stating the facts as they stood. When Papak saw the letter he became melancholy. He wrote in reply to Ardashir as follows: "You did not act wisely in disputing with great men on a matter from which no harm could have reached you, and in addressing them with rough words in public. Now speak out excuses for thy relief and feel humble repentance, for the sages have said: 'It is not possible for an enemy to do that for an enemy, which is brought on himself by an ignorant man from his own actions.' This, too, is said: 'Do not be grieved narrow-mindedly from a person at the time when you can not pass your life happily without him.' And you yourself know that Artabanus is a king more powerful than I, thou, or many people in this world, with reference to our bodies, lives, riches, and estates. And now, too, such is my strictest advice unto thee that thou shouldst act in unison with and obediently toward them, and not deliver up thy own glory to annihilation."

Chapter II

Artabanus had in his service an accomplished maiden, whom he regarded with greater respect and affection than the other maidens under him; and this maiden took part in every service that was meant to do honor to Artabanus. One day, while Ardashir was seated by the horse-stalls, playing a tune on a drum, singing, and making other kinds of merriment, she beheld Ardashir, became enamored of him, and afterward frequently visited him, and formed friendship and love. Always regularly at every night, when the unfortunate Artabanus went to sleep, the maiden would clandestinely approach Ardashir, stay with him till the dawn, and then return to Artabanus.

One day Artabanus invited to his presence the sages and astrologers, who belonged to his court, and put them the following question: "What do you observe regarding the seven planets and the twelve signs of the zodiac, the position and the motion of the stars, the condition of the contemporary sovereigns of different kingdoms, the condition of the peoples of the world, and regarding myself, children, and our family?"

The chief of the astrologers said in reply as follows: "The Nahazig [*Capricorn*] is sunk below; the star Jupiter has returned to its culminating point and stands away from Mars and Venus, while Haptoirang [*Ursa Major*] and the constellation of Leo descend to the verge and give help to Jupiter; whereupon it seems clear that a new lord or king will appear, who will kill many potentates, and bring the world again under the sway of one sovereign." A second leader of the astrologers, too, came in the presence of the King and spoke to the following effect: "It is so manifest that any one of the male servants who flies away from his king within three days from to-day, will attain to greatness and kingship, obtain his wish, and be victorious, over his king."

The maiden, when she returned to Ardashir at night, recounted to Ardashir the words as they were told by the astrologers to Artabanus. Ardashir, when he heard these words, resolved upon departing from that place. He spoke to the maiden thus: "First of all, if thou art sincere and unanimous with me, and, secondly, if any one who runs away from his king within the three fixed days which the sages and astrologers have spoken of, attains to greatness and kingship, we should run away from here as far as this world goes, and escape. If by the grace of God, the glory of the kingdom of Iran falls to our help, and we be delivered and both attain to virtue and goodness, I shall treat thee so that no one in the world will be regarded as more fortunate than thee." The maiden consented and said: "I regard you as a nobleman, and shall obey you in every matter."

As it was nearly dawn, the maiden returned to her own room near Artabanus's chamber. At night, when Artabanus was asleep, she took from the treasury of Artabanus an Indian sword, golden saddles, belts of fine leather, golden crowns, golden goblets full of jewels, dirhems and dinars, coats-of-mail, highly engraved weapons of war, and many other precious things, and she brought them to Ardashir.

Meanwhile Ardashir saddled two of Artabanus's horses that ran seventy *frasangs* a day. He seated himself on one and the maiden on the other, took the road leading to Pars, and rode on with speed. . . .

Chapter III

When the day commenced Artabanus called for the maiden, but she was not to be found. The horse-keeper came and spoke to Artabanus as follows: "Ardashir and two of your steeds are not to be found in their places." Artabanus thereby became aware that one of his maidens, too, had run away and gone with Ardashir. And when he heard the information regarding his treasures his heart burst with grief. He invited the chief of the astrologers, and said: "Make the best of your time, and observe carefully as to the place where that offender [Ardashir] has gone with that dissolute harlot, and as to the time when we shall be able to get hold of them." . . .

Afterward [Artabanus] got his forces and heroes equipped, and dispatched them with one of his sons to Pars, in order to catch Ardashir.

Chapter IV

Ardashir had now taken the road to the seashore, and so resumed his journey. Several of the inhabitants of Pars, who had been distressed by Artabanus, placed their wealth, property, and themselves at his disposal, and expressed to him their unanimity and submission.

When he reached the place which they call *Ramishne Ardashir* ["Delight of Ardashir"] a magnanimous hero of the name of *Banak,* an inhabitant of Spahan, who had escaped from the hands of Artabanus and settled himself there, came personally to Ardashir with his six sons, many soldiers and heroes. Ardashir was at first afraid of Banak, lest the latter, having captured him, would deliver him up to Artabanus. Afterward Banak approached Ardashir, took an oath, and gave him confidence in these words: "As long as I live, I myself with my sons will remain submissive to thee."

Ardashir became glad, and on that site he ordered a town to be built, which was called *Ramishne-i-Artakhshir.* He left Banak there with a detachment of cavalry, and himself marched toward the sea-coast. When in his march onward he saw the ocean before his eyes, he offered thanksgiving to God, called that place the city of Bokht Ardashir, and ordered an Atash-i-Vahram to be enthroned on that sea-coast. From that place Ardashir returned to Banak and his cavalry, and prepared an army.

Thence he went to the threshold of the sacred fire Frobag, which is meritorious, and solicited spiritual gifts from it. Then he came to battle with Artabanus, killed the entire army of the latter, seized their wealth, property, horses, and portable lodges, and settled himself in Stakhar [Ancient *Persepolis,* the capital of Pars]. He collected soldiers in large numbers from Kerman, Mokristan, Spahan, and different districts of Pars, and came to fight with Artabanus himself. So Artabanus sent for soldiers and provisions from different frontiers, such as Rai [near Tehran, the Arsacid capital], Demavand [the mountain range near Rai], Delman [modern Gilan], and Patash-khvargar [an offshoot of the Aparsen Range].

But as the Glory of the Kayanians was with Ardashir, the latter gained success. He killed Artabanus, whose entire wealth and property fell into the hands of Ardashir, who married Artabanus's daughter, and went back to Pars. He built a city which was named Ardashir Gadman, wherein a large tank was dug, from which water was conveyed by means of four canals; and near that tank an Atash-i-Adaran was established.

Further, Ardashir excavated a high mountain, and turned the course of a river into the city through subterranean canals. He bestowed his patronage on many cities, made them very prosperous, and ordered that several Atash-i-Vahrams should also be enthroned.

Chapter V

Afterward he (Ardashir), having collected many soldiers and heroes of Zavul, proceeded to battle against Madig, the King of the Kurds. There were much fighting and bloodshed, in which the army of Ardashir finally sustained a defeat. Ardashir became anxious on account of his own army. On his way back he came at night through a desert which contained neither food nor water, so he himself with all his troops and horses came to hunger and thirst.

Marching onward he saw, from a distance, a fire belonging to some shepherds, and there Ardashir went and beheld an old man living with his cattle on a mountain-steppe. Ardashir passed the night there, and the next day he asked them (the shepherds) about the road. They said: "Three *frasangs* hence there is a very fertile village which has many inhabitants and plenty of food." Ardashir went to that village, and dispatched a person to send to his capital his entire cavalry.

The army of Madig boasted thus: "Now there should be no fear of Ardashir, as on account of his defeat he has returned to Pars." Meanwhile Ardashir, having prepared an army of four thousand men, rushed upon them, and surprised them with a night attack.

He killed one thousand of the Kurds, while others were wounded and taken prisoners; and out of the Kurds that were imprisoned he sent to Pars their king with his sons, brothers, children, his abundant wealth and property.

Source: "Ancient History Sourcebook: The Karnamik-I-Ardashir, or The Records of Ardashir," Fordham University, https://sourcebooks.fordham.edu/ancient/ardashir.asp.

31. The Persian Capture of the Roman Emperor Valerian (r. 253–260): Accounts by John Zonaras and Zosimus

Introduction

Emperor Valerian was the first Roman emperor to be captured alive by his enemies, as opposed to dying in combat. A number of accounts of this event and of his subsequent fate survived. One version given here, written by the 12th-century Byzantine official and scholar John Zonaras, who published an account of the Roman Empire in the 3rd century based on earlier sources, suggests that Valerian, fearing overthrow in a coup, may have deserted to Shapur I of Persia. This unflattering view of Valerian may have reflected a bias against him among Christian historians, including Zonaras, due to the emperor's persecution of Christians during his reign. A second version, by the pagan historian Zosimus writing in the late 4th and early 5th centuries CE, condemns Valerian for being so unwary as to be taken prisoner during peace negotiations intended to buy off Shapur I. Other accounts of Valerian's capture and its sequel differ, though most concur in considering it a great humiliation for Rome. The kindest account is that of the *Historia Augusta,* according to which Valerian was an admirable character "whose life, praiseworthy for sixty years long, finally rose to such glory, that after holding all honours and offices with great distinction he was chosen emperor, not, as often happens, in a riotous assemblage of the people or by the shouting of soldiers, but solely by right of his services, and, as it were, by the single voice of the entire world. In short, if all had been given the power of expressing their choice as to whom they desired as emperor, none other would have been chosen." Various rulers, according to this account, urged Shapur I to return Valerian to his family in Rome. Another source, Book 9 of the *Abridgment of Roman History* by Eutropius, stated that "Valerian, while he was occupied in a war in Mesopotamia, was overthrown by Sapor king of Persia, and being soon after made prisoner, grew old in ignominious slavery among the Parthians." The *Breviarium of the Accomplishments of the Roman People* found it "disgusting to report the fate of the unfortunate *princeps* Valerian . . . [who], having contended against the Persians in Mesopotamia, was defeated by Sapor, King of the Persians, and, having been captured, wasted away in shameful servitude." The *Epitome de Caesaribus* went further, claiming that "Valerianus, waging war in Mesopotamia, was defeated by Sapor, King of the Persians, immediately captured, too, and among the Persians grew old in ignoble servitude. For he lived a long while, and the king of the same province was accustomed, with him bent low, to place his foot on his shoulders and mount his horse." The most sensational accounts of Valerian's death claim that Shapur either killed him by pouring molten gold down his throat or, alternatively, had the emperor flayed alive, with his skin then stuffed with straw and displayed for many years in a Persian temple. More mundane versions have the emperor living out the rest of his life in honorable and pleasant captivity and dying of natural causes. While it is impossible at this distance in time to judge which of these specific narratives is the most accurate, in the lengthy power struggle between Rome and Persia that would continue for almost another four centuries, Shapur I's capture of Valerian—an event commemorated on various Persian monuments—and the permanent detention of the emperor undoubtedly constituted humiliating symbolic blows inflicted on Rome.

Documents

Valerian then with his son Gallienus took over the Roman Empire and persecuted Christians more violently. Many of them in diverse countries became martyrs suffering in many ways for their faith in Christ. In his reign, the nations rose up and the Romans fared badly. The Scyths crossed the Ister and again enslaved the land of Thrace, besieging the illustrious city of Thessalonica, though they did not conquer it. Everyone was inspired with fear of them, such that the Athenians rebuilt their own city wall in ruins since the days of Sulla, while the Peloponnesians walled off the Isthmus from sea to sea. In addition, the Persians, when Shapur was king, overran Syria, ravaged Cappadocia, and besieged Edessa. Valerian hesitated to fight his enemies. However, on learning that soldiers in Edessa had sallied forth from the city and attacked the barbarians slaying many of them and taking a great number of the dogs captive, he took heart and left with the army loyal to him and fought the Persians. They encircled the Romans all in their squares and the greater part fell, some fled, and Valerian along with the men about him was taken captive by his enemies and borne off to Shapur. . . . Cruel he was before, afterwards he became much worse.

Thus is how they have told the story of how Valerian was captured by the Persians. They are willing to say that Valerian submitted to the Persians because as he was fleeing to Edessa, starvation broke out among his soldiers, who because of this rebelled and sought to kill the emperor. Fearing the rebellion of his soldiers, he fled to Shapur, so that he would not be destroyed by his own men, and surrendered himself up to his enemy as well as the Roman troops under him. However, the soldiers were not lost, not learning of the treachery they fled, only a few being slain. Whether the emperor [From here on Zonaras begins to use "basileus" for emperor] was taken in war by the Persians or he willingly handed himself over to them, he was treated dishonorably by Shapur.

The Persians then fearlessly attacked and seized the cities of Antioch by the Orontes, that most illustrious of the cities Tarsus, and Caesarea in Cappadocia. And as for the multitude of captives led off, they did not give them food unless they were about to die, nor did they permit them their fill of water, but only once a day their captors drove them to water like sheep. Caesarea, which was well populated said to have 400,000 inhabitants and had not previously been conquered, nobly had its inhabitants resisted them led by Demosthenes, a brave and wise man, before a doctor was taken captive, who unable to bear the tortures inflicted on him revealed a place from which the Persians entered and killed everyone. Their commander Demosthenes, surrounded by many Persians ordered to take him alive, got on his horse with his sword out and charged into the midst of the enemy. He cut down many of them before he got out of the city and was able to flee.

Thus was how things came about with the Persians, as they scattered about the Roman lands in the east and pillaged fearlessly. The Romans who took flight, as it was said, declared themselves to their commander one Callistus, who on seeing the Persians scatter about and attacking the lands thoughtlessly not supposing anyone would stand against them, he attacked a mob of them killing a great number of barbarians and conquered Shapur's brave young men along with much riches. Shapur, who was much pained for them, returned home leading along Valerian, who died in Persia, a prisoner abused and mocked.

Source: "Zonaras: Alexander Severus to Diocletian, 222–284," Internet Archive, https://web.archive.org/web/20080521191250/http://www.ancientsites.com/aw/Post/1049415.

Valerianus had by this time heard of the disturbances in Bithynia, but his district would not allow him to confide the defence of it to any of his generals. He therefore sent Felix to Byzantium, and went in person from Antioch into Cappadocia, and after he had done some injury to every city by which he passed, he returned homeward. But the plague then attacked his troops, and destroyed most of them, at the time when Sapor made an attempt upon the east, and reduced most of it into subjection. In the mean time, Valerianus became so effeminate and indolent, that he dispaired of ever recovering from the present ill state of affairs, and would have concluded the war by a present of money; had not Sapor sent back the ambassadors who were sent to him with that proposal, without their errand, desiring the emperor to come and speak with him in person concerning the affairs he wished to adjust. To which he most imprudently consented, and going without consideration to Sapor with a small retinue, to treat for a peace, was presently laid hold of by the enemy, and so ended his days in the capacity of a slave among the Persians, to the disgrace of the Roman name in all future times.

Source: "The History of Count Zosimus: Book the First," The Tertullian Project, http://www.tertullian.org/fathers/zosimus01_book1.htm.

32. Queen Zenobia of Palmyra

Introduction

One of the most serious challenges to Roman imperial rule over Syria and Egypt came from Queen Zenobia of Palmyra (r. 267–272). Following the assassination in 267 of her husband Oedenathus and his designated heir, Zenobia became regent for her infant son, defeating the armies of Roman emperor Gallienus. By 270 she had conquered Egypt, Syria, Mesopotamia, and much of Anatolia. Her ascendancy was brief; the following year, the new emperor Aurelian mounted a campaign that decisively destroyed Zenobia's power and kingdom. In 272 CE, she was taken captive by Aurelian. During her reign, Zenobia represented herself as the heir to Queen Cleopatra VII of Egypt of the first century BCE, who had allied herself first with Julius Caesar and then with his younger colleague, Marcus Antonius, before her eventual defeat by Emperor Augustus at the Battle of Actium (31 BCE). As this account reveals, even her Roman enemies displayed grudging admiration for the defeated Queen Zenobia's abilities, courage, and character. Her very inclusion in Aurelian's triumphal procession in Rome, despite her gender, was a backhanded tribute to the respect that her accomplishments won this formidable woman.

Document

Now all shame is exhausted, for in the weakened state of the commonwealth things came to such a pass that, while Gallienus conducted himself in the most evil fashion, even women ruled most excellently. For, in fact, even a foreigner, Zenobia by name, about whom much has already been said, boasting herself to be of the family of the Cleopatras and the Ptolemies, proceeded upon the death of her husband Odaenathus to cast about her shoulders the imperial mantle; and arrayed in the robes of Dido and even assuming the diadem, she held the imperial power in the name of her sons Herennianus and Timolaus, ruling longer than could be endured from one of the female sex. For this proud woman performed the functions of a monarch both while Gallienus was ruling and afterwards when Claudius was busied with the war against the Goths, and in the end could scarcely be conquered by Aurelian himself, under whom she was led in triumph and submitted to the sway of Rome.

There is still in existence a letter of Aurelian's which bears testimony concerning this woman, then in captivity. For when some found fault with him, because he, the bravest of men, had led a woman in triumph, as though she were a general, he sent a letter to the senate and the Roman people, defending himself by the following justification: "I have heard, Conscript Fathers, that men are reproaching me for having performed an unmanly deed in leading Zenobia in triumph. But in truth those very persons who find fault with me now would accord me praise in abundance, did they but know what manner of woman she is, how wise in counsels, how steadfast in plans, how firm toward the soldiers, how generous when necessity calls, and how stern when discipline demands. I might even say that it was her doing that Oedaenathus defeated the Persians and, after putting Sapor to flight, advanced all the way to Ctesiphon. I might add thereto that such was the fear that this woman inspired in the peoples of the East and also the Egyptians that neither Arabs nor Saracens nor Armenians ever moved against her. Nor would I have spared her life, had I not known that she did a great service to the Roman state when she preserved the imperial power in the East for herself, or for her children. Therefore let those whom nothing pleases keep the venom of their own tongues to themselves. For if it is not meet to vanquish a woman and lead her in triumph, what are they saying of Gallienus, in contempt of whom she ruled the empire well? What of the Deified Claudius, that revered and honoured leader? For he, because he was busied with his campaigns against the Goths, suffered her, or so it is said, to hold the imperial power, doing it of purpose and wisely, in order that he himself, while she kept guard over the eastern frontier of the empire, might the more safely complete what he had taken in hand." This speech shows what opinion Aurelian held concerning Zenobia.

Such was her continence, it is said, that she would not know even her own husband save for the purpose of conception. For when once she had lain with him, she would refrain until the time of menstruation to see if she were pregnant; if not, she would again grant him an opportunity of begetting children. She lived in regal pomp. It was rather in the manner of the Persians that she received worship and in the manner of the Persian kings that she banqueted; but it was in the manner of a Roman emperor that she came forth to public assemblies, wearing a helmet and girt with a purple fillet, which had gems hanging from the lower edge, while its centre was fastened with the jewel called cochlis, used instead of the brooch worn by women, and her arms were frequently bare. Her face was dark and of a swarthy hue, her eyes were black and powerful beyond the usual wont, her spirit divinely great, and her beauty incredible. So white were her teeth that many thought that she had pearls in place of teeth. Her voice was clear and like that of a man. Her sternness, when necessity demanded, was that of a tyrant, her clemency, when her sense of right called for it, that of a good emperor. Generous with prudence, she conserved her treasures beyond the wont of women. She made use of a carriage, and rarely of a woman's coach, but more often she rode a horse; it is said, moreover, that frequently she walked with her foot-soldiers for three or four miles. She hunted with the eagerness of a Spaniard. She often drank with her generals, though at other times she refrained, and she drank, too, with the Persians and the Armenians, but only for the purpose of getting the better of them. At her banquets she used vessels of gold and jewels, and she even used those that had been Cleopatra's. As servants she had eunuchs of advanced age and but very few maidens. She ordered her sons to talk Latin, so that, in fact, they spoke Greek but rarely and with difficulty. She herself was not wholly conversant with the Latin tongue, but nevertheless, mastering her timidity she would speak it; Egyptian, on the other hand, she spoke very well. In the history of Alexandria and the Orient she was so well versed that she even composed an epitome, so it is said; Roman history, however, she read in Greek.

When Aurelian had taken her prisoner, he caused her to be led into his presence and then addressed her thus: "Why is it, Zenobia, that you dared to show insolence to the emperors of Rome?" To this she replied, it is said: "You, I know, are an emperor indeed, for you win victories, but Gallienus and Aureolus and the others I never regarded as emperors. Believing Victoria to be a woman like me, I desired to become a partner in the royal power, should the supply of lands permit." And so she was led in triumph with such magnificence that the Roman people had never seen a more splendid parade. For, in the first place, she was adorned with gems so huge that she laboured under the weight of her ornaments; for it is said that this woman, courageous though she was, halted very frequently, saying that she could not endure the load of her gems. Furthermore, her feet were bound with shackles of gold and her hands with golden fetters, and even on her neck she wore a chain of gold, the weight of which was borne by a Persian buffoon. Her life was granted her by Aurelian, and they say that thereafter she lived with her children in the manner of a Roman matron on an estate that had been presented to her at Tibur, which even to this day is still called Zenobia, not far from the palace of Hadrian or from that place which bears the name of Concha.

Source: "Historia Augusta: The Lives of the Thirty Tyrants," University of Chicago, http://penelope.uchicago.edu/Thayer/E/Roman/Texts/Historia_Augusta/Tyranni_XXX*.html#Zenobia.

33. Shapur II the Great and Emperor Constantius: Correspondence (358 CE)

Introduction

After four decades of peace, Persian Sassanid king Shapur II renewed his country's warfare with Rome, seeking to force Emperor Constantius to cede to Persian rule all of Armenia, Mesopotamia, and Macedonia. Shapur launched one war with Rome in 337 that continued until 350, when threats from Scythian forces led to the conclusion of a truce. After defeating the Scythians, in 358

Shapur II renewed his warfare against Rome. This exchange of letters between Shapur II and Emperor Constantius marked the resumption of hostilities between the two empires. Shapur succeeded in battle against Rome, defeating Roman emperor Julian at the Battle of Ctesiphon in 363, an encounter in which Julian was killed. His successor, Jovian, concluded a highly disadvantageous peace, under which Rome ceded massive amounts of its eastern territories and paid a heavy indemnity to Persia. By the time of his death Shapur had won back most of Mesopotamia, Macedonia, and modern Afghanistan and Pakistan. His efforts to subdue Christian Armenia, by contrast, proved unsuccessful.

Document

In the consulship of Datianus and Cerealis, when all arrangements in Gaul were made with more careful zeal than before, and while the terror caused by past events still checked the outbreaks of the barbarians, the king of the Persians, being still on the frontiers of those nations which border on his dominions, and having made a treaty of alliance with the Chionitae and the Gelani, the most warlike and indefatigable of all tribes, being about to return to his own country, received the letters of Tamsapor which announced to him that the Roman emperor was a suppliant for peace.

And he, suspecting that Constantius would never have done so if the empire had not been weakened all over, raised his own pretensions, and embracing the name indeed of peace, offered very unwelcome conditions. And having sent a man of the name of Narses as ambassador with many presents, he gave him letters to Constantius, in which he in no respect abated of his natural pride. The purport of these letters we have understood to be this:

"I, Sapor, king of kings, partner of the stars, brother of the sun and moon, to Constantius Caesar my brother send much greeting. I am glad and am well pleased that at last thou hast returned to the right way, and hast acknowledged the incorruptible decree of equity, having gained experience by facts, and having learnt what disasters an obstinate covetousness of the property of others has often caused.

"Because therefore the language of truth ought to be unrestrained and free, and because men in the highest rank ought only to say what they mean, I will reduce my propositions into a few words; remembering that I have already often repeated what I am now about to say.

"Even your own ancient records bear witness that my ancestors possessed all the country up to the Strymon and the frontier of Macedonia. And these lands it is fitting that I who (not to speak arrogantly) am superior to those ancient kings in magnificence, and in all eminent virtues, should now reclaim. But I am at all times thoughtful to remember that, from my earliest youth, I have never done anything to repent of.

"And therefore it is a duty in me to recover Armenia and Mesopotamia, which were wrested from my ancestor by deliberate treachery. That principle was never admitted by us which you with exultation assert, that all successes in war deserve praise, without considering whether they were achieved by valour or by treachery.

"Lastly, if you are willing to be guided by one who gives you good advice, I would bid you despise a small part of your dominions which is ever the parent of sorrow and bloodshed, in order to reign in safety over the rest. Wisely considering that physicians also sometimes apply cautery or amputation, and cut off portions of the body that the patient may have good use of the rest of his limbs. Nay, that even beasts do the same: since when they observe on what account they are most especially hunted, they will of their own accord deprive themselves of that, in order henceforth to be able to live in security.

"This, in short, I declare, that should my present embassy return without having succeeded in its object, after giving the winter season to rest I will gird myself up with all my strength, and while fortune and justice give me a well-founded hope of ultimate success, I will hasten my march as much as Providence will permit."

Having given long consideration to this letter, the emperor with upright and wise heart, as the saying is, made answer in this manner:

"Constantius, always august, conqueror by land and sea, to my brother Sapor much health. I congratulate thee on thy safety, as one who is willing to be a friend to thee if thou wilt. But I greatly blame thy insatiable covetousness, now more grasping than ever.

"Thou demandest Mesopotamia as thine own, and then Armenia. And thou biddest me cut off some members from my sound body in order to place its health on a sound footing: a demand which is to be rejected at once rather than to be encouraged by any consent. Receive therefore the truth, not covered with any pretences, but clear, and not to be shaken by any threats.

"The prefect of my praetorian guard, thinking to undertake an affair which might be beneficial to the state, without my knowledge discoursed about peace with thy generals, by the agency of some low persons. Peace we should neither regret nor refuse—let it only come with credit and honour, in such a way as to impair neither our self-respect nor our dignity.

"For it would be an unbecoming and shameful thing when all men's ears are filled with our exploits, so as to have shut even the mouth of envy; when after the destruction of tyrants the whole Roman world obeys us, to give up those territories which even when limited to the narrow boundaries of the east we preserved undiminished.

"But I pray thee make an end of the threats which thou utterest against me, in obedience to thy national habit, when it cannot be doubted that it is not from inactivity, but from moderation, that we have at times endured attacks instead of being the assailants ourselves: and know that, whenever we are attacked, we defend our own with bravery and good will: being assured both by thy reading and thy personal experience that in battle it has been rare for Romans to meet with disaster; and that in the final issue of a war we have never come off the worst."

The embassy was therefore dismissed without gaining any of its objects; and indeed no other reply could be given to the unbridled covetousness of the king. And a few days afterwards, Count Prosper followed, and Spectatus the tribune and secretary; and also, by the suggestion of Musonianus, Eustathius the philosopher, as one skilful in persuading, bearing a letter from the emperor, and presents, with a view to induce Sapor to suspend his preparations, so that all our attention might be turned to fortifying the northern provinces in the most effective manner.

Source: Ammianus Marcellinus, *Roman History*, translated by C. D. Yonge (London: Bohn, 1862), Book 17, 133–136.

34. Belisarius Wins the Battle of Dara (530)

Introduction

The early years of Byzantine emperor Justinian's reign (r. 527–565) brought major wars with Persia. Persian shah Kavadh I had tried but failed to persuade Justinian's uncle and predecessor, Emperor Justin I, to adopt his own son Khosrow, a procedure that Kavadh presumably hoped would enable Persia to annex the Byzantine Empire without a fight. The Persian campaign was only the first of many wars and other military ventures that Belisarius, his most accomplished military commander, would wage on Justinian's behalf throughout his long reign, which expanded the empire's territorial extent by around 45 percent. The two men died within months of each other. The Battle of Dara, a major victory over the Persians that persuaded the new king Khosrow to sign the Eternal Peace in 532, albeit a peace that lasted only eight years, was the first of many triumphs for Belisarius. As was often the case, he was able to defeat enemies whose forces greatly outnumbered those of the Romans. The general's adviser Procopius of Caesarea, who began the first of many years of service under Belisarius during the Persian campaign, left an account of the battle. One notable feature of Belisarius's strategy was that he frequently sought negotiations rather than combat and apparently regarded war as only a last resort when other avenues had failed.

Document

When Belisarius and [his fellow commander] Hermogenes... saw the Persians advancing against them, they hastily drew up the soldiers in the same manner as before. And the barbarians, coming up before them, took their stand facing the Romans. But the mirranes [Persian commander] did not array all the Persians against the enemy, but only one half of them, while he allowed the others to remain behind. These were to take the places of the men who were fighting and to fall upon their opponents with their vigour intact, so that all might fight in constant rotation. But the detachment of the so-called Immortals alone he ordered to remain at rest until he himself should give the signal. And he took his own station at the middle of the front, putting Pityaxes in command on the right wing, and Baresmanas on the left. In this manner, then, both armies were drawn up. Then Pharas came before Belisarius and Hermogenes, and said: "It does not seem to me that I shall do the enemy any great harm if I remain here with the Eruli; but if we conceal ourselves on this slope, and then, when the Persians have begun the fight, if we climb up by this hill and suddenly come upon their rear, shooting from behind them, we shall in all probability do them the greatest harm." Thus he spoke, and since it pleased Belisarius and his staff, he carried out the plan.

But up to midday neither side began battle. As soon, however, as the noon hour was passed, the barbarians began the fight, having postponed the engagement to this time of the day for the reason that they are accustomed to partake of food only towards late afternoon, while the Romans have their meal before noon; and for this reason they thought that the Romans would never hold out so well, if they assailed them while hungry. At first, then, both sides discharged arrows against each other, and the missiles by their great number made, as it were, a vast cloud; and many men were falling on both sides, but the missiles of the barbarians flew much more thickly. For fresh men were always fighting in turn, affording to their enemy not the slightest opportunity to observe what was being done; but even so the Romans did not have the worst of it. For a steady wind blew from their side against the barbarians, and checked to a considerable degree the force of their arrows. Then, after both sides had exhausted all their missiles, they began to use their spears against each other, and the battle had come still more to close quarters. On the Roman side the left wing was suffering especially. For the Cadiseni, who with Pityaxes were fighting at this point, rushing up suddenly in great numbers, routed their enemy, and, crowding hard upon the fugitives, were killing many of them. When this was observed by the men under Sunicas and Aigan, they charged against them at full speed. But first the three hundred Eruli under Pharas from the high ground got in the rear of the enemy and made a wonderful display of valorous deeds against all of them and especially the Cadiseni. And the Persians, seeing the forces of Sunicas too already coming up against them from the flank, turned to a hasty flight. And the rout became complete, for the Romans here joined forces with each other, and there was a great slaughter of the barbarians. On the Persian right wing not fewer than three thousand perished in this action, while the rest escaped with difficulty to the phalanx and were saved. And the Romans did not continue their pursuit, but both sides took their stand facing each other in line. Such was the course of these events.

But the mirranes stealthily sent to the left a large body of troops and with them all the so-called Immortals. And when these were noticed by Belisarius and Hermogenes, they ordered the six hundred men under Sunicas and Aigan to go to the angle on the right, where the troops of Simmas and Ascan were stationed, and behind them they placed many of Belisarius' men. So the Persians who held the left wing under the leadership of Baresmanas, together with the Immortals, charged on the run upon the Romans opposite them, who failed to withstand the attack and beat a hasty retreat. Thereupon the Romans in the angle, and all who were behind them, advanced with great ardour against the pursuers. But inasmuch as they came upon the barbarians from the side, they cut their army into two parts, and the greater portion of them they had on their right, while some also who were left behind were placed on their left. Among these happened to be the standard bearer of Baresmanas, whom Sunicas charged and struck with his spear. And already the Persians who were leading the pursuit perceived in what straits they were, and, wheeling about, they stopped the pursuit and went against their assailants, and thus became exposed to the enemy on both sides. For those in flight before them understood what was happening and turned back again. The Persians, on their part, seeing the standard inclined and lowered to the earth, rushed all together against the Romans at that point with Baresmanas. There the Romans held their ground. And first Sunicas killed Baresmanas and threw him from his horse to the ground. As a result of this the barbarians were seized with great fear and thought no longer of resistance, but fled in utter confusion. And the Romans, having made a circle as it were around them, killed about five thousand. Thus both armies were all set in motion, the Persians in retreat, and the Romans in pursuit. In this part of the conflict all the foot-soldiers who were in the Persian army threw down their shields and were caught and wantonly killed by the enemy. However, the pursuit was not continued by the Romans over a great distance. For Belisarius and Hermogenes refused absolutely to let them go farther, fearing lest the Persians through some necessity should turn about and rout them while pursuing recklessly, and it seemed to them sufficient to preserve the victory unmarred. For on that day the Persians had been defeated in battle by the Romans, a thing that had not happened for a long time. Thus the two armies separated from each other. And the Persians were no longer willing to fight a pitched battle with the Romans. However, some sudden attacks were made on both sides, in which the Romans were not at a disadvantage. Such, then, was the fortune of the armies in Mesopotamia.

Source: *Procopius with an English Translation by H. B. Dewing: History of the Wars, Books I and II* (London: William Heinemann, 1914), Book 1, chap. 14, 121–129.

35. The Nika Revolt, Constantinople (January 532)

Introduction

Much of the politics of the Byzantine Empire revolved around the sport of horse racing, with different factions, known as the Blues and Greens, supporting specific opposed theological and political positions, including rival candidates for the imperial throne. In the early years of his reign Emperor Justinian became extremely unpopular, as he imposed high taxes while fighting a war with Persia. The arrest and sentencing to death on charges of murder of a number of faction members was enough to trigger major riots against Justinian, with much of the city of Constantinople burned down in five days of disorder. For some time both Greens and Blues united to demand that Justinian be replaced as emperor by Hypatius, an aristocrat with ties to the Greens. Eventually the Blues were won back to supporting Justinian, and the emperor's military forces brutally suppressed the remaining insurgents. This account, taken from the Chronicle of the Greek monk Theophanes, gives a lively picture of the initial verbal exchanges between the Greens and the herald who represented the emperor, sitting in his box as the games began.

Document

In this year, the 5th of Justinian's reign, in January of the 10th indiction, occurred the so-called Nika revolt. The members of the circus factions crowned as emperor Hypatios, the relative of the emperor Anastasios. A large part of the city was burned, including the Great Church, St Eirene, the hospice of Sampson, the Augustaion, the portico of the Basilica, and the Bronze House of the palace. There was great panic and many of those found in the Hippodrome with Hypatios perished—the number reported is 35,000.

The Nika riot occurred in the following way. The factions went up into the Hippodrome and the Greens began to shout acclamations about Kalopodios the cubicularius and spatharios.

Greens: Long may you live, Justinian Augustus! Tu vincas [May you triumph]. I am wronged, O paragon of virtue, and cannot endure it, as God knows. I am afraid to give his name in case he prospers the more, and I put myself in danger.

Herald: Who is he? I do not know.

Greens: My oppressor, thrice-august, can be found in the shoemakers' quarter.

Herald: No one does you wrong.

Greens: One man and one man only does me wrong. Mother of God, may he not hold his head up high.

Herald: We do not know who he is.

Greens: You and you alone know, thrice-august, who oppresses me today.

Herald: Come now, if there is someone, we do not know him.

Greens: Kalopodios, the spatharios, does me wrong, O lord of all.

Herald: Kalopodios is not at fault.

Greens: Whoever he is, he will share the fate of Judas. God will speedily exact a penalty from my oppressor.

Herald: You have not come here to watch, but only to insult your rulers.

Greens: Surely anyone who wrongs me will share the fate of Judas.

Herald: Silence, you Jews, Manichaeans, and Samaritans!

Greens: Do you call us Jews and Samaritans? May the Mother of God be with everyone.

Herald: How long are you going to curse yourselves?

Greens: If anyone denies that our lord is orthodox, let him be anathema, like Judas.

Herald: I am telling you: Get baptized in one [God].

The Greens shouted above each other and chanted, as Antlas demanded, "I am baptized in one [God]."

Herald: Surely, if you do not keep quiet, I shall behead you.

Greens: Everyone tries to get office for security. So whatever we say in our distress, Your Majesty should not get angry, for deity endures everything. We have a case, emperor, and we shall now name everything. We do not know even where the palace is, thrice-august, nor where is the state ceremonial. I come only once to the City, when I am seated on a mule. And I would rather not then, thrice-august.

Herald: Every free man can go where he likes in public without danger.

Greens: To be sure, I am a free man, but I am not allowed to show it. For if a free man is suspected of being a Green, he is sure to be punished in public.

Herald: Are you ready to die then, and will you not spare your own lives?

Greens: Let this colour be removed and justice disappears. Stop the murdering and let us face punishment. See here a gushing fountain: punish as many as you like. Truly, man's nature cannot bear these two things. Would that Sabbatios had not been born, so he would not have had a murderer for a son. It is the twenty-sixth murder that has taken place in the Zeugma. A spectator in the morning and murdered in the afternoon, lord of all.

Blues: The only murderers in the whole stadium are yours.

Greens: You kill and run away.

35. The Nika Revolt, Constantinople

Blues: You kill and walk about [freely]. The only murderers in the stadium are yours.

Greens: Lord Justinian, they are asking for it and yet no one is killing them. Whoever wants to will understand. The woodseller, the one in the Zeugma—who killed him, emperor?

Herald: You yourselves killed him.

Greens: Who killed the son of Epagathos, emperor?

Herald: You yourselves killed him, and now you are involving the Blues.

Greens: Now, now, have pity O Lord. Truth is being suppressed. I want to quarrel with those who say events are controlled by God. For what is the source of this misery?

Herald: God cannot be tempted with evil.

Greens: God cannot be tempted with evil? But who does me wrong? If there is a philosopher or hermit here, let him explain the difference.

Herald: You God-hated blasphemers, will you never be silent?

Greens: If it pleases Your Majesty, I shall keep quiet, but against my will, thrice-august. I know it all, every bit of it and I say nothing. Farewell, Justice, you exist no more. I shall turn and become a Jew. Better to be a pagan than a Blue, God knows.

Blues: I hate it. I do not want to see it. Your malice is galling.

Greens: Let the bones of the spectators be dug up!

The Greens departed and left the emperor and the Blues as spectators. And immediately a pretext for a faction riot was offered by some officials in the following way. The prefect arrested three partisans among the trouble-makers and had them hanged. One died immediately, but the other two fell from the gibbet. They were hanged again, and again fell. The crowd of bystanders saw them and chanted, 'Get them to the church!' The monks of St Konon heard, carried them to a small boat and took them across to St Laurence, as that church had the privilege that no one was to be ejected from it until such time as he had suffered sufficiently. On hearing of this, the prefect sent soldiers to guard them.

When the partisans learned of this, they went off to the Praetorium and asked the prefect to remove the soldiers on guard at St Laurence. They got no reply from him, so, enraged, they set fire to the Praetorium. The porticoes from the arch of the Forum to the Chalke were burned, and also the shops of the silversmiths and the whole palace of Lausos were destroyed by fire. They killed unsparingly the soldiers who attacked them. Then they broke into houses and began to loot their contents. They set fire to the entrance of the palace (the one with the bronze roof), the portico of the Protectores, and the senate house by the Augustaion. The partisans went down to the Julian harbour (I mean that of Sophia), to the palace of Probus in search of weapons, crying 'Another emperor for the city!' They set fire to the palace of Probus which was gutted. Next they went and burned the baths of Alexander, the great hospice of Sampson (where the patients perished), and the Great Church along with all its columns. It collapsed entirely on all four sides.

The emperor, in terror, wanted to load his moneys on to a dromon and get away as far as Herakleia in Thrace, leaving the magister militum Moundos to guard the palace, along with Moundos' son, 3,000 men, Konstantiolos and the cubicularii. The partisans dragged away the corpses and tossed them into the sea, also killing a large number of women.

When a rumour had got around that the emperor had taken the Augusta and left for Thrace, they proclaimed the patrician Hypatios emperor, and as he sat in the Hippodrome, he was acclaimed by the partisans and listened to the insulting jeers directed against the emperor Justinian. Two hundred young Greens in armour came from Flacillianai intending to open the palace and bring Hypatios in. The emperor, when he heard of these bold moves by the partisans and by Hypatios, went into the palace and up to the Pulpita (as they are called), behind the Kathisma of the Hippodrome, to the dining-room with the bronze doors. He had with him Moundos, Konstantiolos, Belisarius, and other senators plus a detachment of armed soldiers, cubicularii, and spatharioi. The cubicularius Narses went out and won over some of the Blue faction by a distribution of money. They began chanting, 'Justinian Augustus, tu vincas! Lord, preserve Justinian the emperor and Theodora the Augusta!' The crowd was split and people began attacking one another. Those in the palace went out with their forces, detached some people from the partisans, and rushed into the Hippodrome, Narses by the gates, Moundos' son by the Sphendone, others by the narrow passage from the imperial box into the arena. They started slaying the partisans, some with their bows, others with their swords: in the end not one of the citizens, either of the Greens or of the Blues, who were in the Hippodrome, survived. Belisarius ran into the Kathisma with a number of spatharioi, arrested Hypatios, led him to the emperor, and had him put in prison. The day's casualties amounted to 35,000. No partisan was to be seen any longer; indeed on that day peace was restored. On the next day Hypatios and his brother Pompeius were executed. Their bodies were thrown into the sea and their estates were confiscated. A further eighteen patricians, illustres, and consulars had their property confiscated as associates of Hypatios. This produced considerable fear and the city calmed down. The chariot races were not held for a long time.

Source: *The Chronicle of Theophanes Confessor: Byzantine and Near Eastern History, AD 284–813*, translated by Cyril Mango and Roger Scott (Oxford, UK: Clarendon, 1997), 275–279. By permission of Oxford University Press.

36. The Battle of al-Badr (March 13, 624)

Introduction

The Battle of al-Badr, fought in the Hejaz, was the first major victory of Prophet Muhammad and his forces over their Qurayshi opponents in Mecca. Following a number of smaller raids, the battle gave the Muslims hope that they might eventually prevail over their opponents in Mecca and win control there. Due to internal rivalries, by no means all the Qurayshi forces engaged the Muslims. The Battle of Badr was one of the few military engagements mentioned in the Quranic scriptures. It was also the source of detailed traditional Arab accounts, which make it clear that the outnumbered Muslims felt that this was a crucial confrontation, since if they were defeated they would be eradicated not just as a significant fighting force but also as a viable religious movement. Failure would in all probability have reduced Islam to the status of a short-lived schismatic sect. The historian Abu Ja'far Muhammad bin Jarir al Tabari later collected various accounts to provide a composite narrative of what became a key moment in Muslim tradition. To the regret of some of his men, Muhammad would not permit the killing of many of the defeated because he believed that some of the Banu Hashīm tribe and others had been forced under duress to fight and could subsequently be won over to Islam. The fighting was nonetheless bitter and personalized, because many of those engaged in combat were battling against friends or family members whom they knew extremely well, prompting complicated feelings during and after the combat.

Document

When it was the day of Badr, and the Messenger of God [Muhammad] looked at the polytheists and their number, and then looked at his companions, who were something over three hundred, he turned toward the Qiblah and began to pray, saying, "O God, fulfil what you have promised me, O God, if this band of Muslims perishes, you will not be worshipped on the earth." He continued to say this until his cloak fell off. Abū Bakr picked it up and put it back on him, then grasped him from behind and said, "O Prophet of God, whom I value more than my father and mother, this is enough of calling upon your Lord. He will assuredly fulfil what he has promised you." Then God revealed, "When ye sought help of your Lord and he answered you (saying): I will help you with a thousand of the angels, rank on rank."

Abu Bakr took his hand and said, "This is enough, O Prophet of God. You have tired the Lord with your importuning." He was in his coat of mail, and he went out saying, "The hosts will all be routed and will turn and flee. Nay, but the Hour [of doom] is their appointed tryst, and the Hour will be more wretched and more bitter [than this earthly failure]."

Then the Messenger of God [Muhammad] went out to his men and urged them to battle. He promised every man that he could keep all the booty that he took, and then said, "By him in whose hands Muhammad's soul rests, if any man fights them today and is killed, fighting steadfastly and with resignation, going forward and not turning back, then God will cause him to enter Paradise."

When the armies met and drew close to one another, [the Meccan clan leader] Abū Jahl said, "O God, whichever of us has severed the ties of kinship more, and has committed more unacceptable acts, destroy him today." He was thus asking God to give the victory against himself.

Then the Messenger of God picked up a handful of gravel and faced Quraysh with the words, "May their faces be deformed!" A rout followed, in which God killed many chiefs of Quraysh and caused many of their nobles to be taken captive. While the Muslims were taking captives, the Messenger of God was in his shelter. Sa'd b. Mu'ādh was standing at the door, girt with his sword, along with a few of the Ansār, guarding the Messenger of God, since they were afraid that the enemy would wheel round and attack him. The Messenger of God, I have been told, saw in the face of Sa'd b. Mu'ādh that he disapproved of what the people were doing, and said, "It seems, Sa'd, that you disapprove of what the people are doing." "Yes, by God, O Messenger of God," he replied. "This was the first defeat inflicted by God on the polytheists, and killing the prisoners would have been more pleasing to me than sparing them."

When the Messenger of God ordered the dead to be thrown into the well, 'Utbah b. Rabī'ah was taken and dragged to the well. As I have been informed, the Messenger of God looked into the face of his son Abū Hudhayfah, which was dejected and altered, and said, "Abū Hudhayfah, perhaps some sadness has entered you on account of your father," or words to that effect. "No, by God, O Messenger of God," he replied, "I had no doubts about my father, nor about his death. But I knew my father to be a judicious, forbearing, and virtuous man, and I used to hope that these qualities would lead him to Islam. When I saw what had happened to him and remembered the state of unbelief in which he died, after the hopes which I had had for him, it saddened me."

Source: Abu Ja'far Muhammad b. Jarir al Tabari, *The History of al-Tabarī*, Vol. 7, *The Foundation of the Community*, translated by W. Montgomery Watt and M. V. McDonald (Albany: State University of New York Press, 1987), 54–56, 63. Reprinted with permission.

37. The Battle of Nineveh (December 12, 627)

Introduction

The Battle of Nineveh was a key turning point in the Byzantine-Sassanid War waged from 602 to 698. In an unusual winter campaign, Emperor Heraclius invaded Mesopotamia, laying waste as he went, and lured the Persians into attacking him near the former Assyrian capital of Nineveh. Heraclius then marched deep into enemy territory, ravaging the favorite palaces of the beleaguered Shah Khosrow II, who fled before him, loading onto his elephants all the treasure that could be carried, and was overthrown in a coup shortly afterward. His son, who succeeded him, concluded a treaty on terms highly favorable to the Byzantines, returning their lost territories. Following this victory Heraclius began styling himself "King of Kings," a title he commandeered from his Persian rival. He had little time to rest on his laurels, however. In 629, the peoples of the Arab peninsula, united under Muslim leadership, began to pose a serious challenge to Byzantine power, one that would soon absorb all the energy of Heraclius until his death in 641.

Document

In this year the emperor Herakleios, by invading Persia together with the Turks starting in the month of September—an unexpected move, since it was winter—threw Chosroes into a state of distraction when the news had reached him. But the Turks, in view of the winter and the constant attacks of the Persians, could not bear to toil together with the emperor and started, little by little, to slip away until all of them had left and returned home. Now the emperor addressed his troops, saying: 'Know, O brothers, that no one wishes to fight with us, except God and His Mother who bore Him without seed, and this that He may show His might, since salvation does not lie in the abundance of soldiers and weapons, but to those who trust in His mercy, He sends down His aid.'

As for Chosroes, he collected all his armies and appointed Razates commander over them, a most warlike and brave man, whom he sent against Herakleios. The emperor meanwhile was burning the towns and villages of Persia and putting to the sword the Persians he captured. On 9 October of the 15th indiction he reached the land of Chamaetha, where he rested his army for one week. As for Razates, he came to Gazakos, in the emperor's rear, and followed him, while the Romans, in front, were destroying the crops. Trailing behind, like a hungry dog, he fed with difficulty on the emperor's crumbs. On 1 December the emperor reached the Great Zabas river, which he crossed and encamped near the town of Nineveh. Following him, Razates, too, came to the ford and, going another three miles downstream, found another ford which he crossed. The emperor sent out the commander Baanes with a small body of picked soldiers; the latter encountered a company of Persians and, after killing their captain, brought back his head and his sword, which was all of gold. He killed many more and made twenty-six captive, among whom was the sword-bearer of Razates. This man announced to the emperor that Razates was intending to give battle on orders from Chosroes, who had sent him 3,000 armed men; but these had not yet arrived. When the emperor had been informed of this, he sent ahead his camp equipment and himself followed, seeking a place in which to give battle before the 3,000 had joined the enemy. And when he had found a plain suitable for fighting, he addressed his troops and drew them up in battle order. Upon arriving there, Razates also drew up his army in three dense formations and advanced on the emperor.

Battle was given on Saturday, 12 December. The emperor sallied forward in front of everyone and met the commander of the Persians, and, by God's might and the help of the Theotokos, threw him down; and those who had sallied forth with him were routed. Then the emperor met another Persian in combat and cast him down also. Yet a third assailed him and struck him with a spear, wounding his lip; but the emperor slew him, too. And when the trumpets had sounded, the two sides attacked each other and, as a violent battle was being waged, the emperor's tawny horse called Dorkon, was wounded in the thigh by some infantryman who struck it with a spear. It also received several blows of the sword on the face, but, wearing as it did a cataphract made of sinew, it was not hurt, nor were the blows effective. Razates fell in battle, as did the three divisional commanders of the Persians, nearly all of their officers, and the greater part of their army. As for the Romans, fifty were killed and a considerable number wounded, but they did not die, save for another ten. That battle was waged from morning until the 11th hour. The Romans captured twenty-eight standards of the Persians, not counting those that had been broken, and, having despoiled the dead, took their corselets, helmets, and all their arms. And the two sides remained at a distance of two bowshots from one another, for there was no retreat. The Roman soldiers watered their horses at night and fed them. But the Persian horsemen stood until the 7th hour of the night over the bodies of their dead; and at the 8th hour of the night they set forth and returned to their camp; and taking it up, they went away and encamped in fear at the foot of a rugged mountain. The Romans took many gold swords and gold belts set with pearls, and the shield of Razates, which was all of gold and had 120 laminae, and his gold breastplate; and they brought in his caftan together with his head, and his bracelets and his gold saddle. And Barsamouses, the prince of the Iberians who are subject to Persia, was taken alive. [No one can remember such a battle being waged between Persians] and Romans inasmuch as it did not cease all day; and if the Romans won, they did so only by God's help.

After encouraging his army, the emperor pushed on against Chosroes with a view to frightening him and making him recall Sarbaros from Byzantium [from Chalcedon]. On 21 December the emperor was informed that the army of Razates—as much of it as had escaped from the battle—had been joined by the 3,000 men dispatched by Chosroes and had reached Nineveh in pursuit of him. After crossing the Great Zabas, the emperor [dispatched the turmarch George with 1000 men to ride forward and seize the bridges of the Lesser Zabas] before Chosroes had become aware of it. After riding forty-eight miles, George seized the four bridges of the Lesser Zabas in the night and captured the Persians he found in the forts. On 23 December the emperor reached the bridges, crossed them, and encamped in the mansions of Iesdem; he rested both his army and his horses and celebrated the feast of Christ's Nativity in that place. When Chosroes was informed that the Romans had seized the bridges of the Lesser Zabas, he sent a message to the army that had been under Razates that they should try very hard to overtake the emperor so as to join him. Making haste, they crossed the Lesser Zabas in another place and overtook the emperor, in front of whom they now marched. As for the emperor, he came upon [a palace called Dezeridan, which he destroyed and burnt, while the Persians crossed the bridge of the river Tornas and encamped there. The emperor came upon] a second palace of Chosroes called Rousa and this, too, he destroyed. He suspected that the enemy were going to fight him at the bridge of the river Tornas; but when they saw him, they abandoned the bridge and fled. So the emperor crossed without hindrance and reached another palace called Beklal; here a hippodrome had been built, and he destroyed it.

Several of the Armenians who accompanied the Persians came to the emperor [at night] and said: 'Chosroes with his elephants and his own army is encamped five miles on this side of the palace called Dastagerd, in a place called Barasroth, and he has given instructions that his forces should assemble there and fight you. There is a river there that is difficult to cross, and a narrow bridge, and many cramped spaces between buildings, and fetid streams.' After taking counsel with his officers and his army, the emperor remained in the palace of Beklal. He found therein in one enclosure 300 corn-fed ostriches, and in another about 500 corn-fed gazelles, and in another 100 corn-fed wild asses, and all of these he gave to his soldiers. And they celebrated 1 January there. They also found sheep, pigs, and oxen without number, and the whole army rested contentedly and gave glory to God. They caught the herdsmen of these cattle and were exactly informed by them that Chosroes had learnt on 23 December that the emperor had crossed the bridge of the Tornas and forthwith set out from the palace of Dastagerd [making all speed for Ctesiphon, and all the money he had in the palace he loaded on the elephants, camels, and mules that were in his service, and he wrote to the army of Razates that they should enter that same palace and the houses of the noblemen and take away anything they found therein. So the emperor sent one half of his army to Dastagerd], while he himself went by a different road to another palace called Bebdarch. This, too, they destroyed and burnt, and they thanked God for having wrought such wonders by the intercession of the Theotokos. For who had expected that Chosroes would flee before the Roman emperor from his palace at Dastagerd and go off to Ctesiphon, when, for twenty-four years, he would not suffer to behold Ctesiphon, but had his royal residence at Dastagerd? In his palace of Dastagerd the Roman army found 300 Roman standards which the Persians had captured at different times. They also found the goods that had been left behind, namely a great quantity of aloes and big pieces of aloes wood, each weighing 70 or 80 lbs., much silk and pepper, more linen shirts than one could count, sugar, ginger, and many other goods. Others found silver, silken garments, woolen rugs, and woven carpets—a great quantity of them and very beautiful, but on account of their weight they burnt them all. They also burnt the tents of Chosroes and the porticoes he set up whenever he encamped in a plain, and many of his statues. They also found in this palace an infinite number of ostriches, gazelles, wild asses, peacocks, and pheasant, and in the hunting park huge live lions and tigers. Many of the captives from Edessa, Alexandria, and other cities—a great throng of them—sought refuge with the emperor. The emperor celebrated at Dastagerd the feast of the Epiphany; he gladdened and restored his army while he destroyed the palaces of Chosroes. These priceless, wonderful and astonishing structures he demolished to the ground so that Chosroes might learn how great a pain the Romans had suffered when their cities were laid waste and burnt by him.

Source: *The Chronicle of Theophanes Confessor: Byzantine and Near Eastern History, AD 284–813*, translated by Cyril Mango and Roger Scott (Oxford, UK: Clarendon, 1997), 448–452. By permission of Oxford University Press.

38. The Conquest of Mecca (630)

Introduction

Mecca, the birthplace of Prophet Muhammad, was the holiest shrine of Islam, where he had experienced some of his most important revelations of the nature of God. Making a pilgrimage to Mecca became one of the central observances of the religion of Islam. Mecca was held by the Quraysh tribe, to which Muhammad himself traced his origins. In 628, the Quraysh negotiated a 10-year treaty with Muhammad, granting his followers the right to visit the Kaaba shrine without disturbance. Two years later this agreement broke down, and Muhammad launched a campaign against Mecca. Islamic chroniclers recounted how, although some limited fighting occurred, the prophet succeeded in reaching a peaceful understanding with Abu Sufyan, head of the Quraysh of Mecca, who converted to Islam and surrendered the city to Muhammad. Muslim leaders then removed all traces of pagan worship from the city.

Document

According to 'Abd al-Wārith b. 'Abd al-Samad b. 'Abd al-Wārith—his father ['Abd al-Samad b. 'Abd al-Wārith]—Abān al-'Attār—Hishām b. 'Urwah—'Urwah [b. al-Zubayr], who wrote [the following letter] to 'Abd al-Malik b. Marwān: To proceed: You wrote to me asking about Khālid b. al-Walīd, whether he fought on the day of the conquest, and under whose command he fought. As regards Khālid on the day of the conquest, he was on the side of the Prophet. When the Prophet traveled the Marr basin heading for Mecca, Quraysh had already sent Abū Sufyān and Hakīm b. Hizām to meet the Messenger of God, not knowing, when they sent the two, where the Prophet was heading, whether to them or to al-Tā'if—that was at the time of the conquest. Abū Sufyān and Hakīm b. Hizām asked Budayl b. Warqā' to follow—they wanted him to accompany them. They were only Abū Sufyān, Hakīm b. Hizām, and Budayl. When [Quraysh] sent them to the Messenger of God, they said to them, "Let us not be approached from behind you, for we do not know against whom Muhammad intends to go, whether he intends to go against us, against Hawāzin, or against Thaqīf." Between the Prophet and Quraysh there was a peace made on the day of al-Hudaybiyah, with a pact and a fixed period of time. The Banū Bakr were in that peace on the side of Quraysh. Then a group of the Banū Ka'b and a group of the Banū Bakr fought with each other. Among the terms on which the Messenger of God and Quraysh had made peace was that there should be neither betrayal nor clandestine theft. Quraysh aided the Banū Bakr with weapons, and the Banū Ka'b suspected Quraysh. That is why the Messenger of God attacked the people of Mecca. During this expedition of his, he met Abū Sufyān, Hakīm, and Budayl at Marr al-Zahrān. They had no idea that the Messenger of God had encamped at Marr until they suddenly came upon him. When they saw him at Marr, Abū Sufyān, Budayl, and Hakīm went before him in his dwelling at Marr al-Zahrān and swore allegiance to him. After they swore allegiance to him, he sent them ahead of him to Quraysh, to summon them to Islam. I have been told that he said, "Whoever enters the house of Abū Sufyān shall be safe"—his house was in the upper part of Mecca—"and whoever enters the house of Hakīm"—it was in the lower part of Mecca—"shall be safe, and whoever locks his door and withholds his hand shall be safe."

After Abū Sufyān and Hakīm left the presence of the Prophet heading for Mecca, he sent al-Zubayr after them, gave him his banner, and appointed him commander over the horsemen of the Emigrants and Ansār. He commanded him to plant his banner in the upper part of Mecca at al-Hajūn. He said to al-Zubayr, "Do not depart from where I have commanded you to plant my banner until I come to you." (The Messenger of God entered [Mecca] from there.) He commanded Khālid b. al-Walīd, along with those of [the tribe of] Qudā'ah and the Banu Sūlaym who had become Muslims and some people who had become Muslims only a short time before, to enter through the lower part of Mecca—that was where the Banū Bakr were, whom Quraysh had called on for aid, the Banū al-Hārith b. 'Abd Manāt, and the Ahābīsh whom Quraysh had commanded to be in the lower part of Mecca. So Khalid entered against them by the lower part of Mecca.

I have been told that the Prophet said to Khālid and al-Zubayr when he dispatched them, "Fight only those who fight you." When Khālid came upon the Banū Bakr and the Ahābīsh in the lower part of Mecca, he fought them, and God put them to flight. That was the only fighting that took place in Mecca. However, Kurz b. Jāhir, one of the Banū Muhārib b. Fihr, and Ibn al-Ash'ar, a man from the Banū Ka'b—the two were among al-Zubayr's horsemen—took the road to Kadā'. They did not take the route that al-Zubayr took, which he had been commanded to take. They encountered a squadron of Quraysh on the slope of Kadā' and were killed. There was no fighting by al-Zubayr in the upper part of Mecca. The Prophet arrived from there. The people stood before him to swear allegiance to him, and so the people of Mecca became Muslims. The Prophet stayed among them half a month, no more....

Source: Abu Ja'far Muhammad b. Jarir al Tabari, *The History of al-Tabarī*, Vol. 8, *The Victory of Islam: Muhammad at Medina, A.D. 626–630*, translated by Michael Fishbein (Albany: State University of New York Press, 1997), 174–176. Reprinted with permission.

39. Abu Bakr Launches the Ridda Wars (632)

Introduction

When the Islamic prophet Muhammad died in 632, Abu Bakr, his father-in-law and one of his earliest disciples and most trusted advisers, was elected as the first Muslim caliph. Bakr had fought in many of the earliest Muslim battles against the Quraysh tribes from which the first adherents came, including among others the Battle of Badr; the Battle of the Trench, when Muslim forces took the city of Medina; and the conquest of Mecca. His caliphate lasted only 27 months, but during this time Abu Bakr faced major uprisings against Islam from numerous tribes across the Arabian Peninsula, many of whom wished to return to their earlier polytheistic faith. Abu Bakr refused to allow any such backsliding, which he and other dedicated Muslims characterized as apostasy, and dispatched 11 armies to suppress these rebellions. Each commander carried a letter from the caliph, to be delivered to the insurgent leaders, promising that if they repented and returned to the fold of Islam they would be welcomed back into the faith. If they refused to do so, the renegades could expect only ruthless military repression and conquest. Repudiation of Islam would not be tolerated.

Document

[Abu Bakr's Letter to the Apostates]

According to al-Sarī—Sayf—'Abdallāh b. Sa'īd—'Abd al-Rahmān b. Ka'b b. Mālik: Qahdham participated with [Abu Bakr] in commissioning [the armies] and in writing [the letter to the apostates], so that the letters to the apostate tribes of the Arabs were identical:

In the name of God, the Compassionate, the Merciful. From Abū Bakr, caliph of the Apostle of God, to whomever this letter of mine may reach among the commoners and notables who has stood fast in his Islam or who has turned back from it: Peace upon those who follow the [true] guidance and who have not turned back to error and blindness after [having received] the [true] guidance. Verily I praise to you God, other than Whom there is no god. I bear witness that there is no god but God alone, Who has no associate, and that Muhammad is His Servant and His Apostle; we affirm that which he brought, and that which he denied we declare to be unbelief and strive against it. Now then: Verily God, may He be exalted, sent Muhammad with His truth to His creation as a bearer of good tidings and as a warner and as one calling [others] to God, with His permission, and as a light-bringing lamp, so that he might warn [all] who live, and so that the saying against the unbelievers might be fulfilled. So God guided with the truth whoever responded to Him, and the Apostle of God, with His permission, struck whoever turned his back to Him until he came to Islam, willingly or grudgingly. Then God took His Apostle to Him, he having carried out God's command, and counseled His community, and carried out [the duty] that was upon him; for God had made that clear to him and to the people of Islam in the book that was sent down. Thus He said, "You are dead, and they are dead"; and he said, "We have not made any man before you immortal; so, if you die, should they then be immortal?" And to the believers He said, "Muhammad is only an apostle. The apostles before him have passed away; so, if he dies or is killed, will you turn on your heels? For he who may turn on his heels will not harm God one whit, but God will reward the grateful." So whoever worshiped Muhammad, indeed Muhammad has died; but whoever worshiped God alone, Who has no associate, indeed God is always with you, Living, Eternal. He does not die, nor do slumber or sleep take Him; He guards His cause, takes vengeance on His enemy, and punishes him.

I recommend to you the fear of God and your right share and portion of God and of that which your Prophet brought you; and that you let yourselves be guided by His guidance, and cleave to the religion of God. For indeed, whomever God has not guided is astray, and whomever He has not made safe is afflicted, and whomever God has not helped is forsaken. Whomever God guides is on the right way, and whomever He allows to go astray is lost. God said, "Whomever God guides is on the right way, but whomever He lets get lost, you will find no friend to guide him"; nor will any work of his in the world be accepted until he acknowledges Him; and neither repentance nor ransom will be accepted from him in the afterlife.

I have learned that some of you have turned back from your religion after you had acknowledged Islam and labored in it, out of negligence of God and ignorance of His command, and in compliance with the devil. God said, "When We said to the angels, 'Bow down before Adam,' they bowed down except for Iblīs. He was one of the *jinn;* so he strayed from the command of his Lord. Do you then wish to take him and his offspring as friends to the exclusion of Me, even though they are your enemy? How bad an exchange [that is] for the transgressors!" And He said, "The devil is an enemy to you, so take him for an enemy. He only calls his party that they may be among the people of the flame." I have sent to you someone at the head of an army of the *Muhājirūn* and the *Anṣār* and those who follow [them] in good works. I ordered him not to fight anyone or to kill anyone until he has called him to the cause of God; so that those who respond to him and acknowledge [Him] and renounce [unbelief] and do good works, [my envoy] shall accept him and help him to [do right], but I have ordered him to fight those who deny [Him] for that reason. So he will not spare any one of them he can gain mastery over, [but may] burn them with fire, slaughter them by any means, and take women and children captive; nor shall he accept from anyone anything except Islam. So whoever follows him, it is better for him; but whoever leaves him, will not weaken God. I have ordered my messenger to read my letter to you in all gathering places. The invitation [to God's cause] shall be the call to prayer. If, when the Muslims make the call to prayer, they do likewise [in response], leave them alone; but, if they do not make the call to prayer [with the Muslims], then grant them no respite. And, if they do make the call to prayer [with the Muslims], ask them what has come over them; then, if they deny [God], grant them no respite, but, if they acknowledge [God], He will accept them and bring them to what they should do.

Source: Abu Jaʿfar Muhammad b. Jarir al Tabari, *The History of al-Tabarī*, Vol. 10, *The Conquest of Arabia: The Riddah Wars, A.D. 632–633*, translated by Fred M. Donner (Albany: State University of New York Press, 1993), 55–58. Reprinted with permission.

40. The Battle of Ajnadain (July/August 634)

Introduction

The first major military encounter between Byzantine and Muslim forces was the Battle of Ajnadain, fought in July or August 634 at an unknown location somewhere in modern-day Israel. Arab chroniclers left accounts of this battle, which undoubtedly greatly exaggerate the size of the forces involved on both sides. Present-day historians suspect that each army probably numbered no more than somewhere between 10,000 and 20,000. Although the battle ended in a major defeat for the Byzantines, the first real indication that the new Rashidun caliphate represented a formidable enemy for the Romans, the Arabs also suffered major casualties, as the extract given here indicates. The battle was a prelude to more sweeping Arab victories, including the successful siege and capture of the Syrian capital of Damascus shortly afterward.

Document

The enemy routed. The battle of Ajnâdîn ensued. In this battle about 100,000 Greeks took part, the majority of whom were massed one band after the other by Heraclius [Hiraḵl], the rest having come from the neighboring districts. On that day, Heraclius was in Hims [Emesa]. Against this army, the Moslems fought a violent battle, and Khâlid ibn-al-Walîd particularly distinguished himself. At last, by Allah's help, the enemies of Allah were routed and shattered into pieces, a great many being slaughtered.

The martyrs. Those who suffered martyrdom on that day were 'Abdallâh ibn-az-Zubair ibn-'Abd-al-Muttalib ibn-Hâshim, 'Amr ibn-Sa'îd ibn-al-'Âsi ibn-Umaiyah, his brother Abân ibn-Sa'îd (according to the most authentic report. Others, however, claim that Abân died in the year 29), Tulaib ibn-'Umair ibn-Wahb ibn-'Abd ibn-Kusai (who fought a duel with an "unbeliever" who gave him a blow that severed his right hand making his sword fall down with the palm. In this condition he was surrounded and killed by the Greeks. His mother Arwa, daughter of 'Abd-al-Muttalib, was the Prophet's aunt. His surname was abu-Adi), and Salamah ibn-Hishâm ibn-al-Mughîrah. According to others, Salamah was killed at Marj as-Suffar. Other martyrs were: 'Ikrimah ibn-abi-Jahl ibn-Hishâm al-Makhzûmi, Habbâr ibn-Sufyân ibn-'Abd-al-Asad al-Makhzûmi (who, according to others, was killed in the battle of Mu'tah), Nu'aim ibn-'Abdallâh an-Nahhâm al-'Adawi (who, according to others, was killed in the battle of al-Yarmûk), Hishâm ibn-al-'Âsi ibn-Wâ'il as-Sahmi (who is also supposed by others to have been slain in the battle of al-Yarmûk), Jundub ibn-'Amr ad-Dausi, Sa'îd ibn-al-Hârith, al-Hârith ibn-al-Hârith, and al-Hajjâj ibn-al-Hârith ibn-Kais ibn-'Adi as-Sahmi. According to Hishâm ibn-Muhammad al-Kalbi, an-Nahhâm was killed in the battle of Mu'tah.

Sa'îd ibn-al-Hârith ibn-Kais was slain in the battle of al-Yarmûk; Tamîm ibn-al-Hârith, in the battle of Ajnâdîn; his brother, 'Ubaidallâh ibn 'Abd-al-Asad, in al-Yarmûk; and al-Hârith ibn-Hishâm ibn-al-Mughîrah, in Ajnâdîn.

Heraclius flees to Antioch. When the news of this battle came to Heraclius, his heart was filled with cowardice and he was confounded. Consequently, he took to flight to Antioch

[An âkiyah] from im [Emesa]. It was mentioned by someone that his flight from Hims to Antioch coincided with the advance of the Moslems to Syria. This battle of Ajnâdîn took place on Monday twelve days before the end of Jumâda I, year 13. Some, however, say two days after the beginning of Jumâda II, and others two days before its end.

After that, the Greeks massed an army at Yâkûsah which was a valley with al-Fauwârah at its mouth. There the Moslems met them, dispelled them and put them to flight with a great slaughter. Their remnants fled to the cities of Syria.

Source: Philip Khûri Hitti, trans., *The Origins of the Islamic State: Being a Translation from the Arabic Accompanied with Annotations, Geographic and Historic Notes of the Kitâb Futûh al-Buldân of al-Imâm abu-l 'Abbâs Ahmad ibn-Jâbir al-Balâdhuri* (New York: Columbia University Press, 1916), 174–175.

41. Al-Baladhuri: The Battle of the Yarmuk (August 20, 636)

Introduction

Byzantine emperor Heraclius spent his entire reign fighting successive military challenges. His sweeping victory over Persian king Khosrow II at the Battle of Nineveh in 627 brought little respite. Almost immediately Heraclius began fighting the Muslim Arabs who, energized by the teachings of Prophet Muhammad, embarked on conquests of much of Western and Central Asia. At the Battle of the Yarmuk in 636, Arab forces inflicted a crushing victory on the Byzantines, winning control of Syria. The Arab chronicler al-Baladhuri described the battle and its aftermath. Al-Baladhuri emphasized the hostility that the Syrian inhabitants felt toward Byzantium, leading them to welcome the new invaders. This may have been true, but it is equally possible that the local population was doing its best to accommodate the new overlords.

Document

A description of the battle. Heraclius gathered large bodies of Greeks, Syrians, Mesopotamians and Armenians numbering about 200,000. This army he put under the command of one of his choice men and sent as a vanguard Jabalah ibn-al-Aiham al-Ghassani at the head of the "naturalized" Arabs [*musta'ribah*] of Syria of the tribes of Lakhm, Judham and others, resolving to fight the Moslems so that he might either win or withdraw to the land of the Greeks and live in Constantinople. The Muslims gathered together and the Greek army marched against them. The battle they fought at al-Yarmuk was of the fiercest and bloodiest kind. Al-Yarmuk [Hieromax] is a river. In this battle 24,000 Moslems took part. The Greeks and their followers in this battle tied themselves to each other by chains, so that no one might set his hope on flight. By Allah's help, some 70,000 of them were put to death, and their remnants took to flight, reaching as far as Palestine, Antioch, Aleppo, Mesopotamia and Armenia. In the battle of al-Yarmuk certain Moslem women took part and fought violently. Among them was Hind, daughter of 'Utbah and mother of Mu'awiyah ibn-abi-Sufyan, who repeatedly exclaimed, "Cut the arms of these 'uncircumcised' with your swords!" Her husband abu-Sufyan had come to Syria as a volunteer desiring to see his sons, and so he brought his wife with him. He then returned to al-Madinah where he died, year 31, at the age of 88. Others say he died in Syria. When the news of his death was carried to his daughter, umm-Habibah, she waited until the third day on which she ordered some yellow paint and covered with it her arms and face saving, "I would not have done that, had I not heard the Prophet say, 'A woman should not be in mourning for more than three days over anyone except her husband.'" It is stated that she did likewise when she received the news of her brother Yazid's death. But Allah knows best.

Those who lost an eye or suffered martyrdom. Abu-Sufyan ibn-Harb was one-eyed. He had lost his eye in the battle of at-Ta'if. In the battle of al-Yarmuk, however, al-Ash'ath ibn-Kais, Hashim ibn-'Utbah ibn-abi-Wakkas az-Zuhri (i.e., al-Mirkal) and Kais ibn-Makshuh, each lost an eye. In this battle 'Amir ibn-abi-Wakkas az-Zuhri fell a martyr. It is this 'Amir who once carried the letter of 'Umar ibn-al-Khattab assigning abu-'Ubaidah to the governorship of Syria. Others say he was a victim of the plague; still others report that he suffered martyrdom in the battle of Ajnadin; but all that is not true.

Habib ibn-Maslamah pursues the fugitives. Abu-'Ubaidah put Habib ibn Maslamah-al-Fihri at the head of a cavalry detachment charged with pursuing the fugitive enemy, and Habib set out killing every man whom he could reach.

The story of Jabalah. Jabalah ibn-al-Aibam sided with the Ansar saying, "Ye are our brethren and the sons of our fathers," and professed Islam. After the arrival of 'Umar ibn-al-Khattab in Syria, year 17, Jabalah had a dispute with one of the Muzainah and knocked out his eye. 'Umar ordered that he be punished, upon which Jabalah said, "Is his eye like mine? Never, by Allah, shall I abide in a town where I am under authority." He then apostatized and went to the land of the Greeks. This Jabalah was the king of Ghassan and the successor of al-Harith ibn-abi-Shimr.

According to another report, when Jabalah came to 'Umar ibn-al-Khattab, he was still a Christian. 'Umar asked him to accept Islam and pay sadakah [a Muslim alms tax] but he refused saying, "I shall keep my faith and pay sadakah." 'Umar's answer was, "If thou keepest thy faith, thou hast to pay poll-tax". The man refused, and 'Umar added, "We have only three alternatives for thee: Islam, tax, or going whither thou willest." Accordingly, Jabalah left with 30,000 men to the land of the Greeks [Asia Minor]. 'Ubadah ibn-as-Samit gently reproved 'Umar saying, "If thou hadst accepted sadakah from him and treated him in a friendly way, he would have become Moslem."

In the year 21, 'Umar directed 'Umair ibn-Sa'd al-Ansari at the head of a great army against the land of the Greeks, and put him in command of the summer expedition which was the first of its kind. 'Umar instructed him to treat Jabalah ibn-al-Aiham very kindly and to try and appeal to him through the blood relationship between them, so that he should come back to the land of the Moslems with the understanding that he would keep his own faith and pay the amount of sadakah he had agreed to pay. 'Umair marched until he came to the land of the Greeks and proposed to Jabalah what he was ordered by 'Umar to propose; but Jabalah refused the offer and insisted on staying in the land of the Greeks. 'Umair then came into a place called al-Himar—a valley—which he destroyed putting its inhabitants to the sword. Hence the proverb, "In a more ruined state than the hollow of Himar."

Heraclius' adieu to Syria. When Heraclius received the news about the troops in al-Yarmuk and the destruction of his army by the Moslems, he fled from Antioch to Constantinople, and as he passed ad-D'arb he turned and said, "Peace unto thee, O Syria, and what an excellent country this is for the enemy!"—referring to the numerous pastures in Syria.

The battle of al-Yarmuk took place in Rajah, year 15.

Hubash loses his leg. According to Hisham ibn-al-Kalbi, among those who witnessed the battle of al-Yarmuk was Hubash ibn-Kais al-Kushairi, who killed many of the "uncircumcised" and lost his leg without feeling it. At last he began to look for it. Hence the verse of Sauwar ibn-Aufa:

> Among us were ibn-'Attab and the one who went seeking his leg; and among us was one who offered protection to the quarter,

—referring to dhu-l-Rukaibah.

Christians and Jews prefer Moslem rule. Abu-Hafs ad-Dimashki from Sa'id ibn-'Abd-al-'Aziz:—When Heraclius massed his troops against the Moslems and the Moslems heard that they were coming to meet them at al-Yarmuk, the Moslems refunded to the inhabitants of Hims the *karaj* [tribute] they had taken from them saying, "We are too busy to support and protect you. Take care of yourselves." But the people of Hims replied, "We like your rule and justice far better than the state of oppression and tyranny in which we were. The army of Heraclius we shall indeed, with your *'amil's* help, repulse from the city." The Jews rose and said, "We swear by the Torah, no governor of Heraclius shall enter the city of Hims unless we are first vanquished and exhausted!" Saying this, they closed the gates of the city and guarded them. The inhabitants of the other cities—Christian and Jew—that had capitulated to the Moslems, did the same, saying, "If Heraclius and his followers win over the Moslems we would return to our previous condition, otherwise we shall retain our present state so long as numbers are with the Moslems." When by Allah's help the "unbelievers" were defeated and the Moslems won, they opened the gates of their cities, went out with the singers and music players who began to play, and paid the kharaj.

Source: *The Origins of the Islamic State,* being a translation from the Arabic of the *Kitab Futuh al-Buldha* of Ahmad ibn-Jabir al-Baladhuri, translated by P. K. Hitti and F. C. Murgotten (New York: Columbia University Press, 1916 and 1924), I:207–211.

42. The Battle of al-Qādisiyyah (November 16–19, 636)

Introduction

After defeating Roman forces at Yarmuk in August 636, the Muslim armies faced a further challenge from the Persians. The forces of the young Sassanid Persian shah Yazdegerd III (r. 632–651), an army of probably 50,000–100,000, commanded by one of his top generals, Rostam Farrokhzād, confronted a much smaller Muslim force, estimated to have been around 30,000. For three months negotiations took place between the two sides, with Muslim caliph Umar demanding that the Persians should convert to Islam, terms that the Persians rejected. Following the breakdown of truce talks, the Persian Army, which had been in place since July 636, and the Muslims finally began hostilities, fighting inconclusively for three days. On the fourth day the Muslim troops launched a final attack in the course of which, as numerous Arab chroniclers related, Rostam was killed and the Persians fled. The Battle of al-Qādisiyyah opened the way for the Muslim conquest of Iraq over the following years. Yazdegerd III survived a further 15 years but was the last of the Sassanid dynasty in Persia.

Document

According to al-Sarī—Shuayb—Sayf—Talhah and Ziyād: In the morning that followed the Night of al-Qādisiyyah [which is (also) the morning of the Night of Howling; of these battle days, this was the night called the Night of al-Qādisiyyah], the Muslims were exhausted, for they did not close their eyes throughout the night. Al-Qa'qā walked among the men, saying: "He who resumes the fight against the Persians will defeat them in an hour. Endure for [another] hour and launch the attack, because victory comes with endurance. Prefer endurance to fear." A group of commanders gathered around him and stood up against Rustam, until they became entangled at sunrise with the Persians who were protecting him. When the tribes saw this, some of their men rose [to speak]. Qays b. 'Abd Yaghūth, al-Ash'ath b. Qays, 'Amr b. Ma'dīkarib, Ibn Dhī al-Sahmayn al-Khath'amī, and Ibn Dhī al-Burdayn al-Hilāli—all stood up and said: "Let not these men be more earnest than you in complying with God's orders, and let them [meaning the Persians] not be more daring when facing death. Let their souls not be more generous in giving up this world, and compete with each other [for martyrdom]."

They launched an attack from the area adjacent to them and became entangled with (the Persians) opposite them. A number of men rose up among the tribe of Rabī'ah and said: "You know the Persians best, and you were the most courageous against them in the past. What is it, then, that prevents you from being [even] more courageous today?" The first Persians to retreat at noon were al-Hurmuzān and al-Bayruzān; they retreated but made a stand in the place that they reached. At noon a gap was opened in the center [of the Persian army] and dust covered them. A violent westerly wind blew away the sunshade from Rustam's throne, and it fell into al-'Atīq. The dust blew against the Persians.

Al-Qaʿqāʿ and his companions reached Rustam's throne and toppled it. Rustam vacated it when the wind had blown the sunshade away and transferred to some mules which had brought to him certain possessions on that day and were standing [nearby], taking shelter in the shade of one of the mules and of its litter. Hilāl b. ʿUllafah hit the litter under which Rustam was (hiding) and cut its ropes. One of the half-loads fell on Rustam, so that Hilāl did not see him and did not notice him. The load hit Rustam and displaced a vertebra in his spine. His [sleeves] diffused scent. He moved toward al-ʿAtīq and threw himself into it, but without any hesitation, Hilāl went after him and caught him after Rustam had already started to swim. Hilāl stood upright, seized Rustam's leg, and dragged him out to the river's bank, and then struck his forehead with the sword and killed him. Then he dragged him farther and threw him at the feet of the mules. He seated himself on Rustam's throne and exclaimed: "By the Lord of the Kaʿbah, I have killed Rustam! Come to me!" Men gathered around him without noticing or seeing the throne, proclaiming "God is most great!" and calling out to each other.

At this point the polytheists lost heart and were defeated. Al-Jālnūs stood on the barrier and called upon the Persians to cross it. The dust settled. As for those who were chained together, they panicked and threw themselves, one after the other, into al-ʿAtīq. The Muslims stabbed them with their spears, and none of them escaped to tell the story. They numbered thirty thousand. Dirār b. al-Khaṭṭāb seized the royal flag and was given thirty thousand [dirhams] in exchange for it; its value was one million and two hundred thousand. The Muslims killed in the battle ten thousand men, over and above those whom they had killed on the previous day....

According to al-Sarī—Shuʿayb—Sayf—Muhammad, Talhah and Ziyād: When the Persians were defeated, none of them remained between the moat and al-ʿAtīq, and the dead covered the area between al-Qudays and al-ʿAtīq; Saʿd ordered Zuhrah to pursue the [fleeing] Persians. Zuhrah summoned the vanguard; he ordered al-Qaʿqāʿ to pursue those who fled downstream and ordered Shuraḥbīl to pursue those who fled upstream. He ordered Khālid b. ʿUrfuṭah to plunder the dead and to bury the martyrs. Two thousand five hundred martyrs who were killed on the Night of Howling and on the Day of al-Qādisiyyah were buried around Qudays, across al-ʿAtīq, opposite [the valley of] Musharriq, and the martyrs killed before the Night of Howling were buried in Musharriq. The spoils and the wealth were gathered, a quantity such as this had never been gathered, neither before al-Qādisiyyah nor after it.

Saʿd sent for Hilā (b. ʿUllafah), blessed him, and said: "Where is your man?" He replied: "I threw him under [the feet of] the mules." Saʿd said: "Go and bring him here." When Hilal brought the corpse, Saʿd said: "Strip it of everything, except that which you want to leave on it." Hilāl took Rustam's spoils and did not leave on him anything.

Source: Abu Jaʿfar Muhammad b. Jarir al Tabari, *The History of al-Tabarī*, Vol. 12, *The Battle of al-Qādisiyyah and the Conquest of Syria and Palestine*, translated by Yohanan Friedmann (Albany: State University of New York Press, 1992), 122–125. Reprinted with permission.

43. Emperor Heraclius Concludes Peace with Persia (628) and Contemplates the Muslim Threat (ca. 636–638)

Introduction

Byzantine emperor Heraclius (r. 610–641) spent his entire reign fighting off military threats, confronting first the Persians and, after their defeat at Roman hands, the newly emerged armies of Islam. After he inflicted a massive defeat on Persia at the Battle of Nineveh in 627, prompting a coup against King Khosrow II, he negotiated a peace treaty with the new Persian ruler that was highly advantageous to Constantinople. The Byzantine Empire regained territories in Asia Minor that had earlier been ceded to Persia, including Edessa, Palestine, and Jerusalem. On his return the people of Constantinople gave Heraclius a hero's welcome, "dancing with joy" as he entered the city.

Unfortunately, years of protracted fighting had gravely weakened both the Romans and the Sassanid Persians, making them vulnerable prey to a new and unexpected threat from the newly united and expansionist Muslims of the Arabian peninsula.

43. Emperor Heraclius Concludes Peace with Persia and Contemplates the Muslim Threat

Arab chroniclers recounted how in the final years of his reign, after Arab forces inflicted major defeats on both the Byzantines and the Persians within a few months of each other, Heraclius could foresee that it was probably only a matter of time before the Byzantine Empire lost Syria to the Muslims. He could only hope for the appearance of the "ill-fated one," the false Messiah predicted in eschatological prophesy who was expected to wage war against the Muslims but ultimately lose. While in reality Heraclius may not have been familiar with the Muslim scriptures, it seems likely that he did take a gloomy view of the future of the domains he had fought so hard to defend. He nonetheless resolutely pursued a scorched-earth policy intended to deny encroaching Muslim forces the resources of the lands they invaded.

Documents

Excerpt from *The Chronicle of Theophanes*

In this year [628], peace having been concluded between the Persians and the Romans, the emperor sent his brother Theodore bearing letters and accompanied by emissaries of Siroes, emperor of Persia, with a view to sending back peacefully to Persia those Persians who were at Edessa, in Palestine, Jerusalem, and in other Roman towns: those were to cross Roman territory without harm. Now the emperor, having defeated Persia in the course of six years, made peace in the seventh and returned with great joy to Constantinople, thereby fulfilling a certain mystical allegory: for God completed all of creation in six days and called the seventh a day of rest. So the emperor also, after undergoing many toils for six years, returned in the seventh to the City amid peace and joy, and took his rest. When the people of the City had learnt of his coming, all of them, with unrestrained eagerness, went out to meet him at Hiereia, together with the patriarch and the emperor Constantine, his son, holding olive branches and lights and acclaiming him with tears of joy. Coming forward, his son fell at his feet and embraced him, and they both shed tears on the ground. At the sight of this, all the people sent up to God hymns of thanksgiving. After receiving the emperor in this fashion, they entered the City dancing with joy.

The Departure of Heraclius for Constantinople

Then Heraclius set out for Constantinople. There is disagreement concerning the date of his arrival there and of his departure from Syria; Ibn Isḥāq said that it had been in the year 15/636–37 whereas Sayf said that it had been in the year 16/637–38.

According to Sayf—Abū al-Zahrā' al-Qushayrī—a man from Qushayr: When Heraclius set out from al-Ruhā' and asked its inhabitants to follow him, they said: "We are better off here than with you," and they refused to follow him and separated themselves both from him and from the Muslims.

The first man to cause the dogs of al-Ruhā' to bark and its fowls to be scared was Ziyād b. Hanzalah, who was a Companion of the Prophet. [In this expedition?] he was with 'Umar b. Mālik; they were taking turns in commanding the troops. . . .

Before [this incursion] Heraclius set out for Shimshāt. When the Muslims reached al-Ruhā', he entered the Byzantine territory and moved toward Constantinople.

A man of the Byzantines who had been a prisoner of the Muslims caught up with Heraclius. Heraclius said to him: "Inform me about these people." The man said: "I shall tell you, and it will be as if you yourself were looking at them. They are horsemen during the day and monks at night. In the area under their responsibility they do not eat except for a price and do not enter a house except with a greeting of peace. They stand up to those who fight them until they destroy them." Heraclius said: "If you have spoken the truth, they will, indeed, inherit the land on which I stand."

According to 'Ubādah and Khālid: Whenever Heraclius made the pilgrimage to Jerusalem, left Syria behind [on his way back], and entered into the land of the Byzantines, he used to turn back and to say: "Peace be upon you, O Syria! This is the farewell of a man who takes leave of you without fulfilling his desire and will return." When the Muslims moved on Hims, he crossed the Euphrates and camped at al-Ruhā'. He remained there until the people of al-Kūfah appeared, Qinnasrīn was conquered, and

Mīnās was killed. When this happened, he retreated to Shimshāt. When he left Shimshāt in order to cross into the Byzantine territory, he ascended to an elevated place, turned back, looked in the direction of Syria, and said: "Peace be upon you, O Syria! This is a farewell after which there will be no reunion. No Byzantine man will ever return to you except in fear until the ill-fated one is born; would that he would not be born! How sweet will be his deeds and how bitter will be their outcome with regard to the Byzantines."

According to Abū al-Zahrā' and 'Amr b. Maymūn: When Heraclius left Shimshāt and entered the Byzantine territory, he turned back toward Syria and said: "I used to greet you in the manner of a traveler. Today I am greeting you in the manner of one who departs. No Byzantine man will ever return to you except in fear until the ill-fated one is born; would that he would not be born!" Heraclius moved onward and reached Constantinople, taking with him the people of the fortresses located between Alexandretta and Tarsus so that the Muslims should not be able to move within any populated territory between Antioch and the Byzantine land. He laid the fortresses waste so that the Muslims would not be able to find any one there. At times Byzantines lay in ambush near the fortresses and launched surprise attacks on those who were lagging behind, and the Muslims had to take precautions against this.

Source: Abu Ja'far Muhammad b. Jarir al Tabari, *The History of al-Tabarī*, Vol. 12, *The Battle of al-Qādisiyyah and the Conquest of Syria and Palestine*, translated by Yohanan Friedmann (Albany: State University of New York Press, 1992), 181–183. Reprinted with permission.

44. The Battle of Akroinon (May 740)

Introduction

The Battle of Akroinon, fought between armies of the Byzantine Empire and the Umayyad Caliphate in 740, was the first occasion on which Byzantine military forces overcame Arab troops in a pitched battle. Details of this encounter, described below by a Byzantine chronicler, who almost certainly exaggerated the numbers involved, are somewhat sketchy. It appears that Emperor Leo and his son, the future emperor Constantine V, won a crushing victory over the smaller of two Arab invasion force, one led by Suleiman, son of Umayyad caliph Hisham ibn abd-al Malik, and the second by two able and experienced Arab generals. Both of these commanders were killed in the engagement, as were many of their troops, though the survivors retreated in good order and joined Muslim forces at Sinnada. Arab pressure on the Byzantine Empire subsequently declined, though this may have been due less to the empire's own military performance than to threats from the rival Abbasids, who overthrew the Ummayad Caliphate in 750.

Were one to believe the Byzantine and Muslim chroniclers, the Battle of Akroinon was a mere blip in centuries of constant conflict between the two opposing sides. Arab chroniclers, preoccupied with the internecine wrangling and warfare among their own community at this time, simply ignored this battle, which was won by Byzantine forces commanded by the elderly Emperor Leo III and his son and chosen successor, Constantine V (r. 741–775). The Byzantine chronicler Theophanes, a fanatical opponent of Leo III on theological grounds, particularly Leo's objection to the use of icons, managed to include a brief and grudging mention of it, given below, in his lengthy history of the Byzantine Empire and its enemies. From Theophanes's account, none would have guessed that the outcome of the battle, a major success for the Byzantines, was the cessation of Arab raids against Byzantine territory for the next three decades.

Document

In this year, in the month of May [740], indiction 8, Souleiman invaded the Roman country with 90,000 men under four commanders. One of these, Gamer, led the van with 10,000 scouts and set up ambushes in the region of Asia. He was followed by Melich and Batal with 20,000 cavalry as far as the area of Akroinos and, after them, Souleiman with 60,000 men advanced to the area of Tyana in Cappadocia. Those in Asia and Cappadocia captured many men, women, and animals and returned home unharmed, whereas the contingents of Melich and Batal were fought and defeated by Leo and Constantine at Akroinos. Most of them, including the two commanders, perished by the sword. About 6,800 of their warriors, however, fought on and [Or possibly, "About 800 of their warriors, after standing up to 6,000"] fled to Synada. They safely joined Souleiman and returned to Syria. In the same year many [of them] were killed by [the Berbers] in Africa as well, including the commander called Damaskenos.

Source: *The Chronicle of Theophanes Confessor: Byzantine and Near Eastern History AD 284–813*, translated by Cyril Mango and Roger Scott (Oxford, UK: Clarendon, 1997), 571. By permission of Oxford University Press.

45. Harun al-Rashid at War with the Byzantine Empire (803–806)

Introduction

Under Abbasid caliph Harun al-Rashid, hostilities erupted between Baghdad and the Byzantine Empire when a new emperor, Nikephoros I (802–811), seized power in 802. Nikephoros withheld the annual tribute that his predecessor, Empress Irene, had agreed to pay the caliphate. His reneging on this bargain incensed the caliph, who mounted a series of punitive expeditions against the Byzantine Empire and its territories in Asia Minor. These climaxed in 806 when an Arab army of 135,000 men invaded the empire, forcing Nikephoros to back down and pay a humiliating indemnity and annual tribute. With hostilities between them ended, the correspondence between the two rulers resumed a tone of civility, and the two exchanged lavish gifts, with the caliph returning unharmed a young Byzantine woman captured by the Arabs in this campaign who was already affianced to the son of Nikephoros.

Document

In this year, al-Qāsim b. al-Rashīd entered the Byzantine lands in the month of Shaʿbān (July–August, 803). He halted before Qurrah and then laid siege to it, and he sent forward al-ʿAbbās b. Jaʾfar b. Muhammad b. al-Ashʿath, who then halted before the fortress of Sinān, and they made strenuous attacks. The Byzantines sent messages to him offering to hand over 320 Muslim captives if he would depart from them. He agreed to these terms, and fell back from Qurrah and the fortress of Sinān according to the terms of the peace treaty. ʿAlī b. ʿĪsā b. Mūsā died on this raid into the Byzantine lands whilst accompanying al-Qāsim.

In this year, the Byzantine Emperor broke the peace agreement concluded between his predecessor and the Muslims and withheld the tribute which the preceding monarch had undertaken to pay the Muslims.

The reason for the Byzantines' breaking that peace agreement was that there had been a peace agreement in operation between the Muslims and the ruler of Byzantium, their ruler being at that time Irene [*Rīnī*] (we have already mentioned previously the occasion of the peace agreement which existed between her [or, between the Byzantines, *al-Rūm*] and the Muslims). Then the Byzantines turned on Irene and deposed her, and raised to power in her place Nicephorus [*Nigfūr*]. The Byzantines mention that this Nicephorus was a descendant of Jafnah of the house of Ghassān and that, before achieving royal power, he had been in charge of the exchequer. Then, five months after the Byzantines had deposed her, Irene died. It has been mentioned that when Nicephorus had achieved royal power and had received the obedience of all the Byzantines, he wrote to al-Rashīd thus:

From Nicephorus, ruler of the Byzantines, to Hārūn, ruler of the Arabs. As follows: The queen who was my predecessor set you up in the position of a rook (i.e., in chess), and herself as merely a pawn, and she paid over to you from her treasuries the amount whose equivalent you should by right have handed over to her, but that (arose from) the weakness and deficient sense of women.

Now, when you have perused my letter, send back what you received of the money which she sent, and ransom yourself by (disgorging) what you are receiving by means of exaction; if not, then the sword will inevitably be set between us!

He related: When al-Rashīd read the letter, violent anger took hold of him, so that there was no one who dared to look at him, much less speak to him. His boon-companions dispersed, fearful lest they let slip any further words or actions. The vizier's power of judgement was too paralyzed either for him to offer the Caliph any advice or to leave him to make up his own mind unilaterally. The Caliph then sent for an inkstand and wrote on the back of the letter:

In the name of God, the Merciful, the Compassionate, from Hārūn the Commander of the Faithful to Nicephorus the dog of the Byzantines: O son of an infidel woman, I have read your letter, and the reply is what you will see, without you having to hear it. Farewell!

Then he set off immediately and travelled on until he halted before the gates of Heraclia, and then captured it; he took plunder, he selected the best items for himself, he slaughtered people, he destroyed, he burnt and he extirpated. Hence, Nicephorus sought to make peace, on the basis of an annual tribute, and al-Rashīd agreed to this. When he returned from this expedition of his, and reached al-Raqqah, Nicephorus broke the agreement and went back on the covenant. The weather was extremely cold; hence Nicephorus was confident that al-Rashīd would be unable to march back against him....

Among the events taking place during this year [Year 188, December 20, 803–December 4, 804] was Ibrāhīm b. Jibrīl's leading the summer expedition and his invading the Byzantine lands by the pass [*darb*] of al-Ṣafṣāf. Nicephorus marched out to confront him, but some event took place at his rear which deflected him from encountering Ibrāhīm. Hence, he turned back, but came into contact with a Muslim force; he suffered three wounds personally and was put to flight. According to what has been mentioned, 40,700 of the Byzantine troops were killed and 4,000 riding beasts captured....

In this year [806], al-Rashīd conquered Heraclia and sent out contingents of troops and detachments of cavalry to spread through the land of Byzantium. According to what has been said, he entered it with a force of 135,000 regularly paid troops [*murtaziq*], in addition to camp-followers, volunteers, and those not registered on the stipends list [*dīwān*]. ʿAbdallāh b. Mālik (al-Khuzāʿī) halted at Dhū al-Kulāʿ, and sent forward Dāwūd b. ʿĪsā b. Mūsā with 70,000 men to range about within the land of Byzantium. Shurāhīl b. Maʿn b. Zāʾidah captured iṣn al-Ṣaqālibah and Dabasah, and Yazīd b. Makhlad captured al-Ṣafṣāf and Malāqūbiyah. Al-Rashīd's conquest of Heraclia took place in Shawwāl (August–September, 806). He reduced it to ruins and enslaved its people after a thirty days' siege of the town. He gave charge of the Levant coastlands of the eastern Mediterranean as far as Egypt to Humayd b. Maʿyūf (al-Hajūrī). Humayd raided as far as Cyprus, where he razed buildings, burnt property, and enslaved 16,000 of its people. He despatched them to al-Rāfiqah; the judge Abū al-Bakhtarī took charge of selling them, and the bishop of Cyprus fetched two thousand dinars. Al-Rashīd set out for the Byzantine lands on the twentieth of Rajab (June 11, 806)....

After this, al-Rashīd went on to al-Tuwānah and encamped there. Then he travelled away from there, and left behind over it ʿUqbah b. Jaʿfar (al-Khuzāʿiī) ordering him to build a residence there. Nicephorus sent to al-Rashīd tribute and poll-tax (*al-kharāj wa-al-jizyah*), the latter for his own head, that of his designated successor and those of his nobles (*baṭāriqah*) and the rest of the people of his realm, a total of fifty thousand dīnārs, at a rate of four dīnārs on his own head and two dīnārs on that of his son Istabrāq (i.e., Stauracius). Nicephorus also sent a letter, via two of his most prominent nobles, concerning a slave girl from among the captives from Heraclia, and its text was as follows:

To the servant of God Hārūn, Commander of the Faithful, from Nicephorus, ruler of the Byzantines, greetings! As follows: O King, I have a request to make of you which will not cause any damage either to your faith or to your temporal welfare and which is a trifling and insignificant matter: that you grant to my son a slave girl, one of the maidens of Heraclia whom I had sought in marriage for my son. If you deem it expedient to fulfill for me the object of my requirement, then I would be grateful if you would do it. Peace be upon you, and God's mercy and blessing!

Nicephorus also sought from him presents of perfume and one of his (royal) tents [*surādiqātihi*].

Al-Rashīd ordered the slave girl to be sought out; she was brought back, adorned with finery and installed on a seat in the tent in which he himself was lodging. The slave girl and the tent, together with its contents—vessels and fittings—were handed over to Nicephorus's envoy. He also sent to Nicephorus the perfume which he had requested, and he further sent to him dates, dishes of *khabīṣ*, raisins and healing drugs (or: opium, *tiryāq*). Al-Rashīd's envoy handed over all these to Nicephorus. The latter, in return, gave al-Rashīd a load of Islamic dirhams on the back of a chestnut-colored hack [*birdhawn*], amounting to fifty thousand dirhams, one hundred satin brocade garments, two hundred garments of fine brocade [*buzyūn*], twelve falcons, four hunting dogs, and three hacks. Nicephorus further contracted not to destroy Dhū al-Kulāʿ, Ṣumālū or iṣn Sinān, whilst al-Rashīd guaranteed not to resettle and fortify Heraclia—this on the basis that Nicephorus would hand over three hundred thousand dīnārs [annually].

Source: Abu Jaʿfar Muhammad b. Jarir al Tabari, *The History of al-Tabarī*, Vol. 30, *The ʿAbbāsid Caliphate in Equilibrium*, translated by C. E. Bosworth (Albany: State University of New York Press, 1992), 238–241, 248, 262–264. Reprinted with permission.

46. The Siege of Baghdad (August 812–September 813)

Introduction

Following the death of Abbasid caliph Harun al-Rashid in 809, civil war soon broke out between Muhammad al-Amin, his chosen successor, and his slightly older son, al-Amin's half brother Abdallāh al-Mamun. A lengthy and complicated civil war ensued, with portions of the elite Abnā group within the military eventually switching sides from the incumbent al-Amin to al-Mamun, who had won control of Egypt, Mosul, and the Hejaz by 812. The army of al-Mamun, commanded by his general Tahir bin al-Husayn, arrived outside Baghdad, the capital of the caliphate, in August 812 and settled down to besiege the city. While elites by this time increasingly favored al-Mamun, Baghdad's urban proletariat refused to surrender to the invaders and mounted a fierce resistance for 13 months, establishing their own militias. The radical and uncontrollable behavior of the poor—including, it seems, a significant contingent of African slaves—became a growing threat to the well-to-do, further weakening the allegiance of elites to the incumbent al-Amin. An Arab chronicler described those who fought on as "street vendors, naked ones, people from the prisons, riffraff, rabble, cutpurses, and people of the market" who had been "given permission to plunder." After 13 months Baghdad was finally captured, a victory due in part to assistance that the invading forces received from some of the city's richer citizens. A subsequent Arab account of the siege described both the devastation and the social upheavals that Baghdad experienced at this time, events that inspired observers to poetry.

Document

After the battle of Qasr Sālih, Muhammad turned to diversion and drink. He entrusted matters to Muhammad b. ʿĪsā b. Nahīk and [al Hasan] al-Hirsh [a leader of irregular forces]. From the streets and gates near them, the two of them placed their agents in the city gates, suburbs, al-Karkh market, the Tigris quays, al-Muhawwal Gate, and al-Kunāsah. The thieves and criminals of these areas despoiled anyone they were able to lay hands on—men, women, and infirm people from the [Muslim] community and non-Muslims. They did things the likes of which we have never heard to have happened in any other countries at war.

When this had gone on a long time for the people and Baghdad had become oppressive for its inhabitants, those who had the strength to do so left the city after the oppressive exactions, painful affliction, and great danger. Tāhir admonished his forces to behave quite differently: he was strict in this and treated suspicious characters roughly. He commanded Muhammad b. Abī Khālid to protect the weak and women and to give them gifts and relief. When a man or a woman escaped from the hands of al-Hirsh's forces and reached Tāhir's forces, their fear would depart and they would feel secure. The woman would display whatever gold and silver, goods, or fine clothing she had. People therefore said that [the situation of] Tāhir's forces, the forces and companions of al-Hirsh, and the people who had escaped was like the parable of the wall, concerning which God, whose Name is exalted, said: "And a wall shall be set up between them, having a door on whose inward side is mercy, and on whose outward side is chastisement." After the people's tribulation had gone on a long time, their condition became very bad and they were unable to endure it any longer. Concerning this, one of the young men of Baghdad said:

> I wept blood over Baghdad, when
> I lost the ease of a pleasant life.

We have been given sorrow in exchange for joy,
and in exchange for plenty we have been given scarcity.
The [evil] eye of the envious has afflicted Baghdad,
and has caused its people to perish by the *manjaniq*.
Here are people who have been overcome and burned by the fire,
and here a woman is mourning for a drowned man.
Here a woman is shouting, "Alas the day!"
and here one is crying over the loss of someone dear.
Here a dark-eyed woman, pleasing of mien,
in a shift anointed with perfume,
Is fleeing from the fire into the looting,
while her father is fleeing [from the looting] into the fire.
One who stole [the beauty of] her eyes from the gazelle,
and whose teeth are like the flash of lightning—
[All these], as bewildered as beasts being led to the sacrifice, pensive,
wearing necklaces around their throats,
Call on someone to take pity, but there is none to take pity:
brother has lost brother.
Here are people who have been expelled from the shade of this world:
their property is being sold in every market.
Here a stranger, whose home is close,
lies headless in the middle of the road.
He was caught in the middle of all their fighting,
and people do not know to which party [he belonged].
Child does not remain to care for his father,
and friend has fled without friend.
Whatever I may forget of the past,
I will always remember [the battle of] Dār al-Raqīq. . . .

One of the poets of Baghdad said concerning this:

These wars have brought out men
who belong neither to war's Qahtān nor to its Nizār.
A company in woolen coats of mail
who go into battle like ravenous lions.
Upon them are neck protectors made of palm fronds,
which serve instead of helmets, and shields of reed mats.
They do not know what flight is, when
even heroes seek refuge from the spears in flight.
One of them rushes to attack
two thousand—naked, not having even a waist wrapper.
They young fellow says, when he strikes
a spear thrust, "Take that from the vagrant lad (*'ayyār*)!"
How many a noble (*sharif*) has war rendered of no repute!
How many a gambler and cutpurse has it exalted!

Source: Abu Ja'far Muhammad b. Jarir al Tabari, *The History of al-Tabarī*, Vol. 31, *The War between Brothers*, translated by Michael Fishbein (Albany: State University of New York Press, 1992), 152–156. Reprinted with permission.

47. The Zanj Slave Revolts: An Account of the Zanj Leader's Advance on al-Basra with His Army (October 22–24, 869)

Introduction

The Zanj slave Rebellion, which began in 869 and lasted 14 years, was a major challenge to the authority of the Abbasid Caliphate. Led by Ali ibn Muhammad, a man of uncertain background and possibly of mixed race, the uprising mobilized Bantu-speaking African slaves known as Zanj who had been transported to modern-day Iraq to undertake agricultural labor and a variety of other discontented social elements. Ali promised the slaves freedom if they followed him. His first major triumph came at the Battle of Basra in 869, when an initial defeat of the insurgent forces was transformed into a bloody victory the following day. The contemporary chronicler Abu Ja'far Muhammad b. Jarir al Tabari, who lived through these events, provided an account of the battle in which he drew on the eyewitness testimony of Zanj supporters who took part in it. Both sides demonstrated great brutality toward the other, a pattern that would continue throughout the revolt. After winning this battle the Zanj settled in the area, conducting guerrilla warfare and taking Basra itself two years later.

Document

After the Zanj leader had mustered his troops, they reportedly set out for al-Baṣrah from the salt flats stretching beside the Dīnārī canal, the farthest reaches of which extended to the Nahr al-Muhdath. When they had arrived opposite the Nahr al-Riyāḥī, a party of blacks arrived and informed him that they had seen armed men in the al-Riyāḥī area itself. Moments later the Zanj assembled at a call to arms, and the Zanj leader ordered 'Alī b. Aban to cross the canal against the foe, who were on the eastern side of the Dinari canal. 'Alī b. Abān took about three thousand men with him while the Zanj leader collected together his remaining troops, telling 'Alī [at the same time] that, if he required reinforcements, he need only ask for them. After 'Alī b. Abān had left, the Zanj called for their weapons, for they had spotted another movement [of troops] from a direction different from the one 'Alī had taken. The Zanj leader inquired about the troop movement and was told that they were coming from the direction of the village of al-Ja'fariyyah, which lay beside the Nahr Harb. So he despatched Muhammad b. Salm in that direction.

It was reported from Rayhān (b. Ṣāliḥ), one of 'Alī b. Muhammad's followers, that he said, "I was among those accompanying Muhammad (b. Salm) when we set out at the time of the noon prayer. We confronted the enemy in al-Ja'fariyyah, and a fierce battle developed between us, which lasted until the late afternoon." The blacks next led a ferocious assault, forcing the enemy to turn heel and flee. Around five hundred persons were killed from among the soldiers, the Arab tribesmen, and the Baṣran factions of the Bilāliyyah and the Sa'diyyah. . . .

Rayhān said, ". . . The Zanj had resorted to recovering spoils as I made my way along the Nahr al-Dīnārī. . . ."

Moments later the cry "God is greatest" was heard, and 'Alī b. Abān appeared in possession of the head of one of the Bilāliyyah called Abū al-Layth al-Qawārīrī (Muhammad b. al-Hasan—Shibl said that Waṣif al-Zuhrī was the person who killed Abū al-Layth al-Qawārīrī, one of the celebrated members of the Bilāliyyah) and [in possession of] the head of another Bilāliyyah member named 'Abdān al-Kasibī who had a voice among them, as well as the heads of a number of others from them. 'Alī b. Muhammad queried 'Alī b. Abān about the incident, and he told him that no one had fought him more tenaciously than these two men, meaning Abū al-Layth and 'Abdān. 'Alī b. Abān forced them to flee and finally drove them into the Nahr Nāfidh, where they had a barge, which he capsized. . . .

'Alī and the Zanj next made for the salt flats of al-Ja'fariyyah. He remained there that night among the slain. The following morning he gathered together his troops and cautioned them [again] against their entering al-Baṣrah. Regardless, some of them, including Ankalwayh, Zurayq, Abū al-Khanjar—who had not yet been made a commander—Salīm, and Waṣīf al-Kūfī hastened on ahead. When they reached the Nahr al-Shādhānī, a number of Baṣrans came out to meet them, the number swelling quickly into a multitude. 'Alī b. Muhammad received news of this and sent off Muhammad b. Salm, 'Alī b. Abān, and Mushriq, Yahyā's slave, with a large contingent. He went along with them, accompanying the boats that were loaded with pack animals and the wives of the slaves. He established camp at the bridge on the Nahr Kathīr.

Rayḥān continued: "I joined 'Alī b. Muḥammad, having received a wound on my leg from a rock. He asked about developments and I told him that the battle was well underway. He then ordered my return and accompanied me until I reached the high ground overlooking the Nahr al-Sabābijah. He said to me, 'Go to our troops and tell them to disengage and fall back.' I told him that he should get as far away from the place as possible, for I was unsure of his safety from the enemy's slave troops. So he withdrew.

I myself went and informed the commanders of his orders, and they retreated. The Baṣrans pressed the Zanj hard, and a complete rout was the result. That happened in the late afternoon. Many fell into the Kathīr and Shayṭān canals. 'Alī b. Muḥammad called to his followers to come back, but they could not return. A number of them drowned in the Nahr Kathīr and many were slain on the canal bank as well as on the Shādhānī. Among the commanders who drowned that day were Abū al-Jawn, Mubārak al-Bahrānī, 'Aṭā' al-Barbarī, and Salām al-Shāmī. The slave of Abū Shīth, Ḥārith al-Qaysī, and Suhayl caught up with 'Alī b. Muḥammad, and together they mounted the arched bridge (*qanṭarah*) over the Nahr Kathīr. 'Alī then turned back to [challenge] them, and they retreated before him until they were back on the ground. On this day 'Alī was wearing a woolen tunic, a turban, sandals, and a sword, and he carried a shield. When he had left the bridge, the Baṣrans mounted it again in pursuit. 'Alī turned back and killed a man on the fifth step of the bridge. He called out to his men to alert them to his position, but none of them remained in that spot save for Abū al-Shawk, Muṣlī, and Rafīq, Yaḥyā's slave."

Rayḥān said, "I was with 'Alī b. Muḥammad at the time. He fell back to al-Muʿallā and camped on the western side of the Shayṭān canal."

Rayḥān continued: "'Alī b. Muḥammad returned to al-Muʿalla on the western side of the Nahr Shayṭān and camped there. He discovered upon inquiry that many of the men had fled and, after an inspection, he found there were a total of only five hundred men left.

A horn was blown, the sound of which used to be the signal for the slaves to assemble, but no one returned. 'Alī b. Muḥammad spent the night there, in the course of which Jurbān arrived. He had escaped in the general flight, taking with him thirty slaves. 'Alī asked him where he had vanished to, and he replied that he had made a reconnaissance of al-Zawāriqah."

Rayḥān continued: "'Alī b. Muḥammad sent me to find out for him who was still at the Nahr Ḥarb bridge. I found no one around. The Baṣrans had plundered the boats that 'Alī had brought there, removing the pack animals and taking possession of his other goods, his letters and astrolabes. The following morning, when 'Alī b. Muḥammad inspected the troops again, he discovered that a thousand men had made their way back during the night."

Muḥammad b. al-Ḥasan—Muḥammad b. Simʿān al-Kātib: On Monday, the 14th of Dhū al-Qaʿdah (October 24, 869), the people of al-Baṣrah assembled together and went forth in the wake of what they regarded as a triumph over the Zanj the previous day. The man selected to lead the expedition was a Baṣran by the name of Ḥammād al-Sājī, a sailor experienced in operating and fighting from barges. The force comprised volunteers, archers, people from the main mosque, those from the Bilāliyyah and Saʿdiyyah factions prepared to follow Ḥammād, and onlookers from the Hāshimites, Qurayshites, and other sections of the populace. Three barges were loaded with archers who crowded on board, eager to get to the scene of battle. A mob proceeded on foot, some bearing arms while others were mere spectators without weapons. The barges and boats entered the Umm Ḥabīb canal on the tide after sunset that same day. The procession of foot soldiers and spectators along the canal bank was so dense and numerous that they blocked from view everything in front of them. The Zanj leader had stationed himself on the canal known as al-Shayṭān.

Muḥammad b. al-Ḥasan said the Zanj leader told him that, when his scouts had arrived and he knew of the approaching crowd, he sent off Zurayq and Abū al-Layth al-Iṣbahānī with a detachment of troops along the east bank of the [Shayṭān] canal, and Shibl and Ḥusayn al-Ḥammāmī with another detachment along the western bank. Both parties were to set up ambushes. 'Alī

47. The Zanj Slave Revolts: An Account of the Zanj Leader's Advance on al-Basra with His Army

b. Abān was ordered to take the remainder of his troops to intercept the enemy. They should, however, crouch down facing the enemy, guarding themselves with their shields, allowing no one to attack until the adversaries were close enough to brandish swords at them. When the situation had developed in this way, the Zanj attacked the enemy. The Zanj leader gave orders to the two ambuscades that when the throng [on the banks] were abreast of them and they heard their own troops on the attack, they should emerge on both sides of the canal shouting at the enemy. The Zanj women were ordered to gather bricks and keep the men supplied with them.

Muhammad b. al-Hasan said that after this incident the leader of the Zanj told his followers, "That day, as I beheld the mob approaching, I was gripped by a terrible fear, such an overwhelming terror that I appealed [to God] for help. I was accompanied by only a few troops, among them Muṣliḥ, and there was not one among us who did not imagine that he was going to meet his doom. Muṣliḥ marveled at the size of the multitude and I motioned to him to contain himself. As the enemy neared, I cried out, 'Oh God, this is the hour of trial, so come to my aid!' I had scarcely finished saying this when I saw white birds sweep down upon the enemy, and one of the galleys overturned, and all on board were drowned. The barges met the same fate. My troops then fell upon the enemy they were heading for, shouting at them." The ambushers emerged from their hiding places on the canal banks behind the boats and the foot soldiers, clubbing those among them and onlookers on shore who tried to flee. A group here was drowned, a group there was killed, while others who fled toward the canal seeking rescue were overtaken by the sword. Those who resisted were slain, while those who ventured into the water were drowned. The foot soldiers on the canal's edge who sought escape in the water were either killed or drowned until most of the enemy forces had been annihilated. None but the odd fugitive was saved. The numbers of Baṣrans missing soared as their wives raised a chorus of lament.

People spoke of this day as the Day of the Barges (*yawm alshadhā*). They were horrified by the number killed that day. Among the innumerable host killed were a number of sons of the Hāshimite Ja'far b. Sulaymān and forty famous archers.

The abominable one ['Alī b. Muhammad] had the heads [of the slain] collected. He displayed them so that relatives of the deceased who came to him could claim those they recognized. For the rest, which no one claimed, he put aboard a flat-bottomed boat (*jarībiyyah*), filling it up. The boat was released on the falling tide from the Umm Habīb canal, where it drifted toward al-Baṣrah, stopping at Mashra'ah al-Qayyār. People came and recovered the heads of those they recognized.

After this day the enemy of God became ever more powerful as fear of him gripped the Basrans' hearts. They abstained from further battle with him, but the central authorities were informed of his escapades, and Ju'lān al-Turkī was sent with reinforcements to the Baṣrans. Ju'lān ordered Abū al-Ahwaṣ al-Bāhilī to proceed to al-Ubullah as governor, sending as support a Turk called Jurayh.

The abominable one alleged that his followers had boasted to him the wake of this [recent] battle that they had slaughtered the entire fighting force of al-Baṣrah save for the weak and incapacitated. "Give us permission to storm the city," they demanded. 'Alī b. Muhammad berated them and decried their request. "On the contrary," he scolded, "get as far away from al-Baṣrah as possible; we have instilled fear and terror in them, and now you are safe. The thing to do now is forsake war with them until they come looking for you." Then he withdrew his forces to a salt flat at the farthest edge of the network of canals and then went on to the al-Hājir canal.

Shibl said that this place was the salt flats of Abū Qurrah, which lay between the Nahr Abū Qurrah and the Nahr al-Hājir. 'Alī b. Muhammad stationed himself there and gave the command to his troops to construct huts from the reeds (*akwākh*). These salt flats were surrounded by palm groves, villages, and cultivated fields. The Zanj soldiers spread out right and left, raiding the villages, murdering the farmers, stealing their property, and leading their livestock away.

Source: Abu Ja'far Muhammad b. Jarir al Tabari, *The History of al-Tabarī*, Vol. 36, *The Revolt of the Zanj*, translated by David Waines (Albany: State University of New York Press, 1992), 59–67. Reprinted with permission.

48. Urban II: Speech at the Council of Clermont (November 27, 1095), Recounted by Fulcher of Chartres

Introduction

The crusades were launched on the initiative of Byzantine emperor Alexios I Komnenos. Alarmed by pressure from the Seljuk Turks, who had seized almost all of Asia Minor, previously under Byzantine rule, in 1094 or 1095, the emperor sent emissaries to Pope Urban II asking for assistance from Western Christians. At the subsequent Council of Clermont, a gathering of several hundred clerics and noblemen in France that he summoned, Urban spoke to a massive crowd, whom he urged to respond to the Greek request and undertake to free Palestine from Muslim rule. The chronicler Fulcher of Chartres, who was present at the meeting, gave an account of Urban's speech in which he promised that anyone who died while engaged in this quest would win immediate remission of their sins and, presumably, instant entrance into Heaven. Urban's appeal led directly to the launching of the First Crusade, in which between 60,000 and 100,000 people joined, that took the city of Jerusalem in 1099.

Document

Most beloved brethren: Urged by necessity, I, Urban, by the permission of God chief bishop and prelate over the whole world, have come into these parts as an ambassador with a divine admonition to you, the servants of God. I hoped to find you as faithful and as zealous in the service of God as I had supposed you to be. But if there is in you any deformity or crookedness contrary to God's law, with divine help I will do my best to remove it. For God has put you as stewards over his family to minister to it. Happy indeed will you be if he finds you faithful in your stewardship. You are called shepherds; see that you do not act as hirelings. But be true shepherds, with your crooks always in your hands. Do not go to sleep, but guard on all sides the flock committed to you. For if through your carelessness or negligence a wolf carries away one of your sheep, you will surely lose the reward laid up for you with God. And after you have been bitterly scourged with remorse for your faults, you will be fiercely overwhelmed in hell, the abode of death. For according to the gospel you are the salt of the earth [Matt. 5:13]. But if you fall short in your duty, how, it may be asked, can it be salted? O how great the need of salting! It is indeed necessary for you to correct with the salt of wisdom this foolish people which is so devoted to the pleasures of this world, lest the Lord, when He may wish to speak to them, find them putrefied by their sins unsalted and stinking. For if He shall find worms, that is, sins, in them, because you have been negligent in your duty, He will command them as worthless to be thrown into the abyss of unclean things. And because you cannot restore to Him His great loss, He will surely condemn you and drive you from His loving presence. But the man who applies this salt should be prudent, provident, modest, learned, peaceable, watchful, pious, just, equitable, and pure. For how can the ignorant teach others? How can the licentious make others modest? And how can the impure make others pure? If anyone hates peace, how can he make others peaceable? Or if anyone has soiled his hands with baseness, how can he cleanse the impurities of another? We read also that if the blind lead the blind, both will fall into the ditch [Matt. 15:14]. But first correct yourselves, in order that, free from blame, you may be able to correct those who are subject to you. If you wish to be the friends of God, gladly do the things which you know will please Him. You must especially let all matters that pertain to the church be controlled by the law of the church. And be careful that simony does not take root among you, lest both those who buy and those who sell [church offices] be beaten with the scourges of the Lord through narrow streets and driven into the place of destruction and confusion. Keep the church and the clergy in all its grades entirely free from the secular power. See that the tithes that belong to God are faithfully paid from all the produce of the land; let them not be sold or withheld. If anyone seizes a bishop let him be treated as an outlaw. If anyone seizes or robs monks, or clergymen, or nuns, or their servants, or pilgrims, or merchants, let him be anathema [that is, cursed]. Let robbers and incendiaries and all their accomplices be expelled from the church and anathematized. If a man who does not give a part of his goods as alms is punished with the damnation of hell, how should he be punished who robs another of his goods? For thus it happened to the rich man in the gospel [Luke 16:19]; he was not punished because he had stolen the goods of another, but because he had not used well the things which were his.

"You have seen for a long time the great disorder in the world caused by these crimes. It is so bad in some of your provinces, I am told, and you are so weak in the administration of justice, that one can hardly go along the road by day or night without being attacked by robbers; and whether at home or abroad one is in danger of being despoiled either by force or fraud. Therefore it is necessary to reenact the truce, as it is commonly called, which was proclaimed a long time ago by our holy fathers. I exhort and demand that you, each, try hard to have the truce kept in your diocese. And if anyone shall be led by his cupidity or arrogance to break this truce, by the authority of God and with the sanction of this council he shall be anathematized."

After these and various other matters had been attended to, all who were present, clergy and people, gave thanks to God and agreed to the pope's proposition. They all faithfully promised to keep the decrees. Then the pope said that in another part of the world Christianity was suffering from a state of affairs that was worse than the one just mentioned. He continued:

"Although, O sons of God, you have promised more firmly than ever to keep the peace among yourselves and to preserve the rights of the church, there remains still an important work for you to do. Freshly quickened by the divine correction, you must apply the strength of your righteousness to another matter which concerns you as well as God. For your brethren who live in the east are in urgent need of your help, and you must hasten to give them the aid which has often been promised them. For, as the most of you have heard, the Turks and Arabs have attacked them and have conquered the territory of Romania [the Greek empire] as far west as the shore of the Mediterranean and the Hellespont, which is called the Arm of St. George. They have occupied more and more of the lands of those Christians, and have overcome them in seven battles. They have killed and captured many, and have destroyed the churches and devastated the empire. If you permit them to continue thus for a while with impurity, the faithful of God will be much more widely attacked by them. On this account I, or rather the Lord, beseech you as Christ's heralds to publish this everywhere and to persuade all people of whatever rank, foot-soldiers and knights, poor and rich, to carry aid promptly to those Christians and to destroy that vile race from the lands of our friends. I say this to those who are present; it is meant also for those who are absent. Moreover, Christ commands it.

"All who die by the way, whether by land or by sea, or in battle against the pagans, shall have immediate remission of sins. This I grant them through the power of God with which I am invested. O what a disgrace if such a despised and base race, which worships demons, should conquer a people which has the faith of omnipotent God and is made glorious with the name of Christ! With what reproaches will the Lord overwhelm us if you do not aid those who, with us, profess the Christian religion! Let those who have been accustomed unjustly to wage private warfare against the faithful now go against the infidels and end with victory this war which should have been begun long ago. Let those who for a long time have been robbers, now become knights. Let those who have been fighting against their brothers and relatives now fight in a proper way against the barbarians. Let those who have been serving as mercenaries for small pay now obtain the eternal reward. Let those who have been wearing themselves out in both body and soul now work for a double honor. Behold! on this side will be the sorrowful and poor, on that, the rich; on this side, the enemies of the Lord, on that, his friends. Let those who go not put off the journey, but rent their lands and collect money for their expenses; and as soon as winter is over and spring comes, let them eagerly set out on the way with God as their guide."

Source: From Bongars, *Gesta Dei per Francos*, 1, pp. 382ff, translated in Oliver J. Thatcher and Edgar Holmes McNeal, eds., *A Source Book for Medieval History* (New York: Scribner, 1905), 513–517.

49. The Siege of Antioch (1197–1198): Count Stephen of Blois to His Wife Adèle (March 29, 1098)

Introduction

Among the original reasons cited for launching the First Crusade was the need to regain the city of Antioch, which the Seljuk Turks had taken from the Byzantine Empire in 1084. In October 1097 the crusader forces arrived at Antioch, which they eventually took in May 1098. They themselves were then besieged for most of June by the forces of Turkish emir Kerbogha of Mosul until Prince Bohemund of Taranto, who had ambitions to become the prince of Antioch, led a crusader assault against the besiegers, who were defeated and fled. The capture of Antioch was the first major achievement of the crusade, a landmark event in terms of demonstrating that the troops summoned from abroad could have an impact on the situation. While the siege was still in progress, Count Stephen of Blois, one of the aristocratic leaders of the enterprise, sent an account of the situation to his wife.

Document

Count Stephen to Adèle, his sweetest and most amiable wife, to his dear children, and to all his vassals of all ranks—his greeting and blessing:

You may be very sure, dearest, that the messenger whom I sent to you left me before Antioch safe and unharmed and, through God's grace, in the greatest prosperity. And already at that time, together with all the chosen army of Christ, endowed with great valor by him, we had been continuously advancing for twenty-three weeks toward the home of our Lord Jesus. You may know for certain, my beloved, that of gold, silver, and many other kinds of riches, I now have twice as much as you, my love, supposed me to have when I left you. For all our princes, with the common consent of the whole army, though against my own wishes, have made me, up to the present time, the leader, chief, and director of their whole expedition.

You have assuredly heard that after the capture of the city of Nicaea we fought a great battle with the perfidious Turks and, by God's aid, conquered them. Next we conquered for the Lord all Romania and afterwards Cappadocia. And we learned that there was a certain Turkish prince, Assam, dwelling in Cappadocia; thither we directed our course. All his castles we conquered by force and compelled him to flee to a certain very strong castle situated on a high rock. We also gave the land of that Assam to one of our chiefs, and in order that he might conquer the above-mentioned Assam, we left there with him many soldiers of Christ. Thence, continually following the wicked Turks, we drove them through the midst of Armenia, as far as the great river Euphrates. Having left all their luggage and beasts of burden on the bank, they fled across the river into Arabia.

The bolder of the Turkish soldiers, indeed, entering Syria, hastened by forced marches night and day, in order to be able to occupy the royal city of Antioch before our approach. The whole army of God, learning of this, gave due praise and thanks to the omnipotent Lord. Hastening with great joy to the aforesaid city of Antioch, we besieged it and had many conflicts there with the Turks. Seven times we fought with the citizens of Antioch and with the innumerable troops coming to their aid; we rushed to meet them and we fought with the fiercest courage under the leadership of Christ; and in all these seven battles, by the aid of the Lord God, we conquered and most assuredly killed an innumerable host of them. In those battles, indeed, and in very many attacks made upon the city, many of our brethren and followers were killed, and their souls were borne to the joys of paradise.

We found Antioch a very great town, fortified with incredible strength and almost inpregnable. In addition, more than five thousand bold Turkish soldiers had entered the city, not counting the Saracens, Publicans, Arabs, Turcopolitans, Syrians, Armenians, and other different races, of whom an infinite multitude had gathered together there. In fighting against these enemies of God and of our own we have, by God's permission, endured many sufferings and innumerable evils up to the present time. Many also have already exhausted all their resources in this very holy passion. Very many of our Franks, indeed, would have met a temporal death from starvation, if the clemency of God and our money had not succored them. Moreover before the above-mentioned city of Antioch we suffered for our Lord Christ, throughout the whole winter, from excessive cold and enormous torrents of rain. What some say about the impossibility of bearing the heat of the sun throughout Syria is untrue, for the winter there is very similar to our winter in the west.

When Caspain (Bagi Seian), the emir of Antioch, perceived that he was hard pressed by us, he sent his son, Sensadolo by name, to the prince who holds Jerusalem, and to the prince of Calep Rodoam, and to Docap, prince of Damascus. He also sent into Arabia to Bolianuth, and into Carathania to Hamelnuth. These five emirs, with twelve thousand picked Turkish horsemen, suddenly came to aid the inhabitants of Antioch. We, ignorant of all this, had sent many of our soldiers away to the other cities and fortresses—for there are one hundred and sixty-five cities and fortresses throughout Syria which are in our power. But a little before we reached the city we attacked them, at three leagues distance, with seven hundred soldiers, on a certain plain, near the "Iron Bridge."

God fought for us, his faithful servants, against them; for on that day, fighting in the strength that God gives, we conquered them and killed an innumerable multitude—God continually fighting for us—and we also carried back to the army more than two hundred of their heads, in order that the people might rejoice on that account. The emperor of Babylon also sent Saracen messengers to our army with letters, and through these he established peace and concord with us.

I am glad to tell you, dearest, what happened to us during Lent. The city of Antioch is about five leagues distant from the sea. Our princes had commanded a fortress to be built before one of the city gates, which was between our camp and the sea; for the Turks, issuing daily from this gate, killed some of our men on their way to the sea. For this reason they sent the excellent Bohemond and Raymond, count of St. Gilles, down to the sea, with only sixty horsemen, in order that they might bring mariners to aid in this work. When, however, they were returning to us with those mariners, the Turks collected an army, fell suddenly upon our two leaders, and forced them to a perilous flight. In that unexpected fight we lost more than five hundred of our foot soldiers—to the glory of God. Of our horsemen, however, we lost only two, for certain.

On that same day, ignorant of our brethren's misfortunes, we went out joyfully to meet them. When, however, we approached the above-mentioned gate of the city, a mass of horsemen and foot soldiers from Antioch, elated by the victory which they had won, rushed upon us in the same manner. Seeing these, our leaders sent to the camp of the Christians to order all to be ready to follow us into battle. In the meantime our men gathered together, and the two leaders, namely Bohemond and Raymond, with the remainder of their army, came up and narrated the great misfortune which they had suffered.

Our men, full of fury at these most evil tidings, prepared to die for Christ, and, deeply grieved for their brethren, rushed upon the sacrilegious Turks. They, enemies of God and of us, hastily fled before us and attempted to enter their city. But by God's grace the affair turned out very differently; for, when they attempted to cross a bridge built over the great river Moscholum, we followed them as closely as possible, killed many before they reached the bridge, forced many into the river, all of whom were killed, and we also slew many upon the bridge and very many at the narrow entrance to the gate. I am telling you the truth, my beloved, and you may rely upon it, that in this battle we killed thirty emirs (that is, princes) and three hundred other Turkish nobles, not counting the remaining Turks and pagans. Indeed, the number of Turks and Saracens killed is reckoned at twelve hundred and thirty, while of our own troops we did not lose a single man.

On the following day (Easter), while my chaplain, Alexander, was writing this letter in great haste, a party of our men, lying in wait for the Turks, fought a successful engagement with them and killed sixty horsemen, whose heads they brought to the army.

I can write to you only a few, dearest, of the many things which we have done. Although I am not able to tell you all that is in my mind, I trust that all is going well with you, and urge you to watch carefully over your possessions and to treat as you ought your children and your vassals. You will certainly see me just as soon as I can possibly return to you. Farewell.

Source: "Stephen of Blois to His Wife," in *Readings in European History*, Vol. 1, *From the Breaking Up of the Roman Empire to the Protestant Revolt*, ed. James Harvey Robinson (Boston: Ginn, 1904), 321–325.

50. The Fall of Jerusalem (July 1099)

Introduction

One of the greatest symbolic as well as military triumphs of the First Crusade was the capture on July 15, 1099, of the city of Jerusalem following a lengthy siege. The unknown chronicler who wrote the *Gesta Francorum* (Deeds of the Franks) gave a detailed account of this event. As was customary with such victories there was a heavy death toll on both sides, with sacred religious sites becoming scenes of mass slaughter and with the winners looting and plundering the defeated city. The city of Jerusalem would remain in Western hands until 1187, when it was recaptured by Saladin.

Document

At length, our leaders decided to beleaguer the city with siege machines, so that we might enter and worship the Saviour at the Holy Sepulchre. They constructed wooden towers and many other siege machines. Duke Godfrey made a wooden tower and other siege devices, and Count Raymond did the same, although it was necessary to bring wood from a considerable distance. However, when the Saracens saw our men engaged in this work, they greatly strengthened the fortifications of the city and increased the height of the turrets at night. On a certain Sabbath night, the leaders, after having decided which parts of the wall were weakest, dragged the tower and the machines to the eastern side of the city. Moreover, we set up the tower at earliest dawn and equipped and covered it on the first, second, and third days of the week. The Count of St. Gilles erected his tower on the plain to the south of the city.

While all this was going on, our water supply was so limited that no one could buy enough water for one *denarius* to satisfy or quench his thirst. Both day and night, on the fourth and fifth days of the week, we made a determined attack on the city from all sides. However, before we made this assault on the city, the bishops and priests persuaded all, by exhorting and preaching, to honor the Lord by marching around Jerusalem in a great procession, and to prepare for battle by prayer, fasting, and almsgiving. Early on the sixth day of the week we again attacked the city on all sides, but as the assault was unsuccessful, we were all astounded and fearful. However, when the hour approached on which our Lord Jesus Christ deigned to suffer on the Cross for us, our knights began to fight bravely in one of the towers—namely, the party with Duke Godfrey and his brother, Count Eustace. One of our knights, named Lethold, clambered up the wall of the city, and no sooner had he ascended than the defenders fled from the walls and through the city. Our men followed, killing and slaying even to the Temple of Solomon, where the slaughter was so great that our men waded in blood up to their ankles....

Count Raymond brought his army and his tower up near the wall from the south, but between the tower and the wall there was a very deep ditch. Then our men took counsel how they might fill it, and had it proclaimed by heralds that anyone who carried three stones to the ditch would receive one *denarius*. The work of filling it required three days and three nights, and when at length the ditch was filled, they moved the tower up to the wall, but the men defending this portion of the wall fought desperately with stones and fire. When the Count heard that the Franks were already in the city, he said to his men, "Why do you loiter? Lo, the Franks are even now within the city." The Emir who commanded the Tower of St. David surrendered to the Count and opened that gate at which the pilgrims had always been accustomed to pay tribute. But this time the pilgrims entered the city, pursuing and killing the Saracens up to the Temple of Solomon, where the enemy gathered in force. The battle raged throughout the day, so that the Temple was covered with their blood. When the pagans had been overcome, our men seized great numbers, both men and women, either killing them or keeping them captive, as they wished. On the roof of the Temple a great number of pagans of both sexes had assembled, and these were taken under the protection of Tancred and Gaston of *Beert*. Afterward, the army scattered throughout the city and took possession of the gold and silver, the horses and mules, and the houses filled with goods of all kinds.

Rejoicing and weeping for joy, our people came to the Sepulchre of Jesus our Saviour to worship and pay their debt [i.e. fulfil crusading vows by worshiping at the Sepulchre]. At dawn our men cautiously went up to the roof of the Temple and attacked Saracen men and women, beheading them with naked swords. Some of the Saracens, however, leaped from the Temple roof. Tancred, seeing this, was greatly angered.

Source: Excerpt from Gesta francorum et aliorum Hierosolymytanorum (*The Deeds of the Franks*), in August C. Krey, *The First Crusade: The Accounts of Eyewitnesses and Participants,* (Princeton, NJ: Princeton University Press, 1921), 256–257.

51. Joscelin I of Courtenay on His Deathbed (1131)

Introduction

Perhaps the most durable of the original crusader leaders was Joscelin of Courtenay, who arrived in the late 1090s, becoming lord of Caesarea and then count of Edessa, and remaining active until his death in 1131. During his final illness he insisted on taking the field once more, against Sultan Qilij Arslan II of Rum, being borne to the field on a litter. On hearing of Joscelin's approach, the sultan prudently retreated. A careful and imaginative strategist who could plan several moves ahead, the Count of Edessa was no armchair general and had the reputation of being an exceptional fighter in the field.

Document

At this time, Joscelin, count of Edessa, exhausted by a long illness, was lying on his bed awaiting the day of his death, which was imminent. In the year that had just passed, while he was in the country near Aleppo, a tower built of sundried bricks had fallen upon him. To facilitate the capture of the place with some of the enemy who were shut up within it, he had ordered it to be undermined. But, since he did not exercise due caution, he was himself caught in its sudden fall and almost buried alive. His people rescued him with much difficulty, and he was found to be suffering from many fractures. For a long time he had been ill from his injuries, but as yet had succeeded in detaining his spirit, which was struggling to depart. One day a messenger arrived in haste. He brought the news that the sultan of Iconium had laid siege to Cresson, one of Joscelin's fortresses. At this, the high-spirited man, feeble and weak of body but still strong of heart, at once ordered his son to be called. He bade him take all the forces of the country and go forth to meet the enemy valiantly in the place of his helpless father. The son, however, began to make excuses. He urged, as an objection, that the above-mentioned sultan was reported to be advancing at the head of a great host, in comparison with which his own soldiers were but few. The father reflected with bitterness on his son's pusillanimity, well understanding from his reply what manner of man he would be in the future. Then he himself ordered the army and all the people of the locality to be called out. When this had been done, he directed that a litter be made ready for himself. Regardless of his suffering and weakness, he placed himself upon it and advanced against the foe. He had accompanied the army in this manner for some distance when one of the great barons of the land, Geoffrey, surnamed the Monk, came to him with the information that the sultan, on hearing of his advance, had abandoned the siege of Cresson and beat a hasty retreat.

On learning this, the count ordered the litter on which he was being carried to be placed on the ground. He then raised his hands toward heaven and, with tears and sighs, gave fervent thanks to God that in his last days the Lord, in His gracious mercy, had visited him with such favor; that he, though half dead and on the very verge of the grave, was still formidable to the enemies of the Christian faith. While in the very act of giving thanks thus, he rendered up to heaven his last breath. His son, who bore the same name but was far inferior to his father in glory, was left as the sole heir to all his property.

Source: William Archbishop of Tyre, *A History of Deeds Done beyond the Sea: Volume Two*, trans. Emily Atwater Babcock and A. C. Krey (New York: Columbia University Press, 1943), 51–52. Copyright © 1943 Columbia University Press. Reprinted with permission of the publisher.

52. Manuel I Komnenos (r. 1143–1180)

Introduction

Byzantine emperor Manuel I Komnenos (r. 1143–1180) was a protean and subtle ruler who was determined to preserve his empire from the manifold threats its territories faced from both Asian potentates in the East and covetous Western rivals. Doing so involved playing all parties against each other, often with the assistance of lavish bribes. Would-be crusaders from the West represented a particular threat to Byzantine power, as the nobles who embarked on these ventures often hoped to carve out principalities for themselves from portions of past or present Byzantine domains. Manuel was widely suspected of encouraging Sultan Qilij Arslan II of Rum (Iconium) to attack the armies of King Conrad III of Germany and King Louis VII of the Second Crusade (1147–1148) as they crossed Asia Minor en route for the Holy Land. He nonetheless offered the visiting monarchs lavish hospitality once they reached Constantinople. Following a divide-and-rule policy, Manuel also, as the contemporary Byzantine chronicler Niketas Choniates recorded, assisted Italian states that contemplated rebellion against the Holy Roman emperor, Frederick I Barbarossa, another potential opponent of Byzantium. Manuel likewise supported the pope in his conflicts with Frederick. Manuel's employment of these indirect methods did not indicate that he himself was fundamentally averse to military action. Choniates recounted how the emperor, inclined to enjoy a sybaritic lifestyle of extravagant luxury and self-indulgence with multiple mistresses in times of peace, abandoned these excesses and followed a demanding and austere regime when on military campaign with his soldiers in the field.

Document

The following must also be recorded. This emperor, unable to undertake military operations against those nations that dwell around the Ionian gulf or, rather, ever having before his eyes their assaults against the Romans which he deemed formidable and difficult to withstand, realized that the Roman forces were unequal to the task of standing up against the Western armies, that they were like earthern pots striking kettles. He also realized it was possible that the nations would enter into a compact against the Romans, suspecting they would actually join in a conspiracy.

Safeguarding himself from afar in all kinds of ways, he contended that it was permissible to lead on the barbarians in the East, to buy their friendship with money and to convince them by feats of arms not to pour over his borders. But the Western nations which were scattered over many places he viewed with suspicion, for these men were boastful, undaunted in spirit, lacking all humility, and trained to be ever bloodthirsty. They all dressed in great opulence and wore armor into battle; and they also nurtured an unsleeping hostility against the Romans, a perpetual, raving, hatred as they looked askance at them.

And so to Venice, Genoa, Pisa, Ancona, and the other nations spread along the sea, he offered friendship ratified with sworn compacts and won them over with sundry friendly gestures as he provided them with quarters in the queen of cities. Anxious lest one of their so-called kings should muster a large military force and then attack the Romans, he plied them with gifts of money; and he exercised his influence over those peoples who were in danger of falling under the sway of a more powerful ruler and roused them to take up arms.

Time and again he armed the Italians against Frederick, the king of Germany. The latter demanded that they should submit and turn their affairs over to him, while the emperor dispatched envoys who emboldened the Italians, enjoining them to prevail against Frederick and to beware of the king's crafty ways. Frederick attempted several times to enter elder Rome to be crowned, but Manuel thwarted the move by writing to the pope [1167–68], "Do not bestow your glory upon another, and do not repeat the restrictions of the fathers, lest you discover later that your soul is smitten with regret thanks to the unforeseen in these actions and to unreasonable negligence, at which time the evil will be wholly incurable." Consequently, the king was shut out of Rome the very glorious as though he were an unarmed commander boasting of myriads of troops.

When the walls of Milan were destroyed by the Germans [March 1, 1162], the city's inhabitants outwitted those who forced them to swear never to rebuild them, first by protecting themselves behind a deeply dug trench, contending that they had not therefore perjured themselves, and then by restoring the walls with the help of the emperor....

[Manuel] withstood the toils of war exceedingly well, enduring the hardships which the times demanded of him; he suffered the cold, abided the stifling heat, and resisted sleep; but when he was not campaigning he indulged himself in luxuries and took pleasure in recreation. If one carefully observed how much he relished savory dishes and enjoyed the playing of the small lyre and cithara with harmonious singing, one would have said that he had grown up only in such amusements and that pleasure was the primary purpose of life; if, on the other hand, one considered how, in difficult times, he set aside his readiness to indulge in every kind of trivial luxury, one marveled how he moved back and forth between the two.

Source: Harry J. Magoulias, trans., *O City of Byzantium, Annals of Niketas Choniatēs* (Detroit: Wayne State University Press, 1984), 113, 117. Reprinted with permission.

53. Conrad III: Letters to the Abbot of Corvey on the Germans' Crusade (1148)

Introduction

In 1146 Holy Roman emperor Conrad III, together with King Louis VII of France, was inspired by the preaching of the influential cleric Bernard of Clairvaux to embark on the Second Crusade to the Holy Land. The expedition proved disastrous, as mounted

53. Conrad III: Letters to the Abbot of Corvey on the Germans' Crusade

Seljuk Turk squads of archers led by Sultan Mesud I harassed the German invaders for several days in October 1147 as they tried to make their way overland through Anatolia to Palestine. After having journeyed three days beyond the city of Dorylaion, the site of an earlier military encounter during the First Crusade just over 50 years earlier, the Germans decided to turn back. They subsequently joined forces with the French king's army at Nicaea and took the coastal route through western Anatolia, which proved equally difficult. On reaching Ephesus Conrad fell ill, and he and his top officers boarded a ship for Constantinople, where they enjoyed the hospitality of Byzantine emperor Manuel I Comnenos, before sailing on to Acre and Jerusalem. Conrad then joined the crusaders in a futile siege of Damascus and prepared for an abortive expedition against the city of Ascalon, which failed to materialize. Writing what were effectively official bulletins of these campaigns to the abbot of Corvey back home in his native Germany, the emperor struggled to put the best spin possible on the German contributions to a fruitless campaign.

Documents

Conrad III to Wibald, Abbot of Corvey, 1148

Conrad, by the grace of God, king of the Romans, to venerable Wibald, abbot of Corvey and Stavelot his most kind greeting.

Because we have very frequently realized your faithfulness, proven in many trials, to us and to our kingdom, we do not doubt that you will rejoice greatly, if you hear of the state of our prosperity. We, therefore, announce to your faithfulness that we had reached Nicaea with our army entire and strong, wishing to complete our journey quickly, we hastened to set out for Iconium under the guidance of men who knew the road. We carried with us as many necessities as possible. And behold when ten days journey were accomplished and the same amount remained to be traversed, food for the whole host had almost given out, but especially for the horses. At the same time the Turks did not cease to attack and slaughter the crowd of footsoldiers who were unable to follow the army. We pitied the fate of our suffering people, perishing by famine and by the arrows of the enemy; and, by the advice of our princes and barons, we led the army back from that desert land to the sea, in order that it might regain its strength. We preferred to preserve the army for greater achievements rather than to win so bloody a victory over archers.

When, indeed, we had reached the sea and had pitched our tents and did not expect quiet amid so great a storm, to our delight the king of France came to our tents, wholly unexpectedly. He grieved, indeed, that our army was exhausted by hunger and toil, but he took great delight in our company. Moreover, he himself and all his princes offered their services faithfully and devoutly to us and furnished for our use their money especially, and whatever else they had. They joined themselves, therefore, to our forces and princes. Some of the latter had remained with us, and others, either sick or lacking money, had not been able to follow and had accordingly withdrawn from the army.

We proceeded without any difficulty as far as St. John's, where his tomb with the manna springing from it is seen, in order that we might there celebrate the Nativity of our Lord. Having rested there some days to recover our health, inasmuch as sickness had seized on us and many of our men, we wanted to proceed; but weakened by our illness we were wholly unable to do so. The king, therefore, departed with his army, after having waited for us as long as possible; but a long sickness detained us.

When our brother, the emperor of Greece, heard of this, he was greatly grieved, and with our daughter, the most beloved empress, his wife, he hastened to come to us. And, liberally giving to us and our princes his money and the necessities for our journey, he led us back, as it were by force, to his palace at Constantinople, in order that we might be the more speedily cured by his physicians. There he showed to us as much honor as, to our knowledge, was ever shown to any one of our predecessors.

Thence we hastened to set out for Jerusalem on Quadragesima Sunday, in order to collect there a new army and to proceed to Rohas.

Moreover, that God may deign to make our journey prosperous, we ask that you and your brethren will pray for us and will order all Christians to do the same. And we entrust our son to your fidelity.

Conrad III to Wibald, Abbot of Corvey, 1148

Conrad, by the grace of God, august king of the Romans, to venerable Wibald, abbot of Corvey, his most kind greeting.

Because we know that you especially desire to hear from us and to learn the state of our prosperity, we think it fitting first to tell you of this. By God's mercy we are in good health and we have embarked in our ships to return on the festival of the blessed Virgin in September, after having accomplished in these lands all that God willed and the people of the country permitted.

Let us now speak of our troops. When following the advice of the common council we had gone to Damascus and after a great deal of trouble had pitched our camps before the gate of the city, it was certainly near being taken. But certain ones, whom we least suspected, treasonably asserted that the city was impregnable on that side and hastily led us to another position where no water could be supplied for the troops and where access was impossible to any one. And thus all, equally indignant and grieved, returned, leaving the undertaking uncompleted. Nevertheless, they all promised unanimously that they would make an expedition against Ascalon, and they set the place and time. Having arrived there according to agreement, we found scarcely anyone. In vain we waited eight days for the troops. Deceived a second time, we turned to our own affairs.

In brief therefore, God willing, we shall return to you. We render to you the gratitude which you deserve for your care of our son and for the very great fidelity which you have shown to us. And with the full intention of worthily rewarding your services, we ask you to continue the same.

Source: Bouquet: *Recueil des historiens des Gaules et de la France,* xv p. 533–534, Latin original, translated in Dana C. Munro, "Letters of the Crusaders," in *Translations and Reprints from the Original Sources of European History,* Vol. 1:4 (Philadelphia: University of Pennsylvania, 1896), 12–14.

54. Account of Conflict between the Muslims and the Georgians (1162–1163)

Introduction

From the 11th to the 13th centuries the Seljuk Turks and the Georgians waged intermittent warfare against each other, both sides mounting raids against the other at irregular intervals and neither able to win a decisive victory. This account by the Arab chronicler Ibn al-Athīr of two such campaigns in the mid-12th century, one in retaliation for its predecessor, suggests that chronic warfare had become an accepted way of life for all on both sides, with no expectation of genuine peace.

Document

In Sha'bān this year [July 16–August 13, 1162] the Georgians gathered in great numbers, amounting to 30,000 warriors, and entered Islamic territory. They aimed for the city of Dvin in Azerbayjan, which they took and sacked. They killed about 10,000 of the inhabitants and the surrounding peasantry. They enslaved the women and took many captives. They stripped the women and led them away naked and bare footed. They burnt the congregational and the district mosques.

When they returned home, the Georgian women condemned what had been done to the Muslim women, saying, 'You have obliged the Muslims to treat us in the same way as you have treated their women' and they gave the women clothes.

When news of this reached Shams al-Dīn Īldikiz, lord of Azerbayjan, the Uplands and Isfahan, he called up his troops and was joined by Shāh Arman ibn Sukmān al-Qutbī, lord of Khilāt, and Ibn Āqsunqur, lord of Marāgha and other places. They gathered in a large force of more than 50,000 fighting men and marched into Georgian territory in Safar of the year 558 [January 9–February 6, 1163]. They plundered, enslaved women and children and made prisoners of the men. The Georgians confronted them and very fierce fighting followed in which both sides held firm. The hostilities continued between them for more than a month. Victory went to the Muslims and the Georgians were defeated with many of them killed or captured.

The reason for their defeat was that one of the Georgians went to Ïldikiz and accepted Islam at his hands. He said to him, 'Will you give me a force to lead on a route I know and come upon the Georgians from the rear without their knowledge.' He had trust in him and sent a force with him, having named a day when he himself would move against the Georgians. When that day came, the Muslims engaged the Georgians and while they were fighting, the Georgian convert arrived with his force. They shouted 'God is great' and charged the Georgians in the rear, who fled and many were killed or captured. The Muslims took their baggage as booty that was too abundant to be counted. They had been confident that their numbers would give them victory but God frustrated their expectations. The Muslims pursued them, killing and taking captives, for three days and nights and then returned victorious and triumphant.

Source: D. S. Richards, ed. and trans., *The Chronicle of Ibn al-Athīr for the Crusading Period from al-Kāmil fī'l-ta'rīkh*, Part 2, *The Years of Nur-al-Din and Saladin* (Aldershot, UK: Ashgate, 2007), 135. Reprinted with permission from Taylor & Francis UK.

55. King Amalric of Jerusalem: Letters to King Louis VII of France (1163–1165)

Introduction

Amalric, king of Jerusalem (r. 1163–1174), succeeded his brother Baldwin III, who died on February 10, 1163. Amalric was crowned one week later. As soon as he took the throne, Amalric launched ambitious plans to take Egypt from the Fatimid caliphate. He sought assistance from European rulers and the pope in this venture. To win support, Amalric embarked on a letter-writing campaign, deluging the pious King Louis VII of France with missives requesting that the monarch visit the Holy Land and aid the Christian rulers there against troubles that included a recent devastating earthquake in the crusader principality of Antioch, compounded by the capture in 1160 by Saracen forces of its ruler, who remained imprisoned for the next 16 years. Amalric's repeated appeals to Louis were reinforced by similar imploring letters to the king from leading prelates, notably the master of the Knights Templar, praising the achievements of the king of Jerusalem in Egypt. They also sought succor for beleaguered Antioch and the other crusader possessions against the wrath of Nur al-Din, the Zengid sultan of Damascus and Aleppo and an uncompromising and dedicated opponent of the Christian presence in the region who would not tolerate its extension into Egypt. Amalric's repeated campaigns against Egypt met with success in 1167 but ultimately proved fruitless, partly because Nur al-Din refused to sanction any compromises by the Fatimid caliphate of Egypt. Louis, who had already undertaken one disappointing crusade in 1148, remained deaf to Amalric's pleas for his return but sent substantial financial subsidies to the ambitious king of Jerusalem, an antagonist whose abilities even his enemies respected. According to the Arab chronicler Ibn al-Athīr, Amalric's "like for bravery and subtle cunning the Franks had not had since they appeared in Syria." On Amalric's death in 1174, al-Athīr commented that the "king of the Franks (God curse him) had died at the beginning of this year. He was one of the bravest of their kings, the most outstanding for policy, cunning, and intrigue."

Documents

Amalric, King of Jerusalem, to Louis VII, King of France (April 8, 1163), Springs of Saffuriya

To Louis, by the grace of God most glorious King of the French, highest and incomparable hero, most beloved, Amalric, by the grace of the same God King of Jerusalem, greetings and affection. Alas, alas, by this present letter we inform you of the sad and pitiful news of the death of our brother and lord, our famous King Baldwin. God called him to heaven on the Feast of the Saint Scholastica the Virgin. We now rule his kingdom as of hereditary right and are firmly established on the throne of our kingdom. There was no impediment (sine omni impedimento) and all our subjects showed their good will. Because, most illustrious, the whole of Christendom in the East is greatly depleted and under more pressure than usual, it is struggling even more seriously from the misfortune that befell Reynald, the once famous prince of Antioch, who, as you no doubt have already heard, was returning from an expedition when he was captured. Virtually all who were with him were either killed or captured. Then there was the earthquake of last August [1162] that destroyed and razed to the ground almost all of the castles, towers and townships of the principality of Antioch. Hence we ask your serene highness, while it is still possible, to be mindful of that land which the

Lord deigned to visit in the flesh, and consecrate with His Light. It is obvious that your kingdom was strong enough to wrench it from the hands of the filthy infidels and reclaim it for God. Please make it known to everybody how great is the affection, the conviction and the heartfelt sympathy you have shown up to now towards the Holy Sepulchre. Know that from the very beginning, as the bearer of this letter will confirm, there has never been such a great need of your advice and rapid help. And if you should decide to visit the Lord's Sepulchre you can be sure that you will not be entering a foreign country, but indeed one that is totally yours and will be as long as I am alive, for we honour and love you as a great and sublime lord and all that is and was under your rule. Given at the Springs of Saffuriya, six days before the ides of April.

Amalric, King of Jerusalem, to Louis VII, King of France (September 1163)

To Louis, by the grace of God most glorious King of the French, Amalric, by the same grace King of Jerusalem, greetings. Dearest friend, we believe it has come to the notice of your serenity through the true reports of many that after our sins had caused the capture of the prince of Antioch by the Turks and the captivity or death of all his men, there suddenly appeared another, unexpected disaster. An earthquake of unheard-of severity razed to the ground almost all the castles, towers, and townships of the plains and mountainous areas, in Antioch and the adjacent regions, mountains and plains alike, causing the untimely death of a countless number of Christians of both sexes. The earthquake extinguished them—or more accurately swallowed them up in the earth. All this misery and desolation of all kinds culminated, alas, in the death of the famous and distinguished King Baldwin, the symbol of our protection and bravery. After God he was the unique hope and guarantee of safety for the Eastern Church and the kingdom of Jerusalem in particular, a true friend of yours and your kingdom, our lord and brother, the most Christian of kings. His death is all the more brutally disheartening, painfully dispiriting, because God had made him the ready source of help for all Christians everywhere, the remedy for each and every trouble. That is why, most beloved, like tassels hanging from your headdress, we bow to your majesty, recognising that your serenity will be our support and the solid base of the divine faith in Christ. We proclaim that, in our humility, we are your particular care in the Lord. The quality and the quantity of the true charity and its perfection in your aforementioned friend the king of Jerusalem of pious memory in the cause of God and His unconquerable love may now be brought home to everyone in the desolation of ourselves and the Eastern Church. As your inborn holiness has truly learned from the most pious intentions of your predecessors and all your lineage, the kingdom you govern in the Lord has long had the laudable practice of protecting, cherishing, supporting and strengthening the Holy City, its kingdom and all the region around it, as well as all the people characterised by the Catholic faith. If, therefore, the spirit of advice has inspired in your magnificent serenity the will to visit again in person the place on which the feet of Christ stood, this will give you a greater crown. Do not refuse or even hesitate to come now when Christendom's needs are great and its problems many. All our prayers reside in your Holiness, and we and all our kingdom will strive together worthily for God for the approval of yourself and your friend the emperor. For the rest we commend to you, father, the bearer of this letter, a man of great honesty, the venerable archbishop of Mamistra, who is energetic in doing the right thing. Receive him kindly and believe him as you would me. To keep the letter short we have told him our confidential information so that he can impart it to you personally. Farewell.

Amalric, King of Jerusalem, to Louis VII, King of France (September 1163)

Louis, by the grace of God most glorious king of the French and his most serene friend, Amalric, by the same grace King of Jerusalem, greetings. Because we hold your person and your kingdom in great affection and are ready to serve you, but particularly because we put our hopes in you and your kingdom we have thought fit to notify to your majesty our successes. Be it known therefore to your excellency that we have entered Egypt with the force we could muster [c. September 1, 1163], for we left our country as protected as we could on account of Nuredin [Nūr al-Dīn] who had mobilised all the men he could from Baldac, the Euphrates and their borders. We joined battle before the most noble Egyptian city of Bilbeis with the Egyptian squadrons positioned on both wings and in the centre. However, God whose victory does not lie in numbers, put to flight a huge number of his enemies. An infinite number were killed and many of the best and greatest of them were captured. We camped that night on the battlefield. The next day we launched a marvellous attack on the city and it would have been captured or else surrendered as we hoped, if the River of Paradise [the Nile] had not suddenly begun to flow again as it does every year and impeded our advance. If therefore your magnificent force was willing to help us as usual, with God's approval Egypt could easily be marked by the sign of the Holy Cross. Farewell.

Amalric, King of Jerusalem, to Louis VII, King of France (Beginning of 1164)

To Louis, by the grace of God most illustrious king of the French, for a long time most beloved, Amalric, through the same grace King of Jerusalem, greetings and a token of his sincere affection. Since we know that you have long held a great affection for the Holy Land and Jerusalem and a high esteem for the kingdom of Jerusalem, your serenity, we humbly entreat your pious affection; please put into action what you have long cherished in your heart. Put your mind and your efforts to provide assistance for the Holy Land and recall the reason that brought the venerable archbishop of Mamistra to the regions of the Gauls, for the situation now is more critical than can be described. Since the archbishop of Mamistra left here, every day brings us the news that the emperor is about to arrive, and when that happens, all the Christians of the East (Orientales) with us fear that he will certainly take Antioch, as it has fallen into such a weak state. If help does not come from elsewhere Antioch cannot help but fall to the Greeks and the Turks. So, out of devotion and compassion hurry to reach here before the emperor that we fear the most, because you will not come to a foreign land but to one that will totally and wholeheartedly welcome you. All of us, including ourselves, will obey your commands.

Amalric, King of Jerusalem, to Louis VII, King of France (January 12, 1165), Antioch

To Louis, by the grace of God most excellent King of the French and most dear Father in Christ, Amalric, by the same grace King of Jerusalem, greetings, and also from Him who is king to the king of all kings. Since we know that your royal majesty is able to and are convinced that your religious desire incites you to come to the aid of all who are in need of it, we therefore have thought fit to expose in this letter to your highness, even if you have already heard the news, the lamentable oppression of the Christians in the Holy Land of Jerusalem now that the horns of the Turks are raised. While we were fighting Shirkuh in Egypt and driving him out through the virtue of the Cross of the Lord—if he had remained there he would have been a great danger to the whole of Christendom—it happened that the count of Tripoli and the prince of Antioch led a large army to liberate the castle of Harenc, near Antioch, which Nur al-Din had besieged with a multitude of armed men. Thanks to the intervention of divine help the enemy fled before the advancing army, but not content with God's great help the count and the prince arrogantly pursued them to a region that nature had made impregnable, and there the leaders were captured. All of the army was either captured or slaughtered. Another catastrophe has now been added to this one, for while we were in Egypt traitors handed over to Nur al-Din, Panudium, which is called Belinas in the vernacular. Therefore, the struggling Holy Land implores the maximum help from you and your people which we hope will be most efficacious in counter-balancing its weaknesses. Farewell. Given at Antioch the second day before the ides of January.

Source: Translated from *Recueil des Historiens des Gaules et de la France*, Vol. 16, ed. M. Bouquet et al. (Paris, 1878), in Malcolm Barber and Keith Bate, eds., *Letters from the East: Crusaders, Settlers, and Pilgrims in the 12th–13th Centuries* (London: Routledge, 2016), 52–57, 62.

56. The Leper King: Baldwin IV of Jerusalem (r. 1174–1185)

Introduction

Bishop William of Tyre, who was Baldwin IV's tutor, left a description of the ruler of Jerusalem who became king at the age of 13. As a child Baldwin contracted leprosy, with symptoms that William was the first to notice. William obviously felt deep affection for the young king, who died at the age of 24. For most of his reign, Baldwin was an energetic and deeply conscientious monarch who made what must have been herculean efforts to fulfill his hereditary duties. In 1182 the king, then 21, transferred most of his responsibilities to a regent, his brother-in-law, Guy of Lusignan. Even when Guy showed himself incompetent, the king acted forcefully to remedy the situation, ensuring that before his own death Guy's young son was crowned Baldwin V and working to install an alternative and more able regent. Ultimately these maneuverings proved fruitless. Guy bore much of the responsibility for the massive Latin defeat in 1187 at the Battle of Hattin. One can only speculate whether the history of the Kingdom of Jerusalem would have been different had Baldwin IV enjoyed good health.

Document

It is impossible to refrain from tears while speaking of [his] great misfortune. For, as he began to reach years of maturity, it was evident that he was suffering from the terrible disease of leprosy. Day by day his condition became worse. The extremities and the face were especially attacked, so that his faithful followers were moved with compassion when they looked at him. Nevertheless, he continued to make progress in the pursuit of letters and gave ever-increasing promise of developing a lovable disposition. He was comely of appearance for his age, and far beyond the custom of his forefathers he was an excellent horseman and understood the handling of horses. He had a retentive memory and loved to talk. He was economical but always remembered both favors and injuries. In every respect he resembled his father [King Amalric], not alone in face but in his entire mien; even his walk and the tones of his voice were the same. His intellect was keen, but his speech was somewhat halting. Like his father he eagerly listened to history and was well disposed to follow good advice. . . .

[In 1182], the king was suffering from a severe attack of fever at Nazareth. In addition, the leprosy which had begun to trouble him at the beginning of his reign—in fact, in very early youth—became much worse than usual. His sight failed and his extremities became completely deadened so that his hands and feet refused to perform their office. Yet up to this time he had declined to heed the suggestion offered by some that he lay aside his kingly dignity and give up the administration of the realm, so that, with a suitable provision for his needs from the royal revenues, he could lead a tranquil life in retirement.

Although physically weak and impotent, yet mentally he was vigorous, and, far beyond his strength, he strove to hide his illness and to support the cares of the kingdom. When he was attacked by the fever, however, he lost hope of life. He summoned his nobles before him and, in the presence of his mother and the patriarch, he appointed as regent of the realm Guy de Lusignan, count of Jaffa and Ascalon, his sister's husband. . . . He retained the royal dignity, however, and kept for his own use only the city of Jerusalem, with an annual revenue of ten thousand gold pieces.

Source: William Archbishop of Tyre, *A History of Deeds Done beyond the Sea: Volume Two,* trans. Emily Atwater Babcock and A. C. Krey (New York: Columbia University Press, 1943), 398, 492. Copyright © 1943 Columbia University Press. Reprinted with permission of the publisher.

57. Guy of Lusignan, King of Jerusalem (r. 1186–1192)

Introduction

Guy of Lusignan came from a noble French family with strong links to the Holy Land. In 1180 he married one of the sisters of King Baldwin IV of Jerusalem. Baldwin, who was in declining health due to leprosy, of which he died in 1185, named Guy regent for his kingdom in 1182. Guy continued to hold this position after Baldwin's death, acting as regent on behalf of his wife Sibylla's infant son, Baldwin V, who died one year later. Baldwin IV apparently quickly became disillusioned with Guy's performance as regent and in 1183 and 1184 tried but failed to annul his marriage with Sibylla. The account given by Robert of Clari, a soldier in the later Fourth Crusade, is fundamentally true. Sibylla's nobles pressed her to divorce her husband, whom they considered incompetent, and select a spouse who would be a more effective king but left the selection of her new partner to her. Sibylla then chose to remarry Guy. Her barons' misgivings proved prescient. Whatever his merits as a husband, Guy was a decidedly unsuccessful monarch. The following year in July 1187, he engaged the forces of Saracen emir Salah al-Din at the Battle of Hattin, a disaster for the Franks. Saladin took Guy prisoner, and Sibylla surrendered Jerusalem to him in October 1187, begging in return for her husband's release, which Saladin granted. This chronicle suggests that Guy bought his freedom by surrendering to Saladin the crusader coastal fortress of Ascalon, taken by Baldwin III of Jerusalem in 1150. He and Sibylla were clearly not in good odor with other crusaders, who in 1188 refused to allow them to take refuge in Tyre, which had withstood a siege by Saladin and was the one remaining crusader redoubt. Two years after the death of Sybilla and their two daughters in 1190, the barons rejected Guy's claims to continue as king and selected Conrad of Montferrat, who had been hastily married to Sibylla's younger sister, as the new king of Jerusalem. Guy's cousin and supporter King Richard of England, who had joined the Third Crusade, compensated him by making him ruler of the island of Cyprus, conquered by Richard in 1191.

Document

Chapter 33: . . . How Guy of Lusignan Became King of Jerusalem

Now it had already come to pass, or ever yet that whole land was lost [by the Christians], that the King of Jerusalem died, and all the kingdom of Jerusalem was indeed lost; nor was there any other city that still held out, save Tyre and Ascalon. And the king that had died had two married sisters: a knight, my Lord Guy of Lusignan, had wedded the elder, to whom the kingdom had escheated; and my Lord Humphrey of Thoron had the younger. And on a certain day there came together in Jerusalem all the high barons of the land, and the Count of Tripoli, and the Temple, and the Hospital in Jerusalem, to the temple. And they said among themselves that they would divorce my Lord Guy from his wife, because the kingdom had escheated to his wife, and that they would give her another husband who would be more competent to be king than was my Lord Guy. And so did they. They divorced them; but when they had divorced them, then could they never agree to whom they should marry her, until at last they left the whole matter to the queen, who had been wife to my Lord Guy. To her, then, did they deliver the crown, and she should give it to whomsoever she desired to be made king.

Then they came together again on another day—all the barons, and the Temple, and the Hospital; and there also was the Count of Tripoli, who was the goodliest knight in the land, and who verily thought that the lady would give him the crown. And there too was my Lord Guy, he that had had the queen to wife. When, therefore, they were all come together, the lady held up the crown, and she looked this way and that. Then she espieth him who had been her husband, and she went forward and set the crown on his head. Thus did my Lord Guy become king.

But when the Count of Tripoli saw this, he was so grieved that he departed unto his own land, even unto Tripoli, in high dudgeon.

Chapter 34: How King Guy Gave Battle to the Saracens and Was Taken Captive; How He Purchased His Enlargement; and How the Marquis Conrad and the Men of Tyre Defied Him

Not long thereafter the king gave battle to the Saracens, and he was taken captive, and all his people routed, and the land was so utterly lost that there was now not a city that held out, save only Tyre and Ascalon. And when Saladin saw that he held the land in his hand he came to the King of Jerusalem, whom he was keeping in captivity, and he said to him that if he would cause Ascalon to be given up to him, then would he let the king go, and a great part of his people also. And the king answered him, "Only lead me now thither, and I will cause it to be given up to you."

And Saladin led him thither. When they were come thither, then the king spoke to them of the city and told them that they should give up the city, for such was his will. And they came and delivered the city to him. When Saladin had the city in his hand, then did he let the king go, and a part of his people with him; and the king, being escaped from captivity, departed with such of his people as he had and came to Tyre.

And now, while the king had been accomplishing these things, the marquis [Conrad of Montferrat] in the mean time had all the men of Tyre, and the Genoese who were there, both in full accord with him. And they had all sworn fealty to him and vowed by holy relics that they would hold in all things to him as their lord, and he, that he would help them to defend the city. And the marquis had found so great a famine in the city that one measure of corn (of the measure of that city) was sold for an hundred bezants, which would not amount to more than a setier and a half at Amiens.

When the king came to Tyre, then his serjeants began to cry: "Open ye! Open ye the gate! Lo, the king cometh!"

And they that were within the city answered that they should not enter. Likewise the marquis came to the walls and said that the king should not enter.

"Bah!" quoth the king. "How so! Am I not in sooth lord and master of them that are within?"

"As God liveth," quoth the marquis, "neither lord nor king are ye, nor shall ye enter here! For ye have brought us all to shame and utterly lost the land; furthermore, so great is the famine here within that if ye and your people should come in, the whole city would perish of hunger. And I would rather," quoth the marquis, "that ye should perish, both ye and your people, who are of no great use, than that we who are within should perish, or the city itself."

When the king perceived that he could not enter there, he turned about and departed toward Acre, and he went up into a little hill and encamped there. And there was it that the King of France and the King of England found him.

Source: "Robert of Clari's History of the Fourth Crusade," De Re Militari, http://deremilitari.org/2014/01/robert-of-claris-account-of-the-fourth-crusade/.

58. King Richard I the Lionheart of England (September 3, 1189)

Introduction

King Richard I of England, one of the foremost warriors of his age, was eager to embark on the Third Crusade. For him the lure of fighting in an exotic land against strange adversaries was too strong to resist, even after he became king of England in 1189 upon the death of his father, and prudence might have suggested that he remain there and consolidate his hold on the country. Great fighters often catch the popular imagination. A chronicler of the Third Crusade described Richard in eulogistic terms that nonetheless suggest what a charismatic figure contemporaries found the new king of England to be.

Document

Therefore in the same year, after the death of his father, Richard, count of Poitou, having arranged his affairs in Normandy, in about two months crossed over to England, and on St. Giles's day he was received at Westminster, with a ceremonious procession; and three days afterwards, viz., on the 3rd of September, the day of the ordination of St. Gregory the pope, which was a Sunday, he was solemnly anointed king by the imposition of hands, by Archbishop Baldwin, in virtue of his office, who performed the service, assisted by many of his suffragans. At his coronation were present his brother John, and his mother Eleanor, who, after the death of King Henry, had been, by the command of her son Richard, the new king, released from prison, where she had been ten years; and there were also present counts and barons, and an immense crowd of men and soldiers; and the kingdom was confirmed to the hands of King Richard. On the 3rd day of September, in the year of our Lord 1189, Richard was anointed king, on a Sunday, with the dominical letter A., viz., in the year after leap year. Many were the conjectures made, because the day above that was marked unlucky in the calendar; and in truth it was unlucky, and very much so to the Jews of London, who were destroyed that day, and likewise the Jews settled in other parts of England endured many hardships. Having therefore celebrated the occasion by a festival of three days, and entertained his guests in the royal palace of Westminster, King Richard gratified all, by distributing money, without count or number, to all according to their ranks, thus manifesting his liberality and his great excellence. His generosity, and his virtuous endowments, the ruler of the world should have given to the ancient times; for in this period of the world, as it waxes old, such feelings rarely exhibit themselves, and when they do, they are subjects of wonder and astonishment. He had the valour of Hector, the magnanimity of Achilles, and was equal to Alexander, and not inferior to Roland in valour; nay, he outshone many illustrious characters of our own times. The liberality of a Titus was his, and, which is so rarely found in a soldier, he was gifted with the eloquence of Nestor and the prudence of Ulysses; and he shewed himself pre-eminent in the conclusion and transaction of business, as one whose knowledge was not without active good-will to aid it, nor his good-will wanting in knowledge. Who, if Richard were accused of presumption, would not readily excuse him, knowing him for a man who never knew defeat, impatient of an injury, and impelled irresistibly to vindicate his rights, though all he did was characterized by innate nobleness of mind. Success made him better fitted for action; fortune ever favours the bold, and though she works her pleasure on whom she will, Richard was never to be overwhelmed with adversity. He was tall of stature, graceful in figure; his hair between red and auburn; his limbs were straight and flexible; his arms rather long, and not to be matched for wielding the sword or for striking with it; and his long legs suited the rest of his frame; while his appearance was commanding, and his manners and habits suitable; and he gained the greatest celebrity, not more from his high birth than from the virtues that adorned him. But why need we take much labour in extolling the fame of so great a man? He needs no superfluous commendation, for he has a sufficient meed of praise, which is the sure companion of great actions. He was far superior to all others both in moral goodness, and in strength, and memorable for prowess in battles, and his mighty deeds outshone the most brilliant description we could give of them. Happy, in truth, might he have been deemed had he been without rivals who envied his glorious actions, and whose only cause of enmity was his magnificence, and his being the searcher after virtue rather than the slave of vice.

Source: "Richard of Holy Trinity: Itinerary of Richard I and Others to the Holy Land (Formerly Ascribed to Geoffrey de Vinsauf)," York University, http://www.yorku.ca/inpar/richard_of_holy_trinity.pdf.

59. The Siege and Capture of Acre (July 1191)

Introduction

The siege and capture of the city of Acre by the invading western forces was one of the high points of the Third Crusade, in which King Richard I of England was one of the most prominent protagonists. His rival, King Philip II of France, who arrived with his fleet and an army in April 1191, also took a leading role in the final months of the protracted siege, which began in 1189. The protracted siege began in 1189, but the city held out because its defenders were able to bring in supplies by sea. The Saracen army led by Emir Saladin was also harassing the besiegers on land. The appearance of the British king's ships and forces in late June 1191, shortly after they had taken the island of Cyprus, finally tipped the balance in favor of the besiegers. For the next century, Acre would form part of the Latin Kingdom of Jerusalem.

Document

At dawn the anchors were raised and the sails were hoisted. King Richard had not gone far when ... Scandelion appeared. Then, after he had passed by Casal Imbert, the highest towers of the city of Acre appeared in the distance. Little by little the other defensive works of the town came into view.

Acre was hemmed in on all sides, besieged by an infinite multitude of people, people from every Christian nation under heaven, people chosen from all the Christians, people well fitted for war and unremitting labor. The people had now besieged Acre for a very long time and they had been troubled by many afflictions, by constant labors, by shortages of food, and by many adversities, as has in part been pointed out above.

There appeared beyond them, furthermore, an innumerable army of Turks, who covered the mountains and valleys, hills, and plains. Here and there they fixed their tents, made of various patterns of flowing colors.

They also saw the pavilions of Saladin and the tents of his brother, Saif ad Din, and of Taki ad Din, the steward of paganism. The latter superintended the sea and the fort, and he frequently set up assaults and serious attacks against the Christians.

King Richard seemed to be sizing up all their armies. When he put into port, the King of France and the magnates, commanders, and great men of the armies there marched out to him. They received him with joy and exultation, for they had very much desired his arrival. . . .

The King of France, loathing so much delay in making an attack, signified to King Richard that the time was now opportune for making an assault and for having the criers order the army to move forward to attack. King Richard informed him, however, that he was not yet able to undertake this project, both because he was grievously sick and because of the absence (due to adverse winds) of some of his men. They hoped that the latter would arrive with the next fleet of ships and would bring material for building siege machinery.

The King of France, however, was unwilling to give up his project. He ordered the criers to announce throughout the army that an assault was to be made. On the Monday next after the feast of St. John the Baptist [July 1, 1191, but probably the Monday before the feast is meant—i.e. June 17] the French King had his engines set up and ordered his men to be armed. You could see there an incomprehensible multitude of armed men, outfitted respectably with weapons. There were so many shining coats of mail, so many glittering helmets, so many noble horses neighing, so many white-colored mantles, so many select knights, so many assistants of great probity and daring, so many banners of various kinds that never had so many appeared to be reckoned with. When the men stationed at the barricades had organized their defenses, because of the threat of an attack by Saladin and the outer Turkish army, the armed men approached the city walls and delivered a terrific assault, firing stones and missiles without interruption from their balistas and engines. But, when they perceived that they were surrounded, the Turks made such a tumult with their shouting and the sounding of their trumpets that their yells must have reached the stars, for the air resounded with a clamor such as follows a lightning flash. Some of them were appointed by the officers to strike upon the timbrels and pots, to beat the drums, and in other diverse ways to make noise and send up smoke from the fires to let Saladin and the outer army know that, as arranged, they were supposed to come to the help of the town.

When they had seen and heard all this, the outer Turks attacked in groups. The Turks assembled all kinds of material in order to cover the barricades so that they could more easily cross over to attack our men, but they were unable to carry this into effect. Geoffrey of Lusignan, an exceptionally worthy knight, resisted them and very quickly drove them out of the barricades which they had occupied above us. Wielding a twoedged sword with his hand he killed more than ten of them and none whom he struck escaped alive. He captured many alive. He bore himself with such agility and perseverance that everyone said that no one, since the time of those famous knights Roland and Oliver, had been so deserving of praise. He recovered one of the barricades, though with great labor and travail, because of the great multitude of Turks who were fighting doggedly against him. They fought a dual contest for a long time. The violent battle was joined and an insufferable conflict ensued. The contending parties clashed horribly and with great clamor. Those who were fighting against the city, after leveling the barricades, made a hot assault outside the city walls, but they were forced to retreat and to give up the attack altogether. They were unable both to attack the city and, at the same time, to keep up their defense in the face of an attack by the Turks outside the town. Many of the Franks were killed there by the spears, by the missiles and stones of the balistas, and by the spreading of Greek fire. There was great mourning among the people, with wailing and lamentation. . . . After the French had laid down their arms, the Turks vilely reproached our men, taunting them with the fact that the Franks were unable to finish what they had begun. They furthermore shot Greek fire and, little by little, destroyed the engines as well as the other implements of war which the French king had had made with such tender care.

On this account the French king was so overcome with wrath and rage that, so it is said, he fell into a fit of melancholy and, in his confusion and desolation he would not even mount a horse. . . .

King Richard had not yet fully recovered from his illness. He was anxious to be doing things and he was free especially to attend to the capture of the city. He saw to it therefore that the city was attacked by his men so that, perchance, by divine grace the deed might be accomplished in accord with his vow. He had a latticework shed (commonly called a "cercleia") made. It was made solid with many joints, and when it had painstakingly been put together, he ordered it to be taken to the trench outside the city walls. When his most experienced balistarii were in position, he had himself carried out on a silken litter, so that the Saracens might be awed by his presence and also so that he could encourage his men for the fight. His balista, with which he was experienced, was then put into action and many were killed by the missiles and spears which he fired. His miners also made an underground passage to the tower at which his siege engines were firing. The miners sought out the foundations of the tower and hacked out part of it. They filled up the hole with timbers which they set afire. Then the repeated hits of the stone missiles suddenly knocked the tower to bits.

The King pondered the difficulties of proceeding in this enterprise and the great bellicosity of his opponents. He decided that, since in the business world work makes progress through excellence, he might more readily attract the spirits of the young by posting a reward than by giving orders through the commanders. Who, indeed, is not attracted by the scent of money?

The King ordered the criers to proclaim that anyone who removed a stone from the wall next to the aforesaid tower would receive two pieces of gold from the King. Later he promised three gold pieces and then four, so that however many stones anyone removed, he received a payment of four gold pieces for each. Then you could see the young men rush forward and the courageous followers swarm to the wall. When the stones were taken out they would go on eagerly, greedy for praise as well as for payment. Even in the midst of the enemy's missiles they worked on bravely at tearing down the wall. Many of them were wounded, however, and were put out of action. Others, in fear of death, stayed away from danger. But some of them manfully pushed the Turks back from the wall and some of these men were protected neither by shields nor weapons. The wall was extremely high and immoderately thick. The men, however, inspired with courage, overcame danger and removed a great many stones from the massive wall....

Saladin concluded that further delay would be dangerous. He therefore agreed to the requests of the besieged men [to allow them to surrender]. He was persuaded to take this course especially by his emirs, satraps, and powerful friends, some of whom were parents, relatives, and friends of the besieged.... He also recalled the wives of the besieged men and the sorrows of their families whom they had not seen now for the three years during which the siege had continued. They said, further, that he would only be losing a city, rather than such upright people.

Saladin's princes persuaded him on these and similar scores and, lest their last state be worse than the first, he agreed that they should make peace on the best terms they could get. It was therefore provided and declared that they would agree to the better peace terms. When the messengers [from the garrison of the town] announced the decision of Saladin and his counsellors, the besieged men were overjoyed. The principal men among them came out to our Kings. Through an interpreter they offered to give up the city of Acre, free and clear, and to give up the Holy Cross and two hundred of the Christians whom they held captive and to surrender fifty men.

When our people found these terms unacceptable, the Muslims offered two thousand noble Christians and five hundred lesser captives, whom Saladin would seek out throughout his domains. The Turks were to leave the city, each man taking with him nothing except his clothing. They were to leave behind their weapons, food, and everything else. As ransom for their captives, moreover, they were to give two hundred thousand Saracen talents to the two Kings. To assure faithful performance of these terms they were to give as hostages the more noble and important Turks who were to be found in the city.

Our Kings conferred with their wiser men and with each other over whether they should allow these terms to be granted. The universal decision on the matter was that the offer was to be received and the conditions accepted. Oaths were taken and the agreement was put into writing as security. Then, when the hostages had been handed over, the Turks left the city empty-handed.

On the Friday next after the feast of the translation of St. Benedict, [The feast is July 11, the Friday next would be July 12] the hostages, that is, the wealthier and more noble emirs, were delivered and accepted. It was arranged that the Holy Cross was to be delivered at the end of the month; also, the captives who were being sought out were to be delivered at the same time. When these arrangements for the city's surrender were made known by rumor (since they affected everyone) the ignorant mob was inflamed with anger. The wiser men, however, were filled with a not unmerited joy, because they had obtained expeditiously and without danger the aim which they had previously been unable to obtain for such a long time.

It was then announced by the criers that it was forbidden for anyone, by word or deed, to revile the Turks with insults or to injure the conquered men. Nor was anyone to hurl missiles at the wrecked walls or at the Turks whom they might happen to see atop the fortifications. On this critical day the probity of these Turks was admirable, as was their great bravery, for they were most vigorous in military enterprises, distinguished in their magnificence. Now, as they crossed over their high walls on their way out of the city, they were regarded by the deeply curious eyes of the Christians, who admired them especially as soldiers and who recalled their memories. Their appearance, as they emerged almost emptyhanded from the city was, nonetheless, amazing in its gracefulness and dignity. They were unconquered by their adversities. Although extreme necessity had just vanquished them, reducing them almost to beggary, the defeated men who emerged were not broken up by gnawing worry nor dejected by the loss of their possessions. Their constancy had not disappeared; rather, in their spirited appearance they seemed victorious. Their lying, superstitious cult, however, had perverted their powers as men. Their miserable error was corrupted into idolatry.

When all the Turks had left the city, the Christians, on the orders of the two Kings, opened the gates and freely entered the city, joyfully dancing and exulting at the top of their voices. They glorified the Lord and gave thanks, for God had showed his great mercy to them and he had visited and worked redemption for his people. The banners and manifold flags of the Kings were run up atop the walls and towers. The city was equally divided by the two Kings. They also made a proportionally equal distribution of the supplies of arms and of food. The captives of the highest degree of nobility were divided between them by lot. . . . The King of France, moreover, for his part had the noble palace of the Templars with all its appurtenances. King Richard got the royal palace, to which he sent his queens with the children and their servants. Thus each of the Kings peacefully secured his position. The army was housed throughout the city. After the prolonged day by day agonies of the siege, they now quietly refreshed themselves in much desired peace. On the night following our entry, Saladin and his army, out of fear of our people, left the place where they had camped and occupied a mountain further away.

Source: *Itinerarium Peregrinorum et Gesta Regis Ricardi,* ed. William Stubbs, Rolls Series (London: Longmans, 1864) III, 1, 5, 13, 17–18 (pp. 210–211, 214–217, 224–226, 231–234), translated by James Brundage, *The Crusades: A Documentary History* (Milwaukee: Marquette University Press, 1962), 175–181. For this text see also *The Crusade of Richard the Lionhearted,* ed. and trans. John L. LaMonte (New York: Columbia University Press, 1941).

60. Assassins Kill Marquis Conrad of Montferrat (April 28, 1192)

Introduction

The Hashshashin, members of the Syrian-based Ismaili Nizari Muslim sect, a breakaway Shiite movement founded in 1094, were much feared by their contemporaries due to their fondness for committing political murder. Their objective was apparently to extend their territories in Syria. Assassinations, as these murders became known, in tribute to the sect's name, took place across religious lines, with prominent Christians and Muslims of various political affiliations, including Saladin himself, being selected as targets. Myths proliferated about the assassins, with their leader known as the Old Man of the Mountains. A contemporary account of the murder of Marquis Conrad of Montferrat a few days after he had been selected as king of Jerusalem gives some insight into popular beliefs about the assassins. In the 1250s, the assassins came into conflict with the Mongol Ilkhanate leader Hulegu, whose response was to suppress them with great brutality.

Document

For it happened one day that [Conrad of Montferrat] was returning, in a very cheerful and pleasant humour, from an entertainment given by the bishop of Beauvais, at which he had been a guest, and had reached the custom-house of the city, when two young men, assassins, without cloaks, suddenly rushed upon him, and having drawn two poniards, which they carried in their hands, stabbed him to the heart, and ran off at full speed. The marquis instantly fell from his horse, and rolled dying on the ground; one of the murderers was slain directly but the second took shelter in a church; notwithstanding which he was captured, and condemned to be dragged through the city until life should be extinct. One of them was closely questioned before expiring, at whose instigation, and for what reason, they had done the deed, when he confessed that they had been sent a long time before to perpetrate the crime, and that they had done it by the command of their superior, whom they were bound to obey. This turned out to be true; for these very young men had been some time in the service of the marquis, waiting for a favourable opportunity to complete the deed. The old man of Musse had sent them over to assassinate the marquis, whom he thought worthy of death, within a certain space of time; for every one the old man judged deserving of death, he caused to be assassinated in the same manner. The old man of Musse, according to hereditary custom, brought up a large number of noble boys in his palace, causing them to be taught every kind of learning and accomplishment, and to be instructed in various languages, until they could converse in them without the aid of an interpreter, in any nation of the known world. Cruelty of the greatest degree was also inculcated with profound secrecy; and the pupils were carefully and anxiously trained to follow it up. When they reach the age of puberty, the senior calls them to him, and enjoins on them, for the remission of their sins, to slay some great man, whom he mentions by name; and for this purpose he gives to each of them a poniard, of terrible length and sharpness. From their devoted obedience, they never hesitate to set out, as they are commanded; nor do they pause until they have reached the prince, or tyrant, who has been pointed out to them; and they remain in his service until they find a favourable opportunity for accomplishing their purpose; for by so doing they believe they shall gain the favour of heaven. Of this sect were the persons who slew the marquis.

Source: "Richard of Holy Trinity: Itinerary of Richard I and Others to the Holy Land (Formerly Ascribed to Geoffrey de Vinsauf)," York University, http://www.yorku.ca/inpar/richard_of_holy_trinity.pdf.

61. Henry VI of Germany and the Byzantine Empire (1196–1197)

Introduction

King Henry VI of Germany succeeded his father Frederick I Barbarossa as emperor following the latter's death by drowning in 1190 while on crusade. Before dying, Frederick had sent Henry complaints of the hostility and suspicion that Byzantine emperor Isaac II Angelos had displayed toward the crusaders and the Western powers, which, Frederick forcefully argued, justified a major future attack on the Byzantine Empire by their family. As emperor Henry followed his father's advice, submitting complaints of Byzantine behavior to Isaac's successor, his brother Alexios III Angelos, and demanding a huge sum in compensation. Alexios acceded to these demands, but Henry himself, as a Byzantine chronicler happily recounted, died before the funds could be dispatched. The episode was nonetheless a demonstration that predatory Western rulers and crusaders now regarded the Byzantine Empire as a potentially lucrative field for exploitation.

Document

Henry, the ruler of the Germans, was the son of Frederick, who . . . died on his way to Palestine while bathing for the last time in a river's stream. He took hold of his father's kingdom, and after bringing Sicily to terms [autumn of 1194] and subjugating Italy, he turned his attention to the Romans, for he was unnaturally fond of revolutionary movements and an intractable evildoer. He forthwith lay in wait for the opportunity to attack the Romans, but not without hesitation, as he was daunted by the difficulty of the undertaking: the brave deeds performed by the Romans against the Sicilians when they had invaded our lands were still fresh in his mind, and he was no less restrained in his purpose by the pope of elder Rome [Celestine III].

Therefore, he dispatched envoys to Emperor Isaakios [February 1196] (for Isaakios had not yet been banished from the throne) and lodged complaints with the intent of creating an unjustifiable breach. As present ruler of Sicily, he laid claim to all the Roman provinces between Epidamnos and the celebrated city of Thessaloniki, which had recently bowed under the yoke of the Sicilian army by force of arms; its defeat and rout were due to Roman deceit. Henry was not the least of all those who spin pleasant fables. He enumerated the afflictions endured by his father, not only his recent troubles but also those with which he had had to contend over a long period of time because he had been removed from elder Rome, thanks to the cunning Emperor

Manuel, and expelled from Italy as well. Unabashedly recalling events of the distant past, he demanded that the Romans purchase peace at a huge price or prepare to meet him in battle at once. In addition, he wanted to be designated lord of lords and proclaimed king of kings and insisted on succor for his compatriots in Palestine with the dispatch of naval forces. The emperor replied in writing and sent a distinguished envoy; two envoys arrived in turn [before Christmas 1196], one of whom had bushy eyebrows and was remarkable for having been given the responsibility for the king's education as a child. Their negotiations centered around the payment of huge sums of money, false pretensions and boasts, and lists of their countrymen's glories with which they hoped to intimidate their audience.

Because the emperor whose reign we are now recounting could not dismiss the envoys empty-handed, he consented to pay money in return for peace, something which had never been done up to this time. Alexios, intent on extolling the wealth of the Roman empire, undertook no task suited to the times but did that which was neither worthy of respect nor seemly and which appeared almost ridiculous in the eyes of the Romans. On the feast of Christ's Nativity [December 25, 1196], he donned his imperial robe set with precious stones and commanded the rest to put on their garments with the broad purple stripe and interwoven with gold. So astonished were the Germans by what they saw that their smoldering desire was kindled into a flame by the splendid attire of the Romans, and they longed the sooner to conquer the Greeks, whom they thought cowardly in warfare and devoted to servile luxuries. To the Romans who stood among them urging them to gaze upon the full bloom of the precious stones with which the emperor was adorned like a meadow, to pluck the delights of springtime in the middle of winter and enjoy a feast for the eyes, they responded, "The Germans have neither need of such spectacles, nor do they wish to become worshipers of ornaments and garments secured by brooches suited only for women whose painted faces, headdresses, and glittering earrings are especially pleasing to men." To frighten the Romans they said, "The time has now come to take off effeminate garments and brooches and to put on iron instead of gold." Should the embassy fail in its purpose and the Romans not agree to the terms of their lord and emperor, then they would have to stand in battle against men who are not adorned by precious stones like meadows in bloom, and who do not swell in pride like beads of pearls shimmering in the moonlight; neither are they like the intoxicating amethysts, nor are they colored in purple and gold like the proud Median bird [the peacock], but being the foster sons of Ares [the Greek god of war], their eyes are inflamed by the fire of wrath like the rays of gemstones, and the clotted beads of sweat from their day-long toil outshine the pearls in the beauty of their adornment.

In return for peace, the Germans demanded the payment of five thousand pounds of gold. Spent by these negotiations, the emperor dispatched as his envoy to the king Eumathios Philokales, the eparch of the City [beginning of 1197], the wealthiest in the empire. Philokales willingly accepted the role of envoy and asked the emperor that with the insignia of eparch he also be granted those of envoy. The emperor was pleased to provide whatever traveling supplies he requested, but he must set out for the proposed journey at his own expense. Thus he stood out as an odd and eccentric envoy; not only was he not held in esteem compared with former envoys but he also drew derision down upon himself because of the strangeness of his dress.

Since the monies to be paid in exchange for peace came to about sixteen hundredweight of gold, Philokales waited in expectation of the gold's arrival in Sicily, where he met with the king. The emperor contended that he was in need of money and taxed the provinces, imposing the so-called Alamanikon [the German tax] for the first time. Convening the full number of citizens, the senate, and the clergy, as well as all those divided into different trades and professions, he demanded that contributions be made and that everyone pay down a portion of his property. But he soon saw that he was accomplishing nothing and that his words were only empty talk. The majority deemed these burdensome and unwonted injunctions to be wholly intolerable and became clamorous and seditious. The emperor, blamed by some for squandering the public wealth and distributing the provinces to his kinsmen, all of whom were worthless and Alexios Angelos benighted, quickly discarded his proposal, as much as saying that it was not he who had introduced the scheme. Devising another plan, he claimed all the gold and silver votive offerings outside the sanctuary, as well as those that were not used to receive the Divine Body and Blood of Christ. When many recoiled from this, saying that he wished to defile the sacred, he resolved to rob the deaf and dumb tombs of the emperors, since they had no one to take up their cause. The tombs were opened, and they were stripped of every precious ornament. The only things left of those Roman emperors of old who boasted of glorious deeds were their coats of stone, those cold and last garments. Even the sepulcher of Constantine the Great would not have been spared, and the thieves would have stolen the splendid cover interwoven with gold which lay over it had they not been stopped by imperial decree. Collecting thence more than seventy hundredweight [seven thousand pounds] of silver and an amount of gold, the emperor consigned them to the smelting furnace as though they were profane matter. Two men from the imperial court who had been entrusted with the collection of these precious metals died shortly afterwards: one was consumed by a burning fever and the other, swelling up like a wineskin, succumbed to dropsy.

As for what followed—but who can worthily speak of the mighty deeds of the Lord or who shall cause His praises to be heard? News of the death of the king of Germany arrived before the dispatch of the monies [September 28, 1197]. His death was received with great satisfaction by the Romans, and the Western nations were thrice-pleased, especially those that he had won over by force rather than by persuasion and those he was preparing to attack. He was ever racked by cares and opposed to all pleasures in his desire to establish a monarchy and become lord of the nations round about. Reflecting on the Antonines and the Augusti Caesars, he aspired to extend his rule as far as theirs and all but recited the words attributed to Alexander, "All things here and there are mine." Wan and solemn in aspect, he partook of nourishment only late in the day; to those who argued that it was his duty to take food to avoid cachexia, he replied that for a private citizen any time is suitable for eating, especially that which is accustomed, but as for a careworn emperor, if he wishes not to give a lie to his appellation of beloved, evening is time enough for indulging the body.

The death of the king of Germany, therefore, was, as I have said, prayed for by all the nations and more so by the Sicilians because when their island fell he inflicted a host of evils on them which cannot be easily set down in writing. They endured slaughter, suffered the confiscation of their monies, underwent the misfortune of banishment from their country, and became subject to such excruciating tortures that death was preferable to life; in addition, many Sicilian cities were razed to the ground and important fortresses were demolished. To make sure that the Sicilians should never again long for freedom and rebel, Henry dashed their every fair hope, that which reposes in money, or chariots, or horses, and that which trusts in well-fortified city walls, in brave men, and in strong defenses.

Henry, who lived in dread of the future and was unable to stave off the present, was plotted against by certain men but bested them. He did not avenge himself by putting them to the sword; rather, he first tortured them in many ways and then most pitiably took their lives. One he lowered into a cauldron of boiling water, placed in a basket like wheat, and then sent him on to his family; another he cast into a fire heated seven times more than usual; a third he placed in a sack and sent down into the deep. The initiator of the conspiracy, who was also chosen leader, he condemned to a much more violent punishment; ordering a crown made of copper with diagonal holes of equal size along the rim, he placed it with his hands on the rebel. He affixed the diadem with four huge pegs driven right through into the head, and as he walked away he said, "O man, you have the crown which you wanted; I begrudge you not. Enjoy that which you so eagerly sought." The man reeled from dizziness and fell on his face and died soon afterwards, the thread of his life snapped by this pitiable crown.

Source: Harry J. Magoulias, trans., *O City of Byzantium, Annals of Niketas Choniatēs* (Detroit: Wayne State University Press, 1984), 261–264.

62. Emperor Alexios V Doukas Mourtzouphlos (r. January–April 1204)

Introduction

In 1203, forces embarked on the Fourth Crusade diverted to Constantinople. They did so at the request of Byzantine Prince Alexios Angelos, son of former Emperor Isaac II Angelos, who had been overthrown and blinded in 1195 by his younger brother, who then took the throne as Emperor Alexios III Angelos. Following the arrival of the crusaders in summer 1203, Alexios III fled Constantinople, and in August 1203 his nephew became emperor as Alexios IV Angelos. The unruly crusaders, ensconced in the city from July 1203 while they awaited the lavish financial rewards the new emperor had promised in return for their support and protection, soon made themselves extremely unpopular with most of the inhabitants. While

Alexios went on progress around his domains, conflict broke out between the Byzantines and the occupying Latins, resulting in a major fire. The occupiers moved out to an encampment beyond the city limits. On his return, Alexios refused them the lucrative payments he had once promised, possibly because the crusaders had indulged in large-scale looting of his capital. The crusaders then began open war against the Greeks of Byzantium. On January 28, 1204, after just over six months as emperor, Alexios IV was ousted and subsequently murdered by a relatively obscure member of the imperial family who became Emperor Alexios V Doukas Mourtzouphlos. The new incumbent set about preparing his capital city to resist the crusaders' demands. Less than three months after seizing power, the latest usurper was himself overthrown. Before that year ended he too would suffer a brutal death. The historian Niketas Choniates, whom Alexios V dismissed from his court job, admired his courage but had reservations as to his character.

Document

Once Doukas had clearly won the throne by a cast of the die, he longed painfully for changes in the affairs of the state and thought to stir up everything. He was extremely clever by nature and arrogant in his manner, and he believed dissembling to be the mark of shrewdness. He shirked the role of benefactor in all things for as long as the cycle of Meton, saying that he did not deem it prudent in an emperor to allow things to happen on their own and in a haphazard fashion, but that his actions should be characterized by protracted circumspection. He was impelled toward such judgment of his own accord, contending that nothing that needed to be done escaped him, that he had well in hand all issues. Following him about as his assistant was the feeble shadow of his father-in-law Philokales, and in order to place him at the head of the senate, he dismissed me as logothete of the sekreta, without even the benefit of a specious excuse, and promoted him in my place. This man, wholly unprepared to make himself known and precariously exceeding propriety because of inordinate ambition, did not sit together with men of high rank. Some he fooled by affecting the gout, as if his brain had flowed down into his feet with the disease, and so, with his wits wandering, he neglected his duties.

Because the emperor Doukas found the imperial treasury neither full nor half-full, but completely emptied out, he reaped where he sowed not and gathered where he had not strawed, grievously afflicting those who were formerly girded with the highest offices under the Angelos family, who were elevated as sebastokrators and kaisars to exalted dignities, and their confiscated monies he applied to public needs.

In rashly resisting the Latins, he surpassed all others; he shored up the City's sea walls with beams, provided the land walls with fortifications, and rekindled the army's courage with his own example. Moreover, clasping sword in hand and armed with a bronze mace, he would beat back the enemy's sallies, and when they made sporadic sorties in search of provisions, he would appear suddenly before them of his own free will.

Such deeds endeared him to the citizens, although he was extremely distrustful of, and uncompromising towards, his blood relations; nurtured in stupidity and reared in softness, spurning uplifting austerity and prudent behavior even as sick bodies avoid medical treatment, they exalted themselves and were hardened. They turned away from Doukas's rebuke and indignation (for he had by nature a hoarse but resounding bass voice) as they would from the taste of raw octopus, or a meal of hellebore, or a drink of bull's blood, and they deemed his destruction a matter of divine retribution....

When Doukas saw that he could prevail nothing, he was fearful lest he be apprehended and put into the jaws of the Latins as their dinner or dessert, and he entered the Great Palace. He put on board a small fishing boat the Empress Euphrosyne, Emperor Alexios [III]'s wife, and her daughters, one of whom he loved passionately [Evdokia] (for he had frequently engaged in sexual intercourse from the first appearance of hair on his cheek, and he was a proven lecher in bed, having put away two wedded wives) and sailed away from the City [night of April 12–13, 1204], having reigned two months and sixteen days....

... Alexios [III Angelos], for what cause I know not, took [Doukas] captive by deceit [summer 1204] and perversely maimed the pupils of his eyes. A wanderer himself, he despised the wanderer; a deserter from the throne, he opposed him who was cast down therefrom.

Not long after his blinding [end of November 1204], Doukas fell into the hands of the Latins and was returned to Byzantion, where he was brought to trial for having seized his lord and emperor and put him to death by strangulation. His defense was that he looked upon the emperor as a traitor to his country who justly deserved his punishment, not only he alone for the crimes he had committed but others as well, as many partisans and kinsmen who had joined him. But no heed was paid to the words he had spoken, and the Latins refused to lend an attentive ear to the further arguments of this anguished man who was then condemned to an unprecedented and most violent death: placing him atop the lofty column standing in the Forum of the Bull, the Latins cast him down; falling feet first and then tumbling headlong, he shortly crashed aslant and died a most pitiable death.

Source: Niketas Choniatēs, *O City of Byzantium: Annals of Niketas Choniatēs*, trans. Harry J. Magoulias (Detroit: Wayne State University Press, 1984), 311, 313–314, 334. Reprinted with permission.

63. The Crusader Siege and Capture of Constantinople (April 8–13, 1204)

Introduction

At Easter 1204, Western forces from the Fourth Crusade who had intervened in a dispute between rival claimants to the Byzantine throne were encamped outside Constantinople. Their leaders were determined not to leave before they had taken the city, ousted the new emperor, Alexios V Doukas Mourtzouphlos, and made one of their own number emperor in his place. In April, the French and the Venetians engaged in this venture reached agreement on the subsequent division of the spoils, both booty and also the fiefdoms and honors that the emperor controlled. The assault lasted six days before the crusaders were victorious. During the fighting much of the city was burned down, the third major fire since the arrival of the crusaders. The crusaders' takeover of the city was marked by massive looting and pillaging of the various palaces, churches, and private homes as well as large-scale violence and rape against the population, something that the account of the Latin chronicler Geoffrey of Villehardouin largely ignored but Byzantine historians understandably emphasized.

Documents

The fleet was very well prepared and armed, and provisions were got together for the pilgrims. On the Thursday after mid-Lent (April 8, 1204), all entered into the vessels, and put their horses into the transports. Each division had its own ships, and all were ranged side by side; and the ships were separated from the galleys and transports. A marvellous sight it was to see; and well does this book bear witness that the attack, as it had been devised, extended over full half a French league.

On the Friday morning the ships and the galleys and the other vessels drew near to the city in due order, and then began an assault most fell and fierce. In many places the pilgrims landed and went up to the walls, and in many places the scaling ladders on the ships approached so close, that those on the towers and on the walls and those on the ladders crossed lances, hand to hand. Thus lasted the assault, in more than a hundred places, very fierce, and very dour, and very proud, till near upon the hour of nones.

But, for our sins, the pilgrims were repulsed in that assault, and those who had landed from the galleys and transports were driven back into them by main force. And you must know that on that day those of the host lost more than the Greeks, and much were the Greeks rejoiced thereat. And some there were who drew back from the assault, with the ships in which they were. And some remained with their ships at anchor so near to the city that from either side they shot at one another with petraries and mangonels.

Then, at vesper time, those of the host and the Doge of Venice called together a parliament, and assembled in a church on the other side of the straits—on the side where they had been quartered. There were many opinions given and discussed; and much were those of the host moved for the mischief that had that day befallen them. And many advised that they should attack the city on another side[,] the side where it was not so well fortified. But the Venetians, who had fuller knowledge of the sea, said that if they went to that other side, the current would carry them down the straits, and that they would be unable to stop their ships. And you must know that there were those who would have been well pleased if the current had borne them down the straits, or the wind, they cared not whither, so long as they left that land behind, and went on their way. Nor is this to be wondered at, for they were in sore peril.

Enough was there spoken, in more than a hundred places, but the conclusion of their deliberation was this: that they would repair and refit on the following day, which was Saturday, and during the whole of Sunday, and that on the Monday they would return to the assault; and they devised further that the ships that carried the scaling ladders should be bound together, two and two, so that two ships should be in case to attack one tower; for they had perceived that day how only one ship had attacked each tower, and that this had been too heavy a task for the ship, seeing that those in the tower were more in number than those on the ladder. For this reason was it well seen that two ships would attack each tower with greater effect than one. As had been settled, so was it done, and they waited thus during the Saturday and Sunday.

Before the assault the Emperor Mourzuphles had come to encamp, with all his power, in an open space, and had there pitched his scarlet tents. Thus matters remained till the Monday morning, when those on the ships, transports, and galleys were all armed. And those of the city stood in much less fear of them than they did at the beginning, and were in such good spirits that on the walls and towers you could see nothing but people. Then began an assault proud and marvellous, and every ship went straight before it to the attack. The noise of the battle was so great that it seemed to rend the earth.

Thus did the assault last for a long while, till our Lord raised a wind called Boreas which drove the ships and vessels further up on to the shore. And two ships that were bound together, of which the one was called the *Pilgrim* and the other the *Paradise*, approached so near to a tower, the one on the one side and the other on the other—so as God and the wind drove them—that the ladder of the *Pilgrim* joined on to the tower. Immediately a Venetian, and a knight of France, whose name was Andrew of Urboise, entered into the tower, and other people began to enter after them, and those in the tower were discomfited and fled.

When the knights see this, who are in the transports, they land, and raise their ladders against the wall, and scale the top of the wall by main force, and so take four of the towers. And all begin to leap out of the ships and transports and galleys, helter-skelter, each as best he can; and they break in some three of the gates and enter in; and they draw the horses out of the transports; and the knights mount and ride straight to the quarters of the Emperor Mourzuphles. He had his battalions arrayed before his tents, and when his men see the mounted knights coming, they lose heart and fly; and so goes the emperor flying through the streets to the castle of Bucoleon.

Then might you have seen the Greeks beaten down; and horses and palfreys captured, and mules, and other booty. Of killed and wounded there was neither end nor measure. A great part of the Greek lords had fled towards the gate of Blachernae. And vesper-time was already past, and those of the host were weary of the battle and of the slaying. And they began to assemble in a great open space that was in Constantinople, and decided that they would take up their quarters near the walls and towers they had captured. Never had they thought that in a whole month they should be able to take the city, with its great churches, and great palaces, and the people that were in it.

As they had settled, so was it done, and they encamped before the walls and before the towers by their ships. Count Baldwin of Flanders and Hainault quartered himself in the scarlet tents that the Emperor Mourzuphles had left standing, and Henry his brother before the palace of Blachernae; and Boniface, Marquis of Montferrat, he and his men, towards the thickest part of the city. So were the host encamped as you have heard, and Constantinople taken on the Monday after Palm Sunday (April 12, 1204). . . .

Thus did those of the host, who were very weary, rest that night. But the Emperor Mourzuphles rested not, for he assembled all his people, and said he would go and attack the Franks. Nevertheless he did not do as he had said, for he rode along other streets, as far as he could from those held by the host, and came to a gate which is called the Golden Gate, whereby he escaped, and avoided the city; and afterwards all who could fled also. And of all this those of the host knew nothing.

During that night, towards the quarters of Boniface Marquis of Montferrat, certain people, whose names are unknown to me, being in fear lest the Greeks should attack them, set fire to the buildings between themselves and the Greeks. And the city began to take fire, and to burn very direfully; and it burned all that night and all the next day, till vesper-time. And this was the third fire there had been in Constantinople since the Franks arrived in the land; and more houses had been burned in the city than there are houses in any three of the greatest cities in the kingdom of France.

That night passed and the next day came, which was a Tuesday morning (April 13, 1204); and all armed themselves throughout the host, both knights and sergeants, and each repaired to his post. Then they issued from their quarters, and thought to find a sorer battle than the day before, for no word had come to them that the emperor had fled during the night. But they found none to oppose them.

The Marquis Boniface of Montferrat rode all along the shore to the palace of Bucoleon, and when he arrived there it surrendered, on condition that the lives of all therein should be spared.... Of the treasure that was found in that palace I cannot well speak, for there was so much that it was beyond end or counting.

At the same time that this palace was surrendered to the Marquis Boniface of Montferrat, did the palace of Blachernae surrender to Henry, the brother of Count Baldwin of Flanders, on condition that no hurt should be done to the bodies of those who were therein. There too was found much treasure, not less than in the palace of Bucoleon. Each garrisoned with his own people the castle that had been surrendered to him, and set a guard over the treasure. And the other people, spread abroad throughout the city, also gained much booty. The booty gained was so great that none could tell you the end of it: gold and silver, and vessels and precious stones, and samite, and cloth of silk, and robes vair and grey, and ermine, and every choicest thing found upon the earth. And well does Geoffrey of Villehardouin, the Marshal of Champagne, bear witness, that never, since the world was created, had so much booty been won in any city.

Every one took quarters where he pleased and of lodgings there was no stint. So the host of the pilgrims and of the Venetians found quarters, and greatly did they rejoice and give thanks because of the victory God had vouchsafed to them, for those who before had been poor were now in wealth and luxury. Thus they celebrated Palm Sunday and the Easter Day following (April 25, 1204) in the joy and honour that God had bestowed upon them. And well might they praise our Lord, since in all the host there were no more than twenty thousand armed men, one with another, and with the help of God they had conquered four hundred thousand men, or more, and in the strongest city in all the world—yea, a great city—and very well fortified.

Source: Geoffrey de Villehardouin [1160–1213], *Memoirs or Chronicle of the Fourth Crusade and the Conquest of Constantinople,* trans. Frank T. Marzials (London: J. M. Dent, 1908), 59–65.

64. Baldwin I of Constantinople (r. 1204–1206): A Byzantine View

Introduction

After the crusader forces attacked and took Byzantium in April 1204, the following month they selected an emperor from their own ranks to replace Alexios V Doukas Mourtzouphlos, who had fled. The successful candidate, the relatively youthful Count Baldwin of Flanders, was chosen in preference to the older and far more experienced Count Boniface of Montferrat. The Byzantine historian Niketas Choniates, who personally endured the sack of Constantinople by the invading crusaders, left an account of the young and perhaps somewhat naive young emperor's brief reign. He exercised power for slightly less than a year before his capture in battle by the forces of King Ioannitsa of Bulgaria and Walacia, who ultimately condemned his distinguished prisoner to a horrific death. The hostile Choniates was far more explicit than the crusader chronicler Geoffrey de Villehardouin in describing Baldwin's fate. Rather gruesomely, another Byzantine historian, George Akropolites, later recounted that "after John [Ioannatsa] killed Baldwin, his head served as a goblet for the barbarian, after it had been cleaned of all its contents and decorated all round with ornament."

Document

When it was time to anoint an emperor, they assembled in the Great Church of the Apostles of Christ [May 9, 1204], where they deliberated on what should be done. At first, according to an ancestral custom, they considered arranging four chalices in a row, one of which would contain the Bloodless Sacrifice; these would then be given to the priests, who, at the calling of each candidate's name for the throne, would take up one of the cups and bring it to him. He would be selected before the others to whose lot fell the chalice that held the Sacred Body and Blood of Christ.

However, it was the opinion of Dandolo, doge of Venice, that the selection should be left to a vote. The five noblest candidates from among the French and Lombard nations were chosen, and likewise five from among the Venetians. The vote of the majority prevailed, and the lot of empire fell to Baldwin, count of Flanders, but it was common knowledge that Dandolo had manipulated the outcome through fraud and deceit.

Since he himself was maimed of sight and for this reason was excluded from the list of imperial candidates, Dandolo wanted the empire to be administered by someone who would be complaisant in his ways, and not too ambitious in his determination to rule. His greatest concern was that the future emperor's allotted lands be extremely remote from the borders of Venice, so that should emperor and Venetians ever have a falling out, the emperor would not be able to summon his greater forces from nearby and easily penetrate Venice's borders, overrunning and plundering these with impunity; he knew that Marquis Boniface, who came from Lombardy, had the power to do all these things. Lombardy lies on the seaboard, and one can easily sail thence to the Roman Empire. Since Lombardy borders on Venice, it could easily inflict grievous injuries on the Venetians. Thus, Dandolo was motivated by such thoughts which were not wholly unreasonable, and those things which the many with sight could not clearly perceive, he who was sightless discerned through the eyes of his mind and foiled Marquis Boniface. With the joint support of the Venetians and the French, he chose Baldwin, knowing that he came from lower France, and that the borders of France and Venice were as far removed from one another as Venice was distant from the Roman empire.

Baldwin, moreover, accorded Dandolo absolute deference and behaved towards him as towards a father. He did not have long experience in affairs of state, for which reason Dandolo distrusted the marquis. Baldwin was not yet thirty-two years old. He was, furthermore, devout in his duties to God, and was reported to be temperate in his personal conduct; for as long as he was separated from his dear wife, he never so much as cast a glance at another woman. In singing the praises of God and in the face of every distress, he was unwavering. Most important, twice a week in the evening he had a herald proclaim that no one who slept within the palace was to have sexual intercourse with any woman who was not his legal wife.

After he had become emperor [May 16, 1204], Baldwin marched out to the western regions [summer 1204]. He did not intend to subjugate them (for he thought that everything was there for the taking, asserting in a high-spirited manner that verged on boasting, "Give me a place to stand and I shall move the earth with my spear"), but to pass through them as through friendly provinces and to be proclaimed emperor of the Romans by all. Consequently, he did not design to receive certain Romans who represented both the military and the civil bureaucracy. He resolved to do the same with the other commanders and counts of the army; the Latins, who appropriated and claimed valor as their very own as an innate and inborn habit of life, could not tolerate that the martial deeds of other nations should be compared with theirs. And of the related virtues, not one of the Graces or Muses was ever entertained as a guest by these barbarians. I believe, moreover, that they were savage by nature and that their wrath ran ahead of reason....

[At the Battle of Adrianople on April 14, 1205, Baldwin and his forces were lured into an ambush by the lightly-armed horsemen of King Ioannitsa of Wallachia and Bulgaria, who was profiting from the disorder that had descended upon the Byzantine Empire.]

The Latins, exhausted from the exertion of the chase, with horses thoroughly spent, were ensnared by the unwearied Cuman troops, cut off, and encircled. Overpowered by the multitude of Cumans in hand-to-hand combat, they were thrown from their horses. One was surrounded by many; the throats of the stiff-necked were exposed to the scimitar or to the noose, and many of their horses were mutilated. As the Cumans fell upon them like a never-ending black cloud, they could not disentangle themselves from the horses or find any means of escape. So fell the flower of the Latin host and those who were far-famed for their prowess with the lance. Count Louis of Blois also fell, and Baldwin was taken alive and led captive to Mysia, whence he was conducted to Trnovo, where he was cast into prison and bands were clamped upon his neck.

When that most ancient and pernicious evil and chief cause of the horrors that befell the Romans, Dandolo, the doge of Venice, who brought up the rear, learned of the army's defeat from those who fled, he forthwith drew in his reins and rode back to the camp. As night had fallen (for the battle had taken place towards evening), he ordered lights brought to the tents and large numbers of torches set up so that it would not appear that the entire army had been crushed or that they were afraid to give battle. In the middle of the night he set out for maritime Rhaidestos, where he met with Henry, Baldwin's brother, who had just arrived from Atramyttion with the Armenians of Troy with whom he had been campaigning and then returned to Byzantion; because of the many parasangs he had covered during his flight on horseback, he suffered a rupture in which his intestines herniated into the scrotal sac, which became greatly swollen....

Baldwin's death took place in the following manner. Captured in the Cuman War and put in chains, as I have recounted, he was confined for a long time in Trnovo. When Aspietes defected and was joined by his companions and partisans, Ioannitsa seethed with anger against the Latins, and his wrath grew in intensity, nearly driving him to distraction. Removing Baldwin from prison, he gave orders that his legs be summarily chopped off at the knees and his arms at the elbows before being cast headlong into a ravine. For three days Baldwin lay as food for the birds before his life ended miserably.

Source: Niketas Choniatēs, *O City of Byzantium: Annals of Niketas Choniatēs*, trans. Harry J. Magoulias (Detroit: Wayne State University Press, 1984), 327–328, 337–338, 353. Reprinted with permission.

65. Emperor Frederick II to Henry III of England (March 17, 1229)

Introduction

After years of procrastination, delays so lengthy that they had caused Pope Gregory IX to excommunicate him, in 1228 Holy Roman emperor Frederick II arrived at Acre and embarked on the Sixth Crusade. Commanding only a small army and denied assistance by the local authorities and most of the military orders of knights due to his excommunication, he soon turned to negotiations with Ayyubid sultan al-Kamil. Following his marriage in 1225 to Queen Isabella II of Jerusalem, Frederick enjoyed the status of king of the Latin State of Jerusalem, which had lost control of the city of Jerusalem and other territories to the Ayyubid Saladin in 1187. Isabella died in childbirth in May 1228, aged 16, leaving a son, Conrad, as the kingdom's heir, but Frederick had a good claim to be regent during his minority. In February, Frederick arranged a truce with the Ayyubids that restored the city of Jerusalem, together with Nazareth, Bethlehem, and a coastal strip, to the Latin Kingdom. Sacred Islamic sites in Jerusalem, the Dome of the Rock and the al-Aqsa Mosque, would remain under Muslim control, and the city was to remain unfortified. The sultan would also release a number of Christian captives he had taken earlier and not returned. Frederick wrote to his fellow monarch, the pious King Henry III of England, defending these arrangements and proclaiming his intention to rebuild Jerusalem. Frederick's distrustful critics, who resented his readiness to pursue his own interests in the region, were deeply skeptical as to just how long the treaty would last.

Document

Frederic, by the grace of God, the august emperor of the Romans, king of Jerusalem and Sicily, to his well-beloved friend, Henry, king of the English, health and sincere affection.

Let all rejoice and exult in the Lord, and let those who are correct in heart glorify Him, who, to make known His power, does not make boast of horses and chariots, but has now gained glory for Himself, in the scarcity of His soldiers, that all may know and understand that He is glorious in His majesty, terrible in His magnificence, and wonderful in His plans on the sons of men, changing seasons at will, and bringing the hearts of different nations together; for in these few days, by a miracle rather than by strength, that business has been brought to a conclusion, which for a length of time past many chiefs and rulers of the world amongst the multitude of nations, have never been able till now to accomplish by force, however great, nor by fear.

Not, therefore, to keep you in suspense by a long account, we wish to inform your holiness, that we, firmly putting our trust in God, and believing that Jesus Christ, His Son, in whose service we have so devotedly exposed our bodies and lives, would not abandon us in these unknown and distant countries, but would at least give us wholesome advice and assistance for His honor, praise, and glory, boldly in the name set forth from Acre on the fifteenth day of the month of November last past and arrived safely at Joppa, intending to rebuild the castle at that place with proper strength, that afterwards the approach to the holy city of Jerusalem might be not only easier, but also shorter and more safe for us as well as for all Christians. When therefore we were, in the confidence of our trust in God, engaged at Joppa, and superintending the building of the castle and the cause of Christ, as necessity required and as was our duty, and whilst all our pilgrims were busily engaged in these matters, several messengers often passed to and fro between us and the sultan of Babylon; for he and another sultan called Xaphat, his brother, were with a large army at the city of Gaza, distant about one day's journey from us; in another direction, in the city of Sichen, which is commonly called Neapolis, and situated in the plains, the sultan of Damascus, his nephew, was staying with an immense number of knights and soldiers also about a day's journey from us and the Christians.

And whilst the treaty was in progress between the parties on either side of the restoration of the Holy Land, at length Jesus Christ, the Son of God, beholding from on high our devoted endurance and patient devotion to His cause, in His merciful compassion of us, at length brought it about that the sultan of Babylon restored to us the holy city, the place where the feet of Christ trod, and where the true worshippers adore the Father in spirit and in truth. But that we may inform you of the particulars of this surrender each as they happened, be it known to you that not only is the body of the aforesaid city restored to us, but also the whole of the country extending from thence to the seacoast near the castle of Joppa, so that for the future pilgrims will have free passage and a safe return to and from the sepulchre; provided, however, that the Saracens of that part of the country, since they hold the temple in great veneration, may come there as often as they choose in the character of pilgrims, to worship according to their custom, and that we shall henceforth permit them to come, however, only as many as we may choose to allow, and without arms, nor are they to dwell in the city, but outside, and as soon as they have paid their devotions they are to depart.

Moreover, the city of Bethlehem is restored to us, and all the country between Jerusalem and that city; as also the city of Nazareth, and all the country between Acre and that city; the whole of the district of Turon, which is very extensive, and very advantageous to the Christians; the city of Sidon, too, is given up to us with the whole plain and its appurtenances, which will be the more acceptable to the Christians the more advantageous it has till now appeared to be to the Saracens, especially as there is a good harbor there, and from there great quantities of arms and necessaries might be carried to the city of Damascus and often from Damascus to Babylon. And although according to our treaty we are allowed to rebuild the city of Jerusalem in as good a state as it has ever been, and also the castles of Joppa, Cesarea, Sidon, and that of St. Mary of the Teutonic order, which the brothers of that order have begun to build in the mountainous district of Acre, and which it has never been allowed the Christians to do during any former truce; nevertheless the sultan is not allowed, till the end of the truce between him and us, which is agreed on for ten years, to repair or rebuild any fortress or castles.

And so on Sunday, the eighteenth day of February last past, which is the day on which Christ, the Son of God, rose from dead, and which, in memory of His resurrection, is solemnly cherished and kept holy by all Christians in general throughout the world, this treaty of peace was confirmed by oath between us. Truly then on us and on all does that day seem to have shone favorably, in which the angels sing in praise of God, "Glory to God on high, and on earth peace, and goodwill toward men." And in acknowledgment of such great kindness and of such an honor, which, beyond our deserts and contrary to the opinion of many, God has mercifully conferred on us, to the lasting renown of His compassion, and that in His holy place we might personally offer to Him the burnt offering of our lips, be it known to you that on the seventeenth day of the month of March of this second indiction, we, in company with all the pilgrims who had with us faithfully followed Christ, the Son of God, entered the holy city of Jerusalem, and after worshipping at the holy sepulchre, we, as being a Catholic emperor, on the following day, wore the crown, which Almighty God provided for us from the throne of His majesty, when of His especial grace, He exalted us on high amongst the princes of the world; so that whilst we have supported the honor of this high dignity, which belongs to us by right of sovereignty, it is more and more evident to all that the hand of the Lord hath done all this; and since His mercies are over all His works, let the worshippers of the orthodox faith henceforth know and relate it far and wide throughout the world, that He, who is blessed for ever, has visited and redeemed His people, and has raised up the horn of salvation for us in the house of His servant David.

And before we leave the city of Jerusalem, we have determined magnificently to rebuild it, and its towers and walls, and we intend so to arrange matters that, during our absence, there shall be no less care and diligence used in the business, than if we were present in person. In order that this our present letter may be full of exultation throughout, and so a happy end correspond with its happy beginning, and rejoice your royal mind, we wish it to be known to you our ally, that the said sultan is bound to restore to us all those captives whom he did not in accordance with the treaty made between him and the Christians deliver up at the time when he lost Damietta some time since, and also the others who have been since taken.

Given at the holy city of Jerusalem, on the seventeenth day of the month of March, in the year of our Lord one thousand two hundred and twenty-nine.

Source: Translation taken from Roger of Wendover, Bohn edition, Vol. II, p. 5224. Original text in Rolls Series, Roger of Wendover, Vol. II, pp. 365ff. Latin, translated in Dana C. Munro, "Letters of the Crusaders," in *Translations and Reprints from the Original Sources of European History,* Vol 1:4 (Philadelphia: University of Pennsylvania, 1896), 23–31.

66. Gerold of Lausanne, Latin Patriarch of Jerusalem, to All the Faithful (1229)

Introduction

Holy Roman emperor Frederick II, who embarked on the Sixth Crusade in September 1228, soon decided that negotiations with the Ayyubid rulers of Egypt, who controlled much of the Holy Land, were likely to prove more fruitful than fighting. In February 1229, he reached a peace agreement with Sultan al-Kamil that imposed a truce and restored Jerusalem, Bethlehem, Nazareth, and some coastal territory to the Latin Kingdom of Jerusalem. On March 18, 1229, Frederick was crowned in Jerusalem, possibly as emperor, to reinforce the authority of his imperial title, or else as king of Jerusalem, by virtue of his marriage in 1225 to Queen Isabella II of that kingdom, who had since died in childbirth. Gerold of Lausanne, the Latin patriarch of Jerusalem, refused to attend the ceremony, placed the city of Jerusalem under an interdict the following day, and published an open letter condemning Frederick's conduct. Gerold pointed out that the sultan of Damascus, nephew of Sultan al-Kamil, had not made himself a party to the treaty. Gerold also deplored Frederick's hasty exit from the Holy Land and his donation of assorted siege machines from the city of Acre to Sultan al-Kamil. The emperor's efforts to impose his authority on the Latin Kingdom of Jerusalem, to which his infant son Conrad, born in May 1228, was the rightful heir, were largely unsuccessful, as the barons of the state demonstrated obdurate resistance to imperial control. Frederick's habitual absence from the kingdom gave him little leverage over its affairs. His treaty also proved short-lived, as Muslim forces recaptured Jerusalem in 1244 following another siege.

Document

Gerold, patriarch of Jerusalem, to all the faithful greeting.

If it should be fully known how astonishing, nay rather, deplorable, the conduct of the emperor has been in the eastern lands from beginning to end, to the great detriment of the cause of Jesus Christ and to the great injury of the Christian faith, from the sole of his foot to the top of his head no common sense would be found in him. For he came, excommunicated, without money and followed by scarcely forty knights, and hoped to maintain himself by spoiling the inhabitants of Syria. He first came to Cyprus and there most discourteously seized that nobleman J. [John] of Ibelin and his sons, whom he had invited to his table under pretext of speaking of the affairs of the Holy Land. Next the king, whom he had invited to meet him, he retained almost as a captive. He thus by violence and fraud got possession of the kingdom.

After these achievements he passed over into Syria. Although in the beginning he promised to do marvels, and although in the Presence of the foolish he boasted loudly, he immediately sent to the sultan of Babylon to demand peace. This conduct rendered him despicable in the eyes of the sultan and his subjects, especially after they had discovered that he was not at the head of a numerous army, which might have to some extent added weight to his words. Under the pretext of defending Joppa, he marched with the Christian army towards that city, in order to be nearer the sultan and in order to be able more easily to treat of peace or obtain a truce. What more shall I say? After long and mysterious conferences, and without having consulted any one who lived in the country, he suddenly announced one day that he had made peace with the sultan. No one saw the text of the peace or truce when the emperor took the oath to observe the articles which were agreed upon. Moreover, you will be able to see clearly how great the malice was and how fraudulent the tenor of certain articles of the truce which we have decided to send to you. The emperor, for giving credit to his word, wished as a guarantee only the word of the sultan, which he obtained. For he said, among other things, that the holy city was surrendered to him.

He went thither with the Christian army on the eve of the Sunday when "*Oculi mei*" is sung [third Sunday in Lent]. The Sunday following, without any fitting ceremony and although excommunicated, in the chapel of the sepulchre of our Lord, to the manifest prejudice of his honor and of the imperial dignity he put the diadem upon his forehead, although the Saracens still held the temple of the Lord and Solomon's temple, and although they proclaimed publicly as before the law of Mohammed to the great confusion and chagrin of the pilgrims.

This same prince, who had previously very often promised to fortify Jerusalem, departed in secrecy from the city at dawn on the following Monday. The Hospitalers and the Templars promised solemnly and earnestly to aid him with all their forces and their advice, if he wanted to fortify the city, as he had promised. But the emperor, who did not care to set affairs right, and who saw that there was no certainty in what had been done, and that the city in the state in which it had been surrendered to him could be neither defended nor fortified, was content with the name of surrender, and on the same day hastened with his family to Joppa. The pilgrims who had entered Jerusalem with the emperor, witnessing his departure, were unwilling to remain behind.

The following Sunday when "*Laetare Jerusalem*" is sung [fourth Sunday in Lent], he arrived at Acre. There in order to seduce the people and to obtain their favor, he granted them a certain privilege. God knows the motive which made him act thus, and his subsequent conduct will make it known. As, moreover, the passage was near, and as all pilgrims, humble and great, after having visited the Holy Sepulchre, were preparing to withdraw, as if they had accomplished their pilgrimage, because no truce had been concluded with the sultan of Damascus, we, seeing that the holy land was already deserted and abandoned by the pilgrims, in our council formed the plan of retaining soldiers for the common good, by means of the alms given by the king of France of holy memory.

When the emperor heard of this, he said to us that he was astonished at this, since he had concluded a truce with the sultan of Babylon. We replied to him that the knife was still in the wound, since there was not a truce or peace with the sultan of Damascus, nephew of the aforesaid sultan and opposed to him, adding that even if the sultan of Babylon was unwilling, the former could still do us much harm. The emperor replied, saying that no soldiers ought to be retained in his kingdom without his advice and consent, as he was now king of Jerusalem. We answered to that, that in the matter in question, as well as in all of a similar nature, we were very sorry not to be able, without endangering the salvation of our souls, to obey his wishes, because he was excommunicated. The emperor made no response to us, but on the following day he caused the pilgrims who inhabited the city to be assembled outside by the public crier, and by special messengers he also convoked the prelates and the monks.

Addressing them in person, he began to complain bitterly of us, by heaping up false accusations. Then turning his remarks to the venerable master of the Templars he publicly attempted to severely tarnish the reputation of the latter, by various vain speeches, seeking thus to throw upon others the responsibility for his own faults which were now manifest, and adding at last, that we were maintaining troops with the purpose of injuring him. After that he ordered all foreign soldiers, of all nations, if they valued their lives and property, not to remain in the land from that day on, and ordered count Thomas, whom he intended to leave as bailiff of the country, to punish with stripes any one who was found lingering, in order that the punishment of one might serve as an example to many. After doing all this he withdrew, and would listen to no excuse or answers to the charges which he had so shamefully made. He determined immediately to post some crossbowmen at the gates of the city, ordering them to allow the Templars to go out but not to return. Next he fortified with crossbows the churches and other elevated positions and especially those which commanded the communications between the Templars and ourselves. And you may be sure that he never showed as much animosity and hatred against Saracens.

For our part, seeing his manifest wickedness, we assembled all the prelates and all the pilgrims, and menaced with excommunication all those who should aid the emperor with their advice or their services against the Church, the Templars, the other monks of the holy land, or the pilgrims.

The emperor was more and more irritated, and immediately caused all the passages to be guarded more strictly, refused to allow any kind of provisions to be brought to us or to the members of our party, and placed everywhere crossbowmen and archers, who attacked severely us, the Templars and the pilgrims. Finally to fill the measure of his malice, he caused some Dominicans and Minorites [Franciscans] who had come on Palm Sunday to the proper places to announce the Word of God, to be torn from the pulpit, to be thrown down and dragged along the ground and whipped throughout the city, as if they had been robbers. Then seeing that he did not obtain what he had hoped from the above-mentioned siege he treated of peace. We replied to him that we would not hear of peace until he sent away the crossbowmen and other troops, until he had returned our property to us, until finally he had restored all things to the condition and freedom in which they were on the day when he entered Jerusalem. He finally ordered what we wanted to be done, but it was not executed. Therefore we placed the city under interdict.

The emperor, realizing that his wickedness could have no success, was unwilling to remain any longer in the country. And, as if he would have liked to ruin everything, he ordered the cross-bows and engines of war, which for a long time had been kept at Acre for the defense of the Holy Land, to be secretly carried on his vessels. He also sent away several of them to the sultan of Babylon, as his dear friend. He sent a troop of soldiers to Cyprus to levy heavy contributions of money there, and, what appeared to us more astonishing, he destroyed the galleys which he was unable to take with him. Having learned this, we resolved to reproach him with it, but shunning the remonstrance and the correction, he entered a galley secretly, by an obscure way, on the day of the Apostles St. Philip and St. James, and hastened to reach the island of Cyprus, without saying adieu to any one, leaving Joppa destitute; and may he never return!

Very soon the bailiffs of the above-mentioned sultan shut off all departure from Jerusalem for the Christian poor and the Syrians, and many pilgrims died thus on the road.

This is what the emperor did, to the detriment of the Holy Land and of his own soul, as well as many other things which are known and which we leave to others to relate. May the merciful God design to soften the results! Farewell.

Source: Rolls Series, M. Paris, *Chron. maj.* iii, 179184. Latin., translated Dana C. Munro, "Letters of the Crusaders," in *Translations and Reprints from the Original Sources of European History*, Vol 1:4 (Philadelphia: University of Pennsylvania, 1896), 23–31.

67. Richard, Earl of Cornwall and Count of Poitou, to Baldwin of Reviers, Earl of Devon, the Abbot of Beaulieu, and Robert, Clerk (July 1241)

Introduction

Richard, earl of Cornwall (1227–1272), the second son of King John of England and brother of King Henry III, one of the wealthiest men in Europe, embarked on crusade in 1240 after the death of his first wife. He arrived shortly after two earlier noble crusaders from Europe, Theobald of Champagne, king of Navarre, and Duke Peter I of Brittany, together with their accompanying retinue, had left the Holy Land. Their accomplishments had been minimal: following the Egyptian defeat at the November 1239 Battle of Gaza of an errant detachment of crusaders who were too eager to see action and became separated from the main army, the following month the emir of Transjordan successfully besieged the crusaders in the citadel of Jerusalem, which fell on December 7, 1239. Rather than embarking on further fighting, Richard, as he reported in this letter to his secular and religious backers back in England, sought to negotiate a peace treaty between the warring parties. He succeeded in winning the release of the prisoners taken at Gaza, whom he ransomed, and obtaining the return of much of the territory seized by the Muslims, including the city of Jerusalem. Richard also made some rather perceptive remarks as to the prevalence of internal dissension, rivalries, and conflicts among the Christian inhabitants of the Holy Land, which were undercutting their ability to withstand external attack. Predictably, these criticisms had little impact: squabbling and bickering among the Latin nobility continued unabated until the final fall of the crusader territories several decades later.

Document

Richard, Earl of Cornwall and Poitou, to the venerable nobles, dearest in Christ, Baldwin of Reviers, Earl of Devon, the abbot of Beaulieu, and Robert the clerk, greetings, all good wishes sent in genuine affection. Intelligent people recognise the great desolation and grief that have long afflicted the Holy Land and the difficulties involved in rebuilding and raising it up again after the disaster at Gaza dampened men's spirits, since those living nearby have had reliable information and those farther afield have heard rumours. Because our innermost thoughts might be made known through the opening of the present letter en route, giving rise to some sinister interpretation, many things that would have been written therein have had to remain concealed in the depth of our heart. Since the time that kings and kingdoms abandoned Jerusalem it has been divided and ruled by evil usurpers, and in our great grief we can no longer keep silent. Indeed, despite the fact that the subject is not pleasant, we are forced to give tongue to our bitter thoughts, for the sword of compassion has so pierced our soul that it must speak out. For a long time now in the Holy Land discord has replaced peace, schism unity, hate love. These rule in the absence of justice. Many planters of such seeds existed in the Holy Land, and several of them have collected the fruits of these seeds, but if only they could now be uprooted! Among all her lovers she hath none to comfort her. Two brothers in discord in the lap of their mother whom they are supposed to protect have become too rich and arrogant. It is they who have fed and nourished the roots with these humours so that their shoots spread far and wide. For the abundance of wealth creates such an appetite for conflict that they ignore the punishment of the Father who presides over the see of Peter, intent as they are on increasing their reputation in the world. We have spent much effort in trying to calm them, but the paths of peace have not yet been trodden; lovers of discord do not listen to words of peace. They willingly attract those who bring money with them—but only as long as it lasts. But come the time to avenge their mother, they quickly abandon those with good intentions and feigning secret impediments show no desire to console their mother. For this reason and the fact that the huge number of Gallic knights (twice as many as the Saracen army) was so pitifully weakened by bad habits, the enemies of the Cross have unexpectedly become so confident that, despite their small numbers, they have little or no fear of our numerical superiority. Hence the seriousness of the difficulty in bringing relief to the country on our arrival when we saw the nobles who were likely to help us leaving for home. However, when divine clemency so wills, it allows misfortunes to go without remedy, grief without consolation.

On our journey we were hoping to put all our efforts, as required by our vow, to join up with the other Christians to avenge militarily the disgrace that the enemies of the Cross had inflicted on it, by attacking and restoring the lands they have occupied. However, the king of Navarre, who was the leader of the army, and the count of Brittany, had left for home because they had heard we were to arrive in fifteen days' time. In order to look as though they had achieved something before they left they had signed some sort of truce with Nazer, the lord of Kerak, to the effect that he would give up the prisoners he was not in fact holding after the capture of Gaza, along with some lands mentioned in the truce document. As security he would hand over his son and his brothers as hostages, the truce to be operational in forty days' time. Before that date the said king and count left, with no thought of the date of the truce. Meantime, we landed at Acre on the eve of St Denis as we indicated to you previously, and by a unanimous decision we quickly sent an envoy to Nazer to ask if the truce he had made with the king could be maintained with us. He replied that because of his respect for the king he would indeed maintain it if he could, even though it brought him little. So, on the advice of the nobles we awaited the end of the said period to see what the result would be. At that point our envoy reported to us that he was totally unable to keep to the aforesaid agreement. On hearing this, a unanimous decision was taken to go to Jaffa with all possible caution to restore the condition of the land that had deteriorated because of the aforementioned vices. A very powerful magnate of the sultan of Babylon came to us there to tell us that his lord the sultan was willing to agree a truce with us if we so wished. When we had heard and analysed what he explained to us in greater detail, and sincerely renewed our appeal to the grace of God, on the advice of the duke of Burgundy, Count Walter of Brienne, the master of the Hospitallers and the other nobles, that is the major part of the army, we agreed to the terms of the truce below. Although at the time of our arrival this appeared to be a difficult achievement, it is nevertheless commendable and advantageous to the Holy Land, since it offers peace and security to the poor and the pilgrims, useful and welcome to the ordinary inhabitants, useful and honourable to the rich and the religious. When we considered the suffering and conditions around us, it did not seem that we could find a better occupation than that of buying the liberty of the miserable prisoners, since there was a shortage of men and goods and we alone had money. Taking advantage of the truce, we decided to strengthen and fortify against the Saracens the cities and castles that had been destroyed. We have thought fit to list the names of the places and territories surrendered under the terms of the truce, even though this may appear tedious, so that no malicious interpreter may ascribe our achievements to the glory of others, nor malevolently suggest that we did it for perverse reasons. For there were a few who were against the terms of the truce which are as follows: These are the lands that are to be given up according to the terms of the truce with Earl Richard, namely the mountains of Beirut with its dependent lands and boundaries, the whole of the land of Sidon with its appurtenances, the castles of Beaufort, Cozenis, Chastel Neuf with their appurtenances, Scandelion, Lebet, Becheed, St George [al-Ba'ina] with all their appurtenances and lands, flat or mountainous. They have also given up the demesne town of Toron with its appurtenances, Tiberias with its appurtenances, the castle of Benaer, the castles of Mirabel, Rama, Amoat, Alaw and the castle of Hybilis with its appurtenances which is on the other side of the river towards the east. The castle of Safad, Nazareth, Mount Tabor, al-Lajjun, Ascalon, the castle of Bait Jibrin with their appurtenances and all the casalia which belong to the Hospital of St John and are known to belong to it in the dependencies of Jerusalem and Bethlehem, and all the lands on the road from Jerusalem to Bethlehem and from Jerusalem to St George of Ramla [Lydda] and from St George to Jaffa with all the casalia are to be in the hands of the Christians. The city (villa) of Jerusalem has been returned to the Christians. Bethlehem and all the lands around Jerusalem with all the casalia named in the truce have been returned to the Christians, that is St Lazarus of Bethany and Brihaida, 'Isawiya, Shu'fat, Bait Ta'mir, Betheles, Bait 'Anan, al-Qubaiba, Nabi Samwil, Bait Kika (Maqiqa), Bethame, Bait Iksa, Bait Suriq, Qatanna, Lifta, Bait Tulma, Argahong, Bertapsa, Bait Safafa, Khirbat Tabaliya, Sur Bahir, with all their appurtenances and lands named in the divisions of Jerusalem together with the appurtenances on the road to it. More details are to be found in the great truce document. The Christians can, if they wish, fortify all these lands with their castles during the period of the truce. The nobles who were taken prisoner at Gaza and all prisoners on both sides taken in the war with the French are to be freed. As soon as the truce was arranged we went to Ascalon, and so as to put the time to good use we followed the general view and began to build a sizeable castle. While there we sent our envoys to the sultan of Babylon to get him to agree to swear to observe the aforesaid truce and free those prisoners often mentioned. For some reason unknown to us he detained our envoys without sending us any reply, from St Andrew's Day until the Thursday after Candlemas. We learned afterwards from his letters that during that time he took the advice of his nobles and swore to observe the truce. As we were still in Ascalon we put so much effort into the construction of the said castle that by the grace of God even within such a short time it has progressed enormously. At the moment of writing this letter it is totally protected by a double wall with high towers and ramparts made of cut stone. The columns are of marble. It has everything a castle should have apart from a fosse around it, and with the Lord's consent that will be completed without fail a month after Easter. There was a good reason for this; as we were not certain that the truce would be ratified we chose to construct and fortify the castle in the meantime so that if the truce was broken we would have a secure stronghold in the march on the edge of their territory, previously held by them, to which we could retreat if necessary. Its inhabitants need have no fear of a siege, for even if the besiegers could prevent all reinforcements or provisions coming to them by land, the besieged could receive all their goods by sea. The said castle is also useful in times of peace, since it is the key and protector of the kingdom of Jerusalem by land and sea, while it threatens danger to Babylon and the southern regions. On St George's Day at last we received all our prisoners, according to the terms of the truce. At the same time the peace and the treaty were reconfirmed. On completion of all these details we left the Holy Land in peace with the Lord's approval, and on the Feast of the Finding of the Holy Cross we sailed from Acre for home. However, we lacked a following wind and put in to Trapani in Sicily in the octaves of St John the Baptist, thoroughly worn out. There we heard the news of the capture and detention of some of our bishops and other lamentable events for the Church, and so as to do the best in our power to restore peace among those in discord and to bring about the liberation of the captive bishops we made a detour to the Curia at Rome to console our Mother. When the Lord has caused the problems to be resolved as He thinks fit we propose to return home to English soil as quickly as we can.

Source: Matthew Paris, *Chronica Majora*, vol. 4, RS 57 (London, 1877), 138–144, in Malcolm Barber and Keith Bate, eds., *Letters from the East: Crusaders, Settlers, and Pilgrims in the 12th–13th Centuries* (London: Routledge, 2016), 136–140.

68. The Battle of Köse Dağ (June 26, 1243)

Introduction

From the time of their first irruption into Central Asia in 1220, the Mongols employed a combination of tactics to secure their dominance, including fierce fighting resulting in outright conquest and the acceptance of tribute and alliance relationships from potential client states. Over time their demands on these territories became more onerous, with more ostentatious displays of subjugation expected. By the early 1240s the Seljuk Sultanate of Rum, which initially settled for a conciliatory status of friendship toward the Mongols, lubricated with suitable financial offerings, was under Mongol pressure to give further proof of subordination by dispatching Sultan Kaykhusraw II on a visit to the Mongol capital and providing well-connected hostages as a guarantee of good behavior. When the sultan balked at these conditions, in the winter of 1242–1243 Mongol forces commanded by Baiju, one of their leading generals, attacked Rum, capturing the city of Erzurum. The sultan requested assistance from his allies, including the Byzantine successor empire of Trebizond. An Armenian history of these events recounted how due to poor military tactics on the part of the Seljuks and bad decisions by Kaykhusraw, the Mongol armies enticed the Seljuks and their allies into pursuing them and then successfully encircled their opponents. The battle inflicted a major blow on Seljuk power. Kaykhusraw fled, while the Mongols took his cities of Sivas and Kayseri and devastated much of his territory. Armenia and Trebizond both accepted Mongol suzerainty and vassal status, while Kaykhusraw was eventually forced to make peace with the Mongols and agreed to pay considerably increased tribute in the future. The battle and its aftermath triggered the disintegration of the Seljuk sultanate over the next 10 to 15 years, as the Mongol Khan Hulegu took over its territory for use as a springboard for his conquests in Iran, Mesopotamia, and Syria as he captured Baghdad and Damascus.

Document

While the T'at'ar army was securely settled throughout all the plains of Armenia and Aghbania, ambassadors arrived from the sultan [of Rum], Ghiyath al-Din [Kai Khusrau II, r. 1236–1245 (Ghiat'adin)] bearing boastful and threatening words, as is the Tachik custom: "You consider that by destroying one city you have conquered me and my power. Well, my cities are without limit and my troops are innumerable. So stay where you are and I shall come to battle against you." Greatly puffed up, [the ambassadors] said many similar things, including [the information that] "Next winter the sultan shall come to the Mughan plain with his women and soldiers to winter here."

When [the Mongols] heard this, in no way did they become aroused or boast [to the ambassadors]. Baiju-*noyin*, their head, merely replied: "You speak grandly; however, the victory will go to whomever God grants it."

Thus one after another ambassador arrived to make [the Mongols] hasten to war, though they did not hurry in any way; rather, they peacefully gathered their troops and those under their domination, and came to a lush place in the land of Armenia with all their bags and baggage in order to fatten their horses. Then they tranquilly approached the camp of the sultan. The latter had left his accustomed place and had come to that part of Armenia which was under his domination, [to an area near Erzinjan] close to a village named Ch'man-katuk [Kose Dagh]. He came with a countless multitude, with women and concubines, gold and silver and all the valuable possessions he had. For diversion, he also brought along wild animals and many other creeping things, even mice and cats, for he wanted to show himself as fearless to the troops.

General Baiju, consistent with his deep [military] knowledge, divided his soldiers into many groups, putting them under the foremost brave commanders, while the foreign troops, comprising various nationalities, were divided up among [the loyal troops] so that they not work any treachery. Then selecting the valiant and brave from all of them, he made a vanguard which went and battled with the sultan's troops and put them to flight. The sultan himself fled, escaping by a hairsbreadth and leaving his throne and belongings there. [The Mongols] pursued the fugitive troops and mercilessly cut them down, putting them to the sword; then they turned to loot the fallen.

As soon as the main body of the army arrived and saw that the sultan had fled and his army was beaten, they spread throughout the area raiding and looting. They pulled apart many districts and gathered gold and silver and expensive garments, as well as camels, horses, donkeys and countless animals. They came and besieged the city of Caesarea in Cappadocia. Because the inhabitants did not surrender, they took it forcibly and put the population to the sword, ravishing whatever was in the city and leaving it deserted. Then they came to Sebastia, and since the inhabitants of the city had surrendered in advance (coming out to them with gifts and presents) the people were not punished, although part of the city was looted. Conquering the city in their own name, they set up overseers and left.

They came and besieged Eznka (Erzinjan) and fought numerous battles for it. The inhabitants of the city dealt many blows to the T'at'ar army. Then [the Mongols] started to treacherously call the people out of the city on the pretext of frienship; and since the inhabitants had no aid from any quarter, they agreed to come. [The Mongols] fell upon them and cut them down, man and woman, sparing only a few lads and girls whom they took into captivity and slavery.

Thus after destroying and enslaving many districts and lands, they came to the city called Divrigi (Tiwrike/Tephrike). Once the inhabitants knew that it was impossible to resist them militarily they wished to surrender. [The Mongols] took many goods from them, but [left] the city unharmed, while they themselves returned with much booty and in high spirits to their winter camps in Armenia and Aghbania/Aghuania, since the wrecking and destruction of all peoples had come from the Lord. The Christians among their troops freed many people from captivity, both openly and in secret, priests and clerics. This was especially true of the grandee princes Awag, Shahnshah, Vahram and his son Aghbugha, the Xach'ents'is Hasan Jalal and his forces and relatives Grigor, Jalal's mother's sister's son, Dop'i, and other princes and their troops [who freed as many] as they were able. This occurred in 692 A.E. [1243].

Once this [battle] had occurred, when Het'um (king of Cilicia and other states) saw that the sultan had been defeated by [the Mongols] he sent ambassadors and valuable gifts to them to make peace and to place himself in submission. Through the intercession of prince Jalal, those who came to the great court were presented to Baiju-*noyin*, to Elt'ina *khatun* (Chormaghun's wife) and to the other grandee nobles. When [the Mongols] heard the king's message and saw the gifts they asked him to hand over to them the mother, wife and daughter of the sultan, who had fled to him for refuge.

When King Het'um heard this, he was deeply saddened and said: "It would have been better for me had they asked for my own son Lewon than for those others." However, since he was afraid [of the Mongols] and so that a refusal would not occasion any great harm, he reluctantly handed them over with many presents besides to those who had come to take them. [The sultan's relatives] were taken and exhibited to Baiju and to the other chiefs. As soon as [the Mongols] saw them, they were happy and greatly honored the ambassadors of the king, establishing stipends and horses for them during the winter, so that when spring came they could return to their own land. Thus friendship was established with the king. They gave him a written ordinance according to their religion which they call *el-tamgha*.

Source: Kirakos Ganjakets'i, *History of the Armenians*. Translated from Classical Armenian by Robert Bedrosian (New York: Sources of the Armenian Tradition, 1986), 243–247. Reprinted with permission from Robert Bedrosian.

69. The Battle of La Forbie (October 17–18, 1244): Robert, Patriarch of Jerusalem and Papal Legate, and Other Prelates in the Holy Land to the Prelates of France and England (November 25, 1244)

Introduction

Following the Battle of Forbie (Harbiyah) in October 1244, the Christians in the East were in a state of shock and panic. The battle was prompted by the capture and sack of the city of Jerusalem in August 1244 by Khwarezmian Muslim forces allied with the Ayyubid sultan of Egypt, a loss that greatly alarmed not just the Latins of the Middle East but also the maverick Syrian Ayyubid rulers of Damascus, Homs, and Kerak. The military crusading orders and the surviving troops of the kingdom of Jerusalem joined forces with those of the Syrian emirs to take the field against the Egyptian army of Sultan as-Salih Ayyub, commanded by Emir Baybars, who would himself seize power as sultan in 1260. Both sides confronted each other near the village of La Forbie, close to the town of Gaza. Although the Christians fought with dogged courage and persistence they were ultimately defeated, with over 5,000 killed and another 800 taken prisoner. Bishop Robert, patriarch of Jerusalem, writing on behalf of other leading Latin prelates in the Holy Land to the pope and other Roman Catholic clergy in Europe, described the recent defeats and the damage that these losses represented to the ability of the remaining Latin outposts and churches in Palestine to survive. This letter and similar appeals for help prompted Pope Innocent IV to proclaim a new crusade at the First Council of Lyon, held in France in June 1245, a cause in which a number of prominent western princes and nobles, including the young king of France, Louis IX, enlisted. Despite their efforts, these ventures proved incapable of reversing the long-term damage the recent Muslim conquests had inflicted on the Christian position, which would gradually be further eroded.

Document

To the revered fathers in Christ and all friends, archbishops, bishops, abbots, and other prelates in the kingdoms of France and England who will read this letter, Robert, by the grace of God Patriarch of the church of Jerusalem and Legate of the Apostolic See, Henry, Archbishop of Nazareth, Joscelin, elect of Caesarea, Ralph, Bishop of Acre, and the Bishop of Sidon, brother William of Rochefort, second in command (vicemagister) in the house of the Knighthood of the Temple, the convent of the said house, H., Prior of the Lord's Sepulchre, the abbot of St Samuel of the Premonstratensian Order, and the abbots, B. of the Mount of Olives, J. of the Temple of the Lord, P. of Mount Tabor and R. of Mount Sion, send greetings and a positive result to your prayers. From the realms of the East the cruel beast has come to invest the province of Jerusalem. Although the province has often been troubled in the past by the neighbouring Saracens, in recent times the latter have been quiet so that the peaceful conditions have afforded it a breathing space. However, the sins of the Christian population have caused an unknown people from far away to wield the sword of destruction against it. Indeed, the furious onslaught of the Tartars has struck the entire Eastern region several calamitous blows. They have pursued everybody, making no distinction between Christians and infidels, and from the remotest regions have taken captive the would-be capturers of the Christians. These same Tartars destroyed the whole of Persia before adopting an even crueller form of warfare in hunting the cruellest of men, the Khwarazmians, driving them out of their own regions as though they were dragons being dragged from their lairs. Lacking fixed abodes, they were unable to obtain any refuge among Saracens. Only the sultan of Babylon, the persecutor of the Christian faith, offered these Khwarazmians a home, but not in his own land; he invited these unbelievers to settle in the Promised Land, that is the land the Most High promised and gave to those who believed in Him. Trusting in the protection of the sultan many thousands of armed horsemen came with wives and children to the Lord's legacy which the sultan had given them. Their arrival was so sudden that neither we nor our neighbours were able to foresee and prepare against the attack before they entered the province of Jerusalem around Safad and Tiberias. While we were spending a great deal of time and effort in trying to work out how to restore the former peaceful state of affairs which the new enemy had broken, in view of the fact that the Christians were not strong enough to drive them out, these Khwarazmians took possession of all the territory between Toron of the Knights, near Jerusalem, and Gaza. By a common and unanimous desire, including that of the masters of the religious houses of the Knighthood of the Temple and that of the Hospital of St John and of the preceptor of Holy Mary of the Teutons and the nobles of the kingdom, it was decided to call to the aid of the Christians the sultans of Damascus and Homs, who were bound by the peace treaty they had made with us. They were particularly motivated against the Khwarazmians whose arrival they considered to be a danger, and furthermore were held by the terms of the treaty to defend the land occupied by the Christians against all other Saracens. They solemnly promised on oath to help us, but their help was very slow in coming, and while the Christians, very few in number, were hesitating to go into battle alone, those infidel Khwarazmians launched frequent attacks against the almost unprotected city of Jerusalem. In fear of their savagery, more than six thousand of the Christian inhabitants assembled to leave for Christian territory, with only a few remaining behind. With their families and possessions they started out through the mountainous country, trusting in the treaty they had made with its local inhabitants and the sultan of Kerak, but these cruel inhabitants killed some of them and captured others—men, women and even nuns—to sell to other Saracens. Some of the captives, however, escaped into the plain of Ramla where they were slaughtered by the Khwarazmians in an attack that left barely three hundred of the original large number more or less alive. Afterwards the Khwarazmians entered the almost empty city of the Israelites and in front of the Sepulchre of the Lord they disembowelled all the remaining Christians who had sought refuge inside its church. They decapitated the priests while they were in the act of officiating at the altars, saying, "Here we shed the blood of the Christian people where they have drunk wine in honour of their god who they say was suspended on the cross." Worse, we inform you with sighs and cries, that they laid sacrilegious hands on the Sepulchre of the Lord's Resurrection, defiling it in many ways. They totally destroyed its marble surround. As for the Mount of Calvary, where Christ was crucified, and its church, it is not possible to describe all the filthy means they employed to foul it. They removed the sculpted pillars that were placed in front of the Lord's Sepulchre as decoration and transferred them to the sepulchre of the most evil Mahomet where they stand as a sign of their victory and Christian shame. They violated the sepulchres of the blessed kings which were placed in the same church and scattered the bones as an insult to Christians. They irreverently profaned the most revered Mount Sion, polluted in ways unfit to relate the Temple of the Lord, the church of the Valley of Jehoshaphat, home of the Sepulchre of the Blessed Virgin, the church of Bethlehem and the place where the Lord was born. Their wickedness was greater than that of all Saracens who had always shown the utmost reverence for our holy sites during their numerous occupations of the land of the Christians. But these Khwarazmians were not content with all this; they aspired to take and destroy the whole land. These great misfortunes, which were enough to cause grief and bitterness in the heart of any righteous, zealous person of the Catholic faith, could no longer be tolerated. We were so incensed by these many grievous insults that we, the Christian people, by common consent, decided that the strength of the aforesaid sultans should be engaged in joint resistance to the Khwarazmians. On 4 October the Christian army with all its allies began to move along the coast from Acre, and proceeded via Caesarea and the other maritime regions. The Khwarazmians, however, anticipated our approach and retreated gradually until they fixed their camp at Gaza to await reinforcements to be sent to them by the sultan of Babylon, the leading light of sacrilege. These arrived in the shape of many thousands of armed men. Meanwhile, the armies of the Christians and the aforementioned sultans got nearer and nearer to them, and on the Vigil of St Luke we discovered their innumerable forces drawn up for battle at Gaza. Our leaders ordered our armies ready for the battle, whereupon the patriarch and other prelates, under the auspices of the Almighty God and the Holy See, gave remission of their sins to all who repented. Everyone sent heavenwards such signs of contrition and tearfulness! They considered death of the body as insignificant. They hoped for the reward of eternity, thinking that death in Christ was life. Even if destruction should come to our body because of our sins, we ought to have believed that the Almighty, who searches our hearts and knows our secrets, preferred to receive the gift of our souls rather than of our bodies. When both forces joined battle the Saracens on our side were completely routed by the enemy and put to flight, many of them being killed or taken prisoner. Consequently, only the Christians remained to fight. The Khwarazmians and Babylonians attacked the Christians together, and the latter battled against both, resisting bravely, like athletes of God and defenders of the Catholic faith, united in brotherhood by the same passion and beliefs. Alas, their numerical inferiority meant that they fell in battle, victims of the enemy blows. Of the convents of the house of the Temple, the Hospital of St John and Holy Mary of the Teutons only thirty-three Templars, twenty-six Hospitallers and three Teutonic brothers escaped, the others being killed or captured. The majority of the nobles and knights of the country were either captured or killed, not to mention the incalculable slaughter of the ballistarii and the foot-soldiers. As there has been no sign of the archbishop of Tyre, the bishop of St George, the abbot of St Mary of Jehoshaphat, the master of the Temple, the preceptor of St Mary of the Teutons, or of many other monks and clergy, the only real doubt concerning them is whether they died in the battle or were taken prisoner. We have not been able so far to establish the reality. The master of the Hospital and Count Walter of Brienne have been taken to Babylon with many other captives. We, the patriarch, whose sins have brought every calamity on us, have been deemed unworthy of martyrdom by the Lord and so have escaped half-dead to Ascalon with the nobles, the Constable of Acre, Philip of Montfort, and those knights and foot-soldiers who also escaped from the battle. Although having lost everything in the battle there is nothing to console us in such difficult circumstances we are doing what we can at the present. We have sent out letters and special envoys to the illustrious king of Cyprus and the prince of Antioch to ask and exhort them with all affection to send knights and armed men to the defence of the Holy Land at this moment of such dire necessity, though we do not know what they will do about it. At last returning to stay at Acre we found the city and the whole maritime province full of grief, wailing and endless suffering; there is not a single house or person without a death to mourn. As the past brought great grief, so the future brings great fear. The whole of [Eastern] Christendom that was acquired by the sword has had its support cut off and the number of its defenders depleted, the survivors are few and on the verge of extinction. As a result, the enemies of the Cross see their wishes fulfilled; in arrogant fashion they have pitched a two-mile long camp in the plain near the city of Acre. As there is no resistance to them they are roaming at will throughout the whole territory as far as the regions of Nazareth and Safad and distributing the land amongst themselves as though they owned it. They are appointing legates and bailiffs among the villas and the casalia of the Christians, collecting from the peasants the rents and tributes normally paid to the Christians. In fact the peasants have become enemies of the Christians and have *en bloc* joined the Khwarazmians. The result is that all the churches at Jerusalem have no other land in the Christian province at present except for fortresses which they have great difficulty in defending. It is even rumoured that the large number of Babylonians who are at Gaza are going to move on the region of Acre to join up with the Khwarazmians to besiege the city. On 22 November we received envoys and letters from the castellan and brothers of the Hospital in the fortress of Ascalon saying that the Saracen army from Babylon had already laid siege to the fortress and was blockading it. They requested urgent help and support from us and Christendom. In order that your piety may arouse your compassion over the ruin of the Holy Land for which the responsibility lies on the shoulders of us all, we have thought fit to inform you of Christ's cause, humbly entreating you to pray and devoutly worship the Most High so that He grant His compassion for the Holy Land. May He who consecrated the Holy Land with His own blood to redeem us all also show His pity and foresight in support of its defence. Dearest fathers, may you bring whatever positive advice and help you can to the problem so that you may earn a reward for yourselves in Heaven. You can be sure of one thing, that if help is not forthcoming in the next March passagium through the hand of God and of the faithful, the ruin and loss of the land will be quick. Since it would take too long to detail for you all our other needs and the overall state of the land in this letter, we are sending you our venerable father, the bishop of Beirut, and Arnulf, a man from the religious order of the Preachers, who will give you an accurate and full account of the true situation. We humbly entreat you all to receive with generosity and listen to the said envoys who have faced the great dangers of a winter crossing on behalf of the church of God. Given at Acre on 25 November in the year of the Lord 1244.

Source: Matthew Paris, *Chronica Majora*, Vol. 4, pp. 337–344, in Malcolm Barber and Keith Bate, eds., *Letters from the East: Crusaders, Settlers, and Pilgrims in the 12th–13th Centuries* (London: Routledge, 2016), 142–146.

70. Jamal ad-Din ibn Wasil (ca. 1282) on the Battle of Fariskur (April 8, 1250)

Introduction

The Battle of Fariskur, which effectively brought the Seventh Crusade launched by King Louis IX of France in 1248 to a humiliating end, was the culminating act of a two-month siege of French forces in the Egyptian city of al-Mansurah. In early February 1250 the French had taken the town with little opposition, only to find themselves imprisoned there by Egyptian Mamluk troops, who mercilessly harried the hungry defenders. At the beginning of April the French began a retreat back to the strategic port of Damietta, at the mouth of the Nile River, which they had taken in June 1249. Muslim forces followed, surrounded, and trapped them, capturing King Louis IX himself, his brothers, numerous high-ranking officers, and around 20,000 French officers and soldiers. The Arab chronicler Jamal ad-Din ibn Wasil, writing around 30 years later, triumphantly recounted this French humiliation at Arab hands, an event that subsequent Arab writers likewise loved to recall. To win freedom for himself and his fellow prisoners, Louis was compelled to negotiate a cease-fire, pay an immense ransom, and return the captured city of Damietta.

Document

On the night before Wednesday, 3 Muharram 648 [April 7, 1250], the resplendent night that had disclosed a great victory and a stupendous triumph, the Franks marched out with all their forces toward Damietta, which they counted on to defend them, and their ships began to move downstream in convoy. When the Muslims heard the news they set out after them, crossed to the Frankish bank of the river and were soon at their heels. As Wednesday dawned the Muslims had surrounded the Franks and were slaughtering them, dealing out death and captivity.

Not one escaped. It is said that the dead numbered 30,000. In the battle the Bahrite mamluks of al-Malik as-Salih distinguished themselves by their courage and audacity: they caused the Franks terrible losses and played the major part in the victory. They fought furiously: it was they who flung themselves into the pursuit of the enemy; they were Islam's Templars.

The accursed king of France and the great Frankish princes retreated to the hill of Munya, where they surrendered and begged for their lives. They were given assurances by the eunuch Jamal ad-Din Muhsin as-Salihi, on the strength of which they surrendered. They were all taken to Mansura, where chains were put on the feet of the king of France and his companions. They were imprisoned in the house where the secretary Fakhr ad-Din ibn Luqman was living, and the eunuch Sabih al-Mu'ázzami, a servant of al-Malik al-Mu'azzam Turanshah, son of al-Malik as-Salih Najm ad-Din Ayyub, was set to guard them; he had come with his master from Hisn Kaifa and had been promoted and shown great honor....

When agreement was reached between the king of France and the Muslims on the surrender of Damietta, the king sent to order his henchmen in Damietta to hand the city over. They, after objections, and the messengers coming and going between them and the king, finally obeyed, and handed the city over to the Muslims. The sultan's standards entered the city on Friday, 3 Safar 648 [May 1250], and were raised on the walls, proclaiming once again the rule of Islam. The king of France was set free and went, with the remains of his army, over to the western shore. The next day, Saturday, he went aboard and set sail for Acre. He stayed some time in Palestine and then returned home. So God purified Egypt of them, and this victory was many times greater than the first [in the Fifth Crusade], because of the large number of the enemy killed and captured; so many that the prisons of Cairo were full of Franks. The joyful news spread to all the other countries, and the public manifestations of joy and happiness were seen.

After the king of France left, the army marched straight to Cairo and entered the city. There, for many days on end, rolls of drums announced the glad tidings of the Muslim victory over the Franks and the recovery of the province of Damietta, pearl of Islam and frontier of Egypt. This was the second time that the infidels had taken it and lost it again and had fled in defeat and disarray.

Source: Jessalyn Bird, Edward Peters, and James M. Powell, eds., *Crusade and Christendom: Annotated Documents in Translation from Innocent III to the Fall of Acre, 1187–1291* (Philadelphia: University of Pennsylvania Press, 2013), 360–363. Reprinted with permission of the University of Pennsylvania Press.

71. The Siege and Capture of Baghdad (January–February 1258)

Introduction

In early 1258 the forces of the Ilkhanate Mongols besieged and sacked Baghdad, the seat of the Abbasid Caliphate for over 500 years. A contemporary Arab chronicler provided a vivid picture of the siege and its brutal aftermath. The caliph and most of his family and high officials were executed and many of the city's inhabitants were massacred as the conquerors indulged in an orgy of violence and looting. Much of the city was burned, including cultural monuments. Hulegu Khan, brother of the supreme Khagan Mongke Khan, directed the military campaign. The caliph, refusing to believe that Baghdad could be captured, had refused to come to terms with the Mongols. Even though the Mongols had already taken Persia, across the Middle East the taking of Baghdad shocked Muslims and Christians alike. The expansion of Mongol power seemed relentless and irresistible.

Document

The Year 656

We reported in the year 655 that Hülegü Khan had left his land and set out to Baghdad and that he had sent Bayğu to Irbil in order to cross the river Tigris there and then to approach Baghdad from the west, which he did. When the caliph heard of his arrival, he sent the lesser *dawīdār*, Muğahid al-Dīn Aybak, with a group of emirs to go to confront him. They crossed the Tigris, and when they had passed the bridge by the Basra gate by one parasang they saw the Mongol troops approaching like a spreading [swarm of] locusts. They met and engaged in battle on Wednesday, muharram 9. The Mongol soldiers feigned defeat purposefully and cunningly. The *dawīdār* pursued and killed a great number of them and carried their heads back to Baghdad. He continued to follow them until the end of the day. The emir Fath al-Dīn b. Kurr then advised him to stay put and pursue them, but he did not heed his advice. He was overtaken by nightfall and he had crossed the Bašīr canal in the region of Duğayl, so they spent the night there. When they awoke in the morning Mongol troops attacked them; and they fought a bloody battle. The troops of the *dawīdār* could not hold [against the attack] and were defeated. They ran fleeing back towards Baghdad but found that the Bašīr canal had been flooded overnight inundating the desert. The horses could not cross it and got stuck in the mud. Only those who had strong horses survived. Most of the soldiers threw themselves into the river Tigris, and so many of them died. Those who survived returned to Baghdad with the *dawīdār* in a most disgraceful way. The emir Bayğū and his troops followed them, killing them, capturing the majority, and taking all that they had as booty. They [*i.e.* the Mongols] took up quarters in the west side, which had been emptied from its inhabitants. They then began throwing arrows against the east side, and their arrows reached the house on the river bank. At this time, the caliph was sitting in his quarters (*riwāq*), and in his presence was his daughter named 'Arafa, a spoiled, temperamentful, and humorous child born of a Bedouin slave mother. An arrow entering from one of the widows hit and killed her. The caliph was distraught by what had happened and had the arrow brought in front of him; on it was written: "If God wanted his will carried out, he would strip the sensible of their senses". Upon this he ordered that the windows be made impermeable to the marksmen [arrow shooters], so screens were built out of wooden panels.

As to the sultan Hülegü Khan, he arrived behind the outskirt of Baghdad on muharram 12 [January 19], with soldiers whose numbers cannot be counted and whose supply lines never ended. The gates of the [city] wall had been closed, from which he understood that they were too weak to meet him. He ordered to dig a trench and to build a wall with the earth [from the trench] around Baghdad. Gates were then put in and the Mongol emirs positioned over them. They then built shields for the mangonels and set up the mangonels and catapults. Then they showed all they had, while the inhabitants observed them from the wall, upon which they had also installed mangonels. However, these were faulty and useless. The sultan [Hülegü Khan] then ordered to build a bridge to the south of Baghdad in order to prevent anyone from escaping to Wāsit. The bridge was to the south of the village of al-'Uqāb. The inhabitants of Baghdad were unaware of the bridge. When ships reached the bridge, the people on board were captured and killed. A great number of people perished there. On muharram 14 [January 21], the *wazīr*, Mu'ayyad al-Dīn b. al-'Alqamī, went out with a group of his mamluks and followers in the service of the sultan, calling the people of Baghdad to refrain from throwing arrows, saying: "Peace will soon take place, God willing, so do not fight," this while the Mongol soldiers exaggerated shooting arrows. A large number of them [*i.e.* Mongols] gathered close to Burğ al-'Ağamī that was located to the right of the Halba gate. They set up mangonels and proceeded to throw stones at it, so that they destroyed it. They climbed the wall on muharram 21 [January 28] whence they took over the city and ceased to throw arrows. The *wazīr* then returned to Baghdad on Sunday, muharram 17 [January 24], and said to the caliph: "The sultan has ordered that you come out to him." The caliph sent out his middle son Abū l-Fadl 'Abd al-Rahmān immediately, however, he was not accepted. The caliph and the *wazīr* then went out on Monday, muharram 18 [January 25], with a large group. As they reached the outside of the wall, they prohibited his companions from continuing with him and housed him in a separate tent. The lesser *dawīdār* Muğahid al-Dīn Aybak, Sulaymānšāh and the rest of the commanders went out on safar 1 [February 7]. Then followed the caliph's eldest son Abū l-'Abbās Ahmad on Friday, safar 2 [February 8]. The caliph reentered Baghdad on Sunday, safar 4 [February 10], accompanied by several Mongol emirs and Hwāğa Nasīr al-Dīn Tūsī. The caliph brought out for them money, precious stones, jewelry, brocade, fine clothes, gold and silver vases and other splendid objects. He then returned with the group outside the city wall where he spent the rest of the day. The sultan then ordered him to be put to death; he was killed on Wednesday, safar 14 [February 20]. His blood was not shed; instead he was put in a sack and trampled to death. He was then buried and traces of his tomb effaced. He was 46 years and 4 months old. His caliphate had lasted for 15 years, 8 months, and a few days. His son Abū l-ʿAbbās Ahmad was then put to death. He was born in the year 631[/1233]; his children were Abū l-Fadl Muhammad, Sitt al-Mulūk, and Rābiʿa, who was later married to Hwāǧa Hārūn, the son of the *sāhib al-dīwān* Šams al-Dīn al-Ǧuwaynī. She was born on the day of the Feast of the Sacrifice, 655. His middle son, Abū l-Fadl ʿAbd al-Rahmān was then put to death. He was born in the year [6]33[/1235] and had a son, Abū l-Qāsim Muhammad, and a daughter. As to the caliph's youngest son, Mubārak, and his sisters Fātima, Hadīǧa, and Maryam, they were not put to death, but they were imprisoned.

Hülegü Khan then appointed some emirs and entered Baghdad with a retinue and the deputy of the *ustād al-dār* [chamberlain] Ibn al-Ǧawzī. They went to the caliph's uncles and relatives who were in the *dār al-sahar* and *dār al-šaǧara*. They called them one by one, and so they came with their children and slave girls and were taken to al-Hallāl cemetery, opposite the tower, where they were all put to death. Then they killed lesser *dawīdār*, Muǧāhid al-Dīn Aybak, the *amīr al-haǧǧ*, Falak al-Dīn Muhammad b. ʿAlāʾ al-Dīn al-Tubrusī, the greater *dawīdār*, Šihāb al-Dīn Sulaymān Šāh b. Barǧam, Falak al-Dīn Muhammad b. Qayrān al-Zāhirī, Qutb al-Dīn Sanǧar al-Baklakī who was the *šihna* of Baghdad and had also led the people on the *haǧǧ* several years, ʿIzz al-Dīn Abqara, also the *šihna* of Baghdad, Muhyī l-Dīn b. al-Ǧawzī, the *ustād al-dār*, his son Ǧamāl al-Dīn ʿAbd al-Rahmān, his brother, Šaraf al-Dīn ʿAbd Allāh, and his brother Tāǧ al-Dīn ʿAbd al-Karīm, then the *šayh al-šuyūh*, Sadr al-Dīn ʿAlī b. Nayyār, Šaraf al-Dīn ʿAbd Allāh, his nephew, Bahāʾ al-Dīn Dāʾūd b. al-Muhtār, the *naqīb* al-Zāhir Šams al-Dīn ʿAlī b. al-Muhtār, Šaraf al-Dīn Muhammad b. Tāwūs, and finally Taqī l-Dīn ʿAbd al-Rahmān b. al-Tabbāl, the *wakīl* [representative] of the caliph.

He [Hülegü Khan] then ordered the heads of the *dawīdār* and the son the greater *dawīdār* as well as the head of Sulaymānšāh be brought to Mosul and hung outside the city wall. The inhabitants of Baghdad were put under the sword on Monday, safar 5 [February 11], and were subjected to 40 days of continuous killing, pillaging, enslavement; and they tormented the inhabitants using different ways to torture and extort their wealth with severe punishment. They killed men, women, youth and children, so that only a few of the city's inhabitants and those that had come to seek refuge there from the Sawād survived. An exception were the Christians. They were assigned guards (*šihna*s) to protect their houses. Many Muslims had sought refuge with them and were saved. There was a group of merchants in Baghdad that used to travel to Hurāsān and other places that had contacted the Mongol emirs earlier and obtained letters of safe conduct. So when Baghdad was conquered, they went to the emirs and returned with guards to secure their homes. Some of their neighbors also found refuge with them and were saved. This was the case with the house of the *wazīr* Muʾayyad al-Dīn b. al-ʿAlqamī, in which a great number of people were saved, as well as the houses of the *sāhib al-dīwān*, Ibn al-Dāmǧānī, and that of the chamberlain, Ibn al-Dawāmī. Other than in these places, nobody was safe unless they hid in wells or canals. A great part of the city, including the caliph's mosque and its surrounding were burnt, and the city was laid in ruins. The dead lay as mounds in the streets and the markets. Rain fell on them, horses trampled down upon them, their faces were disfigured, and they became an example to anyone who saw them. Then, peace was proclaimed and those that were left came out from hiding. Their color had changed, their minds shocked by the sight of the horror that no words can describe. They were like the dead emerging from their graves the day of resurrection fearful, hungry, and cold.

As for the inhabitants of Hilla and Kūfa, they had left together with their children and what they could carry of their belongings to al-Bataʾih. Their leading Shiites and theologians (*fuqahāʾ*) came together with Maǧd al-Dīn b. Tāwūs al-ʿAlawī to his highness the sultan and asked to spare their blood. He granted their wish and assigned them a contingent [to guard them]. They returned to their city and they sent to the people in al-Bataʾih informing them about that, and they returned to the city with their families and their belongings and gathered a lot of money to give to Hülegü upon which he granted them their lives.

As for Wāsit, the emir Bugʿatimur descended upon the city with his troops and reached the vicinity of Basra. He killed, pillaged, and took prisoners. The governors and their deputies (*al-wulāt wa-l-nuqabāʾ*) and the leading figures had gone to Basra and al-Bataʾih with their families and belongings, and hence they were saved.

It is said that there were more than 800,000 dead in Baghdad, not including the children thrown in the mud, those who perished in the canals, wells, and basements, and those who died of hunger and fear. Those that survived the killing were struck by an epidemic from breathing the odor of corpses and drinking contaminated water. The inhabitants frequently smelled onions because of the strong smell. The number of flies increased, filling the air; they would fall on food and spoil it. The inhabitants of Hilla, Kūfa, and Sīb used to bring food to Baghdad. These people benefitted from selling food for the [exorbitant] price of gemmed books, inlayed brassware or other valuable objects. Many of them enriched themselves this way.

Source: Hend Gilly-Elewy, "*Al-Hawādit al-ğāmi'a:* A Contemporary Account of the Mongol Conquest of Baghdad, 656/1258," *Arabica* 58, no. 5 (October 2011): 363–368. *Arabica* by Levi-Procenval, Evariste. Reproduced with permission of Brill Academic Publishers via Copyright Clearance Center.

72. Baybars (r. 1260–1277)

Introduction

Sultan Baybars of Egypt, of Caucasian origin, began his career as a Mamluk slave in Egypt, where he became a leading military commander. In 1250, he played a major role in defeating the crusading forces of King Louis IX of France at the Battle of Mansurah. After winning the Battle of Ain Jalut against the Mongols in 1260, Baybars reputedly assassinated Sultan Qutuz of Egypt and took his throne. The Western chronicler known as the Templar of Tyre retold this tale, alleging that the sultan's other emirs or military commanders were complicit in his death at the hands of Baybars. Egypt's new sultan proved to be a ruthlessly efficient ruler, capturing the principality of Antioch and most of the other remaining crusader citadels in the Middle East. He also encouraged the resumption of warfare between the Mongols of the Golden Horde and the Ilkhan Mongols of Persia and in 1277 defeated a Mongol army at the Battle of Abulustayn (Elbistan). Shortly afterward he died, reputedly by drinking poison intended for another recipient. This account of his rise to power suggests that even his Frankish enemies found it difficult not to admire him.

Document

This sultan [of Egypt] received news through his spies that the Tartars were widely dispersed across the region. So he left the plain of Acre and went out against them, and he appointed this same emir Baibars as captain of the *izeq,* that is to say of the vanguard, of his host. Baibars had been his mamluk, bought with his own money, and he carried the sultan's *arc de mot.* Because of this he was called *Bendocdar,* because among the Saracens an *arc de mot* is called a *Caus Bondoc.*

This Baibars was most hardy and valiant, and he went out first against the Tartars, and got the better of them, and mauled them badly and killed many. The Tartars rallied, but just then the sultan came up against them with his great army, and the battle between them was very fierce. The onslaught of the Saracens was so great that the Tartars were unable to withstand it, and they were put to flight, and their captain Kitbogha was killed in battle. Of those who fled the disaster, many were killed by the local peasants of the villages. Those who were able to rally themselves went to Armenia, where they found safety.

This battle took place on the third day of September in the said year [1260], on the plains of Tiberias.

After this battle, as you have heard, the sultan of Babylon prepared to go back to Egypt with great pomp and rejoicing. But this did not last long, for on the way back, the emir Baibars killed the sultan, with the approval of the other emirs (who were mostly in his confidence and of his faction). He and some of the emirs who were his associates immediately set off and went to Babylon, and entered the citadel of Cairo. There he found the person who commanded the citadel, called the Atabeg, who was named *Ferès Cataie* [Faris al-Din Aktay al-Mustarib], a wise and very old pagan, and one who was wise in the ways of the world. This Baibars let him know how the sultan had died along the way, and that he knew of no one amongst the pagans who was wiser or more worthy than he, and that he should be invested with the office. And thereupon he drew his sword and wanted to place it in his hand, after the manner of one being invested with a lordship. But the Atabeg was wise and did not wish to take the sword, and said that the sultanate would be better given to him than to anybody else that he knew of in the world, because he had such great valour and potential. Baibars replied, "Since it seems to you that I would be worthy to be sultan, and that you have made another sultan, called ... [lacuna] ... al-Malik al-Zahir," which translated comes out as "the visible king" (the sultans had a custom of calling themselves by whatever name they wished, other than their proper name, as the popes do).

And thus he was made sultan, and had it proclaimed throughout the land. And all the Saracens of the host came flocking in, one emir after another, coming to the new sultan to swear fealty to him and do him reverence.

Source: Paul Crawford, ed., *The 'Templar of Tyre': Part III of the 'Deeds of the Cypriots'* (Aldershot, UK: Ashgate, 2003), 38–39. Reprinted with permission from Taylor & Francis UK.

73. The End of the Latin Empire of Constantinople: The Taking of Constantinople (July 25, 1261)

Introduction

In 1261 the forces of Emperor Michael VIII Palaiologos, an able soldier and administrator who had become coruler of the Nicaean Byzantine state three years earlier, captured the city of Constantinople. Regaining the former imperial capital from the Latin overlords who had taken it in 1204 was one of Michael's major ambitions, which symbolized the regeneration of Byzantine power. A year earlier, Michael had already mounted an unsuccessful campaign against the city. By sheer luck, at least for the Byzantines, in 1261 most of Constantinople's defenders were absent on military operations elsewhere. Michael's general, Alexios Strategopoulos, took advantage of the unexpected opportunity. What had been intended as a preparatory move in pursuit of a long-term objective suddenly metamorphosed into a relatively peaceful takeover of the disputed city. The returning Latin forces took to their ships and evacuated those who wished to leave, including Emperor Baldwin II. This marked the end of the Latin Empire of Constantinople.

Document

The emperor [Michael VIII Palaiologos], having made arrangements, sent forth Alexios Strategopoulos, the caesar, to the western regions with some troops to join battle with the enemies of the Romans there. He gave orders that as he was passing through—since the road which leads to that place is near the city of Constantine—he should make an assault against it and the army should run up to its very gates so that they might instil terror in the Latins inside. But it happened then that something occurred by the providence of God. A large Latin hollow ship from Venice arrived at the city of Constantine and there was a young potentate on it whom they call a podestà. He was, as became apparent, an energetic man and bold in matters of war, urging all Latins in Constantinople to go to battle and advising that, 'We should not only stay inside the city, guarding the city and ourselves, but we should also take some action against the Romans so that they will not be altogether contemptuous of us in their attacks on us.' He persuaded them, therefore, to embark on as many triremes as they had and some other ships, such as lembadia and dromons, and to proceed against the island of Daphnousia, to see if they might be able somehow to bring it to terms and obtain a good share of its spoils. The city was therefore emptied of its men and it was administered and protected by women, children, and the man who supposedly ruled over it as emperor, Baldwin, with a modest number of men.

Suddenly, then, the caesar Alexios Strategopoulos approached the city of Constantine at night. Since he had with him also some men who had come from the city and who had precise information about it, he asked them and learned that there was an opening in the wall of the city through which an armed man could pass inside; he did not delay but set to work. A man passed through it and another followed him, and then another one, and so on up to 15 men, perhaps even more, entered the city in this manner. But since at the wall they found one of the men who had been entrusted with keeping watch, some of them climbed up, and taking him by the legs, hurled him out of the city. Others, taking hold of axes and breaking the bars on the gates, made the entrance to the city free for the army. It was in this way that the Caesar Strategopoulos and all the Romans and Scyths with him (for the army under him was composed of such men) came within the city. The people inside were shaken by the suddenness of the event; everyone sought his salvation as best he could. Some went to the monasteries and were dressed in monks' garments in order to escape slaughter, while women cowered at the openings of the walls and hid in dark passageways and concealed places. The ruler of the city, Baldwin, rushed to the Great Palace.

The Latins who had gone to Daphnousia and the podesta with them, knowing nothing of what had happened, were returning to the city, since they had not been able to accomplish anything against the island of Daphnousia—for God held them back. They got as far as the church of the Archgeneral of the Heavenly Forces, Michael, near Anaplous, without learning anything at all of what had happened. But when they arrived there and learned this, they rushed to come to the city. However, the Roman army, aware of this, set fire to the houses of the Latins which were by the shore and burned them—first the houses of the Venetians, then those of the other races—they call them campi. When the Latins saw the city in flames, striking their cheeks with their hands and taking as many people as they could into their triremes and other ships, they left, while one trireme went to the Great Palace and took Baldwin who had come close to being captured. And these things happened in this way, and by the providence of God the city of Constantine again became subject to the emperor of the Romans, in a just and fitting way, on the 25th of July, in the fourth indiction, in the 6769th year [1261] since the creation of the world, after being held by the enemy for 58 years.

Source: Ruth Mackrides, trans. and ed., *George Akropolites: The History* (Oxford: Oxford University Press, 2007), 375–376. By permission of Oxford University Press.

74. Hulegu, Ilkhan of Persia, to Louis IX of France (April 10, 1262)

Introduction

In 1262, soon after the Egyptian Mamluk sultan defeated Mongol forces at the Battle of of Ain Jalut, Hulegu, the ilkhan of Persia, dispatched envoys to King Louis IX of France, Pope Urban IV (1261-1264), and other prominent leaders of Christian Western Europe. Hulegu suggested that they and the Mongols should form an alliance against the Egyptians, proposing that Louis impose a naval blockade on the Mamluks so they could not escape when the Mongols launched a land offensive. Louis does not appear to have been responsive. This was by no means the last Mongol attempt to forge an alliance with one or more Christian powers against the Mamluks. Hulegu's son Abagha or Abaqa Khan, who married an illegitimate daughter of Byzantine emperor Michael VIII Palaiologos, made similar overtures to Pope Clement IV and King Edward I of England and also dispatched a legation to the Second Council of Lyons, summoned by Pope Gregory X in 1274. Western leaders were generally unreceptive. Both Louis IX and Edward I went on crusade, but neither did so in association with the Mongols.

Document

Some time ago God spoke to our forefathers through prophets concerning these last days variously and in many ways. He spoke to our grandfather Chinggis Khan through his blood relative Teb Tngri (a name which is interpreted as "prophet of God"), miraculously revealing to him events of future times, signifying by making known to the said Teb Tngri: "In the heavens I alone am the omnipotent God, and I appoint you ruler over all peoples and kingdoms, and you will become king of the entire globe, so that you will 'uproot and demolish, scatter and destroy, build up and plant.' I therefore proclaim to you that you ought to make known my commission to you to every generation and tongue and tribe of the north, south, east, and west. And you ought to declare it to every single region of the entire globe in which rulers or kings reign, governors govern, lordship is exercised and wherever horses' hooves may tread, ships may sail, messengers may arrive, and letters be heard, so that those with ears might hear, those hearing might comprehend, those comprehending might believe. In fact, anyone who does not believe in my divine commission ought to consider how those who do not believe in my mandates may be humbled afterward."

We, however, in the Might of the Everlasting Heaven (that is, of the living God) Hülagü Khan, commander of the army of the Mongols, zealous devastator of the faithless people of the Saracens, benevolent exalter of the Christian faith, vigorous conqueror of enemies, and assuredly the loyal friend of his allies the illustrious king of the Franks Louis and also the princes, dukes, counts, barons, knights, and others, send our greetings to each and every person in the entire kingdom of France in the

74. Hulegu, Ilkhan of Persia, to Louis IX of France

mercy of God. We made these things known to you by announcing the aforementioned revelation so that you might choose to ally with us without hesitation. For we are fulfilling the mandate of the living God, which if you reflected upon it attentively (as you ought), you would see that our power was conferred by the Lord Messiah himself (that is, the living God). However, lest we perhaps have caused a message of this nature to be written to you in vain, we will explain succinctly a few of the many things which in our times not long ago befell those of our opponents who did not believe in our mandates, or rather those of the living God.

For it pleased our majesty to begin by announcing the divine command to the kings and rulers of the East, that is: the king of the Kästimi, the king of the Naiman, the king of the Merkid, the king of Kirgis, the king of the Nangyaz, the king of the Kitai, the king of the Kangut, the king of the Töbed, the king of the Uihur, the king of Quamul, the king of Ulbäri, the leader of the Quarasan, the sultan of the Persians, the leaders of the Cumans, and in addition to the kings and sultans, princes and leaders of the southern region (that is, those ruling India and the surrounding areas), and also to the rest and countless others, whose names it would breed disgust to enumerate in writing. Contrary to the divine edict, they contemptuously resisted the lordship conferred upon us by God, and in their pride, trusting in their own armed forces, they were not the least bit afraid to draw up their battle lines against us in combat. And so that we might summarily pass over these matters, we caused these noxious pests to be destroyed by slaughter. We vigorously attacked their kingdoms, possessions, cities, and fortresses, laying waste each and every one of them as we pleased. However, some of their more prominent men, bolstered by our kindness, allied themselves to our excellency in a friendly manner.

And we spared them with all those who looked to them for leadership, and the more prominent of them rejoiced that without hesitation on our part they were permitted to remain there.

And in the other intervening years, the might of the living God leading the way toward the eastern zone, we sent a resolution first to the sultan of the Assassins, that is, the murderer of the circumcised. And we intimated to him that after previously reflecting upon the nature of our authority, he ought speedily to make himself subject to us. However, applauding their fortresses situated on the peaks of the loftiest mountains, and believing himself to possess a vast army and sufficiency of supplies, he instead rashly desired to do battle with us. But we erased the name of Rukn-ad-din [Khurshah] from this earth together with all of his generation, and also his most mighty fortresses, that is, the fortress of Maimundiz, the fortress of Alamut, and each and every fortress we razed to the foundations, nearly one hundred and fifty.

And once this was accomplished, we sent the foresaid mandate to the kings and princes of the circumcised, and fourteen kings and princes who were reported to be disobedient to us we caused to be destroyed with all their men in the same manner. In fact, when these things were completed, after some time had passed, it pleased us to send the original mandate, as described above, to the caliph of Baghdad. Contemptibly boasting of himself, he by no means hesitated to swear most firmly that he was assuredly the pope, head of the world for the race of the aforementioned Muhammad, that most wicked pseudo-prophet, and that he himself was the all-powerful creator for the aforesaid Muhammad and his entire race, that he had created the heaven and the earth and everything contained in them. And so trusting in his noble eminence and boundless riches, countless fortresses, and the most powerful hosts of his armies, he chose rather to battle against us than graciously to submit to our mandate. However, so that by publicly fighting against him we might subdue other rebels, by the power of the omnipotent God we slew from his forces by our reckoning two thousand of thousands fighters, omitting others, of whom there was a countless multitude. We commanded that a certain patriarch of the Nestorians dwelling in the aforementioned city of Baghdad with his bishops, monks, priests, clerics, and all of the same Christians be separated out from the Saracens one by one and that they be granted enlarged possessions and be permitted to reside in that city quietly and without molestation of their possessions.

After we hanged the sultan of Aleppo and Damascus, his terror-stricken son conveyed to us his wish to become our subject. Pleased by his submission, we sent officials to the same [ruler] throughout his lands and privileges written upon golden tablets, which were a sign of fuller preferment. However, after a little while, incited by the instigation of fate, he reneged on his solemn promise and contrary to himself, proved himself hostile to us. Therefore, when the same person fled, we vigorously assaulted his lands and fortresses and destroyed the cities of Aleppo and Damascus, Haman and Haniz, Baalbek, Harran and Baya. After capturing him in flight, we commanded his head to be hung above the gate of the city of Tabriz as an example to other traitors.

We understood without a doubt through John of Hungary that certain Latin slaves had come to the Holy Land for the sake of devotion, against the infidels on behalf of the holy city of Jerusalem. And we do not believe that we ought to conceal from your lordship that through the same John we caused them to be restored to their former liberty. Moreover, you ought to recognize that our excellency is not unacquainted with the fact that, although there are ever so many kings of the western Christians, you nonetheless are distinguished before all others by the splendor of your exceptional zeal, such that, of everyone who is reckoned worthy of the Christian name you are the most assiduously intent upon salvation. For although we had not already sent to you our messengers, as a sign of our particular friendship in honor of the most omnipotent and living God, you took pains to dispatch to our predecessor Güyük through your trustworthy messengers a portable chapel dedicated to the divine name as a special refreshment.

If at that time, as we said, you were not yet intent whatsoever upon these things which were signified by us, you were much more so intent concerning the rest, since not only by letters, but also by our trusty messengers we have taken care to visit Your Majesty. And touched previously by your friendship, we do not fail to believe that you wish to renew such an alliance with us by reforging a stronger bond between us. Moreover, we wished to reveal ourselves in a friendly manner to your lordship. And at first we believed the highest priest, the pope, to be the king of the Franks or the emperor. But after making a more careful investigation, we realized that he was a holy man praying devotedly to God on behalf of all peoples, taking the place upon earth of the Lord Messiah himself, son of the living God, and that he was the head of all those believing in Christ and calling upon him. And once we understood these things we commanded that the holy city of Jerusalem, detained for so long by sacrilegious men, be given back to him, with all the other things pertaining to that entire kingdom, through our faithful and devoted servant John the Hungarian, follower of the aforesaid Christian faith. And we believe without a doubt that this news has already resounded in your ears at various times.

However, because we are accustomed to retire more gladly to the cooler places of the snowy mountains during the summer heat, after the aforementioned cities of Aleppo and Damascus had been laid waste, and both provisions and forage were for the most part consumed, it pleased us to withdraw to the mountains of Greater Armenia for a little while. And we dispatched a few of our men to the aforesaid places in order to destroy the remnants of the Assassins' fortresses, in which they were stealthily hiding after contemplating the scarcity of their surviving numbers, and our men fell upon those Babylonian dogs when they crept out of their holes like mice. Yet some of our men, as their offenses deserved, were gnawed to pieces by the aforementioned mice, because they had been deceitful about obeying our commands by invading the possessions of the Franks. Although the vengeance wreaked upon those faithless men was not entirely displeasing to us, nor did it even inflict detectable damage upon us, nonetheless our intention is to fulfill utterly and in a short period our plan against the aforesaid Babylonian dogs of the infidel race, just as we also plan against other rebels. Because, however, if they are attacked by land they might find a refuge by the waters of the sea, as we understand it, we have taken pains to inspire Your Eminence so that you might exert your power from the opposite quarter upon the shores of the sea. For through your assiduous precaution with armed vessels in the sea you might check the aforesaid infidel dogs, enemies to us and to yourself equally, and you might take care to obstruct the aforesaid refuge, lest due to a lack of sea defenses they might be able to escape our assaults in any respect.

May you prosper in the Lord Messiah, that is, in the living God, eternally without end. If it pleases you, make known your intentions upon these and other matters with timely dispatch, through your special messengers together with ours. Given in the city of Maragheh in the tenth year of Hülagü's reign, in the Year of the Dog, on the tenth day of the month of April.

Source: Jessalyn Bird, Edward Peters, and James M. Powell, eds., *Crusade and Christendom: Annotated Documents in Translation from Innocent III to the Fall of Acre, 1187–1291* (Philadelphia: University of Pennsylvania Press, 2013), 342–347. Reprinted with permission of the University of Pennsylvania Press.

75. Abu l-Fida' on the Fall of Acre (June 12, 1291)

Introduction

The Western capture of the city of Acre in 1191 had given new heart to the embattled Latin states in the Holy Land, encouraging them to fight on. Its fall exactly a century later had the reverse effect, beginning a cascade of surrenders of major fortified crusader-held cities that effectively brought the end of the crusader kingdoms. The Arab conquerors exulted in their victory. As a young man, Abu l-Fida' (ca. 672/1273–732/1331), the Ayyubid lord of Hama, fought at Acre at around the level of a modern platoon leader. He later compiled a world history that included his own recollections of notable events of his own time. His account of the siege of Acre demonstrates the deep pride that many Arabs felt over the final expulsion of the Western crusaders from Palestine.

Document

In 690/1291 the sultan al-Malik al-Ashraf marched on Acre with his Egyptian troops and sent word to the Syrian army to join up with him and to bring the siege engines. The ruler of Hama, al-Malik al-Muzaffar, set out with his uncle, al-Malik al-Afdal and the whole of Hama's army for Hisn al-Akrad, where we collected a huge catapult called "the Victorious"; a hundred wagons were needed to transport it. (It was dismantled and the pieces distributed through the army. The part consigned to me was only one wagonload, since at the time I was an "emir of ten.") It was the end of the winter when we marched off with the wagons; rain and snowstorms struck us between Hisn al-Akrad and Damascus, causing great hardship, for the wagons were heavy and the oxen weak and dying of cold. Because of the wagons it took us a month to march from Hisn al-Akrad to Acre, usually an eight-day ride. The sultan ordered all the other fortresses to send catapults and siege-engines to Acre, and in this way a great number of large and small artillery concentrated under its walls, more than had ever before been assembled in one place.

The Muslim troops mustered at Acre in the first days of Jumada I 690/beginning of May 1291, and the battle raged furiously. The Franks did not close most of the gates; in fact, they left them wide open and fought in front of them in their defense.

The Hama army was in its usual position on the extreme right wing. This meant that we were on the seashore, with the sea on our right when we faced Acre. We were attacked by troops landing from boats protected by wood-faced frames covered with buffalo hides, from which they shot at us with bows and ballistas. Thus we found ourselves fighting on two fronts, the city and the sea. A ship came up with a catapult mounted on it that battered us and our tents from the sea. We were severely hindered by it, but one night when a fierce wind blew up, the ship was buffeted on the waves and the catapult broke up and was not rebuilt.

One night during the siege the Franks made a sortie, put the outposts to flight and reached the tents, where they became tangled up with the guy ropes. One knight fell into the latrine trench of one of the emir's detachments and was killed.

Our troops turned out in overwhelming numbers and the Franks turned tail and fled back to the city, leaving a number of dead accounted for by the Hama army.

The next morning al-Malik al-Muzaffar, lord of Hama, had a number of Frankish heads attached to the necks of horses we had captured and presented them to the sultan al-Malik al-Ashraf.

The blockade was continually reinforced, until God granted to the attackers victory over the city on Friday, 10 Jumada II [June 17, 1291]. As the Muslims stormed the city some of the citizens took to the sea in boats. Within the city was a number of well-fortified towers, and some Franks shut themselves inside them and defended them. The Muslims killed vast numbers of people and gathered immense booty. The sultan forced all those in the towers to surrender, and they submitted to the last man, and to the last man were decapitated outside the city walls. At the sultan's command the city was razed to the ground.

An amazing coincidence occurred: the Franks seized Acre from Saladin at midday on 17 Jumada II 587 [July 12, 1191], and captured and then killed all the Muslims therein; and God, in his prescience destined that this year it should be reconquered at the hand of another Saladin, the sultan al-Malik al-Ashraf.

After the conquest of Acre God put despair into the hearts of the other Franks left in Palestine; they abandoned Sidon and Beirut, which (the emir) ash-Shuja'i took over at the end of Rajab [end of July]. The population of Tyre also abandoned the city and the sultan sent troops to occupy it. They received the surrender of 'Atlit on the first of Shaban [July 30], and that of Tortosa on fifth of Shaban of the same year. So this sultan had the good fortune, granted to none other, to conquer without effort and without striking a blow these great, well-fortified cities, all of which were at his command demolished.

With these conquests the whole of Palestine was now in Muslim hands, a result that no one would have dared to hope for or to desire. Thus the whole of Syria and the coastal zones were purified of the Franks, who had once been on the point of conquering Egypt and subduing Damascus and other cities. Praise be to God!

Source: Jessalyn Bird, Edward Peters, and James M. Powell, eds., *Crusade and Christendom: Annotated Documents in Translation from Innocent III to the Fall of Acre, 1187–1291* (Philadelphia: University of Pennsylvania Press, 2013), 486–489. Reprinted with permission of the University of Pennsylvania Press.

76. Osman I (r. ca. 1299–1326), as Described by Nikolaos Sekoundinos

Introduction

Little that is definite is known about Osman I, the founder of the Turkish Ottoman dynasty. The first Turkish account of his life only appeared in the 15th century and remains decidedly vague. Around 1456 the Greek-born Nikolaos Sekoundinos, a skilled linguist and scholar who served both the Venetian state and the papacy as a diplomat and negotiator and had spent over a year as an Ottoman captive in 1430, produced a brief history of the Ottoman dynasty. He did so at the request of Bishop Aeneas Sylvius Piccolomini of Siena, who would become Pope Pius II two years later and wished to know more about the menacing Ottomans, following Sultan Mehmed II's recent capture and sack of Constantinople. Sekoundinos, an experienced, knowledgeable, and shrewd observer, who gave detailed accounts of the reigns of subsequent Ottoman sultans, was only able to provide a very general description of the career of Osman I.

Document

Six hundred years ago and more the nation of the Turks originated from the Scythians [Mongols], who had been accustomed to live across the Don, everywhere in Asia, in no specific capital, no cities, and no firm or long-term homes but wandered over the open fields; like a stream flowing from its spring, it seems to have spread. To illustrate the point, they first moved through the Pontus and Cappadocia and gradually infiltrated the other neighboring parts. In addition, the same point is argued by the similarity of [style of] life, customs, clothing, care of the body, way of riding horses and of using the bow, the identical way of waging war, their native discipline, and the greatest proof of all: the related languages and manner of speaking. At first they were a small band and operated like robbers, going on clandestine forays and trying to flex their muscles; they flocked together, as it were, and they occupied appropriate mountains and gorges, from which they could easily make sorties and, with inflated courage, they then waged war openly and were no longer afraid to compete with their immediate neighbors about the possession of fields.

Finally, with the passage of time, because the Greeks were careless about this matter, because Fate and the uncertainty of human affairs decreed it necessary, or because the Gods chose to command it otherwise, they succeeded with such amazing speed (in the opinion of all) that they occupied and subjugated not only the Pontus and Cappadocia but also Galatia, Bithynia, Pamphylia, Persia, farther Phrygia, the Cilicians, the Carians and that [part of] Asia that is known as Minor, all the way to the shores of Ionia and the coast of the sea named "Greek." They did not follow any one leader but there were various groups under numerous lords and commands, divided into factions.

And so about one hundred and fifty years later a certain Osman of this tribe, born to a modest and undistinguished family, hastily assembled private soldiers and with this small band, brought together through sedition, he was able to move about widely and launch plundering and devastating raids at will; he indiscriminately harried and ruined both Christians and members of his own tribe [Moslems] in war, spread destruction wherever he could, and began his annexations. Then the lords and princes of the Turks became upset by his desire to dominate and his passion to acquire riches and gradually turned against him; driven by their eagerness to prevail they stirred up so much trouble that they seemed prepared to enter upon an internal conflict and a civil war with all their might. Osman took advantage of this opportunity (which suited his customs and his desires), provided the suitable means, and, with the general approval of all those eager by nature to plunder and pillage and of those whose passion was to amass booty and spoils, he assumed power in a brief span of time. Some towns he seized by luck and others by force; some surrendered to him; quite a few he devastated and wiped out in order to create terror; thus he laid the foundations of a state that would grow and be envied in the future.

Source: Nikolaos Sekoundinos, "An Epitome on the Family of the Ottomans," in Marios Philippides, ed., *Mehmed II the Conqueror and the Fall of the Franco-Byzantine Levant to the Ottoman Turks: Some Western Views and Testimonies* (Tempe: Arizona Center for Medieval and Renaissance Studies, 2007), 57–59.

77. The Crusade of Smyrna (1344)

Introduction

The Crusade of Smyrna was the result of a Holy League proclaimed in 1343 by Pope Clement VI, with the objective of checking the piratical depredations of the Aydin Turkoman emirate led by Umur Pasha, which was based at the city of Smyrna on the Anatolian coast. A secondary objective of this enterprise, as recounted by an official history of the Knights Hospitaller written in the early 18th century, was to reform this military order, which was alleged to have abandoned both its original austere lifestyle and its mission of providing maritime protection to Christian vessels. The crusading forces succeeded in capturing Smyrna on October 28, 1344, and held it against repeated efforts by Umur Begh to retake it that continued until 1347. Responsibility for its defense was then handed to the Knights Hospitaller, who held the port until 1402, when the Mongol emir Tamerlane drove them out.

Document

Rhodes and the other isles of the order enjoyed a profound peace for several years. This security proved in the end prejudicial to the order: they fitted out fewer vessels; their sea affairs were neglected; most of the knights, finding no employment for their arms, returned into their own country; and several commanders, those especially of the kingdoms of the north, under pretence of this apparent calm, neglected to pay their responsions.... The people who used to see their predecessors like true religious, were soon scandalized at a life so entirely secular. Some good men complained of it to pope Benedict XII. Who had lately succeeded John XXII. They represented to him that the hospitallers, by inheriting the immense revenues of the templars, had like them fallen into luxury, and been infected with the dangerous and contagious corruptions that arise from great riches.... The pope, ... to reanimate the courage of the hospitallers, designed to bring them into a league he was forming against the Turks, who were growing every day more formidable; but his death, which happened a little time afterwards, prevented the execution of his project.

Some African corsairs having at the same time made descents upon the coasts of the isles of Cyprus and Candia, and ravaged those of the Archipelago, which were less able to make a defence, furnished occasion for new complaints against the hospitallers. They represented to Clement VI, successor to Benedict XII, that the Christians of the Levant were abandoned as a prey to the infidels, whilst most of the knights being retired in the west, either upon their commandries, or at the courts of Christian princes, were taken up with nothing but their pleasures, or the care of amassing wealth; and that the grand master and the knights that continued with him at Rhodes, secured from the insults of the Barbarians by the fortifications of the place, lived in an utter indifference of what passed at sea. What gave weight to these complaints and murmurs of the public, was, that some chaplains, religious of the order, and some of its Esquires or serving brothers, had sent secret memorials to the court of Avignon against the grand master and the knights, complaining, that in midst of the luxury and effeminacy wherein they lived, they were not ashamed to let them want cloaths, and the necessary sustenance of life. The pope teazed with these complaints, wrote about them to the grand master in sharp and reproachful terms.

"We are informed," says the pontiff to him, "by persons of merit and distinction, that it is the common sentiment of the clergy, and indeed of all the Christian world, that you and your brother companions scarce make any good use of the immense estates you possess, as well on this side as beyond the sea. Those who have the administration of them ride, say they, fine horses, make good chear, are richly dressed, are served in gold and silver, keep abundance of dogs and hawks for hunting and game, lay up great treasures, give little alms, and neglect the defence of the Christians, especially of those beyond sea...."

The pope in the same letter adds, that he had advice, the Turks were making great preparations for the conquest of all Romania. 'Tis not clear, whether by that term he meant only the province which bears that name, or whether, according to the Turkish and Arabian use of the expression, he comprehended under that name all the states which composed at that time what they called in the east the Roman empire; an enterprise, says the pontiff, which would draw along with it the utter ruin of the Christian religion. The pope added farther, that in order to prevent so terrible a calamity, he had formed the plan of a naval armament, composed of the gallies of several princes, that should keep the sea, and might join and act in concert, either to hinder the descent of the Barbarians, or to carry succours to such places as should be attacked; that the king of Cyprus had agreed to furnish for his quota four gallies, and the republic of Venice five; that he ordered the knights of Rhodes to put six to sea, and the holy see would maintain four. "Though," says the pontiff, "we have had remonstrances made us by several of our brethren the cardinals, that your order was rich and powerful enough, not only to save the holy see the charges of this armament, but also to put a whole fleet to sea at their own expence; and that there was in your treasury more gold and silver than could be found in that of any Christian prince whatever, without reckoning the considerable sums which your priors and commanders are scraping together for themselves." The pope concluded this letter with telling the grand master, that the church was but sorrily edified with the particular enmities of the knights between one another; adding at last, that complaints had been made to the holy see that they were negligent in providing for the subsistence of the chaplains and serving brothers.

Tho' the grand master saw plainly they had imposed on the pope's zeal for religion, by the exaggeration made of the riches of the order, yet, like a true religious, he resolved to obey. They fitted out immediately six gallies in the port of Rhodes; and for their maintenance and expence, he, by the advice, and in concert with the sovereign council, appropriated a particular fund . . . arising from the succession of commanders deceased, viz. the rights of mortuaries and vacancies.

The grand master and council made afterwards several regulations for the reformation of manners, especially in respect to the provinces of the west....

The pope was exceedingly moved and affected with the grand master's ready obedience; and to show the like generous care of the common cause, he fitted out the four gallies that he was to furnish for his quota, to which those of the king of Cyprus, the order of St. John and republic of Venice joined themselves, under the general command of a Genoese captain, Gingarria by name. This little fleet kept the sea all the summer, but without attempting any thing answerable to their strength, and the expence the allies were at for this armament. The Genoese general, more mindful of his interest than his glory, made use of his authority to load the gallies with divers sorts of merchandize, and employed the money confided to him for the charges of the campaign, to his own private advantage. Henry, titular patriarch of Constantinople, legate of the holy see, mounted on board the admiral galley, and in that quality had the supreme command, according to the politics of the popes, who always assumed it in those wars that were raised for the sake of religion. This prelate, in imitation of the Genoese general, acted more like a merchant than a delegate of the sovereign pontiff. The year following, the allies, full of indignation against the Genoese, chose for their general brother John de Biandra, knight of Rhodes, prior of Lombardy, who had the particular command of the gallies of the order.

The new general formed a design worthy of his valour. The port of Smyrna, a considerable city of Anatolia, served often for a retreat to the Turkish corsairs who were masters of the city. Biandra having, besides the soldiers on board his fleet, taken in at Rhodes a great number of troops commanded by valiant knights, formed the siege of the place and took it by storm. Some historians pretend that he took only the castle, which was seated by the sea side, and commanded the entrance of the port. All the soldiers in the fort both Turks and Arabians, were cut to pieces. The grand master having advice of it, knowing the importance of that fortress, sent fresh troops immediately thither, with arms and provisions to reinforce the garison. There are still to be seen upon the gates of the castle, tho' fallen to ruin, the arms of the church, which were placed there as a monument of this conquest, the whole honour of which they ascribed to the pope, as head of the league, tho' the knights of Rhodes had the greatest share in it. A Turk called Morbassan, who commanded in the higher town and over all the country, attempted a year after to drive the Christians out of the place. He laid siege to it, but after three months spent in smart attacks and a gallant defence, he made a feint of abandoning his enterprise, or at least of turning the siege into a blockade. The greatest part of his troops drew off, and only a small number was left in his camp. The Christians having notice of his retreat, made a furious sally, easily forced the intrenchments, which were ill defended, broke into the camp, and put to the sword or took prisoners all that made resistance, or did not save themselves by a speedy flight. They celebrated this victory upon the same spot on which they had obtained it, with the sound of military instruments, with feastings, and a joy which was so much the more dangerous as the enemy was not far off.

Morbassan, whom they fancied a great way up in the country, but who only lay concealed with his troops behind the neighbouring mountains, having notice of it by certain signals, marched down, and finding the Christians in disorder, made a cruel slaughter of them in his turn. The greatest loss fell upon the knights of Rhodes: and the pope's legate who was come into the Camp to partake in the public joy, lost there his life, as well as most of the officers and ecclesiastics of his household. The knights who escaped the fury of the Barbarians got back to the fort, and held it out, by help of a new reinforcement, against all the efforts of the Turks and other infidels.

The dismal news of this disgrace, passing into Europe, the pope to repair it published a crusade with all the indulgences annexed to the first. . . . The great business was to find out funds to supply the expence of so long an expedition.

Source: Abbé René-Aubert de Vertot, *The History of the Knights Hospitallers of St. John of Jerusalem*, Vol. 2 (Edinburgh, UK: R. Fleming, 1757), 120–126.

78. Philippe de Mézières on the Fall of Alexandria (October 10, 1365)

Introduction

The crusade that resulted in the capture of Alexandria in 1365 owed its success to two men, both of whom were close to obsessed with the desire to fight and overcome the Ottoman Turks. One was King Peter I of Cyprus, who since boyhood had wished to organize a crusade. The second was the papal legate Peter Thomas, to whom the pope had assigned responsibility for the remaining Christian holdings in the eastern Mediterranean. Their joint efforts succeeded in overcoming initial indifference and bringing together a military force strong enough to take the city of Alexandria in 1365. Those who took part gained immense booty. The sequel proved to be embarrassing when the victorious army, which included contingents from the Knights Hospitaller of Jerusalem and Rhodes, declined to stay and hold Alexandria indefinitely. Even the Knights Hospitaller preferred to use the profits they had gained from Alexandria to shore up their existing commitments. The French soldier of fortune Philippe de Mézières, chancellor of Cyprus since 1360 and a friend and admirer of both King Peter and Peter Thomas, wrote a biography of the latter in which he described the passionate commitment of both monarch and churchman to this undertaking, his participation in the siege of Alexandria, and the profound disappointment of king and legate when the conquest of Alexandria proved impermanent.

Document

The king of Cyprus visited the emperor of the Romans and other western kings and princes for close on a year and a half [in 1363–1364], with great dangers, [hard] work, and expense, constantly asking for assistance for the passage. But alas, the world was sunk in sin and governed by the envy of princes, and he found nobody who would praise God and be concerned about the passage. There were lots of words but no deeds. Nobody, alas, had pity on the Holy Land, or sympathized with its shame. They all made excuses to the king of Cyprus, and sent him away empty-handed and tearful. Then the king, despairing of

Christendom's princes, the deadline having long since elapsed, without any help save that of God, returned to Venice with just a few men, all having lost hope for the crusade. At Venice he was splendidly received....

Then [in April 1365] the king, rejoicing for the crusade's sake that peace [between Venice and Genoa] had been made, assembled at his own expenses all the faithful whom he could find, without the help of a single Christian prince or community. The legate piously preached to the king's little army on the mystery of the cross and the Lord's passion, and gave the venerable sign of the cross to all who were setting out. He absolved sinners, and with continual prayer and through the divine office, he piously and devoutly instructed those setting out in the dictates of the faith. For his part, the king was profoundly moved by the legate's constant encouragement. Trusting in God, he made a public vow that he would never return to his kingdom until he had led his army into the territory of the enemies of the faith, even if it cost him his life. Then those who scorned the passage, seeing the king's preparations and the legate's firm resolve, were taken aback and to some extent fell silent.

[On October 9, 1365, the crusading forces arrived at the Old Harbour of Alexandria.]

I cannot refrain from mentioning the vigour of my father the legate and his ardent desire for martyrdom. The Saracens had gathered their forces together and deployed them astutely and energetically along the shoreline outside the gate, and were yelling and awaiting our arrival on land. Bursting with enthusiasm, and ignorant of the reason for the delay in our engaging the enemy, the legate shouted at me: 'My brother, most sweet chancellor, let's get going with our galley in memory of the Lord's passion. Let's get onto land, because I can't stand the way they insult the cross. Let's smash the cross.' I was struck by his daring and his willingness to die for Christ, and no little impressed by it. Smiling, I replied: 'My father, this is not the hour of your death, not the hour to disembark; with respect I will not do it.' He was more saddened than I can describe. But I was in charge of my father's galley, and I had to comply with the king's commands.

[On October 10, 1365, the Christian forces took Alexandria, with the customary bloodshed, looting, and brutality of fighting in the fourteenth century. The aftermath proved more problematic.]

When the city had been taken, the most victorious king held a general council to discuss its defence, but found few or no helpers and servants of God. In tears the king piously implored knights of every rank to stay with him, but they refused. He found that they were discarding their crosses and awaiting departure. Anybody who had witnessed my father the legate grieving, weeping, almost beside himself, appealing to Heaven, beseeching the knights to stay, and heard them refusing, would certainly have lamented the scandal to the Christian faith. He showed clearly how God's honour, the good of Christendom, and the acquisition of the city of Jerusalem, [all] hung on the retention of Alexandria; and with countless arguments he portrayed the harm and shame which would ensue for the Christians should they abandon [the city]. Some in our army did readily volunteer to stay with the king and the legate, but by the Devil's work the majority stood in their way. What more is there to say? Their hearts were hardened and they were overwhelmed by wickedness. The grief-stricken king and the legate, who was almost dying of anguish, were overcome by the wicked. They decided on withdrawal. They had no trust in God and no confidence in His might, and entirely forgot his incredible victories.

[Following this disappointment, Peter Thomas wrote to Pope Urban V and the Holy Roman Emperor Charles IV, condemning the reluctance of the Christian powers and peoples to make the sacrifices necessary for a holy war against the Muslims, and urging the Western world's two foremost religious and secular leaders to make renewed efforts to accomplish this. His letter began with an appropriate quotation from the Christian Bible's Book of Isaiah. De Mézières reproduced this letter in his biography of Peter Thomas.]

"Hear, O heavens, and give ear, O earth, for the Lord has spoken. I have nourished and brought up children, and they have rebelled against me. The ox knows his own, and the ass his master's crib, but Israel knows me not." [Isaiah 1:2–3.] "Israel seeing God" means the people of the Christians, which had witnessed [His] miracles in a sea crossed without danger, in the flight of a defeated people, and in the capture of a city virtually without hindrance. "Hear, O heavens, and give ear, O earth," refers to the prelates who rule the Church and the princes who have charge of the earth in the Lord's name.

For your part, high priest, you should proceed by exhorting the people, granting indulgences, and contributing from the Church's treasure. In a sense this disaster is your fault, because if enough people had come, if the Church had done enough, there would have been no excuse for [failing to] hold on to [Alexandria]. Behold, my lord, our disgrace in the abandonment of the city. Yet consider God's power, for although we were few, indeed none by comparison with the enemy, the Lord handed over to you a city surrounded by walls and embellished with towers. This was home to Egypt's riches and Egypt's delights, and here the Agarenes suffered a terror which they will never forget. Plead opportunely and inopportunely, because there remains no option for us except to raise our eyes to you. Assist us, and quickly, because fear has weakened the race of the Agarenes, the present time favours our people, and God is helping us.

As for you, unconquered emperor, the eyes of all Israel turn to you for help, and you must take the matter in hand. King of kings, and lord of lords, to you God gave wisdom greater than Solomon's, power greater than Pharaoh's, and, so they say, money enough. The kings will provide you with help, the Venetians, Genoese and other maritime [powers] sufficient shipping, and the lord pope the assistance of indulgences. The people, touched by devotion, will co-operate, the clergy by fasting and praying, the whole world by donations. Lord, put forth your power and come to free us. Free the holy city of Jerusalem which has been a slave-girl for such a long time. She calls, calls, calls to you, and her cry reaches the ears of the Lord of Sabaoth. If you do not hear it and listen to it, I fear, and not just me but many others with me, that the Lord will be angry with you, and that you will perish before your time.

Source: J. Smet, ed., *The Life of Saint Peter Thomas by Philippe de Mézières* (Rome, 1954), 121, 124, 130, 133–134, 139–140, in Norman Housley, ed., *Documents on the Later Crusades, 1274–1580* (Houndmills, UK: Macmillan, 1996), 86–89.

79. Murad I and the Battle of Kosovo (June 15, 1389)

Introduction

The beginning of Ottoman efforts to seize and rule the Balkans came in the late 1380s, when Sultan Murad I waged war on Serbia, events recounted by the chronicler Doukas, a member of a Byzantine noble family with family ties to the Ottomans, with whom his grandfather Michael Doukas had taken refuge in 1345 during the Ottoman Civil Wars. Beginning in the early 1420s, the younger Doukas, who was fluent in Italian and Turkish as well as Greek, served as an official functionary and diplomat for the neighboring Italian enclaves of New Phokaia and Lesbos, which became Ottoman targets following the fall of Constantinople. He died in 1462 during the Turkish siege of Mytilene, leaving unfinished the last sentence of his history of the final decades of the Byzantine Empire. The history included a brief account of Murad I's invasion of Serbia, a campaign during which the sultan himself died at the Battle of Kosovo in 1389. For several centuries his successors continued his initiative to subjugate the Balkans.

Document

Since [Sultan Murad I] now held practically all the lands of the Romans, he advanced to the Triballi [Serbs]. He destroyed many of their fortresses and towns and took their inhabitants captive; he then transported them to the Asiatic shore over the straits of the Chersonese. When Lazar, the son of Stefan, kral [king] of Serbia, and himself kral of Serbia at that time, beheld these things, he assembled all his forces and joined battle with the tyrant; many fell on both sides [June 15, 1389]. There took place afterwards an incredibly novel stratagem. A young Serb nobleman, who was more daring than any other man of his time, separated himself from the Christian phalanx, as though he were deserting, and fell into the midst of the Turkish ranks. When the Turks immediately laid hands on him, he called out the ruler's name, saying, "I wish to see him and tell him something secretly so that he can win this battle; this is the reason I have deserted." They presented him to the ruler. As Murad motioned with his hand for the youth to approach, he rushed forward and, when near enough, mortally wounded Murad by plunging a sword into his heart; he then was hacked to pieces by Murad's axe-bearers and bodyguards.

When the Turks beheld this unexpected and novel deed, they could not allow such an evil suddenly to befall them before their eyes without retaliating. They conceived a clever and very deceptive plan. Pitching a tent in the center of the battle formations, they placed the half dead Murad within and, undaunted by the many dangers, fought their way like rabid dogs to the front ranks. The Serbs, on the other hand, were ignorant of the great deed accomplished on their behalf by the brave youth which had resulted in the loss to the Turks of their ruler. Because their worthy commander was losing the anticipated victory, they despaired and faintheartedly resisted the Turks and the battle came to an end. Lazar was captured with most of the nobles. The Turks led Lazar and all his subordinates into the tent where Murad lay breathing his last and slew them. Thus both they and Murad suffered death together.

Neither the right wing nor the left was aware of what was happening since these actions took place in the rear. The commander of the right wing was Sawdji, the eldest of Murad's sons, while the left wing was led by his second son Bayazid, terrifying and mighty above all others. Bayazid was recalled by Murad's chief counselors, called viziers in their tongue, who revealed to him what had happened and showed him his father's corpse. Neither weeping nor displaying any signs of mourning, he summoned Sawdji his brother, pretending that he was being summoned by their father to discuss more effective tactics. Sawdji, ignorant of what had happened, came willingly to see his father, but was seized by his brother, who gouged out his eyes.

Bayazid was acclaimed ruler of the Turks. He was a feared man, precipitate in deeds of war, a persecutor of Christians as no other around him, and in the religion of the Arabs a most ardent disciple of Muhammad, whose unlawful commandments were observed to the utmost, never sleeping, spending his nights contriving intrigues and machinations against the rational flock of Christ.

On assuming the rule after the fall of Lazar and Murad, as mentioned above, this Bayazid first made the Serbs subjects and tributaries, taking hostages and making treaties. He stipulated that Stefan, Lazar's son, consecrated kral by Serbia following that calamity, accompany Bayazid when on campaign with his Serbian troops. He further stipulated that Stefan give him in marriage his sister Maria, Lazar's daughter, a tender virgin, as well as many talents of silver from the silver mines of Serbia.

Source: Doukas, *Decline and Fall of Byzantium to the Ottoman Turks,* trans. and ed. Harry J. Magoulias (Detroit: Wayne State University Press, 1975), 60–62. Reprinted with permission.

80. Bayezid I (r. 1389–1403)

Introduction

The Ottoman ruler Bayezid I was a major threat to all his neighbors, expanding his dominions into Christian and Muslim territories alike. His ambitions included the taking of Constantinople from its Byzantine rulers who, though in effect vassals of the Ottomans since the 1340s, nonetheless retained a degree of autonomy. Bayezid, as his Christian opponents recognized, possessed great talents, determination, and physical stamina, all of which facilitated his ruthless efforts to expand Ottoman power. Only in 1402 would he meet his match in the person of the Mongol khan Tamerlane. The accomplished Greek diplomat Nikolaos Sekoundinos, writing half a century later on the Ottoman dynasty at the request of the future Pope Pius II, provided an accurate assessment of Bayezid's character and attainments.

Document

... Bayezid became the sole ruler; he was brash, had a passion to achieve greatness, and was bold in his hard tasks; he exhibited cunning in adversity and was indefatigable in bringing matters to completion; he was sharp and perceptive of advantageous situations, swift to action, courageous, strong, warlike, restless in peace, hungry for glory, ready to embrace danger, and admirably skilled in deceiving his enemy. His speciality was to wipe out his enemy by employing stratagems and ambush; by contrast, he could predict and evade his enemy's plans skillfully and wisely. His superior intellect, endurance, talent, discipline, way of life, habits, as well as fortune's favor so extended and magnified the boundaries of his new state in a brief span of time that he occupied and brought under his control all of Thrace, Thessaly, Macedonia, Phocis, Boeotia, and Attica; in addition, he reduced and weakened the Mysians [Bulgarians], the Illyrians [Albanians], and the Triballians [Serbs] with frequent raids, sieges, and battles. He conquered some and exacted annual tribute from others; from others he demanded soldiers for his expeditions and weapons. He added so many rich provinces to the kingdom of his father and grandfather. He finally plundered the countryside and the pleasant suburbs of Byzantium [Constantinople], the imperial city, which he tormented with such a long and cruel siege that the emperor, with almost all the princes of the state, set out for a voyage abroad to seek help from the faithful [Christians] in Italy and even went so far as to reach Upper Gaul [France]. Abandoned, unprotected, and driven by extreme famine and the most cruel war which increased daily as the enemy pressed his advantage on all sides, the citizens began to negotiate a surrender; they would have incurred widespread death and would have become subjects to a most cruel enemy, if that renowned Tamburlaine, the overlord of the Scythians [Mongols] had not appeared like a torrent which destroys and devastates everything in its forceful path, sweeping along its path Bayezid himself with all his troops and forces; he [Tamburlaine] summoned him [Bayezid] to fight in Asia [Minor]; the battle lines were formed; there were many standards; and the two sides fought courageously during that famous battle. Bayezid had less strength and his courage proved lacking; he lost the battle, was defeated in an enormous slaughter, was finally released, and died shortly thereafter.

Source: Nikolaos Sekoundinos, "An Epitome on the Family of the Ottomans," in Marios Philippides, ed., *Mehmed II the Conqueror and the Fall of the Franco-Byzantine Levant to the Ottoman Turks: Some Western Views and Testimonies* (Tempe: Arizona Center for Medieval and Renaissance Studies, 2007), 65–71.

81. The Crusade of Nikopolis (September 25, 1396)

Introduction

The Crusade of Nikopolis, one of the last large-scale crusades of the Middle Ages, ended in humiliation at the Battle of Nikopolis. By the 1390s the Byzantine Empire was under ever-increasing pressure from Ottoman sultan Bayezid I, who seemed likely to capture the Byzantine capital of Constantinople in the near future. The pope urged Western rulers, nobles, and fighting men to undertake the rescue of the beleaguered Christians of the Near East. A multinational force of Christian troops from Hungary, Bulgaria, Walacia, Croatia, Germany, England, France, and Burgundy plus a Venetian naval contingent laid siege to the Danubian fortress of Nikopolis, lost by Bulgaria to the Ottomans in 1390, with the objective of winning it back. The European forces included some of the leading nobility of Western Europe as well as the king of Hungary. The French chronicler Sir John Froissart recounted how Ottoman sultan Bayezid I stealthily brought up his army to attack the besiegers, who gave battle before the troops of the king of Hungary could arrive to reinforce them. Overwhelmed by a numerically superior Turkish army, the would-be crusaders went down to defeat, with many killed and others captured and held for ransom, while Bayezid proclaimed his intention of overrunning all of Europe.

Document

The Christians were besieging Nicopoli, and as yet nothing had been heard of any assistance from Bajazet. During the whole summer he had been busily employed in raising a large army of Saracens and infidels, and had even sent to Persia for succor. These, to the amount of 200,000, crossed the Hellespont, and advanced so secretly, that they were close to Nicopoli before the Christians knew that they had begun their march. Bajazet was as well acquainted as most persons with the stratagems of war, and marched to raise the siege in the following order. His army was drawn up in the form of a harrow, and occupied about a league of ground; in front of the main body were 8,000 Turks, to mask the body of the army, which was divided into two wings, and Bajazet was in the midst of the main body.

It happened on the Monday preceding Michaelmas Day in the year 1396, about ten o'clock, as the King of Hungary and his lords were seated at dinner, news was brought that the Turks were at hand. This was agreeable information to many who were desirous of arms; they instantly arose, pushed the tables aside, and demanded their horses and armor. Being somewhat heated with wine, they hastened to the field, and banners and pennons were displayed. The banner of the Virgin Mary was unfurled, and the guard of it given to that valiant knight, Sir John de Vienne, admiral of France. The French were the first in the field, and seemingly fearless of the Turks, for they were ignorant of their immense numbers, and that Bajazet commanded them in person. The King of Hungary sent to entreat them not to begin the battle before they heard from him again; but the Count d'Eu, the constable of France, was impetuous, and determined to fight the enemy.

The infidels were now fast approaching, and in such numbers that the Christians became completely surrounded, and found it impossible to retreat. Many knights and squires, who were used to arms, knew that the day must be lost; nevertheless they advanced. The French lords were so richly dressed out in their emblazoned surcoats, that they looked like little kings; but, as I was told, when they met the Turks they were not more than 700 in number. Had they waited for the Hungarian army, they might, perhaps, have gained the victory; to their pride and presumption was the whole loss owing—a loss which was so great, that never, since the defeat of Roncesvalles, when twelve peers of France were slain, did the French suffer so considerably. However, before they were overcome they made a great slaughter of the Turks; indeed, they defeated the van battalion, and put it to flight, pursuing it into a valley where Bajazet was posted with the main army. The French would have returned, but could not, for they were now enclosed on all sides. The battle raged with fury, and lasted a considerable time.

The King of Hungary, when informed of the engagement, was very angry that his orders had not been obeyed: "We shall lose the day from the vanity of the French," he said to the Grand Master of Rhodes, who was beside him. "If they had waited for us to join them, we should have had sufficient strength to cope with the enemy." As he thus spoke, he looked back, and saw his men flying panic-struck, and the Turks pursuing them. It was a most unfortunate day for the Hungarians and French. As they fled, in the greatest confusion, the Turks followed, killing them, or making prisoners at pleasure. God assisted the King of Hungary and the Grand Master of Rhodes, for, on arriving at the banks of the Danube, they fortunately found a small vessel, into which they entered, and, by means of it, crossed to the opposite shore.

Sir William de la Tremouille and his son displayed great feats of valor before they were slain. Sir John de Vienne, also, who bore the banner of our Lady, in spite of his deeds of arms, was killed, grasping the banner in his hands, and was thus found after the battle. Very many of the French were saved from the extreme richness of their armor—they were dressed like kings: and the Saracens and Turks, who are very avaricious, thought, by saving their lives, that they should gain large ransoms; for they believed them to be much greater lords from their appearances than they really were. The Count de Nevers was made prisoner, as were also the counts d'Eu and de la Marche, the lords de Coucy, Boucicaut, and others. The battle lasted three hours; more were killed in the pursuit than in the battle, and numbers were drowned. Happy indeed was he who could escape from such danger by any means. When the business was over, the Turks, Persians, and others retired to the tents and pavilions, which they had conquered from the Christians, and enjoyed themselves.

Bajazet dismounted at the sound of many minstrels, at the principal tent that had belonged to the King of Hungary, which was very large and richly adorned. When he was disarmed, to cool and refresh himself, he sat on a silken carpet in the middle of the tent, and sent for his principal friends to chat and joke with them. He began the conversation by saying that he would now conquer Hungary, and all the rest of Christendom; and that, as he was descended from his blood, he would reign like Alexander of Macedon, who for twelve years governed the whole world. He then gave three orders: first, that everyone who had made prisoners should produce them before him next day; secondly, that the dead should be carefully examined, and the nobles and great lords set apart and left untouched until he had seen them; thirdly, that exact inquiries should be made after the King of Hungary, that he might know whether he was dead or alive.

When Bajazet had refreshed himself he resolved to visit the dead on the field of battle, where, to his great surprise and anger, he found that the victory had cost him dear; for where one Christian lay dead, there were thirty of their enemies around them. The next morning, before Bajazet was risen, great numbers came to his tent to learn his will respecting the prisoners. It had been rumored that he intended having them all put to death without mercy; this, however, was not the case: his orders were, "Let those alone be spared who are nearly related to the King and willing to pay for their liberty a great sum of money, and all others be put to death."

Shortly after, the Sultan made his appearance to his people before the tent; who, bowing down, made him obeisance. The army was drawn up in two wings. The Sultan with his nobles, the Count de Nevers, and all those prisoners who were to be spared, were in the centre; for he would they should witness the execution of their companions, which the Saracens were eager to perform. Many excellent knights and squires of France and other nations were brought forth in their shirts one after another before Bajazet, who eyed them a little as they were led on, and as he made a signal they were instantly cut to pieces by men waiting for them with drawn swords. Such was the cruelty of Bajazet this day, when upward of 300 gentlemen were piteously murdered. It was a cruel case for them to suffer for the love of our Saviour, Jesus Christ, and may he receive their souls!

Source: Sir John Froissart, *Chronicles of England, France, Spain and the Adjoining Countries,* trans. Thomas Johnes, rev. ed. (New York: Colonial Press, 1901), 158–161.

82. The Battle of Ankara (July 20, 1402)

Introduction

Ottoman sultan Bayezid I broke off his seven-year assault on the city of Constantinople in the summer of 1402, to confront the Mongol khan Tamerlane at the Battle of Ankara (Angora). The sultan, who had never met defeat up to that time, undoubtedly expected to emerge victorious. Instead, as this account by a Greek chronicler relates, he experienced a shattering defeat. Not only were his forces routed, but he himself was taken prisoner by Tamerlane's forces. Accounts of Bayezid's fate varied, with sensational but quite possibly fictional stories of his abuse at the Mongol ruler's hands during his captivity circulating widely. The Elizabethan playwright Christopher Marlowe enshrined these tales in a play about Tamerlane's career in which Bayezid and his wife were displayed in cages that accompanied Tamerlane on his travels. Some sources state that Bayezid committed suicide, and others suggest that he died of a stroke during his imprisonment. Conspicuous cruelty to the defeated was, however, a standard feature of war across the Middle East, and Bayezid himself had often indulged in comparable brutality.

Document

Fearing Timur, the king of Great Tataria, Bayezid lifted the siege of the City [of Constantinople], marched with his troops to Anatolia, and besieged and took Ertzika, a city commanded by a Turkish duke. Then he moved on and subdued other Turkish lords, whom he deprived of their territories. Then all the lords of Anatolia gathered, came, and complained to Timur in the following manner: "Sultan Bayezid has invaded and robbed us of our lands and commands. You are a great king, your Lordship, and you have great power. Let us join forces and fight him, since it was he who decided to spare neither ourselves nor our cities." Timur consented and made preparations for war. He dispatched his *çavuş* to Bayezid, bearing a woman's gown; it was his custom to send this gift with his envoys to other kings. He gave the following instructions to his *çavuş*: "Take this message to Bayezid: since you are waging war upon the Turks, who have the same faith as yourself, you are not a good man. You should have attacked foreigners, not Turks, the children of the Prophet, who have never wronged you. You are committing an injustice."

Bayezid listened quietly to the words of the messenger-*çavuş*. He was greatly offended by the dress that Timur had sent him. Then he addressed the *çavuş*: "Go tell Timur, your king, that I am liked neither in the east nor in the west, because I fight for the faith. Since my actions and conquests are not to his liking and since he wishes to force me out of the places that I took with my sword, I will be his enemy; tell him to refrain, next time, from sending such presents, because I am the scion of kings and possess more riches than he does." Then the envoy-*çavuş* returned and related Bayezid's response to Timur. When the *çavuş* had done with his report, Timur became greatly angered. He called the Turkish lords together and related Bayezid's reply. Once more the same envoy-*çavuş* was dispatched to Bayezid, telling him to give up the lands and the cities that he had seized from the Turkish lords; if he refused to restore them, he would be declared Timur's foe: "I will lead my forces against you. I will also conquer your territories in Anatolia." When Bayezid heard this message, he laughed and ridiculed Timur's words.

Then Timur took his forces, marched, seized the districts of Sebasteia and Cappadocia, and continued with the conquest of Anatolia. He even came near to Constantinople. As soon as Bayezid, who was in Rumeli, was told that Timur had conquered Sebasteia and was advancing through Anatolia, he took his forces and crossed over to Anatolia. Then he was told again that Timur had conquered Sebasteia, had put all inhabitants to the sword, had enslaved many, and had even captured Bayezid's son alive, whom he had then beheaded. On top of this, another message reached Bayezid: he was told to restore the territories that he had subdued to their former lords, to give 2,000 measures of butter and 2,000 tents, to proclaim throughout his realm that Timur was a great king, to add Timur's name to all newly minted aspers and florins, and to send one of his sons to Timur's court to be a servant. If he refused to send him and to act accordingly, he would be a great enemy. Bayezid issued no response to this ultimatum.

So Timur marched to find him with an army of 800,000; he passed through Phrygia and Lydia. Then Bayezid, too, went to find and confront him with an army of 120,000; his forces included 10,000 Bulgarian and Serbian Christians, who had come to help Bayezid; on them he had placed all hope since they had experience in warfare. He marched as far as Phrygia, where he encountered Timur. . . .

Timur was amazed at the boldness of Bayezid, who had dared to confront him with few troops. Then Timur mounted his horse and approached Bayezid's camp; after he looked at it, he laughed and said: "Truly this man could be called Lightning." Then Timur divided his army into two sections, put his son in charge of half and kept the other half for himself. Bayezid, too, divided his troops into three parts: to the left wing he assigned the pasha of Anatolia, to the right the pasha of Rumeli, while Bayezid positioned himself in the center with the janissaries and all the picked regiments of the seraglio.

On the following day he advanced in battle order; he was accompanied by Sakoukos, a Persian lord, and by other Persian lords, who were in his retinue. Then the two armies began fighting and a hard conflict ensued. The Bulgarians and Serbs fought bravely against their opponents. When Bayezid saw that he was being defeated by his foe, because his troops from Rumeli were being routed, he became apprehensive, in case the Persian Sakoukos came and forced him in the front. He cried out to his men to turn back but they did not hear him. He kept threatening them, until they managed to get free; they tried to reach his position. On their way back the enemy intercepted them and they were butchered. When Bayezid saw the rout and slaughter of his troops—by now whoever could flee did so—he mounted a fast mare and he, too, fled with all his might to save himself. Even before Timur had entered the struggle, he had seen that Bayezid had been routed. As soon as he realized this, he issued orders not to kill or enslave the Turks, because he felt pity for them; they were to be stripped and released. But Bayezid was fleeing on the mare; then his mare became thirsty, sought and found water, and stopped. Bayezid was unable to dissuade her with the reins. While she was bending to water herself, Timur's men reached him, took him prisoner, and escorted him to their lord. . . .

When they brought Bayezid, a bound prisoner, to Timur, he rejoiced greatly and addressed him: "Unfortunate man! Why did you throw your family into unhappiness? Why did you fail to listen? My men's servants alone could have defeated you and overturned your good fortune, yet you dared to march against me with falconers, *zağarcı,* and hounds, as if you were dealing with a child." It is reported that Bayezid had 7,000 falconers and *zağarcı* hunters, in addition to 6,000 hounds. When Bayezid heard Timur's mocking words, he answered as follows: "King, you are a Tatar, i.e., a Scythian. You are greedy; you seize, you live as befits a thief and you are not aware of the value of falcons and hounds. But I, Murad's son and Orhan's descendant, the scion of kings, must maintain hunters, falcons, and hounds." This response enraged Timur; he ordered his prisoner bound, thrown on top of a mule, and paraded through the entire camp to be ridiculed by the troops. Then he put him in prison.

Next he ordered Bayezid's dear wife to be brought to him; he had her dresses cut from the knee to the thigh. In addition to the other indignities, whenever Timur sat to dinner with his officers, he had Bayezid brought in and kept at a distance in chains, so that the servants could throw bones at him. After such indignities, Bayezid spoke to him: "Rude and ignorant man, you are as befits your parents' race; they were villains of peasants, crude, rough, and obscure stock. It is not right that you should have contempt for the wives and children of kings. You do not listen; you cannot tell friend from foe." Timur laughed at his words and said: "You are ignorant."

He had Bayezid's neck bound with a golden chain and he had him paraded throughout Anatolia, Syria, and the regions that he visited, until Bayezid died. Whenever Timur was about to mount, he would force Bayezid upon the ground and use his back for a stool. Bayezid died in a place called Ionia.... Bayezid had been a prisoner for one year. Some people maintain that Bayezid perished in prison, when, out of bitterness, he struck his head against the wall and expired. He was a stubborn man. He reigned for twenty-five years. He was brave. On account of his speed, he was nicknamed "Lightning."

Source: Marios Philippides, ed. and trans., *Byzantium, Europe, and the Early Ottoman Sultans: An Anonymous Greek Chronicle of the Seventeenth Century* (Codex Barberinus Graecus 111) (New Rochelle, NY: Aristide D. Caratzas, 1990), 29–32. Reprinted with permission from Marios Philippides.

83. A Muslim View of the Death of Tamerlane (1405)

Introduction

In 1405 the Mongol khan Tamerlane (1336–1405) finally succumbed to illness and old age. In the words of his biographer, the Islamic chronicler and historian Ahmed ibn Arabshah, who took a highly critical view of Tamerlane's depredations against the Muslims, "God Almighty in His mercy took from men the punishment of shame and the stock of the race which had done wickedly was cut off; praise be to God, Lord of the ages!" Although Tamerlane styled himself a Muslim (while indulging copiously in alcohol, according to the accounts of foreign envoys who visited his court in Samarkand), his conquests had been driven primarily by geography and opportunity and were conducted without respect to religion or ethnicity. Having defeated Ottoman sultan Bayezid II at the Battle of Ankara in 1402, Tamerlane then proceeded to capture the city of Smyrna from the Knights Hospitaller, who had held it ever since Christian forces seized it in 1344. He also undertook skirmishes against the Byzantine Empire and its offshoot in Trebizond. Although several Christian powers made overtures to him, regarding him as a useful counter to the growing Ottoman threat, Tamerlane's ambitions were so insatiable that had he lived longer, he might well have proved as dangerous to Western interests as he had to the Ottomans and other Muslim rulers.

Ahmed ibn Arabshah wrote a rather extraordinary poem on Tamerlane's death, one that closely resembled the biblical psalms in style. The poem took an extremely hostile approach to the ravages that Tamerlane's military conquests had wreaked on the Muslim world. Yet many of Arabshah's reflections on the transience of earthly power and glory could have applied to almost any of the grandiloquent warlords who for millennia featured so prominently in the history of the Middle East.

Document

The earth is a water-wheel turning joy and adversity.
A man reaches the topmost peak; soon thou mayest see him crushed beneath the stones of the tomb.
How many suns that have climbed in the sky to the zenith, each with its moons,
When they have touched the zenith of their glory, have failed and waning light has brought them eclipse!
The kings of the world have burned seas with the fire of their injustice;
They rule countries and their peoples; their sway spreads far and wide.
The deceitful world drives them, kindled by greed, and the Deceiver fills them with vain hope concerning God.
Fortune regards them with smiling mouth and they hold strong places on the frontiers.
Soon like wolves they go forth to ravage and prowl like lions.
They abound in wealth and dance like black shadows without knowledge.
They present in their courts the ghost of fancy when it wanders.
They picture Fortune ever complaisant to them, so that it would never flee away,
Or their share of this world overflowing, so that it would never decrease.
They rush one on the other, they fight, they leap like panthers,

83. A Muslim View of the Death of Tamerlane

They struggle, and provoke one another and smite like lions.
They stab each other, they rend, they pierce like eagles;
Madness! Oh that they had fostered mutual peace and forgiven each other lies and cunning!
But like moths they have flown into the fire, thinking the fire a light.
While they hold the peak of their glory, Fortune deceitful, jealous,
Swoops on them from above like a hawk on petty birds.
They become unfortunate and each of them is thrown like food to the hawks.
No king or kingdom or house has repelled from them the hand of destruction—
Nothing, neither army nor children nor armies of allies.
Then their footprints are destroyed, as rain destroys lines of tracks.
Their time leaves naught of them but a blurred memory.
Like them all are the calamities of Timur, like dark seas,
That lame impostor, who broke skulls and backs,
Subdued countries and homes therein, in the revolving fortunes of this world.
God the Merciful prolonged his life, but he added iniquity to iniquity.
And He gave him aid, permitting to him progress in things that pass and perish,
That He might see whether in his rule he would follow justice or tyranny.
He rooted out all men among Arabs and barbarians,
He destroyed right custom and went forth wicked with insolent sword that moved hither and thither.
He destroyed kings and all the noble and learned,
And strove to put out the light of Allah and the pure Faith,
With the tenets of Jengizkhan, that wicked tyrant and unbeliever;
He permitted the shedding of blood of all the constant and grateful,
He made it a free right to take captive chaste believers from the harem;
He threw children upon the fire as if burning incense,
He added to fornication the drinking of wine.
Now he saw treaties violated, now vows broken;
And against noble matrons among the chaste and grave
They let loose every ravening wolf and fierce dog;
They rushed in and sundered hearts, after rending the curtains.
They branded their brows while they prostrated themselves before God the Forgiver;
They dragged men from pleasant beds and branded their sides and backs;
They violently snatched wealth from men's hands
And gave them to drink a draught of the simoom and to suck a draught of scorching wind;
They took for slaves the people of the Prophet, the elect, the purest one;
They sold them to Turks in the country of unbelievers
And so also the only son of every mother of one son alone.
And in these crimes they continued and went forward constantly
Crossing through the countries between Iran and Turan;
And he advanced further, penetrating from the Khatas to the furthest regions.
When his raids reached their height and that evil-doing was completed,
The onset of Fate seized him; for in every consummation is decrease;
The hands of death snatched him from those sins to the tomb;
His nobility was exchanged for contempt and hatred;
He departed to the house of punishment with a heavy load of crimes;
Those hosts were scattered and oblivion destroyed what he had built.
His deeds brought on him curses, so long as the ages revolve,
And the monuments of his evil-doing are committed to perpetual memory.

83. A Muslim View of the Death of Tamerlane

Look therefore, brother! and consider this evening and this dawn!
Death distinguishes not between the grateful pious and the infidel.
Where are they whose faces shone, like the star Zubur?
The fortunate, the clever, famed for dominion and majesty,
Who obscured the moon in the sky and put to shame the abundant seas?
They were great among leaders and leaders among warriors;
Trampling ground down those great ones and shattered those leaders;
And the wind of destruction scraped them as the hand of the storm scrapes the sands.
Where are the sons and those who brought the heart joy and light?
When the curtain was parted and the hangings removed from them,
Thou wouldst see a new splendour, like the sun, rise from the darkness of the curtains,
Beyond any buck or doe with beautiful eyes, that surpasses the houris.
Elegance clad them with the robe of comfort over coloured tunics.
Everyone would have wished with his last heart's blood to redeem them from the evil of calamities.
The place in which they rested they altered because of joy;
They were eyes in the face of this world and a light to the eyes
And gardens for its pleasaunces and in its pleasaunces flowers.
And while they are drunk with their sweet fortune, pride the wanton mixing them drink,
And their life is blooming and fortune favouring,
Lo! the cupbearer of death, who brings them cups of destruction.
Then the cup, which comes to every evil one, waters the gardens of their life.
Reluctant they leave their noble palaces for the narrow tomb,
And perforce drink the cups of their departure to every sad and jealous one,
Who rends his bosom with grief and beats his breast for desire of them.
If bribery availed aught or gifts according to vows profited,
The careful shepherd would redeem, defend and guard them.
They dwell in the tomb, their splendours and joys altered,
And the consuming worm devours them and rends like a butcher;
They rot in the tomb and abide there till the day of resurrection.
The friend dutifully visits their tombs and addresses them,
And wails, and lamenting, asks of the tomb what it easily forgets
And stains with dust his cheeks, which stream with tears.
They call, but they answer them not, except the echo of the dumb rocks.
He who visits now is soon himself visited—
By the will and providence of God which works slowly.
The world is a bridge, whence take an example by which to be warned; seek money for the journey
And seek the sound kernel; all the rest is shell.
Were not the world with its goods a smoke, which easily vanishes,
Its plain would not be withdrawn from every constant and faithful one.
This one and most of those who go proudly on the earth, are lame and blind;
Yet they suffer not themselves to be guided, but bear themselves too proudly:
They fight against the truth and turn from it to lying and iniquity.
O Lord, make us constant in those things that please Thee!
Forgive us the sins well known to Thee, O Forgiver!
Confer blessedness upon us, with which we may match the malice of Satan
And give us from the gate of Thy bounty the merchandise that will never perish.

Source: Ahmed ibn Arabshah, *Tamerlane or Timur the Great Amir*, trans. J. H. Sanders (London: Luzac, 1936), 233–237.

84. The Battle of Khirokitia (July 7, 1426)

Introduction

In 1426 the new Mamluk sultan Barsbay of Egypt mounted an offensive against Cyprus, which had become a base for corsairs of several different nationalities. King Janus of Cyprus had also recently mounted a raid against Syrian territory. Mamluk forces landed on the island, taking the city of Limassol, and inflicted a crushing defeat on Janus at the Battle of Khirokitia, where he was captured. The Mamluks proceeded to sack Nicosia, the capital of Cyprus. Together with around 6,000 Cypriots, Janus was taken to Egypt, to be ransomed eight months later for 200,000 ducats after agreeing to become the sultan's vassal and pay an annual tribute. Most of his ransom was provided by the military order of the Knights Hospitaller, which maintained a large base and extensive estates on Cyprus. As an official history of the order first published in 1728 explained, these events had major ramifications not just for Cyprus but also for the order itself, leading its grand master to send out a wide call for reinforcements for its headquarters on the island of Rhodes.

Document

Whilst the knights and the Turks, equally animated against one another, were roving up and down the seas, ravaging the coasts, where they could make any descent, and labouring to surprise one another, there started up a new enemy to the order, who was almost as near Rhodes as the Turks, but more formidable, on account of his maritime forces, his fleets, and particularly from the skillfulness of his subjects in navigation, in which they excelled, especially since he began his reign. I speak of the famous sultan of Egypt Alnazer-al-Daher [Barsbay], a Circassian by birth, whom the Mamelukes had raised to the throne. They admitted none into that body, which was the strongest in Egypt, but foreign slaves; and these generally were young children that had either been taken by the Tartars in their incursions, or else sold to them by their unnatural parents. The Egyptians bought all they could, and brought up these young men in exercises suitable to the profession they destined them for; and when they were able to bear arms, they incorporated them into the body of the Mamalukes. 'Twas in this manner, that Daher, whom were are speaking of, was admitted into that body; and after many long years of service, and a great series of glorious actions and distinguished valour, was at last advanced to the sovereign power, which by the laws of that body could never devolve from father to son, or descend to his heirs.

Daher in order to maintain himself in a dignity subject to frequent revolutions, from the inconstancy and seditious temper of the Mamalukes, and also to find employment for their courage, declared war against Janus of Lusignan king of Cyprus. His fleet landed a considerable army in their land. The king immediately applied to the order for assistance; and tho' the knights were then at peace with the Saracens, the grand master and council could not see their arms so near the isle of Rhodes, without fearing some unhappy consequences to the order from that war. As the territories belonging to it were situated between those of the Turkish emperor and the sultan of Egypt, the council was always so politic as to maintain peace with one of those infidel princes, while it was engaged in war with the other. Agreeable to this maxim they could have wished to have had no quarrel with the Saracens, whilst they were at war with the Turks. The grand master, in this view, omitted nothing that might contribute to the bringing about a peace between the sultan of Egypt and the king of Cyprus; but as the Egyptian regulated his pretensions by his forces, he insisted that the king of Cyprus should acknowledge himself his vassal, and as such, pay him and his successors an annual tribute, and should likewise reimburse him all the expence he had been at in that armament and expedition.

These conditions were too hard to be accepted; so that there was a necessity of deciding the dispute by arms. Acts of hostility were begun on both sides. The order, as an ally of the crown of Cyprus, sent over considerable succours at different times. The war proved long and bloody. At last they came to a battle, the particulars of which we are unacquainted with. We only know in general, that the Christians lost it, and that a great number of Cypriot lords and gentlemen, and several knights of St. John, were slain at the same time. The Saracens had a compleat victory, and the king, to make the misfortune still greater, fell into the hands of the infidels, who carried him to Alexandria.

The grand master hearing this bad news, and fearing the infidels might seize on the whole island, sent over new succours of men and money, and gave secret assurances to the principal lords of the kingdom, that the order would never abandon them, provided they would not abandon themselves; and that they should take up a noble resolution to die sword in hand rather than submit to the Mahometans. But those lords, divided among themselves, and effeminated by pleasures, not discovering any great courage and resolution, sent, by the grand master's advice, embassadors to Egypt, to the sultan's court, to treat for the ransom of their sovereign. The negotiation was spun out a great length. The sultan, in hopes that his troops would soon reduce the whole island, was every day starting new difficulties; but the Egyptian general soon found a stop put to the progress of his arms by the valour of the knights. By way of revenge, he ravaged the great commandry or bailliage which the order possessed in that island, demolishing the houses, cutting down the trees, and rooting up the vines; so that this great commandry, which was reckoned the richest of the order, was entirely ruined. The sultan too resolved to turn the efforts of his arms against the isle of Rhodes, hoping that if he could make himself master of it, that of Cyprus, being left destitute of the succours of the knights, would of course fall into his hands. And as ambitious princes seldom let any bounds to their projects, the sultan flattered himself, that the conquest of the isles of Rhodes and Cyprus would pave the way to that of all the isles of the Archipelago; and that after this, Asia minor could never resist a power so formidable as his would then be. Full of such vast designs, the dangers and difficulties of which his ambition concealed from him, he again set the negotiation on foot with the embassadors of Cyprus. His ministers set a price upon the king's liberty, and demanded an hundred and twenty thousand florins of gold for his ransom. The prince rejected this proposal, not only because he looked on the sum as too extravagant, but also because he wanted money, his exchequer being quite exhausted by the war. But the grand master, who was afraid lest the Saracens should at last seize on the isle of Cyprus, advised him to get out of the hands of those barbarians at any rate; and the order, to facilitate his liberty, supplied him with the greatest part of his ransom. Peace was made on these conditions.

The sultan, to amuse the grand master, and under pretence of desiring to maintain a lasting peace with the order, renewed at the same time the treaty which the sultan his predecessor had made during the mastership of Naillac. But the grand master, who paid for good intelligence, and kept spies in Alexandria, and even in that prince's council, was soon informed of his most secret designs. To prevent being surprised by the Barbarian, he immediately sent advice of it to pope Eugenius IV. and to most of the Christian princes, transmitting at the same time a general summons into all parts of the Christian world, with express injunctions to the priors to send away forthwith 25 knights or commanders out of each priory to Rhodes. But a much greater number of them arrived, whom zeal and courage had drawn thither; part of them were kept at Rhodes, and the rest distributed into the isles belonging to the order. Brother Hugh de Sarcus, grand prior of France, sent to the capital of the order a ship laden with cross-bows, arrow-heads, and other arms necessary for the defence of the place. The grand master took care to supply it with corn and all sorts of provisions; in time, this worthy chief, by his vigilance and activity, put himself in so good a posture to receive the enemy, that the news of his armament soon passed into Egypt; and the sultan flattering himself that the order could not long maintain so great a number of knights, saw fit to suspend his enterprise.

Source: Abbé René-Aubert de Vertot, *The History of the Knights Hospitallers of St. John of Jerusalem*, Vol. 2 (Edinburgh, UK: R. Fleming, 1757), 236–240.

85. The Fall of Constantinople (1453): A Muslim Account

Introduction

The high-ranking Ottoman official Tursun Beg, a government secretary and surveyor who spent much of his career in the service of Grand Vizier Mahmud Pasha, was present at the siege of Constantinople and also took part in several subsequent military operations led and directed by Mehmed II, including campaigns in Serbia, Walacia, Lesbos and the Morea, Bosnia, and Albania. A poet and writer, in retirement Tursun Beg wrote memoirs of the reign of Mehmed II, intended to be presented to the new sultan, Bayezid II. Tursun Beg drew closely on his own direct knowledge of contemporary events and personalities, providing an intimate portrait of Mehmed II, including what seems to have been a near addiction on the sultan's part to warfare that even his soldiers sometimes found excessive. Tursun Beg's history took virtually for granted the brutality, slaughter, and plunder that routinely accompanied Ottoman warfare. His depiction of the siege of Constantinople provides an Ottoman perspective on an event retold many times in Western accounts but less often from the viewpoint of the triumphant conquerors.

Document

Mehmed was possessed with the idea of conquering Istanbul and constantly insisted on the necessity of taking the city without delay. Senior statesmen spoke of the strength of the fortifications and of the bad consequences that would arise from a prolonged siege of the city, but Mehmed would not listen and immediately began preparations for the siege.... It was intolerable that Istanbul, surrounded by the lands of Islam, should survive under a Christian ruler, the so-called *Kayser-i Rūm*, especially since he gave protection within the city walls to pretenders to the Ottoman throne and constantly tried to stir up conflict in the Ottoman territories....

In the spring of 857 [1453], he left Edirne [Adrianople] with the intention of capturing Istanbul. He ordered the large cannons to be dragged by the *yayas*. The master *nakkābs*, stoneborers from the mines in Rumeli, joined the army while the naval forces waited in Gelibolu. The Sultan proceeded by land and the navy by sea. According to custom, the day that camp was to be made near Istanbul the army was ordered by regiment into rows. He ranged at the center of the army around his own person the white-capped Janissary archers, the Turkish and European crossbowmen, and the musketeers and cannoneers (*darbzen*). The red-capped '*azebs* were placed on his right and left, joined at the rear by the cavalry. Thus organized, the army marched in formation on Istanbul.

On the other side, the Byzantine emperor had received reinforcements from Christian rulers in Europe. He sent these armoured, mounted knights in front of the gates to meet the approaching army of the Sultan. The Muslim forces pushed them back within the walls, and finally the Sultan arrived on the scene at the outer walls. According to Ottoman practice, the Sultan pitched his large tent in the middle of the ranks. The Janissaries set up their tents in the form of a circle surrounding the Sultan's. The *Beglerbegi* of Anatolia, Ishak Beg, formerly one of the vizirs of Sultan Murād, took up his place on the right wing of the Anatolian forces, while the *Beglerbegi* of Rumeli, Dayı Karaca Beg, uncle of Prince 'Alāeddīn, was on the left. Trenches were dug for emplacing the cannon, and catapults were set up in several places. They set up barricades and vaulted bunkers (*mancu-yerleri* and *toÐuz-damları*) and showed the miners their places. Hostilities immediately broke out in front of the gate.

One difficulty, however, was the fact that the Golden Horn was closed off. Sultan Mehmed ordered that some of the smaller ships and galleys should be dragged over the hill behind Galata into the Golden Horn. Thus forced to guard the sector of the walls on the Golden Horn as well, the enemy forces would necessarily be spread out. So, as ordered, the ships and galleys were decked out with banners of every color and dragged overland to the Golden Horn. By lashing the boats together a secure bridge was formed over which the soldiers could cross, and the fortress was surrounded on three sides.

Meanwhile, the cannons and catapults continued to bombard the walls. The shock of the balls shook and rent the walls. Fighting continued every day from sunrise to sunset, but the defenders placed their trust in the firmness of the fortifications even after several towers were completely destroyed by cannon fire. At this stage, two coques (*köke*) filled with arms and reinforcements arrived from Europe. At that point the soldiers and naval troops of the Sultan were busily making preparations for the dragging of the ships over to the Golden Horn. With the aid of a favorable wind, the coques began to approach very quickly. The admiral Balta-oÐlu Süleymān Beg sent against them all the ships he could gather, and a great battle took place in which the Ottomans were defeated. The Greeks opened up the barrier across the Golden Horn and let in the coques.

After this naval defeat the Muslims were distressed and lost hope, but in fact the arrival of the coques turned out to be a helping factor in the Ottomans' final victory. By that time, the walls facing the Janissaries and the Sultan's soldiers had been destroyed and paths prepared to the trenches. The Greeks feared that the fortress would be taken from this direction and wished to be responsible themselves for its defense. However, the European troops who had come as reinforcements demanded that the defense of this area be given to them, otherwise threatening to withdraw their support. Fearing that they would indeed desert the cause if he did not give in, the Emperor granted their wish. This, in turn, caused discontent among the Greeks in the city and the forces defending the city fell into disunity.

The Sultan proclaimed a general assault and gave the troops permission to take booty in the city. At night the soldiers reached the walls from the trenches and, against the defenders on the walls, attempted to climb up under the protection of their shields. At daybreak the Sultan approached on horseback and the attack on the fortress began in earnest. The cannons began to fire, then the battle cry was sounded and the general assault was underway. The attackers proceeded to rain arrows on the defenders. In the breaches which had been opened by the cannon fire, soldiers fought breast to breast and sword to sword. The enemy threw Greek fire on the attackers. As the battle proceeded in this fashion, in the section where the cannon had opened breaches in the walls, the European troops met the Ottoman troops in front of the smaller outer walls. The enemy commander arrived at this place and, while he was struggling with an Ottoman soldier on top of the tower, another soldier pierced his belly from below. When they saw that their commander had been wounded, the enemy troops were overcome. They tried to escape by fleeing into the inner fortresses, but the defenders had barred the gate. Left trapped between the walls, they were all put to the sword. The Ottoman troops immediately stormed the inner walls and pushed back the defenders. The rest of the army then began to spread out into the city by means of the breach in the wall while the enemy troops fled before them.

While the Sultan's standing army, the *kapu kulu,* was achieving this victory, the Anatolian, Rumelian, and navy troops continued to fight unaware of the new developments. The Byzantine Emperor and his retinue were reduced to panic when they saw the Janissaries so close behind them, and they too began to flee. Some of them shut themselves in a tower while others perished charging their horses desperately against the Ottoman troops. Still others were taken prisoner.

At that juncture the Emperor was stealthily fleeing towards the Golden Horn with the intention of escaping in one of the ships. He was met on the way by a group of *'azebs.* This group of *'azebs* had entered the city with a band of Janissaries, and later, becoming separated from them, had wandered into a side street where they met the Emperor with his retinue. A desperate battle ensued. The Emperor's horse slipped as he was attacking a wounded *'azeb,* whereupon the *'azeb* pulled himself together and cut off the Emperor's head. When they saw this, the rest of the enemy troops lost hope and the *'azebs* managed to kill or capture most of them. A great quantity of money and precious stones in the possession of the Emperor's personal retinue was also seized.

After having completely overcome the enemy, the soldiers began to plunder the city. They enslaved boys and girls and took silver and gold vessels, precious stones, and all sorts of valuable goods and fabrics from the imperial palace and the houses of the rich. In this fashion many people were delivered from poverty and made rich. Every tent was filled with handsome boys and beautiful girls.

Then the gates of the fortress were opened and Sultan Mehmed toured the city with a group of commanders and religious dignitaries in his retinue. He visited the great buildings and bazaars and particularly expressed his desire to see Hagia Sophia. Over the years this church had deteriorated so that at this time only its dome was standing.

When the Sultan returned to his headquarters from this tour, a council was held. There the prominent Byzantines were brought into his presence. He ordered some of them executed while others were spared for practical purposes. He appointed Karıştıran Süleymān Beg governor of Istanbul and entrusted to him the work of reconstructing the city.

Source: Tursun Beg, *The History of Mehmed the Conqueror,* ed. and trans. Halil Inalcik and Rhoads Murphey (Minneapolis: Bibliotheca Islamica, 1978, 33–37). Reprinted with permission.

86. Sultan Mehmed II (r. 1450–1481), as Described by Nikolaos Sekoundinos (January 24, 1454)

Introduction

Within two years of succeeding his father, Murad II, as sultan, the Ottoman ruler Mehmed II had finally achieved the long-cherished Turkish goal of taking Constantinople from the Byzantines. The fall to Muslim rule of the much-diminished Byzantine

Empire's capital, a symbol of Christian power for more than 1,000 years, was a huge symbolic blow to Western prestige. It also prompted great curiosity about the youthful Mehmed II and his ambitions. Nikolaos Sekoundinos, a Greek-born diplomat and outstanding linguist who served both the Venetian government and the papacy, spent two months at Mehmed's court in late 1453 as part of a Venetian deputation that sought to negotiate the release of prisoners taken in the siege of Constantinople. On his return Sekoundinos addressed audiences in Venice and Rome, providing an insightful portrait of the young Ottoman ruler. It was clear that Mehmed represented a formidable new threat to all his neighbors, Arab and Christian alike.

Document

[T]he king [sultan] of the Turks, Mehmed by name, is twenty-three years old; he has a melancholy nature; he is average in stature, is presentable in appearance, and possesses the rudiments of kindness and mildness (notwithstanding his instincts), although he is apparently cruel to Christians. I would attribute it not to his character but to hatred, as he seems to express wrath towards our faith and the name of Christ vehemently. He is very clever and sharp. After the death of his father, he painstakingly took over the [Ottoman] kingdom and, as I mentioned, has focused all his attention on its internal conditions; with great diligence did he educate himself about the court and the palace; he eliminated and canceled trivial affairs that seemed a waste of time to him, but he adjusted and corrected many conditions, before he chartered innovations and issued orders to attend to them.

His life and habits do not exhibit the temperance, the modesty and gravity, which should accompany a somber and responsible prince but they match the habits of his forefathers and are appropriate for a young man, proud by nature, addicted to pleasures and luxury, and accustomed to taking advantage of his royal power to fulfill his desires; instead of serving him under control, they urge and press him on, and result in corruption rather than legislation; they lead him headlong, "with free rein," as the saying goes, to crime and perdition. Yet I suggest that if you study his ways, you would conclude that he does exhibit self-control and sane judgment. Day and night he is energetically involved with the ship of such an extensive and rich state, avoiding the appearance of being eagerly addicted to pleasure, to sex, to food, to hunting, to fowling, to dancing, and to singing. He evades ridicule and superficiality, does not indulge in banquets and in drinking (an addiction of their race), and is not involved in such lazy games. Something always occupies him and he is always on the move, planning, thinking out, and pondering how to carry out all designs he has decided upon, with admirable speed, incredible care, and diligence. This does not apply only to the royal resources and the management, but also in his own life: he is very frugal for the most part; he desires and demands to participate in everything, regardless of the difficulty of a march, of inclement weather, or of local foods; he is deterred by nothing: not by mountains, not by hot weather, not by cold, not by hunger, not by thirst; he seems not to run but to fly, in my opinion.

In spite of being busy with all administrative matters, as I was saying, he finds time for literature and philosophy: he is learned in Arabic. Daily, at a prescribed time, the prince devotes time to hear or read something worthwhile. In addition, he employs two physicians, one educated in Latin, the other in Greek. Under their attentive tutelage he wants to learn ancient history and he particularly pays attention to the deeds of the Lacedaemonians, of the Athenians, of the Romans, of the Carthaginians, and of kings and princes. He has particularly chosen to emulate Alexander of Macedon and Gaius Caesar, whose deeds he has arranged to be translated into his own language. He is delighted when he hears or reads about them. He is determined to challenge their fame and he seems to be ardently inspired by their glory and praises.

Source: Nikolaos Sekoundinos, speech, January 25, 1454, translated in Marios Philippides, ed., *Mehmed II the Conqueror and the Fall of the Franco-Byzantine Levant to the Ottoman Turks: Some Western Views and Testimonies* (Tempe: Arizona Center for Medieval and Renaissance Studies, 2007), 9–11.

87. The Fall of Trebizond (August 1461)

Introduction

After seizing Constantinople, Ottoman sultan Mehmed II proceeded to mop up the last surviving enclave of Byzantine power, the empire of Trebizond, established in 1204 after Western nobles and Venetians enlisted in the Fourth Crusade captured the city of Constantinople and set up their own kingdom there. An unknown Greek chronicler, writing in the 17th century but relying on earlier sources, left an account of the siege of Trebizond, which lasted over a month before Emperor David Komnenos came to terms. Initially, David accepted a fief consisting of assorted villages in the nearby Black Mountains. Most of Trebizond's nobility were likewise deported. Perhaps predictably, the settlement between David and Mehmed II, who had initially sought the emperor's unconditional surrender, proved transient, only lasting until sometime in 1263. The former Byzantine official George Sphrantzes, writing in the 1280s, recounted that "After a short while, the sultan took all [David's] property and strangled him for an insignificant and false reason." He probably suspected the former emperor of conspiring against him with David's relative by marriage, Emir Uzun Hasan of Armenia. David and most of his family were executed, though one son who converted to Islam apparently survived, and a daughter reputedly entered Mehmed's harem.

Document

Next [Mehmet II] moved against Trebizond and Emperor David for the following reason: his young nephew had placed a charge against him to the sultan with these words: "My uncle has taken my empire, even though my father was its lord and emperor." Then the sultan found a pretext and moved his armada from Sinope; it came to Trebizond and plundered the environs. The sultan arrived by land later. His pasha fought for thirty-two days. When the sultan, too, had arrived, the lord of Trebizond sent him a message, stating that he would surrender his entire lordship if he were granted another region, as he had given to Despot Demetrios from the Morea. He would also give him his daughter in marriage and: "My entire revenue which comes from the place called Kolkhis." When the sultan heard this, he did not agree and decided to fight. Earlier, before the armada arrived to fight, Emperor David's wife had gone and met her brother-in-law, Malkias, who was a good friend of the sultan, and she asked him to go to the sultan to conclude a peace treaty with Emperor David. He concluded the peace treaty because they agreed and he gave him the entire lordship and the places ruled by David. So a peace treaty was arranged and the war ceased. He received Emperor David and his entire family with honor and grace and sent them to Constantinople by sea, the fastest route. The sultan's armies went by land. He commanded Emperor David to go to Adrianople and live there with his family. When the sultan returned to Constantinople, he celebrated with numerous festivals, on account of his victory. He had seized the empire of the Romans, that of Trebizond, that of the Morea, and numerous other places. He had uprooted the pitiable Romans. Glory be to God! Lord, wise is Your judgment! The sultan seized and divided the inhabitants of the city; some became *sihladar*, some *sipahi-oğlanı* of the seraglio, and others janissaries to remain in the City. He took 800 young men and made them janissaries. In a similar way, he apportioned the women and distributed them among the members of the seraglio.

Source: Marios Philippides, ed. and trans., *Byzantium, Europe, and the Early Ottoman Sultans: An Anonymous Greek Chronicle of the Seventeenth Century* (Codex Barberinus Graecus 111) (New Rochelle, NY: Aristide D. Caratzas, 1990), 84. Reprinted with permission from Marios Philippides.

88. Brother Jacopo dalla Castellana: The Loss of Negroponte (June–July 1470)

Introduction

For over 100 years, in the late 15th and 16th centuries the Ottomans waged a steady war of attrition against Venice's Mediterranean and Aegean territorial possessions, which successive Turkish rulers gradually annexed. Lengthy periods of war were punctuated by intermittent truces following the negotiation of rather unreliable treaties of peace. The results were economically disastrous for Venice, eroding the foundations of its commercial empire and its ability to protect vital trade routes. Victories over Venetian strongholds in the Morea in the 1470s, including the island of Negroponte (Khalkis), were the first steps in a progression that ultimately, a century later, saw the Turks conquer Cyprus and Crete. Treachery among the defenders was far from unknown, as demonstrated by this eyewitness account written by a cleric who escaped the sack of Negroponte due to his fluency in both Greek and Turkish. In the case of Negroponte, the indecision and unwillingness to take action and engage the enemy displayed by Admirale Nicolo da Canale, commander of the Venetian fleet sent to assist the besieged island, apparently also played a crucial part. On the orders of the infuriated Venetian government, da Canale was arrested, put on trial for dereliction of duty, and sentenced to internal exile.

Document

In the year of our Lord Jesus Christ 1470, . . . on the 15th day of this month [of June], the armada of the Turk reached Negroponte by the region of Karystos and the harbor of Porto Leone [Piraeus] and entered the channel, approaching the Bridge of San Marco that measures three miles from the mainland. On the same day and hour came the Grand Turk himself [Mehmed II] over land with three hundred thousand men (not counting the men of the fleet who amounted to sixty thousand); *in toto* there were 360,000 individuals with the army and navy.

On the 24th day of the aforesaid month the Turk ordered that a wooden bridge be built over boats; it measured one hundred paces, i.e., it was as long as the distance from the mainland to the island. Its width measured forty paces. It was positioned in the area near the bridge of San Marco, by the army's bivouac. From the same spot passed the Grand Turk and his younger son, as well as the pasha of Romania [Rumeli], as the pasha of Anatolia was the general captain of the armada [admiral]. The Grand Turk passed into the island with two hundred and fifty thousand individuals; they were all horsemen, outside of 14,000 *Tanengarii* [janissaries], i.e., Christian renegades.

He had his tent erected below Santa Chiara, opposite Furcae on the mainland. There he deployed a bombard over the hill, which pounded the Gate of Christ. This Gate is the middle of the region of Beccaria, facing east. The pasha erected his tent within the area of San Francesco, by the fountain. There were deployed thirty mortars, i.e., bombards, which had the same width and length and are placed upright when they are about to be fired; they cast stone missiles of two hundred *rotoli* each weighing six hundred pounds, which they fired into the air so they could tumble down into our territory. They damaged many houses and killed many people. His young son, who was not yet an adult, erected his tent under Falegriza [Kalograia], i.e., in Santa Mari[n]a, on top of the hill. From there to the fountain, that is to say within San Francesco, the entire region was full of the tents of the Turks, stretching, from one side to the other, to a distance of five miles.

At Fornaki, i.e., within the city, at the left side to the south, two very large bombards of the Turks were deployed and bombarded the Gate of the Church, specifically the very gate that had been repaired by the former commander, Sir Bondinieri [Bondumier]. The two bombards against Fornaki were protected by a huge rampart in front of them, and could not be destroyed by those within our territory. On the mainland, i.e. the region from Furcase to Figher, where the fountain is located, the territory was covered by the tents and pavilions of the Turks. This section is situated above the channel and near the walls, between the bridges and the Gate of Christ; on this wall San Marco is depicted, facing Turkish territory [Boeotia]. The Grand Turk deployed ten bombards on top of that small hill, on the road to Stives [Thebes], that fired their missiles over the sea against the Giudecca and Vourkos, i.e. the arsenal. These ten cannons fired 24 missiles each, day and night.

On the last day of the aforementioned month, the Grand Turk realized that the city was not going to surrender and dispatched three thousand horsemen with his standard throughout the island, as far as Rio, and they put everyone, men and women, to the sword. Boys, up to the age of 15, were sent to Constantinople to be slaves; infants in the cradle were killed, as if they were puppies. The same three thousand horsemen captured, though treachery, a fort named Touppa [La Cuppa]. In that fortress there were three thousand Christians, i.e., Greeks. They were all slaughtered before the walls of Negroponte in order to inspire fear and terror among the besieged and compel them to surrender.

On the same day came a vessel, a cargo ship from Venice carrying war supplies and soldiers to the aid of our territory. The ship entered the channel from where the armada of the Turk was, as they did not suspect that it would be there. So the Grand Turk ordered the execution of soldiers and sailors, all of them in full view from our territory. On the same day a young bombardier who was in Negroponte struck with his bombard two bombardiers of the Turk, who were his best.

On the 5th day of the month of July the Grand Turk issued orders to fill the ditches with timber on the side that the walls had been destroyed, i.e., from the church to the Gate of Christ. As soon as the aforementioned ditches had been filled, the Turk began an assault, intending to gain entrance into the territory. The defenders poured gunpowder on the aforementioned timber and,

88. Brother Jacopo dalla Castellana: The Loss of Negroponte

when the Turks were in the middle of the moat, the defenders set fire to the timber. In the course of this first battle more than 14,000 Turks were burned or drowned, as we were informed by a slave who managed to escape from the Turks. On the 8th day of the month the Turks launched their second assault against the island and, during the attack, the defenders erected a Turkish standard on the collapsed walls, in order to deceive the enemy and lure them across the moat. The Grand Turk saw his standard on the collapsed walls and concluded that it had been erected by those who advocated surrender, i.e., by Tommaso Schiavo. Then the Grand Turk dropped his silver baton under the impression that the city was already being sacked. As they believed that the city was being sacked, about 200 Turkish regiments hastened to enter. The defenders resisted bravely. In this second battle 16 thousand Turks were killed, i.e., casualties from the first and second battles together amounted to thirty thousand Turks.

On the same day the plot engineered within our territory by the cursed soul of Tommaso Schiavo was discovered by the wife of the aforementioned Tommaso, who went and revealed it to an old Greek lady. In turn, this old lady went to inform the lord *bailo* of the plot. The lord *bailo* then summoned Tommaso Schiavo and Commander Fioredinardo [Fiorio di Nardo], along with the other commanders, including Giorgio Albanese, who confessed the reality of the conspiracy. When Tommaso Schiavo realized that Giorgio Albanese had revealed the whole plot without the application of torture, he was forced to admit his treacherous plans, according to which he was going to surrender the territory at night to the Grand Turk and become a pasha. Then Sir Loiso Dolfini [Alvise Dolfin], in the presence of the lord *bailo*, stabbed Tommaso in the chest with a dagger; then the *bailo* ordered that the aforementioned Tommaso and Fioredinardo be quartered and the sections thrown into the camp of the Turk. Master Enrico, the bombardier, was blinded and his scribe Master Petro Albanese was thrown off the walls but managed to go over to the Turks.

On the 9th day of the same month the Grand Turk launched his third assault upon Negroponte from the side of the island; it was a Thursday. In this third battle five thousand Turks perished; I mean to say that *in toto* 35,000 Turks had been killed. On the 10th day of the aforementioned month the pasha launched the fourth assault, in which three thousand Turks perished; *in toto* 38,000 had been killed.

On the 11th day of the aforementioned month the Grand Turk issued orders to fill in the ditches with barrels and with corpses. He then began a frontal attack upon the island, where he had destroyed the walls, i.e., from the region of the Church, from the region of Christ, and from the sea. He commanded his fleet to approach the same parts from the sea, where the walls were in ruins, i.e. from the Giudecca. When the fleet approached the city to enter our territory, our bombardier, a young man, struck thirty Turkish galleys.

Our fleet from Venice entered from the part of the channel by the Bridge of Santa Clara [Chiara] to the east and was in good position to help our territory. But they were apprehensive of the four bombards of the Turk that had been deployed by the second bridge, which was on the side of the armada of the *Signoria*. This bridge had been constructed over 30 *fuste* of the Turk; it offered a passage to the Turk and his engines from the Bridge of San Marco to the Bridge of Santa Clara [Chiara], i.e., a distance of 5 miles. His Magnificence, the Captain General Nicolo da Canale, made an error, as His Magnificence would not allow some ships of the Genoese that had been enlisted in Candia to attack and besiege the bridge or the two galleys from Cyprus and two galleys from Rhodes that volunteered to sail to the aid of the city. His Magnificence would not issue permission to attack. The cause of this is not known but, consequently, our territory received no assistance. We within the territory realized that we were not going to receive any help; yet we fought on bravely until the second hour of the day. By the second hour of the day the Turks assumed command of all the walls of Negroponte; at noon the fighting went on in the main square. From the gate that bore the image of San Marco to the Gate of the Church the streets had been barricaded with beams and barrels. The women put to death a large number of Turks by pouring boiling water and lime on them from windows. On that day Negroponte was plundered, i.e., the entire territory, with the exception of the bridge that fell the following Saturday.

Those found in Negroponte, men and women 15 years and over, were slaughtered; the infants in swaddling clothes were killed like puppy dogs. The Grand Turk called an assembly to see how many of his men had perished in the last battle. They discovered that 39,000 Turks had fallen; I mean to say that together with the others 77,000 Turks perished. The Captain General of the Venetians announced that about 30,000 Christians had perished, young and old.

Stato, Scopulo, Orto, and Carasco dispatched their keys [surrendered] to the Turks. It was also said that in a similar way Dolimbro, Castalimoni, and Fittilto also surrendered their keys to the Turks.

On that day arrived the vice-captain of the Venetians, Lorenzo Loredano, with sixteen galleys, five ships, and two *galeazi*. Also came Sir Giacomo Veneri, the Captain General of the ships, with 12 ships and four *galeaze*. In sum, 59 ships set sail from Porto Leone.

I, Brother Jacopo dalla Castellana, saw all these events, and escaped from the island because I speak both Turkish and Greek.

> **Source:** Fra Giacomo Pugliese, "The Loss of Negroponte by Brother Jacopo dalla Castellana," in Marios Philippides, ed., *Mehmed II the Conqueror and the Fall of the Franco-Byzantine Levant to the Ottoman Turks: Some Western Views and Testimonies* (Tempe: Arizona Center for Medieval and Renaissance Studies, 2007), 251–259.

89. Giovan Maria Angiolello: The Battle of Otlukbeli (August 11, 1473)

Introduction

Uzun Hasan (r. 1453–1478), ninth shahanshah of the Turkoman White Sheep Confederation of Central Asia, was an unreliable Ottoman ally, with expansionist ambitions of his own that brought him into conflict with Ottoman sultan Mehmed II. Uzun Hasan's fourth marriage to the niece of Emperor David of Trebizond, whom Mehmed displaced and subsequently killed, was a further source of friction. Venetian relatives of Uzun Hasan's wife encouraged him to attack the Ottomans, promising him support of their own that in practice never eventuated. Initially, Uzun Hasan restricted himself to stirring up trouble for Mehmed among his fractious neighbors. In 1473, he embarked on open warfare against the Ottoman sultan and his sons, a campaign that ended in August that year in wholesale defeat for Uzun Hasan at the Battle of Otlukbeli. Thereafter, Uzun Hasan refrained from further challenges to Ottoman power. The Venetian soldier and official Giovan Maria Angiolello, captured and enslaved by the Turks at the siege of Negroponte in 1470, served in the Turkish armies for several years and became personally close to Prince Mustafa, heir apparent to Mehmed II. Angiolello later returned to Venice and wrote a memoir that included an account of the Battle of Otlukbeli.

Document

Chap. VII.—The Grand Turk, arriving at the river Euphrates, determines to cross, and orders Asmurat to force a passage with his men, whereupon he is defeated by the Persians.

Now on arriving at the river Euphrates, and marching north-east along its bank, we perceived that Ussuncassano [Uzun Hasan] had arrived with his army on the other side, at the spot where he thought that the Turk would cross. The river was wider in this place—divided into many streams by banks of mud; here the armies encamped opposite each other, with the stream separating them. Ussuncassano had an immense army, and with him were three of his sons, the first named Calul, the second Ugurlimehemet, and the third Zeinel, and also Pirahomat, the prince of Caramania, and many other lords and men of various nationalities, namely, Persians, Parthians, Albanians (?), Georgians, and Tartars. On Ussuncassano's seeing the Turkish army encamped, he was quite astonished at the multitude, and stood some time without speaking, and then said in the Persian language, "Baycabexen nede riadir," which means, "O, son of a whore, what a sea," comparing the Turkish army to an ocean. On the same day that the armies encamped in this place, about nine, it was decided to attempt a passage and to attack the enemy, and that Asmurat, Beglerbeg of Romania should attempt it with all his men, and, as he was young, Mahumut Bassa was given him as a colleague. Then having raised the standards, sounded the drums, the naccare, and other warlike instruments, they began to cross, swimming over certain streams, and going from sandbank to sandbank, and so arrived nearly at the other side of the river.

Ussuncassano, seeing that the Turkish troops began to cross, and were already near his bank, sent a body of his own men against them, who also entered a good way into the river; but as a deep stream separated them, they began the fight with arrows. Still the Turks, wishing to cross, made great exertions; and a part of them crossing the stream, came to blows with the Persians, the fight lasting more than three hours, with great slaughter on both sides. The Persians being nearest their bank of the river, easily received support from their own people; while the Turks, being only able to cross by a narrow ford, arrived a few at a time, swimming over with their horses, many also being drowned by the rush of water which carried them away from the ford. At length the Turks were overcome by the Persians, and made to retreat, recrossing the stream in their flight. Mahumut Bassa, who was on a bank, half a mile distant from the place where they were fighting, not only did not give them assistance, but retreated across several streams to another sandbank. The Persians pursued the Turks, killing and taking prisoners; and the Turks in their flight got into disorder, and blocked up the passage, many being drowned by falling into the whirlpools of which there are a great many in this river, and among others Asmurat, Beglerbeg of Romania. When he, with many others, fell into a large whirlpool, the Turks, and in particular his slaves and retainers, endeavouring to assist him, made head, and attacked the Persians again. And numbers of them being killed and drowned, the Persians crossing several streams in pursuit of the Turks, arrived at a muddy bank on which Mahumut Bassa had formed many squadrons, and where the contest was renewed.

But the Persians, with all their efforts, could gain no ground in the hand to hand fight that ensued with the troops of Mahumut, neither party gaining the least advantage. And as the evening began to come on, and the day to close, the Turk, who the whole time with all the rest of the army had been under arms on the bank of the river, sounded a retreat, and Ussuncassano, who had been also under arms on the other bank, did the same. And the retreat being sounded on both sides, each withdrew without any further attack; still Ussuncassano had the best of the fight, as of his men fewer were killed, but few drowned, and not one taken prisoner. But on our side, when the muster was made, there were twelve thousand men missing, among whom were several persons of note. Sentinels were posted on the banks of the river, the Persians doing the same, as both parties were apprehensive of an attack....

Chap. VIII.—Ussun Cassano pursues the Turk, who, after his defeat, returns to his country, and a battle takes place, in which, by the flight of Ussun Cassano from the army, the Persians are routed, and the Grand Turk remains victorious.

Having suffered this defeat, the Turk became very apprehensive, and determined to lead his army back to his country by the shortest route; and, to console his soldiers, besides their usual pay, he gave them another advance, making them a present of the former one which he had given at his departure. Also he liberated all his slaves that were in the camp, on the condition that none should abandon him, but should serve him like the other troops, who are not slaves, and who can do what they like with their own; he made many other concessions to the captains. The army having started, we marched along the bank of the river, and the Persians did the same on the other side, not attempting to cross, but keeping on their guard, seeing that the Turkish army was still larger than theirs; nevertheless, as was afterwards reported, Ussuncassano was incited by his sons and the other commanders to cross the river and attack us, as we were in flight in consequence of the defeat we had sustained, many consultations being held about it. At the end of about ten days the Turkish forces, having turned away from the river, with the city of Baybret on their right, among the mountains which separate Greater and Lesser Armenia, took their way towards the northwest, entering a valley on the route to Trebizond. At the second halt we made after entering the valley, at the end of August, at the fourteenth hour of the day, behold the Persians appeared on the mountains on our right.

Then the Turk faced round towards the enemy, and gained the heights, but first fortified the camp, leaving the brother of the ruler of Scandeloro, named Eustraf, to guard it and the bagage-waggons. All the arrangements being made, he marched by the mountains towards the enemy, placing Daut Bassa Beglerbeg of Natolia, with his whole column, and all those of Romania who remained from the first rout in the van, Bajesit, the Grand Turk's eldest son, being on the right of his father, and Mustafa, the second, on the left. Thus marching over mountains and rocky ground, we arrived at a valley on the other side of which the Persians were drawn up, with a very extended line, opposite which the Grand Turk had his men arrayed. Then both sides sounded a countless number of naccare, drums, and other warlike instruments, the noise and din being so great that one had to hear it to imagine it. The slopes of the valley where the armies fronted each other were easy of ascent and descent; it was a quarter of a mile wide and rather long, in a wild situation among mountains.

Here began a stubborn contest, first one party and then the other repulsing the enemy, each giving assistance to their own side wherever the need was greatest, until Pirahomat, prince of Caramania, who was on Ussuncassano's right, after a fierce resistance, was defeated by Mustafa, son of the Grand Turk, and recoiling on the flank of Ussuncassano, who, fearing to be surrounded, which might easily have happened, from the superiority of the Turks on every side, and principally on the right, where the great captain Mustafa fought, began to get very much afraid, mounted an Arab mare, and in a very short time took to flight. In this way they were routed and chased as far as the tents, which were nearly ten miles off in a plain, and some of the prisoners taken at the rout of the fords were rescued. The tents were also plundered and an immense booty taken, and among the slain was a son of Ussuncassano named Zeinel, whose head was presented to the Turk by a foot-soldier who had killed him in the battle; since this prince Zeinel, leaving his father when he mounted the mare, entered among the infantry, and was surrounded and slain with many of his followers. This was a great rout, about ten thousand of the Persians being killed, and many more taken prisoners, of whom some were put to death each day.

The night was all spent in rejoicing, with bonfires, and music, and shouting. But because Mustafa the Sultan's son had pursued Ussun Cassano, and it was now the second hour of the night, the Turk became anxious, and sent some couriers after him, with whom he returned. His father came out of his tent with a cup of gold full of julep, which he presented to him with his own hand, kissing him and commending him greatly for his bearing and valour. This battle lasted eight continuous hours before the Persians were put to rout, and if it had not been for Mustafa and Ussun Cassano's cowardly flight, they might not have lost. In this battle, of Turks there were in all about one thousand killed. There were found in the baggage-waggons of Ussun Cassano some vases of gold, with their sheaths covered with copper, and other vases of gold and silver; there were also some fine suits of armour, made at Syras, quite masterpieces, like mirrors, with gilt borders wonderfully polished and a marvel to behold. They also captured a thousand horses and a great number of camels. I must not omit to mention that in this battle Ugurlimehemet, Ussun Cassano's second son, came with a great number of men to assail our camp, but he also was repulsed by the lord Cusers [Eustraf?] and the rest of the garrison, and so much so that he narrowly escaped being taken prisoner, but got away through his acquaintance with the country. Thus if Ussun Cassano had remained content with his first victory, the Turk would have gone away ignominiously, and he would not have lost the territories he did.

Source: Giovan Maria Angiolelli, "Life and Acts of King Ussun Cassano," in Charles Grey, ed. and trans., *A Narrative of Italian Travels in Persia in the Fifteenth and Sixteenth Centuries* (London: Hakluyt Society, 1873), 86–92.

90. The Poetry of Shah Ismail I of Persia: Mathnavi No. 3 (ca. 1500–1510)

Introduction

The charismatic young monarch of Persia, Shah Ismail I (r. 1500–1524), a red-haired grandson of Uzun Hasan and his Christian fourth wife from Trebizond, whose forebears included Muslim, Georgian, Turkish, and Byzantine royalty and nobility, reestablished Persia as a state and Great Power in the early 16th century and founded the Safavid dynasty. After establishing himself as ruler of Azerbaijan at the age of 13, with the help of Turkoman tribesmen who adhered to Shia Islam, by the time Ismail was in his late 20s he had conquered Iran, Mesopotamia, Armenia, much of Anatolia, and Uzbekistan. Highly educated and literate and a prolific poet, in his writings Ismail rather grandiloquently expressed his boundless ambitions and his pride in his family as well as his views on religion, theology, philosophy, and, on occasion, love. The translator of his lengthy poem "Mathnavi No. 3," which was probably composed when Ismail was still very young, considered both its grammar and vocabulary "original" but bluntly stated that "Its poetical merits are nil; but the leisurely epic metre and the unconventional flow of oratory gave the poet much more freedom than the shorter poems on religious and love subjects." Modesty was clearly not characteristic of its author, who grandiloquently complained that he lacked worthy adversaries and longed to test himself against some of the greatest heroes of the past.

Document

1. In the name of God, Living and Bountiful, for His is might and His nature is old.

2. It is He who exalts the "Nine Heavens" and purifies the face of the earth.

90. The Poetry of Shah Ismail I of Persia: Mathnavi No. 3

3. He produces the storm like unto Simoom; by the wind of the Day of Resurrection he softens stones to wax.

4. He makes some superior to others, some is suspense (?) and some lowly;

5. Some like Solomon, and some like ants, some vilified and some strong.

6. He makes some superior to the whole world, and some a refuge to men.

7. He makes some lords of the world, and while He flowers, He creates others as thorns.

8. He makes some (sit on) the throne and (wear) a crown; others needy of half-a-farthing.

9. He makes some awful like Rustam, and others [with] less hair (muichak?);

10. Some endowed with courage (lit. liver), others without and carrion-like.

11. To some He gives swords and good horses, while He checkmates others on their carpet.

12. He creates some (as if) to stand (lit. fall) as Alexander's wall, and some as if to flee like deserters (or "like swift stallions"?).

13. God is the Creator of all, He is cognizant of everybody's affairs.

14. Has He not created five fingers to a narrow hand so that each of them (?) should know its way?

15. Were all the world equal, how would the affairs of the world be successful?

16. Surely there is a difference between slave-girls and a man; Heaven and Earth are not equal.

17. A man must know his perfection and do what work he can do.

18. A mouse in the desert says: "I am wicked," but when it is confronted (with an enemy) it loses its way.

19. Do not believe such (pretensions) before you have scanned them, do not lean on the wall of an unmanly person.

20. God (Haqq) is the Helper in this world; in bad days He shares the sorrow of his slaves.

21. A brave beg (bag-igit) will conquer all lands: all Asia Minor (Rum), China, Khorasan, and Syria.

22. Is he a man, he who marches with an army against a (single) man? Is an army (necessary) to crush an enemy?

23. In a fight, lads (aran) would crush one single man, but in an army the beg becomes the leader of men (ar-sarvari).

24. I am he who will fight a crocodile, and wage war with the tiger and the panther.

25. I am such that should I meet Afrasiyab, I will smite his head with my mace and stun him.

26. I am he who will march without fear against the foe; do not be afraid that on looking (at him) I shall show hesitancy.

27. I shall smash the fortress of Khaybar with my fist; shall I (ever) fear cannon and guns?

28. I shall conquer Asia Minor and Syria, and then think of the Franks.

29. Should Afrasiyab be my foe, I shall take it for a dishonour to come to blows with him.

30. Should something happen to you in a fight, turn not your back, run not with shouts towards your companion.

31. A pity! Would that there were a suitable occasion, should see a man better than himself!

32. A pity! Would that Isfandiyar existed now, that I might spare neither his throne, nor his kingdom, nor his country.

33. A pity! Would that Afrasiyab were there, that I might answer (his challenge) with my sword.

34. A pity! Would that Giv lived nowadays, that I might appear to him like a male divinity.

35. A pity! Would that Zal were alive now, that he might see what a struggle is like.

36. A pity! Would that the hero Sohrab were now in existence! He would not be striking with his sword in his hand.

37. A pity that (on the battlefield) I am tied to females, that I encounter but effeminates and cowards.

38. A pity, that there is no longer a price for a man, for a hero breaking through the enemy line, for a male lion.

39. Neither Rustam nor Bijan are my opponents, a female wanted (?) to command me.

40. I wish there were a great fight that I might encounter the foe face to face.

41. They would know that a Man has been born of a mother; every one would hear news of his talents.

42. "A hero eats (his) bread in a manly way." This word was said by the best of the braves (or "by one of the braves").

43. How can one eat bread without labour; every piece of bread is in a dragon's mouth.

44. Go and annihilate the dragon, snatch that bread from his mouth.

45. O God, sharpen my sword that it should smite the foe seeking my life.

46. Exalt my sire through my hand, let my sire run at the envious (enemy). Let not the foe spit into my face, but rather at my dead body.

48. Let thirty thousand men be my enemies, and each one of them be Rustam-like.

49. When I make up my mind to take the field, let them come and let me fight them alone.

50. Let me smite them all with the sword so that they should forget their designs and their attack.

51. Are the braves annoyed by death? Shall I keep (this) bag of ungnawed bones?

52. Nobody says to the one devoid of energy "This is a Man"; better is death for a liar lacking ardour.

53. Do not associate me with cowards, who, in the eyes of an Alan, are less than females.

54. Lengthen my sword that I reach the enemy and scatter before me his array and his right flank.

55. Even for an Isfandiyar I shall make the field too narrow; lion or panther will stand my blows.

56. O Lord, show me Thy friendliness and, though the foe be a Rustam, I will smash him.

57. O God, accept my prayer for my needs, my supplication at Thy gate, and my appeal to Thee,

58. Through the merits of my Prophet who is the Miracle of Speech, (?) and of 'Ali, who is the Perfect Imam.

59. (They?) did not turn away their faces, but on this path made sacrifice of their beings.

60. Pray, let me work havoc in (the) ranks (of the foe), for only by the sword can the foe be abashed.

Source: Translated by Victor Minorsky, in V. Minorsky, "The Poetry of Shāh Ismā'īl I," *Bulletin of the School of Oriental and African Studies* 10, no. 4 (1942): 1050a–1053a.

91. Letters between Ottoman Sultan Selim I and Shah Ismail I of Persia (1514)

Introduction

In 1514 Shah Ismail I (r. 1501–1524), founder of the Safavid dynasty of Persia who had reestablished Iran as a major power in the Middle East, and the Ottoman sultan Selim I came into conflict. Both rulers were bent on territorial expansion. Ismail I, an Azerbaijani ruler of exotic mixed descent whose grandparents included a Byzantine princess and the Turkoman Sheikh Uzun Hasan, established his hold on power and massively extended his domains with the help of Turkoman Shia Islamic tribes, conquering both Iran and Iraq as well as Armenia, Eastern Anatolia, and Uzbekistan and reducing the rulers of Georgia to vassal status. Originally a Sufi leader, Ismail made Shia Islam the official religion of Iran, aggressively destroying Sunni sacred sites. Both his territorial ambitions and his religious affiliation brought him into conflict with the Ottoman Empire, the champion of Sunni Islam. Before going to war in 1514, the two rulers—both of them well known for their poetry—exchanged a long series of belligerent and bombastic letters that highlighted their religious differences and also their determination not to back down.

Documents

Letter from Selim to Ismail, 1514

"It is from Solomon: 'In the Name of God, the Compassionate, the Merciful. Do not exalt yourselves above me, but come to me in all submission.'" (Qur'an 27: 30–31) God's blessings upon the best of his creatures, Muhammad, his family, and his companions all.

And now We have revealed this Scripture truly blessed. Observe it and keep from evil, so that you may find mercy. (Qur'an 6: 156)

This missive, which is stamped with the seal of victory and which—like inspiration descending from the heavens—is witness to the verse "We do not punish a nation until We have sent forth a messenger to forewarn them." (Qur'an 17: 15) has been graciously issued by our most glorious majesty—we who are the Caliph of God Most High in this world, far and wide; the proof of the verse "that which profits men remains on the earth" (Qur'an 13: 17); the Solomon of Splendor, the Alexander of eminence; haloed in victory, Faridun triumphant; slayer of the wicked and the infidel, guardian of the noble and the pious; the warrior in the Path, the defender of the Faith; the champion, the conqueror; the lion, son and grandson of the lion; standard-bearer of justice and righteousness, Sultan Selim Shah son of Sultan Bâyezid, son of Sultan Mehmet Khan—and is addressed to the ruler of the kingdom of the Persians, the possessor of the land of tyranny and perversion, the captain of the vicious, the chief of the malicious, the usurping Darius of the time, the malevolent Zahhak of the age, the peer of Cain, Prince Isma'il.

As the Pen of Destiny has drawn up the rescript "You bestow sovereignty on whom You will" (Qur'an 3: 26) in our sublime name and has signed it with the verse "The blessings God bestows on men none can withhold" (Qur'an 35: 2), it is manifest in the Court of Glory and the Presence of Deity that we, the instrument of Divine Will, shall hold in force upon the earth both the commandments and prohibitions of Divine Law as well as the provisions of royal proclamations. "Such is the grace of God: He bestows it on whom He will." (Qur'an 57: 21).

It has been heard repeatedly that you have subjected the upright community of Muhammad (Prayers and salutations upon its founder!) to your devious will, that you have undermined the firm foundation of the Faith, that you have unfurled the banner of oppression in the cause of aggression, that you no longer uphold the commandments and prohibitions of the Divine Law, that you have incited your abominable Shi'i faction to unsanctified sexual union and to the shedding of innocent blood, that—like they "Who listen to falsehood and practice what is unlawful" (Qur'an 5: 42)—you have given ear to idle deceitful words and have partaken of that which is forbidden:

> He has laid waste to mosques, as it is said,
> Constructing idol temples in their stead,

that you have rent the noble fabric of Islam with the hand of tyranny, and that you have called the Glorious Qur'an the myths of the Ancients. The rumor of these abominations has caused your name to become like that of Harith deceived by Satan.

Indeed, as both the legal rulings of distinguished religious scholars who base their opinion on reason and tradition alike and the consensus of the Sunni community agree that the ancient obligation of extirpation, extermination, and expulsion of evil innovation must be the aim of our exalted aspiration, for "Religious zeal is a victory for the Faith of God the Beneficent": then, in accordance with the words of the Prophet (Peace upon him!) "Whosoever introduces evil innovation into our order must be expelled" and "Whosoever does anything against our order must be expelled," action has become necessary and exigent. Thus, when the Divine Decree of Eternal Destiny commended the eradication of the infamously wicked infidels into our capable hands, we set out for their lands like ineluctable fate itself to enforce the order "Do not leave a single unbeliever on the earth." (Qur'an 71: 26) If God Almighty wills, the lightning of our conquering sword shall uproot the untamed bramble grown to great heights in the path of the refulgent Divine Law and shall cast them down upon the dust of abjectness to be trampled under the hooves of our legions, for "They abase the mightiest of its inhabitants and these will do the same" (Qur'an 27: 34); the thunder of our avenging mace shall dash out the muddled brains of the enemies of the Faith as rations for the lionhearted ghazis. "The wrongdoers will realize what a reversal they shall have." (Qur'an 26: 227)

> When I draw my keen-edged weapon from its sheath,
> Then shall I raise up doomsday on the earth;
> Then shall I roast the hearts of lion-hearted men,
> And toast the morning with a goblet of their blood.
> My crow-fletched shaft will fix the eagle in his flight;
> And my bare blade will shake the orb of day.

> Ask of the sun about the dazzle of my reign;
> Inquire of Mars about the brilliance of my arms.
> Although you wear a Sufi crown, I bear a trenchant sword,
> And he who holds the sword will soon possess the crown.
> O Mighty Fortune, pray grant this my single wish:
> Please let me take both crown and power from the foe.

But "Religion is Counsel." Therefore, should you turn the face of submission toward our angelic threshold—the refuge of the noble, the qibla of felicity, and the Ka'ba of certainty—and lift the hand of oppression from the heads of your subjects bowed by oppression and sedition, take up a course of repentance and become like one blameless, return to the sublime straight path of the Sunna of Muhammad (Prayers and salutations upon him and God's satisfaction upon his immaculate family and his rightly-guided companions all!)—for "My companions are like the stars: whomever you choose to follow, you will be guided aright."—and consider your lands and their people a part of the well-protected Ottoman state, then shall you be granted our royal favor and our imperial condescension.

> He whose face touches the dust of my threshold in submission
> Will be enveloped in the shadow of my favor and my justice.

> How great the happiness of him who complies with this!

On the other hand, if your evil and seditious habits have become ingrained in your nature, then that which has become essential can never again be accidental.

> Of what avail are sermons to the black-hearted?

Then, with the support and assistance of God, I will crown the head of every gallows tree with the head of a crown-wearing Sufi and clear that faction from the face of the earth—"God's followers are sure to triumph" (Qur'an 5: 56); I will break the oppressors' grip with the power of the miraculous white hand of Moses, for "The Hand of God is above their hands." (Qur'an 48: 10) Let them remove the cotton of negligence from the ears of their intelligence and, with their shrouds on their shoulders, prepare themselves for "That which you are threatened with is sure to come." (Qur'an 6: 134) The triumphant troops "As firm as a mighty edifice" (Qur'an 61: 4) crying out like fate evoked "When their hour is come, not for one moment shall they hold it back, nor can they go before it" (Qur'an 7: 34) and maneuvering in accordance with "Put them to death wherever you find them" (Qur'an 4: 89), will wreak ruin upon you and drive you from that land. "Such being the will of God before and after, and on that day the believers will rejoice in God's help." (Qur'an 30: 4) "Thus were the evil-doers annihilated. Praise be to God, Lord of the Universe." (Qur'an 6: 45)

Response from Ismail to Selim, 1514

May his godly majesty, the refuge of Islam, the might of the kingdom, he upon whom God looks with favor, the champion of the sultanate and of the state, the hero of the faith and of the earth, Sultan Selim Shah (God grant him immortal state and eternal happiness!) accept this affectionate greeting and this friendly letter, considering it a token of our good will.

Now to begin: Your honored letters have arrived one after another, for "No sooner has a thing doubled than it has tripled." Their contents, although indicative of hostility, are stated with boldness and vigor. The latter gives us much enjoyment and pleasure, but we are ignorant of the reason for the former. In the time of your late blessed father (May God enlighten his proof!) when our royal troops passed through the lands of Rum to chastise the impudence of 'Ala' al-Dawla Dhu'l-Qadr, concord and friendship was shown on both sides. Moreover, when your majesty was governor at Trebizond there existed perfect mutual understanding. Thus, now, the cause of your resentment and displeasure yet remains unknown. If political necessity has compelled you on this course, then may your problems be soon resolved.

> Dispute may fire words to such a heat
> That ancient houses be consumed in flames.

The intention of our inaction in this regard is twofold:

(1) Most of the inhabitants of the land of Rum are followers of our forefathers (May God the All-Forgiving King have mercy upon them!).
(2) We have always loved the ghazi-titled Ottoman house and we do not wish the outbreak of sedition and turmoil once again as in the time of Timur.

Why should we then take umbrage at these provocations? We shall not.

> The mutual hostility of kings is verily an ancient rite.
> Should one embrace the bride of worldly rule too close,
> His lips will kiss those of the radiant sword.

Nevertheless, there is no cause for improper words: indeed, those vain, heretical imputations are the mere fabrications of the opium-clouded minds of certain secretaries and scribes. We therefore think that our delayed reply was not completely without cause for we have now dispatched our honored personal companion and servant Shah Quli Aqa (May he be sustained!) with a golden casket stamped with the royal seal and filled with a special concoction for their use should they deem it necessary. May he soon arrive, so that with assistance from Above, the mysteries concealed behind the veil of fate might be disclosed. Keeping in view that regrets are of no avail in the end, one should always exercise free judgment and not be bound solely by the words of others.

At this writing we were engaged upon the hunt near Isfahan. We now prepare provisions and our troops for the coming campaign and in all friendship we say, "Do what you will."

> Bitter experience has taught that in this world of trial
> He who falls upon the house of 'Ali always falls.

Kindly give our ambassador leave to travel unmolested for "No soul shall bear another's burden." (Qur'an 6: 164; 53: 38) When war becomes inevitable, hesitation and delay must be set aside, and one must think on that which is to come. Farewell.

Source: John E. Woods, trans., *Asnad va namaha-yi tarikhi va ijtima'i-yi dawrayi safaviya*, ed. by Z. Sabitiyan (Tehran: Ibn Sina, 1964), 112–117, http://www.fas.nus.edu.sg/hist/eia/documents_archive/selim.php.

92. The Battle of Chaldiran (August 23, 1514)

Introduction

Ottoman sultan Selim I (r. 1512–1520), facing discontent among his janissary troops and Shia uprisings by dissident Muslims in his domains, decided to move against Shah Ismail I of Persia, the great patron of Shia Islam. In the summer of 1514 Selim led an army that invaded Persian-held territories, encountering and defeating Ismail's hitherto invincible troops at the Battle of Chaldiran. Much about this engagement remains unclear. The Venetian official, geographer, and historian Giovanni Battista

92. The Battle of Chaldiran

Ramusio (1485–1557), who collected and edited several narratives written by Italian travelers to Persia including that of the Venetian ambassador Caterino Zeno, claimed in the extract included below that Ismail was not present in person at the Battle of Chaldiran. The Persian chronicler Eskandar Beg Monshi (ca. 1560–ca. 1632), writing in the early 17th century, gave a dramatic account describing how Ismail "entered that frightful field in person, supervising the course of the battle and performing deeds of valor" that included attacking the Ottoman gun carriages and engaging in personal combat, until prevailed upon by his closest companions to flee the field after he had been wounded and almost captured.

The Battle of Chaldiran marked a decisive Ottoman blow against what had until then been the steadily expansionist policies of Safavid Iran under its charismatic founding ruler, Ismail I, who had embraced Shiite Islam, the inspiration for many of his dedicated *qezelbāš* [red-turbaned] fighters. Selim took Mesopotamia and Eastern Anatolia, the beginning of several decades of contention between Persia and Turkey over these territories, ultimately resolved well over a century later in Turkey's favor. Ismail, demoralized by the temporary capture of his capital, Tabriz, and the capture of most of his harem and treasure, never took the field again, finding refuge in alcohol until his death in 1524 at the age of 36.

Document

… Selim, the Grand Turk, having heard that Ismail was engaged with the war waged against the city of Samarcant [Samarkand], which was the largest in the possession of the Tartar prince, brought together an immense army of Turks, and advanced in person against Persia, in the year 1514; he marched towards the river of Sivas, which is six hundred miles distant from Constantinople and six hundred and forty from Tauris: so that one may say that it is about half way between the two cities, and having passed the river Lai, he marched forward quickly through the country of Arsenga [Erzincan]. Ismail, who was in Tauris without his regular troops, who were engaged in besieging Samarcant, hearing of this, began to levy other forces in haste, and having collected a tolerably good army placed it under two of his most valiant captains, one named Stacalu Amarbei and the other Aurbec Samper, and sent them against Selim, in order, by skirmishing, to retard his advance until he had assembled sufficient men to oppose his enemy openly in the field. This army consisted of fifteen thousand horsemen, all good soldiers, and, so to speak, the flower of the Persian people, as the kings of Persia are not accustomed to give pay on the occasion of war, but to a standing force, which is called the "porta" of the king. Thus it is that the Persian gentlemen, to be well brought up, pay great attention to horsemanship, and when necessity calls, go willingly to war, and bring with them, according to their means, a certain number of servants as well armed and mounted as themselves; nevertheless, they do not come out except for the defence of the country; so that, if the Persian soldiery were paid, as is the Turkish, there is no doubt but that it would be far superior to that of the Ottoman princes.…

Now, the two captains, Amarbei and Samper, marched ahead, and hearing that Selim had crossed the Euphrates and was advancing by forced marches, retreated to Coi [Khoi], where Ismail, who had come from Tauris, was in person. Being informed of the large forces Selim was bringing with him on this enterprise, he caused his army to be strongly entrenched, and returned to Tauris to collect more troops, and then to show front to the enemy. Coi is a city which they say was built on the ruins of the ancient Artasata, not more than three days' journey distant from Tauris; on this account, it appeared likely to Ismail, from its proximity, that he might in a very short time find himself engaged in a battle, and therefore expressly commanded the above-mentioned captains to wait, and when he arrived with fresh forces they would drive back the enemy together. However, shortly after the departure of Ismail, the Turkish army came up in array, on the 24th of August, and spread itself over the plains called Calderane, where the Persians also had their encampment.

The latter, seeing the enemy behave with such audacity and provoke them to battle, could not refrain from attacking them, as they had been victorious in so many past wars under the auspices of the greatest monarch of the East: hence, having been joined the night before by some bands of horse from Tauris, making them in all twenty-four thousand men, divided in two deep columns, of which one was led by Stacalu Amarbei and the other by Aurbec Samper, signal of battle being given, they attacked the enemy bravely.

Amarbei, who was foremost, assaulted the troops of Natolia with such a terrific rush, that he broke and routed them utterly, and the Persians made such a slaughter of the Turks, that in that quarter they already had the victory in their hands, if it had not been that Sinan Pasha, to aid that side of the conflict advanced the Caramanian troops, and, taking the Persian force in flank, enabled those who were routed and preparing to fly to make head again. The Persians, resisting Sinan, bore themselves as valiantly as before; nor even when Amarbei was cut to pieces did they fail to keep up the fight courageously.

Samper, seeing the Caramanians change their positions and attack Amarbei, also closed his column and attacked Sinan on his flank, routed the Caramanians, and in a moment was on the royal forces, and the cavalry, though in disorder and badly led, cut to pieces the foremost ranks of the janissaries, and cast into confusion that famous infantry, so that it appeared a thunderbolt cleaving that large and mighty army. The monarch, seeing the slaughter, began to retreat, and to turn about, and was about to fly, when Sinan, coming to the rescue at the time of need, caused the artillery to be brought up and fired on both the janissaries and Persians. The Persian horses hearing the thunder of those infernal machines, scattered and divided themselves over the plain, not obeying their riders' bit or spur any more, from the terror they were in. Sinan, seeing this, made up one squadron of cavalry from all that which had been routed by the Persians, and began to cut them to pieces everywhere, so that, by his activity, Selim, even when he thought all lost, came off the victor. It is certainly said, that if it had not been for the artillery, which terrified in the manner related the Persian horses which had never before heard such a din, all his forces would have been routed and put to the edge of the sword; and if the Turk had been beaten, the power of Ismail would have become greater than that of Tamerlane, as by the fame alone of such a victory he would have made himself absolute lord of the East.

As it happened, the Persians being discomfited, in the manner related, by Selim, not without great loss on his side, Aurbec Samper was led before him covered with wounds, and on his hearing that Ismail had not been in the action, he said to him, full of indignation, "Dog that thou art, thou hast had the audacity to come against me, who am in the place of a prophet, and hold the post of God on earth." To this, without any sign of fear, Samper replied, "If you held the post of God on earth, you would not come against my master; but God has saved you from our hands, that you may fall alive into his, and then he will avenge his and our wrongs." Selim, being greatly enraged by his words, said,

"Go and kill this dog." And he replied, "I know that this is my hour; but do you prepare your soul to pay the sacrifice of mine; since my master will meet you in a year, and will do the same to you, which you order to be done to me"; whereupon he was immediately cut to pieces. Having done this, Selim raised the camp and came to Coi, in which city he rested with his whole army some days; he then published abroad, and wrote in many letters sent to different places, that he had gained the victory, and that Ismail had been in person in the battle which had taken place in the Calderani plains. This, however, was written falsely, as Ismail was not there in person, nor even the corps of his veteran soldiers, who were then round Samarcant, investing that city.

Source: Caterino Zeno, "Travels in Persia," in Charles Grey, ed. and trans., *A Narrative of Italian Travels in Persia in the Fifteenth and Sixteenth Centuries* (London: Hakluyt Society, 1873), 58–63.

93. The Ottoman Conquest of Egypt (1516–1517)

Introduction

The Ottoman sultan Selim I (r. 1512–1520), after overcoming the forces of Shah Ismail I of Persia at the Battle of Chalderan in 1514, turned his attention to a campaign against the Mamluk Sultanate of Egypt. The enterprise was brief and conclusive. On August 24, 1516, at the Battle of Marj Dabiq, Ottoman forces equipped with modern guns encountered and defeated Mamluk troops who relied largely on bows and arrows. Sultan Khansuh al-Ghuri died in combat, and the Ottomans promptly overran Syria. The Battle of Yaunis Khan on October 28, 1516, inflicted a second defeat on the Mamluks. Selim I then joined his troops and advanced on the Egyptian capital of Cairo, defeating the new Egyptian sultan, Tuman Bey, at the Battle of Ridaniya on January 24, 1517, and then capturing and sacking Cairo. Tuman Bey continued guerrilla operations but was defeated once more in late March. Fleeing the field, he took refuge with former supporters, who eventually betrayed him into Ottoman hands. Kazi Asker (Cadi Lascher), a high-ranking military officer in the Ottoman Army, sent the account of this campaign given below to a friend shortly after its end.

Document

Chap. XX.—The Turk makes an expedition against the Soldan, and meeting him in battle, defeats him, the Soldan being slain.

In the year 1516, the Turk hearing of the agreement between the Soldan [of Egypt] and the Sophi [Ismail I of Persia], and seeing that Ismael was hard pressed by those of the green caftans, determined to set out with a large army against the Soldan. In the same year, in the month of May, he sent his troops across the strait into Natolia under his general Sinan Bassa, with a number of arquebusiers and artillerymen, commanding him to march towards Caramania. Traversing the country of the Turcomans he arrived at a place named Albustan, and remained there several days to refresh his troops. The Sophi hearing this sent envoys to the Sultan of the Mamelukes, Campson, named the Gauri, to tell him that he would advance from one quarter and that the Gauri should do the same from the other, and together crush Sinan Pasha. The Soldan agreed to all, and, having assembled a great number of soldiers, leaving Cairo, went to Aleppo; the Turk hearing this, set out from Constantinople on the 5th June, 1516, to join Sinan Bassa, and while on the journey sent forward as his envoys the Cadi Lascher [Kazi Asker], and Zachaia Bassa to enquire of the Soldan his reasons for coming in this unexpected way to Aleppo. But he received no satisfactory answer, which plainly shewed an understanding with the Sophi. Therefore the Turk summoned all the Doctors and learned men, and enquired of them the will of God. They answered that it was his duty first to root out that obnoxious thorn, and then to follow the path in which God would guide him. Hearing the reply he marched toward Aleppo with an immense army, and great rejoicings, and on his arrival there encamped in a beautiful plain near the venerated tomb of the prophet David, sending the vanguard in advance in four divisions; so that the troops were under arms both night and day. The Mamelukes, arriving the following day, arrayed themselves in order of battle.... Arrayed in this manner on the 24th of August, at the third hour of the day they joined in a fierce and sanguinary contest which lasted till mid day. Opposed to the Greeks was the ruler of Damascus, a great chief named Sibes, and opposed to the Natolians was Caierbec the ruler of Aleppo; Sinan Bassa fighting bravely drove back those opposed to him as far as their standards, and the other troops seeing the valour of the Bassa followed up their success, both parties bearing themselves bravely, and repulsing the enemy in turn five or six times. At last the ruler of Aleppo turned his back, and fled with all his troops, when the Bassa turned his arms against the ruler of Damascus, who was not able to resist any longer and fled to the great Soldan. He was pursued by one of the Grecian warriors, who cut off his head, and shortly afterwards the Soldan Campsonthe Gauri [Khansuh al-Ghuri] was slain....

Chap. XXI.—Tomombei [Tuman Bay], the new Soldan, hearing of the victory of the Turk, sends Algazeli against the Turks in Gazzara; but Sinan Bassa going to their assistance, confronts and defeats him. The Turk leaves Damascus and goes to Jerusalem, where he gives alms and offers sacrifices.

The new Soldan of Cairo, the great Diodar surnamed Tomombei, was quickly informed of this victory; and Algazeli who was a brave General, on his arrival at Cairo asked permission to go and attack this force. The Turks who had arrived at Gazzara [Gaza] stood firm, and this Algazeli, setting out from Cairo with five thousand well armed Mamelukes, hurried through the country raising troops. The Turks at Gazzara became apprehensive, but nevertheless determined to perish sword in hand; the Grand Turk, on receiving the news, determined to reinforce the troops at Gazzara, and for this purpose send Sinan Bassà with fifteen thousand men. Algazeli having left Cairo arrived at Catia, and after crossing the sandy desert and coming to a caravanserai or villa where he halted, received intelligence of Sinan's arrival at Gazzara; though this was to his great disgust, as it prevented him accomplishing his object, he nevertheless plucked up spirits, and exhorted his men to fight valiantly, promising them the victory. Having arranged an assault on the Turks during the night, news of this determination came to the ears of the enemy, and Sinan Bassà arrayed his troops for the battle, and resolved to conquer or die; there being no other alternative left them, as they were surrounded by such a number of Moors. That night they held great rejoicings with salutes and bonfires, praying to Allah for victory, and set out on their march; hence the people of Gazzara imagined that they were retreating to join their sovereign, the Grand Turk, and therefore they put to death all the wounded in Gazzara, and informed Algazeli that our troops had fled. This caused him great satisfaction, but at the third hour of the day, seeing the dust made by the army which he thought had fled, coming to meet him in battle, his satisfaction was turned to disgust, and he seemed struck with astonishment. Our men drawing near, dismounted, tightened the girths of their horses, and then asking forgiveness one of another, they shook hands, embraced, and commenced praying to God for the sake of his prophet Mahomet, and his four vicars, Abu Beker, Omar, Osman, and Ali, and all the other prophets, his predecessors, that he would give the victory to the army of the true Mussulmans.

Then Sinan Bassà, turning to the army, exhorted them all, saying that they had often before routed larger armies and gained more important battles than these; telling them that they should stand firm, as he who was destined to die would perish even if he fled, and he who was not destined to fall would not do so even if he fought on; and that as male wethers are proper for sacrifices, so ought they to fight for their sovereign. "Let us avenge our friends, whom these dogs have slain at the first outset, whose corpses, if they could speak, would cry, 'Slay, slay'; if you conquer you will receive great rewards from our ruler, and obtain great fame, as many of you who are now of low rank will be promoted." They all replied, saying: "God give long life to our sovereign; may the whole earth be subjected to him; and let him who does not submit be put to death. Forward! Forward!"

Having marched, therefore, and the two armies having met, the Circassians resisted our attack with great courage and daring, each side repulsing the other in turn several times from the third hour till noon, numbers being slain. At last the Circassians were routed, while our troops were highly elated with the victory and immense booty; the Mamelukes fled to Cairo, pursued by some of our men. The others returned to Gazzara with Sinan Bassà, stuffing with straw the heads of the dead chiefs, while the others they fixed to the palm trees in memory of the battle.

The great monarch [Selim I] sent two hundred Solacchi to meet Sinan Bassà, and request him to ride forward and meet him in a certain place. . . . Then he met Sinan Bassà, and thanked him, the army, and the Spachi, which means noblemen, and made them many presents. . . .

Chap. XXII.—The Turk marches on Cairo, and the Soldan, with Algazeli, confronts him; but in the battle is defeated and flies in disguise; while the Turk enters the capital of the Soldan.

We then set out on the straight route to Cairo, where the newly created Soldan Tomombei was making preparations by digging moats and raising embankments of earth with a great number of labourers. He also posted pieces of artillery with the design when our army appeared of sweeping it all away, and by a sally of fourteen thousand Mamelukes and twenty thousand auxiliaries to rout it utterly. When we arrived in the country six thousand Mamelukes deserted, and informed the Grand Turk of everything. Therefore he turned suddenly into another road, which was unguarded, and in which he could not be molested by the enemy's artillery. The Circassians and the Soldan seeing that the Sultan was advancing by another route, attacked us with great shouts and yells: Algazeli against the Greek troops, a vizier named Allem against those of Natolia, and the Soldan against the Grand Turk himself; so that, from the morning till mid-day, there was a fierce fight. And in the battle, unfortunately, Sinan Bassà was killed, and with him a great number of his retainers who had partaken of his bread and salt, and who, clad in garments he had given them, devoted themselves to death with their master. They bathed him with their tears, and having enveloped him in a fine cloth, and having sprinkled him in some water called Abzenzom found at Mecca, they buried him in a grave they dug for him. Mustafa Bassà, seeing that all depended on him, with loud shouts and great valour began the combat, which being seen by the men of Natolia, at the head of whom he was, they got so enraged that they cut down the Circassians like grass in the most marvellous manner. The troops of the monarch and of Greece also fought bravely, but at the hour of evening prayers each retired from fatigue, and the Circassians, wearied out, were put to flight, part into Cairo and part to the open country. The Greeks pursued them till night, plundering and slaughtering them; the monarch remained that night on the field of battle, and ordered all the prisoners to be put to death, which was done. They remained here three days, and on the fourth reached the river Nile at a place called Bichieri, where they halted two days. The Mamelukes who had advanced joined the Soldan to the number of nine thousand, planning a night attack; but the Sultan, hearing this, ordered the troops to remain under arms all night. But the enemy, hearing this, changed their plan and determined to attack us by day, and thus came on with fearful yells. The janizzaries fought bravely, and the troops of Greece mounted and fought on horseback. Still, not being able to conquer the enemies that day, both armies retreated. The following morning the great monarch rose with the dawn, and, having returned thanks to God, ordered all the army to be put in array, all mounting, moving with great solemnity and display against the Circassians, who, with their usual cries, began the battle, one side being soon hidden from the other by the dust. The Mamelukes were desperate, and wished for nothing better than to die sword in hand, it appearing to them a disgrace to escape and leave all their possessions in the hands of the enemy, a calamity from which God preserve every one, and more especially all good Mahometans. The monarch, seeing that he could not destroy the Circassians, ordered the city to be set on fire, which the janizzaries did in several places. The Mamelukes, seeing this, cried out for quarter with loud and terrible yells; and the Sultan, having pity on them, ordered the fire to be extinguished, it being almost by a miracle that the whole city was not burnt down. The Circassians renewed the contest with such vigour that the arrows fell like rain; and so many fell on both sides, that the streets of Cairo ran blood, the fight continuing the entire day. At night, the Circassians, being faint and exhausted, retired into a mosque, in which as a citadel they kept up a gallant defence for three days and three nights. But at length, a grand attack being made, the mosque was taken by storm. The Soldan Tomombei escaped in disguise, when the great monarch went to rest and his followers to get booty and prisoners; the heads of these prisoners were afterwards cut off by the banks of the Nile....

Chap. XXIII.—The Turk sends Ambassadors to the Soldan, who had fled, advising him to submit; but, these men being killed by the Circassians, he sends Mustafa with an army to revenge them. The Soldan is defeated; and, being pursued by Mustafa, is taken prisoner, and brought to the Grand Turk, who causes him to be impaled by one of the gates of Cairo.

[A few days later, the Ottoman forces pursued the Mamluk army and a further battle ensued]

... The monarch [Selim] ordered Mustafa to mount and set the army in array. The Circassians charged and drove back our troops as far as the standard, but, being reinforced, we repulsed them; the Circassians, seeing this, again closed and drove us back with such slaughter that the blood ran in rivers. The Moors fought only to give the Circassians time to rest, so that our men were at a great disadvantage, fighting on bravely still, but with immense loss. The Bassa, who was in attendance on the Sultan, seeing this, and that the day was in a way to be lost, seized his scimitar and bosdocan furiously, and rushed towards the Soldan, intending to cut the life out of his body before dying himself. The Greeks, seeing this act of valour, struggled on to assist their chief. And it is certain that if their courage had failed them then, they would have lost their lives, as they would all have been cut to pieces. But their bravery showed the Soldan that they would gain the victory, and, seeing that from a great and rich monarch he would become a poor and solitary outcast, looking up to heaven he bewailed his sad lot with such bitter words as to make all who heard him pity him. After many words, accompanied with tears, he took to flight, riding night and day till he reached a bridge, where he rested a short time. Mustafa and the Greeks pursued him, but he managed to keep in advance of them. The Turk set out from Cairo, and halted half a day's journey distant from Mustafa, who had pursued the Soldan for four days and as many nights, till he forced him from fatigue to take refuge in a Casal of the Moors.... Tomombei and the Circassians were surrounded by the Moors, so that they could not escape till the arrival of our men, who soon got them into their power. The Circassians threw themselves into a neighbouring lake, while our soldiers cut some of them to pieces and made prisoners of the others. Tomombei was taken standing up to his knees in water, and conducted to the Bassa.... After this there was another battle with the Moors in another fortress near the Nile; the inhabitants and some Mamelukes were continually killing and robbing our men. Mustafa set out and destroyed the fortress, and, after remaining four days, returned to the Turk, who was holding a court, and had commanded that Tomombei Soldan should be led through the country of Cairo on a mule, with a chain round his neck, and that at a gate of the city called Bebzomele he should be impaled, which was immediately done. This was the termination of the kingdom of the Mamelukes and the commencement of the greater power of Selim Sultan. The history of this last expedition of Selim against the Soldan and the Mamelukes was carefully written by a Cadi Lascher [Cazi Asker], who was with the army, to a Cadi in Constantinople, and translated from the Turkish into Tuscan on the 22nd October, 1517.

Source: Giovan Maria Angiolelli, "Life and Acts of King Ussun Cassano," in Charles Grey, ed. and trans., *A Narrative of Italian Travels in Persia in the Fifteenth and Sixteenth Centuries* (London: Hakluyt Society, 1873), 124–137.

94. Ottoman Sultan Selim I (r. 1512–1520): Poem on His Conquests

Introduction

The Ottoman sultan Selim I, in an eight-year reign, enormously expanded the Ottoman Empire, annexing all the territories of the Mamluk Sultanate of Egypt. Under his rule, the Sunni Ottoman state assumed the role of protector of the two holy Muslim cities of Medina and Mecca, effectively taking over the caliphate from Egypt. A little earlier, Selim also beat back the efforts of the Shiite Muslim shah Ismail I of Persia to expand his dominions into Ottoman territory, decisively defeating his enemy at the Battle of Chaldiran in 1514. Selim, a dedicated fighter who won his way to power through civil war, dethroning and exiling his father, Sultan Bayezid II, and his half brother Ahmet, whom Bayezid had expected to be his heir, celebrated his victories over Persia and Egypt in a blunt and straightforward poem that nonetheless expressed his pride in these achievements.

Document

Gazel

> From Istambol's throne a mighty host to Iran guided I;
> Sunken deep in blood of shame I made the Golden Heads to lie.
> Glad the Slave, my resolution, lord of Egypt's realm became:
> Thus I raised my royal banner e'en as the Nine Heavens high.
> From the kingdom fair of Iraq to Hijaz these tidings sped,
> When I played the harp of Heavenly Aid at feast of victory.
> Through my saber Transoxania drowned was in a sea of blood;
> Emptied I of kuhl of Isfahan the adversary's eye.
> Flowed adown a River Amu from each foeman's every hair—
> Rolled the sweat of terror's fever—if I happed him to espy.
> Bishop-mated was the King of India by my Queenly troops,
> When I played the Chess of empire on the Board of sov'reignty.
> O Selimi, in thy name was struck the coinage of the world,
> When in crucible of Love Divine, like gold, that melted I.

Source: Charles F. Horne, ed., *The Sacred Books and Early Literature of the East*, Vol. 6, *Medieval Arabic, Moorish, and Turkish* (New York: Parke, Austin, & Lipscomb, 1917), 283, https://sourcebooks.fordham.edu/source/turkishpoetry1.asp#Gazel5.

95. The Ottoman Capture of Rhodes (1522)

Introduction

In 1480 Ottoman sultan Mehmed II, who had spent his entire reign expanding his domains at the expense of the Christian powers, taking both Constantinople and the empire of Trebizond, unsuccessfully sent his fleet to besiege the island of Rhodes, which was held by the Knights Hospitaller, the Christian military order. Repelled on his first attempt, the sultan planned a second siege but died in 1481. His successors regarded the capture of Rhodes as unfinished business. An Ottoman naval history recounted how Selim I (r. 1512–1520) contemplated an assault against the island, but more pressing military campaigns against Persia and Egypt and then ill health prevented him from undertaking this. Suleiman the Magnificent, the son who followed him as sultan, regarded the capture of Rhodes, which he accomplished in December 1522 after a lengthy siege, as an act of filial duty.

Document

On the decease of Sultan Selim, Suleiman Khan coming to the throne, began to subjugate all those places which he thought proper should be annexed to the Ottoman dominions; and opening both by land and sea the gates of war, he terminated that armistice which from necessity had been adopted during the reign of his illustrious father, and in his second expedition succeeded in the capture of Rhodes.

Preparation of a Fleet for Rhodes

In the year 923 (A.D. 1517), during the reign of Sultan Selim the First, the countries of Egypt having been subdued and added to the Ottoman dominions, in 925 it was considered necessary to open a road for the importation of the productions of that country. For this purpose the capture of Rhodes, the seat of pirates, was suggested to the victorious Sultan, who immediately began to prepare a fleet; but although for a long time reports of an intended expedition were heard from the ministers and nobles, yet from the movements of the Sultan nothing to that effect could be perceived, till one day with his nobles and attendants he went out to visit the tomb of Abi Aiub Ansari, and standing on his usual spot beside the high dome near his nurse's tomb, he read the *Fatihat* [the first chapter of the *Koran*]. Looking towards the channel, he saw one of the newly built vessels cruising about, and in a rage demanded to know by whose authority they had put it to sea, before an expedition had been determined upon; at the same time giving orders for the execution of the Capudan Jafar Aga. Piri Pasha with some difficulty satisfied him, by saying that the vessel had been put to sea merely to try it. On his majesty's return he severely reprimanded the veziers, saying, "Whilst I am accustomed to subdue kingdoms, you waste the means in taking a single castle, the requisite for which is ammunition. How many months will your ammunition last? and are the necessary stores in readiness?" The veziers informed him of what stores they had, but declined giving any account of their ammunition till the next day, and thus they departed with many reproaches. The next morning they reported to his majesty that their ammunition was sufficient for four months. His majesty in a scornful manner replied, that whilst his grandfather Sultan Mohammed Khan's disgrace with respect to Rhodes was not yet forgotten, they wished to double it on him, especially as four months' ammunition was by no means sufficient for the reduction of a fortress like Rhodes, which, if it were taken in double that time, would be highly creditable: that he was determined to undertake no expedition on such vain counsel, nor by the advice of any one; and concluded by saying, that for himself he had no voyage in view, except the one to eternity. According to his prediction, the fortress was with difficulty taken in the time he specified; and about six months after this conversation he departed to the world of spirits.

The Expedition to Rhodes

Sultan Soleiman Khan, of happy memory, ascended the throne in 926 (A.D. 1520).... After the capture of Belgrade, the subjugation of Rhodes being considered most important, the emperor, in the month of Rajab 928, came to the capital and issued orders for the preparation of an immense fleet; and a great number of sailors and azabs being collected, the second vizier, Mustaffa Pasha, was appointed commander. On an auspicious day they set out, and with about seven hundred vessels of various sorts sailed for the Mediterranean. The Capudan Pasha also joined them with the ships he had prepared at Gallipoli; and in the month of Rajab 928 the illustrious emperor passed over to Skutari, whence he pursued his journey by land. The Roumeili troops, having marched by different routes, joined the royal camp in the vales of Moghala; and on the third of Rajab his majesty crossed over to a small island opposite Marmaross. Previously to this, the fleet having arrived in the vicinity of Rhodes, the commander, Kara Mahmūd Reis, sent a few vessels to an island called Herka, and reduced its fortress. After this the fleet touched opposite Jam-Baghche. The heavy vessels were stationed to guard the channel; whilst the pasha, with three hundred galleys, proceeded to the fortress of Rhodes, and entered the harbour of Cape Oghuz. Having arranged their cannon, on the fifth of Ramazan [July 29, 1522] they blockaded the fortress: a week after, Bâli Beg, one of the Egyptian begs, arrived, and with twenty-four galleys, which had sailed before him, brought additional ammunition and stores. They continued to have sharp battles, and to make brave assaults, till the end of *Sheval;* and the *Arab* tower being the occasion of much molestation to the troops, orders were given to attack it. In doing this, although they succeeded in passing the trench, and raised their flag on the walls and towers, yet the enemy bore down and repelled them; and Bâli Beg, the beg of Seké, and Ali Beg, the beg of Avlona, fell as martyrs. As they could not thus effect any thing, they began, with the approbation of the experienced among them to raise a mound, and after five months of continued warfare they raised it to a level with the walls. The infidels within the castle, helpless and confounded, and not being able to screen themselves from the cannons and muskets, on the fifth of Seffer 929

[December 20, 1522], they surrendered the fortress. Its governor, Mighali Masturi [the grand master], was permitted to go out, and accordingly he went over to Malta. The islands subject to Rhodes, such as Takhtalu, Londas, Istanco, and Bodrum, being also subdued and all necessary arrangements completed, the victorious emperor, on the fourteenth of the same month, with honor and dignity proceeded to Mantesha, whence by hasty marches he returned to the capital.

Source: James Mitchell, *The History of the Maritime Wars of the Turks, Translated from the Turkish of Haji Khalifeh, Chapters I to IV* (London: Printed for the Oriental Translation Fund, by A. J. Valpy, 1831), 24–26.

96. Hayreddin Barbarossa and the Battle of Preveza, September 28, 1538

Introduction

Hayreddin Barbarossa (ca. 1478–1546), also known as Khair-ad-din, grand admiral of the Ottoman Fleet, was an outstanding example of the mixed ethnic heritage of many on both sides of the early modern Christian-Muslim divide. He and his three brothers, the sons of an Albanian who had converted to Islam and a Greek Orthodox widow, began their careers as privateers, eventually in 1516 capturing Algiers from Spain, whereupon they thought it advisable to seek Ottoman political and military backing of their continued rule of this territory in return for their acceptance of Ottoman overlordship and suzerainty. Following the death of his brother Oruç in 1517, Hayreddin inherited his position as ruler of Algiers, together with his hostility toward the Habsburg Empire. A remarkably able naval commander and a formidable Ottoman military asset, he became grand admiral of the Ottoman fleet, declining periodic invitations from Habsburg emperor Charles V to switch his allegiance to the West. Hayreddin's most spectacular achievement was the Battle of Preveza of 1538 that, as an Arab naval historian recounted, assured Ottoman predominance in the Mediterranean for the next generation.

Document

Third Expedition of Khair-ad-Din Pasha

The winter season being nearly over, Soltan Soleiman gave orders to his veziers to equip a hundred and fifty vessels, and to send Khair-ad-din to sea. Accordingly, although the ships were not ready, the veziers pressed Khair-ad-din to sail; and he not consenting, they had recourse to stratagem, saying that Andrea Doria had gone with forty vessels to Candia, where he was waiting to intercept Saleh Reis, who with twenty vessels had gone to bring Indian merchandise from Egypt. Khair-ad-din therefore with the forty ships that were in readiness (the other ninety being ordered to follow) sailed on the ninth of Moharrem, 945 (June 8th, 1538), accompanied by three thousand janissaries; and Ali Beg, the beg of Kogia-eili, Khorrem Beg, the beg of Tekké, Ali Beg, the beg of Seida, and Mustaffa Beg, the beg of Alanieh, having joined him, they proceeded to Imbro, where some time previously a vessel containing seventeen pieces of cannon had been wrecked, and having possessed themselves of these, they sailed to an island called Ishkatos (Skiathos), which had a strong castle and harbour. In consequence of the complaint of the governor of Negropont that the pirates were in the habit of lying there and carrying on their depredations in the vicinity, they conveyed their artillery from a distance of seven miles, and blockaded the castle for six days and nights, taking it by assault on the seventh day. A great number of the infidels were slain, and three thousand eight hundred taken prisoners.

The ninety vessels from Constantinople, and Saleh Reis, with the twenty under his command, had now arrived; so that, according to the royal command, the fleet now consisted of a hundred and fifty vessels; but the equipment and manning of the ninety from the Porte not being quite complete, Khair-ad-din emptied and sent back twelve of them to Gallipoli; the rest he despatched to the Negropont. . . .

The heat at this time became very oppressive, and hot winds like the Sam beginning to blow, and the sailors suffering much, the fleet went over to the island of Ilki (Piscopia), where they rested for some time. Sailing thence to Stanko, they broke up the

96. Hayreddin Barbarossa and the Battle of Preveza

levend frigates, and manned the galleys with the sailors they found on board. Besides these, they also took in a great number of infidel sailors from the islands and the Anatolian coasts. They then reduced an island called Stanpalia, which the pasha left to be plundered by the volunteer ships. This year the Venetians possessed twenty-five islands, each having one, two, or three castles; all of which were taken; twelve of the islands being laid under tribute, and the remaining thirteen plundered.

After this the fleet sailed towards Roumelia, and having broken up the heavy sailing vessels at Kuzil Hissar, put into the harbour of Negropont. They then took over the light sailing vessels by night to Kara-Ata, where they oiled their sides, and returned to Negropont to take in provisions. At this time Saleh Reis, who was a most valiant commander, arrived at Negropont with thirty vessels; on which occasion numerous salutes were fired.

The Grand Battle of Khair-ad-Din Pasha

About this time information was received that the Spanish, Papal, and Venetian fleets had assembled at Corfu, and attacked Prevesa; whereupon Khair-ad-din sent twenty small privateers to that quarter, which, on reaching Zante, came in sight of forty guard ships. These latter immediately returned to their fleet and gave information that Barbarossa was in the neighbourhood. The enemy then left Prevesa; which circumstance being made known to Khair-ad-din, when he was near Motone, he took in water at Helomej, and proceeded thence to Cephalonia, where he landed his men and plundered the surrounding villages. Crossing thence to Prevesa, the castle of which had been much injured by the enemy's cannon, he was preparing to besiege it, when he received reinforcements during the night from Santa Maura. With this assistance he entered the fortress, many of the infidels being slain in the assault: and having planted his great guns, the infidels, exhausted and terrified, left the place. The pasha then ordered his troops to repair the fortress; and in the mean time sent over a few private vessels to the infidel coasts to obtain information. These on their return reported that the Spanish, Papal, Portuguese and Venetian fleets had assembled at Corfu. This intelligence was immediately forwarded to the sultan, who was then on an expedition into Boghdan (Moldavia). About the middle of the month Jemazi-al-avul the fleets of these accursed infidels arrived and anchored about two miles from Prevesa.

The Return of the Infidels' Ships

Andrea Doria had fifty-two galleys; the Venetian general, seventy; the Pope's admiral, thirty; and the lieutenant of the Grand-Master of Rhodes, ten. The Spaniards and Portuguese had eighty barges, and the Venetians ten krakas, each of which contained two thousand arms of different sorts, and was equal to fifty galleys. Andrea Doria's own ship was a huge galleon, with arms and ammunition beyond computation. Besides these there were a few barges from different places; the whole amounting to one hundred and sixty-two galleys, one hundred and forty barges, and three hundred other ships, which, with the small privateers, formed a fleet of upwards of six hundred sail.

The Moslem fleet consisted of only one hundred and twenty-two light galleys. Khair-ad-din having held a consultation, and encouraged his troops, began to make preparations for an engagement. He then lowered the masts, giving strict injunctions to his officers to keep a constant eye upon his movements. The private vessels he ordered to take a position by themselves out of the line, and when they came in contact with the enemy's ships to fire their bow-guns. The begs, seeing the number of infidel ships, recommended the landing of the men and artillery. Khair-ad-din however did not consider this advisable; but having afterwards ascertained that the plan of the enemy was to enter the bay of Prevesa by night, he landed his men and stationed his artillery on the shore. The infidels shortly afterwards landed, when he commenced a fire upon them, whilst Mourad Agha, of the line of privateers, Tourghoudjé, Kouzloujé Mohammed, Sadek Reis, and several others, attacked them in the rear, and filled them with terror. Two days after several of the enemy's light vessels came up the strait of Prevesa, where the arrogant wretches opened a fire upon the Moslem vessels. The brave and experienced pasha, unable to bear this insolence any longer, beat his drum and cymbals, hoisted his flags, and sailed out of the bay, with the intention of there meeting the fleet of the despicable infidels. Casting anchor about six miles from land, he waited until the rest of the Moslem vessels should join him; and when they were all assembled, and had taken their proper positions, gave a signal, at which each of the hundred and twenty-two ships fired three guns, and coming forward to the attack, the brave Moslems filled the air with their shouts. This struck dismay into the hearts of the infidels, who, as evening approached, weighed anchor and fled towards Corfu. The pasha then returned to his former position. That night, whilst praying for direction, he saw in a dream great numbers of fishes issuing out of the harbour; and rising up at midnight, he sailed in that direction.

Attack and Flight of the Infidels

On the third of Jamazi-al-avul, as Andrea Doria was preparing to enter the gulf of Lepanto, Khair-ad-din sailed to Bahshiler, and having reached that place, he sent men to the mast-heads, who descried masts in the neighbourhood of Santa Maura and the harbour of Ingir. He therefore immediately weighed anchor, and sailed, prepared for an engagement. The infidels observing them, came out to meet them; and the wind being in their favour, the Moslems were overwhelmed with fear, for galleys are not able to compete with barges under such circumstances. Khair-ad-din however wrote two verses of the Koran, and threw one on each side of his vessel; when the wind immediately fell, and the barges lay motionless. This occurrence teaches that commanders, however celebrated, ought not to trust in human means alone, but also to pay all possible regard to spiritual means for ensuring success. The unfortunate infidels, stationing themselves in regular lines, now began to discharge their artillery; which, however, wanted strength to make it efficient. A galleon first came out and opened a heavy fire, but was driven back by the fire of the fleet. Khair-ad-din succeeded in taking several of the barges by attacking them from a distance, and thus gradually weakening them. Andrea Doria and the general having now come up with their galleys, were about to commence an attack, when the brave pasha bore down upon them, and commenced a heavy fire, which obliged them to bring round their barges. The balls from the barges now fell like rain, and the two fleets were so enveloped in smoke, that they could not see each other. The enemy's galleys several times attempted to take the Moslem vessels in the rear, that so they might take up a position between them and the other ships and barges. The latter, which from their size resembled floating castles, were dashing against each other with great violence; nor was it possible to separate them. At length, after nine of the barges had been driven back by the strength of the Moslem vessels, the pasha (of lion-like courage) redoubled his exertions, and keeping up a brisk fire, sunk several, and clearing a way through them, passed on to the galleys, strictly prohibiting his men from plundering a single barge. The infidels were astonished, and overwhelmed with terror at the impetus of the warriors: and their small galleys being unable any longer to maintain the fight, they turned their faces to flight. The slaughter continued during the whole of the interval between the two hours of prayer, and most of the barges were either destroyed or sunk by the cannon. Andrea Doria seeing this tore his beard, and took to flight, all the smaller galleys following him. The Moslems, supposing the barges were of less value than the galleys, pursued the latter, and succeeded in capturing two of them.

In the evening the wind fell, which obliged them to remain on the scene of action; whilst the unfortunate infidels set fire to the remaining barges, which continued to burn till morning. Such wonderful battles as those fought between the forenoon and sunset of that day were never before seen at sea.

Next morning the pasha went to Santa Maura, where he gave his son charge of two captains he had taken, and despatched him to the sultan with the news of the victory. He then proceeded to Prevesa, where the begs kissed his hand and congratulated him. Sultan Soleiman Khan was at this time hunting at Ianboli, where the pasha's son on his arrival was received with the greatest honors; and a divan being assembled, the proclamation of the victory was read, all present standing, and thanksgiving and praise were offered to the Divine Being. The Capudan Pasha then received orders to make an advance of one hundred thousand pieces of money to the principal officers, to send the proclamation of the victory to all parts of the country, and to order public rejoicings in all the towns.

Andrea Doria after his flight made Corfu his place of rendezvous; whilst the pasha on the 14th of the same month started from Prevesa by night, and on the evening of the following day arrived at Bahshiler; but finding no traces of the infidels there, he returned to Prevesa. The privateers having obtained his permission to plunder Cephalonia, proceeded thither, and left nothing behind them but the bare fortress. On the other hand, whilst the pasha was engaged in repairing the fortress of Prevesa, information was brought him that the infidels had attacked Durazzo; upon which he cleared his galleys, and stood out to sea the same night. Next morning he attacked the fort of Parga, put the inhabitants to flight, took four hundred prisoners, and plundered and set fire to the castle. On his way to Bahshiler he took two barges; and after resting there two days, on the morning of the third, he again sailed to the channel of Corfu, where he was overtaken by a violent storm, which obliged him to put into Avlona, where he was detained for ten days until the weather cleared up. During this time the army suffered greatly. While there the pasha received orders either to winter there, or to return to Constantinople, as he might think most advisable. He chose the latter alternative, and immediately sailed for Constantinople. On their way the fleet had to encounter another dreadful storm at the strait of Beberjek, but succeeded in reaching Gallipoli, and thence proceeded to Constantinople, which they entered amidst the firing of numerous salutes.

Source: James Mitchell, *The History of the Maritime Wars of the Turks, Translated from the Turkish of Haji Khalifeh, Chapters I to IV* (London: Printed for the Oriental Translation Fund, by A. J. Valpy, 1831), 59–65.

97. Kâtib Çelebi, Precious Gifts from the Expeditions in the Seas: The Ottoman Conquest of Cyprus (1570–1571)

Introduction

The conquest of the island of Cyprus, under Venetian rule since the death of its last king in 1473, was a top priority for Ottoman sultan Selim II, who succeeded his father Suleiman the Magnificent in 1566. For over a year beginning in 1570, Ottoman forces waged a protracted and costly war to capture the strategically and commercially important island, picking off its fortresses one by one. The stronghold of Famagusta held out for 11 months against what became an Ottoman army numbering over 200,000 before finally surrendering on August 1, 1571. Ottoman casualties apparently amounted to 50,000. While the siege was in progress, Pope Pius V organized a Holy League that gathered a multinational fleet to come to the assistance of Venice and Cyprus, but Famagusta fell before it could take action. The 17th-century Turkish scholar Kâtib Çelebi (1609–1657) wrote a history of the Ottoman conquests that included a lengthy description of the invasion and capture of Cyprus, which remained an Ottoman possession from then until it became a British protectorate in 1882.

Document

The Expedition for the Conquest of Cyprus

This island was, since many years, in the hands of Venice, but, although an agreement had been achieved in the meantime, the ships with pilgrims and merchants going to Egypt were always damaged by the brigands of this island. Each time this issue was arisen, they refused and claimed that this was done by the ships of Mesina and Malta, which were fighting in the sea. Meanwhile, when it was confirmed that when the ship of the *Defterdar* of Egypt was passing by, they took and plundered it and there was a need for an expedition against them. *Sheikhulislam* Ebu'ssuud Efendi was asked and he gave a fatwa on this matter. . . .

After this, according to the firman, ships were built and supplies were collected in the ports of the imperial dominions. Lala Mustafa Paşa, the fifth of the viziers, was appointed as the chief of the entire army, in which also participated the governor of Anatolia İskender Paşa, the governor of Caraman Hasan Paşa, the governor of Sivas Behram Paşa, the governor of Mara Mustafa Paşa, the governor of Aleppo Derviş Paşa, Mazul Muzaffer Paşa from Şehrizul and from the rulers of Rumelia the commanders of the provinces of Trikala, Yanena, Morea, Elbasan and Prizrin with their army and five thousand Janissaries with their colonel named Yahya, also armorers, artillerymen and a number of cavalry troops. The third vizier, Piyale Paşa, was also ordered to go with them, to guard the side of the sea. During the middle ten days of month *Zilhicce*, nine hundred seventy seven, Kapudan Ali Paşa, left from Beşiktaş and sailed to the Mediterranean, with one hundred and eighty galleys, ten barges and one hundred and seventy smaller ships of different kinds, all together three hundred and sixty vessels. Even His Highness the Sultan, escorted the army of Islam with a ship, up to Yedi Kule. The imperial fleet reached Phoenicia, they waited there twenty days, because the Anatolian army had not yet come. After this they left and on the twentieth day of month Safer, seventy eight, they anchored at the south coast of Cyprus, at Tuzla. Even though Piyale Paşa was son-in-law of the sultan and third vizier, he followed the chief of the army and he never opposed him. In accordance with his orders, he went first out on the island and he prepared the tent for the chief. The other generals and rulers also went out and pompously they carried the chief of the army to his tent. Piyale Paşa returned to the fleet ships and took his position.

The Besieging of Lefkosia

There, a consultation took place, where the chiefs and the officials agreed that firstly, the fortress of Lefkosia, which is located in the center of the island and was the old capital, should be seized. The governor of Sivas, Behram Paşa, remained at the port of Tuzla, in order to guard the ships with the supplies and the ammunition while Piyale Paşa with the fleet undertook the task to obstruct the infidels coming through the sea to help and to transfer to the island the troops from Aleppo and Damask. Kapudan Ali Paşa, being capable and senior, was appointed for the besieging of the fortress. The rulers of Kırşehir and Akşehir first reached Lefkosia carrying the tents, and the infidels came out and began the battle. But when the governor of Caraman[,] Hasan Paşa, arrived and attacked them from behind, the infidels were scattered and they ran back into the castle. The next day the famous chief together with the great army arrived, they settled and immediately the same day, the entrenchments were prepared. On the one wing entered the trenches the slaves of the great army chief, on the other wing the janissaries, on the other wing İskender Paşa on the other wing Kapudan Ali Paşa, on the other wing the governor of Aleppo Derviş Paşa and Mazul Muzaffer Paşa together with the rulers of Rumelia and on the other wing, the governor of Caraman Hasan Paşa. Artillery was placed on the four sides and the fortress was surrounded. And that day, the governor of Mara, Mustafa Paşa, was sent with the army of his province to besiege the fortress of Famagusta. On the thirty third day of the siege of Lefkosia, the thirteenth day of month *Rebiyülevvel,* at noon, the infidels came out of the fortress and attacked the army from Caraman. The ghazis were prepared and they fought bravely. In this battle many infidels were killed and captured and the rest of them ran into the fortress.

The Conquest of Lefkosia

Meanwhile, a captain named Kara Hoca came, sent by the governor of Algiers Uluc Ali Paşa. Earlier, in month *Şevval* of nine hundred seventy seven, Tunis was taken by its ruler Ahmet Hafsî, the state of Hafsîs was demolished and an independent province formed. On the eighth of month *Safer,* the abovementioned Ali Paşa, went out to the sea, with the intention to be united with the fleet. He encountered ships from Malta and seized four of their galleys. He announced that he was going to return to Tunis, in order to repair the ships which had been damaged during the battle and he sent the flags taken from the galleys. When these flags were placed opposite Mangosa fortress, the infidels were terrified. After this, day by day, the signs of victory and conquest became more and more evident. The fifty fifth day of the besieging, on the eighth day of month *Rebiülâhir,* the braves from Anatolia and Caraman entered the fortress from the east side. Other ghazis also entered from the breaches opened, they killed many infidels and captured others. Their army chiefs withdrew into a stronghold in a palace like a castle, but with the great efforts of Derviş Paşa, they were also arrested and executed. With the help of God, this fortress was conquered by the ghazis and its churches were transformed into mosques. The fortress was measured and it was established that its perimeter was eight thousand eight hundred and eighty yards.

The Submission of the Inhabitants of Kyrenia and Paphos

After the conquest of Lefkosia, envoys were sent to the inhabitants of Kyrenia and Paphos fortresses, with the head of the ruler of Lefkosia, and when they were asked to surrender, they thought of their lives and they asked to submit and to surrender their castles and their land. In that way, they saved the lives of their army chiefs. Soldiers were appointed as guard. When the governor of Maraş, who was charged earlier with the besieging of Famagusta fortress, arrived there and was preparing the siege and the battle, the army chief of the castle came out unexpectedly one night and attacked. Since sentry was at opposite side and everyone was resting, a confusion was created among the army. But the famous general was capable and experienced, he remained at his position, he opposed the enemy and he avoided any losses. When the infidels did not achieve what they wanted, they turned and ran into the fortress. Approximately two hundred of them were captured and another two hundred became prey to the swords. The **moral lesson** from this incident is that, during a battle or a night attack, army chiefs should remain stable at their positions. Where the chiefs did not move, the attackers turned and ran away. When Grand Vizier Hafiz Ahmet Paşa was at the siege of Baghdad, Shah Abbas attacked with the Kızılbaş army and even though the greater part of the army was scattered, the general stayed at his position, he did not run away, so he was not defeated. The deserters returned back, under the flag and the army of the Shah withdrew.

The Besieging of Famagusta

After the conquest of Lefkosia, on the fifteenth of month *Rebiülâhir*, the army chief and army of Islam reached and besieged the fortress of Famagusta. Piyale Paşa, together with the ships of the fleet, after plundering the coasts of Crete island, returned and with approximately two hundred ships besieged the aforementioned fortress from the sea. This fortress was a strong castle built on a huge rock at the side of the sea. From the land they had excavated a big ditch and they cut the way to those going and coming. Meanwhile, the galley of the Grand Vizier Mehmet Paşa, which had unloaded on the island the supplies it carried was loaded with different booties and slaves. It was ready to take off, when the gunpowder inside it exploded. The galley was destroyed, together with two big ships which were at both of its sides. Apart from the famous spahis and tradesmen who were inside it, around eight hundred female slaves died, and countless riches and supplies were spoiled. Meanwhile, autumn came and since there was no port near by, for the fleet to winter, Piyale Paşa and Kapudan Ali Paşa appointed the ruler of Rhodes Arap Ahmet with forty galleys at the post of the army chief and they came to Istanbul.

The Chief of the Army Pertev PaÐa

Mustafa Paşa passed that winter in Cyprus. In spring, second vizier from the Sublime Port[e] Pertev Paşa was appointed as chief of the imperial fleet and, during the second ten days of month *Zilkade* of nine hundred seventy eight, sailed with two hundred and fifty galleys and barges. Since the army was around Famagusta and in order to be there before the fleet of the infidels, the fleet left earlier than usually, and for this reason there were a lot of deficiencies among the oarsmen and the warriors. And all the ships with warriors were approximately three hundred. Within the first ten days of month *Zilhicce* they reached Famagusta and anchored. They unloaded to the land the cannons and the supplies, and after delivering them to the chief of the army, they returned to the passage of Rhodes and remained there to prevent the passing of the ships of the infidels.

The Battle of Famagusta's Fortress

On the twentieth day of month *Zilhicce*, the army of Islam prepared again trenches and they opened fire from several positions. From each side they dug a lot of earth and they created underground tunnels. On the thirty third day of the siege, which was the third day of month *Muharrem* of seventy nine, the ruler of Kilis Canpolat beg, dug a tunnel towards the castle which was on the sea side and blew it up from its foundations. While there was still smoke and dust, the ghazis attacked and there was a great battle from the daybreak until noon. Even captain Arap Ahmet Paşa was with forty galleys from the side of the sea, but that day conquest was not achieved. On the sixth day of month *Safer*, they dug a tunnel from the wing of Muzaffer Paşa and from the breach opened, the soldiers of Islam attacked. They fought and they tried a lot, but on that day also victory was not achieved, because of the fortress' strength and the abundance of the infidels inside. Once more a tunnel was dug from the wing of the governor of Anatolia İskender Paşa and they attacked, but they did not succeed and they returned.

The Death of the Ghazis during the Attack

After all these, the great army chief ordered the soldiers to dig earth and fill the ditch towards the breaches and to move ahead. But the infidels from the inside had dug a tunnel and had put gunpowder under the earth with which they filled the ditch. While the ghazis were going forward, they blew it up and around three thousand ghazis on and close to it were killed. From the officers martyred for the religion the ruler of Malatya Ferhad beg, the rulers of Ayıntap, Kars and Divriği, fief holders and many other persons. Never before so many people died because of a tunnel. The **moral lesson** is that before each attack against a fortress, the ground should be controlled very well in order to prevent this kind of losses, because they create aversion among the army.

The Next Attack of the Army and the Conquest of the Fortress of Famagusta

On the twenty seventh day of month *Safer,* the ghazis attacked from the wing of the Anatolian army and they entered the fortress. With great efforts they pulled out eight cannons and day by day tunnels were dug and breaches were created from every side. After this, the infidels were disparate. The great army chief, gave instructions to the army and on the eighth of month *Rebiyülevvel,* the fighters attacked the fortress from everywhere. The infidels understood that no help could reach them. Having no other option, they sent envoys to the army chief and they surrendered the same day. The keys of the fortress came and it was agreed that the remaining infidels would be allowed to return to their countries, with the condition that they would not harm the Muslim captives. The infidels came out of the fortress and they pitched their tents at a place separate from the army. The soldiers entered the fortress and with this the order for conquest was carried out. The island became a province and was appointed to Muzzafer Paşa. Famagusta and Kyrenia were registered as *sandjacks* and to this province the *sandjacks* of Içel, Tarsus and Sis from the mainland were added. The seven hundred and sixty cannons of the fortress were recorded. The chief [Marco Antonio Bragadin] of the around four thousand infidels that came out from the fortress, the infidel named Pragadi, who was a cursed obstinate person, killed the Muslim captives and did not want to give the pledge determined for the ships and because of this he was tortured and flayed. The four thousand infidels were distributed as oarsmen to the galleys. The great army chief left and came to the capital by land where he was honored.

Source: Translation of Kâtib Çelebi, *Tuhfetü'l-kibâr fî esfâri'l bihâr* [Precious Gifts from the Expeditions in the Seas], 1656 [published 1729], in Eftihios Gavriel, "The Expedition for the Conquest of Cyprus in the Work of Kâtib Çelebi," in *Ottoman Cyprus: A Collection of Studies on History and Culture,* ed. Michalis N. Michael, Matthias Kappler, and Eftihios Gavriel (Wiesbaden: Harrassowitz Verlag, 2009), 31–36.

98. Sebastian Veniero Describes the Battle of Lepanto (October 7, 1571)

Introduction

The Battle of Lepanto, fought at sea in 1571 between the Ottoman fleet and a Holy League naval force from Europe's Catholic powers, organized by Pope Pius V, was crucial in terms of checking the further expansion of Ottoman naval power in the Mediterranean, which greatly benefited the Spanish and the Austrian Habsburgs. It came too late, however, to save Christian—especially Venetian—interests in the eastern Mediterranean and the Aegean. After an 11-month siege, on August 1, 1571, Ottoman troops captured the citadel of Famagusta in Cyprus, the last remaining redoubt of Venetian power on that island, which remained a Turkish possession for the next three centuries. The Venetians contributed one of the most significant contingents of ships to the combined fleet, but it was under the command of Don John of Austria, illegitimate son of Habsburg Holy Roman emperor Charles V and half brother of King Philip II of Spain, who provided most of the funding for the expedition. The Venetian captain general of this force, Sebastian Veniero, wrote a report on Lepanto for the Venetian Senate, which he submitted over a year later after undertaking various additional naval operations independently of the Habsburg forces. Besides the description of the actual fighting at Lepanto, included below, and of his fleet's subsequent activities, Veniero's official report included lengthy diatribes against his Habsburg allies, whom he accused of being reluctant to engage the Turkish ships. He also complained bitterly that the Venetians did the great bulk of the fighting and suffered by far the most casualties but received a disproportionately small amount of the booty and prisoners captured in the battle, with the lion's share going to the Spanish and Austrians. Veniero's attitude was characteristic of other prominent Venetian leaders in the Holy League naval force. The acrimonious relations between the Venetians and their allies were evidence of the deep disunity among Western powers that had often proved advantageous to Ottoman invaders. When he finally returned to Venice, Veniero received a hero's welcome.

Document

Extracts from the Report presented to the Doge and Senate of Venice, by Sebastian Veniero, Captain-General of the Fleet of the Republic at Lepanto, on his return from service, 29th December 1572

At 2 or 3 o'clock we sailed towards the Curzolari [islands], and on the morning of the 7th at dawn, near the point of a rock called Vilamarin and the point of Mal-canton, armed vessels were perceived. As the day broke the whole Turkish fleet came into view. Don John [of Austria] [soon afterwards] came to astern of me, and said: 'Are we to give battle?' I [replied]: 'We must, we cannot do otherwise.' His Highness then went through the fleet. We placed the heavy ships two and two together, a little in front; the galleys could not be got into a correct line, and this gave me a little annoyance. On the left side, towards the rocks, was Barbarigo with the two Proveditori; on the right side, towards the sea, was [Giovanni] Andrea Doria; in the centre we three chiefs, the Signor Marc Antonio [Colonna] on the right [of Don John of Austria] and I on the left. Next to [me on] my left there ought to have been three of His [Highness's], the flag galley of Genoa [commanded by] Hettor Spinola, the Granada of Spain, and the [galley of] Captain Gil de Andrade, but I saw none of them; then Hieronimo Veniero and Francesco Bon (these two were slain), and next Gabriel da Canal, who received four wounds. One of the heavy ships, which was first I do not know, but every one claimed to have been first, fired a gun into the midst of the enemy's fleet, and all the rest followed [her example]; whereupon the [enemy's] fleet divided itself, and avoiding the heavy vessels, bore down upon us, and we upon them. In front of us chiefs were four galleys bearing the lamps of principal officers. Don John [of Austria] attacked that of the Pasha Ali, prow to prow, and I at midships. Four galleys then came to attack me on the left side, but by God's will all went by my stern, and turned back towards my right, on which they were met by those two most gallant gentlemen, Messer Chatarin Malipiero and Messer Zan Loredan, whom I had sent to call, and they attacked two of these galleys and, most valiantly fighting, were both of them slain. My galley with its artillery, arquebuses, and bows, prevented the passage of a single Turk from the poop of the Pasha's vessel to the prow, by which means Don John [of Austria] had a fair field in which to board and vanquish the Pasha, who was slain in the battle; and I can say with truth that if it had not been for my galley he would not so easily have conquered the Pasha. Besides fighting from the prow I fought with one galley on my right quarter, and with another somewhat further astern. At length my people boarded, when Zan Battista Inverardo, one of my household, planted my banner upon one, and upon the other Captain Zan Battista Belacato, as I myself saw, bore himself most valiantly, who to my great sorrow was afterwards killed at Santa Maura. Of the Turks, part were brought on board my galley, and part chained and shut up in their own. My flag captain and lieutenant desired to tow them off; but seeing Don John of Austria fighting at a little distance, I wished to go and help him, but in the meanwhile he beat off his assailants, and so ended the battle, which had lasted 3 hours and more. His Highness steered towards the Curzolari [islands], and I seeing I cannot tell how many Turkish galleys with their sails set, escaping in the direction of Santa Maura, desired to attack them but could not, some of our galleys being entangled by their prows. The two galleys which I had conquered were towed away by their sterns by two other Spanish galleys. When I arrived at the Curzolari [islands] His Highness sent his launch for me, with two of his gentlemen, to bring me [on board the flagship], and when I went [thither] he made me a world of caresses, embracing me, and so did all those captains and gentlemen, greatly extolling to one another the gallant battle, and the honourable deeds which our galleys had done, and the truth was seen in the killed and wounded; my flag captain, boatswain, colonel, purser, bombardier, and others to the number of 106 being wounded, and the chief of the soldiers, a bombardier, and other 4 being killed. I was slightly [wounded] in one of my knees....

Source: Translated in William Stirling-Maxwell, *Don John of Austria or Passages from the History of the Sixteenth Century 1547–1578*, 2 vols. (London: Longmans, Green, 1883), 2:399–401.

99. The Battle of Sarab (September 10, 1618)

Introduction

War between the Ottoman sultanate and Safavid Persia was in progress from 1603 to 1618. After squelching internal opposition to his rule, Shah Abbas I of Persia (r. 1588–1629) sought to regain some of the territories lost to Persia during the reign of his grandfather Tahmasp (r. 1524–1576) and his immediate successors. In the summer of 1618 peace negotiations between the Ottomans and Persians broke down, and an Ottoman army invaded Persia. Abbas pursued a scorched-earth policy, evacuating territory and drawing the Ottomans farther into Persian territory. According to the Italian composer and diplomat Pietro della Valle, who had arrived at the Persian court several months earlier, Qarachaqay Khan, the commander of Abbas's army, took advantage of an unexpected opportunity to entrap the advancing Ottoman troops and defeated them at the Battle of Sarab. The Turks then sued for peace, offering appreciably less onerous terms than they had a few weeks earlier and requesting provisions from the Persians. Della Valle did not mention that as the Turkish forces withdrew from Persian territory, Qarachaqay Khan's troops and those of other Persian commanders rather ominously shadowed them, escorting them peacefully but not without menace back to their own lands.

Document

And on the 3d September, by couriers from Carchica Bey [Qarachaqay Khan], the King learnt that, the Turks having advanced, he had demolished and quitted the fortress of Tebriz, of which they had taken possession, after its having been abandoned by its inhabitants, who had carried off every thing, and that all the neighbouring country had been previously desolated.

The King, upon this intelligence, ordered Ardebil to be evacuated in effect; which took place, and was a most afflicting scene.

On the next morning, Bahadu Khan appeared at court; his government lays between Ardebil and the Caspian Sea. He came before the King in the same condition in which he arrived, booted, his bow in his hand and quiver at his waist. To this person, a descendant from the Pagan Kings of Persia of the dynasty of Cofrhoè, and governor of various fortresses and ports on the Caspian Sea, but of no cities, the care of protecting the emigrants was delegated by the Shah; recommending to him to see that they met with succour and friendly reception on their way. At the same time he issued orders that such of the inhabitants as could bear arms should remain; and that the various banditti on the frontiers, the commanders of whom are known to the King, under promise of pardon, should hover on the flanks of the Turkish army, which is never entrenched, and serve as light troops to cut off their supplies, and pillage their camp in the night.

On the 10th of September a Tatar spy arrived, bringing intelligence, that a division of the Turkish army, consisting it was said of forty thousand, with six days provisions, had been detached from Tebriz, under command of the Georgian Prince Teimuraz, expectedly to fall on a sudden on Ardebil. The King immediately gave directions, that such inhabitants in the city and neighbouring villages as had not yet left should quit them, and take the road to Mazanderan, or some more distant part of Media or Irak: that every thing at Casvin should be in readiness for the inhabitants quitting that place, if it should appear requisite, and in the mean time, that all the merchandize and property there belonging to His Majesty should be transported thence, as safely as possible to Ferhabad and Hispahan: that everyone in Ardebil should hold himself in readiness to leave the city on the following day for the strong fort where the King had placed his baggage to wait for the enemy; and that preparation should be made for setting fire to every part of the city upon our evacuation, as well as the various towns and villages in its neighbourhood.

On the 11th September, just as we were about to mount our horses, and fire the city, intelligence of the most grateful description was received from Carchica Bey, giving account of a victory most unexpectedly obtained over the Turks. This Corchi Basha, on the Turks entering Tebriz, had withdrawn to Ugiun, one day's journey from that city, on the direct road to Casvin, leaving the way open as preconcerted to Ardebil, under expectation that they would in course direct their march thither. The Turks, however, conceiving that this step was a mark of weakness; and understanding from the [Turkish] ambassador who had been at Ardebil that no pillage would be obtained there; and that the King himself, with the small army he had with him, was in the greatest consternation, and had resolved on flying before them, determined on attacking Carchica Bey; after routing whom, they might easily pursue their plan of ruining Ardebil, without having any apprehension from him in their rear. As, however, they knew from the orders he had received, it would be difficult to induce the Corchi Basha to hazard a pitched battle, they attempted to take him by surprize. With this intent, they selected their best troops, as well Turks as Tatars, to the amount of from forty to fifty thousand, as we had before heard, which were detached lightly equipped, and calculated for dispatch, to fall upon Carchica Bey in the night-time or by dawn of day. In stating Ardebil as their destination, the spy was deceived, as well as in their being commanded by Teimuraz Khan, who at that time was indisposed and not with the army. Unfortunately for the Turks, while on their march, a Persian in their army of the name of Ali Bey, influenced by that *amor patriae* so natural to man, when mounted with the rest, clapped spurs to his horse, and favoured by darkness and the speed of his animal, quickly reached the camp of Carchica Bey.

This nobleman found the army completely off its guard, and, passing the drowsy centinels, reached the very tent of Carchica Bey entirely unperceived. Here, after making a great noise, he succeeded in gaining admittance to the general, to whom he succinctly related his danger. The general immediately issued orders for the troops to saddle their horses, and load the baggage waggons, not to create disorder or a panic amid the soldiers; so that before day-break, this prodigious body of cavalry was in readiness to march in military array, and divided in four immense squadrons at some distance from the baggage, and a row of tents which formed the market or bazar; leaving from a thousand to fifteen hundred horse, who were directed, in case of the enemy appearing, to engage their van, and draw them, as they retreated, among the baggage and the tents, which were left standing.

So orderly was every thing managed, that none of the soldiers had any idea of their having to engage, but merely imagined that they were about to decamp for some other spot, as was frequent with them. But Carchica Bey seeing a favourable opportunity had so contrived, that he was apparently reduced either to comply with the King's injunctions and abandon in disgrace his camp and baggage, or attempt to deliver them from the enemy by an engagement.

The enemy came up shortly after day break, and the Tatars made a furious charge on the troops of Shiraz Imaunculi Khan, by whom they were valiantly received, and a desperate conflict ensued. Carchica Bey, who was in the rear, upon this stated, that he could not in conformity to the King's orders hazard an engagement, but should entrench himself. Upon this Imaunculi Khan sent word that he was unavoidably drawn into battle, and that the Corchi Basha must think seriously of fighting and immediately join him, as notwithstanding the bravery of his troops they must otherwise be overpowered, enjoining him if he would not fight to draw up his forces, as their appearance might intimidate the enemy and encourage his men. In the mean time, the fifteen hundred men of the van who had done their duty, agreeable to the orders received, pretended to fly, and drew the enemy among the tents, where they immediately began pillaging and massacreing such as they found in the bazar, giving over the pursuit. At this instant, Carchica Bey seeing things in the state he wished them, and holding himself justified with respect to his orders in the opinion as well of Imaunculi Khan as the rest of the nobles in the army who blamed him for his inertness, joined his forces to those of the Khan of Shiraz, and fell with the utmost fury on the Tatars with his four squadrons. The Tatars bravely sustained the shock, but finding themselves at length overpowered by the Persians and not supported by the Turks, who came up but slowly, owing to some impediment on the road, or their cowardice, which induced them rather to be spectators of the battle than actors in the field, were at length obliged to give way in disorder; the Khan of Caffa, who had behaved himself bravely, and was wounded in several places, retiring at the entreaty of his people.

The Persians, upon the Tatars being put to the rout, followed up their advantage closely for several miles, driving before them not only the Tatars but also the dilatory Turks whom they met on the road, putting to the sword most of those whom the want of fleetness of their horses put within their reach, and making very few prisoners. Of these, the only ones of condition were the Basha of Van, a grey-haired old man, a Captain of Tatars, and a Georgian of note in his own country, a Captain of Janissaries. Among the dead, the number of which is uncertain, were seven or eight Bashas, whose names are mentioned. On the side of the Persians, no one is spoken of as killed of any consequence; such a victory, however, cannot have been purchased without great loss. In his account of the battle Carchica Bey excused himself for his disobedience of His Majesty's orders by the singularity and urgency of the case, and stated, that if His Majesty disapproved of his conduct, he was ready to lay his head at his feet. The Shah expressed himself satisfied with what he had done, and commended him for his skill.

This intelligence occasioned the revocation of the former orders. The whole day long nothing was heard but music and rejoicing, and an infinite number of people repaired to the mosque in order to return thanks for the victory. Ali Bey, who was nobly rewarded by the Corchi Basha and his officers, had apartments assigned him in the house of Bahadur Khan.

His Majesty pardoned the Tatars and his chief prisoners, but ordered all the Turks to be put to death, as well as some of their spies who were taken; their execution was barbarous, it consisted in cutting off their feet or legs, and leaving them in the different streets to bleed to death and be trampled on by passengers.

On the 16th September, Emir Gunch Erouan Khan came to confer with the Shah, and after a promise from the King that he would not conclude peace without hearing more from the army, he returned to join the Corchi Basha.

The Turkish ambassador appeared again at court with new proposals. These went, that the Turks were willing to make peace without restitution of any conquests, upon condition only of the annual present being sent, or in lieu of it a certain quantity of scarlet cloth, some horse trappings and other trifles, provided the army were allowed to return by the road of Maraga and Curdistan, the country through which they came being exhausted, and that the King would furnish them with a quantity of corn, straw, and shoes for their horses, with other articles of which they stood in need. The wary King, while he consented to the tribute, refused to allow them a passage through Curdistan, and insisted on their return by the same way they came; upon their agreeing to which he would furnish them with the requisite provisions. With this answer the ambassador returned, accompanied by Bouroun Casum Bey for the conclusion of peace on these terms on the part of the Serdar.

Source: Pietro della Valle, Letter V, Hispahan, 22nd April and 6th May, 1619, in "Extracts from the Travels of Pietro delle Valle in Persia," in *A General Collection of the Best and Most Interesting Voyages in All Parts of the World*, ed. John Pinkerton, Vol. 9 (London: Longman, Hurst, Lees, Orme, and Brown, 1811), 88–91.

100. The Ottomans Fail to Capture Baghdad from Persia: Letter of a Senior Ottoman Officer to Moṣlī Čelebī (1626)

Introduction

In 1624, the forces of Shah Abbas I of Persia captured the strategically important city of Baghdad in Iraq from the Ottomans and soon took much of the rest of Iraq as local tribes and rulers quickly switched allegiance to Abbas. Eager to repair this major blow to Ottoman prestige, in 1625 an Ottoman army led by Grand Vizier Hafiz Ahmed Pasha marched into Iraq with the objective of besieging and retaking Baghdad. In November Hafiz Ahmed reached Baghdad, and his troops invested the city on three sides. Shah Abbas then dispatched a relief army, but the Ottomans took refuge in a heavily fortified camp, continuing the siege. Abbas then cut the invaders' supply lines, starving them out and forcing them to attack the Persian forces, who repulsed them, inflicting heavy losses. In July 1626 the Ottomans abandoned the siege, a major humiliation for their empire albeit a loss that they reversed 12 years later, in 1638, after which the Ottomans held Baghdad until 1917. During the siege, the Persians captured an Ottoman courier carrying an assortment of dispatches and letters from high-ranking military officers to their superiors in Constantinople. Most were fairly businesslike, but among them was a rather more revealing personal letter by one senior Ottoman officer to a friend, possibly a well-placed administrative official, that vividly conveyed the hardships, frustrations, and dangers that the besieging forces endured and the panicked loss of confidence that these caused. The officer in question clearly anticipated his own death in the near future.

Document

To proceed: if you inquire about what took place on this regrettable expedition and about cruel Baghdad, the abode of affliction, what can we say? May this expedition not end in favor of our adversary! We have now been laying siege to the stronghold for nine months and not a breach has been made in its stones. At the beginning of our siege, while there was still not a sign of those evil *qezelbāš* who were like a fox lying hidden in a valley, breastworks were made, mines constructed, and palisades erected. Many times attacks took place—in each attack several thousand of the (Ottoman) Household troops and *enfants perdus* [lost children] perished. From day to day those accursed ones in the stronghold were triumphant and every enterprise ended in defeat for the army of Islam (i.e., the Ottomans). Meanwhile a troublemaker named Zeynal Khan who was in command on behalf of the Shah of Iran appeared with probably forty thousand evil *qezelbāš*, full of cunning and good for nothing. He crossed the Diāla River and advanced upon us. Many times he drew up his regiments in order of battle. Under cover of their movements, the Shah of Iran advanced step by step with the bloodthirsty force which was with him, paying no attention to us. He assigned a part of his force to attack the fortress of Mandalī. By force of arms he drove the army of Islam together with Mehemmed Aqa, the *qapibāšī* of the grand vizier, Jestānlū Mostafā Pasha and others, out of the abovementioned fortress; some were captured, some fell prey to the sword, and some he made unbelieving *qezelbāš* like himself. Afterward, when the army of Islam which was in the Lak fort was overcome, a great fear took possession of the Army of Islam at this news.

While they were in the stage of concerting measures as to whether it was feasible to go out and confront the enemy, the Shah of Iran made a general advance on us with his household troops. That worthless commander who has been mentioned earlier joined him. While he was beginning to set up a bridge across the Diāla, the grand vizier sent fifteen thousand valiant youths under Morād Pasha, the *beglerbeg* of Diār Bakr, with six guns to drive him off. By chance that accursed trickster swiftly eluded us and established his bridge. While three or four thousand *qezelbāš* were alighting at Šahrabān, Morād Pasha arrived and made an assault with cannon and musket fire on the *qezelbāš* who were there. They were forced to fight. One or two attacks took place (but) the Divine Wisdom of the Seventy Saints (*Rejāl al-Geyb*) decided in favor of the *qezelbāš*. With dust and wind and the sharp sword they made the army of Islam retreat.

In short, with our complete defeat in the above-mentioned battle, the flower of our fine and cheerful young men from the *sanjaqs* of Diār Bakr, Qaramān, Aleppo, and Anatolia tasted of the drought of martyrdom and what remained wet on the poisoned blade. Morād Pasha, intervening in the battle in the evening, came and sought sanctuary in the camp with many of his followers severely wounded. After that the Shah of Iran came and set up a bridge at the place where the Šatt-e Qādīšān [sic!] joins the Diāla River and dispatched part of his army against us and part against Old Baghdad. Attacking us like a wolf rushing on its prey, he appeared sometimes on this side and sometimes on that. In short, we were besieging Baghdad and the *qezelbāš* were besieging us so we returned to the right wing, which was galled by artillery fire. If we direct our efforts against the fortress, the *qezelbāš* will attack us unexpectedly out of the redoubt once more, so we should simply persevere in the siege of the stronghold. In the hope that the stronghold might be reduced through hunger and that we might bring them to terms, we had the fortress surrounded on four sides. When the Shah of Iran became aware of these measures, he was not unduly perturbed but dispatched ten thousand *qezelbāš* to Old Baghdad two nights ago. Three thousand loads of provisions and more arrived near the Qūš castle with camels and mules. When the army of Islam attacked them, fortune was not favorable to us. Then many of our *sekbāns* were cast into the water of the Šatt and many died a prey to the sword. In short, it was early in the morning when we were watching with our keen eyes this immense quantity of provisions ranging from sheep to butter and fowls being landed from boats at the fort. For that reason the army of Islam was defeated and at one blow all our hopes of taking the stronghold were dashed.

While we were engaged in these melancholy thoughts about our perplexing situation, the Shah of Iran, gaining assurance from these events, told the *qezelbāš* to cut us off on all four sides from the Šatt and the Euphrates. Truly a bird could not escape by land or sea. Waters such as the Šatt and the Euphrates—both like the Danube in fury and turbulence—seemed like a brook under the horses' hooves of those cruel *qezelbāš*. They attacked in the direction of Hella, Karbala, Fallūja, and Mosayyeb. It all seemed alike in those places—the army of Islam was of no more account than a dog, the Pasha than a horse and his followers than stableboys. The *qezelbāš* overcame Aslan Pasha at Hella and the household troops and the Arabs in such a manner that the tongue fails in reporting it and the pen snaps in recording it. In all there were periods when not a single *oke* (2.82 lbs) of provisions came from this direction; if we engage the *qezelbāš*, the garrison of the fortress from behind us will dash our hopes. At length there was nothing for it but to dig trenches, and we made a redoubt, but they paid no heed to the redoubt. Many times they approached our redoubt and drew themselves up in battle order.

On 27 Šaʿbān 1035/24 May 1626, when they came with the intention of attacking our redoubt, the grand vizier proclaimed among the army of Islam a general levy for all those able to bear arms—men of high and low degree, horse and foot—apart from the Janissaries, who were at their posts in the earthworks before the stronghold. We went forth and confronted them in battle. From early morning until late afternoon fighting went on under cannon and musket fire. Their commander, Zeynal

100. The Ottomans Fail to Capture Baghdad from Persia: Letter of a Senior Ottoman Officer to Moṣlī Čelebī

Khan, put up a fierce resistance. No sooner had he set up the awning (for the Shah) on the *terre-plain* of the fort than those accursed ones beat the kettledrums of rejoicing at the sight of this. Those of humble and high degree (in the Ottoman army) were vexed; the *qezelbāš*, undismayed by the cannon and musket fire, launched an attack which, if the Elborz Range had been in front of them, would have pushed it aside! In short, with this attack the army of Islam was thrown into utter confusion. Such of our *sekbāns* as left the redoubt for the most part became trampled under the horses' hooves.

When the *sepāhī* detachment saw that the battle was going against them, they did not stay any longer in the grand vizier's regiment but changed their resolution to stand to one of flight, and their heads fell upon desert and plain. Losing their way to the redoubt, most of them from that day forth were never seen again. So-and-so of us were overthrown and beaten down like a moth without wings. We sought refuge in the redoubt and decided to take shelter.

After this engagement, the grand vizier took counsel with the high-ranking officers. They decided that there was no chance of breaking into the Ottoman camp. Whoever had acquired a great deal of provisions earlier on, now had some of it confiscated and some sold. By this means a time of abundant and cheap food has come about in our camp which we shall mention—1 *oke* of flour cost 1 piaster, 1 *oke* of butter 2 piasters, 1 *oke* of dates 1 piaster, 1 *kīle* (bushel) of barley 8 piasters, 3 dirhems (3.21 grams) of bread 1 asper (*aqča*), and 1 *oke* of horseflesh was sold for 40 piasters. Those of delicate constitution who were dainty in their food now are thankful when they see horseflesh! Those conceited heroes who in the coffeehouses have mocked at the *qezelbāš* for their cowardice now when they behold the most insignificant of them three miles away on the road, compare him with Rostam son of Zāl; and those brave lads who have come in the hope of taking booty from the *qezelbāš* now abandon their tents and gear and are thankful to save their lives! Those dignitaries living in luxury who rode horses with silver trappings and used to go with their retinue to the bath now are filled with longing and regret when they see a pack-saddled ass!

Since of the four parts of our army only one part remained mounted (i.e., only one quarter of the Ottoman army had horses) the survivors of the army of Islam are dismounted and disorganized. If we receive false reports and are forced to withdraw, there are neither men to bring away the Janissary regimental transport horses nor to protect any member of our armory or artillery train. We were reflecting that they have brought the *balyemez* and *sengendāz* guns which have been in Bīrejīk and Basra since the time of Sultan Sülaymān to reduce the stronghold. The grand vizier is tormented by the thought that it would be a dishonor for the House of ʿOsmān if they were abandoned. On many occasions men were sent expressly for assistance and money. No trace of them was ever seen again. We do not know whether they fell into the hands of the *qezelbāš*—not that the Sultan wished for the muster roll of the army of Islam to be obliterated from the face of the earth, only there is a ballad which is being sung among the Turks (i.e., as opposed to the Ottoman educated class) to the effect that 'Neither from Baghdad nor Basra is anything coming. There is no help coming to us from those Ottoman rascals.' Now if money and help came up to this month, there would be a chance for us; but henceforth even if the Sultan came in person, it would not be enough to help us.

Why has Fate treated us so unkindly? On one side of us the Dīāla, on another side the Šātt, behind us Shah ʿAbbas and in front of us Baghdad. Perhaps help will come to us from God. In a word, nobody since Adam has fallen into such peril. None knows our plight; and well I know that whatever measure the Shah of Iran undertakes, it will turn out in his favor—there is absolutely no doubt that the miracles of ʿAlī have some effect. We do not know why the Emām-e-Aʿzam (i.e., Abū Ḥanīfa) is so much weaker in exerting his miraculous power on our behalf or else we could turn for help to the saint on account of his sacred resting place and kindly spirit. When my heart is so troubled about this question, I do not say these strange things aloud but only in a way which can be kept secret between ourselves. You will then be safe from the evil insinuations of those who care only for their own interests. *Amen, O Helper.*

I expect you know that there is a disease associated with the climate of province prevalent in our camp—it cuts just like the curved sword of the *qezelbāš*. It is only possible to go back again if one is fortunate enough to escape such sufferings and calamities as colic, dropsy, catarrh, sudden death, and the simoom wind. You are asking pardon and conveying our message of farewell to true friends—let them freely give up any claims against us in the Hereafter. *The judgment belongs to God, the One, the Irresistible.* We should only be thankful that we spent the rest of our life on the ground where the Emām-e Aʿzam lies. We have sent letters secretly to our true friends. If they see any mistakes in them it is only because when I was writing a line, three or four times the alarm arose that the enemy was coming. Those ruthless *qezelbāš* have completely overawed the army of Islam; like the wolf rushing after the sheep, they charged on our redoubt killing all they could find right up to our trenches just as well by night as by day—there were some occasions when they forced their way into our camp at night bearing lanterns. It is all up with us. We have neither been able to loosen our belts from our loins nor our two hands from our weapons—each one has to take care of himself. Apart from God none knows our plight. If all I have to tell you were written down it would not go into a hundred such letters! Truly the calamity of the Day of Resurrection will not equal these days of our sufferings here—you can draw your own conclusion from this—so farewell!

Source: Eskandar Beg Monshi, *History of Shah 'Abbas the Great (Tārik-e 'Ālamārā-ye 'Abbāsī)*, Vol. 2, trans. Roger M. Savory (Boulder, CO: Westview, 1978), 1275–1280. Reprinted with permission.

101. Grand Vizier Köprülü Mehmed Pasha (ca. 1583–1661)

Introduction

Within the Ottoman Empire the grand vizier, the sultan's highest administrative official, often possessed enormous authority, which was delegated to him by the grand signior. For much of the latter 17th century this power was exercised by grand viziers drawn from the Köprülü family, a clan of Albanian origins that produced six highly effective viziers known both for their administrative skills and their military successes. The first and founding grand vizier was Köprülü Mehmed Pasha, a retired official who took office in 1656 at a time of military and political crisis. This enabled Köprülü to insist that he be assigned unquestioned authority, while he relegated Sultan Mehmed IV to a life of hunting and pleasure, when possible well away from the capital in the city of Adrianople (Edirne), which Mehmed greatly preferred to Constantinople. In his five years as grand vizier, Köprülü reorganized the Ottoman Army, rooted out corruption, and won major military victories against the Cossacks, the Hungarians, and Venice, significantly expanding Ottoman territory. The diplomat and historian Sir Paul Rycaut, who came to Constantinople in 1660 as secretary to the Earl of Winchilsea, who had just been appointed as British ambassador to the Supreme Porte, arrived in time to observe the elderly grand vizier's final days. Rycaut later wrote an unsparing assessment of Köprülü, whose undoubted ability was matched by his ruthlessness toward his enemies, domestic and foreign.

Document

At the arrival [in early 1661] of this Embassadour [the Earl of Winchelsea, ambassador of Great Britain], the important affairs of this vast and still growing Empire, were governed by the Great Vizier *Kuperlee;* a person decrepit and infirm in body, by reason of his great Age, but of a solid and subtle judgment; by Nature cruel, and by Years froward; which disposition was singularly well fitted to do service to his Master, against the impetuous storms of the Faction of those times, in which the Pashaws, and Chiefs of the Souldiery (as often it happens in Empires, whose Body is grown too vast to be ruled by a weak Head) became rich and powerful, and by the long Vacations of Peace, insolent and wanton; for as then the Wars with *Venice* were carried on faintly, only by sending forth an Armata of Gallies in the Spring; and the preparations became rather accustomary, returning with the Year, and made for exercise of the Arsenal, and amusement of the people, than designed with any probable expectation of success or Victory, proportionable to that Treasure and trouble which maintained them. So that to encounter so many difficulties, and predominancy of Ambition and Avarice, the Prince himself being young, the Fortune of his Empire had more than urgent necessity of such a rough and cruel disposition as was found in *Kuperlee;* who so seasonably made use of it, to the destruction of all such, who might either endanger his Prince, or himself; that in two or three Years time he became Master of the Lives, and Estates, of the Grand Mutiniers; confiscating their richesse and fortunes to the use and security of his Master; having in his time put to Death, thirty six thousand persons, whom he proscribed in several Countries; and privately strangled in the City, by vertue of his absolute and uncontroulable Authority, without giving the Offenders liberty of Processes, or Pleas for their Lives, or the solemnity of Scaffolds, or applause of a Funeral Oration at the Gallows, whereby to win the affections and compassions of the vulgar, but went through with his bloody and tragical business, without noise, or rumour, or knowledge almost of all the Souldiery, or the people; whilst the great Personages, whose rapine and pride had contracted them envy and hatred from their inferiours, stood confused and amased, not having power to rebel, nor Sanctuary to fly unto.

Such is the effect of an absolute, and arbitrary power, which is Master of times and affairs, and rather fits and squares Enterprizes to Counsels, than Counsels to Enterprizes. *Reges Hercule non liberi solum impedimentis omnibus, sed Domini rerum, temporum{que} trahunt Consiliis cuncta, non sequuntur. Liv. lib. 9.* [Now consider kings: not only are they free from all impediments, but they are lords of time and circumstance, and in their counsels carry all things with them, instead of following in their train. Livy, *History of Rome,* Book 9.] The Grand Signior in the mean time applauded the diligence and circumspection of his Minister; and though yet trembling with the memory of late sollevations amongst the Janizaries; yet being young, and active, addicted himself wholly to the delight of Hunting, and to follow the Chace of fearful, and flying Beasts; whilst his Vizier so closely followed his game of bloud, that he left no person considerable in the Empire, who was not a Creature made by, or depending on him. . . .

It was now towards the Winter, when this Vizier *Kuperlee,* finding himself mature with Age, and ready to fall like Autumn Fruit, sent for his Son from *Constantinople* to bear a share with him in the Burden of the Empire. This he did with the consent of the Grand Signior, for he alledged, that being now feeble and decayed, he could not make his personal Addresses as formerly, nor attend at the Court to render his Majesty an account of his Affairs; and therefore had need of so trusty a Messenger as his Son, to carry his advices and directions, and faithfully to communicate what he should encharge to his Relation; all others being on some consideration or other suspected, and at least Enemies to him, or to the Grand Signior. The Sultan accepting the proposition and the Person, had often occasions of discourse and familiarity with the Son, called *Ahmet,* who deported himself with that faith and prudence in the management of all his Affairs, that the old Vizier had no great difficulty to procure a Grant of succession for him in that Office: For though there were many obstacles therein, as the abhorrency of the Turkish Policy from all hereditary succession in places of trust; and the Youth of his Person not exceeding 32 years of Age, and some emulous, powerful, and ancient Competitors, who hated the Father; Yet the old Fox had so ingratiated himself with his Master, for (to speak truly) he had been the only instrument that had preserved him and his Empire from falling into as many Divisions as there are Pashalicks, or Governments, that the Grand Signior gave credit to him as to an infallible Oracle, assuring him that before any other, who might either pretend merit, Age, or Precedency, his Son should be preferred to the Succession. The old man acknowledged the favour with all humility and thankfulness, declaring, that he had now served his Majesty faithfully for the space of five years, a longer proportion than commonly Viziers had managed that Office, in such tempestuous and distracted times, who either for their own offences, or want of Providence, or good Conduct have made shipwrack of their own lives, and the Charge they piloted: But he had lived in the worst of times, when the spirits of men with discontent were enflamed round about him, and threatned the ruine of their Prince and Empire; and yet had reduced things to composure, and to the obedience of the Ottoman Yoke, that now he that was the Sultan might incline his head to rest with security, and enjoy his pastimes and pleasures, without being interrupted by those Conspiracies, which destroyed his Father, and endangered him in his years of Infancy. And because the continuance of his Security and Glory depended on the execution of certain Maximes, which he had framed to himself, he was chalking out to his Son such undoubted Rules and Doctrines of Government, as would certainly tend to the glory and prosperity of the Empire, being abundantly satisfied that his Son was faithful, prudent, and active. But three things he particularly recommended to his Majesty.

1. Never to give Ear to the Counsels and Advices of Women.
2. To amass what Treasure he could possible into his Coffers, though with Oppression, and impoverishment of his people.
3. To be continually on horse-back, and keep his Armies in constant Action.

On the 19*th* of *October Kuperlee* having ended his days, whose Disease was Old Age, and a Gangrene in his Legs, his Son by Hattesheriff, or the Grand Signior's Patent under his hand, taking the Seal was constituted Vizier in the place of his Father, to the admiration and disappointment of the graver Seniors, who were discontented, not only to perceive themselves neglected, but that person also to supplant them, who was judged uncapable of the office, according to the Canon, and ancient Precedents of this Government.

The Body of *Kuperlee* was transported to *Constantinople,* where in his life time he had erected a very stately and magnificent Structure, as his Monument over the Grave, or Vault, where he designed to be interred. In his life time he had filled it with Corn, which daily was distributed to the poor, and being emptied after his death, received his Corps, over which a small Mosch was endowed with Oyl for Lamps, and maintenance of certain Talismans and Softaes, to make Prayers and Offerings for his Soul.

Source: Paul Rycaut, *The History of the Turkish Empire from the Year 1623 to the Year 1677 Containing the Reigns of the Three Last Emperours, viz., Sultan Morat or Amurat IV, Sultan Ibrahim, and Sultan Mahomet IV, His Son, the XIII Emperour Now Reigning* (London: J. M. for John Starkey, 1780), 68, 82–83, https://quod.lib.umich.edu/e/eebo/A57996.0001.001?view=tocpp.

102. Evliyá Efendí Describes the Austro-Ottoman Wars (1660–1664)

Introduction

For several years beginning in 1658, the Ottoman hegemony over Transylvania was threatened, first by the refusal of George II Rakoczy, prince of Transylvania and king of Poland, to accept the Ottoman overlordship established in 1526 and then, following Rakoczy's death from wounds received in battle in 1660, by the obduracy of his successor, János Temény. In 1663–1664, this simmering conflict developed into full-scale war between the Habsburg emperor and an alliance of German princes, which ultimately checked an Ottoman campaign directed against the Austrian capital of Vienna. The Ottoman official and travel writer Evliyá Efendí, a loyal follower and client of Melek Ahmed Pasha, governor first of Bosnia and then of Rumelia, took part in these destructive and bitterly fought wars and the peace negotiations that followed. He later gave an account of them written from the perspective of a midlevel Ottoman functionary who profited financially from every victory in terms of the booty gained.

Document

Defeat of Rakoczy.

[Prince George II] Rakoczy [of Transylvania], who had been named King of Poland by the grand vezír Boyúní, Egrí, but was not acknowledged as such by his successor Kopreïlí, assembled two hundred thousand men, in order to support his claim against the Poles, who had sent an envoy to request the assistance of the Ottoman arms. In consequence of this application, the Tátár Khán, Melek Mohammed Gheráï, and Melek Ahmed Pasha, the governor of Oczakov, took the field against Rakoczy, who was defeated, and fled with three hundred horsemen to the mountains of Szeklers in Transylvania. In the engagement, forty thousand infidels were slain, and seventeen princes, with Rakoczy's minister, taken prisoners, after which, the armies of the Tátár Khán, and Melek Ahmed Páshá, marched victoriously to Ak-kermán. I, the humble Evliyá, who composed a chronograph for this occasion, received seventeen prisoners, twenty horses, ten sable pelisses, a pair of silver stirrups, and other silver articles, as my share of the booty. The Hungarians seeing the defeat of Rakoczy, assembled an immense army composed of various nations, with which they attacked Temisvar, Lippa, Cianad, Gulia, and Fecsat. Complaints from these places having reached the Porte, the governor of Buda, Kana'án Páshá, received orders to march against the invading enemy. On the banks of the Maros, between Lippa and Arád, the Páshá encountered eighty thousand of the hostile army and was routed, but saved himself and some thousands of his cavalry by a flight to Slankament. In this defeat the Ottoman army lost no less than eleven thousand men. Kana'án Páshá was in consequence removed from Buda, and the government was given to Seidí Ahmed Páshá of Bosnia; whilst the government of Bosnia was conferred upon Melek Ahmed Páshá. In the same year, Seidí Ahmed Páshá, with twelve thousand brave horsemen, entered the province of Transylvania by Demir-kapu (the Iron Gate), gave battle to the detested Rakoczy's army, who defended the castle of Koljovar, and defeated them, with the assistance of Husain Pasha, the brother of the governor of Temisvar, Siavush Pasha. The white bodies of the infidels were strewed upon the white snow; and the carriages, cannon, and tents were sent to Constantinople; where, however, no thanks were voted to Seidí Páshá for the victory, nor was even a "well done" said on the occasion, although it was a victory not less brilliant than that of Erla by Mohammed III; for Seidí Páshá had no more than eleven thousand men opposed to a hundred and sixty thousand infidels, now inhabitants of hell. The vile Rakoczy escaped to the castle of Koljovar, where he began to collect a new army.

The emperor having heard of the depredations committed by the infidels in Bosnia, appointed Melek Ahmed to the command of an army against Zara. The Páshá assembled his troops under the walls of this fortress, but not being able to reduce it, he plundered the neighbouring country, attacked the castle of Rinjisi, which he took after a storm of seven hours, and carried off the inhabitants.

In the same year (1660) Rakoczy having refused to pay the tribute due by Transylvania, and having encamped with two hundred thousand men under Koljovar, was attacked a second time by Seidí Páshá with forty thousand chosen troops of Buda, Erla, Temisvar, and Kanisa. Rakoczy was beaten, wounded, and obliged to fly to Kalova, where he expired, calling out, "Receive me, O Jesus!" Jesus however would not receive him, but he was seized by the angel Azraïl. Seidí Páshá carried an immense booty, with several thousand heads to Constantinople; but even by this signal exploit he could not gain the emperor's favour.

The fortresses of Lippa, Jeno, and Logos were conquered by Kopreïlí Mohammed Páshá, who also repaired the fortifications of Arád and Jeno, and was on the eve of undertaking an expedition against the Transylvanian fortresses, when he received repeated imperial rescripts, intimating that it was not the emperor's wish to continue the war any longer in that country, and that should the Páshá even bring the king of Transylvania or the emperor of Germany prisoners to Constantinople, it would not meet his Majesty's approbation; but he was desired to proceed with all possible speed to the Porte [to deal with a major internal Ottoman rebellion].... Sinán Páshá and Seidí Páshá were left to protect the castle of Jeno, whilst Kopreïlí marched with the greatest possible haste towards Constantinople....

In the same year (1660) Melek Ahmed Páshá of Bosnia sent seven thousand heads to the Porte, and announced the reduction of the fortresses of Kámín, Kirád, and Rinja. Alí Páshá, who had the government of the Dardanelles, was removed, and sent against the castle of Arad, which surrendered.

The rebellion of Mehneh Beg in Valachia being evident, Fazlí Páshá, Ján Arslán Páshá, and several Begs were sent against him. The two armies met at Gurgivo, and the Ottoman army was defeated. At the same time the prince of Moldavia, Búrúnsiz Kostantin (Constantine without a nose) erected the standard of rebellion at Yassy, began to coin new *zolotas* (money), and took possession of Moldavia. The Tátár Khán of the Crimea, and the Tátárs of Búják, were ordered against him; whilst young Stefano, son of Lipul, the late prince of Moldavia, a prisoner in the Seven Towers, was nominated prince.

On this occasion Kemánkesh Ahmed Aghá was appointed *Iskemla-Aghá* (aghá of the chair), and Siláhshúr Ahmed Aghá, the Sanjak-ághá (ághá of the banner.) The army reached Yassy on a severe winter day, when a battle ensued, the result of which was the flight of Búrúnsiz Kostantin, the loss of ten thousand men on the part of the infidels, and the establishment of prince Stefano. The flying Moldavians were pursued by the Tátárs as far as Valachia, and the whole country was ravaged by fire. Fazlí Páshá and Ján Arslán Páshá, who at this time were shut up in the fortress of Gurjivo, were in the greatest distress, and had already resolved to drown themselves, when the infidels being afraid of the Tátárs, left the trenches and fled to Bucharest. The Ottomans pursued them, and took a great number of prisoners and immense booty. The Tátárs, also, continued their pursuit after the infidels as far as the mountains of Prashova (Kronstadt) on Irshova (Orsova), and took prisoners twenty thousand Valachians and sixty-seven thousand Moldavians. Thus, God be praised! In twenty days Valachia and Moldavia were reduced; and I, the humble writer, who was present, received as my share the value of twenty prisoners. Young Stefano presented me with a purse of gold, six saddle-horses, and a robe; and Ghazá-Zádeh, the Aghá of the Sanjak, gave me a purse, one horse, and a fine boy. On the forty-second day we entered Adrianople. God be praised that I was in this brilliant expedition! I then proceeded to join my lord. Melek Ahmed Páshá, whom I found at Halúna. Were I, however, to describe the Bosnian victories, my list would be extended to an inconvenient length. To be brief, my lord, Melek Ahmed Páshá, was removed from the government of Bosnia, and on a Monday, the 12th of Rabiul-evvel 1071 (1660), was promoted to the government of Rúmeïlí. The province of Bosnia was given to Alí Páshá, the conqueror of Arad, who, in the year 1072 (1661) was also appointed commander of the army against [János] Kemeny, in Transylvania....

This year (1071/1660), during our stay near the castle of Sázmajár, at Sibín, we received intelligence of the death of Kopreïlí Mohammed, and of the promotion of his son to the vazírat. A great battle, also, on a severe winter's day, was fought at Forgrash: the army returned by the Demir kapú, with forty thousand wagons and a hundred thousand prisoners, and were sent into winter quarters. My lord, Melek Ahmed Páshá, took up his winter quarters at Belgrade, whence, by the express command of the emperor, he repaired to Constantinople, to be present at the marriage of Fátima, the daughter of Sultán Ahmed. My lord had been a vezír of the cupola for three months when he died, and was buried in the burial-ground of Eyúb, at the feet of his late master, Kechí Mohammed Efendí. Thus the unfortunate Evliya was left without a patron; but God is merciful!

The following castles were also conquered: Uivár, Litra, Novígrád, Lowa, Sikían, Kermán, Deregil, Holaúk, and Boyák, and many thousands of prisoners were taken. But forty-seven days earlier the famous victory of Gran was won, which might be compared to the victories of Erla and Moháj. It was followed by the fall of the castles of Kiskúivár, Kemenvár, Egervál, Egerzek, Balashka, Washún, and forty others, which were all burnt. All these belonged to Zerín Oghlí (Zriny). Before Kiskúivár was conquered, it was necessary to deliver from the hands of the infidels the castles of Essek, Lippova, Siklos, Beks, Kapushvár, Kopen, Nadas, Berebisinj, Siget, and Kaniza, which were all besieged by the German Electors. When, however, they heard of the arrival of the grand vezír, they raised the siege of Kanisa, and fled to the new castle (Kiskúivár), which was also subsequently conquered. Croatia was ravaged, thirty-six castles were burnt, and the inhabitants carried away captives. Elated with such success, the Moslem army advanced to the river Raab, where, after the conquest of Kiskúivár, it was defeated by the mismanagement of the grand vezír, Ismail Páshá, and Gurjí Mohammed Pasha. Many thousands of Moslems were drowned in the Raab; the Sipahís were deceived by a retrograde motion of the Janissaries, and these, seeing the retreat of the Sipahís, also took to flight, in consequence of which the bridge broke down, and an immense number of men were drowned. The vezír defended himself bravely for twenty-four hours longer, but at last retreated to Stuhlweissenburg, whence he sent proposals of peace. He then took up his winter quarters at Belgrade, and an envoy having been sent from the German emperor, Kara Mohammed Páshá was dispatched as ambassador to Vienna, and the humble author received orders to accompany him in the embassy. The peace being concluded at Vienna, I travelled, with the emperor's patent, through Germany to Dunkirk, thence to Denmark, Holland (where I saw Amsterdam), Sweden, and Cracovie, in Poland, making, in three years and a half, the tour of the countries of the seven infidel kings (the seven Electors). In the year 1668, on the night of the Prophet's ascension, I found myself on the Ottoman frontier, at the castle of Toghan-kechid, on the Dneister. Conducted by my guides, who were Kozaks, I saw lights in the minaret, and, for the first time, after so long an absence, I heard the sound of the Mohammedan call to prayer.

Source: Evliyá Efendí, *Narrative of Travels in Europe, Asia, and Africa in the Seventeenth Century*, trans. Ritter Joseph von Hammer (London: Parbury, Allen & Co. for the Oriental Translation Fund, 1834), 159–163.

103. Ottoman Sultan Mahmud IV's Declaration of War on Emperor Leopold I, Signed at Adrianople (February 20, 1683)

Introduction

For several centuries, from 1529 until the late 18th century, hostility and conflict between Ottoman Turkey and the Habsburg Empire were endemic features of the international scene. The persistent rivalry between the two empires was characterized by intense competition for territorial and political dominance in the Balkans, Central and Eastern Europe, and the Mediterranean. In 1683, Ottoman sultan Mehmed (Mahmud) IV (r. 1648–1687) launched a new war against Austrian emperor Leopold I, supporting a major Hungarian uprising against Habsburg rule. From July 17 until September 12, 1683, a massive Ottoman army led by Grand Vizier Kara "Black" Mustapha besieged Vienna, the third such assault since 1529. The siege was defeated by a combined Western force led by King John III Sobieski of Poland that inflicted a major rout on the Ottoman forces. The unsuccessful siege marked a major check to the further extension of Ottoman power, as the western armies of the Holy League began a successful campaign to push Ottoman power back to the Balkans, culminating in the Second Battle of Mohács in 1687, a crushing Turkish defeat. At this point, Mehmed IV was deposed and replaced by his brother. Following this, Ottoman dominance in its Balkan and West Asian territories would in the course of more than two centuries be gradually but steadily eroded. The sultan's ominously bombastic and threatening declaration of war in 1683, redolent of hostility to Christianity, was evidence of the degree to which religious hostility and the quest for territorial and political expansion reinforced each other in the long-running Turkish-Habsburg competition.

Document

The Great Turks Declaration of War against the Emperour of Germany (At his Pallace at Adrinople, February 20, 1683)

Mahomet Son of Emperours, Son to the famous and glorious God, Emperour of the *Turks,* King of *Graecia, Macedonia, Samaria,* and the Holy-land, King of Great and Lesser *Egypt,* King of all the Inhabitants of the Earth, and of the Earthly Paradise, Obedient Prince and Son of *Mahomet,* Preserver of the Towns of *Hungaria,* Possessour of the Sepulcher of your God, Lord of all the Emperours of the World, from the rising of the Sun to the going down thereof, King of all Kings, Lord of the Tree of Life, Conquerour of *Melonjen, Itegly,* and the City *Prolenix* [Podolia, Ukraine], Great Pursuer of the Christians, Joy of the flourishing World, Commander and Guardian of the Crucified God, Lord of the Multitude of Heathens.

We Command you to greet the Emperour Leopold *(in case he desire it) and you are our Friends, and a Friend to our Majesty, whose Power we will extend very far. Thus,*

You have for some time past acted to our prejudice, and violated our Frendship, although we have not offended you, neither by War, or any otherwise; but you have taken private advice with other Kings, and your Councils how to take off your Yoke, in which you have acted very Indiscreetly, and thereby have exposed your People to fear and danger, having nothing to expect but Death, which you have brought upon your selves. For I declare unto you, I will make my self your Master, pursue you from *East* to *West,* and extend my Majesty to the end of the Earth; in all which you shall find my Power to your great prejudice. I assure you that you shall feel the weight of my Power; and for that you have put your hope and expectation in the strength of some Towns and Castles, I have given command to overthrow them, and to trample under feet with my Horses, all that is acceptable and pleasant in your Eyes, leaving nothing hereafter by which you shall make a friendship with me, or any fortified places to put your trust in: For I have resolved without retarding of time, to ruin both you and your People, to take the *German* Empire according to my pleasure, and to leave in the Empire a Commemoration of my dreadful Sword, that it may appear to all, it will be a pleasure to me, to give a publick establishment of my Religion, and to pursue your Crucified God, whose Wrath I fear not, nor his coming to your Assistance, to deliver you out of my hands. I will according to my pleasure put your Sacred Priests to the Plough, and expose the Brests of your Matrons to be Suckt by Dogs and other Beasts.

You will therefore do well to forsake your Religion, or else I will give Order to Consume you with Fire. This is enough said unto you, and to give you to understand what I would have, in case you have a mind to know it.

Source: "The Great Turks Declaration of War against the Emperour of Germany (At his Pallace at Adrinople, February 20, 1683)" London: Printed by G. C. for John Mumford, 1683. Reprinted in C. A. Macartney, ed., *The Habsburg and Hohenzollern Dynasties in the Seventeenth and Eighteenth Centuries* (New York: Harper & Row, 1970), 57–58. Introduction, editorial notes, chronology, translations by the editor; and compilation copyright © 1970 by C. A. Macartney. Used by permission of HarperCollins Publishers.

104. Napoleon Bonaparte: Proclamations to His Troops and to the People of Egypt (June–July 1798)

Introduction

In the late 1790s, the revolutionary government of France launched an invasion of Egypt, a province of the Ottoman Empire. By this juncture the Ottoman rulers enjoyed the informal protection of Great Britain, the world's greatest naval power and a determined opponent of revolutionary France. As the French Army embarked for Egypt, General Napoleon Bonaparte issued a proclamation to his troops. He highlighted how much damage a successful campaign in Egypt would inflict on England, which sought to monopolize commerce with Egypt. He expressed total confidence that his men would succeed. Perhaps most important of all, he exhorted his men to display respect and toleration for the Muslim religion of Egypt, no matter how alien it might seem to them, and for other Egyptian customs that differed greatly from those of France. On arriving in Egypt Napoleon issued another proclamation, this time to the Egyptian people, in which he declared his veneration for Islam. Claiming that the French intended to rescue the people from oppression, he also attacked the existing Mamluk administration as inequitable and asked the people of Egypt to remain neutral in the coming conflict and refuse to fight for the Mamluks. Contemporaries later recalled how for the rest of his life Emperor Napoleon remained fascinated by Egypt and what he might have been able to accomplish there had the Battle of the Nile later in 1798 and his siege of Acre in 1799 had more favorable outcomes for him.

Documents

Proclamation to the Troops on Embarking for Egypt, June, 1798

Headquarters on Board the Orient, the 4th Messidor, year 6.
Bonaparte, member of the National Institute, General-in-Chief.

Soldiers:—You are about to undertake a conquest the effects of which, on civilization and commerce, are incalculable. The blow you are about to give to England will be the best aimed, the most sensibly felt, she can receive until the time arrives when you can give her her death-blow.

We must make some fatiguing marches; we must fight several battles; we shall succeed in all we undertake. The destinies are with us. The Mameluke beys, who favor exclusively English commerce, whose extortions oppress our merchants, and who tyrannize over the unfortunate inhabitants of the Nile, a few days after our arrival will no longer exist.

The people amongst whom we are going to live are Mahometans. The first article of their faith is this: 'There is but one God and Mahomet is His prophet.' Do not contradict them. Behave to them as you behaved to the Jews, to the Italians. Pay respect to their muftis and their imams, as you did to the rabbis and the bishops. Extend to the ceremonies prescribed by the Koran and the mosques the same toleration which you showed to the synagogues, to the religion of Moses and of Jesus Christ.

The Roman legions protected all religions. You will find customs different from those of Europe. You must accommodate yourselves to them. The people amongst whom we are about to mix differ from us in the treatment of women; but in all countries he who violates is a monster. Pillage only enriches a small number of men; it dishonors us; it destroys our resources; it converts into enemies the people whom it is our interest to have for friends.

The first town we shall come to was built by Alexander. At every step we shall meet with grand recollections, worthy of exciting the emulation of Frenchmen.

Proclamation to the Egyptians, July 1798

People of Egypt: You will be told by our enemies that I am come to destroy your religion. Believe them not. Tell them that I am come to restore your rights, punish your usurpers, and raise the true worship of Mahomet. Tell them that I venerate, more than do the Mamelukes, God, His prophet, and the Koran. Tell them that all men are equal in the sight of God; that wisdom, talents, and virtue alone constitute the difference between them. And what are the virtues which distinguish the Mamelukes, that entitle them to appropriate all the enjoyments of life to themselves? If Egypt is their farm, let them show their lease, from God, by which they hold it. Is there a fine estate? It belongs to the Mamelukes. Is there a beautiful slave, a fine horse, a good house? All belong to the Mamelukes. But God is just and merciful, and He hath ordained that the Empire of the Mamelukes shall come to an end. Thrice happy those who shall side with us; they shall prosper in their fortune and their rank. Happy they who shall be neutral; they will have time to become acquainted with us, and will range themselves upon our side. But woe, threefold woe, to those who shall arm for the Mamelukes and fight against us! For them there will be no hope; they shall perish.

Source: *Selections from the Proclamations, Speeches and Correspondence of Napoleon Bonaparte,* ed. Ida M. Tarbell (Boston: Joseph Knight, 1897), https://www.history.ubc.ca/faculty/friedrichs/sites/default/files/Napoleon%20in%20Egypt%20texts.pdf.

105. The Battle of the Pyramids (July 21, 1798): Napoleon Bonaparte, Letter to the Directory in Paris (July 24, 1798)

Introduction

Three days after the Battle of the Pyramids, General Napoleon Bonaparte sent a detailed report on the engagement to the members of the Directory in Paris. He praised the courage shown not just by his own men but also by the Egyptian Mamluk cavalry. Conditions in Egypt were clearly extremely trying for the French troops, who had been deprived of wine for some time. Ambush and assassination by Egyptian guerrillas was an ever-present risk to which several of his officers had already fallen victim. Napoleon was also shocked by the country's abject poverty and backwardness. Yet he still believed that its fertile soil and the abundance of food it produced would make it an excellent colony for France.

Document

Headquarters, Cairo, 6 Thermidor, year 4. (24 July, 1798)

Citizen Directors:—On the morning of the 2nd Thermidor we caught sight of the Pyramids.

On the evening of the 2nd, we were within six leagues of Cairo, and I learned that the twenty-three beys, with all their forces, were entrenched at Embâbeh, and that their entrenchments were armed by more than sixty pieces of cannon.

BATTLE OF THE PYRAMIDS.

On the 3rd, at dawn, we encountered their vanguard, which we drove from village to village. At 2 o'clock in the afternoon we arrived before their entrenchments and found ourselves in the presence of the enemy.

I ordered the divisions of Generals Desaix and Reynier to take up their position on the right, between Giza and Embâbeh, in such a manner as to cut off the enemy's communication with upper Egypt, which is their natural retreat. The position of the army was the same as at Battle of Chobiâkhyt.

No sooner had Mourad-Bey perceived General Desaix's movements, than he resolved to charge them. He despatched one of his bravest beys with a corps of picked men, who, with lightning rapidity, charged the two divisions. They were allowed to get within fifty feet, then we greeted them with a shower of balls and grape-shot which left many of their number dead on the battle-field. They dashed into the space formed by the two divisions, where they were received by a double fire which completed their defeat.

I seized the opportunity and ordered General Bon's division, which was on the Nile, to prepare for an attack on the enemy's entrenchments. I ordered General Menon's division, which was commanded by General Vial, to bear down between the corps that had just charged us and the entrenchments, in such a manner as to accomplish the triple end of,—

> Preventing this corps re-entering their entrenchments.
> Cutting off the retreat of those who occupied them.
> And finally, if necessary, of attacking the entrenchments on the left.

Directly the generals, Vial and Bon, were in position, they ordered the first and third divisions of each battalion to draw up in columns of attack, while the second and fourth retained their former position, forming a square battalion, now only three deep, while they advanced to support the columns of attack.

General Bon's columns of attack, commanded by the brave General Rampon, threw themselves upon the entrenchments with their usual impetuosity, in spite of the fire from a large quantity of artillery, when suddenly the Mamelukes made a charge. They

105. The Battle of the Pyramids: Napoleon Bonaparte, Letter to the Directory in Paris

emerged from their entrenchments on a full gallop, but our columns had time to come to a halt, to face all sides, and receive them on the points of their bayonets, or by a shower of balls. In an instant the field was strewn with the enemy.

Our troops soon razed their entrenchments. The Mamelukes fled, precipitating themselves *en masse* upon their left, but General Vial was ready for them. They were obliged to pass within five feet of a battalion of our riflemen, and the butchery was awful. A large number threw themselves into the Nile and were drowned.

After the numerous combats and battles that my troops have gained over superior forces, I should not think of praising their conduct and their *sang-froid* on this occasion, were it not that this new method of warfare has required, on their part, a patience which contrasts with French impetuosity. Had they given way to their ardor they could not have gained the victory, which was obtainable only by great coolness and patience.

The Mamelukes' cavalry displayed great bravery; they defended their fortunes, and upon every one of them our soldiers found from three to five hundred louis.

It would be difficult to find a land more fertile, and a people more miserable, more ignorant, more abject. They prefer one of our soldiers' buttons to a six-franc piece.

In the villages they do not even know the sight of a pair of scissors. Their houses are made of a little mud. Their sole furniture is a mat of straw and two or three earthen pots. They eat and burn very little as a general thing. They do not know the use of mills; consequently, we frequently bivouacked on stalks of wheat without being able to obtain any flour. We live on vegetables and cattle. The little grain they do use, they grind into flour with stones, and in some of the large villages they have mills turned by oxen.

We are constantly annoyed by clouds of Arabs; they are the greatest robbers and the greatest rascals on the face of the earth, assassinating alike Turks and French, or anyone who falls in their way.

Brigadier-General Mireur and several aides-de-camp and officers of the staff have been assassinated by these wretches. They lie in ambush behind banks and ditches on their excellent little horses, and woe to him who ventures to wander a hundred feet from the columns.

By a fatality that I have often observed to attend men whose last hour approaches, General Mireur went alone, in spite of the remonstrances of the main-guard, to a little elevation about two hundred feet from the camp. Behind it were stationed three Bedouins who murdered him.

The Republic has met with a real loss. He was one of the bravest generals I have ever known.

There is very little coin in this country, not enough to pay the army. There is plenty of wheat, rice, vegetables, and cattle. The Republic could not have a colony better suited to its needs, nor of a richer soil. The climate is very healthy, owing to the cool nights.

In spite of fifteen days' march, and all kinds of fatigue, the absolute deprivation of wine, in fact, of everything that could alleviate fatigue, we have no one on the sick list. The soldiers have found a great resource in the *postèques,* a kind of watermelon that is very abundant here.

Source: *Selections from the Proclamations, Speeches and Correspondence of Napoleon Bonaparte,* ed. Ida M. Tarbell (Boston: Joseph Knight, 1897), https://www.history.ubc.ca/faculty/friedrichs/sites/default/files/Napoleon%20in%20Egypt%20texts.pdf.

106. Sir Edward Berry: Report on the Battle of the Nile (August 1, 1798)

Introduction

Shortly after the Battle of the Nile, Captain Edward Berry wrote an account of the engagement. He did so on the instructions of Admiral Horatio Nelson, who commanded the British fleet in this engagement but had been wounded in the head, and therefore delegated to Berry, who served Nelson as an aide on his own flagship, the task of describing the battle in detail. Berry's report was included with Nelson's dispatch to the Admiralty reporting his victory and was widely reproduced in the contemporary press. It was also included in printed editions of Nelson's letters published after his death. Although effectively an official dispatch, it conveyed much of the atmosphere of the encounter between the British and French fleets that took place at night, watched from the shore by Arab and Mamluk spectators who subsequently celebrated the British victory. Nelson had been determined to track down and, if possible, destroy the French ships that had carried General Napoleon Bonaparte's army to Egypt. Uncertain as to the destination of Bonaparte and his troops, ever since July 15, 1798, the British had been doggedly hunting for the French fleet, gleaning intelligence from local sources on its whereabouts.

Document

We saw the Pharos of Alexandria at noon on the 1st of August. The Alexander and Swiftsure had been detached ahead on the preceding evening, to reconnoitre the ports of Alexandria, while the main body of the squadron kept in the offing. The enemy was first discovered by the Zealous, Captain Hood, who immediately communicated by signal the number of ships, sixteen, lying at anchor in line of battle, in a bay along the larboard bow, which we afterwards found to be Aboukir Bay. The Admiral hauled his wind that instant, a movement which was immediately observed and followed by the whole squadron; and at the same time he recalled the Alexander and Swiftsure. The wind was at this time N.N.W., and blew what seamen call a top-gallant breeze. It was necessary to take in the royals when we hauled upon a wind. The Admiral made the signal to prepare for battle, and that it was his intention to attack the enemy's van and centre, as they lay at anchor, and according to the plan before developed. His idea in this disposition of his force was, first to secure the victory, and then to make the most of it, as circumstances might permit. A bower cable of each ship was immediately got out abaft, and bent forward. We continued carrying sail and standing in for the enemy's fleet in a close line of battle. As all the officers of our squadron were totally unacquainted with Aboukir Bay, each ship kept sounding as she stood in. The enemy appeared to be moored in a strong and compact line of battle, close in with the shore, their line describing an obtuse angle in its form, flanked by numerous gun-boats, 4 frigates, and a battery of guns and mortars on an island in their van. The situation of the enemy seemed to secure them the most decided advantages, as they had nothing to attend to but their artillery, in their superior skill in the use of which the French so much pride themselves, and to which indeed their splendid series of land victories are in great measure to be imputed.

The position of the enemy presented the most formidable obstacles; but the Admiral viewed these with the eye of a seaman determined on attack, and it instantly struck his eager and penetrating mind, that where there was room for an enemy's ship to swing, there was room for one of ours to anchor. No further signal was necessary than those which had already been made. The Admiral's designs were as fully known to the whole squadron, as was his determination to conquer, or perish in the attempt. The Goliath and Zealous had the honour to lead inside, and to receive the first fire from the van ships of the enemy, as well as from the batteries and gun-boats with which their van was strengthened. These two ships, with the Orion, Audacious, and Theseus, took their stations inside the enemy's line, and were immediately in close action. The Vanguard anchored the first on the outer side of the enemy, and was opposed within half pistol-shot to the Le Spartiate, the third in the enemy's line. In standing in, our leading ships were unavoidably obliged to receive into their bows the whole fire of the broadsides of the French line, until they could take their respective stations; and it is but justice to observe, that the enemy received us with great firmness and deliberation, no colours having been hoisted on either side nor a gun fired, till our van ships were within half gun-shot. At this time the necessary number of our men were employed aloft in furling sails, and on deck in hauling the braces, &c., preparatory to our casting anchor. As soon as this took place, a most animated fire was opened from the Vanguard, which ship covered the approach of those in the rear, which were following in a close line. The Minotaur, Defence, Bellerophon, Majestic, Swiftsure, and Alexander came up in succession, and, passing within hail of the Vanguard, took their respective stations opposed to the enemy's line. All our ships anchored from the stern, by which means the British line became inverted from van to rear. Captain Thompson, of the Leander, of 50 guns, with a degree of skill and intrepidity highly honourable to his professional character, advanced towards the enemy's line on the outside, and most judiciously dropped his anchor athwart hause of Le Franklin, raking her with great success, the shot from the Leander's broadside which passed that ship all striking L'Orient, the flag ship of the French Commander in Chief.

The action commenced at sunset, which is at 31 minutes past 6 p.m., with an ardour and vigour which it is impossible to describe. At about seven o'clock total darkness had come on, but the whole hemisphere was illuminated by the first of the hostile fleets. Our ships, when darkness came on, had all hoisted their illuminating lights, by a signal from the Admiral. The van ship of the enemy, Le Guerrier, was dismasted in less than twelve minutes; and in ten minutes after, the second ship, Le Conquérant, and the third ship, Le Spartiate, very nearly at the same moment were also dismasted. L'Aquilon and Le Souverain Peuple, the fourth and fifth ships of the enemy's line, were taken possession of by the British at half past eight in the evening. Captain Berry, at that hour, sent Lieutenant Galwey, of the Vanguard, with a party of marines, to take possession of Le Spartiate, and that officer returned by the boat, the French captain's sword, which Capt. Berry immediately delivered to the Admiral, who was then below, in consequence of the severe wound which he had received in the head during the heat of the attack. At this time it appeared that victory had already declared itself in our favour; for although L'Orient, L'Heureux, and Tonnant were not taken possession of, they were considered as completely in our power, which pleasing intelligence Captain Berry likewise communicated in person to the Admiral. At ten minutes past nine a fire was observed on board L'Orient, the French Admiral's ship, which seemed to proceed from the after part of the cabin, and which increased with great rapidity, presently involving the whole of the after part of the ship in flames. This circumstance Capt. Berry immediately communicated to the Admiral, who, though suffering severely from his wound, came up on deck, where the first consideration that struck his mind was concern for the danger of so many lives, to save as many as possible of whom he ordered Captain Berry to make every practicable exertion. A boat, the only one that could swim, was instantly dispatched from the Vanguard, and other ships that were in a condition to do so immediately followed the example; in which means from the best possible information, the lives of about seventy Frenchmen were saved. The light thrown by the fire of L'Orient upon the surrounding objects enabled us to perceive with more certainty the situation of the two fleets, the colours of both being clearly distinguishable. The cannonading was partially kept up till about ten o'clock, when L'Orient blew up with a most tremendous explosion. An awful pause and death like silence for about three minutes ensued, when the wreck of the masts, yards, &c., which had been carried to a vast height, fell down into the water and on board the surrounding ships. A port fire from L'Orient fell into the main royal of the Alexander, the first occasioned by which was, however, extinguished in about two minutes by the active exertions of Captain Ball.

After this awful scene the fire was recommenced with the ships to leeward of the centre, till twenty minutes past ten, when there was a total cessation of firing for about ten minutes; after which it was revived till about three in the morning, when it again ceased. After the victory had been secured in the van, such British ships as were in a condition to move had gone down upon the fresh ships of the enemy. At five minutes past five in the morning, the two rear ships of the enemy, Le Guillaume Tell and Le Généreux, were the only French ships of the line that had their colours flying. At fifty-four minutes past five a French frigate, L'Artemise, fired a broadside and struck her colours; but such was the unwarrantable and infamous conduct of the French captain, that after having thus surrendered, he set fire to his ship, and with part of his crew, made his escape on shore. Another of the French frigates, La Serieuse, had been sunk by the fire from some of our ships; but, as her poop remained above water, her men were saved upon it, and were taken off by our boats in the morning. The Bellerophon, whose masts and cables had been entirely shot away, could not retain her situation abreast of L'Orient, but had drifted out of the line to the lee side of the bay, a little before that ship blew up. The Audacious was in the morning detached to her assistance. At eleven o'clock Le Généreux and Guillaume Tell, with two frigates, La Justice and La Diane, cut their cables and stood out to sea, pursued by the Zealous, Captain Hood, who, as the Admiral himself has stated, handsomely attempted to prevent their escape; but as there was no other ship in a condition to support the Zealous, she was recalled. The whole day of the 2nd was spent in securing the French ships that had struck, and that were now completely in our possession, Le Tonnant and

Timoleon excepted; as these were both dismasted, and consequently could not escape, they were the last taken possession of. On the morning of the 3rd the Timoleon was set fire to, and Le Tonnant had cut her cable and drifted on shore; but that active officer, Captain Miller of the Theseus, soon got her off again, and secured in the British line. The British ships engaged consisted of 12 ships of 74 guns, and the Leander of 50. . . .

The Admiral, knowing the wounded of his own ships had been well taken care of, bent his attention to those of the enemy. He established a truce with the Commandant of Aboukir, and through him made a communication to the Commandant of Alexandria, that it was his intention to allow all the wounded Frenchmen to be taken ashore to proper hospitals, with their own surgeons to attend them—a proposal which was assented to by the French, and was carried into effect on the following day. He communicated with the shore, and had the address to procure a supply of fresh vegetables, onions, &c., which were served out to the sick and wounded, and which proved of essential utility. On the 2nd of August the Arabs and Mamelukes, who during the battle had lined the shores of the bay, saw with transport that the victory was decisively ours, an event in which they participated with an exultation almost equal to our own; and on that and the two following nights the whole coast and country were illuminated as far as we could see, in celebration of our victory. This had a great effect upon the minds of our prisoners, as they conceived that this illumination was the consequence, not entirely of our success, but of some signal advantage obtained by the Arabs and Mamelukes over Bonaparte.

Source: Lord Nelson, *Dispatches and Letters (The Battle of the Nile and the Years 1798 to 1800)* (Glasgow: Blackie and Son, 1913), 24–33.

107. Admiral Horatio Nelson to Lord Minto (August 29, 1798)

Introduction

After winning the Battle of the Nile, Admiral Horatio Nelson, who commanded the British Mediterranean Fleet, was eager to exploit the victory and drive the French completely out of Egypt. Writing to his friend Lord Minto, at that time the British governor of the island of Corsica and later governor-general of India, Nelson laid out a plan of attacking the French transport vessels that still remained based at Alexandria. This would eliminate any French threat to the British position in India. Nelson hoped to win the cooperation of the Ottoman sultan, of whose domains Egypt was part, and had already sent an envoy to Constantinople in the hope of winning Ottoman support. Nelson's letter illustrates the strategic considerations driving the British decision to oppose the French invasion of Egypt.

Document

Vanguard, Off Rhodes, August 29th, 1798

My Dear Lord, Your affectionate and flattering letter of April 25th, I received on the 14th August, and I assure you that I feel a great comfort on your account that I shall not (I fancy) be thought entirely undeserving of the many handsome things you said of me. You know, my dear Lord, that I have more than once thought that the Mediterranean fleet has been put into our power to annihilate, therefore I had the advantage of my predecessors. I regret that one escaped, and I think, if it had pleased God that I had not been wounded, not a boat would have escaped to have told the tale; but do not believe that any individual in the fleet is to blame. In my conscience, I believe greater exertions could not have been; and I only mean to say, that if my experience could (in person) have directed those exertions of individuals, there was every appearance that Almighty God would have continued to bless my endeavours for the honour of our King, the advantage of our country, and for the peace and happiness (I hope) of all Europe. It is no small regret that L'Orient is not in being to grace our victory. She was completely beat, and I am sure had struck her colours before she took fire; for as she had lost her main and mizzen masts, and on her flagstaff, which Hood cut from her wreck, was no flag, it must be true that the flag was hauled down, or it would have been entangled with the rigging, or some remnant remained at the masthead. She had on board £600,000 sterling, in ingots of gold and diamonds, for the French brought no coin with them. I wish you had succeeded in getting bomb-vessels sent with our fleet; then, in 48 hours, after the victory, every transport, and all the stores in them, would have been destroyed at Alexandria; for the port is so very small, and so crowded, that not one shell or carcass could have fell amiss.

The present situation of the French Army is briefly this: they have Rosetta and Damietta, the principal entrances of the Nile, for they can get nothing by land to Cairo over the desert; and as we are in possession of the anchorage of Bequier, between Alexandria and Rosetta, the army can get nothing by water. Apropos, this being the season of the rising and overflowing of the Nile, it is usual for the different Beys to send their people and open the canals in order to obtain water till the return of this season; and this applies very strongly to Alexandria, where they have no water but what comes by the canal and fills their reservoir. Now, unless the French are able to buy the Beys and Bedouins, Alexandria must perish for want of water; and I do not think it improbable but that the garrison must evacuate it, and an endeavour will be made to get the ships *arme en flute* with the stores out of the harbour; but, as I have left Hood with three ships of the line and three frigates to annoy Buonaparte, I trust the business will be well attended to. The French Admiral and Officers, who we have on board, were not aware of my leaving a Squadron off Alexandria, and freely declare their opinion that their Army is lost by the measure; for that the Transports are in divisions with stores, &c., and were to move along the coast as Buonaparte penetrated into Syria. In short it is hardly possible to calculate what good events may arrive from our victory. I lost not a moment in sending an Officer overland to India; (if you see Mr. Drake, tell him it is his relation, a very clever young man,) for, if Buonaparte should send any troops down the Red Sea, (which now I do not believe he will,) our Settlements will be prepared. And here I would give an opinion on our last Peace with Tippoo, but high respect for the Officers who made it will not allow me.

I have sent an express to Constantinople, and have urged Mr. Jackson to represent to the Grand Signior, that if he will send a few ships and some bombs, all the transports will be destroyed—if 10,000 men, Alexandria may be retaken; and if he will not send anything, he will lose Syria. . . .

. . . If Naples will give me bombs, I will either return or send [Captain] Troubridge to ruin Buonaparte, for his Army may be destroyed if the Grand Signior, Naples, and England do but exert themselves for three months; I wish I had the means in my power.

Source: Lord Nelson, *Dispatches and Letters (The Battle of the Nile and the Years 1798 to 1800)* (Glasgow: Blackie and Son, 1913), 42–44.

108. Napoleon Bonaparte Besieges Acre (March 18–May 18, 1799)

Introduction

Napoleon Bonaparte spent almost a year in Egypt with the objective not just of replacing Mamluk rule and transforming it into a French colony but also using it as a springboard to overthrow the Ottoman Empire and end British rule in India. Crucial to these ambitious plans, he believed, was control of the city of Acre, then ruled by a somewhat bloodthirsty pasha. Bonaparte spent two months fruitlessly besieging Acre before confessing defeat and returning to Cairo. His private secretary, who was accompanying him, left a memoir of this event that highlights both Bonaparte's disappointment at this outcome and his subsequent attempts to conceal his failure at Acre.

Document

About the end of August [1798] Bonaparte wished to open negotiations with the Pasha of Acre, nicknamed the Butcher. He offered Djezzar his friendship, sought his in return, and gave him the most consolatory assurances of the safety of his dominions. He promised to support him against the Grand Seignior, at the very moment when he was assuring the Egyptians that he would support the Grand Seignior against the beys. But Djezzar, confiding in his own strength and in the protection of the English, who had anticipated Bonaparte, was deaf to every overture, and would not even receive Beauvoisin, who was sent to him on the 22d of August. A second envoy was beheaded at Acre. The occupations of Bonaparte and the necessity of obtaining a more solid footing in Egypt retarded for the moment the invasion of that pashalic, which provoked vengeance by its barbarities, besides being a dangerous neighbour....

During our march on St. Jean d'Acre, which was commenced on the 14th of March [1799], the army neither obtained the brilliant triumphs nor encountered the numerous obstacles spoken of in certain works. Nothing of importance occurred but a rash skirmish of General Lannes who, in spite of contrary orders from Bonaparte, obstinately pursued a troop of mountaineers into the passes of Nabloua. On returning, he found the mountaineers placed in ambush in great numbers amongst rocks, the windings of which they were well acquainted with, whence they fired close upon our troops, whose situation rendered them unable to defend themselves. During the time of this foolish and useless enterprise, especially while the firing was brisk, Bonaparte, exhibited much impatience, and it must be confessed, his anger was but natural. The Nablousians halted at the openings of the mountain defiles. Bonaparte reproached Lannes bitterly for having uselessly exposed himself, and "sacrificed, without any object, a number of brave men." Lannes excused himself by saying that the mountaineers had defied him, and he wished to chastise the rabble. "We are not in a condition to play the swaggerer," replied Napoleon.

In four days we arrived before St. Jean d'Acre, where we learned that Djezzar had cut off the head of our envoy, Mailly-de-Chateau-Renaud, and thrown his body into the sea in a sack. This cruel pasha was guilty of a great number of similar executions. The waves frequently drove dead bodies towards the coast, and we came upon them whilst bathing.

The details of the siege of Acre are well known. Although surrounded by a wall, flanked with strong towers, and having, besides, a broad and deep ditch defended by works, this little fortress did not appear likely to hold out against French valour and the skill of our corps of engineers and artillery; but the ease and rapidity with which Jaffa had been taken occasioned us to overlook in some degree the comparative strength of the two places, and the difference of their respective situations. At Jaffa we had sufficient artillery: at St. Jean d'Acre we had not. At Jaffa we had to deal only with a garrison left to itself: at St. Jean d'Acre we were opposed by a garrison strengthened by reinforcements of men and supplies of provisions, supported by the English fleet, and assisted by European Science. Sir Sidney Smith was, beyond doubt, the man who did us the greatest injury.

—[Napoleon, when at St. Helena, in speaking of the siege of Acre, said,—"Sidney Smith is a brave officer. He displayed considerable ability in the treaty for the evacuation of Egypt by the French. He took advantage of the discontent which he found to prevail amongst the French troops at being so long away from France, and other circumstances....

"The chief cause of the failure at Acre was, that he took all my battering train, which was on board of several small vessels. Had it not been for that, I would have taken Acre in spite of him. He behaved very bravely, and was well seconded by Phillipeaux, a Frenchman of talent, who had studied with me as an engineer. There was a Major Douglas also, who behaved very gallantly. The acquisition of five or six hundred seamen as gunners was a great advantage to the Turks, whose spirits they revived, and whom they showed how to defend the fortress. But he committed a great fault in making sorties, which cost the lives of two or three hundred brave fellows without the possibility of success. For it was impossible he could succeed against the number of the French who were before Acre. I would lay a wager that he lost half of his crew in them. He dispersed Proclamations amongst my troops, which certainly shook some of them, and I in consequence published an order, stating that he was *mad,* and forbidding all communication with him." (*Voices from St. Helena,* vol. 4, p. 208).]—

All our manoeuvres, our works, and attacks were made with that levity and carelessness which over-confidence inspires. Kleber, whilst walking with me one day in the lines of our camp, frequently expressed his surprise and discontent. "The trenches," said, he, "do not come up to my knees." Besieging artillery was, of necessity, required: we commenced with field artillery. This encouraged the besieged, who perceived the weakness of our resources. The besieging artillery, consisting only of three twenty-four pounders and six eighteen pounders, was not brought up until the end of April, and before that period three assaults had taken place with very serious loss. On the 4th of May our powder began to fail us. This cruel event obliged us to slacken our fire.

108. Napoleon Bonaparte Besieges Acre

We also wanted shot; and an order of the day fixed a price to be given for all balls, according to their calibre, which might be picked up after being fired from the fortress or the two ships of the line, the 'Tiger' and 'Theseus,' which were stationed on each side of the harbor. These two vessels embarrassed the communication between the camp and the trenches; but though they made much noise, they did little harm. A ball from one of them killed an officer on the evening the siege was raised.

The enemy had within the walls some excellent riflemen, chiefly Albanians. They placed stones, one over the other, on the walls, put their firearms through the interstices, and thus, completely sheltered, fired with destructive precision....

On the 10th of May, when an assault took place, Bonaparte proceeded at an early hour to the trenches....

The siege of St. Jean d'Acre lasted sixty days. During that time eight assaults and twelve sorties took place. In the assault of the 8th of May more than 200 men penetrated into the town. Victory was already shouted; but the breach having been taken in reverse by the Turks, it was not approached without some degree of hesitation, and the men who had entered were not supported. The streets were barricaded. The cries, the howlings of the women, who ran through the streets throwing, according to the custom of the country, dust in the air, excited the male inhabitants to a desperate resistance, which rendered unavailing this short occupation of the town, by a handful of men, who, finding themselves left without assistance, retreated towards the breach. Many who could not reach it perished in the town....

We often bathed in the sea. Sometimes the English, perhaps after taking a double allowance of grog, would fire at our heads, which appeared above water. I am not aware that any accident was occasioned by their cannonade; but as we were beyond reach of their guns, we paid scarcely any attention to the firing. It was seen a subject of amusement to us.

Had our attack on St. Jean d'Acre been less precipitate, and had the siege been undertaken according to the rules of war, the place would not have held out three days; one assault, like that of the 8th of May, would have been sufficient. If, in the situation in which we were on the day when we first came in sight of the ramparts of Acre, we had made a less inconsiderate estimate of the strength of the place; if we had likewise taken into consideration the active co-operation of the English and the Ottoman Porte, our absolute want of artillery of sufficient caliber, our scarcity of gunpowder and the difficulty of procuring food, we certainly should not have undertaken the siege; and that would have been by far the wisest course.

Towards the end of the siege the General-in-Chief received intelligence of some trifling insurrections in northern Egypt. An angel had excited them, and the heavenly messenger, who had condescended to assume a name, was called the Mahdi, or El Mohdy. This religious extravagance, however, did not last long, and tranquillity was soon restored. All that the fanatic Mahdi, who shrouded himself in mystery, succeeded in doing was to attack our rear by some vagabonds, whose illusions were dissipated by a few musket shots.

The siege of St. Jean d'Acre was raised on the 20th of May. It cost us a loss of nearly 3000 men, in killed, deaths by the plague, or wounds. A great number were wounded mortally. In those veracious documents, the bulletins, the French loss was made 500 killed, and 1000 wounded, and the enemy's more than 15,000....

Bonaparte, not having at this time experienced reverses, having continually proceeded from triumph to triumph, confidently anticipated the taking of St. Jean d'Acre. In his letters to the generals in Egypt he fixed the 25th of April for the accomplishment of that event. He reckoned that the grand assault against the tower could not be made before that day; it took place, however, twenty-four hours sooner. He wrote to Desaix on the 19th of April, "I count on being master of Acre in six days." On the 2d of May he told Junot, "Our 18 and 24 pounders have arrived. We hope to enter Acre in a few days. The fire of their artillery is completely extinguished." Letters have been printed, dated 30th Floréal (19th May), in which he announces to Dugua and to Poussielque that they can rely on his being in Acre on 6th Floréal (25th April). Some mistake has evidently been made. "The slightest circumstances produce the greatest events," said Napoleon, according to the *Memorial of St. Helena;* "had St. Jean d'Acre fallen, I should have changed the face of the world." And again, "The fate of the East lay in that small town." This idea is not one which he first began to entertain at St. Helena; he often repeated the very same words at St. Jean d'Acre. On the shore of Ptolemais gigantic projects agitated him, as, doubtless, regret for not having carried them into execution tormented him at St. Helena.

Almost every evening Bonaparte and myself used to walk together, at a little distance from the sea-shore. The day after the unfortunate assault of the 8th of May Bonaparte, afflicted at seeing the blood of so many brave men uselessly shed, said to me, "Bourrienne, I see that this wretched place has cost me a number of men, and wasted much time. But things are too far advanced not to attempt a last effort. If I succeed, as I expect, I shall find in the town the pasha's treasures, and arms for 300,000 men. I will stir up and arm the people of Syria, who are disgusted at the ferocity of Djezzar, and who, as you know, pray for his destruction at every assault. I shall then march upon Damascus and Aleppo. On advancing into the country, the discontented will flock round my standard, and swell my army. I will announce to the people the abolition of servitude and of the tyrannical governments of the pashas. I shall arrive at Constantinople with large masses of soldiers. I shall overturn the Turkish empire, and found in the East a new and grand empire, which will fix my place in the records of posterity. Perhaps I shall return to Paris by Adrianople, or by Vienna, after having annihilated the house of Austria." After I had made some observations which these grand projects naturally suggested, he replied, "What! do you not see that the Druses only wait for the fall of Acre to rise in rebellion? Have not the keys of Damascus already been offered me? I only stay till these walls fall because until then I can derive no advantage from this large town. By the operation which I meditate I cut off all kind of succour from the beys, and secure the conquest of Egypt. I will have Desaix nominated commander-in-chief; but if I do not succeed in the last assault I am about to attempt, I set off directly. Time presses. I shall not be at Cairo before the middle of June. The winds will then lie favourable for ships bound to Egypt from the north. Constantinople will send troops to Alexandria and Rosetta. I must be there. As for the army which will arrive afterwards by land, I do not fear it this year. I will cause everything to be destroyed, all the way to the entrance of the desert. I will render the passage of an army impossible for two years. Troops cannot exist among ruins."

As soon as I returned to my tent I committed to paper this conversation, which was then quite fresh in my memory; and, I may venture to say that every word I put down is correct. I may add, that during the siege our camp was constantly filled with the inhabitants, who invoked Heaven to favour our arms, and prayed fervently at every assault for our success, many of them on their knees, with their faces to the city. The people of Damascus, too, had offered the keys to Bonaparte. Thus everything contributed to make him confident in his favourite plan.

The troops left St. Jean d'Acre on the 20th of May, taking advantage of the night to avoid a sortie from the besieged, and to conceal the retreat of the army, which had to march three leagues along the shore, exposed to the fire of the English vessels lying in the roads of Mount Carmel. The removal of the wounded and sick commenced on the 18th and 19th of May.

Bonaparte then made a proclamation, which from one end to the other offends against truth. It has been published in many works. The season of the year for hostile landing is there very dexterously placed in the foreground; all the rest is a deceitful exaggeration. It must be observed that the proclamations which Bonaparte regarded as calculated to dazzle an ever too credulous public were amplifications often ridiculous and incomprehensible upon the spot, and which only excited the laughter of men of common sense. In all Bonaparte's correspondence there is an endeavour to disguise his reverses, and impose on the public, and even on his own generals. For example, he wrote to General Dugua, commandant of Cairo, on the 15th of February, "I will bring you plenty of prisoners and flags!" One would almost be inclined to say that he had resolved, during his stay in the East, thus to pay a tribute to the country of fables.

—[The prisoners and flags were sent. The Turkish flags were entrusted by Berthier to the Adjutant-Commandant Boyer, who conducted a convoy of sick and wounded to Egypt. Sidney Smith acknowledges the loss of some flags by the Turks. The Turkish prisoners were used as carriers of the litters for the wounded, and were, for the most part, brought into Egypt. (*Erreurs*, tome i. pp. 47 and 160)]—

Thus terminated this disastrous expedition.

Source: Louis Antoine Fauvelet de Bourrienne, *Memoirs of Napoleon Bonaparte*, Vol. 1, ed. R. W. Phipps (New York: Scribner, 1906), 170–171, 199–210.

109. The Treaty of Gulistan (October 2, 1813)

Introduction

The Treaty of Gulistan, signed in 1813, ended the Russo-Persian War of 1804–1813. Iran ceded to Russia the bulk of Iran's Caucasian territories, including present-day Dagestan, eastern Georgia, most of Azerbaijan, and portions of Armenia. Although supposedly designed to end a decade of hostilities between the two states, all sides recognized that the agreement represented only a truce before the resumption of future hostilities, as Iran regrouped with British assistance, while Russia sought a breathing space that would allow it to concentrate on its ongoing war with Emperor Napoleon I of France. Resentment of its terms on the part of Iran prompted a further and equally unsuccessful war from 1826 to 1828. The Treaty of Turkmenchay (1828), which ended that conflict, transferred the remainder of Armenia and Azerbaijan to Russia. Even today, Iran regards these two treaties as humiliating and unequal agreements that were forcibly and unfairly imposed upon it. Current Iranians still consider Fath Ali Shah, the Persian monarch who lost these wars and was compelled to cede these territories, as one of the most incompetent rulers in Iran's history.

Document

In the name of Almighty God

With the intention to cease the horror of the war and re-establish the steady peace and well-wishing friendship neighborhood shared by Russia Empire and the State of Iran since ancient times, The GLORIOUS and GREAT EMPEROR and RULER of All Russia HIS MAJESTY the EMPEROR and the Head of the State of Iran, HIS MAJESTY the King, for the fair purpose of saving and moved by deep love to their servants, appointed the following authorised Representatives:

The Emperor of All Russia HIS MAJESTY appointed HIS General-lieutenant Nikolay Rtishev, Commander in Chief of forces in Georgia and the Caucasus, the Chief of Civil Affairs in the governments of Astrakhan and Caucasus and Georgia, the Chief of all Border Affairs for Georgia, the Commander of the Caspian Navy, the holder of the orders of the Saint Alexander Nevski, the first rank of Saint Anna, the fourth rank of Saint Martyr and the order of Saint Georgy, the owner of the gold sword with the script awarded for courage. His Majesty the king of Iran appointed his highest ambassador to the Turkish and English Palaces, the High-ranking Respectful Mirza Hasan Khan, distinguished among Iranian chiefs, who has been awarded a set of dagger and sword decorated with brilliants, a shawl cloth and horse accessories decorated with brilliants, the Close Servant of his King, the Councillor of Secret Affairs of the Supreme Iran Palace and the second Khan in the Iran Palace from a Vizier family. We met in Karabakh in the village of Gulistan near the river Zeyva, exchanged our credentials, carefully studied everything related to the peace and friendship to be re-established on behalf of our GREAT LEADERS and by the force and the Supreme authority given to us, WE the abovementioned Representatives adopted and forever affirmed the following:

ARTICLE I

This Treaty ends the enmity and disagreement between the Empire of Russia and the State of Iran today and in the future and from henceforth establishes eternal peace, friendship and agreement between HIS MAJESTY THE EMPEROR of All Russia and HIS MAJESTY the king of Iran and the Successors to THEIR Thrones.

ARTICLE II

As both of the Supreme States mutually agreed to re-establish peace based on the existing state of relations, i.e. by preserving lands, khanates and properties they already possess, and today and for the future to identify the borderline between the Empire of All Russia and the State of Iran as follows: Adinabazar—straight through the Mugan lowland—the Yeddibulag passage up to the junction of the river Kapanak with Araz—along the right bank of the river Kapanak to the Mehri chain—along the boundaries of the Karabakh and Nakhchivan khanates—the chain of the Alagoz mountains—the boundary of Daralayaz adjacent to the boundaries of the Karabakh, Nakhchivan and Iravan khanates and part of the Yelizavetpol (former Ganja khanate) region—along the boundary separating the Iravan khanate from the Yelizavetpol district, Gazakh and Shamsaddin lands to the boundary of Eshekmeydan—the mountain chains—the right bank of the river in the direction of the stream—the road of Hamzachiman—the chain of the Pambak mountains—the boundary of Shuragol—the mountain chains up to Arpachay along the passage between Mastaras and Artikin. For the reason that the territory of Talish changed hands during the war, to ensure greater fairness, the boundaries of that khanate at Zinzeley and Ardabil will be determined by mutually selected Commissars (under the Chief Commanders they are to give an exact and detailed description of the lands, villages, valleys, rivers, mountains, lakes and national boundaries under the real control of the parties), after this treaty is concluded and signed. The boundaries of the Talish khanate then should be determined in such a way that each party can remain the owner of the lands it controls. If something remains to be settled outside the above determined boundaries, each party will give guarantees after the Commissars of both Supreme States announce their findings.

ARTICLE III

To demonstrate his friendly attitude to HIS MAJESTY THE EMPEROR of All Russia, on behalf of himself and his royal successors to come HIS MAJESTY the Shah of Iran solemnly accepts that the following belong to the Russian Empire: the Karabakh khanate and Yelizavetpol province (former Ganja khanate), the khanates of Sheki, Shirvan, Derbend, Guba, Baku and Talish (territories under the Russian Empire), Dagestan, Georgia (together with the province of Shuragol), Imperiya, Guriya, Mingrelia and Abkhaziya, and all the properties and lands between the established Caucasus line borderline (with the people and lands pertaining to the Caspian).

ARTICLE IV

To demonstrate his friendly attitude to HIS MAJESTY the Shah of Iran and to confirm his desire to support a stable autocracy and sovereign government in Iran, his neighbor, HIS MAJESTY THE EMPEROR of All Russia, on behalf of himself and his successors, promises not to render any assistance to any claimant to the throne, until he is appointed heir to the throne of Iran by the King, and to render necessary assistance so that no foreign forces may interfere with the State Affairs of Iran and so that the Iran Palace may be strengthened by the help of the Supreme Russian Palace. Should any conflict develop among the sons of the King over the State Affairs of Iran, the Empire of Russia will not interfere until asked to do so by the King in power.

ARTICLE V

Russian commercial vessels will preserve their right to sail near the Caspian shore and to moor there and Iran will help Russia in cases of shipwreck. Iran shares the same rights. As to naval vessels, they may sail under the Russian flag both in war and during peace. In this respect, Russia preserves its former rights and no other country except Russia may show its flag in the Caspian Sea.

ARTICLE VI

Hostages from both sides, Christians and those of other religions, are to be released within three months of the date of conclusion of the Treaty. Each party should supply hostages with food and other necessities until they reach Garakilsa (the place where the border chiefs are creating a joint facility for delivery of the hostages). Any hostage who has escaped under his own volition, or has violated the law despite his nationality, has the freedom to return to his Motherland without any penalty. Both parties shall grant amnesty to escapees or pardon them.

ARTICLE VII

In addition to all the above-mentioned stipulations, HIS MAJESTY THE EMPEROR of All Russia and HIS MAJESTY the King of Iran will mutually receive Ministers or the Ambassadors at THEIR Supreme Palaces of suitable rank for their tasks. The suite of Representatives or Consuls appointed to protect urban trade should not exceed ten persons. As authorized officials, they should be treated with the respect and honor their positions deserve. According to the Law, no one may harm them and should any disputes arise, the citizens of both parties shall be fairly judged.

ARTICLE VIII

In regard to commercial relations between the citizens of each state, possessing written documents from their government or its appointed officials, proving that they are merchants or citizens of Russia or Iran, they are free to visit and travel in both Supreme States—the parties to this agreement—by land and across the Sea. They are also free to remain there, to send merchants, to leave the territory without any let or hindrance, and to send and exchange goods brought to Iran from Russia and from Russia to Iran. Arbitration of potential disputes arising between the merchants of both Supreme States over claims relating to duties and other matters, is the responsibility of the Consuls or Representatives and in the case of their absence that of local officials. They shall judge fairly, handle such payments or find appropriate persons to do so, and protect merchants from harm and oppression.

Russian merchants visiting Iran shall have freedom of movement to other states enjoying friendly relations with Iran. For this purpose Iran will supply those merchants with the necessary passport to accord them free travel. The same process is applicable to Iranian merchants in Russia and states friendly with Russia.

If any Russian citizen visiting Iran shall die, all his inheritance and other properties are to be delivered to his family or near relatives. Those relatives have the right to sell those properties for their own profit. Whatever their citizenship, this entire process is to be implemented on a legal basis with no concealment or appropriation of those properties, as regulated in the Russian Empire and other civilized states.

ARTICLE IX

Russian merchants shall pay customs duties only once of not more than 0.05% ad valorem for goods brought to cities or ports in Iran. They shall pay the same amount of customs for goods bought in Iran. They shall not pay any additional taxes, duties or imposts on any pretexts. Iranian merchants shall also pay only once the same amount of customs for goods brought to Russian cities and ports.

ARTICLE X

The merchants of both States (the parties to the treaty) are free to sell their goods and buy or exchange them for other goods at shores, ports or in adjacent cities without permission or supervision from any customs office or obligators. This is intended to promote freedom of commercial circulation and avoid the arbitrary and constant extortion of legal duties from the seller and the purchaser for the state treasury.

ARTICLE XI

After this treaty is signed, the representatives of both Supreme States shall mutually and quickly issue the necessary information and order the cessation of all military operations.

Consisting of two copies (with a translation into Persian), signed by the abovementioned Representatives of the Supreme parties, ratified with their seal and mutually exchanged, this eternal Peace treaty shall be re-established and solemnly Ratified by the hands of his MAJESTY THE EMPEROR of All Russia and HIS MAJESTY THE king of Iran.

The ratified copies of the Treaty shall be mutually delivered from the Supreme Palaces to the abovementioned Representatives within three months.

The Treaty was concluded on the 2nd of October eighteen thirteen, by the Iranian calendar on the 29th of Shavval in twelve twenty-eight at the Russian armed camp in the village of Gulustan near the river Zeyva of Karabakh.

SIGNED BY:

The Representative and the Chief Commander Georgia Nikolay Rtishev
(STAMP)

The Representative of Glorious State of Iran Mirza Abul Hasan Khan
(STAMP)

Source: Republic of Azerbaijan, Ministry of Foreign Affairs, translation adapted by Priscilla Roberts, http://mfa.gov.az/en/content/809.

110. "Fall of Turkey–Treaty of Adrianople," *The Spectator* (October 17, 1829)

Introduction

The Treaty of Adrianople (Edirne) concluded in September 1829 between the Ottoman Empire and Russia ended the Russo-Turkish War of 1828–1829 on terms highly disadvantageous to the Turkish government. The Ottoman government was forced to recognize Georgia and the khanates of Erivan and Nakhichevan, which Persia had ceded to Russia the year before, as Russian possessions. Both Serbia and Greece, which had rebelled against Ottoman rule, were recognized as autonomous. The Dardanelles Straits were opened to all commercial vessels. In addition, Russia was allowed to occupy Moldavia and Walacia until the Ottoman government had paid a large indemnity. Influential British journalists regarded this treaty with great apprehension, arguing that within the Ottoman Empire's European territories, Russian tyranny was simply replacing an equally brutal regime. The following article, published in *The Spectator* and other widely read British periodicals one month after the conclusion of the Treaty of Adrianople, demonstrates widespread fears in elite British circles that Russia, by demanding special privileges for Russian subjects within the Ottoman Empire, intended to reduce its once formidable rival to a puppet state and dominate the making of Turkish policy. During the 19th century, such apprehensions would become crucial in impelling successive British governments to support the Ottomans against tsarist Russia and prevent any further erosion of the beleaguered empire's strength.

Document

THE PRESS, TIMES.—The supplementary and separate articles of that treaty, which has fixed the expectation and attention of Europe for some weeks past, as it may affect her repose directly or indirectly for a much longer period, throw a lurid colouring over the policy of the Government by which they were dictated. We do not now attempt to raise, much less to pronounce upon, the question, whether the virtual transfer of Turkey in Europe to Russia be a sufficient cause of slants for the rest of Europe, to justify measures of combined hostility against that all-grasping Government; but this we assert without fear of contradiction, that by the articles of the treaty, original and supplemental, explaining and enforcing each other, Turkey in Europe no longer exists, but as both in sense and essence a province, or mass of provinces, under the immediate gripe and sway of Russia. A sum of more than £5,250,090 is on the face of it, unless the whole world be deceived as to the financial means of the Turkish Government, far beyond the power of Turkey, whoever may be Sultan, to liquidate within ten years. That the amount has been raised, deliberately, to a level which the resources of the Sultan could never be supposed to reach, there seems, we apprehend, some reason for conjecturing, from certain other stipulations of the same treaty. It was formerly observed in this journal, that the only sovereignty left throughout Turkey, if Russian subjects were to enjoy in the full extent the immunities provided for them by the 7th article, would be that of the Russian Minister and Consuls. Such privileges enjoyed by foreign sovereigns within territories which do not own their formal sway, have ever been regarded as badges of the worst kind of servitude. Suppose a Russian subject should behave with provoking insolence and turbulence to the Turkish authorities,—suppose (since such things are at last conceivable) that, for political purposes, he should be secretly instigated by Russian functionaries to get up a scene of bad example to the Turks, and dangerous to the influence of the native magistrates,—is Turkey to have no means of dealing at once with the offender, except through the medium of his associates or tutors in guilt? Would the Emperor Nicholas permit French or British—least of all, would he suffer Turkish—subjects, to enjoy within the Russian territory an entire exemption from the penalties of Russian law? So, with respect to Russian shipping, a merchantman under that flag may be loaded with merchandise contraband of peace or war, and within the Turkish waters she is to brave the authorities of Turkey, and outrage every principle of the law of nations with impunity! Then comes another and highly illustrative condition of this treaty which, taken in conjunction with the military occupancy of the empire, and with the extraordinary rights conferred on Russian subjects, affords what the lawyers call "cumulative evidence" of the design to ingraft a Russian sovereignty upon—or rather, indeed, to incorporate it with—the whole frame and existence of Turkey. At the close of the 11th article are these words:—"Until the complete evacuation of the territories occupied by the Russian troops, the administration and the order of things there established at the present time, under the influence of the Imperial Court of Russia, shall be maintained, and the Sublime Ottoman Porte shall not interfere with them in any manner." Here, then, is not only a military occupation, but a direct and complete administration of the civil government by Russia. Her Commander-in-Chief, it is known, lets put arms into the hands of all the most disaffected Turks; he has fostered the faction of the broken Janissaries,—the irreconcilable Islahmoud; he has given that faction the administrative power throughout the whole country which his troops have overrun and conquered. Coupling, therefore, this system with the arrangements made for keeping military possession of the Turkish soil, is it too much to say that the manifest policy has been to overthrow all those associations and institutions which led the inhabitants of Turkey in Europe to consider the Sultan as their lawful ruler, and to instil the notion of Muscovite supremacy as the habit and principle of the national mind of Turkey? The revenues, moreover, collected according "to the present order of things, and under the influence of the Imperial Court of Russia," must go indubitably into the pocket of that Imperial Court. So that by this singular adjunct of fiscal and civil government to military occupation, the means of the Sultan to get rid of both must be still further impaired and exhausted, and the military tenure will thus become the dexterous instrument of its own unlimited prolongation. Now we do not say that this Russian imperium in imperio may not be a benefit to the Turks: on the contrary, we are sure that their condition will be much happier, and the progress of their civilization more sensible, by virtue of their transfer to the dominion of the Czar. We beg most distinctly to deny,—and we do so because of the gross misrepresentations which our sentiments have often been exposed to on this subject,—we do most gravely, and in terms, disclaim every wish for the preservation of the Turkish Government in any part of Europe. Its religion is a fraud, its essence is ferocious tyranny, its sceptre is the axe, its people are barbarians. No Christian or civilized being can desire the continuance of such a monarchy, as a thing to be valued for itself. Our only subject of regret or apprehension, or both, is that the downfall of such a brutal power should be qualified by the establishment of another species of monster in the place of it. We do not mean to use the word "monster" offensively in its application to Russia: we would signify merely an unnatural and highly formidable power. It is said that there exists no danger of another universal monarchy; and that we believe. It is said that there exists no chance of the revival of any power which shall threaten seriously to disturb the equilibrium of Europe. Doubtless, that proposition likewise we believe, with the proviso that fit means are taken to arrest the growth of such a power. The chance does not, or did not exist, because there is, or was, a greater chance that such an event would be seasonably and effectually frustrated. If nothing in the shape of resistance to the overgrowth of an immoderate power be attempted, the maxim is a silly one which denies the possibility of such a power. Upon the whole, we consider the state of affairs consequent upon the signature of the treaty in question, as one which may be termed critical in the extreme. Wisdom and firmness are mighty defensive agents against calamities which threaten the general welfare; but they must animate the councils of more states than one, or those who betray the common interest will, unfortunately, not suffer alone.

Source: *The Spectator*, October 17, 1829, 7, The Spectator Archive Website, http://archive.spectator.co.uk/article/17th-october-1829/7/fall-of-turkeytreaty-of-adrianople.

111. British Foreign Minister Palmerston to Viscount Beauvale, British Ambassador in Vienna (June 28, 1839)

Introduction

By the 1830s, European powers realized that the Ottoman Empire was in decline. Ottoman Turkey's weakness quickly became a factor in international power politics. After a long and bitter rebellion, in 1832 the Greeks won independence from Ottoman rule, an event that encouraged other states to seek to partition further Ottoman territories. Tsarist Russia, which considered itself the spiritual heir of the Byzantine Empire, sought to enhance its position in the Caucasus and the Middle East. Russian leaders cherished designs of regaining the former Byzantine capital of Istanbul (Constantinople), which controlled the strategic Bosporus Straits, the only maritime passage from the Russian-dominated Black Sea to the Mediterranean. France too sought special rights in the Middle East in Lebanon, Syria, Egypt, and Palestine. The Austrian Empire, whose Balkan provinces shared borders with the Ottoman Empire and the likewise hoped to enhance its territorial position. Internally, during the 1830s Pasha Mehmed Ali of Ottoman Egypt, nominally only that province's governor but in reality a virtually autonomous ruler, rebelled against his overlord in Constantinople and sought to control and annex the Sudan, Syria, Arabia, and the Levant. Alarmed by the Ottoman Empire's growing instability, ambitions of their European rivals, whose power they had no wish to strengthen, British statesmen decided that its preservation was in their own country's interests. In collaboration with other European powers, in 1840 Britain moved to check Mehmed Ali's ever-expanding aspirations, forcing him to renounce his quest for territory in Syria and Arabia. In return, Mehmed Ali and his family were granted the right of hereditary rule over Egypt and the Sudan, leaving the Ottoman sultan the largely titular overlord of those provinces. In an 1839 letter to the British ambassador in Vienna, capital of the Austrian Empire, Lord Palmerston, then British foreign secretary and later a Conservative Party prime minister, enunciated his country's position. Protection of the territorial integrity of the Ottoman Empire would remain British foreign policy for at least four decades and was a major reason for Britain's intervention in the 1854–1856 Crimean War.

Document

The general view which Her Majesty's Government, as at present informed, entertain of the affair in question, may be stated as follows:

The Great Powers are justified in interfering in these matters, which are, in fact, a contest between a sovereign and his subject, because this contest threatens to produce great and imminent danger to the deepest interests of other Powers, and to the general peace of Europe. Those interests and that peace require the maintenance of the Turkish Empire; and the maintenance of the Turkish Empire is, therefore, the primary object to be aimed at. This object cannot be secured without putting an end to future chances of collision between the Sultan and Mehemet Ali. But as long as Mehemet Ali continues to occupy Syria, there will be danger of such collision. Mehemet Ali cannot hold Syria without a large military force constantly stationed there. As long as there is an Egyptian force in Syria, there must necessarily be a Turkish army in that part of Asia Minor which borders on Syria. Each party might agree at present to reduce those forces to a given amount, but neither could be sure that the other was not, after a time, secretly increasing his amount of force; and each party would, beyond a doubt, gradually augment his own force; and thus at no distant period, the same state of things which has existed of late, would again recur: for the motives and passions which have led to it would still be in action. Mehemet Ali, or [his son] Ibrahim, would still desire to add more territory to their Pashalics; the Sultan would still burn to drive them back into Egypt.

It appears then to Her Majesty's Government, that there can be no end to the danger with which these affairs menace the peace of Europe until Mehemet Ali shall have restored Syria to the direct authority of the Sultan; shall have retired into Egypt; and shall have interposed the Desert between his troops and authorities and the troops and authorities of the Sultan. But Mehemet Ali could not be expected to consent to this, unless some equivalent advantage were granted to him; and this equivalent advantage might be hereditary succession in his family to the Pashalic of Egypt: Mehemet Ali and his descendants being secured in the Government of that Province in the same way that a former Pasha of Scutari and his family were so secured; the Pasha continuing to be the vassal of the Porte, paying a reasonable tribute, furnishing a contingent of men, and being bound like any other Pasha by the treaties which his sovereign might make. Such an arrangement would appear to be equitable between the parties, because, on the one hand, it would secure the Sultan against many dangers and inconveniences which arise from the present occupation of Syria by the Pasha; while, on the other hand, it would afford to the Pasha that security as to the future fate of his family, his anxiety about which, he has often declared to be the main cause of his desire to obtain some final and permanent arrangement.

It appears to Her Majesty's Government that if the Five Powers were to agree upon such a plan, and were to propose it to the two parties, with all the authority which belongs to the Great Powers of Europe, such an arrangement would be carried into effect, and through its means, Europe would be delivered from a great and imminent danger.

Source: United Kingdom, *Parliamentary Papers*, 1841, 29:117–119.

112. The Rescript of Gülhane, Gülhane Hatt-ı Hümayunu (November 3, 1839)

Introduction

From 1839 to 1876, the Ottoman Empire launched a program of reforms intended to modernize, consolidate, and strengthen its flagging structure. The objective was to rationalize Ottoman financial and civil administration, eradicate corruption, establish a modern banking system, and recruit and build a conscript army. The wearing of Western-style dress was encouraged. One major purpose was to preempt the increasing strength of nationalism across the empire's diverse provinces by improving economic and political conditions within the empire and encouraging a sense of Ottoman pride and identity. Non-Turks and non-Muslims were to be integrated more closely into the existing power structure, enjoying religious and political equality, which it was hoped would prevent them from seeking independence outside the Ottoman state. In November 1839, Sultan Abdulmejid I issued the Edict of Gülhane, setting out the broad principles of this policy. It was followed by a lengthy program of legislation implementing specific policies, including, for example, the introduction of paper banknotes, post offices, reforms of the civil and criminal codes, and the rationalization of the taxation system and of military recruitment.

Document

All the world knows that in the first days of the Ottoman monarchy, the glorious precepts of the Kuran and the laws of the empire were always honored.

The empire in consequence increased in strength and greatness, and all its subjects, without exception, had risen in the highest degree to ease and prosperity. In the last one hundred and fifty years a succession of accidents and divers causes have arisen which have brought about a disregard for the sacred code of laws and the regulations flowing therefrom, and the former strength and prosperity have changed into weakness and poverty; an empire in fact loses all its stability so soon as it ceases to observe its laws.

These considerations are ever present to our mind, and ever since the day of our advent to the throne the thought of the public weal, of the improvement of the state of the provinces, and of relief to the (subject) peoples, has not ceased to engage it. If, therefore, the geographical position of the Ottoman provinces, the fertility of the soil, the aptitude and intelligence of the inhabitants are considered, the conviction will remain that by striving to find efficacious means, the result, which by the help of God we hope to attain, can be obtained within a few years. Full of confidence, therefore, in the help of the Most High, and certain of the support of our Prophet, we deem it right to seek by new institutions to give to the provinces composing the Ottoman Empire the benefit of a good administration.

These institutions must be principally carried out under three heads, which are:

1. The guarantees insuring to our subjects perfect security for life, honor, and fortune.
2. A regular system of assessing and levying taxes.
3. An equally regular system for the levying of troops and the duration of their service.

And, in fact, are not life and honor the most precious gifts to mankind? What man however much his character may be against violence, can prevent himself from having recourse to it, and thereby injuring the government and the country, if his life and honor are endangered? If, on the contrary, he enjoys in that respect perfect security, he will not depart from the ways of loyalty, and all his actions will contribute to the good of the government and of his brothers.

If there is an absence of security as to one's fortune, everyone remains insensible to the voice of the Prince and the country; no one interests himself in the progress of public good, absorbed as he is in his own troubles. If, on the contrary, the citizen keeps possession in all confidence of all his goods, then, full of ardor in his affairs, which he seeks to enlarge in order to increase his comforts, he feels daily growing and bubbling in his heart not only his love for the Prince and country, but also his devotion to his native land.

These feelings become in him the source of the most praiseworthy actions.

As to the regular and fixed assessment of the taxes, it is very important that it be regulated; for the state which is forced to incur many expences for the defense of its territory cannot obtain the money necessary for its armies and other services except by means of contributions levied on its subjects. Although, thanks be to God, our empire has for some time past been delivered from the scourge of monopolies, falsely considered in times of war as a source of revenue, a fatal custom still exists, although it can only have disastrous consequences; it is that of venal concessions, known under the name of "iltizam."

Under that name the civil and financial administration of a locality is delivered over the passions of a single man; that is to say, sometimes to the iron grasp of the most violent and avaricious passions, for if that contractor is not a good man, he will only look to his own advantage.

It is therefore necessary that henceforth each member of Ottoman society should be taxed for a quota of a fixed tax according to his fortune and means, and that it should be impossible that anything more could be exacted from him. It is also necessary that special laws should fix and limit the expenses of our land and sea forces.

Although, as we have said, the defense of the country is an important matter, and it is the duty of all the inhabitants to furnish soldiers for that object, it has become necessary to establish laws to regulate the contingent to be furnished by each locality according to the necessity of the time, and to reduce the term of military service to four or five years. For it is at the same time doing an injustice and giving a mortal blow to agriculture and to industry to take, without consideration to the respective population of the localities, in the one more, in the other less, men than they can furnish; it is also reducing the soldiers to despair and contributing to the depopulation of the country by keeping them all their lives in the service.

In short, without the several laws, the necessity for which has just been described, there can be neither strength, nor riches, nor happiness, nor tranquility for the empire; it must, on the contrary, look for them in the existence of these new laws.

From henceforth, therefore, the cause of every accused person shall be publicly judged, as the divine law requires, after inquiry and examination, and so long as a regular judgment shall not have been pronounced, no one can secretly or publicly put another to death by poison or in any other manner.

No one shall be allowed to attack the honor of any other person whatever.

Each one shall possess his property of every kind, and shall dispose of it in all freedom, without let or hindrance from any person whatever; thus, for example, the innocent heirs of a criminal shall not be deprived of their legal rights, and the property of the criminal shall not be confiscated. These imperial concessions shall extend to all our subjects, of whatever religion or sect they may be; they shall enjoy them without exception. We therefore grant perfect security to the inhabitants of our empire in their lives, their honor, and their fortunes, as they are secured to them by the sacred text of the law.

As for the other points as they must be settled with the assistance of enlightened opinions, our council of justice (increased by new members as shall be found necessary), to whom shall be joined, on certain days which we shall determine, our ministers and the notabilities of the empire, shall assemble in order to frame laws regulating the security of life and fortune and the assessment of the taxes. Each one in those assemblies shall freely express his ideas and give his advice.

The laws regulating the military service shall be discussed by a military council holding its sittings at the palace of Serasker. As soon as a law shall be passed, in order to be forever valid, it shall be presented to us; we shall give it our approval, which we will write with our imperial sign-manual.

As the object of those institutions is solely to revivify religion, government, the nation, and the empire, we engage not to do anything which is contrary thereto.

In testimony of our promise we will, after having deposited these presents in the hall containing the glorious mantle of the prophet, in the presence of all the ulemas and the grandees of the empire, take oath thereto in the name of God, and shall afterwards cause the oath to be taken by the ulemas and the grandees of the empire.

After that, those from among the ulemas or the grandees of the empire, or any other persons whatsoever who shall infringe these institutions, shall undergo, without respect of rank, position, and influence, the punishment corresponding to his crime, after having been well authenticated. A penal code shall be compiled to that effect.

As all the public servants of the empire receive a suitable salary, and as the salaries of those whose duties have not up to the present time been sufficiently remunerated are to be fixed, a rigorous law shall be passed against the traffic of favoritism and bribery (rüşvet), which the Divine law reprobates, and which is one of the principal causes of the decay of the empire.

The above dispositions being a thorough alteration and renewal of ancient customs the imperial rescript shall be published at Istanbul and in all places of our empire, and shall be officially communicated to all the ambassadors of the friendly powers resident in Istanbul, that they may be witnesses to the granting of these institutions, which, should it please God, shall last forever. Wherein may the Most High have us in His holy keeping. May those who shall commit an act contrary to the present regulations be the object of Divine malediction, and be deprived forever of every kind of (protection) happiness.

Source: Boğaziçi University, Atatürk Institute of Modern Turkish History, http://www.anayasa.gen.tr/gulhane.htm.

113. Prince Pyotr Gortschakoff: General Order after the Fall of Sebastopol (August 30, 1855)

Introduction

Throughout the 18th and 19th centuries Russia expanded its territory at the expense of its neighbors, including Poland, China, Persia, and the Ottoman Empire. By the early 19th century, ever-increasing Russian ambitions in Central Asia and the Middle East alarmed both Britain and France. Although Britain allied itself with Russia during the Napoleonic Wars that ended in 1815, the British government also sought to back Persia and the Ottoman Empire in their efforts to restrain further Russian encroachments. Defending the Ottoman Empire also once more became a French priority, as it had traditionally been since the 16th century. In July 1853, the Ottomans met a Russian occupation of the Danubian principalities with military resistance. In

October, Britain and France entered the conflict in support of the Ottomans. The conflict—the first major military confrontation involving European powers since the Napoleonic Wars—was long and brutal, marked by logistical incompetence on both sides, with soldiers inadequately equipped for winter conditions and often denied proper medical treatment. Military engagements during the battles at Inkerman and Balaklava in 1854 inflicted a heavy toll in casualties on all sides, but their outcome was inconclusive. What had become a stalemated war of attrition finally saw movement at the end of August 1855, when Russian troops were forced to abandon the city of Sebastopol, the main Russian naval base in the Black Sea, following an 11-month siege by British, French, and Ottoman forces. Prince Pyotr Gortschakoff's order announcing the Russian decision to abandon Sebastopol praised the fighting prowess of the Russian military but could not disguise the fact that this was a major blow to Russia, one that soon forced the tsarist government to sue for peace.

Documents

Headquarters, Heights of Inkermann, 30 August 1855

Valiant Comrades: On the 12th September last year a strong enemy's army appeared before the walls of Sebastopol. Despite its numerical superiority, despite the absence of obstacles which military science might have opposed to it in the town, that army did not dare attack it openly and undertook a regular siege.

Since then, despite the formidable means at the disposal of our enemies, who by their numerous ships constantly received reinforcements, artillery, and ammunition for eleven months and a half, all their efforts failed before your bravery and firmness. It is a fact unexampled in military annals that a town hastily fortified, in presence of the enemy, should have been able to hold out so long against a force, the means of attack of which have exceeded everything that hitherto could have been foreseen in calculations of this nature.

And with means so enormous, and on such a description, after the ruinous effects of an artillery of colossal dimensions, continued for nine months, the enemy having frequently had recourse to prolonged bombardments of the town, firing on each occasion many hundred thousand rounds, they became convinced of the inadequacy of their efforts, and resolved to take Sebastopol by a combat.

On the 6th of June they made the assault on different sides, entered courageously into the town, but you received them with intrepidity, and they were driven back on all points in the most brilliant manner.

This check forced them to return to a continuation of their first plan of siege, multiplying their batteries, and increasing the activity of their trench works and mining operations.

Since the memorable day upon which you repulsed the assault two months and a half have elapsed, during which, animated by sentiments of duty and love to the throne and to your country, you have heroically disputed each inch of ground, forcing the assailants to advance only foot by foot, and paying with torrents of blood and an incredible loss of ammunition each yard of ground gained.

In this obstinate defence your courage did not flag; on the contrary it rose to the highest degree of self-denial.

But if your intrepidity and your patience were without bounds there are such in the nature of the possibility of defence. As the approaches of the enemy gradually advanced, their batteries were erected nearer the walls. The circle of fire which surrounded Sebastopol grew daily narrower, and sent death and destruction upon the courageous defenders still further into the town.

Taking advantage of the superiority of their fire at short range, the enemy, after the concentrated action of their artillery during thirty days—which cost our garrison from 800 to 1,000 men per day—commenced that terrible bombardment from their innumerable engines of war, and of a calibre hitherto unknown, which destroyed our defences, which has been repaired at night

113. Prince Pyotr Gortschakoff: General Order after the Fall of Sebastopol

with great labor and at great loss, under the incessant fire of the enemy—the principal work, the Kerniloff Redoubt, on the Malakoff Hill, having experienced considerable and irreparable damage.

To continue under these circumstances the defence of the south side would have been to expose our troops daily to a useless butchery, and their preservation is today, more than ever, necessary to the Emperor of Russia.

For these reasons, with sorrow in my heart, but with a full conviction, I resolved to evacuate Sebastopol, and take over the troops to the north side by the bridge constructed beforehand over the bay and by boats.

Meantime the enemy beholding on the 27th of August at 10:30, the half ruined works before them and the Korniloff redoubt with its ditches filled up, resolved upon a desperate assault, first on Bastions No. 2, Korniloff, and No. 3, and after about three hours upon Bastion No. 5, and the Belkin and Schwartz redoubts.

Of these six attacks, five were gloriously repulsed. Some of the points of attack, like that on Bastion No. 2, on which the enemy had succeeded in bringing guns by flying bridges, having at various times been taken and retaken, remained finally ours. But the Korniloff redoubt, more damaged than the others by the bombardment, was taken by the French, who brought more than 30,000 men against it, and could not be retaken after the great losses we had suffered at the commencement of this combat, for it would have been necessary to ascend in the midst of the ruins a very steep incline, and then cross a narrow ridge above a deep ditch of the rear face occupied by the French. Such an undertaking might have prevented us achieving the proposed object, and would have cost us, without the slightest doubt, incalculable losses.

The attempt was the more needless, as for reasons already mentioned I had resolved to evacuate the place. Therefore, as the success of the enemy was confined to the sole capture of the Korniloff Redoubt, I ordered that no attack should be made on that Redoubt, and to remain in front of it to oppose any continuation of the enemy's attack on the town itself, an order which was executed despite all the efforts of the French to get beyond the gorge of the redoubt.

At dusk the troops were ordered to retire according to the arrangements previously made.

The examples of bravery you gave during that day, valiant comrades, aroused such a feeling of esteem in the enemy, that, despite the knowledge they must have had of our retreat by the explosion of our mines, which our troops exploded one after the other as they gradually retreated, they not only did not pursue us in columns, but even ceased firing with their artillery, which they might have continued with impunity.

Valiant Comrades, it is painful, it is hard to leave Sebastopol in the enemy's hands. But remember the sacrifice we made upon the altar of our country in 1812. Moscow was surely as valuable as Sebastopol—we abandoned it after the immortal battle of Borodino. The defence of Sebastopol during 349 days is superior to Borodino, and when the enemy entered Moscow in that great year of 1812, they only found heaps of stones and ashes. Likewise it is not Sebastopol which we have left them, but the burning ruins of the town which we ourselves set fire to, having maintained the honor of the defence in such a manner that our great-grandchildren may recall the remembrance thereof with pride to all posterity.

Sebastopol kept us chained to its walls; with its fall we acquire freedom of movement, and a new war commences, a war in the open field, that most congenial to the Russian soldier. Let us prove to the Emperor, let us prove to Russia, that we are still imbued with the spirit which animated our ancestors in our memorable and patriotic struggle. Wherever the enemy may show himself we will present our breasts to him, and defend our native land as we defended it in 1812.

Valiant warriors of the land and sea forces!—In the name of the emperor, I thank you, for the unexampled courage, firmness and constancy you have displayed during the siege of Sebastopol. . . .

[L]et us also honor, comrades, those who have fallen honorably for our faith and for our country on the ramparts of Sebastopol.

Let us remember the immortal names of Nachimoff, Korniloff, and Istomine, and let us address prayers to the Most High that He will grant them peace and eternalize their memory as an example to the future generations of the Russians.

Source: *New York Times,* October 18, 1855, The Victorian Web, http://www.victorianweb.org/history/crimea/genorder.html.

114. The Bombardment of Alexandria: Report from the *London Weekly Times* (July 16, 1882)

Introduction

In 1876 Khedive Ismail Pasha of Egypt, who had amassed heavy international financial obligations that his country could no longer afford to service, faced bankruptcy. British and French officials forced the khedive, a grandson of Mehmed Ali, to resign, replacing him with his more pliable son, Tewfik Pasha. Much of Egypt's internal administration was by this point in foreign hands. Popular and elite resentment of external dominance prompted a military revolt in 1881 led by Colonel Ahmad Urabi, an Egyptian officer of peasant origin who sought to repudiate foreign rule while demanding democratic elections. In June 1882 following the defeat of an Egyptian army by Mahdist forces in the rebellious Sudan, violent riots targeting foreign businesses and personnel broke out in the city of Alexandria and then spread rapidly throughout Egypt. The British government responded by dispatching a British naval squadron to bombard Alexandria and take over the city. This marked the beginning of the British military administration of Egypt, which would not end until after World War II. Newspaper correspondents who saw action on board the British vessels sent back reports of this engagement and its sequel, when fires—possibly sparked by the bombardment or set by looters—broke out in much of Alexandria.

Document

The threatened bombardment of the forts of Alexandria was carried out on Tuesday [July 11, 1882]. A correspondent on board the *Monarch* writes:—

"The 11th July has avenged the 11th June. The cruel massacre and the subsequent insults have been punished by the destruction of the forts at the entrance to Alexandria Harbour. On Monday evening the Monarch and Invincible were anchored outside the Mole opposite Forts Isalac and Omuk Kubebe, the guns of which were bearing direct on the ships. At 8 o'clock the Monarch threw the electric light over the harbour and forts, and later steamed quietly down to Fort Babelmex in company with the Invincible, the Penelope having already taken up her station there opposite the entrance to the harbour some hours sooner. Nothing of any interest occurred; and no further communication was received from Ragheb Pasha. The order had been given earlier to prepare for action. The topgallant yards and masts were sent down, the rigging staked down, and everything made ready for action. At 4 o'clock on Tuesday morning all hands were astir and eager for the fray; and at 5 a.m. the bugles sounded for action. In an incredible small space of time every man and boy was at his appointed post, and the smallest middies vied with their elder brother officers in their eagerness for action, and their anxiety to do their duty. The Monarch, Invincible, and Penelope were placed in echelon opposite the Babelmex and Tabia Elusura forts under the personal command of Admiral Beauchamp Seymour. The off-shore squadron, consisting of the Sultan, Superb, Temeraire, Alexandra, and Inflexible, were under the command of Captain Hunt Grubbe, of the Sultan. To the in-shore squadron was assigned the destruction of the fort on the west side, and to the off-shore squadron the forts at Ras-el-Tin, the lighthouse, and the eastern forts of Pharos, Ada, and Libsili. The gunboats Helicon and Hecla, from Malta, were stationed outside the breakwater.

"When all was ready, and every eye was watching the signal to commence, an Egyptian boat arrived alongside the Helicon, and everyone was half afraid that it might be some attempt of Ragheb Pasha at further delay and deceit. The messenger brought a

114. The Bombardment of Alexandria: Report from the *London Weekly Times*

letter for the Acting Consul-general from Dervish Pasha in reply to the official communication of Monday, in which Ragheb Pasha affected to be quite surprised at the declaration of hostilities after the fleet had been such a long time at Alexandria, and seeing that the Egyptian question was being settled by the Conference. He expressed, at the same time, regret that any complaint of Admiral Seymour against the Egyptian Government had not been settled amicably. In reference to the Khedive, Dervish Pasha said his Highness was thinking more of the safety of the country than of his own personal safety. Dervish, however, made no request, and his aide-de-camp was merely informed that there was no answer.

"As soon as the boat got clear away, precisely at 7 a.m., the Alexandra fired a shell into the newly-erected earthwork at Fort Ada. In a few moments the firing from the fleet became general, and for some time there was no reply from the forts on shore. It looked as if it were going to be a one-sided affair. At the commencement of the attack the fleet fired only their small guns, with their Nordenfeldt and Gatlings, but as by degrees the forts opened file, the turret guns were brought into play. Splendid practice was made, and the small forts roundabout Babelmex were silenced and set fire to in an hour. The main fort of Bablemax [*sic*] was more difficult to destroy, and although the Arabs [omission as in original] as only to be able to fire occasionally, it was noon before the fort was actually silenced. At 2 o'clock a firing party from the Invincible landed in a pinnace, spiked some of the guns, and blew up the remainder with charges of gun-cotton.

"At 8 a.m. the Condor, Lord Charles Beresford, bore down towards the Marabout fort, the extreme western fort commanding Boghaz Pass, and for some 1700 yards' distance sent a stream of shells into the fort, and, after doing this single-handed for more than an hour, the Condor was joined by the Bittern, Cygnet, and Decoy, whose combined attack soon silenced the guns. Meanwhile the Temeraire was destroying the forts allotted to her off the Central Pass, the Inflexible opened fire on the guns in the Babelmex and Tabia Elusura Forts in support of the in-shore squadron; whilst the Superb, Sultan, and Alexandra flanked the works on Ras-el-Tin. The tremendous guns and appliances of these magnificent ironclads, commanded and served as they were by the elite of the British navy, soon made terrible havoc with the inferior men and guns opposed to them. The Arab gunners, all things considered, fought very well. They did not desert their guns on the approach of the first shell, as some prophesied, and were not routed in half an hour, as some prophets had foretold. The unanimous opinion of the English officers is that the Arabs did all that was possible to do against long odds, and the only cause of regret at their defeat is that those who made the quarrel took no part in the defence, and were not in the way of some of the British shells. The forts at Marabout, Babelmex, and Ras-el-Tin are dismantled. The harem portion of the Kas-el-Tin Palace was on fire. The lighthouse has received several shells, but is still standing. On board the Monarch there was not a single casualty; but I have to report one officer and four men killed, and 27 men wounded in the following ships—viz, one officer killed and two men wounded in the Inflexible, one man killed and one wounded in the Inflexible [*sic*: should be either the Superb or Temeraire], six men wounded in the Invincible, two men killed and seven wounded in the Sultan, one man killed and three wounded in the Alexandra, eight men wounded in the Penelope. The Monarch having a very low freeboard probably accounts for her freedom from accidents.

"At the forts a number of Arabs were no doubt killed and wounded. At Ras-el-Tin there must have been great destruction of life and property, but there being no communication with the shore, it is impossible to form an estimate. The Invincible, Monarch, and Penelope have bombarded the forts towards the inner harbour."

The Egyptian losses cannot of course be yet estimated, but they must have been heavy. The great fact in connection with this engagement is that, though there were several hours continuous firing and many forts were blown to pieces, no injury of importance was received by one of the English ships. This fact is virtually certain, for Admiral Seymour while giving a list of the killed and wounded, does not refer in any way to injuries to his ships. A few other facts in connection with the engagement deserve to be mentioned. Not one of the telegrams says anything about torpedoes, and it may almost be taken for granted that the Egyptians had neither the means nor the opportunity for using these, the most deadly engines of modern warfare. Five gunboats were engaged, not merely as supports to the iron clads, but actually in the serious fighting at Marabout and Meks, and yet there was not a single casualty on board any one of the five. Dynamite was used for blowing up the heavy guns in Fort Meks, the operation being performed, after the silencing of the fort, by a small party from the Invincible. Thus ended the first naval fight in which England has been engaged since the time of the Crimean War, for though we are not as yet masters of Alexandria, and though the statement that the guns of the fleet command the railroad to Cairo requires confirmation, yet with all its outer defences destroyed, Alexandria can scarcely now be called a fortified town. . . .

ABANDONMENT OF THE FORTS.—THE CITY PILLAGED.

At daylight on Thursday flags of truce were flying at the Ras-el-Tin Lighthouse and divan of the Minister of War, and the Arsenal. The Helicon, with a truce flag flying, the Invincible, Monarch, and Penelope steamed into the inner harbour, while the rest of the squadron outside under weigh, steamed up and down. The conflagration in the town extended during the night, the spectacle being grand, but awful. The following telegram was received at the Admiralty from Sir Beauchamp Seymour, at Alexandria, on Thursday at 9.25 a.m.:—"Immense conflagration in Alexandria last night. Forts apparently abandoned, and the entire garrison withdrawn under flag of truce, leaving Bedouins to pillage and fire the town. Invincible, Monarch, Penelope, and gunboats inside harbour. Other ironclads under weigh off the New Port. Decoy gone to Port Said for information. Weather bad. Communication difficult."

THE VESSELS ENGAGED.

The following is a list of the vessels engaged:—Eight ironclads, supported by five gunboats, represented the effective English force. The ironclads were—Inflexible, 11,400 tons, turret ship, mounting four guns of 81 tons each, and carrying armour of from 16 to 24 inches. Temeraire, 8510 tons, mounting eight heavy guns, four of 25 tons each and four 18 tons each, and carrying eight and 10 inch armour; Superb, 9100 tons, mounting four 25-tons guns, and being protected by 10 or 12 inch armour; Sultan, 9290 tons, mounting eight 18-ton guns and four 12-ton guns, and carrying armour of six to nine inches in thickness; Alexandra (Admiral Beauchamp Seymour's flagship), 9490 tons, mounting two guns of 25 tons each, and 10 of 18 tons each, and bearing armour of eight to 12 inches; Monarch, 8320 tons, mounting four 25-ton guns and two of six and a-half tons each, and being armoured with from eight to 10 inches of iron; Invincible, 6010, mounting 10 12-ton guns, and carrying eight to 10 inches of armour; Penelope, 4470, also mounting 10 12-ton guns, and carrying five to six inches of armour. These eight powerful fighting ships were supported by the gunboats Beacon, Bittern, Cygnet, Candor, and Decoy. All the 13 vessels were fully manned, and, in addition to their heavy armament, most of them were fitted with torpedoes and machine guns of the modern Nordenfeldt and Gatling pattern. The whole fleet was under the command of Vice-admiral Sir F. Beauchamp Paget Seymour, G.C.B., the flag officer of the Mediterranean station. The forts against which this naval force was brought to bear have been so recently strengthened and enlarged that no precise idea of the Egyptian strength can yet be formed. The fortifications, however, extend from Pharos Castle on the extreme east to Marsa-el-Kanat and Marabout Island on the west. The chief fortifications between these two extreme points were Fort Ada, on the northern point of the town, a long line of batteries extending from the east of the Ras-el-Tain Palace to the lighthouse at the shore end of the great breakwater, and the row of forts bearing upon the outer harbour and covering the roads by which vessels must steam after passing the shoal by way of either the Corvette Pass, the Boghaz Central Pass, or the Marabout or Western Pass, to get inside the breakwater. The forts presented an almost unbroken line of defences from Fort Tsale to the southwest of the landing place to the fort and battery of Marsa-el-Kanat, situated just where the shore reaches away to the north. Then come the long stretch of low sandhills, terminating in Chersonesus Point, which was protected by Fort Adjemi, and the guns of Marabout Island covering more or less effectually the Marabout Pass, with its five or six fathoms of water. Besides those fortifications the town was protected by Fort Caffarelli or Napoleon, Fort Cretin, and the fort which, from its position in the front of the ruins of Ptolemy's Palace, commands the East Harbour or New Port. There were therefore two distinct systems of defence—those which protected the New Port and Eastern town, and of which Ports Pharos and Ada were the principal, and those which protected the entrances to the outer Western Harbour. Admiral Seymour's plan of attack consisted in dividing his vessels so as practically to simultaneously bombard the whole of the Egyptian position.

GREAT FIRES IN THE CITY.

The Egyptian troops are supposed to have evacuated Alexandria, as since Tuesday morning several fires have been observed on shore, the conflagrations at night assuming large proportions. The town is reported to be almost empty, and is believed to be left to the lowest class of Arabs, and possibly Bedouins, to plunder. During Tuesday night there was a fire at the Harem Palace. The flames rose high from another great conflagration which was also raging in the town. The consternation of the refugees on board the steamers lying off behind the fleet at the destruction which is being wrought in the town, is great indeed. All fear that their property will be ruined by pillage and fire.

Source: Papers Past Website, https://paperspast.natlib.govt.nz/newspapers/ODT18820825.2.27#print.

115. The Earl of Cromer (Evelyn Baring) on the British Takeover of Egypt (1882)

Introduction

In 1882 Great Britain rather reluctantly took over directly the administration of Egypt, which had previously been a semiautonomous Ottoman province, albeit one with a strong admixture of Western administrators in the financial sphere of government. The well-connected Evelyn Baring (1841–1917), a former military officer from a prominent British banking family, became Egypt's British financial controller in 1877, in tandem with a French counterpart. Following the removal from office in 1878 of Khedive Ismail, the Urabi Revolt, a military uprising against foreign rule, developed, to be repressed in 1882 by a British naval attack on Alexandria. The British then took over the government of Egypt, supposedly temporarily, and Baring was appointed the British agent and consul general, expected to implement minor reforms and facilitate the removal of British troops. Instead, he moved to establish a system known as the Veiled Protectorate whereby Egypt had a supposedly independent government, but all effective power rested with British supervisory officials. Baring, who was raised to the peerage in 1892 and became the first earl of Cromer in 1901, effectively directed Egypt's government for 25 years from 1882, finally retiring in 1907. Shortly afterward, he published a lengthy two-volume book describing and defending his policies in Egypt. The preface included a revealing justification of the British takeover of that country and provides considerable insight into the dynamics driving not just British imperialism but also that of other states.

Document

Egypt may now almost be said to form part of Europe. It is on the high road to the Far East. It can never cease to be an object of interest to all the powers of Europe, and especially to England. A numerous and intelligent body of Europeans and of non-Egyptian orientals have made Egypt their home. European capital to a large extent has been sunk in the country. The rights and privileges of Europeans are jealously guarded, and, moreover, give rise to complicated questions, which it requires no small amount of ingenuity and technical knowledge to solve. Exotic institutions have sprung up and have taken root in the country. The capitulations impair those rights of internal sovereignty which are enjoyed by the rulers or legislatures of most states. The population is heterogeneous and cosmopolitan to a degree almost unknown elsewhere. Although the prevailing faith is that of Islam, in no country in the world is a greater variety of religious creeds to be found amongst important sections of the community.

In addition to these peculiarities, which are of a normal character, it has to be borne in mind that in 1882 the [Egyptian] army was in a state of mutiny; the treasury was bankrupt; every branch of the administration had been dislocated; the ancient and arbitrary method, under which the country had for centuries been governed, had received a severe blow, whilst, at the same time, no more orderly and law-abiding form of government had been inaugurated to take its place. Is it probable that a government composed of the rude elements described above, and led by men of such poor ability as Arabi and his coadjutators, would have been able to control a complicated machine of this nature? Were the sheikhs of the El-Azhar mosque likely to succeed where Tewfik Pasha and his ministers, who were men of comparative education and enlightenment, acting under the guidance and inspiration of a first-class European power, only met with a modified success after years of patient labor? There can be but one answer to these questions. Nor is it in the nature of things that any similar movement should, under the present conditions of Egyptian society, meet with any better success. The full and immediate execution of a policy of "Egypt for the Egyptians," as it was conceived by the Arabists in 1882, was, and still is, impossible.

History, indeed, records some very radical changes in the forms of government to which a state has been subjected without its interests being absolutely and permanently shipwrecked. But it may be doubted whether any instance can be quoted of a sudden transfer of power in any civilized or semi-civilized community to a class so ignorant as the pure Egyptians, such as they were in the year 1882. These latter have, for centuries past, been a subject race. Persians, Greeks, Romans, Arabs from Arabia and Baghdad, Circassians, and finally, Ottoman Turks, have successively ruled over Egypt, but we have to go back to the doubtful and obscure precedents of Pharaonic times to find an epoch when, possibly, Egypt was ruled by Egyptians. Neither, for the present, do they appear to possess the qualities which would render it desirable, either in their own interests, or in those of the civilized world in general, to raise them at a bound to the category of autonomous rulers with full rights of internal sovereignty. If, however, a foreign occupation was inevitable or nearly inevitable, it remains to be considered whether a British occupation was preferable to any other. From the purely Egyptian point of view, the answer to this question cannot be doubtful. The intervention of any European power was preferable to that of Turkey. The intervention of one European power was preferable to international intervention. The special aptitude shown by Englishmen in the government of Oriental races pointed to England as the most effective and beneficent instrument for the gradual introduction of European civilization into Egypt. An Anglo-French, or an Anglo-Italian occupation, from both of which we narrowly and also accidentally escaped, would have been detrimental to Egyptian interests and would ultimately have caused friction, if not serious dissension, between England on the one side and France or Italy on the other. The only thing to be said in favor of Turkish intervention is that it would have relieved England from the responsibility of intervening.

By the process of exhausting all other expedients, we arrive at the conclusion that armed British intervention was, under the special circumstances of the case, the only possible solution of the difficulties which existed in 1882. Probably also it was the best solution. The arguments against British intervention, indeed, were sufficiently obvious. It was easy to foresee that, with a British garrison in Egypt, it would be difficult that the relations of England either with France or Turkey should be cordial. With France, especially, there would be a danger that our relations might become seriously strained. Moreover, we lost the advantages of our insular position. The occupation of Egypt necessarily dragged England to a certain extent within the arena of Continental politics. In the event of war, the presence of a British garrison in Egypt would possibly be a source of weakness rather than of strength. Our position in Egypt placed us in a disadvantageous diplomatic position, for any power, with whom we had a difference of opinion about some non-Egyptian question, was at one time able to retaliate by opposing our Egyptian policy. The complicated rights and privileges possessed by the various powers of Europe in Egypt facilitated action of this nature.

There can be no doubt of the force of these arguments. The answer to them is that it was impossible for Great Britain to allow the troops of any other power to occupy Egypt. When it became apparent that some foreign occupation was necessary, that the Sultan would not act save under conditions which were impossible of acceptance, and that neither French nor Italian cooperation could be secured, the British government acted with promptitude and vigor. A great nation cannot throw off the responsibilities which its past history and its position in the world have imposed upon it. English history affords other examples of the government and people of England drifting by accident into doing what was not only right, but was also most in accordance with British interests.

Source: The Earl of Cromer, *Modern Egypt*, Vol. 1 (New York: Macmillan, 1908), xvii–xviii.

116. Sir Frederick Stephenson to William Stephenson (October 13, 1886)

Introduction

Imperial powers often find it easier to begin a military occupation of strategically important foreign territory than to end it. This was true of British rule in Egypt, undertaken primarily to safeguard access to the Suez Canal, the fastest route to India and other British imperial possessions in Asia. For most of the 1880s and 1890s the security of Egypt was jeopardized by an uprising in neighboring Sudan led by a charismatic Muslim cleric known as the Mahdi, whose apocalyptic rhetoric won him many thousands of followers. The professional soldier General Sir Frederick Charles Arthur Stephenson, commander of British occupation forces in Egypt from 1883 to 1887 who defeated incursions by Mahdist Dervish forces at the Battle of Ginnis in 1885, wrote to his brother a year later. With some resignation, Stephenson recognized that the British government wished to cut back on military spending yet felt that it could not leave the frontier between Egypt and the Sudan undefended.

Document

To his Brother

Assouan, October 13, 1886.

My dear William,—I have come up the Nile again, as you will see by above; this seems likely to be an annual occupation, to which I see no immediate end, though I suppose one will come in due time. I am now making an inspection tour, and shall leave in about three days for Korosko and Haifa, returning to Cairo for the present, should I find the Dervishes are not making an immediate advance; but I shall probably have to come up here again, for there is a fair prospect of another winter campaign. In making the necessary preparations my hands are tied to no small extent by considerations both political and financial, for the Government at home are very averse to my sending any English troops at all beyond Assouan. They fear public opinion, which may interpret such a move as implying an intention to go on ultimately to Dongola. I am therefore restricted, except in a case of extreme urgency, to garrisoning both Haifa and Korosko with nothing but Egyptian troops, and these will have to stand the attack of the Dervishes without the immediate support of British troops: it is to be hoped that they will but be steady, for we have made Haifa very strong, and they ought to find no difficulty in holding it. In the meantime the English force in Egypt has been reduced very low, and a large portion of the Egyptian army are newly raised corps; but I have an excellent set of officers, and we shall do very well. The defence of this frontier is, however, a task of some little anxiety, because if the enemy should penetrate it, there is not only the fear of alarm spreading amongst a timid and helpless population, but also there are the foreign communities to be taken into account, who would be up in arms at the very idea that they were running any risk, and some of whom would only be too glad of an excuse to still further abuse the English. The weather has now become very bearable even up here, and the health of the troops is improving accordingly. The financial difficulties of the Government in connection with Egypt are very great; for they will have to pay all excess over the military budget for the Egyptian army for this year; and as our own has also been exceeded, the fear is that unless the army estimates for the next year are very moderate, there may be an outcry in Parliament for our withdrawal from Egypt altogether. Then, again, the Egyptian Government will have to satisfy the International Commission by the 1st April next that their army budget can be met by Egyptian resources. Their army has had to be considerably increased of late to meet the heavy additional duties thrown upon it by the defence of the frontier and Suakin. Economy is therefore strictly the order of the day for both armies, the responsibility of which falls upon my shoulders. I have come in for the cold fit: if only two or three of those millions were forthcoming which have been so shamefully squandered by the mismanagement of Gladstone's Government ever since I have been out here! There are, however, causes for far greater anxieties in Eastern Europe, but I cannot help thinking that the Czar will content himself with what he can gain by carrying the game of bullying to the extreme without actually going to war; the game, however, is a dangerous one and may land him in difficulties, which he will be unable to get clear of without war.

Source: Sir Frederick Charles Arthur Stephenson, *At Home and on the Battlefield: Letters from the Crimea, China and Egypt, 1854–1888* (London: John Murray, 1915), 348–350.

117. Theodor Herzl, *The Jewish State* (1896)

Introduction

The most influential early theoretician and publicist of Zionism was Theodor Herzl (1860–1904), a Hungarian Jew who earned a law degree from the University of Vienna. A journalist who spent much of his life working in Paris, Herzl was greatly affected by the famous Dreyfus case of 1894, when a Jewish French Army captain, Alfred Dreyfus, was wrongly accused of treason. The popular anti-Semitism that this episode stirred up convinced Herzl that ineradicable prejudice meant that Jews could not be assimilated into Western nations but instead must establish a nation of their own. In 1896 he published the book *Der Judenstaat* (*The Jewish State*), setting forth these views and proposing that Jews from around the world raise funds and set up a company to work to create a separate Jewish state, a suggestion that ultimately resulted in the formation of the Zionist Organization. Herzl's call resonated with many relatively poor Jews in Eastern Europe who quickly became dedicated supporters, although some wealthy Jewish leaders such as Baron [Maurice de] Hirsch whose backing he had hoped for were far less enthusiastic. In August 1897 Herzl followed up his book by summoning a Zionist Congress, which met in Basel, Switzerland. The delegates founded the World Zionist Organization and adopted a resolution demanding the establishment of a Jewish national homeland in Palestine. This was the first of six annual Zionist Congresses that Herzl summoned before his untimely death in 1904, a demise many attributed to exhaustion caused by overwork in the Zionist cause.

Document

... The Jewish question still exists. It would be foolish to deny it. It is a remnant of the Middle Ages, which civilized nations do not even yet seem able to shake off, try as they will. They certainly showed a generous desire to do so when they emancipated us. The Jewish question exists wherever Jews live in perceptible numbers. Where it does not exist, it is carried by Jews in the course of their migrations. We naturally move to those places where we are not persecuted, and there our presence produces persecution. This is the case in every country, and will remain so, even in those highly civilized—for instance, France—until the Jewish question finds a solution on a political basis. The unfortunate Jews are now carrying the seeds of Anti-Semitism into England; they have already introduced it into America.

I believe that I understand Anti-Semitism, which is really a highly complex movement. I consider it from a Jewish standpoint, yet without fear or hatred. I believe that I can see what elements there are in it of vulgar sport, of common trade jealousy, of inherited prejudice, of religious intolerance, and also of pretended self-defense. I think the Jewish question is no more a social than a religious one, notwithstanding that it sometimes takes these and other forms. It is a national question, which can only be solved by making it a political world-question to be discussed and settled by the civilized nations of the world in council.

We are a people—one people.

We have honestly endeavored everywhere to merge ourselves in the social life of surrounding communities and to preserve the faith of our fathers. We are not permitted to do so. In vain are we loyal patriots, our loyalty in some places running to extremes; in vain do we make the same sacrifices of life and property as our fellow-citizens; in vain do we strive to increase the fame of our native land in science and art, or her wealth by trade and commerce. In countries where we have lived for centuries we are still cried down as strangers, and often by those whose ancestors were not yet domiciled in the land where Jews had already had experience of suffering. The majority may decide which are the strangers; for this, as indeed every point which arises in the relations between nations, is a question of might. I do not here surrender any portion of our prescriptive right, when I make this statement merely in my own name as an individual. In the world as it now is and for an indefinite period will probably remain, might precedes right. It is useless, therefore, for us to be loyal patriots, as were the Huguenots who were forced to emigrate. If we could only be left in peace....

But I think we shall not be left in peace.

Oppression and persecution cannot exterminate us. No nation on earth has survived such struggles and sufferings as we have gone through. Jew-baiting has merely stripped off our weaklings; the strong among us were invariably true to their race when persecution broke out against them. This attitude was most clearly apparent in the period immediately following the emancipation of the Jews. Those Jews who were advanced intellectually and materially entirely lost the feeling of belonging to their race. Wherever our political well-being has lasted for any length of time, we have assimilated with our surroundings. I think this is not discreditable. Hence, the statesman who would wish to see a Jewish strain in his nation would have to provide for the duration of our political well-being; and even a Bismarck could not do that.

For old prejudices against us still lie deep in the hearts of the people. He who would have proofs of this need only listen to the people where they speak with frankness and simplicity: proverb and fairy-tale are both Anti-Semitic. A nation is everywhere a great child, which can certainly be educated; but its education would, even in most favorable circumstances, occupy such a vast amount of time that we could, as already mentioned, remove our own difficulties by other means long before the process was accomplished.

Assimilation, by which I understood not only external conformity in dress, habits, customs, and language, but also identity of feeling and manner—assimilation of Jews could be effected only by intermarriage. But the need for mixed marriages would have to be felt by the majority; their mere recognition by law would certainly not suffice. . . .

No one can deny the gravity of the situation of the Jews. Wherever they live in perceptible numbers, they are more or less persecuted. Their equality before the law, granted by statute, has become practically a dead letter. They are debarred from filling even moderately high positions, either in the army, or in any public or private capacity. And attempts are made to thrust them out of business also: "Don't buy from Jews!"

Attacks in Parliaments, in assemblies, in the press, in the pulpit, in the street, on journeys—for example, their exclusion from certain hotels—even in places of recreation, become daily more numerous, the forms of persecution varying according to the countries and social circles in which they occur. In Russia, imposts are levied on Jewish villages; in Rumania, a few persons are put to death; in Germany, they get a good beating occasionally; in Austria, Anti-Semites exercise terrorism over all public life; in Algeria, there are traveling agitators; in Paris, the Jews are shut out of the so-called best social circles and excluded from clubs. Shades of anti-Jewish feeling are innumerable. But this is not to be an attempt to make out a doleful category of Jewish hardships.

I do not intend to arouse sympathetic emotions on our behalf. That would be a foolish, futile, and undignified proceeding. I shall content myself with putting the following questions to the Jews: Is it not true that, in countries where we live in perceptible numbers, the position of Jewish lawyers, doctors, technicians, teachers, and employees of all descriptions becomes daily more intolerable? Is it not true, that the Jewish middle classes are seriously threatened? Is it not true, that the passions of the mob are incited against our wealthy people? Is it not true, that our poor endure greater sufferings than any other proletariat? I think that this external pressure makes itself felt everywhere. In our economically upper classes it causes discomfort, in our middle classes continual and grave anxieties, in our lower classes absolute despair.

Everything tends, in fact, to one and the same conclusion, which is clearly enunciated in that classic Berlin phrase: "Juden Raus" (Out with the Jews)!

I shall now put the Question in the briefest possible form: Are we to "get out" now and where to?

Or, may we yet remain? And, how long?

Let us first settle the point of staying where we are. Can we hope for better days, can we possess our souls in patience, can we wait in pious resignation till the princes and peoples of this earth are more mercifully disposed towards us? I say that we cannot hope for a change in the current of feeling. And why not? Even if we were as near to the hearts of princes as are their other subjects, they could not protect us. They would only feel popular hatred by showing us too much favor. By "too much," I really mean less than is claimed as a right by every ordinary citizen, or by every race. The nations in whose midst Jews live are all either covertly or openly Anti-Semitic.

The common people have not, and indeed cannot have, any historic comprehension. They do not know that the sins of the Middle Ages are now being visited on the nations of Europe. We are what the Ghetto made us. We have attained pre-eminence in finance, because mediaeval conditions drove us to it. The same process is now being repeated. We are again being forced into finance, now it is the stock exchange, by being kept out of other branches of economic activity. Being on the stock exchange, we are consequently exposed afresh to contempt. At the same time we continue to produce an abundance of mediocre intellects who find no outlet, and this endangers our social position as much as does our increasing wealth. Educated Jews without means are now rapidly becoming Socialists. Hence we are certain to suffer very severely in the struggle between classes, because we stand in the most exposed position in the camps of both Socialists and capitalists....

Source: Theodor Herzl, *A Jewish State: An Attempt at a Modern Solution of the Jewish Question* (New York: Maccabaeturean Publishing Company, 1904), 4–6, 16–18.

118. The Young Turks: Proclamation for the Ottoman Empire (1908)

Introduction

In 1878 Ottoman sultan Abdulhamid II suspended his empire's constitution, restoring his position as an absolute monarch. By the late 19th century, several modernizing groups of predominantly youthful young progressive reformers had come into being in Turkey. In 1906, they united themselves under the umbrella organization the Committee of Union and Progress. Meanwhile, the peripheries of the Ottoman Empire were crumbling and receding as nationalist movements rejecting Ottoman rule in favor of independence gained strength throughout the Balkans and also in Arabia and present-day Iraq and Syria, while Egypt fell under British control. In 1907 Turkish military officers formed the Ottoman Freedom Committee, which allied itself with the Committee of Union and Progress. In 1908 the insurgents pressured Abdulhamid to restore the long-suspended Turkish Constitution, threatening a military coup and his overthrow unless he did so, and initiating a march on the palace. On winning power, the Committee of Union and Progress, or Young Turks as they were generally known, issued a proclamation establishing a democratic government, ethnic equality, and religious freedom. They also declared their intention of providing free education for all, boosting economic development, and upgrading the military. Implementing these impeccably liberal principles in practice proved to be more difficult than their authors anticipated.

Document

1. The basis for the Constitution will be respect for the predominance of the national will. One of the consequences of this principle will be to require without delay the responsibility of the minister before the Chamber, and, consequently, to consider the minister as having resigned, when he does not have a majority of the votes of the Chamber.

2. Provided that the number of senators does not exceed one-third the number of deputies, the Senate will be named as follows: one-third by the Sultan and two-thirds by the nation, and the term of senators will be of limited duration.

3. It will be demanded that all Ottoman subjects having completed their twentieth year, regardless of whether they possess property or fortune, shall have the right to vote. Those who have lost their civil rights will naturally be deprived of this right.

4. It will be demanded that the right freely to constitute political groups be inserted in a precise fashion in the constitutional charter, in order that article 1 of the Constitution of 1293 A.H. [Anno Hegira] be respected.

7. The Turkish tongue will remain the official state language. Official correspondence and discussion will take place in Turkish.

9. Every citizen will enjoy complete liberty and equality, regardless of nationality or religion, and be submitted to the same obligations. All Ottomans, being equal before the law as regards rights and duties relative to the State, are eligible for government posts, according to their individual capacity and their education. Non-Muslims will be equally liable to the military law.

10. The free exercise of the religious privileges which have been accorded to different nationalities will remain intact.

11. The reorganization and distribution of the State forces, on land as well as on sea, will be undertaken in accordance with the political and geographical situation of the country, taking into account the integrity of the other European powers.

14. Provided that the property rights of landholders are not infringed upon (for such rights must be respected and must remain intact, according to law), it will be proposed that peasants be permitted to acquire land, and they will be accorded means to borrow money at a moderate rate.

16. Education will be free. Every Ottoman citizen, within the limits of the prescriptions of the Constitution, may operate a private school in accordance with the special laws.

17. All schools will operate under the surveillance of the state. In order to obtain for Ottoman citizens an education of a homogeneous and uniform character, the official schools will be open, their instruction will be free, and all nationalities will be admitted. Instruction in Turkish will be obligatory in public schools. In official schools, public instruction will be free. Secondary and higher education will be given in the public and official schools indicated above; it will use the Turkish tongue. Schools of commerce, agriculture, and industry will be opened with the goal of developing the resources of the country.

18. Steps shall also be taken for the formation of roads and railways and canals to increase the facilities of communication and increase the sources of the wealth of the country. Everything that can impede commerce or agriculture shall be abolished.

Source: "The Young Turks," trans. A. Sarrou, in *Civilization since Waterloo*, ed. Rondo Cameron (Paris, 1912), 40–42.

119. The Adana Massacres (April 1909)

Introduction

Within the Ottoman Empire the position of Armenians, most of whom were Christians though some converted to Islam, had always been somewhat precarious. The seizure of political power in 1908 by the modernizing Young Turks emboldened the Armenians to support the new regime, which promised them equality with Muslims, and form political groupings, which then acquired arms. In March 1909 an unsuccessful Ottoman countercoup precipitated a Turkish pogrom against the Armenians, supposedly prompted by rumors that the Armenians were preparing for an insurrection against Sultan Abdulhamid II. From April 13, Turkish mobs attacked Armenian quarters in the cities of Adana, Alexandretta, Mersina, and Tarsus in the province of Cilicia. The attacks continued for a month during which Western missionaries and diplomats also became targets, with some killed. In an effort to quell the disturbances and deliver provisions for the Armenians, British and French warships ostentatiously appeared at the port of Alexandretta. The Ottoman authorities subsequently estimated that 5,243 Christians and 1,186 Muslims died during the riots. Foreign observers believed that the number of Armenians killed was much higher, probably between 20,000 and 30,000. The Princeton-educated American missionary Herbert Adams Gibbons, then age 28 and based in Tarsus, where he and his bride had arrived the previous summer, provided Western journalists with the first eyewitness account of these events.

Document

DAYS OF HORROR DESCRIBED

American Missionary an Eyewitness of Murder and Rapine

ADANA, Asiatic Turkey, via Constantinople, April 27 [1909].—The Rev. Herbert Adams Gibbons of Hartford, Conn., a missionary of the American Board of Foreign Missions stationed here and at Tarsus, was an eyewitness of the scenes of terror and destruction at the centre of the Moslem uprising. He gives the following story of massacre, rapine, and incendiarism:

"The entire vilayet of Adana has been visited during the last five days with a terrible massacre of Armenians, the worst ever known in the history of the district. The terror has been universal, and the Government is powerless to check the disorders. Adana, the capital of the province, has been the storm centre.

"Conditions have been unsettled for some time past, and there has been animosity between Turks and Armenians, owing to the political activity of the latter and their open purchasing of arms.

"Early last Wednesday morning, while I was in the market, I noticed that the Armenians were closing their shops and hurrying to their homes. An Armenian and a Turk had been killed during the night and the corpses were paraded through their respective quarters. The sight of the dead inflamed the inhabitants, and crowds at once began to gather in the streets armed with sticks, axes, and knives. A few young Armenians assembled in the centre of the covered market and began firing revolver shots into the air. By 11 o'clock in the morning the crowd had begun the looting of shops.

Military Commander in Seclusion

"The military commander of Adana was by my side in the market when the firing commenced. He had not the courage to endeavor to disperse the mob; he returned to his residence and did not venture out for two days.

"William Chambers, Field Secretary of the Young Men's Christian Association, and myself proceeded to the Konak and found a howling mob demanding arms with which to kill the Giaours. We then went to the telegraph office to summon the British Consul. On the steps of the building we saw three Armenians who had been killed. Their bodies had been mutilated. While we were in the telegraph office a mob burst into the room where we were and killed two Armenians before our eyes. The unfortunates were supplicating the protection of the Vali when they were struck down.

"We managed to make our way into the next room, where we made representations to the Vali. This official said he could do nothing. He was afraid for his own life, and he made no attempt to protect us. Somehow we managed to get to the interior of the Konak, where we remained at the side of the Government officials for the next forty-eight hours.

"That afternoon the situation grew distinctly worse. The Armenians withdrew to their quarter of Adana, which is situated on a hill, and converted the houses that held advantageous positions into fortresses. Here the fighting went on for two days, during which the Armenians succeeded in beating off their Turkish assailants.

British Woman Cares for Wounded

"Wednesday evening Major Daughty-Wylie, the British Vice Consul at Mersina, arrived at Adana and established headquarters in the house of the dragoman of a wealthy Greek resident, where many refugees had been received. The wife of the British Vice Consul, who was brought into Adana under fire on Thursday, tended personally to many wounded women and children.

"Adana was a hell. The bazaars were looted and set on fire. There was continuous and unceasing shooting and killing in every part of the town, and fires raged in many quarters.

"Moslems from the neighborhood began pouring into the city, and notwithstanding our protests, the Vali distributed arms to these men, alleging that they were Turkish reserves.

"Major Daughty-Wylie, at the head of troops which he compelled the Vali to supply, went to the railroad station of the town and was successful in preventing the villagers from coming into Adana. Later, while the Major was attempting to pacify the town he was shot and disabled.

"Missionaries of the Central Turkey Mission had assembled for a district conference in the centre of Adana on the day of the outbreak. They received and protected hundreds of refugees in the American Seminary for Girls, and courageously endeavored to pacify the warring elements.

Missionaries Treacherously Killed

"On Thursday Daniel Miner Rogers and Henry Maurer, American missionaries, were killed under treacherous circumstances.

"On Friday the Armenians yielded, since when there has been little murdering.

"Adana is in a pitiable condition. The town has been pillaged and destroyed, and there are thousands of homeless people here without means of livelihood. It is impossible to estimate the number of killed. The corpses lie scattered through the streets. Friday, when I went out, I had to pick my way between the dead to avoid stepping on them. Saturday morning I counted a dozen cartloads of Armenian bodies in one-half hour being carried to the river and thrown into the water. In the Turkish cemeteries graves are being dug wholesale.

"The condition of the refugees is most pitiable and heartrending. Not only are there orphans and widows beyond number, but a great many, even the babies, are suffering from severe wounds.

"The situation in Adana itself is unspeakable. On Friday afternoon 250 so-called Turkish reserves, without officers, seized a train at Adana and compelled the engineer to convey them to Tarsus, where they took part in the complete destruction of the Armenian quarter of that town, which is the best part of Tarsus. Their work of looting was thorough and rapid. It is said that they spread with kerosene and fired the great historic Armenian church at Tarsus, the most important building in the city. They demolished marble statues and shattered important historic tablets. Everything portable was carried away, but the church itself resisted their attempts to burn it. Fortunately few persons were killed here. This was owing to the proximity of the American College, where 4,000 destitute and homeless persons had sought and found shelter."

Source: *New York Times*, April 28, 1909.

120. Ottoman Abrogation of the Capitulations (September 9, 1914)

Introduction

From the 17th century onward, Western foreigners enjoyed a variety of special commercial and legal privileges within the Ottoman Empire. On the commercial side, these involved exemption from various tolls, duties, and other charges. In the legal sphere, foreigners accused of crimes or engaged in disputes with Ottoman subjects came under the jurisdiction of their own courts and institutions, and Ottoman law did not apply to them. As nationalist sentiment mounted in Turkey in the late 19th and early 20th centuries, the Capitulations, as these privileges were known, aroused growing resentment not just among the general population but also among the growing number of nationalists in the Turkish elite. The modernizing Committee of Union and Progress that seized power in the Ottoman Empire in 1908 sought to revive national pride, regenerate the empire, and repudiate foreign domination.

World War I, when the major European powers were too occupied with fighting each other to defend their rights overseas, offered an apparently ideal opportunity to jettison the Capitulations. Little more than a month after the conflict began, the Ottoman government announced to each foreign power involved the wholesale abrogation of the Capitulations, to take effect from October 1, 1914. Germany, which had for some years been allied with the Ottoman Empire, constructing railway lines across the Middle East and providing military training to the Ottoman Army, promptly accepted this decision. The British, French, and Russians—the Allied Powers who were all fighting Germany—declined to do so, one factor in the Ottoman decision, announced on October 29, 1914, to join Germany in war against the Allies.

Document

Mr. AMBASSADOR: The Imperial Ottoman Government, in its sentiments of hospitality and sympathy towards the subjects of the friendly Powers, had in former times determined in a special manner the rules to which foreigners coming to the Orient to trade there should be subject, and had communicated those rules to the Powers. Subsequently those rules, which the Sublime Porte had decreed entirely of its own accord, were interpreted as privileges, corroborated and extended by certain practices, and were maintained down to our days under the name of ancient treaties (or Capitulations). Meanwhile these privileges, which on the one hand were found to be in complete opposition to the juridical rules of the century and to the principle of national sovereignty, constituted on the other hand an impediment to the progress and the development of the Ottoman Empire, just as they gave birth to certain misunderstandings in its relations with the foreign Powers; and thus they form an obstacle to the attainment of the desired degree of cordiality and sincerity in those relations.

The Ottoman Empire, surmounting all resistance, continues to march in the path of renaissance and reform which it entered upon in 1255 by the Hatti-Humayoun of Gul-Hané, and, in order to assure for itself the place which was due it in the family of the civilized peoples of Europe, it accepted the most modern juridical principles and did not deviate from the program of supporting the edifice of the State on these foundations. The establishment of the constitutional regime demonstrates with what happy success the efforts of the Ottoman Government in the way of progress were crowned.

However, as consequences deduced from the Capitulations, the intervention of foreigners in the exercise of judiciary power, which constitutes the most important basis of the sovereignty of the State; the limitation of the legislative power, by the claim put forth that many laws could not be applied to foreigners; the fact that a criminal who has committed an offense against public security is screened from the application of the laws on the sole ground of his being of foreign nationality; or again the fact that public action is compromised by the necessity of respecting in regard to the foreign delinquent all sorts of restrictions and conditions; the fact finally that, according to the nationality of the contracting parties, a difference arising from a single contract admits of a different forum and mode of procedure—all these facts and other similar restrictive privileges constitute an insurmountable barrier to all organization of tribunals begun with a view to assuring in the country the perfect working of justice.

Likewise, that consequence of the Capitulations which renders foreigners exempt and free from taxes in the Ottoman Empire renders the Sublime Porte powerless not only to procure the necessary means for providing for the carrying out of reforms, but even for satisfying current administrative needs, without having recourse to a loan. In the same order of ideas, the obstacles raised to the increase of indirect taxes result in raising the quota of direct taxes and in overburdening the Ottoman taxpayers. The fact that foreigners trading in the Ottoman Empire and enjoying there all sorts of immunities and privileges are less heavily taxed than Ottomans constitutes at the same time a manifest injustice and an infringement of the independence and dignity of the State. The Imperial Government, in spite of all these obstacles, was zealously pursuing its efforts at reform when the unforeseen outbreak of the general war brought the financial difficulties in the country to the last degree of acuteness, endangering the accomplishment of all the work which had been begun or the undertaking of which had been decided upon. Now the Sublime Porte is convinced that the only means of salvation for Turkey is to bring into being this work of reform and of development as soon as possible. And it is likewise convinced that all the steps that it takes in this direction will meet with the encouragement of all the friendly Powers.

It is on the basis of this conviction that the decision has been taken to abrogate, reckoning from October 1, 1914, the Capitulations, which up to the present have constituted a hindrance to all progress in the Empire, as well as all privileges and toleration accessory to these Capitulations or resulting from them, and to adopt as the basis of relations with all States the general principles of international law.

While having the honor of communicating the present decision, which as it is to open an era of happiness for the Ottoman Empire will for this reason, I have no doubt, be received with satisfaction by the American Government, I consider it my duty to add that the Sublime Porte, inspired exclusively in its decision by the higher interests of the Ottoman land, does not nourish, in abrogating the Capitulations, any unfriendly thought in regard to any Power and that it is quite disposed to enter upon negotiations with a view to concluding with the American Government treaties of commerce on the basis of the general principles of public international law.

Kindly accept [etc.]

SAID HALIM

Source: U.S. Department of State, *Papers Relating to the Foreign Relations of the United States with the Address of the President to Congress, December 8, 1914* (Washington, DC: U.S. Government Printing Office, 1922), 1092–1093.

121. The Ottoman Empire Declares War on the Allies: Proclamation by Sultan Mehmed (October 29, 1914)

Introduction

After almost three months of wavering and an initial halfhearted attempt at neutrality, in late October 1914 Ottoman Turkey finally opted for war as an ally of the Central Powers, Germany and Austria-Hungary. This decision did not surprise the Allies but did mean that they now felt free to reach agreements among themselves as to the future disposition of various Turkish-ruled territories in the Near and Middle East and Europe. The Allies also encouraged separatist movements in those territories in the Near East and the Balkans that were still under Ottoman rule. World War I would ultimately bring the final breakup of the Ottoman Empire.

Document

To my army! To my navy!

Immediately after the war between the Great Powers began, I called you to arms in order to be able in case of trouble to protect the existence of empire and country from any assault on the part of our enemies, who are only awaiting the chance to attack us suddenly and unexpectedly as they have always done.

While we were thus in a state of armed neutrality, a part of the Russian fleet, which was going to lay mines at the entrance of the straits of the Black Sea, suddenly opened fire against a squadron of our own fleet at the time engaged in maneuvers.

While we were expecting reparation from Russia for this unjustified attack, contrary to international law, the empire just named, as well as its allies, recalled their ambassadors and severed diplomatic relations with our country.

The fleets of England and France have bombarded the straits of the Dardanelles, and the British fleet has shelled the harbor of Akbah on the Red Sea. In the face of such successive proofs of wanton hostility we have been forced to abandon the peaceful attitude for which we always strove, and now in common with our allies, Germany and Austria, we turn to arms in order to safeguard our lawful interests.

The Russian Empire during the last three hundred years has caused our country to suffer many losses in territory, and when we finally arose to that sentiment of awakening and regeneration which would increase our national welfare and our power, the Russian Empire made every effort to destroy our attempts, either with war or with numerous machinations and intrigues. Russia, England, and France never for a moment ceased harboring ill-will against our Caliphate, to which millions of Mussulmans, suffering under the tyranny of foreign dominations, are religiously and wholeheartedly devoted, and it was always these powers that started every misfortune that came upon us.

Therefore, in this mighty struggle which now we are undertaking, we once for all will put an end to the attacks made from one side against the Caliphate, and from the other against the existence of our country.

The wounds inflicted, with the help of the Almighty, by my fleet in the Black Sea, and by my army in the Dardanelles, in Akbah, and on the Caucasian frontiers against our enemies, have strengthened in us the conviction that our sacred struggle for a right cause will triumph. The fact, moreover, that to-day the countries and armies of our enemies are being crushed under the heels of our allies is a good sign, making our conviction as regards final success still stronger.

My heroes! My soldiers! In this sacred war and struggle, which we began against the enemies who have undermined our religion and our holy fatherland, never for a single moment cease from strenuous effort and from self-abnegation.

Throw yourselves against the enemy as lions, bearing in mind that the very existence of our empire, and of 300,000,000 Moslems whom I have summoned by sacred Fetva to a supreme struggle, depend on your victory.

The hearty wishes and prayers of 300,000,000 innocent and tortured faithful, whose faces are turned in ecstasy and devotion to the Lord of the universe in the mosques and the shrine of the Kasbah, are with you.

My children! My soldiers! No army in the history of the world was ever honored with a duty as sacred and as great as is yours. By fulfilling it, show that you are the worthy descendants of the Ottoman Armies that in the past made the world tremble, and make it impossible for any foe of our faith and country to tread on our ground, and disturb the peace of the sacred soil of Yemen, where the inspiring tomb of our prophet lies. Prove beyond doubt to the enemies of the country that there exist an Ottoman army and navy which know how to defend their faith, their country and their military honor, and how to defy death for their sovereign!

Right and loyalty are on our side, and hatred and tyranny on the side of our enemies, and therefore there is no doubt that the Divine help and assistance of the just God and the moral support of our glorious Prophet will be on our side to encourage us. I feel convinced that from this struggle we shall emerge as an empire that has made good the losses of the past and is once more glorious and powerful.

Do not forget that you are brothers in arms of the strongest and bravest armies of the world, with whom we now are fighting shoulder to shoulder. Let those of you who are to die a martyr's death be messengers of victory to those who have gone before us, and let the victory be sacred and the sword be sharp of those of you who are to remain in life.

Source: Charles F. Horne and Warren F. Austin, eds., *The Great Events of the Great War,* Vol. 2 (Washington, DC: National Alumni, 1920), 382–384.

122. The Ottoman Empire: Official Rejection of Treaties of Dependency (October 29, 1914)

Introduction

Simultaneously with its declaration of war against the Allied Powers—the British Empire, France, and Russia—in October 1914, the Ottoman Empire repudiated treaties it had previously signed with Western powers on the grounds that these were unjust to Ottoman Turkey and that the Western powers had in any case never observed those provisions favorable to Ottoman Turkey. Ottoman Turkey's action set a precedent for many similar unilateral abrogations of treaties by once weak nations during the 20th century on the grounds that these were unfair, unequal, and quasi colonial in nature. The Young Turks who came to power in Turkey in 1909 particularly resented the position of tutelage and inferiority that these agreements imposed on the Ottoman Empire.

Documents

The Imperial Ottoman Government had occasion in the course of the second half of the last century to sign, under various circumstances, two important treaties, of Paris of March 10, 1856, and the one of Berlin of August 3, 1878.

The first established a state of affairs, an equilibrium, which the second treaty destroyed to a great extent, but both were violated by the signatory powers themselves, who violated their promises, either openly or secretly, so that after having obtained the application of the clauses which were to the disadvantage of the Ottoman Empire, they did not trouble themselves about those which were in its favor, and they even opposed them constantly.

The Treaty of Paris contained a stipulation "to respect the independence and territorial integrity of the Ottoman Empire," and to guarantee jointly "the strict observation of this agreement." It further excluded all interference in the relations of the Imperial Government "with its subjects and with the internal administration of the empire."

This did not prevent the French Government from exercising in the Ottoman Empire an intervention supported by armed force, and to exact the establishment of a new administration. The other signatory powers were then obliged to associate themselves diplomatically with this act so as not to leave France free in her designs, which were contrary to the above-mentioned stipulations of the Treaty of Paris, and gave rise to fears of aims of annexation.

On the other hand, the Russian Government embarked upon a similar line of conduct by preventing the Sublime Porte in an ultimatum from taking action against the principalities of Serbia and Montenegro which Russia had aroused, and to whom it did not fail to furnish arms, subsidies, officers, and even soldiers, and finally to declare war on the Ottoman Empire, after having demanded that a new internal administration be established in certain Ottoman provinces, and that foreign interference enter into the conduct of their public affairs.

Moreover, the above-mentioned clauses of the Treaty of Paris did not hinder the French Government from occupying Tunis and establishing a protectorate over this dependence of the empire; nor did it prevent the British Government from occupying Egypt and establishing effective domination, nor from making a series of encroachments of Ottoman sovereignty south of Yemen at Nedjid, at Koweit, at El Katr, as well as in the Persian Gulf; nor did these provisions inconvenience the four Governments who are now at war with Turkey in modifying by force the status of the Island of Crete and in creating there a new situation in flagrant contradiction with the integrity which they had undertaken to respect.

Finally, Italy had no scruples in declaring war on the Ottoman Empire without any serious reason, simply with the object of conquest and to obtain compensations as a result of the new political situation in North Africa, and it did not even trouble to comply with its promise that it would "before using force enable the contracting parties to prevent such extreme measures by mediation."

The above makes it unnecessary to enumerate still more circumstances when intervention in the internal affairs of the Ottoman Empire took place.

The Treaty of Berlin, which was signed as a result of the events of 1877–1878, modified considerably the Treaty of Paris by creating new situations in European Turkey; these situations were afterward changed by further conventions, which annulled the stipulations of the international convention referred to.

But not long after the conclusion of this treaty the Russian Government showed the degree of its respect for its own promises. Not having conquered Batoum, it had only been able to annex this fortress by declaring in a solemn international clause its intention to transform it into an essentially commercial free port. The British Government had on this basis consented to renew certain arrangements.

However, the Cabinet of St. Petersburg, after having realized its intentions, simply repudiated this article of the treaty, and made of said city a fortified place. The British Government did not take a single one of the measures which it had promised, thus showing how little importance it attached to the system established by the Treaty of Berlin.

The Imperial Ottoman Government carried out very scrupulously the onerous clauses of the treaty, but the few provisions inserted therein in its favor have remained a dead letter, in spite of its insistence and that of its creditors, owing to the interest which a certain power had in preventing all improvement in the fate of the Ottoman Empire.

The developments set forth show that the Treaties of Paris and Berlin were constantly being violated in their essential and general clauses by certain States which had signed them. But it cannot be conceived that the same international convention should be violated as regards the duties of one of the contracting parties when all provisions of the latter are invariably disregarded. This fact alone renders it already null and void for said party.

Moreover, the situation in which the two above-mentioned treaties were signed has completely changed. The Imperial Ottoman Government is at war with four of the signatory powers, the powers on whose initiative and assistance, and in whose interest said conventions were concluded, a fact which annuls them absolutely as regards the relations between Turkey and those powers.

Furthermore, the Imperial Government has allied itself with two of these powers on a footing of entire equality.

Hence the Ottoman Empire has definitely abandoned its somewhat subordinate position under the collective guardianship of the great powers which some of the latter were interested in maintaining. It therefore enters the group of European powers with all the rights and prerogatives of an entirely independent Government. This new situation also removes all raison d'être for the above-mentioned treaties.

All these different considerations render the said conventions null and void without any contractual value. Nevertheless, in order not to allow any doubts on this point in the minds of those contracting States who have changed their relationship of friendship into an alliance, the Imperial Government has the honor to inform the Imperial Government of Germany and the Imperial and Royal Government of Austria-Hungary that it denounces said treaties of 1856 and 1878.

It deems it useful, however, to declare that it will not fail to appeal to the principles of international law in order to have these rights respected which had been stipulated in its favor by the above-mentioned treaties and which until now have been disregarded.

Source: Charles F. Horne and Warren F. Austin, eds., *The Great Events of the Great War,* Vol. 2 (Washington, DC: National Alumni, 1920), 384–388.

123. General Nikolai Yudenich: Diary Entries on the Early Caucasus Campaign (November 1914–January 1915)

Introduction

On German insistence, in mid-November 1914 Enver Pasha, the Turkish minister of war and de facto commander in chief during World War I, ordered the Ottoman Empire's poorly equipped military forces to mount a major offensive against Russia in the Caucasus. German objectives in pushing their Ottoman allies to undertake this campaign were twofold: Germany's leaders wished to relieve pressure on Germany's eastern front in Poland and Galicia by compelling the Russian military to open a diversionary second front and also wished to ensure that Russia did not gain control of major oil fields around Basra in the Ottoman province of Mesopotamia and in neighboring Persia. Russian Cossack guerrillas began operations in this region in late October 1914, anticipating Turkey's formal declaration of war against the Allied Powers on October 29 and invading Ottoman territory

123. General Nikolai Yudenich: Diary Entries on the Early Caucasus Campaign

in Armenia and northeastern Anatolia. On November 1 the Russian General Staff created the Army of the Caucasus, effectively directed by Major General Nikolai Yudenich, who headed its general staff. The British journalist Morgan Phillips Price, who interviewed Yudenich in February 1916 one day after his forces had taken the crucial fortress of Erzerum, described him as "a short, bullet-headed man with long moustaches.... His voice was sharp and abrupt, his manner that of one who is accustomed to command." His diary entries, reproduced in an official Russian history published in 1916, graphically depicted the ferocity of the two thrusts of the early Caucasus campaign in which around 75,000 Turkish soldiers and perhaps 32,000 Russian troops died, many of cold, exposure, and starvation. The unfortunate inhabitants of the area fared no better.

Document

... The path of Turkish withdrawal was spread with bodies of the frozen soldiers. Defeated Turkish troops hurried to take refuge behind the towers of Deve Boynu and in Erzurum.

... Our officers give further descriptions of Turkish troops: "This enemy is certainly less organized than the Germans, however, they are relatively brave and strong. The misfortune of the Turkish army is their bad clothing, lack of discipline, but, mainly, the lack of inspiration and insight."

... As opposed to the illiteracy of the [Ottoman] soldiers, one can see quite well-educated people among Turkish officers. One of the captured [Ottoman] officers formulated the mood of leading Turkish military circles and the plausible failure of Germans in Turkey: "The 'saving mission' of Germany in Turkey is one thing, but their Germans' treatment of Turkish command contingent is another. Therefore, on this ground, sometimes some serious excesses, which exclude the possibility of real unity, take place."

... In villages and settlements of Zachorokhskiy [Trans-Chorokh kray], where Turks entered and from where they were later repelled by our troops, nobody remained. In Lazistan, where Laz live, and in Ajaria, where Ajars [Acars] live, most of the houses were destroyed by the enemy or burnt. Upon the seizure of villages, Turkish bandits forced the civil population not only to obey them but also to join them actively against our troops. Turkish chetniks [çetes] sent women and children to the Turkish hinterland; men, being threatened, were forced to stay in villages and fight against Russian troops.

... In the meantime, at Oltu, the officers and soldiers knew that they would not have rest, because Turks were actively advancing from Zardanes, Bardus and Jurjurs and huge enemy troops were approaching Oltu.

... After gathering sizeable troops at the upper area of the Çoruh River, Turks penetrated to Oltu through the Narivan mountains. Our army heroically defended the road to Oltu, taking positions over the settlement of Merdenek, between Oltu and Ardahan, where the battle started.

... After defeating the Turks at Merdenek, our troops started approaching to Oltu again, where the major Turkish forces were also approaching through the valley of the Oltu-Çay River.

The population was fleeing—leaving their stocks and property—and joining the [Russian] military carts not only from Oltu, but also from the adjacent villages.

... It was already the evening when our troops entered Oltu. The center and surrounding districts of the town were burning. The Christian population already was not there; all of them left.... When our front lines were straightened, our infantry started slowly withdrawing from Oltu. Turkish artillery and infantry still continued shooting. The civil Muslim people of the town were also firing at our withdrawing troops from the roofs and windows. The mulla of the local mosque climbed to the minaret and started calling for the holy war. He was shot.

... En route, Turkish forces were committing massacres and persecuted the refugees. At one place in the vicinity of Oltu, the Turks gathered a great number of Armenian and Greek children and pushed them in a deep trench where they were crushed to death.

... On December 17 [December 30], the outflanking Turkish troops seized Ardahan, not far from the borders of the Kars and Ardahan oblasts, and retained it in their hands for four days. On December 21 [January 4, 1915], our troops that arrived defeated Turks at Ardahan, where, by the way, the standard of the 8th Turkish regiment was captured.... On December 20 [January 3], the Turks remaining in Ardahan were surrounded by a firm ring from all sides. The Turks withdrew in disorder, ... they ran towards Ardanuch and lost almost the whole Ardahan regiment.

... During their attack against Ardahan, Turkish officers forced their soldiers to advance under the threat of execution, and some cases of execution by machine gun took place.

... In the meantime, an attack was made by a strong Turkish column, supported by rebel Muslim population from the areas of the Panturetskiy and Yagaluzcham mountain passes, in the direction of Ardahan.... During these operations, Turks counted mainly, on the compassion and broad support of local Muslims, organized in advance by Turkish emissaries.... The Turks were shaken and started to withdraw towards the settlement of Upper Sarikamiş. In order to stop the bloodshed, we sent emissaries to Ishan-Pasha, who was commanding Turkish forces, with a proposal to surrender. Our proposal, however, was rejected by them, and [soon] the remains of the Turkish corps started an attack with shouting and wild sighs against us....

The 12-day long Sarikamiş battle, ended by the Turkish loss of two corps—the 9th and 10th—and some regiments of the 8th corps.... During the Sarikamiş battles, 200 officers and up to 20,000 soldiers were captured by us.... In the places where Turks passed, nothing remained on their way.... They did not also have mercy for civil Kurdish population, shooting them without any differentiation.

... The 11th corps of the Turkish army, almost doubled in number vis-à-vis its usual compound, strengthened regularly by people from Erzurum, supported by artillery, continued to attack our vanguard troops in the region of Karaurgan and Horum-Dag....

During the attack on the settlement of Altun-Bulat, almost the whole Turkish regiment, some of its remnants were captured. A strong natural position at Zivin, seized by us, was again conquered by us by a decisive storm.

... The last Turkish efforts of resistance were made at the heights of Upper and Lower Ahalik settlements and Chermuk, but they were all destroyed by our bayonet attacks.

... The 52nd, 92nd and 54th regiments with their commanders, remnants of the 97th, 98th and 99th regiments were captured by our troops; besides, three Turkish camps at the Gelya mountain, Zirin position, and the heights of Lower Abalik were also captured.

... The attack of the Turkestani division from the side of Yeniköy, the advance towards Turkish Mejingert and capture of Zimniy [Winter] Sagot created the situation that allowed our further success of our advancement [at the Iranian-Ottoman border]....

On November 19 [December 2], the troops of the Caucasian army seized the town of Başkale and the village of Saray en route from Dilman and Hoy.

... In the battles at Başkale and Saray, the Russian army received substantial support from the Armenian brigades as well as the local Armenian population. Thus, in one village, an Armenian priest showed our troops the location of Turkish artillery batteries on the mountain peak and offered to provide [us] with Armenian guides.

... Serious battles also held in the Eleşkirt valley. Here, all our troops departed from Iğdir through Bayazit towards Van.... In the meantime, our troops continued to advance towards Van. On December 7 [December 20], a serious battle took place here.

... The villages of the Van vilayet were gradually purged of wild Kurds who were persistently robbing and killing the Armenian population. There were cases, when Kurds left without killing anybody after robbing Armenian houses, but, after some hours, returned especially in order to kill the owners of the robbed houses. Kurds themselves said that they did it upon the orders of Turkish authorities.

Source: Nikolai Yudenich, diary entries included in *The Second Patriotic War According to the Stories of Its Heroes* (Petrograd: Izdaniye pod Vysochayshim Ego Imperatorskago Velichestva Gosudarya Imperatora pokrovitel'stvom Skobelevskago Komiteta, 1916), 184–238, translated in Stanford J. Shaw, *The Ottoman Empire in World War I*, Vol. 2 (Ankara: Türk Tarih Kurumu [Turkish Historical Society], 2008), 830–833.

124. The British Fleet Fails to Force the Dardanelles (March 18, 1915)

Introduction

Early in 1915, the British government decided to mount an expedition to seize from Turkey the strategically important Dardanelles Straits, which controlled access from the Black Sea to the Mediterranean. The British fleet was originally expected to take the straits, but a substantial force of British, Canadian, New Zealand, and Australian troops was dispatched to back up this operation. At the beginning of the Dardanelles/Gallipoli Campaign in February 1915, a British fleet attempted to force a passage through. If the Royal Navy had controlled this passage, it would have been able to send supplies to Russia through the Mediterranean and Black Seas. After suffering losses in earlier attacks, British vessels renewed their attack on March 18, 1915, but finally fell back. Ambassador Henry Morgenthau, the U.S. envoy to Turkey, left this account of the occasion.

Document

[O]n March 18th, the Allied fleet made its greatest attack. As all the world knows, that attack proved disastrous to the Allies. The outcome was the sinking of the *Bouvet*, the *Ocean*, and the *Irresistible* and the serious crippling of four other vessels. Of the sixteen ships engaged in this battle of the 18th, seven were thus put temporarily or permanently out of action. Naturally the Germans and Turks rejoiced over this victory. The police went around, and ordered each householder to display a prescribed number of flags in honour of the event. The Turkish people have so little spontaneous patriotism or enthusiasm of any kind that they would never decorate their establishments without such definite orders. As a matter of fact, neither Germans nor Turks regarded this celebration too seriously, for they were not yet persuaded that they had really won a victory. Most still believed that the Allied fleets would succeed in forcing their way through. The only question, they said, was whether the Entente was ready to sacrifice the necessary number of ships. Neither [German ambassador Baron von] Wangenheim, nor [the Austrian Ambassador the Marquis] Pallavicini believed that the disastrous experience of the 18th would end the naval attack, and for days they anxiously waited for the fleet to return. The high tension lasted for days and weeks after the repulse of the 18th. We were still momentarily expecting the renewal of the attack. But the great armada never returned.

Should it have come back? Could the Allied ships really have captured Constantinople? I am constantly asked this question. As a layman my own opinion can have little value, but I have quoted the opinions of the German generals and admirals, and of the Turks—practically all of whom, except [Brigadier General Ismail] Enver [Pasha, Turkey's Minister of War], believed that the enterprise would succeed, and I am half inclined to believe that Enver's attitude was merely a case of graveyard whistling; in what I now have to say on this point, therefore, I wish it understood that I am giving not my own views, but merely those of the officials then in Turkey who were best qualified to judge.

Enver had told me, in our talk on the deck of the *Yuruk*, that he had "plenty of guns—plenty of ammunition." But this statement was not true. A glimpse at the map will show why Turkey was not receiving munitions from Germany or Austria at that time. The fact was that Turkey was just as completely isolated from her allies then as was Russia. There were two railroad lines leading from Constantinople to Germany. One went by way of Bulgaria and Serbia. Bulgaria was then not an ally; even though she had winked at the passage of guns and shells, this line could not have been used, since Serbia, which controlled the vital link extending from Nish to Belgrade, was still intact. The other railroad line went through Rumania, by way of Bucharest. This route was independent of Serbia, and, had the Rumanian Government consented, it would have formed a clear route from the Krupps to the Dardanelles. The fact that munitions could be sent with the connivance of the Rumanian Government perhaps accounts for the suspicion that guns and shells were going by that route. Day after day the French and British ministers protested at Bucharest against this alleged violation of neutrality, only to be met with angry denials that the Germans were using this line. There is no doubt now that the Rumanian Government was perfectly honourable in making these denials. It is not unlikely that the Germans themselves started all these stories, merely to fool the Allied fleet into the belief that their supplies were inexhaustible.

Let us suppose that the Allies had returned, say on the morning of the nineteenth, what would have happened? The one overwhelming fact is that the fortifications were very short of ammunition. They had almost reached the limit of their resisting power when the British fleet passed out on the afternoon of the 18th. I had secured permission for Mr. George A. Schreiner, the well-known American correspondent of the Associated Press, to visit the Dardanelles on this occasion. On the night of the 18th, this correspondent discussed the situation with General Mertens, who was the chief technical officer at the straits. General Mertens admitted that the outlook was very discouraging for the defense.

"We expect that the British will come back early tomorrow morning," he said, "and if they do, we may be able to hold out for a few hours."

General Mertens did not declare in so many words that the ammunition was practically exhausted, but Mr. Schreiner discovered that such was the case. The fact was that Fort Hamidié, the most powerful defense on the Asiatic side, had just seventeen armour-piercing shells left, while at Kilid-ul-Bahr, which was the main defense on the European side, there were precisely ten.

"I should advise you to get up at six o'clock tomorrow morning," said General Mertens, "and take to the Anatolian hills. That's what we are going to do."

The troops at all the fortifications had their orders to man the guns until the last shell had been fired and then to abandon the forts.

Once these defenses became helpless, the problem of the Allied fleet would have been a simple one. The only bar to their progress would have been the minefield, which stretched from a point about two miles north of Erenkeui to Kilid-ul-Bahr. But the Allied fleet had plenty of mine-sweepers, which could have made a channel in a few hours. North of Tchanak, as I have already explained, there were a few guns, but they were of the 1878 model, and could not discharge projectiles that could pierce modern armour plate. North of Point Nagara there were only two batteries, and both dated from 1835! Thus, once having silenced the outer straits, there was nothing to bar the passage to Constantinople except the German and Turkish warships. The *Goeben* was the only first-class fighting ship in either fleet, and it would not have lasted long against the [British battleship] *Queen Elizabeth*. The disproportion in the strength of the opposing fleets, indeed, was so enormous that it is doubtful whether there would ever have been an engagement.

Thus the Allied fleet would have appeared before Constantinople on the morning of the twentieth. What would have happened then? We have heard much discussion as to whether this purely naval attack was justified. Enver, in his conversation with me, had laid much stress on the absurdity of sending a fleet to Constantinople, supported by no adequate landing force, and much of the criticism since passed upon the Dardanelles expedition has centred on that point. Yet it is my opinion that this exclusively naval attack was justified. I base this judgment purely upon the political situation which then existed in Turkey. Under ordinary circumstances such an enterprise would probably have been a foolish one, but the political conditions in Constantinople then were not ordinary. There was no solidly established government in Turkey at that time. A political committee, not exceeding forty members, headed by [Turkish Minister of Finance Mehmet] Talaat [Pasha], Enver, and Djemal [Turkish Minister of Marine Ismail Cemal Pasha], controlled the Central Government, but their authority throughout the empire was exceedingly tenuous. As a matter of fact, the whole Ottoman state, on that eighteenth day of March, 1915, when the Allied fleet abandoned the attack, was on the brink of dissolution. All over Turkey ambitious chieftains had arisen, who were momentarily expecting its fall, and who were looking for the opportunity to seize their parts of the inheritance. As previously described, Djemal had already organized practically an independent government in Syria. In Smyrna Rahmi Bey, the Governor-General, had often disregarded the authorities at the capital. In Adrianople Hadji Adil, one of the most courageous Turks of the time, was believed to be plotting to set up his own government. Arabia had already become practically an independent nation. Among the subject races the spirit of revolt was rapidly spreading. The Greeks and the Armenians would also have welcomed an opportunity to strengthen the hands of the Allies. The existing financial and industrial conditions seemed to make revolution inevitable. Many farmers went on strike; they had no seeds and would not accept them as a free gift from the Government because, they said, as soon as their crops should be garnered the armies would immediately requisition them. As for Constantinople, the populace there and the best elements among the Turks, far from opposing the arrival of the Allied fleet, would have welcomed it with joy. The Turks themselves were praying that the British and French would take their city, for this would relieve them of the controlling gang, emancipate them from the hated Germans, bring about peace, and end their miseries.

No one understood this better than Talaat. He was taking no chances on making an expeditious retreat, in case the Allied fleet appeared before the city. For several months the Turkish leaders had been casting envious glances at a Minerva automobile that had been reposing in the Belgian legation ever since Turkey's declaration of war. Talaat finally obtained possession of the coveted prize. He had obtained somewhere another automobile, which he had loaded with extra tires, gasolene, and all the other essentials of a protracted journey. This was evidently intended to accompany the more pretentious machine as a kind of "mother ship." Talaat stationed these automobiles on the Asiatic side of the city with chauffeurs constantly at hand. Everything was prepared to leave for the interior of Asia Minor at a moment's notice.

But the great Allied armada never returned to the attack.

About a week after this momentous defeat, I happened to drop in at the German Embassy. Wangenheim had a distinguished visitor whom he asked me to meet. I went into his private office and there was Von der Goltz Pasha, recently returned from Belgium, where he had served as governor. I must admit that, meeting Goltz thus informally, I had difficulty in reconciling his personality with all the stories that were then coming out of Belgium. That morning this mild-mannered, spectacled gentleman seemed sufficiently quiet and harmless. Nor did he look his age—he was then about seventy-four; his hair was only streaked with gray, and his face was almost unwrinkled; I should not have taken him for more than sixty-five. The austerity and brusqueness and ponderous dignity which are assumed by most highly-placed Germans were not apparent. His voice was deep, musical, and pleasing, and his manners were altogether friendly and ingratiating. The only evidence of pomp in his bearing was his uniform; he was dressed as a field marshal, his chest blazing with decorations and gold braid. Von der Goltz explained and half apologized for his regalia by saying that he had just returned from an audience with the Sultan. He had come to Constantinople to present his majesty a medal from the Kaiser, and was taking back to Berlin a similar mark of consideration from the Sultan to the Kaiser, besides an imperial present of 10,000 cigarettes.

The three of us sat there for some time, drinking coffee, eating German cakes, and smoking German cigars. I did not do much of the talking, but the conversation of Von der Goltz and Wangenheim seemed to me to shed much light upon the German mind, and especially on the trustworthiness of German military reports. The aspect of the Dardanelles fight that interested them most at that time was England's complete frankness in publishing her losses. That the British Government should issue an official statement, saying that three ships had been sunk and that four others had been badly damaged, struck them as most remarkable. In this announcement I merely saw a manifestation of the usual British desire to make public the worst—the policy which we Americans also believe to be the best in war times. But no such obvious explanation could satisfy these wise and solemn Teutons. No, England had some deep purpose in telling the truth so unblushingly; what could it be?

"*Es ist ausserordentlich!*" (It is extraordinary) said Von der Goltz, referring to England's public acknowledgment of defeat.

"*Es ist unerhört!*" (It is unheard of) declared the equally astonished Wangenheim.

These master diplomatists canvassed one explanation after another, and finally reached a conclusion that satisfied the higher strategy. England, they agreed, really had had no enthusiasm for this attack, because, in the event of success, she would have had to hand Constantinople over to Russia—something which England really did not intend to do. By publishing the losses, England showed Russia the enormous difficulties of the task; she had demonstrated, indeed, that the enterprise was impossible. After such losses, England intended Russia to understand that she had made a sincere attempt to gain this great prize of war and expected her not to insist on further sacrifices.

The sequel to this great episode in the war came in the winter of 1915–16. By this time Bulgaria had joined the Central Powers, Serbia had been overwhelmed, and the Germans had obtained a complete, unobstructed railroad line from Constantinople to Austria and Germany. Huge Krupp guns now began to come over this line—all destined for the Dardanelles. Sixteen great batteries, of the latest model, were emplaced near the entrance, completely controlling Sedd-ul-Bahr. The Germans lent the Turks 500,000,000 marks, much of which was spent defending this indispensable highway. The thinly fortified straits through which I passed in March, 1915, is now as impregnably fortified as Heligoland. It is doubtful if all the fleets in the world could force the Dardanelles to-day.

Source: Extract from Henry Morgenthau, *Ambassador Morgenthau's Story* (Garden City, NY: Doubleday and Page, 1918), 223–231.

125. The Gallipoli Campaign: Ellis Ashmead-Bartlett to British Prime Minister Herbert Henry Asquith (September 8, 1915)

Introduction

The Gallipoli Campaign, when British troops assisted by Australian, New Zealand, and French forces unsuccessfully sought to seize from Turkey the strategically valuable Dardanelles Straits dividing Europe from Asia and controlling access from the Black Sea to the Mediterranean, proved disastrous. Heavy wartime censorship made frank reporting difficult, so Ellis Ashmead-Bartlett, a British war correspondent accompanying the British forces, arranged to have this letter hand-carried to London by an Australian colleague, Keith Murdoch, for personal delivery to Prime Minister Henry H. Asquith. French police in Marseilles confiscated the letter but could not prevent Murdoch—the father of Rupert Murdoch, himself later a well-known newspaper publisher—reporting its substance to his own government, whose troops had borne much of the brunt of the Gallipoli Campaign. Australian officials in turn passed these complaints on to Asquith, who shortly afterward recalled Sir Ian Hamilton, the British commander in chief, and at the end of the year evacuated all Allied forces from Gallipoli. The operation was seen as a great triumph for the Turkish Army and prompted an upsurge of national pride within Turkey.

Document

Dear Mr Asquith

I hope you will excuse the liberty I am taking in writing to you, but I have the chance of sending this letter through by hand, and I consider it absolutely necessary that you should know the true state of affairs out here. Our last great effort to achieve some definite success against the Turks was the most ghastly and costly fiasco in our history since the Battle of Bannockburn. Personally, I never thought the scheme decided on by Headquarters ever had the slightest chance of succeeding and all efforts now to make out that it only just failed, owing to the failure of the 9th Corps to seize the Anafarta Hills, bear no relation to the real truth. The operations did, for a time, make headway in an absolutely impossible country, more than any general had a right to expect, owing to the superlative gallantry of the Colonial Troops, and the self-sacrificing manner in which they threw away their lives against positions which should never have been attacked. The main idea was to cut off the southern portion of the Turkish Army by getting astride of the Peninsula from Suvla Bay. Therefore, the whole weight of the attack should have been concentrated on this objective; instead of which the main attack with the best troops was delivered against the side of the Turkish positions which are a series of impossible mountains and valleys covered with dense scrub. The Staff seem to have carefully searched for the most difficult points, and then threw away thousands of lives in trying to take them by frontal attacks. A few Gurkhas obtained a lodgement on Chunuk Bair, but were immediately driven off by the Turkish counter-attacks, and the main objective, Koja Chemen Tepe, was never approached. The 9th Corps, miserably mishandled, having failed to take the Anafarta Hills, is now accused of being alone responsible for the ultimate failure of the operations. The failure of the 9th Corps was due not so much to the employment of new and untried troops, as to bad Staff work. The generals had but a vague idea of the nature of the ground in their front and no adequate steps were taken to keep the troops supplied with water. In consequence many of these unfortunate volunteers went three days in very hot weather on one bottle of water, and were yet expected to advance, carrying heavy loads, and to storm strong positions. The Turks, having been given ample time to bring up strong reinforcements to Anafarta, where they entrenched themselves in up to their necks, were again assaulted in a direct frontal attack on August 21st. The movement never had the slightest chance of succeeding and led to another bloody fiasco in which the unfortunate 29th Division, who were brought up especially from Helles, and the 2nd Mounted Division (Yeomanry) were the chief sufferers. As the result of all this fighting our casualties, since August 6th, now total nearly fifty thousand killed, wounded, and missing.

The Army is in fact in a deplorable condition. Its morale as a fighting force has suffered greatly, and the officers and men are thoroughly dispirited. The muddles and mismanagement beat anything that has ever occurred in our military history. The fundamental evil at the present moment is the absolute lack of confidence in all ranks in the Headquarters Staff. The confidence of the Army will never be restored until a really strong man is placed at its head. It would amaze you to hear the talk that goes on amongst the junior commanders of divisions and brigades. Except for the fact that the traditions of discipline still hold the force together, you would imagine that the units were in an open state of mutiny against Headquarters. The Commander-in-Chief and his Staff are openly spoken of, and in fact only mentioned at all, with derision. One hates to write of such matters, but in the interests of the country at the present crisis I feel they ought to be made known to you. The lack of a real Chief at the head of the Army destroys its discipline and efficiency all through, and gives full rein to the jealousies and recriminations which ever prevail amongst the divisional leaders.

At present the Army is incapable of a further offensive. The splendid Colonial Corps has been almost wiped out. Once again the 29th Division has suffered enormous losses, and the new formations have lost their bravest and best officers and men. Neither do I think, even with enormous reinforcements, that any fresh offensive, from our present positions, has the smallest chance of success. Our only real justification for throwing away fresh lives and fresh treasure in this unfortunate enterprise is the prospect of the certain cooperation of Bulgaria. With her assistance we should undoubtedly pull through. But as I know nothing of the attitude of Bulgaria or Greece or Italy, I am only writing to give you a true picture of the state of the army and the problems with which we are faced in the future, if we are left to fight the Turks alone. Already the weather shows signs of breaking, and by the end of this month we cannot rely on any continuous spell of calm for the landing of large bodies of troops at some other point on the coast. In fact the season will soon be too late for a fresh offensive, if another is contemplated. We have therefore to prepare against the coming of the winter or to withdraw the army altogether. I am assuming it is considered desirable to avoid the latter contingency at all costs for political reasons, owing to the confession of final failure it would entail, and the moral effect it might have in India and Egypt. I am convinced the troops could be withdrawn under cover of the warships without much loss, far less in fact than we suffer in any ordinary attack. I assume also that the future of the campaign out here must be largely dependent on the measure of success that attends our fresh offensive, in conjunction with the French, in the West.

It is no use pretending that our prospects for the winter are bright. The Navy seems to think it will be able to keep the army supplied in spells of calm weather provided a sufficient reserve of food, munitions, and ammunition is concentrated while the weather holds at the various beaches. The outlook for the unfortunate troops is deplorable. We do not hold a single commanding position on the Peninsula and at all three points, Helles, Anzac, and Suvla Bay, we are everywhere commanded by the enemy's guns. This means that throughout the winter all the beaches and lines of communication to the front trenches will be under constant shell-fire. Suvla Bay is especially exposed. The Turks are firing a fair amount of ammunition, but it is obvious they are feeling the shortage or else are carefully husbanding their supply, otherwise they could shell us off the Peninsula at some points altogether. But it must be remembered that as soon as they are absolutely certain our offensive has shot its bolt, and that we are settling down in our positions for the winter, they will be free to concentrate their artillery at certain points, and also to bring up big guns from the forts, and therefore we must expect a far more severe artillery fire on the beaches during the winter months than we are exposed to at present.

A great many of the trenches which we hold at present will have to be abandoned altogether during the winter as they will be underwater. This will mean concentrating the Army at certain points on dry ground, and preparing a series of defensive works which will ensure us against sudden surprise attacks. We could thus hold our positions with fewer men and rest some of the divisions from time to time in the neighbouring islands. We ought to be able to hold Helles without much trouble, but even if we commence our preparations in time, we shall be faced with enormous difficulties at Anzac and Suvla Bay. Our troops will have to face the greatest hardships from cold, wet trenches, and constant artillery fire. I believe that at the present time the sick rate for the Army is roughly 1,000 per day. During the winter it is bound to rise to an even higher figure. I know one general, whose judgement is generally sound, who considers we shall lose during the winter in sickness alone the equivalent of the present strength of the Army. This may be an exaggeration, but in any case our loss is bound to be very heavy. The whole Army dreads, beyond all else, the prospect of wintering on this dreary and inhospitable coast. Amongst other troubles, the autumn rains will once more bring to view hundreds of our dead who now lie under a light covering of soil.

But I suppose we must stay here as long as there is the smallest prospect of the Balkan Alliance being revived, and throwing in its lot with us, even if they do not make a move until next Spring. I have laid before you some of the difficulties with which we are faced in order that they may be boldly met before it is too late. No one seems to know out here what we are going to do in the future, and I am so afraid we shall drag on in a state of uncertainty until the season is too far advanced for us to make proper preparations to face the coming winter in a certain measure of comfort and security. At the present time some of our positions, gained by the Colonial Corps high up on the spurs of the hills on which the Turks are perched, cannot be considered secure. A sudden counter-attack, vigorously delivered, would jeopardise the safety of our line, and might lead to a serious disaster. There will have to be a general reshuffling of the whole line, and some of our advanced posts will have to be abandoned during the winter months. I have only dealt with our own troubles and difficulties. The enemy of course has his. But to maintain, as I saw stated in an official report, that his losses in the recent fighting were far heavier than ours, is a childish falsehood which deceives no one out here. He was acting almost the whole time on the defensive, and probably lost about one-third of our grand total.

You may think I am too pessimistic but my views are shared by the large majority of the Army. The confidence of the troops can only be restored by an immediate change in the supreme command. Even if sufficient drafts are sent out to make good our losses, we shall never succeed, operating from our present positions. A fresh landing on a grand scale north of Buliar would probably ensure success, but the season is late, and I suppose the troops are not available. If we are to stay here this winter let orders be given for the Army to start its preparations without delay. If possible have the Colonial troops taken off the Peninsula altogether because they are miserably depressed since the last failure, and, with their active minds, and the positions they occupy in civil life, a dreary winter in the trenches will have a deplorable effect on what is left of this once magnificent body of men, the finest any Empire has ever produced. If we are obliged to keep this Army locked up in Gallipoli this winter large reserves will be necessary to make good its losses in sickness. The cost of this campaign in the East must be out of all proportion to the results we are likely to obtain now, in time to have a decisive effect on the general theatre of war. Our great asset against the Germans was always considered to be our superior financial strength. In Gallipoli we are dissipating a large portion of our fortune, and have not yet gained a single acre of ground of any strategical value. Unless we can pull through with the aid of the Balkan League in the near future, this futile expenditure may ruin our prospects of bringing the war to a successful conclusion by gradually wearing down Germany's colossal military power.

I have taken the liberty of writing very fully because I have no means of knowing how far the real truth of the situation is known in England, and how much the military authorities disclose. I thought, therefore, that perhaps the opinions of an independent observer might be of value to you at the present juncture. I am, of course, breaking the censorship regulations by sending this letter through, but I have not the slightest hesitation in doing so, as I feel it is absolutely essential for you to know the truth. I have been requested over and over again by officers of all ranks to go home and personally disclose the truth, but it is difficult for me to leave until the beginning of October.

Hoping you will therefore excuse the liberty I have taken.

Believe me
   Yours very truly
   E. Ashmead-Bartlett

Source: The Gallipoli Campaign: Ellis Ashmead-Bartlett to British Prime Minister Herbert Henry Asquith, September 8, 1915, Institute of Commonwealth Studies Library, London, Ashmead-Bartlett Papers, ICS 84/B/3/137; also Ellis Ashmead-Bartlett, *The Uncensored Dardanelles* (London: Hutchinson, 1920), 240–243.

126. Sir Henry McMahon, British High Commissioner in Cairo, to Husain Ibn Ali, the Sharif of Mecca (October 24, 1915)

Introduction

As the Turkish sultanate lost its hold on the territories of the Ottoman Empire and exacerbated Muslim sensibilities by allying itself with Christian Germany in the war, Hussein ibn Ali, the high priest or sharif of the Islamic territory of the Hejaz, which contains the holy cities of Medina and Mecca, moved toward independence. He was encouraged by British officials, including Sir Henry McMahon, British high commissioner in Egypt, who promised him and his three sons, Ali, Faisal, and Abdullah, recognition and financial and military assistance if they were willing to rebel against Ottoman rule. Arab nationalists regarded McMahon's pledge as a promise of immediate and complete independence. The territorial delimitations described in McMahon's letter were ambiguous and left unclear whether or not they included what was then Palestine, present-day Israel. The British later claimed that Palestine, which was not mentioned, was implicitly excluded from the regions promised to Hussein. Arab nationalists argued that the territories pledged to them included Palestine and that the subsequent partition of the Ottoman Empire and the 1917 Balfour Declaration promising Jews a national homeland in Palestine contravened McMahon's letter.

Document

I have received your letter of the 29th Shawal, 1333, with much pleasure and your expression of friendliness and sincerity have given me the greatest satisfaction.

I regret that you should have received from my last letter the impression that I regarded the question of limits and boundaries with coldness and hesitation; such was not the case, but it appeared to me that the time had not yet come when that question could be discussed in a conclusive manner.

I have realised, however, from your last letter that you regard this question as one of vital and urgent importance. I have, therefore, lost no time in informing the Government of Great Britain of the contents of your letter, and it is with great pleasure that I communicate to you on their behalf the following statement, which I am confident you will receive with satisfaction.—

The two districts of Mersina and Alexandretta and portions of Syria lying to the west of the districts of Damascus, Homs, Hama, and Aleppo cannot be said to be purely Arab, and should be excluded from the limits demanded.

With the above modification, and without prejudice to our existing treaties with Arab chiefs, we accept those limits.

As for those regions lying within those frontiers wherein Great Britain is free to act without detriment to the interests of her ally, France, I am empowered in the name of the Government of Great Britain to give the following assurances and make the following assurances and make the following reply to your letter:

(1) Subject to the above modifications, Great Britain is prepared to recognise and support the independence of the Arabs in all the regions within the limits demanded by the Sherif of Mecca.
(2) Great Britain will guarantee the Holy Places against all external aggression and will recognise their inviolability.
(3) When the situation admits, Great Britain will give to the Arabs her advice and will assist them to establish what may appear to be the most suitable forms of government in those various territories.
(4) On the other hand, it is understood that the Arabs have decided to seek the advice and guidance of Great Britain only, and that such European advisers and officials as may be required for the formation of a sound form of administration will be British.
(5) With regard to the vilayets of Bagdad and Basra, the Arabs will recognise that the established position and interests of Great Britain necessitate special administrative arrangements in order to secure these territories from foreign aggression, to promote the welfare of the local populations, and to safeguard our mutual economic interests.

I am convinced that this declaration will assure you beyond all possible doubt of the sympathy of Great Britain towards the aspirations of her friends the Arabs and will result in a firm and lasting alliance, the immediate results of which will be the expulsion of the Turks from the Arab countries and the freeing of the Arab peoples from the Turkish yoke, which for so many years has pressed heavily upon them.

I have confined myself in this letter to the more vital and important questions, and if there are any other matters dealt with in your letters which I have omitted to mention, we may discuss them at some convenient date in the future.

It was with very great relief and satisfaction that I heard of the safe arrival of the Holy Carpet and the accompanying offerings which, thanks to the clearness of your directions and the excellence of your arrangements, were landed without trouble or mishap in spite of the dangers and difficulties occasioned by the present sad war. May God soon bring a lasting peace and freedom of all peoples.

I am sending this letter by the hand of your trusted and excellent messenger, Sheikh Mohammed ibn Arif ibn Uraifan, and he will inform you of the various matters of interest, but of less vital importance, which I have not mentioned in this letter.

(Compliments).
(Signed): A. HENRY MCMAHON.

Source: Great Britain, Parliamentary Papers, 1939, Misc. No. 3, Cmd. 5957.

127. The Sykes-Picot Agreement: Sir Edward Grey to Paul Cambon (May 15–16, 1916)

Introduction

As Turkish power crumbled in the Middle East, British and French officials reached tentative agreement as to how to divide influence within that region between their two nations. On May 9, 1916, Paul Cambon, the French foreign minister, wrote to British foreign secretary Sir Edward Grey formally proposing a disposition of the Middle East between France and Britain along lines already agreed by junior French and British diplomats in the area. Sir Edward Grey replied, first briefly, then at greater length. Britain recognized French predominance in Syria, Lebanon, and Palestine (later exchanged for portions of Iraq) in return for French acceptance of British control of Iraq and Jordan. The British and French envisaged permitting Arab states in these former Ottoman provinces but only on the condition that their governments recognize British or French overlordship. At the subsequent 1919 Paris Peace Conference Britain and France retained control of these regions, which were defined as mandates under the new League of Nations. This was a great disappointment to Arab nationalists, who had hoped to establish independent states free of Western colonial rule. During the 1920s, resentment of Anglo-French domination continued to simmer in the newly established kingdoms of Iraq and Transjordan and in the states of Syria and Lebanon.

Documents

Sir Edward Grey to Paul Cambon, May 15, 1916

I shall have the honour to reply fully in a further note to your Excellency's note of the 9th instant, relative to the creation of an Arab State, but I should meanwhile be grateful if your Excellency could assure me that in those regions which, under the conditions recorded in that communication, become entirely French, or in which French interests are recognised as predominant, any existing British concessions, rights of navigation or development, and the rights and privileges of any British religious, scholastic, or medical institutions will be maintained.

His Majesty's Government are, of course, ready to give a reciprocal assurance in regard to the British area.

Sir Edward Grey to Paul Cambon, May 16, 1916

I have the honour to acknowledge the receipt of your Excellency's note of the 9th instant, stating that the French Government accept the limits of a future Arab State, or Confederation of States, and of those parts of Syria where French interests predominate, together with certain conditions attached thereto, such as they result from recent discussions in London and Petrograd on the subject.

I have the honour to inform your Excellency in reply that the acceptance of the whole project, as it now stands, will involve the abdication of considerable British interests, but, since His Majesty's Government recognise the advantage to the general cause of the Allies entailed in producing a more favourable internal political situation in Turkey, they are ready to accept the arrangement now arrived at, provided that the co-operation of the Arabs is secured, and that the Arabs fulfil the conditions and obtain the towns of Homs, Hama, Damascus, and Aleppo.

It is accordingly understood between the French and British Governments—

1. That France and Great Britain are prepared to recognize and protect an independent Arab State or a Confederation of Arab States in the areas (A) and (B) marked on the annexed map, under the suzerainty of an Arab chief. That in area (A) France, and in area (B) Great Britain, shall have priority of right of enterprise and local loans. That in area (A) France, and in area (B) Great Britain, shall alone supply advisers or foreign functionaries at the request of the Arab State or Confederation of Arab States.
2. That in the blue area France, and in the red area Great Britain, shall be allowed to establish such direct or indirect administration or control as they desire and as they may think fit to arrange with the Arab State or Confederation of Arab States.
3. That in the brown area there shall be established an international administration, the form of which is to be decided upon after consultation with Russia, and subsequently in consultation with the other Allies, and the representatives of the Shereef of Mecca.
4. That Great Britain be accorded (1) the ports of Haifa and Acre, (2) guarantee of a given supply of water from the Tigris and Euphrates in area (A) for area (B). His Majesty's Government, on their part, undertake that they will at no time enter into negotiations for the cession of Cyprus to any third Power without the previous consent of the French Government.
5. That Alexandretta shall be a free port as regards the trade of the British Empire, and that there shall be no discrimination in port charges or facilities as regards British shipping and British goods; that there shall be freedom of transit for British goods through Alexandretta and by railway through the blue area, whether those goods are intended for or originate in the red area, or (B) area, or area (A); and there shall be no discrimination, direct or indirect, against British goods on any railway or against British goods or ships at any port serving the areas mentioned.

That Haifa shall be a free port as regards the trade of France, her dominions and protectorates, and there shall be no discrimination in port charges or facilities as regards French shipping and French goods. There shall be freedom of transit for French goods through Haifa and by the British railway through the brown area, whether those goods are intended for or originate in the blue area, area (A), or area (B), and there shall be no discrimination, direct or indirect, against French goods on any railway, or against French goods or ships at any port serving the areas mentioned.

6. That in area (A) the Baghdad Railway shall not be extended southwards beyond Mosul, and in area (B) northwards beyond Samarra, until a railway connecting Baghdad with Aleppo via the Euphrates Valley has been completed, and then only with the concurrence of the two Governments.
7. That Great Britain has the right to build, administer, and be sole owner of a railway connecting Haifa with area (B), and shall have a perpetual right to transport troops along such a line at all times.

It is to be understood by both Governments that this railway is to facilitate the connexion of Baghdad with Haifa by rail, and it is further understood that, if the engineering difficulties and expense entailed by keeping this connecting line in the brown area only make the project unfeasible, that the French Government shall be prepared to consider that the line in question may also traverse the polygon Banias-Keis Marib-Salkhab Tell Otsda-Mesmie before reaching area (B).

8. For a period of twenty years the existing Turkish customs tariff shall remain in force throughout the whole of the blue and red areas, as well as in areas (A) and (B), and no increase in the rates of duty or conversion from ad valorem to specific rates shall be made except by agreement between the two Powers.

There shall be no interior customs barriers between any of the above-mentioned areas. The customs duties leviable on goods destined for the interior shall be collected at the port of entry and handed over to the administration of the area of destination.

9. It shall be agreed that the French Government will at no time enter into any negotiations for the cession of their rights and will not cede such rights in the blue area to any third Power, except the Arab State or Confederation of Arab States, without the previous agreement of His Majesty's Government, who, on their part, will give a similar undertaking to the French Government regarding the red area.
10. The British and French Governments, as the protectors of the Arab State, shall agree that they will not themselves acquire and will not consent to a third Power acquiring territorial possessions in the Arabian peninsula, nor consent to a third Power installing a naval base either on the east coast, or on the islands, of the Red Sea. This, however, shall not prevent such adjustment of the Aden frontier as may be necessary in consequence of recent Turkish aggression.
11. The negotiations with the Arabs as to the boundaries of the Arab State or Confederation of Arab States shall be continued through the same channel as heretofore on behalf of the two Powers.
12. It is agreed that measures to control the importation of arms into the Arab territories will be considered by the two Governments.

I have further the honour to state that, in order to make the agreement complete, His Majesty's Government are proposing to the Russian Government to exchange notes analogous to those exchanged by the latter and your Excellency's Government on the 26th April last. Copies of these notes will be communicated to your Excellency as soon as exchanged.

I would also venture to remind your Excellency that the conclusion of the present agreement raises, for practical consideration, the question of the claims of Italy to a share in any partition or rearrangement of Turkey in Asia, as formulated in article 9 of the agreement of the 26th April, 1915, between Italy and the Allies.

His Majesty's Government further consider that the Japanese Government should be informed of the arrangement now concluded.

Source: *British Documents on Foreign Affairs: Reports and Papers from the Foreign Office Confidential Print; Series H: The First World War, 1914–1918,* Vol. 2 (Bethesda, MD: University Publications of America, 1989), 326–327.

128. Lord Bryce Reports on the Armenian Massacres (June 1916)

Introduction

After compiling a report on German atrocities in Belgium, the respected Liberal British statesman James, Viscount Bryce, turned to Turkish efforts to massacre the Armenians living within the Ottoman Empire. Since the late 19th century, especially since the Young Turks came to power in Constantinople, Armenians had been subject to persecution. From early 1915 such anti-Armenian campaigns redoubled, reaching such an intensity that they might fairly be described as genocide. Although Bryce was unable to visit Turkish territory to confirm his report, which may well have been exaggerated in some respects, overall it provided a sobering picture of the wartime sufferings of minorities, which would be repeated on too many occasions during the rest of the 20th century. Bryce's preface effectively stated the case for the prosecution.

Document

In the summer of 1915 accounts, few and scanty at first, but increasing in volume later, began to find their way out of Asiatic Turkey as to the events that were happening there. These accounts described what seemed to be an effort to exterminate a whole nation, without distinction of age or sex, whose misfortune it was to be the subjects of a Government devoid of scruples and of pity, and the policy they disclosed was one without precedent even in the blood-stained annals of the East. It then became the obvious duty of those who realised the gravity of these events to try to collect and put together all the data available for the purpose of presenting a full and authentic record of what had occurred. This has been done in the present volume. It contains all the evidence that could be obtained up till July 1916 as to the massacres and deportations of the Armenian and other Eastern Christians dwelling in Asia Minor, Armenia and that north-western corner of Persia which was invaded by the Turkish troops. It is presented primarily as a contribution to history, but partly also for the purpose of enabling the civilised nations of Europe to comprehend the problems which will arise at the end of this war, when it will become necessary to provide for the future government of what are now the Turkish dominions. The compilation has been made in the spirit proper to an historical enquiry, that is to say, nothing has been omitted which could throw light on the facts, whatever the political bearing of the accounts might be. In such an enquiry, no racial or religious sympathies, no prejudices, not even the natural horror raised by crimes, ought to distract the mind of the enquirer from the duty of trying to ascertain the real facts.

As will be seen from the analysis which follows, the evidence here collected comes from various sources.

A large, perhaps the largest, part has been drawn from neutral witnesses who were living in or passing through Asiatic Turkey while these events were happening, and had opportunities of observing them.

Another part comes from natives of the country, nearly all Christians, who succeeded, despite the stringency of the Turkish censorship, in getting letters into neutral countries, or who themselves escaped into Greece, or Russia, or Egypt and were there able to write down what they had seen.

A third but much smaller part comes from subjects of the now belligerent Powers (mostly Germans) who were in Turkey when these events were happening, and subsequently published in their own countries accounts based on their personal knowledge....

(i) Nearly all of it comes from eye-witnesses, some of whom wrote it down themselves, while others gave it to persons who wrote it out at the time from the statements given to them orally. Nearly all of it, moreover, was written immediately after the events described, when the witnesses' recollection was still fresh and clear.

(ii) The main facts rest upon evidence coming from different and independent sources. When the same fact is stated by witnesses who had no communication with one another, and in many cases did not even speak the same language, the presumption in favour of its truth becomes strong....

(iii) Facts of the same, or of a very similar, nature occurring in different places, are deposed to by different and independent witnesses. As there is every reason to believe—and indeed it is hardly denied—that the massacres and deportations were carried out under general orders proceeding from Constantinople, the fact that persons who knew only what was happening in one locality record circumstances there broadly resembling those which occurred in another locality goes to show the general correctness of both sets of accounts.

Thus, the two Danish Red Cross nurses (Doc. 62) state that they twice witnessed the massacre, in cold blood, of gangs of unarmed Armenian soldiers employed on navvy work, along the road from Erzindjan to Sivas. In Doc. 7 (written at Constantinople) we find a statement that other gangs of unarmed Armenian soldiers were similarly murdered on the roads between Ourfa and Diyarbekir, and Diyarbekir and Harpout; and the massacre on this latter section of road is confirmed by a German lady resident, at the time, at Harpout (Doc. 23).

Again, there is frequent mention of roads being lined, or littered, with the corpses of Armenian exiles who had died of exhaustion or been murdered on the way. If these allusions were merely made in general terms, they might conceivably be explained away as amplifications of some isolated case, or even as rhetorical embellishments of the exiles' story without foundation in fact. But when we find such statements made with regard to particular stretches of road in widely different localities, and often by more than one witness with regard to a given stretch, we are led to infer that this wholesale mortality by the wayside was in very deed a frequent concomitant of the Deportations, and an inevitable consequence of the method on which the general scheme of Deportation was organised from headquarters. . . .

(iv) The volume of this concurrent evidence from different quarters is so large as to establish the main facts beyond all question. Errors of detail in some instances may be allowed for. Exaggeration may, in the case of native witnesses, who were more likely to be excited, be also, now and then, allowed for. But the general character of the events stands out, resting on foundations too broad to be shaken, and even details comparatively unimportant in themselves are often remarkably corroborated from different quarters. . . .

(v) In particular it is to be noted that many of the most shocking and horrible accounts are those for which there is the most abundant testimony from the most trustworthy neutral witnesses. None of the worst cruelties rest on native evidence alone. If all that class of evidence were entirely struck out, the general effect would be much the same, though some of the minor details would be wanting. One may, indeed, say that an examination of the neutral evidence tends to confirm the native evidence as a whole by showing that there is in it less of exaggeration than might have been expected.

Docs. 7 and 9, for instance, both of which are native reports at second-hand, refer in somewhat rhetorical terms to the corpses of murdered Armenians washed down by the waters of the Tigris and Euphrates. Yet their words are more than justified by many concrete and independent pieces of evidence. The description in Doc. 12 (German material) of how barge-loads of Armenians were drowned in the Tigris below Diyarbekir, renders more fully credible the accounts of how the Armenians of Trebizond were drowned wholesale in the Black Sea. Doc. 12 also contains the statement, from a German employee of the Baghdad Railway, that the Armenian exiles who reached Biredjik were drowned in batches every night in the Euphrates; and similar horrors are reported from almost every section of the Euphrates' course. Docs. 56, 57, 59 and 62 describe how the convoys of exiles from the Vilayet of Erzeroum were cast into the Kara Su (western branch of the Euphrates) at the gorge called Kamakh Boghaz, and were then either shot in the water or left to drown. The author of Doc. 59 was present at such a scene, though she was herself spared, and the information in Docs. 56 and 57 was obtained direct from a lady who was actually cast in, but managed to struggle to the bank and escape. The authors of Doc. 62 received their information from a gendarme who had been attached to a convoy and had himself participated in the massacre. Doc. 24 records the experiences of an Armenian woman deported from Moush, who was driven with her fellow-exiles into the Mourad Su (eastern branch of the Euphrates), but also managed to escape, though the rest were drowned. Doc. 66 describes corpses floating in the river in the neighbourhood of Kiakhta, and Doc. 137 the drowning of exiles in the tributaries of the Euphrates between Harpout and Aleppo. These are evidently instances of a regular practice, and when we find the exiles from Trebizond and Kerasond being disposed of in the same fashion in a comparatively distant part of the Turkish Empire, we are almost compelled to infer that the drowning of the exiles *en masse* was a definite part of the general scheme drawn out by the Young Turk leaders at Constantinople.

Perhaps the most terrible feature of all was the suffering of the women with child, who were made to march with the convoys and gave birth to their babies on the road. This is alluded to in Doc. 12, from a German source, at second-hand, but in Docs. 129 and 137 we have the testimony of neutral witnesses who actually succoured these victims, so far as the extremity of their plight and the brutality of their escort made succour possible. It should be mentioned that in Doc. 68 an Armenian exile testifies to the kindness of an individual Turkish gendarme to one of her fellow-victims who was in these straits.

(vi) The vast scale of these massacres and the pitiless cruelty with which the deportations were carried out may seem to some readers to throw doubt on the authenticity of the narratives. Can human beings (it may be asked) have perpetrated such crimes on innocent women and children? But a recollection of previous massacres will show that such crimes are part of the long settled and often repeated policy of Turkish rulers. In Chios, nearly a century ago, the Turks slaughtered almost the whole Greek population of the island. In European Turkey in 1876 many thousands of Bulgarians were killed on the suspicion of an intended rising, and the outrages committed on women were, on a smaller scale, as bad as those here recorded. In 1895 and 1896 more than a hundred thousand Armenian Christians were put to death by Abd-ul-Hamid, many thousands of whom died as martyrs to their Christian faith, by abjuring which they could have saved their lives. All these massacres are registered not only in the ordinary press records of current history but in the reports of British diplomatic and consular officials written at the time. They are as certain as anything else that has happened in our day. There is, therefore, no antecedent improbability to be overcome before the accounts here given can be accepted. All that happened in 1915 is in the regular line of Turkish policy. The only differences are in the scale of the present crimes, and in the fact that the lingering sufferings of deportations in which the deaths were as numerous as in the massacres, and fell with special severity upon the women, have in this latest instance been added.

The evidence is cumulative. Each part of it supports the rest because each part is independent of the others. The main facts are the same, and reveal the same plans and intentions at work. Even the varieties are instructive because they show those diversities of temper and feeling which appear in human nature everywhere.

The Turkish officials are usually heartless and callous. But here and there we see one of a finer temper, who refuses to carry out the orders given him and is sometimes dismissed for his refusal. The Moslem rabble is usually pitiless. It pillages the houses and robs the persons of the hapless exiles. But now and then there appear pious and compassionate Moslems who try to save the lives or alleviate the miseries of their Christian neighbours. We have a vivid picture of human life, where wickedness in high places deliberately lets loose the passions of racial or religious hatred, as well as the commoner passion of rapacity, yet cannot extinguish those better feelings which show as points of light in the gloom. . . .

This preface is intended to deal only with the credibility of the evidence here presented, so I will refrain from comment on the facts. A single observation, or rather a single question, may, however, be permitted from one who has closely followed the history of the Turkish East for more than forty years. European travellers have often commended the honesty and the kindliness of the Turkish peasantry, and our soldiers have said that they are fair fighters. Against them I have nothing to say, and will even add that I have known individual Turkish officials who impressed me as men of honesty and good-will. But the record of the rulers of Turkey for the last two or three centuries, from the Sultan on his throne down to the district Mutessarif, is, taken as a whole, an almost unbroken record of corruption, of injustice, of an oppression which often rises into hideous cruelty. The Young Turks, when they deposed Abd-ul-Hamid, came forward as the apostles of freedom, promising equal rights and equal treatment to all Ottoman subjects. The facts here recorded show how that promise was kept. Can anyone still continue to hope that the evils of such a government are curable? Or does the evidence contained in this volume furnish the most terrible and convincing proof that it can no longer be permitted to rule over subjects of a different faith?

Source: Lord Bryce, *The Treatment of Armenians in the Ottoman Empire 1915–16: Documents Presented to Viscount Grey of Fallodon Secretary of State for Foreign Affairs* (London: HMSO, 1916), xxi–xxviii.

129. Proclamation Published in Mecca by Sharif Hussein (June 27, 1916)

Introduction

In June 1916 the long-contemplated Arab Revolt finally broke out under the leadership of Sharif Hussein of Mecca and his three sons, Ali, Faisal, and Abdullah. The sharif published a lengthy proclamation accusing the Ottoman overlords of having jettisoned Islamic principles by installing a secular government in Constantinople. This document was widely circulated around the Arab world. Whereas Turkey, then and after World War I, continued on a secularist and modernizing course, for the rest of the 20th century Arab states would remain largely wedded to a traditional Islamic political and social outlook, something that Hussein's proclamation foreshadowed. Such staunch adherence to Muslim principles would later help to promote pervasive Arab and Islamic distaste and suspicion of Western societies and would contribute to the fervor with which Arab leaders and peoples resented Jewish claims on Palestine and, once it was established, the State of Israel.

Document

In the name of God, the Merciful, the Compassionate.

This is our general proclamation to all our Moslem brothers.

O God, judge between us and our people in truth: Thou art the Judge.

The world knoweth that the first of all Moslem princes and rulers to acknowledge the Turkish Government were the Emirs of Mecca the Blessed. This they did to bind together and make strong the congregation of Islam, as they saw the Sultans of the House of Osman (may the dust of their tombs be blessed, and may they dwell in Paradise), how they were upright, and how they fulfilled all the commandments and ordinances of the faith and of the Prophet (prayers be upon him) perfectly. Therefore they were obedient to them at all times.

For a token of this, remember how in 1327 I, with my Arabs, helped them against the Arabs, to save Ebhah from those who were besieging it, and to preserve the name of the Government in honour; and remember how again in the next year I helped them with my armies, which I entrusted to one of my sons; for indeed we were one with the Government until the Committee of Union and Progress rose up and strengthened itself and laid its hands on power. Consider how since then ruin has overtaken the State, and its possessions have been torn from it, and its place in the world has been lost, until now it has been drawn into this last and most fatal war.

All this they have done, being led away by shameful appetites, which are not for me to set forth, but which are open and a great cause for sorrow to the Moslems of the whole world, who have seen this greatest and most noble Moslem Power broken in pieces and led down to ruin and utter destruction. Our lament is also for so many of its subjects, Moslems and others alike, whose lives have been sacrificed without fault on their part. Some have been treacherously put to death, others cruelly driven from their homes, as though the calamities of war were not enough. Of these calamities the heaviest share has fallen upon the Holy Land. The poor, and even the families of substance, have been made to sell their doors and windows, yea, even the wooden frames of their houses, for bread, after they had lost their furniture and all their goods.

Not even so was the lust of the Union and Progress fulfilled. They laid bare all the measure of their wicked design and broke the only bond that endured between them and the true followers of Islam. They departed from their obedience to the precepts of the Book.

With the countenance of the Grand Vizier of the Ottoman Empire, the Sheikh-ul-Islam, the Ulema, the Ministers and the notables, one of their papers called the "Ijtihad" published in Constantinople unworthy things about the Prophet (the Prayer and Peace of God be upon him) and spoke evil of him (God forbid). Then the Union and Progress rejected God's word "A man shall have twice a woman's share" and made them equal. They went further, and removed one of the five corner stones of the faith, even the fast in Ramadan, by causing the soldiers in garrison in Mecca, Medina and Damascus to break their fast for new and foolish reasons, taking no account of the ordinance of God saying: "Those of you who are sick or on a journey. . . ." Yea, they went further. They made weak the person of the Sultan, and robbed from him his honour, forbidding him to choose for himself the chief of his personal cabinet. Other like things they did to sap the foundation of the Khalifate.

For this it had been clearly our part and our necessary duty to separate ourselves from them and renounce them and their obedience. Yet we would not believe their wickedness, and tried to think that they were the imaginings of evildoers to make a division between us and the Government. We bore with them until it was open to all men that the rulers in Turkey were Enver Pasha, Jemal Pasha and Talaat Bey, who were doing whatever they pleased. They made their guilt manifest when they wrote to the Judge of the Sacred Court in Mecca, traducing the verses in the Cow, and laying upon him to reject the evidence of believers outside the court, and to consider only the deeds and contracts engrossed within the court. They made manifest their guilt when they hanged in one day twenty-one of the most honourable and enlightened Moslems, among them Emir Omar El Jezairi, Emir Arif El Shehabi, Shefik Bey Moayad, Shukri Bey El Asli, Abdel Wahab, Tewfik El Bassat, Abdel Hamid El Zahrawi, Abdel Gahni El Areisi and their learned companions.

To destroy so many, even of cattle, at one time would be hard for men void of all natural affection or mercy. And, if we suppose they had some excuse for this evil deed, by what right did they carry away to strange countries the innocent and most miserable families of these ill-fated men? Children, old men and delicate women, bereaved of their natural protectors, were subjected in exile to all foul usage, and even to tortures, as though the woes they had already suffered were not chastisement enough. Did not God say: "No punishment should be inflicted on any one for the sins of another"? Let us suppose they found for themselves some reason for ill-treating the harmless families of their victims. But why did they rob them of their properties and possessions that alone remained to keep them from death by famine? And, if we suppose for this evil deed also an excuse or reason, how shall we find pardon for their shattering the tomb of our most righteous and upright Lord and Brother, El Sayed El Sherif Abd El Kader El Jazairi El Hassani, whose bones they have polluted and whose dust they have scattered abroad?

We leave the judgment of these misdeeds, which we have touched on so briefly, to the world in general and to Moslems in particular. What stronger proof can we desire of the faithlessness of their hearts to the religion and their feelings towards the Arabs than their bombardment of that ancient House, which God had chosen for His House, saying: "Keep My House pure for all who come to it"—a House so venerated by all Moslems? From their fort of Jyad when the revolt began they shelled it. The first shot struck a yard and a half above the Black Stone. The second fell three yards short of it, so that the flame leapt up and took hold upon the Kiswa, which, when they saw, the thousands and thousands of Moslems first raised a lamentable cry, running to and fro, and then shouted in fierce anger, and rushed to save it. They had to burst open the door and mount upon the roof before they could quench the flames. Yet a third shell fell upon the tomb of Abraham, and other shells fell in and about the precincts, which they made a target for their guns, killing every day three or four who were at prayer within the mosque till they prevented the people coming near to worship. This will show how they despised His House and denied it the honour given it by believers.

We leave all this to the Moslem world for judgment.

Yes, we can leave the judgment to the Moslem world, but we may not leave our religion and our existence as a people to be the plaything of the Unionists. God (blessed be He) has made open for us the attainment of freedom and independence, and has shown us a way of victory, to cut off the hand of the oppressors, and to cast out their garrison from our midst. We have attained independence—an independence of the rest of the Ottoman Empire, which is still groaning under the tyranny of our enemy. Our independence is complete, absolute, not to be laid hands on by any foreign influence or aggression, and our aim is the preservation of Islam, and the uplifting of its standard in the world. We fortify ourselves on the noble religion, which is our only guide and advocate in the principles of administration and of justice. We are ready to accept all things in harness with the faith, and all that leads to the Mountain of Islam, and in particular to uplift the mind and spirit of all classes of the people in so far as we have the strength and ability.

This is what we have done in accordance with the dictates of our religion, and on our part we trust that our brethren in all parts of the world will each do his duty also, as is incumbent upon him, that the bonds of brotherhood in Islam may be confirmed.

We beseech the Lord of Lords for the sake of the Prophet of Him who giveth all things, to grant us prosperity, and to direct us in the right way for the welfare of the faith and of the faithful.

We depend upon God the all-powerful, whose defence is sufficient for us.

Sherif and Emir of Mecca, HUSSEIN.
   Shaaban 25, 1334.

Source: *British Documents on Foreign Affairs: Reports and Papers from the Foreign Office Confidential Print; Series H: The First World War, 1914–1918,* Vol. 2 (Bethesda, MD: University Publications of America, 1989), 410–412.

130. Personal Notes of T. E. Lawrence on the Sharifial Family (October 27, 1916)

Introduction

Central figures in the World War I Arab Revolt against Ottoman Rule were the family of Sharif Hussein of Mecca and his three sons, Ali, Faisal, and Abdullah. The British military officer Thomas Edward Lawrence, who joined the Arab forces led by Hussein's sons during the revolt as an adviser and fought with them in extensive guerrilla operations, wrote a shrewd and perceptive description of the various family members in 1916 that was published in the *Arab Bulletin,* a secret publication that the British government's Arab Bureau produced several times a month from June 1916 to August 1918. Its readership was estimated at around 25 people, including the director of military intelligence and members of the British Foreign Office and the Admiralty. No more than 30 copies were normally produced, and its contents were kept highly confidential. Lawrence, the founding editor of this bulletin and a regular contributor, was regarded as something of a maverick by more conventional British military figures. He nonetheless soon established himself as one of the major authorities on the Arabs whose expertise was impossible to ignore.

Document

One can see that to the nomads the Sherif and his three elder sons are heroes. Sherif Hussein (Sayidna as they call him), is outwardly so gentle and considerate as to seem almost weak, but this appearance hides a deep and crafty policy, wide ambitions and an un-Arabian foresight, strength of character and persistence. There was never any pan-Arab secret society in Mecca, because the Sherif has always been the Arab Government. His influence was so strong in the tribes and country districts, as to be tantamount to administration; and in addition he played Arabs' advocate in the towns against the Turkish Government.

Particularly have his tastes and sympathies been always tribal. The son of a Circassian mother, he is endowed with qualities foreign to both Turk and Arab, but he determined to secure the hearts of the nomads by making his sons Bedouins. The Turks had insisted that they be educated in Constantinople, and Sherif Hussein agreed most willingly. They have all had a first-class Turkish education, and profit by their knowledge of the world. However, when they came back from Constantinople as young Levantines, wearing strange clothes and with Turkish manners, Sherif Hussein at once made them change into Arab things, and rub up their Arabic. He gave them Arab companions, and a little later sent for them, to put them in command of some small bodies of Arab camel corps, patrolling the pilgrim roads against the Auf. The young Sherifs fell in with the plan, as they thought it might be amusing, but were rather dashed when they were forbidden to take with them special food, or bedding, or saddle cushions, and still more when they were not given permission to come to Mecca for the Feast, but had to spend all the season out in the desert with their men, guarding the roads day and night, meeting nomads only, and learning to know their country and their manners.

They are now all thorough Bedouins, and as well have from their education the knowledge and experience of Turkish officials, and from their descent that blend of native intelligence and vigour which so often comes from a cross of Circassian and Arab blood. This makes them a most formidable family group, at once admired and efficient. It has, however, left them curiously isolated in their world. None of them seems to have a confidant or adviser or minister, and it is doubtful whether any one of them is fully intimate with another or with their father, of whom they all stand in awe.

Sidi Ali.—Short and slim, looking a little old already, though only thirty-seven. Slightly bent. Skin rather sallow, large deep brown eyes, nose thin and a little hooked, face somewhat worn and full of lines and hollows, mouth drooping. Beard spare and black. Has very delicate hands. His manners are perfectly simple, and he is obviously a very conscientious, careful, pleasant, gentleman, without force of character, nervous and rather tired. His physical weakness makes him subject to quick fits of shaking passion with more frequent moods of infirm obstinacy. Apparently not ambitious for himself, but swayed somewhat too easily by the wishes of others. Is bookish, and learned in law and religion. Shows his Arab blood more than his brothers.

Sidi Abdullah.—Aged thirty-five, but looks younger. Short and thick built, apparently as strong as a horse, with merry dark brown eyes, a round smooth face, full but short lips, straight nose, brown beard. In manner affectedly open and very charming, not standing at all on ceremony, but jesting with the tribesmen like one of their own sheikhs. On serious occasions he judges his words carefully, and shows himself a keen dialectician. Is probably not so much the brain as the spur of his father. He is obviously working to establish the greatness of the family, and has large ideas, which no doubt include his own particular advancement. The clash between him and Feisal will be interesting. The Arabs consider him a most astute politician, and a far-seeing statesman: but he has possibly more of the former than of the latter in his composition.

Sidi Feisal.—Is tall, graceful, vigorous, almost regal in appearance. Aged thirty-one. Very quick and restless in movement. Far more imposing personally than any of his brothers, knows it and trades on it. Is as clear-skinned as a pure Circassian, with dark hair, vivid black eyes set a little sloping in his face, strong nose, short chin. Looks like a European, and very like the monument of Richard I, at Fontevraud. He is hot tempered, proud and impatient, sometimes unreasonable, and runs off easily at tangents. Possesses far more personal magnetism and life than his brothers, but less prudence. Obviously very clever, and perhaps not over scrupulous. Rather narrow-minded, and rash when he acts on impulse, but usually with enough strength to reflect, and then exact in judgement. Had he been brought up the wrong way might have become a barrack-yard officer. A popular idol, and ambitious; full of dreams, and the capacity to realise them, with keen personal insight, and a very efficient man of business.

Sherif Zeid.—Aged about twenty. Is quite overshadowed by the reputation of his half-brothers. His mother was Turkish and he takes after her. Is fond of riding about, and playing tricks. Has not so far been entrusted with any important commission, but is active. In manner a little loutish, but not a bad fellow. Humorous in outlook, and perhaps a little better balanced, because less intense, than his brothers. Shy.

Yenbo, October 27, 1916
    T.E.L.

Source: *The Arab Bulletin*, November 26, 1916, https://wwi.lib.byu.edu/index.php/Personal_Notes_of_T.E._Lawrence_on_the_Sherifial_Family.

131. Copy of Letter from Mustapha Kemal to Enver Pasha (September 30, 1917)

Introduction

Turkish armed forces prevailed at Gallipoli, which the British imperial expeditionary force evacuated in January 1916, and at the siege of Kut, which Ottoman troops captured in April 1916. On other fronts, however, the Turks encountered persistent military disasters, including major defeats in the Caucasus, a stubbornly persistent revolt in Arabia fomented by the British, and the loss of Baghdad. In response, in 1917 General Otto Liman von Sanders, head of the German military mission to Turkey, established a new combat group, the Ottoman Army Yildirim Force, intended to be an efficient elite striking force that would reverse the Ottoman fortunes. General Erich von Falkenhayn, former German chief of staff, was dispatched to Turkey and in September 1917 took command of Yildirim and an additional Ottoman army. Meanwhile, another German officer, General Friedrich Kress von Kressenstein, commanded Ottoman forces in Palestine until mid-1918, when he was transferred to Georgia with the objective of preventing Russian Bolshevik inroads. Ottoman commander Mustapha Kemal, who had been largely responsible for the failure of the Allied offensive at Gallipoli, wrote vehemently to Minister of War Enver Pasha protesting that the predominance of German officers in the highest echelons of the Turkish military meant that Ottoman interests were being subordinated to those of Germany in what was effectively a form of colonial rule.

Document

I beg to forward the following observations about the general situation. They are submitted to Your Excellency, who is responsible for the direction of the country's destiny, after deep consideration and not in any spirit of panic or pessimism.

1. The general state of the country should be considered before everything else. The war has been brought home to our people more than to any other country. The link between the people and its government has been broken. Those that remain in their homes are fortunate in escaping the attention of the central authority, for though the people—women, cripples, or deserters—have not enough to live on, the civil and military administrations are compelled to be more and more severe in their levies of supplies. The Government finds it impossible to control the general situation, which is sinking more and more into anarchy. The measures it takes in the name of the people are opposed to the latter's rights, and the population is becoming more and more discontented.

The weakness of the civil administration has been further increased by want, corruption, profiteering, inferior officials, and the breakdown of justice. The evils are apparent in every part of the country. There are strong indications of disaster in ordinary trade and the provision of supplies. Consequently, if the war continues, the greatest danger by which we are confronted is the probable internal dissolution of the Empire, threatened as it is in every direction.

2. The military situation gives no sign of an early cessation of the war. Our allies are intent on a peace obtained by the aid of military forces, and will have no discussion as to terms. The Germans' possibilities are limited, and they can only say to their enemies: "Come, try and conquer us." The Entente Powers have shown that they will not make peace separately, and it is obvious that they will continue the war, as long as we can hold out, in the hope of saving their own countries and obtaining favourable terms. The war, therefore, is likely to continue for a considerable time. Our side does not hold the key to peace, but somehow we have to win.

3. The military situation of Turkey is as follows. Our forces are very weak. Compared with what they were at the beginning of the war, the strength of many armies has decreased by eighty per cent. The resources of the country in man power cannot bring them up to strength. Fifty per cent. of the 54th Division which was sent to me was composed of immature youths of 17 to 20 or unfit men of 45 to 55.

The battalions of another of the best divisions left Stamboul 1,000 strong and arrived at Aleppo with 500 each. The reason of this is the unsatisfactory lot of the people and the state of the civil administration. My illustration shows that even if all our resources were collected we should not be sufficiently strong. It is unnecessary to mention the deficiencies in the corps of officers in quality and quantity.

The situation at all the points is as follows:

In the West we are not in contact with the enemy. But, as Stamboul is on one of the maritime highways of the world and is our richest province, it is quite probable that the army will strike at it from the west. In the Caucasus the situation is one of stalemate, and it is impossible for us to make headway. The internal situation of Russia and the Russian dependence on Europe makes an offensive impossible. But if for some reason they did advance, we are not in a position to hinder or threaten them. The Russians do what they can with the means at their disposal, and they have halted against their will. In Iraq the British have gained their objectives. Consequently I am of opinion that there is no political, economic or military reason for a further advance on their part. However, if they continue northwards and are successful, the addition of Mosul to our toll of losses would not be a very severe blow the country. It may be said that such an event would not affect the general situation, so on this point we can only wait and see.

On the Hejaz and Sinai fronts the enemy has not yet attained his political and military objectives, and, as we know, is making every preparation to achieve his purpose. To create a Moslem power subservient to Britain, to form a Christian state in Palestine under British influence, to tear from Turkey her most prosperous provinces as well as to destroy her last religious predominance, are the British aims. For us this means that our life itself is to be extinguished. Thus the exigencies of the military situation require us to be ready for an attack in the West and to forestall the enemy's advance which he is preparing on the borders of Syria. In the present state of affairs it is useless to think of the recapture of Baghdad with our last reserves. The nearest enemy, the most powerful and most prepared, is in Sinai. He cannot be ignored.

Secondly, the Baghdad project is physically impossible. The effectives of the divisions which would carry out the venture are weak and low in value. After two months' marching they would be nothing more than a rabble—to use a slight exaggeration. Our *shakturs* and camels cannot compare with the enemy's railways and ships to Baghdad. Finally, one of the surest indications of the futility of the plan is that after two days' marching regiments would melt away.

What are my deductions from this short study of the situation? One stage of the war is finished and we cannot alter the past. I do not see the good of writing of the greatest perils before us out of pure pessimism; while there is life and hope, we must seek for a road out of our troubles.

In my opinion the decisions we should take today are:

(a) Internally strengthen the administration, and security of life. Officers for the gendarmerie, reorganization as far as possible of justice, commerce and food supplies, to check corruption, or at least to confine it to its narrowest limits, so that the country will have a firm and healthy base from which to work. If a prolongation of the war brings more trouble and calamity to us, we shall at any rate have our country and people behind us. We must not allow them to be a broken reed.

(b) Our military policy should be defensive, and every possible reserve should be religiously nursed. Not a single reserve should be permitted to serve outside the Empire. The question as to whether the Sinai front can be best secured by attack or defence cannot be decided to-day. The enemy in that quarter is superior to us in men and means. It is practically impossible to expect all our reinforcements in Sinai before some months have passed. It is probable that the enemy will try to gain a decision against the troops now in front of him before the others arrive. Besides, while we are dispatching troops to the front, the British can also call upon more reinforcements with the aid of their perfected communications. Consequently even if the enemy does not attack now, it is within the bounds of possibility that we should be still more inferior after our concentration. Thus, as it is impossible to say when our troops from Aleppo will arrive at the Sinai front, it is essential that orders should be issued for the immediate despatch of the Seventh Army. To exactly determine at the moment how these troops will be finally employed with the utmost economy is impossible, from a study of maps, from a military point of view. When the Seventh Army has been sent south the best way out of all our difficulties is as follows:

Up to now all Syria and Hejaz have been under the orders of a Musalman, and the Sinai operations have been entrusted independently to another Musalman. The good of the country requires this system of command. I am satisfied that [General Erich von] Falkenhayn's advent, his management of the coming events, the confirmation of von Kress's position, and lastly the dominating influence of the Germans are opposed to the interests of the State. I do not suppose we shall be deprived of a voice in questions regarding the life of the people, nor that, in the execution of his duty, Falkenhayn will do anything prejudicial to the interests of the State. But if the defence of Sinai is carried out by two armies under the orders of von Kress and the Seventh Army Commander respectively, and Falkenhayn is in supreme command, the interests of the country will not be well served. All difficulties would be avoided if General Falkenhayn comes under the orders of the man who is in command of Syria and Hejaz. By this arrangement, the senior official would be a Turk responsible to our Government, and having in his hands all internal political and administrative matters. Falkenhayn would exercise a command restricted to military questions only, while the lines of communication, administration of the districts, supplies, and areas behind the front, would be under one of our own race.

With regard to my remaining in command of the Seventh Army, till now I have been an independent army commander. If the interests of the country require it, I should not object if relegated to an inferior position. But there is a delicate point to be considered first. When the Seventh Army has been despatched, future operations will tend to mingle my troops with those of von Kress. It would be bad policy to allocate troops to each commander and it would be preferable to put them all as they arrive under von Kress. In that case my army Headquarters would become superfluous and von Kress would gradually assume command of all troops in the field. If the situation in the future develops in this way, and the interest of the country requires it, I am resigned to my role as a spectator. My duty will be to command without demur the smallest part of the front where my troops may intervene. That is to say, if my troops are to act independently I shall command. This point must be decided.

If the administration of Syria is not handed over to Falkenhayn, Your Excellency can trust me not to obstruct the Germans in any way. Though it is necessary to escape from the predicament in which we find ourselves in company with Germany, I am opposed to their policy of taking advantage of our misfortune and the prolongation of the war to turn us into a German colony and exploit all our resources. Our Government must be jealous and independent like the Bulgarians. I assure you that when the Germans understand that we mean to guard our independence, they will respect us more than the Bulgarians. To continually keep oneself in the background will not inspire respect or justice in any ally, especially the Germans. The more we give the more they will grasp. Falkenhayn, even now, is bold enough to say that he is a German before everything and that German interests come first. In Aleppo and Syria and on the Euphrates it is impossible to be blind to what German policy and German interests mean. If a German commander is in a position to order Turks to die by thousands, it is obvious that the interests of the State are not being watched. From the day on which Falkenhayn arrived, he sent German lieutenants to the chiefs of the tribes to establish direct relations—"The Arabs are enemies of the Turks. We can gain their friendship as we are neutral," said Falkenhayn to me, an army commander. He understood from the very first that the Iraq project was hopeless, so he has adopted the exploitation of the country as his aim. In truth, he has taken all Arabia under German protection, and has now begun the second phase of his plan. Abandoning his Iraq objective, he now discusses the chances of an offensive in Sinai. What will it be in two months, attack or defence? The talk of an offensive is only an alluring pretext by which the Germans hope to seize Syria and Arabia. If in two months the offensive is unfavourable and the defence of Palestine with all the troops proves feasible, there is no doubt we shall be very indebted to Falkenhayn if he gains a great success. But in that case the Government and country will pass from our hands and we shall become a German colony. To this end Falkenhayn is wanting the gold in our Treasury and shedding the blood of the last Turks whom Anatolia can produce. In fact to-day the most vital question is to enquire what is going on in the civil administration or among the people. Our interest is the protection of the country and if even a corner of it is given over to the influence and administration of the foreigner, the life of the Empire is being destroyed.

Such are my views. I feel a load off my mind now that I have ventilated them.

MUSTAPHA KEMAL
    Commander Seventh Army
    30th September, 1917

Source: Brigadier General F. J. Moberly, *The Campaign in Mesopotamia, 1914–1918*, Vol. 4 (London: HMSO, 1927), 348–351.

132. The Balfour Declaration: Arthur Balfour to Lord Rothschild (November 2, 1917)

Introduction

World War I gave considerable impetus to Zionist demands for the establishment of a Jewish state or homeland in Palestine, then part of the Ottoman Empire. At least some British statesmen were sympathetic, in part because of the romantic fascination that the Zionist idea exercised upon assorted influential individuals, notably British foreign secretary Arthur James Balfour. More practical considerations also impelled them. British leaders were anxious to win support from Jewish elements in countries with which they were at war. They also sought to win over the politically influential Jewish lobby in the United States, initially a key neutral state and eventually a vital ally whose economic and manpower resources proved crucial in bringing about the Allied victory. Lobbying efforts by Chaim Weizmann, a leading Zionist and biochemist whose scientific research was of great value to the Allied efforts, also proved persuasive to British leaders. On November 2, 1917, Balfour wrote an official letter to Lord Rothschild, a prominent British Zionist leader. Although its terms were somewhat ambivalent, this brief communication offered Jews a homeland in Palestine, a development that eventually led to the creation of the State of Israel in 1948. Correctly or not, Sharif Hussein of Mecca, a key Arab leader and British ally in revolt against Turkey, believed that he too had been promised this territory, a source of lasting bitterness among Arab leaders and peoples. After World War I Palestine would become a British mandate under the League of Nations, and Arab and Jewish settlers would begin a lengthy struggle over which element should predominate in this territory.

Document

November 2, 1917

Dear Lord Rothschild,

I have much pleasure in conveying to you, on behalf of His Majesty's Government, the following declaration of sympathy with Jewish Zionist aspirations which has been submitted to, and approved by, the Cabinet.

"His Majesty's Government view with favour the establishment in Palestine of a national home for the Jewish people, and will use their best endeavours to facilitate the achievement of this object, it being clearly understood that nothing shall be done which may prejudice the civil and religious rights of existing non-Jewish communities in Palestine, or the rights and political status enjoyed by Jews in any other country."

I should be grateful if you would bring this declaration to the knowledge of the Zionist Federation.

Signed: Arthur James Balfour

Source: "Letter of Foreign Minister Balfour to Lord Rothschild," *The Times* (London), November 2, 1917.

133. Sir Edmund Allenby on the Fall of Jerusalem (December 9, 1917)

Introduction

A high point of the campaign in Mesopotamia and Palestine waged by Allied forces was the capture of Jerusalem in December 1917. Sacred to Christians, Jews, and Muslims alike, the city carried highly symbolic and emotional significance for the Allies, who felt that their success in taking it gave the seal of divine approval to their cause. Sir Edmund Allenby, commander of the British forces, sent a dispatch to the British War Office describing this military action. The campaign, which began on October

31, culminated in victory on December 9. Two days later, Allenby and other top officials entered the city. To indicate their respect for its special religious significance, they did so on foot. Concerned that his forces should not alienate the Muslim population, Allenby also sought to protect the Islamic holy places in the city.

Document

The date for the attack on Jerusalem was fixed as December 8th.

Welsh troops, with a cavalry regiment attached, had advanced from their positions north of Beersheba up the Hebron-Jerusalem road on the 4th. No opposition was met, and by the evening of the 6th the head of this column was ten miles north of Hebron.

The infantry were directed to reach the Bethlehem-Befit Jala area by the 7th, and the line Surbahir-Sherafat (about three miles south of Jerusalem) by dawn on the 8th, and no troops were to enter Jerusalem during this operation.

It was recognized that the troops on the extreme right might be delayed on the 7th and fail to reach the positions assigned to them by dawn on the 8th. Arrangements were therefore made to protect the right flank west of Jerusalem, in case such delay occurred.

On the 7th the weather broke, and for three days rain was almost continuous. The hills were covered with mist at frequent intervals, rendering observation from the air and visual signalling impossible.

A more serious effect of the rain was to jeopardize the supply arrangements by rendering the roads almost impassable—quite impassable, indeed, for mechanical transport and camels in many places.

The troops moved into positions of assembly by night, and, assaulting at dawn on the 8th, soon carried their first objectives. They then pressed steadily forward. The mere physical difficulty of climbing the steep and rocky hillsides and crossing the deep valleys would have sufficed to render progress slow, and the opposition encountered was considerable.

Artillery support was soon difficult, owing to the length of the advance and the difficulty of moving guns forward. But by about noon London troops had already advanced over two miles, and were swinging northeast to gain the Nablus-Jerusalem road, while the yeomanry had captured the Beit Iksa spur, and were preparing for a further advance.

As the right column had been delayed and was still some distance south of Jerusalem, it was necessary for the London troops to throw back their right and form a defensive flank facing east toward Jerusalem, from the western outskirts of which considerable rifle and artillery fire was being experienced.

This delayed the advance, and early in the afternoon it was decided to consolidate the line gained and resume the advance next day, when the right column would be in a position to exert its pressure.

By nightfall our line ran from Neby Samwil to the east of Beit Iksa, through Lifta to a point about one and a half miles west of Jerusalem, whence it was thrown back facing east. All the enemy's prepared defences west and northwest of Jerusalem had been captured, and our troops were within a short distance of the Nablus-Jerusalem road.

The London troops and yeomanry had displayed great endurance in difficult conditions. The London troops especially, after a night march in heavy rain to reach their positions of deployment, had made an advance of three to four miles in difficult hills in the face of stubborn opposition.

During the day about 300 prisoners were taken and many Turks killed. Our own casualties were light.

Next morning the advance was resumed. The Turks had withdrawn during the night, and the London troops and yeomanry, driving back rearguards, occupied a line across the Nablus-Jerusalem road four miles north of Jerusalem, while Welsh troops occupied a position east of Jerusalem across the Jericho road.

These operations isolated Jerusalem, and at about noon the enemy sent out a *parlementaire* and surrendered the city.

In the operations from October 31st to December 9th over 12,000 prisoners were taken. The total captures of material have not yet been fully counted, owing to the large area covered by these operations; but are known to include about 100 guns of various calibres, many machine guns, more than 20,000,000 rounds of rifle ammunition, and 250,000 rounds of gun ammunition.

More than twenty airplanes were destroyed by our airmen or burned by the enemy to avoid capture.

I entered the city officially at noon, December 11th, with a few of my staff, the commanders of the French and Italian detachments, the heads of the political missions, and the Military Attachés of France, Italy, and America.

The procession was all afoot, and at Jaffa gate I was received by the guards representing England, Scotland, Ireland, Wales, Australia, New Zealand, India, France, and Italy. The population received me well.

Guards have been placed over the holy places. My Military Governor is in contact with the acting custodians and the Latin and Greek representatives. The Governor has detailed an officer to supervise the holy places.

The Mosque of Omar and the area around it have been placed under Moslem control, and a military cordon of Mohammedan officers and soldiers has been established around the mosque.

Orders have been issued that no non-Moslem is to pass within the cordon without permission of the Military Governor and the Moslem in charge.

Source: Charles F. Horne and Warren F. Austin, eds., *The Great Events of the Great War*, Vol. 5 (Washington, DC: National Alumni, 1920), 409.

134. General Liman von Sanders to Major General von Seekt (December 13, 1917): Condition of the Turkish Army Today

Introduction

General Otto Liman von Sanders, head of the German Military Mission in Turkey during World War I, quickly became comprehensively disillusioned with his Turkish allies. In memoirs of his service in Germany written shortly after the war while he was detained on the island of Malta, Liman von Sanders was very frank about his numerous disagreements with the Turkish military high command, especially with Minister of War Enver Pasha. These were the product in part of disagreements over wartime strategy and operations but also of personal incompatibilities, particularly between Liman von Sanders and Enver Pasha. Liman von Sanders sent several scathing reports back to the German high command in Berlin seeking greater authority over Turkish military operations. In June 1918 he even attempted to resign the command of Army Group F in Palestine, which he had taken over at the beginning of March, but the Kaiser commanded him to remain in his position. Detained by the British authorities in Malta for six months at the end of the war, Liman von Sanders used his enforced leisure to write memoirs of his wartime service, which included some of his memoranda from those years.

Document

Panderma 13th December 1917

Condition of the Turkish Army today.

Through a series of errors the numerical strength of the combatant troops of the Turkish Army and their fighting efficiency has sunk to a level so low that it cannot be overlooked. The causes of both defects must be clearly understood in order to devise a remedy.

Any remedial measures must expect to encounter many difficulties from the unsatisfactory condition of transport roads and transport means.

I. Numerical Strength

In the unavoidable battles in the various theatres of war, the Turkish Army has suffered severe losses, which it could not escape. But it suffered further great losses which with some care might have been avoided, and which should be instructive for the future. In the latter class are:

a) The first Caucasus campaign in December 1914 and January 1915. The Third Army (leader, Enver Pasha, chief of the general staff, Major General von Bronsart) numbered about 90,000 good troops at the beginning of December 1914.

It held a favorable position in the mountains near Hassan Kala, near the frontier; the opposing Russians were not superior in numbers.

An offensive against Sarikamisch-Kars was decided upon, against my urgent advice, although in case the army succeeded in forcing a passage through and out of the mountains, it would be unable to take Kars because the Turks had no siege artillery.

The advance by the left with two army corps on snow-covered mountain roads and trails, with inadequate provision for supplies, led to the separate defeat of each corps while the third corps fought without result on the front. According to official reports barely 12,000 men returned, and these in a miserable condition. All the rest were killed, died of hunger or cold, or were captured.

The history of war will never find grounds on which to justify this offensive.

b) The offensive of the Third Army undertaken with inadequate forces against the Russians in the early summer of 1916.

On the retreat a considerable part of the army dispersed.

c) The concentration and fruitless offensive of the Second Army in the summer of 1916, which started from the line Lake Van-Mus-Kighi in the general direction of Erzerum, and collapsed at its beginning.

The contemplated operation against the enemy's flank and rear were quite impracticable, because there were no practicable roads to the front, or usable communications to the rear, and because the trains necessary for mobile war were non-existent.

According to the lowest statements this army lost 60,000 men from hunger and disease, and later from cold, the loss from enemy effect being the smallest.

d) The advance of the Thirteenth Army Corps into Persia in the summer of 1916 and winter of 1916/17, which from a military point of view was a great mistake. This advance should not have begun until the British in Irak were driven back to Gurna, if not to Basra. The loss of Bagdad was an immediate consequence; the corps was absent from the decision in March 1917.

134. General Liman von Sanders to Major General von Seekt: Condition of the Turkish Army Today

I refer here to my report of October 25th or 26th, 1916, handed by General von Chelius to H. E. General von Ludendorff and to my personal report at the headquarters in Pless in December 1916.

e) The hopeless advance of the expeditionary corps against the Suez Canal in August 1916 with an eye to the conquest of Egypt.

This advance of only 18,000 fighting men was condemned to failure from the beginning, and it caused the British to follow through the desert of El Tih, though originally they merely meant to defend the canal. Their progress today in Palestine was initiated through this mistaken measure.

Here also I refer to my report to H. E. General von Ludendorff of October 1916.

I am perfectly aware that one cannot invariably succeed in war, and that even the best are not spared reverses, but I am also aware that one should not sacrifice valuable troops when there is no hope of success, simply because one does not know whether to take the offensive or to remain on the defensive.

f) The desertions from the Turkish Army which exceed all bounds.

The Turkish Army today has more than 300,000 desertions. They are not men that go over to the enemy, but for the most part return to the country in rear where they rob and plunder and make the country insecure. Everywhere detachments had to be formed for the pursuit of these deserters. The reasons for this desertion en masse are stated in part II.

Only those familiar with the events can understand the low combatant strength of the Turks.

The First Army has divisions temporarily attached only, besides the replacements in and near Constantinople, and the labor formations, which are mere paper formations and of no military value.

The Second and Third Army (Caucasus group), Izzet Pasha, commander of the group, told me a few days ago has an effective strength of some 20,000 rifles.

The Fifth Army, charged with the protection of the coast from the Bulgarian frontier to Alaja on the Mediterranean (approximately 2,000 kilometers) has slightly over 26,000 rifles.

The Sixth Army, according to a statement of a few months ago by Major Kretzschmer, the then chief of staff, had about 31,000 rifles.

Of the fighting strength of the armies in Palestine and Syria I have no knowledge at this time.

II. Deterioration of Fighting Efficiency

The Turkish soldier, particularly the Anatolian, is excellent fighting material.

Well looked after, sufficiently nourished, properly trained and calmly led these men will accomplish the highest aims.

A large part of the Arabs may be made into good usable soldiers, if from the very beginning of their service they are treated with strictness and justice.

The diminution of the efficiency of many parts of the army is chiefly due to the mistakes of Turkish headquarters.

For about two years now a great part of the troops have not been granted sufficient time for training. They have been torn apart, before the small and large units have been properly cemented together.

Companies, battalions, machine gun companies, garrisons of batteries have been detached and sent elsewhere. The strength of the departing troops has been complemented at the last moment by slightly trained or wholly untrained troops, or the men were taken from units that had just become effective, and they in turn had to be detached before recovering their efficiency.

When sent to the railroad station, the men for the most part did not know each other or their superiors. They only knew that they were being sent to some bad place. Hence they ran away whenever they could, and risked being shot while running. They jumped from the cars in motion, from the marching column in covered terrain, or from the bivouac, or from their billets.

There is hardly a division that has not lost thousands of men while en route by rail or march to the theaters east or south of the Taurus.

The Turkish soldier needs a certain amount of care, and a certain firmness in his treatment. When he has learned confidence in his superiors, they can accomplish anything with him.

The present phase of inordinate desertion is not a hereditary defect of the Turkish Army. Izzet Pasha, the leader of the Caucasus Group and a wholly reliable man, has told me that this kind of desertion was formerly unknown.

There is no doubt that the unsatisfactory condition of the roads, of the means of transportation, and of subsistence contributes its share.

The present condition of the Turkish Army shows that the road followed is a wrong one, and that another must be taken to gain success. It should not be forgotten that it has become difficult to get replacements.

Sgd. Liman von Sanders

Source: Liman von Sanders, *Five Years in Turkey* (Baltimore: Williams & Wilkins, 1928), 189–192.

135. Emir Faisal: Memorandum to the Supreme Council at the Paris Peace Conference (January 1, 1919)

Introduction

As the Paris Peace Conference began, Emir Faisal of the Hejaz, son of Sharif Hussein ibn-Ali of the Hejaz and a leader of the Arab Revolt, submitted a memorandum detailing his hopes for a greater Arab state headed by his own family. At this time the British, who had conquered and occupied Syria in 1918, had permitted Faisal to establish a short-lived provisional Arab government with its headquarters in Syria. Faisal hoped that a united Arab people would eventually emerge in the Middle East, "if no attempt is now made to force it, by imposing an artificial political unity on the whole, or to hinder it, by dividing the area as spoils of war among great Powers." Until this occurred, he argued, different portions of the region should have somewhat different forms of government but Arabs should predominate in all. Syria, a fairly highly developed urbanized and agricultural province, should, he claimed, be effectively autonomous. Mesopotamia, or Iraq, had only three major cities and otherwise was rather thinly populated and undeveloped, so its government, which he insisted should be Arab, would nonetheless need to seek protection from "the men and material resources of a great foreign Power." Faisal stated that his family's base, the Hejaz, should remain completely independent and "a tribal area" ruled under "patriarchal conditions."

Given the possibility of future conflicts between Arabs and Jews in Palestine, where "the Arabs cannot risk assuming the responsibility of holding level the scales in the clash of races and religions," Faisal sought that province's supervision by a Great Power trustee. He begged all the Great Powers to lay aside rivalries and jealousies and cooperate in ensuring that the various Arab administrations of the region "open internal frontiers, common railways and telegraphs, and uniform systems of education" that would promote their future union. Proclaiming the fundamental Pan-Arab unity of this region's peoples, Faisal warned that "They expect the powers to think of them as one potential people, jealous of their language and liberty, and ask that no step be taken inconsistent with the prospect of an eventual union of these areas under one sovereign government." The Great Powers at Paris ignored most of Faisal's stipulations, effectively dividing the region into spheres of influence and discouraging rather than promoting Arab unity, decisions that would contribute to the deep internecine Arab rivalries that subsequently characterized the Middle East.

Document

The country from a line Alexandretta-Persia southward to the Indian Ocean is inhabited by "Arabs"—by which we mean people of closely related Semitic stocks, all speaking the one language, Arabic. The non-Arabic-speaking elements in this area do not, I believe, exceed one per cent, of the whole.

The aim of the Arab nationalist movements (of which my father became the leader in war after combined appeals from the Syrian and Mesopotamian branches) is to unite the Arabs eventually into one nation. As an old member of the Syrian Committee I commanded the Syrian revolt, and had under me Syrians, Mesopotamians, and Arabians.

We believe that our ideal of Arab unity in Asia is justified beyond need of argument. If argument is required, we would point to the general principles accepted by the Allies when the United States joined them, to our splendid past, to the tenacity with which our race has for 600 years resisted Turkish attempts to absorb us, and, in a lesser degree, to what we tried our best to do in this war as one of the Allies.

My father has a privileged place among Arabs, as their successful leader, and as the head of their greatest family, and as Sherif of Mecca. He is convinced of the ultimate triumph of the ideal of unity, if no attempt is made now to force it, by imposing an artificial political unity on the whole, or to hinder it, by dividing the area as spoils of war among great Powers.

The unity of the Arabs in Asia has been made more easy of late years, since the development of railways, telegraphs, and air-roads. In old days the area was too huge, and in parts necessarily too thinly peopled, to communicate common ideas readily.

The various provinces of Arab Asia—Syria, Irak, Jezireh, Hedjaz, Nejd, Yemen—are very different economically and socially, and it is impossible to constrain them into one frame of government.

We believe that Syria, an agricultural and industrial area thickly peopled with sedentary classes, is sufficiently advanced politically to manage her own internal affairs. We feel also that foreign technical advice and help will be a most valuable factor in our national growth. We are willing to pay for this help in cash; we cannot sacrifice for it any part of the freedom we have just won for ourselves by force of arms.

Jezireh and Irak are two huge provinces, made up of three civilised towns, divided by large wastes thinly peopled by semi-nomadic tribes. The world wishes to exploit Mesopotamia rapidly, and we therefore believe that the system of government there will have to be buttressed by the men and material resources of a great foreign Power. We ask, however, that the Government be Arab in principle and spirit, the selective rather than the elective principle being necessarily followed in the neglected districts, until time makes the broader basis possible. The main duty of the Arab Government there would be to oversee the educational processes which are to advance the tribes to the moral level of the towns.

The Hedjaz is mainly a tribal area, and the government will remain, as in the past, suited to patriarchal conditions. We appreciate these better than Europe, and propose therefore to retain our complete independence there.

The Yemen and Nejd are not likely to submit their cases to the Peace Conference. They look after themselves, and adjust their own relations with the Hedjaz and elsewhere.

In Palestine the enormous majority of the people are Arabs. The Jews are very close to the Arabs in blood, and there is no conflict of character between the two races. In principles we are absolutely at one. Nevertheless, the Arabs cannot risk assuming the responsibility of holding level the scales in the clash of races and religions that have, in this one province, so often involved the world in difficulties. They would wish for the effective super-position of a great trustee, so long as a representative local administration commended itself by actively promoting the material prosperity of the country.

In discussing our provinces in detail I do not lay claim to superior competence. The powers will, I hope, find better means to give fuller effect to the aims of our national movement. I came to Europe, on behalf of my father and the Arabs of Asia, to say that they are expecting the Powers at the Conference not to attach undue importance to superficial differences of condition, and not to consider them only from the low ground of existing European material interests and supposed spheres. They expect the powers to think of them as one potential people, jealous of their language and liberty, and ask that no step be taken inconsistent with the prospect of an eventual union of these areas under one sovereign government.

In laying stress on the difference in the social condition of our provinces, I do not wish to give the impression that there exists any real conflict of ideals, material interests, creeds, or character rendering our union impossible. The greatest obstacle we have to overcome is local ignorance, for which the Turkish Government is largely responsible.

In our opinion, if our independence be conceded and our local competence established, the natural influences of race, language, and interest will soon draw us together into one people; but for this the Great Powers will have to ensure us open internal frontiers, common railways and telegraphs, and uniform systems of education. To achieve this they must lay aside the thought of individual profits, and of their old jealousies. In a word, we ask you not to force your whole civilisation upon us, but to help us to pick out what serves us from your experience. In return we can offer you little but gratitude.

Source: David Hunter Miller, *My Diary at the Conference of Paris*, Vol. 4 (New York: Appeal Printing, 1924), 297–299.

136. A Report on Mesopotamia by T. E. Lawrence, *The Sunday Times* (August 22, 1920)

Introduction

By 1920, the celebrated British Army officer Thomas Edward Lawrence, who had fought with Arab guerrilla forces during the World War I rebellion against Ottoman rule, was highly critical of British policy toward Mesopotamia, or present-day Iraq. He fiercely condemned the fact that having promised the former Ottoman province independence, the British occupation authorities were now treating it almost as conquered territory, subjecting the resentful inhabitants to a brutal and repressive foreign regime that was little if any better than that of Ottoman Turkey. Writing in the influential newspaper the *Sunday Times*, Lawrence broke with official British policy, which was, he charged, a massive betrayal of the pledges of "self-determination" for the area that the British had made during the war.

Document

[Mr. Lawrence, whose organization and direction of the Hedjaz against the Turks was one of the outstanding romances of the war, has written this article at our request in order that the public may be fully informed of our Mesopotamian commitments.]

The people of England have been led in Mesopotamia into a trap from which it will be hard to escape with dignity and honour. They have been tricked into it by a steady withholding of information. The Baghdad communiqués are belated, insincere, incomplete. Things have been far worse than we have been told, our administration more bloody and inefficient than the public knows. It is a disgrace to our imperial record, and may soon be too inflamed for any ordinary cure. We are to-day not far from a disaster.

136. A Report on Mesopotamia by T. E. Lawrence, *The Sunday Times*

The sins of commission are those of the British civil authorities in Mesopotamia (especially of three 'colonels') who were given a free hand by London. They are controlled from no Department of State, but from the empty space which divides the Foreign Office from the India Office. They availed themselves of the necessary discretion of war-time to carry over their dangerous independence into times of peace. They contest every suggestion of real self-government sent them from home. A recent proclamation about autonomy circulated with unction from Baghdad was drafted and published out there in a hurry, to forestall a more liberal statement in preparation in London. 'Self-determination papers' favourable to England were extorted in Mesopotamia in 1919 by official pressure, by aeroplane demonstrations, by deportations to India.

The Cabinet cannot disclaim all responsibility. They receive little more news than the public: they should have insisted on more, and better. They have sent draft after draft of reinforcements, without enquiry. When conditions became too bad to endure longer, they decided to send out as High Commissioner the original author of the present system, with a conciliatory message to the Arabs that his heart and policy have completely changed.

Yet our published policy has not changed, and does not need changing. It is that there has been a deplorable contrast between our profession and our practice. We said we went to Mesopotamia to defeat Turkey. We said we stayed to deliver the Arabs from the oppression of the Turkish Government, and to make available for the world its resources of corn and oil. We spent nearly a million men and nearly a thousand million of money to these ends. This year we are spending ninety-two thousand men and fifty millions of money on the same objects.

Our government is worse than the old Turkish system. They kept fourteen thousand local conscripts embodied, and killed a yearly average of two hundred Arabs in maintaining peace. We keep ninety thousand men, with aeroplanes, armoured cars, gunboats, and armoured trains. We have killed about ten thousand Arabs in this rising this summer. We cannot hope to maintain such an average: it is a poor country, sparsely peopled; but Abd el Hamid would applaud his masters, if he saw us working. We are told the object of the rising was political, we are not told what the local people want. It may be what the Cabinet has promised them. A Minister in the House of Lords said that we must have so many troops because the local people will not enlist. On Friday the Government announced the death of some local levies defending their British officers, and say that the services of these men have not yet been sufficiently recognized because they are too few (adding the characteristic Baghdad touch that they are men of bad character). There are seven thousand of them, just half the old Turkish force of occupation. Properly officered and distributed, they would relieve half our army there. Cromer controlled Egypt's six million people with five thousand British troops; Colonel Wilson fails to control Mesopotamia's three million people with ninety thousand troops.

We have not reached the limit of our military commitments. Four weeks ago the staff in Mesopotamia drew up a memorandum asking for four more divisions. I believe it was forwarded to the War Office, which has now sent three brigades from India. If the North-West Frontier cannot be further denuded, where is the balance to come from? Meanwhile, our unfortunate troops, Indian and British, under hard conditions of climate and supply, are policing an immense area, paying dearly every day in lives for the wilfully wrong policy of the civil administration in Baghdad. General Dyer was relieved of his command in India for a much smaller error, but the responsibility in this case is not on the Army, which has acted only at the request of the civil authorities. The War Office has made every effort to reduce our forces, but the decisions of the Cabinet have been against them.

The Government in Baghdad have been hanging Arabs in that town for political offences, which they call rebellion. The Arabs are not at war with us. Are these illegal executions to provoke the Arabs to reprisals on the three hundred British prisoners they hold? And, if so, is it that their punishment may be more severe, or is it to persuade our other troops to fight to the last?

We say we are in Mesopotamia to develop it for the benefit of the world. All experts say that the labour supply is the ruling factor in its development. How far will the killing of ten thousand villagers and townspeople this summer hinder the production of wheat, cotton, and oil? How long will we permit millions of pounds, thousands of Imperial troops, and tens of thousands of Arabs to be sacrificed on behalf of a form of colonial administration which can benefit nobody but its administrators?

Source: *The Sunday Times*, August 22, 1920, World War I Document Archive, https://wwi.lib.byu.edu/index.php/A_Report_on_Mesopotamia_by_T.E._Lawrence.

137. Mustafa Kemal Ataturk Assails the Treaty of Sèvres (June–October 1921)

Introduction

The Grand National Assembly, the provisional government established in Ankara in March 1920 by Turks who resented the acquiescence of the Ottoman government in the post–World War I Allied occupation and partition of Turkey, repudiated the highly disadvantageous peace terms the Treaty of Sèvres imposed on the Ottoman Empire in August 1920. The pusillanimity of the Ottoman authorities based in Istanbul in signing this agreement was a major reason for the subsequent abolition of the sultanate by the Grand National Assembly in November 1922, following which Sultan Mehmed VI was expelled from Turkey. To a French representative who arrived in Ankara to open negotiations to end the ongoing war between Greece and Turkey, Mustafa Kemal Ataturk, Speaker of the Grand National Assembly and commander in chief of Turkish forces, expounded on the Ankara government's objections to the Sèvres settlement. Following several years of warfare, in July 1923 Turkey and the Allies negotiated the less onerous Treaty of Lausanne, under which the new Turkish republic regained significant portions of Anatolia and other territories.

Document

The French Government had at first unofficially sent M. Franklin Bouillon, the former Minister, to Ankara. For about two weeks I negotiated with him myself in the presence of Fevzi Paşa and Yusuf Kemal Bey, the Foreign Minister, after M. Bouillon had arrived at Ankara on the 9th June.

After a private conversation for the purpose of making our mutual acquaintance, we had our first meeting in my quarters near the railway station at Ankara on Monday, the 13th June. After we had begun to exchange our views at this meeting the question before us was to define what should be the starting of our negotiations. I suggested that on our side it should be the National Pact. M. Bouillon pointed out the difficulties that would arise from a discussion about this and suggested the Treaty of Sèvres. Then he remarked, as though it were a foregone conclusion, that it would be advisable if we took the agreement that had been made in London between Bekir Sami Bey and M. Briand as the basis of our negotiations, reserving discussion on the points which were in contradiction to the Pact. To support this proposal, he asserted that our plenipotentiaries had not spoken about the National Pact in London, and, moreover, that nobody in Europe or even in Istanbul had yet sufficiently grasped the sense and real bearing of the Pact and the national movement. In my reply I remarked that a New Turkish State had arisen from the old Ottoman Empire, that it must be recognised, and that this New Turkey would, in any case, secure for herself the recognition of her rights in the same manner as the rights of any independent nation. "The Sèvres Treaty," I said, "is such a death sentence for the Turkish nation that we demand that its very name shall not be mentioned by anybody who calls himself our friend. Its name must not be referred to in the course of these negotiations. We cannot enter into confidential relations with countries that have not banished the Sèvres Treaty from their minds. In our eyes this Treaty does not exist. If the leader of the Turkish Delegation which went to London has not spoken to this effect, it signifies that he has not acted in accordance with the instructions and within the compass of the full powers which were given him. He has made himself guilty of a mistake. We are well aware that this mistake has led to unfavourable impressions in Europe and particularly in the public opinion of France. If we were to follow the same course as Bekir Sami Bey, we would be committing a similar error. It is impossible that Europe is ignorant about our National Pact. It must have been brought to knowledge. Europe and the whole world, however, witnessing how we have been shedding our blood for years, must surely have reflected on the cause of these sanguinary struggles. There is no truth in the assertion that Istanbul knows nothing about the Pact and the national struggles. The population of Istanbul together with the whole of the Turkish nation are fully informed and entirely approve of these struggles. The persons who seem not to support it, and all those who allow themselves to be influenced by them, are only a small group and are known to the nation."

In reply to my statement that Bekir Sami Bey had exceeded his instructions, M. Franklin Bouillon asked whether he might speak about this subject. I told him that he could do so to whomsoever he wished. Then he tried to make excuses so as not to be obliged to depart from the agreement made with Bekir Sami Bey. He maintained that the latter had never spoken of the existence of the Pact nor of having been instructed to keep within the limits of this Pact. If he had done so, they could have discussed and acted as the necessities of the situation demanded, but considering the present state of affairs the question had become a much more difficult one. He added that public opinion would inquire: "Why have these Turks never had this question put forward by their representative? Now they are trying continually to raise new questions?"

After long negotiations, M. Franklin Bouillon finally proposed that the discussion should be adjourned so that he could read the Pact and grasp its meaning. Then the Articles of the Pact were read, one after the other from the beginning to the end, and after that had been done the negotiations were resumed. The Article that delayed us most was the one that referred to the abolition of the Capitulations and our complete independence. M. Franklin Bouillon remarked that these questions required more thorough study and deeper consideration. My explanations on this point may be condensed thus: "The attainment of our full and complete independence is the very essence of the mission we have taken upon ourselves. It is the duty we have undertaken before the nation and before history. It is certain that before undertaking this obligation we have thought a great deal about the prospects for its fulfilment. But in the end we are convinced that we shall succeed in our enterprise. We are people who have learned how to be practical and to face things in a proper manner. As a result of the faults committed by our predecessors, our nation, nominally independent, found itself in reality subject to numberless restrictions on its actions.

"Everything invented hitherto with the object of depicting Turkey in the eyes of the civilized world as bristling with faults has its origin in this false impression and the consequences produced by it. To be governed by this error can only result in the country and the nation being deprived of their dignity and their vitality. We are a nation that wants to live and that desires to do so in full possession of our dignity and honour. We cannot be content to see ourselves deprived of these attributes because we succumb to an error. All the individuals constituting our nation, whether ignorant or educated, have without exception rallied around one principle, perhaps even without being conscious of the difficulties lying before them, and they have resolved to shed the last drop of their blood to carry out what they have to do in order to defend it. This principle is the attainment and maintenance of our full independence. Whoever speaks of complete and full independence means thereby unlimited independence: political, economic, legal, military, cultural, and the rest. If in any of these spheres of independence there should be something lacking, it would be equivalent to saying that the country has not yet gained its independence in the fullest meaning of the word. We do not believe that we can enjoy peace and rest until we have achieved this aim. We may conclude peace and enter into purely formal agreements; but our nation will never be at rest nor mistress of her own existence under a peace or an agreement which does not bestow complete independence on her. It could never happen that the nation would have given up the material struggle and consented to their destruction. But if they would have been inclined to be satisfied with such conditions as these, why would they have gone on fighting for two years?

"On the day of the Armistice they could have taken refuge behind a condition of inactivity and pacification."

M. Franklin Bouillon's observations in reply to my elucidation showed his seriousness and sincerity. In the end he expressed his conviction that after all it was only a question of time.

Source: *A Speech Delivered by Mustafa Kemal Atatürk* (Ankara: Başbakanlık Basımevi, 1981), 523–526.

138. Ze'ev (Vladimir) Jabotinsky: "The Iron Wall: We and the Arabs" (November 4, 1923)

Introduction

Writing in 1923 a few weeks after Great Britain assumed the mandate for Palestine, the Russian-born Zionist activist Ze'ev Jabotinsky addressed the issue that the Arabs of Palestine might not welcome the presence of new Jewish settlers. Jabotinsky thought it most unlikely that the Arabs would voluntarily accept Jewish immigrants. At the same time, he affirmed the right of the Jews to return to what had once been their homeland and said that it was more than large enough to absorb all the Jews who wished to move there without displacing the existing Arab inhabitants. The wish of the Jews to do so, Jabotinsky stated, was morally justified. He therefore called for Palestine to be administered by a strong outside power, one that would not yield to Arab pressure and would facilitate Jewish immigration while negotiating suitable guarantees to safeguard the rights of the current population. Although Jabotinsky disavowed any ambition to establish a Jewish state, he envisaged that Jews would be in the majority in Palestine. Whether the British would accept the role he implicitly assigned to them in administering Palestine was not a question that Jabotinsky chose to raise.

Document

Contrary to the excellent rule of getting to the point immediately, I must begin this article with a personal introduction. The author of these lines is considered to be an enemy of the Arabs, a proponent of their expulsion, etc. This is not true. My emotional relationship to the Arabs is the same as it is to all other peoples—polite indifference. My political relationship is characterized by two principles. First: the expulsion of the Arabs from Palestine is absolutely impossible in any form. There will always be two nations in Palestine—which is good enough for me, provided the Jews become the majority. Second: I am proud to have been a member of that group which formulated the Helsingfors Program. We formulated it, not only for Jews, but for all peoples, and its basis is the equality of all nations. I am prepared to swear, for us and our descendants, that we will never destroy this equality and we will never attempt to expel or oppress the Arabs. Our credo, as the reader can see, is completely peaceful. But it is absolutely another matter if it will be possible to achieve our peaceful aims through peaceful means. This depends, not on our relationship with the Arabs, but exclusively on the Arabs' relationship to Zionism.

After this introduction I can now get to the point. That the Arabs of the Land of Israel should willingly come to an agreement with us is beyond all hopes and dreams at present, and in the foreseeable future. This inner conviction of mine I express so categorically not because of any wish to dismay the moderate faction in the Zionist camp but, on the contrary, because I wish to save them from such dismay. Apart from those who have been virtually "blind" since childhood, all the other moderate Zionists have long since understood that there is not even the slightest hope of ever obtaining the agreement of the Arabs of the Land of Israel to "Palestine" becoming a country with a Jewish majority.

Every reader has some idea of the early history of other countries which have been settled. I suggest that he recall all known instances. If he should attempt to seek but one instance of a country settled with the consent of those born there he will not succeed. The inhabitants (no matter whether they are civilized or savages) have always put up a stubborn fight. Furthermore, how the settler acted had no effect whatsoever. The Spaniards who conquered Mexico and Peru, or our own ancestors in the days of Joshua ben Nun behaved, one might say, like plunderers. But those "great explorers," the English, Scots and Dutch who were the first real pioneers of North America were people possessed of a very high ethical standard; people who not only wished to leave the redskins at peace but could also pity a fly; people who in all sincerity and innocence believed that in those virgin forests and vast plains ample space was available for both the white and red man. But the native resisted both barbarian and civilized settler with the same degree of cruelty.

Another point which had no effect at all was whether or not there existed a suspicion that the settler wished to remove the inhabitant from his land. The vast areas of the U.S. never contained more than one or two million Indians. The inhabitants fought the white settlers not out of fear that they might be expropriated, but simply because there has never been an indigenous inhabitant anywhere or at any time who has ever accepted the settlement of others in his country. Any native people—it's all the same whether they are civilized or savage—views their country as their national home, of which they will always be the complete masters. They will not voluntarily allow, not only a new master, but even a new partner. And so it is for the Arabs. Compromisers in our midst attempt to convince us that the Arabs are some kind of fools who can be tricked by a softened formulation of our goals, or a tribe of money grubbers who will abandon their birth right to Palestine for cultural and economic gains. I flatly reject this assessment of the Palestinian Arabs. Culturally they are 500 years behind us, spiritually they do not have our endurance or our strength of will, but this exhausts all of the internal differences. We can talk as much as we want about our good intentions; but they understand as well as we what is not good for them. They look upon Palestine with the same instinctive love and true fervor that any Aztec looked upon his Mexico or any Sioux looked upon his prairie. To think that the Arabs will voluntarily consent to the realization of Zionism in return for the cultural and economic benefits we can bestow on them is infantile. This childish fantasy of our "Arabo-philes" comes from some kind of contempt for the Arab people, of some kind of unfounded view of this race as a rabble ready to be bribed in order to sell out their homeland for a railroad network.

This view is absolutely groundless. Individual Arabs may perhaps be bought off but this hardly means that all the Arabs in Eretz Israel are willing to sell a patriotism that not even Papuans will trade. Every indigenous people will resist alien settlers as long as they see any hope of ridding themselves of the danger of foreign settlement.

That is what the Arabs in Palestine are doing, and what they will persist in doing as long as there remains a solitary spark of hope that they will be able to prevent the transformation of "Palestine" into the "Land of Israel."

Some of us imagined that a misunderstanding had occurred, that because the Arabs did not understand our intentions, they opposed us, but, if we were to make clear to them how modest and limited our aspirations are, they would then stretch out their arms in peace. This too is a fallacy that has been proved so time and again. I need recall only one incident. Three years ago, during a visit here, [prominent Zionist activist Nahum] Sokolow delivered a great speech about this very "misunderstanding," employing trenchant language to prove how grossly mistaken the Arabs were in supposing that we intended to take away their property or expel them from the country, or to suppress them. This was definitely not so. Nor did we even want a Jewish state. All we wanted was a regime representative of the League of Nations. A reply to this speech was published in the Arab paper **Al Carmel** in an article whose content I give here from memory, but I am sure it is a faithful account.

Our Zionist grandees are unnecessarily perturbed, its author wrote. There is no misunderstanding. What Sokolow claims on behalf of Zionism is true. But the Arabs already know this. Obviously, Zionists today cannot dream of expelling or suppressing the Arabs, or even of setting up a Jewish state. Clearly, in this period they are interested in only one thing—that the Arabs not interfere with Jewish immigration. Further, the Zionists have pledged to control immigration in accordance with the country's absorptive economic capacity. But the Arabs have no illusions, since no other conditions permit the possibility of immigration.

The editor of the paper is even willing to believe that the absorptive capacity of Eretz Israel is very great, and that it is possible to settle many Jews without affecting one Arab. "Just that is what the Zionists want, and what the Arabs do not want. In this way the Jews will, little by little, become a majority and, ipso facto, a Jewish state will be formed and the fate of the Arab minority will depend on the goodwill of the Jews. But was it not the Jews themselves who told us how 'pleasant' being a minority was? No misunderstanding exists. Zionists desire one thing—freedom of immigration—and it is Jewish immigration that we do not want."

The logic employed by this editor is so simple and clear that it should be learned by heart and be an essential part of our notion of the Arab question. It is of no importance whether we quote Herzl or Herbert Samuel to justify our activities. Colonization itself has its own explanation, integral and inescapable, and understood by every Arab and every Jew with his wits about him. Colonization can have only one goal. For the Palestinian Arabs this goal is inadmissible. This is in the nature of things. To change that nature is impossible.

A plan that seems to attract many Zionists goes like this: If it is impossible to get an endorsement of Zionism by Palestine's Arabs, then it must be obtained from the Arabs of Syria, Iraq, Saudi Arabia and perhaps of Egypt. Even if this were possible, it would not change the basic situation. It would not change the attitude of the Arabs in the Land of Israel towards us. Seventy years ago, the unification of Italy was achieved, with the retention by Austria of Trent and Trieste. However, the inhabitants of those towns not only refused to accept the situation, but they struggled against Austria with redoubled vigor. If it were possible (and I doubt this) to discuss Palestine with the Arabs of Baghdad and Mecca as if it were some kind of small, immaterial borderland, then Palestine would still remain for the Palestinians not a borderland, but their birthplace, the center and basis of their own national existence. Therefore it would be necessary to carry on colonization against the will of the Palestinian Arabs, which is the same condition that exists now.

But an agreement with Arabs outside the Land of Israel is also a delusion. For nationalists in Baghdad, Mecca and Damascus to agree to such an expensive contribution (agreeing to forego preservation of the Arab character of a country located in the center of their future "federation") we would have to offer them something just as valuable. We can offer only two things: either money or political assistance or both. But we can offer neither. Concerning money, it is ludicrous to think we could finance the development of Iraq or Saudi Arabia, when we do not have enough for the Land of Israel. Ten times more illusionary is political assistance for Arab political aspirations. Arab nationalism sets itself the same aims as those set by Italian nationalism before 1870 and Polish nationalism before 1918: unity and independence. These aspirations mean the eradication of every trace of British influence in Egypt and Iraq, the expulsion of the Italians from Libya, the removal of French domination from Syria, Tunis, Algiers and Morocco. For us to support such a movement would be suicide and treachery. If we disregard the fact that the Balfour Declaration was signed by Britain, we cannot forget that France and Italy also signed it. We cannot intrigue about removing Britain from the Suez Canal and the Persian Gulf and the elimination of French and Italian colonial rule over Arab territory. Such a double game cannot be considered on any account.

Thus we conclude that we cannot promise anything to the Arabs of the Land of Israel or the Arab countries. Their voluntary agreement is out of the question. Hence those who hold that an agreement with the natives is an essential condition for Zionism can now say "no" and depart from Zionism. Zionist colonization, even the most restricted, must either be terminated or carried out in defiance of the will of the native population. This colonization can, therefore, continue and develop only under the protection of a force independent of the local population—an iron wall which the native population cannot break through. This is, in toto, our policy towards the Arabs. To formulate it any other way would only be hypocrisy.

Not only must this be so, it is so whether we admit it or not. What does the Balfour Declaration and the Mandate mean for us? It is the fact that a disinterested power committed itself to create such security conditions that the local population would be deterred from interfering with our efforts.

All of us, without exception, are constantly demanding that this power strictly fulfill its obligations. In this sense, there are no meaningful differences between our "militarists" and our "vegetarians." One prefers an iron wall of Jewish bayonets, the other proposes an iron wall of British bayonets, the third proposes an agreement with Baghdad, and appears to be satisfied with Baghdad's bayonets—a strange and somewhat risky taste, but we all applaud, day and night, the iron wall. We would destroy our cause if we proclaimed the necessity of an agreement, and fill the minds of the Mandatory with the belief that we do not need an iron wall, but rather endless talks. Such a proclamation can only harm us. Therefore it is our sacred duty to expose such talk and prove that it is a snare and a delusion.

Two brief remarks: In the first place, if anyone objects that this point of view is immoral, I answer: It is not true; either Zionism is moral and just or it is immoral and unjust. But that is a question that we should have settled before we became Zionists. Actually we have settled that question, and in the affirmative.

We hold that Zionism is moral and just. And since it is moral and just, justice must be done, no matter whether Joseph or Simon or Ivan or Achmet agree with it or not.

There is no other morality.

All this does not mean that any kind of agreement is impossible, only a voluntary agreement is impossible. As long as there is a spark of hope that they can get rid of us, they will not sell these hopes, not for any kind of sweet words or tasty morsels, because they are not a rabble but a nation, perhaps somewhat tattered, but still living. A living people makes such enormous concessions on such fateful questions only when there is no hope left. Only when not a single breach is visible in the iron wall, only then do extreme groups lose their sway, and influence transfers to moderate groups. Only then would these moderate groups come to us with proposals for mutual concessions. And only then will moderates offer suggestions for compromise on practical questions like a guarantee against expulsion, or equality and national autonomy.

I am optimistic that they will indeed be granted satisfactory assurances and that both peoples, like good neighbors, can then live in peace. But the only path to such an agreement is the iron wall, that is to say the strengthening in Palestine of a government without any kind of Arab influence, that is to say one against which the Arabs will fight. In other words, for us the only path to an agreement in the future is an absolute refusal of any attempts at an agreement now.

Source: First published in Russian under the title *O Zheleznoi Stene* in Rassvyet, November 4, 1923. Published in English in the *Jewish Herald* (South Africa), November 26, 1937.

139. Shah Reza Pahlavi and the Roosevelt Administration (August–October 1938)

Introduction

In 1938 Wallace Murray, chief of the U.S. State Department's Division of Near Eastern Affairs who had represented the United States in Tehran in 1924, toured the Near East. Among those leaders he met was Shah Reza Pahlavi of Iran, whom he had known when Pahlavi was prime minister of Iran rather than its monarch. The two men had a lengthy interview during which the shah highlighted his efforts to modernize Iran, comparing these to the New Deal reforms launched by U.S. president Franklin D. Roosevelt in the 1930s. Murray arrived bearing a letter from Roosevelt that praised the shah's construction of a Trans-Iranian Railroad and his recent conclusion of a nonaggression treaty with several neighboring powers. Murray returned to Washington with a reciprocal letter from the shah to Roosevelt. These expressions of mutual goodwill did not suffice to maintain the shah in power during World War II, when his relative imperviousness to Allied demands for support from Iran led Great Britain and the Soviet Union to take over the country's government and eventually force the shah to abdicate in favor of his young son.

Documents

The Chargé in Iran (Moose) to the Secretary of State

Tehran, October 6, 1938—2 p.m.
[Received October 7—11:35 a.m.]

106. Referring to the Legation's telegram No. 105 October 3 [2], noon. From Murray. The Shah received me this morning and the audience lasted nearly an hour to the astonishment of Palace and Foreign Office officials who had informed me that 15 minutes was the maximum that I might expect to remain with His Majesty.

The Shah opened the conversation by expressing his particular satisfaction that the President had seen fit to send me to Persia on the present visit since His Majesty felt I would be better able than any other to appreciate the significance of what has happened in Persia during the years since I was here.

The Shah listened attentively to the reading in Persian translation of the President's letter and expressed profuse thanks for the signed original which he said he expected to answer personally. He seemed particularly impressed with the specific references in the letter to his reforms and said he could observe that President's remarks represented his true sentiments. He added that he fully appreciated the greatness of President Roosevelt and the importance of his program of reform in the United States and could only regret that there was not a more general understanding in the United States of what he, the Shah, was endeavoring to do for Persia. (This was undoubtedly a veiled reference to the American press.) . . .

The above remarks offered a suitable occasion for me to explain to His Majesty the importance which the President attaches to his policy of the Good Neighbor which was evidenced by my present visit to Persia and by the cordial personal message with which the President had entrusted me for delivery in person to His Majesty. I assured the Shah that my Government and the people of my country entertain feelings of warmest regard for him personally and for the Persian people and I expressed the hope that the past might be forgotten and that we might look forward to a future of mutual trust in each other and fruitful cooperation. I referred in that connection to the substance of the Department's triple priority circular telegram of September 27 requesting Persian cooperation during the Czechoslovak crisis and it was clear that our action in that instance had been pleasing to the Shah.

Realizing the pride which the Shah takes in the progress of his program of modernization and reform I took occasion repeatedly during the audience to compare the old Persia that I had known nearly 14 years ago with the new Pahlavi Iran of Reza Shah and stated that even the progress of reform in Turkey had not impressed me more than that in Iran. This remark led the Shah to compare the problems of Persia with those of Turkey and quite properly to state that the difficulties facing him when he started his reforms in Iran were much greater than those facing Atatürk in Turkey by reason of the dark forces of religious fanaticism that were far more powerful and hostile to progress here than they had ever been in Turkey.

As an example of what he had been up against he cited the killing of Vice Consul Imbrie by a fanatic mob in 1924 which he said had been a cause of deep sorrow and humiliation to him personally and to the Persian people. The fact that Reza Shah mentioned the Imbrie incident at all was most surprising but it was gratifying to note that his remarks were not tinged with the slightest sign of resentment or bitterness which I am sure was in the first instance feared by Foreign Office officials as a possible result of my visit.

During the course of the conversation I took the opportunity to refer to the Crown Prince in complimentary terms and to his recent betrothal. The Shah immediately sent for the Prince and presented him.

Before terminating the audience the Shah said he wanted me to feel at home during my stay in Iran and turning to the Acting Foreign Minister who was present instructed him to render me every assistance and to hold himself in readiness for any further conversations I might wish to have at the Foreign Office. I assume that this was intended by His Majesty to authorize his officials to discuss freely with me matters of concern to our two Governments at this time including of course that of diplomatic relations. Since the Moslem weekend started at noon today and lasts until Saturday the Acting Foreign Minister has set Saturday morning for our next conversation which I shall report in due course.

As an obvious indication of the Shah's good will the Government is giving a luncheon in my honor on Sunday and I shall return the honor on Monday.

I may say in conclusion that contrary to current rumors of the Shah's bad state of health and decrepitude I found him in excellent physical shape and quite as alert mentally as when I had much to do with him in 1924. [Murray.]

Moose

President Roosevelt to the Shah of Iran (Reza Shah Pahlavi)

Washington, August 12, 1938.

Your Majesty: I am very happy to avail myself of this opportunity to convey to You in this manner my cordial greetings and an expression of my warm personal regard.

It is with the greatest interest that I have followed the important and far-reaching reforms that have been introduced in Iran under Your Majesty's inspiration and guidance for the improvement of conditions, both social and economic, among Your people. And only recently I have been pleased to learn that the great Trans-Iranian railway linking the Persian Gulf with the Caspian Sea is nearing completion. The accomplishment of this difficult feat of engineering planned by Your Majesty has aroused admiration in the United States, where we had similar obstacles to overcome when we were constructing our great railroad lines spanning the continent from the Atlantic to the Pacific Ocean.

As Your Majesty is doubtless aware, we, also, are faced with problems of a social and economic nature which we are making vigorous efforts to solve through a broad program of reform, which I am happy to say has made steady progress. We are endeavoring at the same time to understand the needs and problems of other peoples as well, and to enlist their cooperation. This we call the policy of the Good Neighbor and it has become the guiding principle in our relations with other countries of the world.

I recall in this connection the fine leadership or Your Majesty in bringing about the conclusion of the Saadabad Pact in 1937, which will, I feel sure, bring lasting benefits to the peoples of the Near and Middle East.

For long years the most cordial and sympathetic relations have existed between our two peoples and the recollection of the confidence reposed in us in past times by the Iranian people is a gratifying one. I am therefore confident that Your Majesty shares with me the desire that our relations shall become steadily closer, not only for the mutual benefit of our two countries, but also in order that we may make a common contribution to the well-being of mankind.

In bidding Your Majesty farewell, I desire to assure you again of my most friendly sentiments and to express my earnest wishes for the welfare and prosperity of the Iranian people.

Your good friend,

Franklin D. Roosevelt

The Shah of Iran (Reza Shah Pahlavi) to President Roosevelt [Translation]

Honorable Friend: We were happy to receive your letter of August 12, 1938. The sentiments you expressed in the letter and through Mr. Wallace Murray have been a source of utmost pleasure and gratitude. Although we have asked Mr. Murray to convey to Your Excellency Our thanks and special greetings, nevertheless We are pleased to repeat those feelings in this letter. We personally as well as the Iranian people value, in the same degree as expressed by Your Excellency, the maintenance and strengthening of the friendship which for long years has existed between the two countries and are interested in having it continue.

In the same manner that Your Excellency has followed the efforts exerted in our country for the achievement of reforms, making particular reference to the happy completion of the Trans-Iranian railway this year, We also have been fully aware of the efforts made by the American people under Your Excellency's guidance towards economic and social reforms, and We admire and appreciate the progress thus achieved for the American people notwithstanding all the difficulties. We have no doubt that you will with equal success achieve the remainder of the program which you have before you.

Understanding the needs and problems of other nations which in your letter you have called the policy of Good-Neighbor has always been Our aim also and we have endeavored in our relations with other nations to take into consideration the principles of humanity and to settle differences in a peaceful manner. It was in the spirit of this policy that we eliminated frontier and other differences with our neighbors and succeeded in concluding the Saadabad Pact. And We hope that this pact will not only prove to be effective in maintaining peace in the Near East, but with the extension of this spirit of good will and cooperation, will make a contribution to world peace of which the American Government is an earnest advocate.

It has always been our intention to maintain warm friendly relations with the American people, and we assure Your Excellency that the Imperial Government will not spare any effort to cooperate (with your Government) to attain this aim.

In concluding this letter we renew our sentiments of friendship and good will and express our most sincere wishes for the happiness and success of Your Excellency and the American people.

Your sincere friend

Reza

Pahlavi Palace, October 9, 1938 (Mehrmah, 17, 1317).

Source: U.S. Department of State, *Foreign Relations of the United States: Diplomatic Papers 1938*, Vol. 2, *The British Commonwealth, Europe, Near East, and Africa* (Washington, DC: U.S. Government Printing Office, 1954), 734–735, 739–742.

140. The Arab Revolt in Palestine: Bernard Montgomery to Sir Ronald "Bill" Adam (December 4, 1938)

Introduction

In November 1938, British major general Bernard Montgomery took over as general officer Commanding the Eighth Division of the British Army, stationed in northern Palestine. The major task facing him was to deal with the Arab Revolt that had begun in 1936 and was still continuing. Shortly after his arrival, Montgomery wrote to an influential friend in the War Office, Lieutenant General Sir Ronald "Bill" Adam, deputy chief of the Imperial General Staff, giving his detailed views of the situation in Palestine following an extended in-depth inspection tour. Montgomery recommended a policy of ruthless repression of the Arab uprising. He described how he and his colleague Major General Richard O'Connor, commander of the Seventh Division, which was responsible for southern Palestine, were already pursuing measures to implement this.

Document

You asked me for my views on the situation here. I have been terribly busy since I arrived and have not been able to write earlier, but I will try and set out the situation as I see it.

1. When I arrived in Palestine I decided that I did not want to take over operational and administrative control of the 8th Div until I had toured the whole Divl area and studied the situation and the problem.

Force HQ agreed to this. So I sent my 'Q' staff to Haifa to get our HQ ready, and I set out with my 'GI' to tour the 8 Div area. This area includes Samaria, Galilee, and the whole of the frontier district. During my tour I visited every single military garrison, detachment and post in the area; interviewed every civil servant; and talked to every single British policeman. It was an immense task and it took me one week; I got up at 5.0 a.m. each morning and went to bed at midnight. My division is in 35 garrisons and detachments, but it was well worth while, and enabled me to take over operational control with a definite and formed policy.

2. Before leaving Jerusalem I said to Force HQ that I wanted the answer to the following question:

Is the campaign that is being waged against us a National movement, or is it a campaign that is being carried on by gangs of professional bandits? Obviously the policy to be adopted must depend on the answer to this question. Force HQ was quite clear that the campaign was definitely a national movement.

3. When I had got about halfway on my tour it began to be clear to me that the campaign was *not* a national movement. I am certain now that this view is correct.

The campaign against us is being waged by gangs of professional bandits; these constitute an Army, with a definite though somewhat crude organisation. There are three 'Army' Commanders and they take their orders from Damascus; there is little cohesion in the rebel forces and the esprit-de-corps is a 'gang' one.

A gang is anything from 50 to 150 men and each 'Army' commander controls the gangs in his area by means of sub-area commanders. There is no higher organization than the gang as far as is known.

The 'Army' commanders are very elusive and it will be difficult to catch them; we know where they keep their women, and that is about all. The gangs operate in the country and live in the hill areas. They move about from place to place and conscript the local peasants—against their will—and force them to take up arms against us; the peasants have to comply, since refusal means death and the destruction of their houses. The gang leaders also have agents in the towns, and by means of them they carry out assassinations and commit other acts of terrorism; this is very difficult to combat, especially in a place like Haifa with a population of over 100,000.

4. The net result is that the British Army in Palestine is at war with a rebel army which is one hundred per cent Arab.

If you now examine the feelings of the general public, including the peasantry, you find it is as follows:

The bulk of the Arab population of the country are 'fed up' with the whole thing; they are very short of food and are hustled about by both sides i.e. the British and rebel armies; they would like to see law and order restored; they would be quite content to live under the British mandate so long as Jewish immigration is limited to a fixed total (say of 500,000).

The Jewish population go on with their work as if there was no war on but they defend their own colonies stoutly with arms which we allow them to have for the purpose; the colonies are all protected by wire obstacles, powerful searchlights operate all night long, and there is a regular system of sentries and patrols in each colony by day and night.

5. The above gives a brief picture of the situation and having read so far I think it is important to realize that we are definitely at war. British soldiers are being killed and wounded in battle with the rebels every day. The enemy army wears uniform when operating by gangs and for movement about the country it resorts to civilian dress. The normal uniform in the North is a high neck polo sweater of a saffron colour, with riding boots and khaki trousers or breeches.

6. I think that what has been lacking out here has been any clear cut statement, defining the situation and saying what was to be done about it. I decided that I must issue such a statement of policy at once in my division so that all efforts would be directed along the same lines. Having briefly defined the situation as it appeared to me, I went on to give the tasks on which we would concentrate. They were as follows, in order of importance:

a) To hunt down and destroy the rebel armed gangs. They must be hunted relentlessly; when engaged in battle with them we must shoot to kill. We must not be on the defensive and act only when attacked; *we* must take the offensive and impose our will on the rebels. The next few weeks, before the winter rains set in, is an opportunity and during them we may well smash the rebel movement given a little luck. We must put forward our maximum effort *now* and concentrate on killing armed rebels in battle; this is the surest way to end the war.
b) To get the dwellers in urban areas, and the peasantry, on our side. To do this we must be scrupulously fair in our dealings with them. We want them to realize that they will always get a fair deal from the British army; but if they assist the rebels in any way they must expect to be treated as rebels; and anyone who takes up arms against us will certainly lose his life.
c) To prepare the police force to take over from us when the rebellion is crushed.

The police are working as soldiers. Large reinforcements are coming in and these are practically all ex-soldiers; they are fitted out in Jerusalem and then drafted straight out to their districts (I am referring to the British police, of whom there are to be some 3000).

It is the British police who will form the backbone of the future Palestine Police Force. They are now being used like soldiers, but we cannot stay here for ever and when we have restored law and order we shall want to hand over control to the police;

we have therefore got to help them to get back gradually to their duties as 'police.' They are under our orders and so we have a definite responsibility in the matter. In order to do this they must receive training; they require instruction in police duties and they must be able to speak Arabic.

The British police are now concentrated in the larger towns and on the Northern frontier; as their numbers increase we must aim at getting them out into the country areas working with our military detachments; it is the British police who will form the backbone of the mounted gendarmerie that will eventually be organized for the control of rural areas, and we must begin to fit them for this role.

1. I started off with this policy in the North and Dick O'Connor is doing much the same in the South. He and I are great personal friends and we are keeping in the closest touch. During the last week in my area the rebels have been brought to battle twice and dealt two smashing blows. On 28th November we cornered a gang of about 60 in the Carmel Range and killed fifty of them; they fought like wild beasts, knowing that they were 'for it' and in one case there was a hand-to-hand conflict between a Corporal of the Irish Fusiliers and an Arab in which the Arab was finally killed. All the killed men were armed and dressed in uniform. Present with the gang was ABU DORRAH, the 'Rebel Army' Commander in the North; it is reported he was killed but we cannot definitely confirm this; the action took place in the afternoon and in the broadcast from Beyrouth that night it was stated he had been killed.

This is the real way to end the war, i.e. to kill the rebels and particularly their leaders. To do this we must take the offensive and hunt them relentlessly.

2. Now for a few comments on things in general. I think there have been 3 main troubles out here.

The first one has been the very high degree of centralisation of everything at Force HQ. Nothing could be done without asking permission; no operation could take place until it had been approved by Force HQ; forecasts of operations a week ahead had to be sent in, thus prejudicing secrecy. In fact Force HQ tried to run the whole country in detail; the result was that they had no time for anything let alone to think, and the staff was frightfully hard worked.

Dick and I had to make it very clear that all this was to cease now that there were two divisional commanders to deal with instead of five infantry brigadiers. I had to do some very plain speaking on the subject! . . .

3. The young regimental officer out here is quite splendid. Of course it is magnificent training; it is a wonderful thing to visit a post of 50 men commanded by a 2/Lieut of one year's service; he will tell you all about his post, his role, and how he carries it out; he has a wireless set and on receiving his orders to act suddenly on some intelligence received, he leaves a defensive garrison in the post and sallies forth with the remainder by day or night to play his part in the operation that is being staged.

It makes a man of him; officers who are supposed to be not much good develop surprisingly good qualities when forced to act on their own in this way.

To my mind it shows that the type of officer we are now taking into the army through our military colleges is of the right type, and just what we want. You could not have a better test than this one out here, and they are coming through it without blemish.

Similarly with the soldier. The British soldier out here is magnificent; there is nothing really curious about this as he always is magnificent anywhere, but this is rather a curious sort of war; you don't often see your enemy but all the time you are exposed to the risk of being murdered or blown up.

It is amazing what a difference it makes to a company or a battalion after it has had a good battle with the rebels in open fight. All the men are on their toes after such a battle and that unit is never likely after that to be caught at a disadvantage by the rebels.

4. The Bren-gun is superb; it is far-and-away superior to the Lewis gun and never stops or becomes clogged up. The rebels dislike it intensely because of its power of maintaining fire. All officers and men speak of it in terms of the greatest admiration.

5. I am strongly of the opinion that the troops out here should be given a medal for Palestine. They are engaged in fighting a rebel army which wears uniform and has a definite organisation. Soldiers are killed and wounded in battle with the rebels; the troops having a very hard time; the work is very hard and arduous, and many of my men get only one night in bed out of two; they are frequently out in the field in operations against the rebels for 72 hours at a stretch.

A medal does not cost very much and the resulting uplift among the troops would be wonderful.

6. . . . .

7. For the future I am full of hope. The situation is definitely in hand and there are very distinct signs that the rebel movement is crumbling. The surest way to complete this crumbling process is to direct all our energies *now* on killing the armed rebels.

I have taken off my brigadiers all the administrative details with which they were cluttered up and have loosed them on the task of killing rebels.

'Dreadnought' Harrison and Jack Evetts require no urging in this respect! During the ten days ending today we have killed a hundred in my divisional areas; there are probably more but I take account only of dead bodies actually collected.

8. There will be some very difficult problems ahead of us when the actual rebellion is crushed. But one thing at a time; for the present I am concentrating on killing the rebels.

9. This letter is private and personal and I know you will treat it as such. I have made certain observations which I would not normally make but you asked me for my views and I have given them at some length.

Source: Miscellaneous War Office file (WO 216/111), UK National Archives, in Nigel Hamilton, *Monty: The Making of a General, 1887–1942* (New York: McGraw-Hill, 1981), 291–297.

141. Haj Amin al-Husseini: Summons to a Jihad against Britain (May 10, 1941)

Introduction

British efforts to conciliate Arab leaders in Palestine during the 1930s proved unavailing. In 1921 Haj Amin al-Husseini became the grand mufti of Jerusalem, the preeminent Islamic religious figure in Palestine, a position he won in part thanks to British influence. Al-Husseini soon became one of the strongest voices urging Arab opposition to the growing Jewish presence in Palestine, a major force behind the Arab riots of 1929 and the Arab Revolt of 1936–1939. Al-Husseini was a leading member of the Higher Arab Committee that directed the Arab Revolt. In the autumn of 1937 after he and others in the group were implicated in the murder of the British high commissioner for Galilee, al-Husseini fled Palestine for Lebanon and then Iraq. He was among those who helped to plan the May 1941 coup whereby four Iraqi generals overthrew the pro-British regent of Iraq and installed a military government friendly to Germany in the hope that this would allow them to win full Iraqi independence from Britain, as opposed to the limited independence granted in 1937. On May 10, 1941, al-Husseini also proclaimed a fatwa (religious ruling) calling on Muslims throughout the world to launch a jihad, or holy war, against Britain and British imperialism. His message was broadcast throughout the Middle East and Europe by Iraqi and German radio stations. Six months later in November 1941, al-Husseini met with German chancellor Adolf Hitler, an encounter in which the grand mufti expressed his strong support for Hitler's anti-Jewish policies and requested German aid for the Arabs in their efforts to win complete independence from Western colonial rule. Hitler promised that when the military situation permitted, he would turn German forces to the task of eliminating Jewish elements in the Middle East, particularly Palestine. Al-Husseini was reputedly related to the later Palestinian leader Yasser Arafat, and the grand mufti's views allegedly had a considerable influence on Arafat's thinking.

Document

In the name of Merciful and Almighty God.

I invite all my Moslem brothers throughout the whole world to join in the Jihad for Allah, for the defense of Islam and her lands against her enemy. O Faithful, obey and respond to my call.

O Moslems!

Proud 'Iraq has placed herself in the vanguard of this Holy Struggle, and has thrown herself against the strongest enemy of Islam certain that God will grant her victory.

The English have tried to seize this Arab-Moslem land, but she has risen, full of dignity and pride to defend her safety, to fight for her honor and to safeguard her integrity. 'Iraq fights the tyranny which has always had as its aim the destruction of Islam in every land. It is the duty of all Moslems to aid 'Iraq in her struggle and to seek every means to fight the enemy, the traditional traitor in every age and every situation.

Whoever knows the history of the East has everywhere seen the hand of the English working to destroy the Ottoman Empire and to divide the Arab countries. British politics toward the Arab people is masked under a veil of Hypocrisy. The minute she sees her chance, England squeezes the prostrate country in her Imperialist grasp, adding futile justifications. She creates discord and division within a country and while feeding it in secret openly she assumes the role of advisor and trusted friend.

The time when England could deceive the peoples of the East is passed. The Arab Nation and the Moslem people have awakened to fight British domination. The English have overthrown the Ottoman Empire, have destroyed Moslem rule in India, inciting one community against another; they stifled the Egyptian awakening, the dream of Mohammed Ali, colonizing Egypt for half a century. They took advantage of the weakening of the Ottoman Empire to stretch out their hands and use every sort of trick to take possession of many Arab countries as happened to Aden, the 9 Districts, the Hadramut, Oman, Masqat and the Emirates of the Persian Gulf and Transjordania.

The vivid proof of the imperialistic designs of the British is to be found in Moslem Palestine which, although promised by England to Sherif Hussein has had to submit to the outrageous infiltration of Jews, shameful politics designed to divide Arab-Moslem countries of Asia from those of Africa. In Palestine the English have committed unheard of barbarisms; among others, they have profaned the el-Aqsa Mosque and have declared the most unyielding war against Islam, both in deed and in word. The Prime Minister at that time told Parliament that the world would never see peace as long as the Koran existed. What hatred against Islam is stronger than that which publicly declares the Sacred Koran an enemy of human kind? Should such sacrilege go unpunished?

After the dissolution of the Moslem Empire in India and of the Ottoman Caliphate, England, adhering to the policy of Gladstone, pursued her work of destruction to Islam depriving many Islamic States both in the East and in the West of their freedom and independence. The number of Moslems who today live under the rule of England and invoke liberation from their terrible yoke exceeds 220,000,000.

Therefore I invite you, O Brothers, to join in the War for God to preserve Islam, your independence and your lands from English aggression. I invite you to bring all your weight to bear in helping 'Iraq that she may throw off the shame that torments her. O Heroic 'Iraq, God is with Thee, the Arab Nation and the Moslem World are solidly with Thee in Thy Holy Struggle!

Source: "The Palestinian Grand Mufti Haj Amin el Husseini: Fatwa—Holy War against Britain—1941," Zionism and Israel Information Center, www.zionism-israel.com. Reprinted with permission.

142. General Bernard Montgomery: Message to the Troops Following El Alamein (November 11, 1942)

Introduction

The Second Battle of El Alamein, fought in late October 1942, was a major British victory, in many respects one of the great turning points of World War II. In fierce fighting that continued for more than a week, the new British commander in chief of the Eighth Army, General Bernard Montgomery, routed the combined German and Italian forces of the charismatic German field marshal Erwin Rommel. Montgomery, an inspirational military leader, ascribed much of his army's success to rigorous training and strict discipline together with the deliberate inculcation of enthusiasm for the coming battle among all ranks from top officers down to ordinary soldiers. The personal message he sent to his entire army in the aftermath of the Battle of El Alamein was a demonstration of his down-to-earth, straightforward style of leadership.

Document

EIGHTH ARMY

    PERSONAL MESSAGE FROM THE ARMY COMMANDER

    To Be Read Out to All Troops

1. When we began the Battle of Egypt on 23 October I said that together we would hit the Germans and Italians for six right out of North Africa.

We have made a very good start and to-day, 12 Nov., there are no German and Italian soldiers on Egyptian territory except prisoners.

In three weeks we have completely smashed the German and Italian Army, and pushed the fleeing remnants out of Egypt, having advanced ourselves nearly 300 miles up to and beyond the frontier.

2. The following enemy formations have ceased to exist as effective fighting formations:

Panzer Army	15 Panzer Div.
	21 Panzer Div.
	90 Light Div.
	164 Light Div.
10 Italian Corps.	Brescia Div.
	Pavia Div.
	Folgore Div.
20 Italian Corps.	Ariete Armd. Div.
	Littorio Armd. Div.
	Trieste Div.
21 Italian Corps.	Trento Div.
	Bologna Div.

The prisoners captured number 30,000, including nine Generals.

The amount of tanks, artillery, anti-tank guns, transport, aircraft, etc., destroyed or captured is so great that the enemy is completely crippled.

3. This is a very fine performance and I want, first, to thank you all for the way you responded to my call and rallied to the task. I feel that our great victory was brought about by the good fighting qualities of the soldiers of the Empire rather than by anything I may have been able to do myself.

4. Secondly, I know you will all realise how greatly we were helped in our task by the R.A.F. [Royal Air Force]. We could not have done it without their splendid help and co-operation. I have thanked the R.A.F. warmly on your behalf.

5. Our task is not finished yet; the Germans are out of Egypt but there are still some left in North Africa. There is some good hunting to be had further to the West, in Libya; and our leading troops are now in Libya ready to begin. And this time, having reached Bengasi [sic] and beyond we shall not come back.

6. On with the task, and good hunting to you all. As in all pursuits some have to remain behind to start with; but we shall all be in it before the finish.

12.11.42
    B. L. Montgomery
    General,
    G.O.C.-in-C., Eighth Army

Source: Nigel Hamilton, *Master of the Battlefield: Monty's War Years, 1942–1944* (New York: McGraw-Hill, 1983), 51–52. Reprinted with permission from Nigel Hamilton.

143. The Declaration of the Establishment of the State of Israel (May 14, 1948)

Introduction

On May 14, 1948, a few hours before the withdrawal of British troops from the Palestine mandate, the National Council, consisting of representatives of Palestine's Jewish inhabitants and the Zionists, met in Tel Aviv and approved the declaration of independence of the new State of Israel, or Eretz Israel. The declaration began by recalling the historic ties of the Jewish people to the land of Israel and recounted the history of more than 50 years of Zionist efforts, beginning with Theodor Herzl's establishment of the First Zionist Congress and the Balfour Declaration, to establish the new state. The declaration invoked the sufferings of Jews in Europe during the Nazi Holocaust and the efforts of Jewish fighters during World War II. After recalling the endorsement that the United Nations (UN) had given to the creation of a Jewish state, the authors proclaimed the existence of the new State of Israel. From midnight that evening, the declaration established the Provisional State Council, based on the existing National Council, to hold authority until elections could be held under a constitution, still to be drawn up. The new State of Israel declared itself ready to welcome all Jews as immigrants, work closely with the UN, and cooperate harmoniously with the Arab inhabitants of Palestine and with all Arab states. The declaration proclaimed Israel's intention of living in peace with all. The authors of this declaration nonetheless undoubtedly knew that the withdrawal of British troops would prove to be the signal for immediate attack by the armed forces of Transjordan, Egypt, Syria, and other neighboring Arab countries and that the attainment of peace would depend on Israel's ability to wield the sword.

Document

ERETZ-ISRAEL [(Hebrew)—the Land of Israel, Palestine] was the birthplace of the Jewish people. Here their spiritual, religious and political identity was shaped. Here they first attained to statehood, created cultural values of national and universal significance and gave to the world the eternal Book of Books.

After being forcibly exiled from their land, the people kept faith with it throughout their Dispersion and never ceased to pray and hope for their return to it and for the restoration in it of their political freedom.

Impelled by this historic and traditional attachment, Jews strove in every successive generation to re-establish themselves in their ancient homeland. In recent decades they returned in their masses. Pioneers, *ma'pilim* [(Hebrew)—immigrants coming to Eretz-Israel in defiance of restrictive legislation] and defenders, they made deserts bloom, revived the Hebrew language, built villages and towns, and created a thriving community controlling its own economy and culture, loving peace but knowing how to defend itself, bringing the blessings of progress to all the country's inhabitants, and aspiring towards independent nationhood.

In the year 5657 (1897), at the summons of the spiritual father of the Jewish State, Theodore Herzl, the First Zionist Congress convened and proclaimed the right of the Jewish people to national rebirth in its own country.

This right was recognized in the Balfour Declaration of the 2nd November, 1917, and reaffirmed in the Mandate of the League of Nations which, in particular, gave international sanction to the historic connection between the Jewish people and Eretz-Israel and to the right of the Jewish people to rebuild its National Home.

The catastrophe which recently befell the Jewish people—the massacre of millions of Jews in Europe—was another clear demonstration of the urgency of solving the problem of its homelessness by re-establishing in Eretz-Israel the Jewish State, which would open the gates of the homeland wide to every Jew and confer upon the Jewish people the status of a fully privileged member of the comity of nations.

Survivors of the Nazi holocaust in Europe, as well as Jews from other parts of the world, continued to migrate to Eretz-Israel, undaunted by difficulties, restrictions and dangers, and never ceased to assert their right to a life of dignity, freedom and honest toil in their national homeland.

In the Second World War, the Jewish community of this country contributed its full share to the struggle of the freedom- and peace-loving nations against the forces of Nazi wickedness and, by the blood of its soldiers and its war effort, gained the right to be reckoned among the peoples who founded the United Nations.

On the 29th November, 1947, the United Nations General Assembly passed a resolution calling for the establishment of a Jewish State in Eretz-Israel; the General Assembly required the inhabitants of Eretz-Israel to take such steps as were necessary on their part for the implementation of that resolution. This recognition by the United Nations of the right of the Jewish people to establish their State is irrevocable.

This right is the natural right of the Jewish people to be masters of their own fate, like all other nations, in their own sovereign State.

ACCORDINGLY WE, MEMBERS OF THE PEOPLE'S COUNCIL, REPRESENTATIVES OF THE JEWISH COMMUNITY OF ERETZ-ISRAEL AND OF THE ZIONIST MOVEMENT, ARE HERE ASSEMBLED ON THE DAY OF THE TERMINATION OF THE BRITISH MANDATE OVER ERETZ-ISRAEL AND, BY VIRTUE OF OUR NATURAL AND HISTORIC RIGHT AND ON THE STRENGTH OF THE RESOLUTION OF THE UNITED NATIONS GENERAL ASSEMBLY, HEREBY DECLARE THE ESTABLISHMENT OF A JEWISH STATE IN ERETZ-ISRAEL, TO BE KNOWN AS THE STATE OF ISRAEL.

WE DECLARE that, with effect from the moment of the termination of the Mandate being tonight, the eve of Sabbath, the 6th Iyar, 5708 (15th May, 1948), until the establishment of the elected, regular authorities of the State in accordance with the Constitution which shall be adopted by the Elected Constituent Assembly not later than the 1st October 1948, the People's Council shall act as a Provisional Council of State, and its executive organ, the People's Administration, shall be the Provisional Government of the Jewish State, to be called "Israel."

THE STATE OF ISRAEL will be open for Jewish immigration and for the Ingathering of the Exiles; it will foster the development of the country for the benefit of all its inhabitants; it will be based on freedom, justice and peace as envisaged by the prophets of Israel; it will ensure complete equality of social and political rights to all its inhabitants irrespective of religion, race or sex; it will guarantee freedom of religion, conscience, language, education and culture; it will safeguard the Holy Places of all religions; and it will be faithful to the principles of the Charter of the United Nations.

THE STATE OF ISRAEL is prepared to cooperate with the agencies and representatives of the United Nations in implementing the resolution of the General Assembly of the 29th November, 1947, and will take steps to bring about the economic union of the whole of Eretz-Israel.

WE APPEAL to the United Nations to assist the Jewish people in the building-up of its State and to receive the State of Israel into the comity of nations.

WE APPEAL—in the very midst of the onslaught launched against us now for months—to the Arab inhabitants of the State of Israel to preserve peace and participate in the upbuilding of the State on the basis of full and equal citizenship and due representation in all its provisional and permanent institutions.

WE EXTEND our hand to all neighbouring states and their peoples in an offer of peace and good neighbourliness, and appeal to them to establish bonds of cooperation and mutual help with the sovereign Jewish people settled in its own land. The State of Israel is prepared to do its share in a common effort for the advancement of the entire Middle East.

WE APPEAL to the Jewish people throughout the Diaspora to rally round the Jews of Eretz-Israel in the tasks of immigration and upbuilding and to stand by them in the great struggle for the realization of the age-old dream—the redemption of Israel.

PLACING OUR TRUST IN THE "ROCK OF ISRAEL," WE AFFIX OUR SIGNATURES TO THIS PROCLAMATION AT THIS SESSION OF THE PROVISIONAL COUNCIL OF STATE, ON THE SOIL OF THE HOMELAND, IN THE CITY OF TEL-AVIV, ON THIS SABBATH EVE, THE 5TH DAY OF IYAR, 5708 (14TH MAY, 1948).

David Ben-Gurion
Daniel Auster
Mordekhai Bentov
Yitzchak Ben Zvi
Eliyahu Berligne
Fritz Bernstein
Rabbi Wolf Gold
Meir Grabovsky
Yitzchak Gruenbaum
Dr. Abraham Granovsky
Eliyahu Dobkin
Meir Wilner-Kovner
Zerach Wahrhaftig
Herzl Vardi
Rachel Cohen
Rabbi Kalman Kahana
Saadia Kobashi
Rabbi Yitzchak Meir Levin
Meir David Loewenstein
Zvi Luria
Golda Myerson
Nachum Nir
Zvi Segal

Rabbi Yehuda Leib Hacohen Fishman
David Zvi Pinkas
Aharon Zisling
Moshe Kolodny
Eliezer Kaplan
Abraham Katznelson
Felix Rosenblueth
David Remez
Berl Repetur
Mordekhai Shattner
Ben Zion Sternberg
Bekhor Shitreet
Moshe Shapira
Moshe Shertok

Source: The Declaration of the Establishment of the State of Israel, May 14, 1948, Israel Ministry of Foreign Affairs, http://www.mfa.gov.il/MFA.

144. Arab League Statement (May 15, 1948)

Introduction

The same night that British forces withdrew from the Palestine mandate and the State of Israel was proclaimed, Arab League forces from Egypt, Syria, Lebanon, Iraq, and Transjordan invaded the new state. The Egyptian foreign minister informed the United Nations (UN) Security Council that their purpose in doing so was to restore law and order. On May 15, 1948, the Arab League issued a statement proclaiming that its forces were entering Palestine to protect the rights of its Arab inhabitants. The statement included a lengthy historical exposition of the Arab case and condemned the British for issuing the Balfour Declaration and allowing large numbers of Jews to enter and settle in Palestine over the previous 30 years. The Arab states demanded that Palestine be governed by Arabs. They argued that a state of disorder, which might spread to Palestine's neighbors, currently prevailed there, with no existing governmental authority capable of restoring order, and that they were intervening to redress this situation and establish a competent government and an independent Palestinian state.

Document

1. Palestine was part of the former Ottoman Empire, subject to its law and represented in its parliament. The overwhelming majority of the population of Palestine were Arabs. There was in it a small minority of Jews that enjoyed the same rights and bore the same responsibilities as the [other] inhabitants, and did not suffer any ill-treatment on account of its religious beliefs. The holy places were inviolable and the freedom of access to them was guaranteed.

2. The Arabs have always asked for their freedom and independence. On the outbreak of the First World War, and when the Allies declared that they were fighting for the liberation of peoples, the Arabs joined them and fought on their side with a view to realizing their national aspirations and obtaining their independence. England pledged herself to recognize the independence of the Arab countries in Asia, including Palestine. The Arabs played a remarkable part in the achievement of final victory and the Allies have admitted this.

3. In 1917 England issued a declaration in which she expressed her sympathy with the establishment of a national home for the Jews in Palestine. When the Arabs knew of this they protested against it, but England reassured them by affirming to them that this would not prejudice the right of their countries to freedom and independence or affect the political status of the Arabs in Palestine. Notwithstanding the legally void character of this declaration, it was interpreted by England to aim at no more than

the establishment of a spiritual centre for the Jews in Palestine, and to conceal no ulterior political aims, such as the establishment of a Jewish State. The same thing was declared by the Jewish leaders.

4. When the war came to an end England did not keep her promise. Indeed, the Allies placed Palestine under the Mandate system and entrusted England with [the task of carrying it out], in accordance with a document providing for the administration of the country, in the interests of its inhabitants and its preparation for the independence which the Covenant of the League of Nations recognized that Palestine was qualified to have.

5. England administered Palestine in a manner which enabled the Jews to flood it with immigrants and helped them to settle in the country. [This was so] notwithstanding the fact that it was proved that the density of the population in Palestine had exceeded the economic capacity of the country to absorb additional immigrants. England did not pay regard to the interests or rights of the Arab inhabitants, the lawful owners of the country. Although they used to express, by various means, their concern and indignation on account of this state of affairs which was harmful to their being and their future, they [invariably] were met by indifference, imprisonment and oppression.

6. As Palestine is an Arab country, situated in the heart of the Arab countries and attached to the Arab world by various ties—spiritual, historical, and strategic—the Arab countries, and even the Eastern ones, governments as well as peoples, have concerned themselves with the problem of Palestine and have raised it to the international level; [they have also raised the problem] with England, asking for its solution in accordance with the pledges made and with democratic principles. The Round Table Conference was held in London in 1939 in order to discuss the Palestine question and to arrive at the just solution thereof. The Governments of the Arab States participated in [this conference] and asked for the preservation of the Arab character of Palestine and the proclamation of its independence. This conference ended with the issue of a White Paper in which England defined her policy towards Palestine, recognized its independence, and undertook to set up the institutions that would lead to its exercise of the characteristics of [this independence]. She [also] declared that her obligations concerning the establishment of a Jewish national home had been fulfilled, since that home had actually been established. But the policy defined in the [White] Paper was not carried out. This, therefore, led to the deterioration of the situation and the aggravation of matters contrary to the interests of the Arabs.

7. While the Second World War was still in progress, the Governments of the Arab States began to hold consultations regarding the reinforcement of their cooperation and the increasing of the means of their collaboration and their solidarity, with a view to safeguarding their present and their future and to participating in the erection of the edifice of the new world on firm foundations. Palestine had its [worthy] share of consideration and attention in these conversations. These conversations led to the establishment of the League of Arab States as an instrument for the cooperation of the Arab States for their security, peace and well-being.

The Pact of the League of Arab States declared that Palestine has been an independent country since its separation from the Ottoman Empire, but the manifestations of this independence have been suppressed due to reasons which were out of the control of its inhabitants. The establishment of the United Nations shortly afterwards was an event about which the Arabs had the greatest hopes. Their belief in the ideals on which that organization was based made them participate in its establishment and membership.

8. Since then the Arab League and its [member] Governments have not spared any effort to pursue any course, whether with the Mandatory Power or with the United Nations, in order to bring about a just solution of the Palestine problem; [a solution] based upon true democratic principles and compatible with the provisions of the Covenant of the League of Nations and the [Charter] of the United Nations, and which would [at the same time] be lasting, guarantee peace and security in the country and prepare it for progress and prosperity. But Zionist claims were always an obstacle to finding such a solution, [as the Zionists], having prepared themselves with armed forces, strongholds and fortifications to face by force anyone standing in their way, publicly declared [their intention] to establish a Jewish State.

9. When the General Assembly of the United Nations issued, on November 29, 1947, its recommendation concerning the solution of the Palestine problem, on the basis of the establishment of an Arab State and of another Jewish [state] in [Palestine] together with placing the City of Jerusalem under the trusteeship of the United Nations, the Arab States drew attention to the injustice implied in this solution [affecting] the right of the people of Palestine to immediate independence, as well as democratic principles and the provisions of the Covenant of the League of Nations and [the Charter] of the United Nations. [These States also] declared the Arabs' rejection of [that solution] and that it would not be possible to carry it out by peaceful means, and that its forcible imposition would constitute a threat to peace and security in this area.

The warnings and expectations of the Arab States have, indeed, proved to be true, as disturbances were soon widespread throughout Palestine. The Arabs clashed with the Jews, and the two [parties] proceeded to fight each other and shed each other's blood. Whereupon the United Nations began to realize the danger of recommending the partition [of Palestine] and is still looking for a way out of this state of affairs.

10. Now that the British mandate over Palestine has come to an end, without there being a legitimate constitutional authority in the country, which would safeguard the maintenance of security and respect for law and which would protect the lives and properties of the inhabitants, the Governments of the Arab States declare the following:

First: That the rule of Palestine should revert to its inhabitants, in accordance with the provisions of the Covenant of the League of Nations and [the Charter] of the United Nations and that [the Palestinians] should alone have the right to determine their future.

Second: Security and order in Palestine have become disrupted. The Zionist aggression resulted in the exodus of more than a quarter of a million of its Arab inhabitants from their homes and in their taking refuge in the neighbouring Arab countries.

The events which have taken place in Palestine have unmasked the aggressive intentions and the imperialist designs of the Zionists, including the atrocities committed by them against the peace-loving Arab inhabitants, especially in Dayr Yasin, Tiberias and others. Nor have they respected the inviolability of consuls, as they have attacked the consulates of the Arab States in Jerusalem. After the termination of the British mandate over Palestine the British authorities are no longer responsible for security in the country, except to the degree affecting their withdrawing forces, and [only] in the areas in which these forces happen to be at the time of withdrawal as announced by [these authorities]. This state of affairs would render Palestine without any governmental machinery capable of restoring order and the rule of law to the country, and of protecting the lives and properties of the inhabitants.

Third: This state of affairs is threatening to spread to the neighbouring Arab countries, where feeling is running high because of the events in Palestine. The Governments of the Member States of the Arab League and the United Nations are exceedingly worried and deeply concerned about this state of affairs.

Fourth: These Governments had hoped that the United Nations would have succeeded in finding a peaceful and just solution of the problem of Palestine, in accordance with democratic principles and the provisions of the Covenant of the League of Nations and [the Charter] of the United Nations, so that peace, security and prosperity would prevail in this part of the world.

Fifth: The Governments of the Arab States, as members of the Arab League, a regional organization within the meaning of the provisions of Chapter VIII of the Charter of the United Nations, are responsible for maintaining peace and security in their area. These Governments view the events taking place in Palestine as a threat to peace and security in the area as a whole and [also] in each of them taken separately.

Sixth: Therefore, as security in Palestine is a sacred trust in the hands of the Arab States, and in order to put an end to this state of affairs and to prevent it from becoming aggravated or from turning into [a state of] chaos, the extent of which no one can foretell; in order to stop the spreading of disturbances and disorder in Palestine to the neighbouring Arab countries; in order to fill the gap brought about in the governmental machinery in Palestine as a result of the termination of the mandate and the non-establishment of a lawful successor authority, the Governments of the Arab States have found themselves compelled to intervene in Palestine solely in order to help its inhabitants restore peace and security and the rule of justice and law to their country, and in order to prevent bloodshed.

Seventh: The Governments of the Arab States recognize that the independence of Palestine, which has so far been suppressed by the British Mandate, has become an accomplished fact for the lawful inhabitants of Palestine. They alone, by virtue of their absolute sovereignty, have the right to provide their country with laws and governmental institutions. They alone should exercise the attributes of their independence, through their own means and without any kind of foreign interference, immediately after peace, security, and the rule of law have been restored to the country.

At that time the intervention of the Arab states will cease, and the independent State of Palestine will cooperate with the [other member] States of the Arab League in order to bring peace, security and prosperity to this part of the world.

The Governments of the Arab States emphasize, on this occasion, what they have already declared before the London Conference and the United Nations, that the only solution of the Palestine problem is the establishment of a unitary Palestinian State, in accordance with democratic principles, whereby its inhabitants will enjoy complete equality before the law, [and whereby] minorities will be assured of all the guarantees recognized in democratic constitutional countries and [whereby] the holy places will be preserved and the rights of access thereto guaranteed.

Eighth: The Arab States most emphatically declare that [their] intervention in Palestine was due only to these considerations and objectives, and that they aim at nothing more than to put an end to the prevailing conditions in [Palestine]. For this reason, they have great confidence that their action will have the support of the United Nations; [that it will be] considered as an action aiming at the realization of its aims and at promoting its principles, as provided for in its Charter.

Source: United Nations Security Council Official Records, S/745, May 15, 1948.

145. United Nations Press Release: General Lundstrom Gives an Eyewitness Account of Bernadotte's Death (September 18, 1948)

Introduction

With war between the Arab states and Israel in progress as soon as Israel was declared an independent state, the United Nations (UN) sought to mediate a settlement. The Swedish diplomat Count Folke Bernadotte was selected as negotiator. As fighting continued, in June 1948 he put forward a proposal for a federated Arab-Jewish state. After all sides rejected this, Bernadotte suggested that Palestine be partitioned into an independent Jewish state and Arab territories, which he suggested might be united with the emirate of Transjordan. The city of Jerusalem would be administered by an international authority. The government of Israel found both proposals unacceptable and rejected them. On September 17, 1948, three members of the extreme Zionist Jewish insurgent Lehi group, often known as the Stern Gang, fearing that the United Nations might pressure Israel to accept these terms, assassinated Bernadotte and a French military officer who was accompanying him. The two men were shot in Bernadotte's car on the streets of Jerusalem. General Aage Lundstrom, a Swedish officer serving as a UN military observer in Palestine, sent an eyewitness account of the murders to UN headquarters in Lake Success, New York.

Document

The following eyewitness account of General Aage Lundstrom of the killing of Count Bernadotte and Colonel Serot has been received today by the Secretary-General from Dr. Ralph Bunche, Chief of the UN Mission in Palestine. Colonel Lundstrom was seated in the rear of the Mediator's car at the time of the murder but escaped unhurt. This account was cabled to UN Headquarters at Lake Success from Paris.

145. United Nations Press Release: General Lundstrom Gives an Eyewitness Account of Bernadotte's Death

"I met Count Bernadotte in Beirut Thursday morning, 16 September, and went with him to Damascus, where we spent the night. We left Damascus Friday morning, the 17th, at 9:30 a.m., Arab time. On our way to Kollundia field, we received a message from Haifa to the effect that all aircraft landing at Kollundia would be fired on. As we had sent advance notice of arrival and received clearance, we discounted the warning as false, and landed at Kollundia without incident.

"At the airfield, we were met by UN observers Colonel Bonnot and Colonel Serot of France, and Major A. F. Petersens of Sweden. With Major Messart, Belgian driver, the Count, Commander Cox, Lieutenant Colonel Flach of Sweden, Major De Jeer of Sweden, and myself, we left the airfield to visit Brigadier Lash of the Arab Legion at Ramallah. The rest of Count Bernadotte's party were ordered to proceed to the American school to meet us there.

"Before we started, I was told that every other jeep or car was fired upon at Mandelbaum Gate. I then asked Count Bernadotte if it would not be wise to proceed from Ramallah or Latrun to Jerusalem. This route would take an hour longer but would be undoubtedly safer. Count Bernadotte answered: 'I would not do that. I have to take the same risks as my observers, and moreover, I think no one has the right to refuse us permission to pass through the lines. If I do not go, I will be admitting they have the right to prevent me from crossing the lines.' I agreed, and it was decided that after meeting with Brigadier Lash, we would return through the lines at Mandelbaum Gate.

"We then left to keep our appointment with Brigadier Lash. After the meeting, I asked Brigadier Lash for a guard to take us to the front lines, and received an armored car which met us on the way to the lines. En route, just past Kollundia, our car was fired on from a short distance (pistol shot). One bullet hit a disk of the rear wheel. We then arrived at the American school, where we collected the rest of the Count's staff, and proceeded to Mandelbaum Gate and on to the Y.M.C.A. without incident of any kind.

"During lunch, at the Y.M.C.A., the program for the afternoon was settled. Count Bernadotte was to see Dr. Joseph, Military Governor of the Jewish part of Jerusalem, at 6:30 p.m., and before that we were to visit the Government House and Agricultural School in the Red Cross area. Three cars were ordered, but I decided that only two would be permitted to pass the lines to the Red Cross area. One car was driven by Colonel Frank Begley, with Commander Cox (US) in the front seat, the Count, Colonel Serot and myself in the back seat. The other car was driven by Major Massart with the Jewish Liaison officer, Captain Hillman, Miss Wessel (Count Bernadotte's secretary), Lieutenant Colonel Flach and Major De Geer as passengers. We went first to the Government House. From the roof of the tower, Commander Cox pointed out different areas where there had been a lot of firing, front lines and neutral zone, etc.

"The question was raised about eighteen Jewish men who had been brought to the Agricultural School, while it was desired that still more should be brought in to clear up. Count Bernadotte would not allow that, of course, as it was against his decision. He asked Swiss Dr. Facel, representing the interest of the International Red Cross Committee of the Government House to come with us to the Agricultural School to speak with women in charge of the school. When we came to the Agricultural School, the woman in charge was away, and Commander Cox was notified about the terms of the agreement. He wanted to look at his papers in the Y.M.C.A. and the doctor was asked to come with us in order that we might get his opinion on how to deal with this situation. The doctor took his own Red Cross car and otherwise the order of the cars remained the same with the Count's car last in the convoy. We went from the neutral zone to the Jewish lines without incident across the check points and went on further into the New City.

"In the Katamon quarter, we were held up by a Jewish Army type jeep placed in a road block and filled with men in Jewish Army uniforms. At the same moment, I saw an armed man coming from this jeep. I took little notice of this because I merely thought it was another checkpoint. However, he put a Tommy gun through the open window on my side of the car, and fired point blank at Count Bernadotte and Colonel Serot. I also heard shots fired from other points, and there was considerable confusion. The Jewish liaison officer came running to our car and told Mr. Begley, who was at that time outside the car, to drive away as quickly as possible. In the meantime, the man was still firing.

"Colonel Serot fell in the seat in back of me, and I saw at once that he was dead. Count Bernadotte bent forward, and I thought at the time he was trying to get cover. I asked him: 'Are you wounded?' He nodded, and fell back. I helped him to lie down in the car. I now understood that he was severely wounded; there was a considerable amount of blood on his clothes, mainly around the heart. By this time, the Jewish liaison officer had got into the car, and was urging Begley to drive quickly to Hadassah Hospital, which was only a short distance away. I have the impression that the Jewish liaison officer did everything he possibly could to assist us to get to the hospital as quickly as possible. It could not have taken more than a couple of minutes to make the journey from the scene of the incident to the hospital.

"When we arrived, with the help of some other people, I carried the Count inside and laid him on the bed. We had sent for a medical officer, but while waiting for him to arrive, I took off the Count's jacket and tore away his shirt and undervest. I saw that he was wounded around the heart and that there was also a considerable quantity of blood on his clothes about it.

"When the doctor arrived, I asked if anything could be done, but he replied that it was too late. Major De Geer went in Dr. Facel's car to fetch the Count's personal physician, Dr. Ullmark. He stayed with the Count and was later joined by Major De Geer, Miss Wessel and Dr. Ullmark. I then left and went to see Colonel Serot, who had been placed in another room. The doctor confirmed that he had died instantly.

"After a while, I went with a car to the Y.M.C.A. and tried to get in touch with Dr. Joseph and Colonel Dayan, military commander of Israel forces in Jerusalem. They arrived at the Y.M.C.A. after a very short time. I said that I would not do anything that would create an impression of panic, but that I had to decide before sunset whether observers should stay at their posts during the night without danger. If in their opinion, there would be considerable danger for observers, they would recall them. They assured me that in their opinion, although of course they could make no guarantee, there was no added danger, and I decided that observers should remain at their posts. However, I asked Colonel Dayan for a guard to be placed around the Y.M.C.A., where it had been decided that the bodies of Count Bernadotte and Colonel Serot would lie in state.

"Later on, General Riley and Mr. Bunche arrived from Kollundia airfield. By that time, it had already been decided that the bodies of Count Bernadotte and Colonel Serot should be taken to the Y.M.C.A. and onwards on Saturday morning, 18 September, to Haifa. The bodies would be accompanied by Colonel Bonnot, Lt. Col. Flach and myself with members of the Count's personal staff. A room in the Y.M.C.A. was beautifully arranged by Mr. Miller, head of the Y.M.C.A., and the bodies of Count Bernadotte and Colonel Serot were laid in state. A short simple service was conducted by two Catholic priests, and a guard of officer observers was mounted inside the room to watch through the night, with an enlisted observer on guard at the door. On reflection after the incident, I am convinced that this was a deliberate and carefully planned assassination. The spot where the cars were halted was carefully chosen, and the people who approached the cars quite obviously not only knew which car Count Bernadotte was in, but also the exact position in the car which he occupied."

Source: United Nations Department of Public Information, https://unispal.un.org/DPA/DPR/unispal.nsf/0/23E5F866FE7393B585256A680061B348.

146. Sir John Bagot Glubb on Arab Refugees (1950–1951)

Introduction

The first Arab-Israeli war of 1948–1949 caused many Arabs to flee what became the territory of Israel, and others were expelled from lands that the Israeli Army seized. Many of them took refuge in the kingdom of neighboring Jordan in camps from which at least some crossed the border into Israel, in some cases to conduct raids against Jewish settlers there and in other cases to smuggle goods of some kind or steal. The Israeli armed forces retaliated with raids against Arabs living close to the border. Writing to Sir Alexander Kirkbride, the British ambassador to Jordan, Sir John Bagot Glubb, the British commander of the Arab

Legion in Jordan, protested bitterly and repeatedly against Israeli policies toward the refugees, which he considered both cruel and counterproductive. Glubb's complaints to British officials over this issue continued until he left Jordan in 1956, if anything intensifying over time.

Documents

Glubb to Sir Alexander Kirkbride, June 28, 1950

There seems to be little doubt Arabs in Israel are subjected to the same torture camps technique as the Jews themselves suffered in Nazi Germany, though on a lesser scale. This however is difficult to prove.

The leading statesmen in Israel are constantly making speeches or statements to the press in which they claim that they are holding out the hand of friendship to the Arabs, but that the Arabs refuse all their advances.

I do not know if the Jews want peace—I daresay they do. Meanwhile however the policy of terrorism and frightfulness towards the Arabs they get hold of goes on. They have a considerable minority in Israel, and I imagine that the Jews want them to emigrate. They therefore try to persuade them with rubber coshes and by tearing out finger nails whenever they get the chance.

I do not know whether this is the policy of the Israel cabinet, but it must certainly be known and winked at on a ministerial level, I think. The brutality is too general to be due only to the sadism of ordinary soldiers. On the other hand, it may be that the Israeli government really want peace, but that they imagine that shootings and torture will cow the Arabs into making peace. If this is the case, then they have entirely misjudged the psychological effect. Indignation in Jordan is mounting. If the Jews really want peace, they are themselves destroying their chances of securing it.

The Jews make a tremendous propaganda about Arabs going over to 'raid' Israel. Arabs are traditionally connected with 'raids' but the world at large do not realise that the 'Arabs' of Palestine are as far removed from the Arabs who used to raid, as a Wimbledon grocer is from the clans of the Scottish Highlands.

We admit that when one of these unfortunates recrosses the line by stealth, a technical breach of the Armistice is committed. We are doing our best to prevent this, and we are constantly asking for Jewish police cooperation with this object. The Israelis, however, instead of cooperating, prefer their own deterrent measures—shooting or torturing the people they catch. This may have a deterrent effect, but it is simultaneously creating so much indignation in Jordan that the chance of peace negotiations is becoming less.

Glubb to Sir Alexander Kirkbride, March 18, 1951

Everybody I speak to seems to agree with you that infiltration is largely an economic question, rather than one of revenge. The economic situation has got much worse lately owing to the all round rise in prices and is likely further to deteriorate owing to bad crops. The prospects of peace and quiet on the Israel armistice line seem therefore to be pretty bad.

The only thing which can help us to reduce infiltration is better economic conditions for the refugees. However at the moment we are going rapidly in the other direction.

The solution of nearly all our problems lies in getting the refugees settled. They do nearly all the infiltrating, and as they get hungrier and more desperate, they will do more. A man can get to the stage when he does not mind if he gets shot and would positively like to go to prison, to get food and three blankets and a roof over his head. When he gets to that stage, you cannot stop infiltrating.

Source: The UK National Archives, FO 371/82205/EE1091/61, FO 816/173, in Tancred Bradshaw, ed., *The Glubb Reports: Glubb Pasha and Britain's Empire Project in the Middle East, 1920–1956* (New York: Palgrave Macmillan, 2016), 133–134, 137–138.

147. Loy Henderson, U.S. Ambassador to Iran: Despatch to the U.S. Department of State Regarding the Coup in Iran (August 23, 1953)

Introduction

By the early 1950s, the United States had taken on commitments that implied that it would oppose the emergence of communist regimes anywhere in the world. Successive Cold War presidents in the United States turned to the Central Intelligence Agency (CIA) to help overthrow foreign governments that appeared unfriendly to the United States due to either their ideological complexion or their antagonism toward U.S. economic or strategic interests. The first occasion when the CIA was instrumental in successfully ousting another government came in Iran in 1953. Until the early Cold War, Iran had been largely under British and Russian influence. The British Anglo-Iranian Oil Company controlled Iran's petroleum resources, and during World War II the British and Russians overthrew the Nazi-oriented monarch, Shah Reza Pahlavi, and jointly occupied Iran to deny these resources to Germany and safeguard supply routes to the Soviet Union. In 1946 British and Russian forces left Iran, the Russians at least reluctantly, as they had hoped to set up a pro-Soviet republic in the north that they had previously controlled.

As early as World War II, U.S. diplomats already believed that their own nation, which they felt that the Iranians knew was untainted by past exploitation of Iran, had an opportunity to win that country's loyalties. In 1951 the Iranian government announced its intention of nationalizing the Anglo-Iranian Oil Company; the British, who controlled the refineries, withdrew their technicians and blockaded all exports of Iranian oil, provoking severe economic difficulties within Iran. The government headed by Prime Minister Mohammed Mossadegh stood firm and eventually, after the young shah Mohammad Reza Pahlavi had made an abortive attempt to replace him, declared a national emergency and took control of the Iranian military. In alliance with radical Muslims and the leftist Soviet-leaning Tudeh Party, in 1952 Mossadegh implemented socialist reforms, especially in agriculture, and broke diplomatic relations with the United Kingdom. Britain turned to the United States for assistance, characterizing Mossadegh as a radical who was turning toward communism and steering Iran into the Soviet orbit.

The administration of Republican president Dwight D. Eisenhower, which took office in January 1953, proved sympathetic and authorized the CIA to spend up to $1 million removing Mossadegh. CIA agents in Tehran spread rumors and disinformation and in some cases acted as agents provocateurs. Economic problems intensified, and Mossadegh suspended parliament and extended his emergency powers. The CIA sought to persuade the indecisive young shah to dismiss Mossadegh, while Mossadegh urged the monarch to leave the country. Eventually in 1953 the shah dismissed Mossadegh, but the latter refused to step down from office, and the shah took refuge in Italy. Major protests for and against the monarchy were held throughout the country, as Iranians of all political stripes assumed that before long Mossadegh would declare Iran a republic and himself head of state. Promonarchy forces, heavily funded by the CIA, gained the upper hand, and Iranian tanks and troops entered Tehran, the Iranian capital, and besieged the prime minister's residence until Mossadegh surrendered. He was subsequently put on trial for treason and sentenced to three years in prison. General Fazlollah Zahedi, one of the military leaders who arrested Mossadegh, became prime minister, and the shah flew back and resumed power. From then until his overthrow in 1979, Iran would be a key U.S. ally in the Middle East.

Speaking to Loy Henderson, the U.S. ambassador in Iran, the shah expressed his fervent gratitude to the Americans for their role in his return, adroitly stressed his wish to carry out social reforms that would benefit the poorest Iranians, and declared that a communist regime was the only alternative to his own. He made it very clear that to carry out such policies he badly needed American aid, and he also discreetly intimated that the Americans should not "interfere in personnel matters of [the Iranian] Government." The shah soon reached an agreement with the British and Americans, under whose terms the foreign oil companies still made substantial profits as large amounts of Iranian oil once more flowed to world markets. These revenues enabled the shah to modernize his country and make it a strong military state, but his authoritarian policies, his persecution of opponents, and the social disruptions caused by his reforms eventually alienated many Iranians and were among the reasons why in 1979 an Islamic fundamentalist revolt ended his rule. Only in the late 1990s did the U.S. government publicly acknowledge the extent of CIA involvement in the overthrow of Mossadegh. The eventual success of this undertaking subsequently emboldened CIA director Allen W. Dulles and other agency officials to try to orchestrate comparable operations against several other foreign governments—in Guatemala, Cuba, the Dominican Republic, and Chile—that U.S. leaders found unpalatable.

Document

At [the] Shah's request that I visit him privately without publicity, I saw him [at] six o'clock this evening. Pirnia, master of ceremonies, who met me [at the] rear entrance [of the] Palace, said I would find [the] Shah [a] changed man. He was right. [The] Shah showed vigor, decisiveness and [a] certain amount [of] clear thinking which I had not found in him before. Only time will determine whether this change [is] merely temporary [as a] result [the] discovery that [the] people of [his] country had [a] deeper sense of loyalty [to] him than he had realized. In any event, I did not find hesitation, brooding, discouragement and [an] air [of] "what can I do" which I had noticed [in] practically all previous conversations.

He greeted me warmly and expressed deep appreciation of [the] friendship which [the] US had shown him and Iran during [that] period. I read [an] oral message from [the] President to which I had taken [the] liberty of adding [an] introductory paragraph as follows: "I congratulate you for the great moral courage which you displayed at a critical time in your country's history. I am convinced that by your action you contributed much to the preservation of the independence and to the future prosperity of Iran." The Shah wept as I read this message and asked me in reply to tell the President how grateful he was for [the] interest which [the] President and Government of [the] US had shown in Iran. He would always feel deeply indebted for this proof of genuine friendship. [The] Miracle of saving Iran which had just been wrought was due to friendship [with the] West, to [the] patriotism [of the] Iranian people and to [the] intermediation [of] God. It [was] impossible for him [to] believe so many factors could have contributed simultaneously to this salvation [of] his country unless Providence had so willed.

[The] Shah dwelt for some time on [the] part which [the] "common people of Iran" had played. People of [the] poorest classes who were ill-clad and hungry had been willing [to] sacrifice their lives on his behalf. He could never forget this and he would never be satisfied until hunger had been eliminated from his country. Iran had been saved but victory would be short-lived unless substantial aid came from [the] US immediately. No time could be lost. This was Iran's last chance to survive as an independent country. I said I agreed that if [the] present government should fail, Communism seemed to be only alternative. He said "if I fail, [there is] no alternative but Communism. People have shown their trust in me and it rests upon me [to] prove their trust merited. I must help [the] new government live up to expectations and I cannot do that without quick aid from the US. How soon can this aid come and in what quantities and form?"

I replied [that the] US [is] prepared [to] extend aid but it must be given in [an] orderly way and in circumstances which would be acceptable [to the] US public as well as [the] Iranian public. I had been endeavoring all day to get in touch with financial and economic experts [in the] new government in order [to] begin conversations. If he wished quick aid, he should take steps [to] see that conversations begin immediately. He promised [to] talk to Zahedi this evening in [an] effort [to] accelerate.

[The] Shah said he [was] not completely happy re [the] Cabinet which Zahedi had presented him on his arrival. [The] Same old faces which had been rotating in office for years. He had hoped for [a] Cabinet which would stimulate [the] country particularly [the] youth. He had been told [that the] Americans had insisted Amini be included as Minister [of] Finance and that [the] Cabinet be selected before his arrival and presented to him as [a] *fait accompli*. I told him [the] information [was] incorrect.

I do not know who had selected Amini. Certainly not [the] Americans. There had been [a] feeling in [the] Embassy that [the] Cabinet should be formed quickly so [that the] Government could begin to function [at the] earliest possible moment, [but] no idea [of] endeavoring [to] have members selected without consultation with him. He said he [was] relieved [to] hear me say this. He [was] sure [the] Americans would not begin trying [to] interfere in personnel matters of [the] Government. They should know from experience this would be [the] surest way [to] change friendship into suspicion. Particularly important [was] no interference in [the] future in his control [of the] armed forces. Neither foreigners nor Iranians should come between him and [the] army. Razmara had been unsuccessful in trying to separate [the] army from [the] Shah. Mosadeq had been able to break down army unity. It was his task and it would be [a] difficult and delicate one to rebuild [the] army as [a] solid block loyal to him. Otherwise there would be no stability in [the] country.

I asked if I [were] to infer [that] he [was] dissatisfied with [the] way Zahedi had been conducting affairs or if he [was] under [the] impression [that] Zahedi [was] attempting [to] exert authority which should be vested in him. He replied negative insisting he had complete confidence in Zahedi. He did not believe Zahedi had ambitions other than [to] serve Iran and its Shah, nevertheless he thought that certain advisers around Zahedi were pressing [the] latter to take actions without proper consultation with him. He had had several discussions with Zahedi and was sure that he had achieved understanding with him re extent [of] consultation in [the] future.

I said Zahedi and many other army officers had risked their lives for Shah and country. I hoped [the] Shah would show in some way his appreciation. He said he intended to do so but he must disappoint many retired army officers expecting [to] resume active service. Most of them [were] outmoded, some corrupt. He could give them decorations and other awards but not jobs.

In discussing [the] failure of plans on [the] night of August 15 he said someone must have betrayed them. Could it have been British agents?

I expressed surprise. I pointed out in various previous conversations he had said if Iran [is] to be saved [it is] necessary for [the] British and Americans to have [a] common policy re Iran and work with mutual confidence. This situation had been achieved and I hoped he would never again make either to British or Americans remarks which might tend [to] undermine that mutual confidence. I knew for [a] fact that [the] British were dealing honestly with him and he should get out of his head once [and] for all [the] idea [that] they [were] engaging in double dealing. He said he [was] relieved [to] hear this and believed me. I told him Communists espionage facilities [were] well developed. They had many dangerous hearing devices. He said perhaps they had broken down code telegrams exchanged between Tehran and Ramsar. I agreed this [was] quite possible.

I said if Iran wanted [the] British and [the] US [to] pursue [a] common policy re Iran [the] Government should not expect [to] receive substantial aid from [the] US while it was making [the] British [a] whipping boy. I worried lest when [the] Majlis reassembled there would again take place long tirades against [the] British. I [was] also concerned re Tudeh press in this respect. He said he would endeavor [to] arrange for those members [of the] Majlis who had not resigned to meet and vote [for] dissolution [of the] Majlis. Elections would then be held in spring so [the] Government could accomplish much without interference [from the] Majlis. It was his intention also not to convene [the] Senate until [the] new Majlis [had been] elected. He intended taking steps also to reward in some way although not with Cabinet positions [a] small band [of] Majlis members who had at risk [of their] lives refused [to] resign. It [was] also his intention [to] completely root out [the] subversive press. He [was] determined [to] completely wreck [the] Tudeh organization while at [the] same time maintaining as correct relations as possible with [the] USSR.

In terminating conversation he again urged me [to] impress on [the] US Government [the] importance [of] receiving substantial and immediate financial and economic aid. In [the] absence [of the] Majlis it would be difficult [to] arrange for [a] loan. Therefore most of this aid must be in [the] form [of a] grant. I said if this [were] true we might be severely hampered in our efforts. For instance it might be easier quickly to obtain funds for road building and similar programs through loans rather than grants. He promised [to] look into legal aspects [of] this problem but said he feared it might be impossible for [the] Iranian Government to accept loans without consent [of the] Majlis.

HENDERSON

Source: U.S. Department of State, *Foreign Relations of the United States, 1952–1954: Vol. 10, Iran, 1952–1954* (Washington, DC: U.S. Government Printing Office, 1989), 762–765.

148. The Baghdad Pact (February 24, 1955)

Introduction

The Baghdad Pact was originally a mutual security agreement, modeled on the North Atlantic Treaty Organization (NATO), that Iraq, Turkey, Pakistan, Iran, and the United Kingdom signed in 1955. The United States encouraged the development of this organization by promising military and economic aid and established a military liaison arrangement with it but initially chose not to join itself, fearing that doing so might lose it the goodwill of various other Middle Eastern states that President Dwight D. Eisenhower's administration also sought to cultivate. The objective was to encourage the signatories to collaborate against potential Soviet expansionism in the area by erecting a bastion of anticommunist states along the Soviet Union's southwestern frontier. The alliance was originally known as the Middle Eastern Treaty Organization. After Iraq, the only Arab member, withdrew in 1958 in the aftermath of a bloody revolution led by the leftist and Moscow-oriented Baath Party, the United States joined as a full member, and the grouping became the Central Treaty Organization (CENTO). The organization proved largely ineffective in preventing the spread of Soviet influence in the Middle East. During the 1960s and 1970s, the Soviet Union simply bypassed the CENTO states to develop close military and economic ties with Egypt, Syria, Iraq, Yemen, Somalia, and Libya, establishing bases in Egypt, Somalia, and Yemen. CENTO lacked a single military command structure, and the links between the member states remained relatively loose. The organization did facilitate American access to bases in Iran with useful communications and intelligence capabilities, while from the late 1950s onward Pakistan allowed the United States to utilize airfields on its own soil to launch U-2 espionage and surveillance flights over Soviet territory. At times Great Britain too made use of bases in Pakistan and, like the United States, also on occasion had recourse to similar Turkish facilities, although the latter arrangements were organized through the NATO alliance. Never a particularly successful alliance, CENTO largely fell into desuetude after Turkey invaded Cyprus in 1974, causing the British to withdraw their forces from CENTO. In 1979 Islamic radicals overthrew the Iranian monarchy, whose collapse brought the formal end of CENTO.

Document

Whereas the friendly and brotherly relations existing between Iraq and Turkey are in constant progress, and in order to complement the contents of the Treaty of friendship and good neighbourhood concluded between His Majesty The King of Iraq and His Excellency The President of the Turkish Republic signed in Ankara on the 29th of March, 1946 which recognised the fact that peace and security between the two countries is an integral part of the peace and security of all the Nations of the world and in particular the Nations of the Middle East, and that it is the basis for their foreign policies;

Whereas Article 11 of the Treaty of Joint Defence and Economic Co-operation between the Arab League States provides that no provision of that Treaty shall in any way affect, or is designed to affect, any of the rights and obligations accruing to the contracting parties from the United Nations Charter;

And having realised the great responsibilities borne by them in their capacity as members of the United Nations concerned with the maintenance of peace and security in the Middle East region which necessitate taking the required measures in accordance with Article 51 of the United Nations Charter;

They have been fully convinced of the necessity of concluding a pact fulfilling these aims and for that purpose have appointed as their Plenipotentiaries . . . who, having communicated their full powers, found to be in good and due form, have agreed as follows:

Article 1

Consistent with Article 51 of the United Nations Charter the High Contracting Parties will co-operate for their security and defence. Such measures as they agree to take to give effect to this co-operation may form the subject of special agreements with each other.

Article 2

In order to ensure the realisation and effect application of the co-operation provided for in Article 1 above, the competent authorities of the High Contracting Parties will determine the measures to be taken as soon as the present Pact enters into force. These measures will become operative as soon as they have been approved by the Governments of the High Contracting Parties.

Article 3

The High Contracting Parties undertake to refrain from any interference whatsoever in each other's internal affairs. They will settle any dispute between themselves in a peaceful way in accordance with the United Nations Charter.

Article 4

The High Contracting Parties declare that the dispositions of the present Pact are not in contradiction with any of the international obligations contracted by either of them with any third state or states. They do not derogate from, and cannot be interpreted as derogating from, the said international obligations. The High Contracting Parties undertake not to enter into any international obligation incompatible with the present Pact.

Article 5

This Pact shall be open for accession to any member state of the Arab League or any other state actively concerned with the security and peace in this region and which is fully recognised by both of the High Contracting Parties. Accession shall come into force from the date on which the instrument of accession of the state concerned is deposited with the Ministry of Foreign Affairs of Iraq.

Any acceding State Party to the present Pact may conclude special agreements, in accordance with Article 1, with one or more states Parties to the present Pact. The competent authority of any acceding State may determine measures in accordance with Article 2. These measures will become operative as soon as they have been approved by the Governments of the Parties concerned.

Article 6

A Permanent Council at Ministerial level will be set up to function within the framework of the purposes of this Pact when at least four Powers become parties to the Pact.

The Council will draw up its own rules of procedure.

Article 7

This Pact remains in force for a period of five years renewable for other five year periods. Any Contracting Party may withdraw from the Pact by notifying the other parties in writing of its desire to do so, six months before the expiration of any of the above-mentioned periods, in which case the Pact remains valid for the other Parties. . . .

Source: "Pact of Mutual Co-Operation between Iraq and Turkey, February 24, 1955," *United Nations Treaty Series* 233, no. 3264.

149. Moshe Dayan: Eulogy for Roi Rotberg (April 29, 1956)

Introduction

On April 28, 1956, Arab marauders killed Roi Rotberg, a 21-year-old security officer in Kibbutz Nahal Oz, close to Israel's border with Gaza. They dragged his body across to Gaza, mutilated it, and handed it over to United Nations observers. General Moshe Dayan, chief of staff of the Israel Defense Forces, who had met Rotberg a few days earlier, delivered the eulogy at his funeral. Dayan wrote it himself in half an hour. He painted a grim picture of the continuing hostilities that he anticipated would characterize relations between the Israeli settlers and the Palestinian refugees they had driven out. To many, his words seemed prophetic. More than two decades later as foreign minister, Dayan helped to draft the 1978 Camp David Accords setting the terms for peace between Egypt and Israel. By then he had come to endorse the idea of direct negotiations between Israel and the Palestinians.

Document

Yesterday with daybreak, Roi was murdered. The quiet of a spring morning blinded him, and he did not see the stalkers of his soul on the furrow. Let us not hurl blame at the murderers. Why should we complain of their hatred for us? Eight years have they sat in the refugee camps of Gaza, and seen, with their own eyes, how we have made a homeland of the soil and the villages where they and their forebears once dwelt.

Not from the Arabs of Gaza must we demand the blood of Roi, but from ourselves. How our eyes are closed to the reality of our fate, unwilling to see the destiny of our generation in its full cruelty. Have we forgotten that this small band of youths, settled in Nahal Oz, carries on its shoulders the heavy gates of Gaza, beyond which hundreds of thousands of eyes and arms huddle together and pray for the onset of our weakness so that they may tear us to pieces—has this been forgotten? For we know that if the hope of our destruction is to perish, we must be, morning and evening, armed and ready.

A generation of settlement are we, and without the steel helmet and the maw of the cannon we shall not plant a tree, nor build a house. Our children shall not have lives to live if we do not dig shelters; and without the barbed wire fence and the machine gun, we shall not pave a path nor drill for water. The millions of Jews, annihilated without a land, peer out at us from the ashes of Israeli history and command us to settle and rebuild a land for our people. But beyond the furrow that marks the border, lies a surging sea of hatred and vengeance, yearning for the day that the tranquility blunts our alertness, for the day that we heed the ambassadors of conspiring hypocrisy, who call for us to lay down our arms.

It is to us that the blood of Roi calls from his shredded body. Although we have vowed a thousand vows that our blood will never again be shed in vain—yesterday we were once again seduced, brought to listen, to believe. Our reckoning with ourselves, we shall make today. We mustn't flinch from the hatred that accompanies and fills the lives of hundreds of thousands of Arabs, who live around us and are waiting for the moment when their hands may claim our blood. We mustn't avert our eyes, lest our hands be weakened. That is the decree of our generation. That is the choice of our lives—to be willing and armed, strong and unyielding, lest the sword be knocked from our fists, and our lives severed.

Roi Rotberg, the thin blond lad who left Tel Aviv in order to build his home alongside the gates of Gaza, to serve as our wall. Roi—the light in his heart blinded his eyes and he saw not the flash of the blade. The longing for peace deafened his ears and he heard not the sound of the coiled murderers. The gates of Gaza were too heavy for his shoulders, and they crushed him.

Source: Translation as given in Mitch Ginsburg, "When Moshe Dayan Delivered the Defining Speech of Zionism," *Times of Israel*, April 28, 2016. Reprinted with permission from Mitch Ginsburg and the Times of Israel.

150. King Faisal II of Iraq: Speech during Luncheon at the Guildhall, London (July 17, 1956)

Introduction

The youthful Faisal II of Iraq (1935–1958), who became king shortly before his fourth birthday following the death of his grandfather, Faisal I, was educated largely in Britain, attending Harrow School. Iraq had originally been established as a British protectorate, and although it had won formal independence, Faisal and his prime minister, Nuri al-Said, maintained the existing orientation toward Britain and increasingly the United States. In 1941 British forces restored the existing royal house to power after an internal coup encouraged by Germany, with which Britain was at war. In 1948 Iraq and Britain negotiated an Anglo-Iraqi Treaty, a defense agreement, and in 1955 Nuri al-Said was a leading architect of the U.S.-backed Baghdad Pact or Middle East Treaty Organization, a security alliance of Iran, Iraq, Pakistan, Turkey, and the United Kingdom intended to counter communist expansion in the region. Iraq's entrance into each of these arrangements prompted widespread popular protests. Faisal used Iraq's oil revenues to fund internal development programs, many of which relied heavily on British personnel. Visiting Britain in the summer of 1956, he spoke at the Guildhall in London, praising Anglo-Iraqi cooperation and describing his plans for Iraq. Two years later on July 14, 1958, the 23-year-old Faisal was killed during a military coup, prompted in part by resentment of his pro-Western orientation.

Document

I cannot tell you how greatly moved I am by the singular honour paid me in this ancient and historic Hall, which was attacked by the enemy, but could not be destroyed, and I should like to pay tribute to the unconquerable spirit of this great City, which is so admirably represented by you, my Lord Mayor, Aldermen and Commons.

It is from your midst that for centuries brave men have gone forth, inspired by adventure, daring the many hazards of the seas, ever seeking new trade routes and furthering the advancement of commercial enterprises as well as the advancement of knowledge.

The two great Rivers, the Tigris and Euphrates, already a source of great blessing to my country, are further being developed to benefit the land and to remove the danger of flood and devastation. Your engineers are at work on vast projects. But it is of tomorrow that we must think today. I look forward to great and impressive plans in which the young men of your country and of mine will together help to give our peoples much needed security and prosperity. Our hope and confidence are high. A youthfulness has come upon my country. The future is bright.

More than a thousand Iraqis, men as well as women, young in years, are at work now in your technical schools and colleges to acquire your new skills; and at the same time your constructional engineers in equal numbers, are in Iraq now helping us with our great new schemes, most urgent of which has been the task of curbing our two mighty rivers so that they shall not, by their rising, bring again the sad havoc and devastation that afflicted us only a year or two ago.

They are helping us to revive our ancient system of canals that for 5,000 years have been the arteries of our fertility. The name of your people stands very high in my country. For centuries your merchant traders have been respected for their integrity. Everyone knows in Iraq, as elsewhere, that the Englishman's word is his bond.

It is our hope that our country will flourish with fresh enterprises and become increasingly prosperous by its own industry, for the prosperity of every country depends, as you know, on the industry of the people, and we are seeking for a fuller and more effective use of our own very great natural resources.

Quite apart from our mineral wealth we have other resources. We have been able by my Government's careful economy to be today the biggest importers of British goods in the Middle East, and yet balance these imports with our exports.

Our Cities are also forging ahead. As boldly as Sir Christopher Wren planned here in London, British experts are now re-designing my capital, whose growth has been hitherto a little haphazard. I hope we may both achieve a new simplicity and convenience of design in our respective Cities.

The new generation, facing the future with young and eager eyes, radiating fresh ideas, will lead us both the people of Iraq and of Britain, to new fields of fulfilment, because neither you nor we wish to recline in the shade and watch the world go by. You have been in the *midst* of this moving throng, as, if I may be allowed to say so—from the earliest times, were *we*.

I trust that we shall continue to go forward in friendship and in prosperous co-operation.

Source: "Visit of H. M. King Faisal II to Guildhall, 17th July 1956," http://media.bufvc.ac.uk/newsonscreen2/BPN/46730/NoS_46730_other.pdf.

151. Egyptian Law Nationalizing the Suez Canal Company (July 26, 1956) and Gamal Abdel Nasser, Speech on Nationalization of Suez Canal Company, Alexandria, Egypt (July 26, 1956)

Introduction

The nationalist Egyptian government that came to power in 1952 found foreign ownership of the commercially valuable canal and its revenues a constant irritant. Even before then, use and operation of the canal had become internationally controversial. From the date of Israel's creation in 1948, Egypt had denied the use of the canal not just to Israeli vessels but also to ships bearing goods bound for Israel on the grounds that since Israel and Egypt—even after the 1949 armistice—were formally at war, the normal stipulations of free navigation by all nations did not apply. In September 1951 the United Nations Security Council passed Resolution 95 demanding that Egypt permit passage through the canal of Israeli ships and goods bound for Israel, a demand that successive Egyptian governments simply ignored. Under Gamal Abdel Nasser, who took power in 1954, demands that ownership of the canal and its revenues pass from the Suez Canal Company to the Egyptian government intensified and by early 1956 were reaching a crisis point. On the symbolically significant fourth anniversary of the Egyptian revolution, just a few days after Britain, the United States, and the World Bank withdrew their pledged funding for the construction of the Aswan High Dam, a project that Nasser regarded as inextricably linked to Egypt's international prestige, Nasser responded by seizing the physical property and administration of the Suez Canal and taking over not just its operation but also all of its revenues. In a heated three-hour speech, he proclaimed that these funds would be used to build the Aswan Dam, while the stock belonging to existing shareholders would be bought out at current prices on the Cairo stock market. Several other neighboring Arab states immediately applauded his audacity in facing up to what they considered neocolonial exploitation, and Nasser became a hero to nationalist movements around the world. His action sparked the Suez Crisis, an abortive effort by Great Britain and France to regain the canal by military force.

Documents

Decree Nationalizing the Suez Canal Company, July 26, 1956

ARTICLE 1

The International Company of the Suez Maritime Canal (Egyptian Joint Stock Company) is hereby nationalized. Its assets and liabilities revert to the State and the councils and committees at present responsible for its administration are dissolved.

The shareholders and holders of founders' shares will be compensated for the stock and shares which they own on the basis of their closing price on the Paris Bourse immediately preceding the date on which this law enters into force.

Payment of this compensation will be made when all the assets of the nationalized company have been fully handed over to the State.

ARTICLE 2

The administration of traffic services through the Suez Canal will be carried out by an independent body with the legal status of a corporation; it will be attached to the Ministry of Commerce. An order of the President of the Republic will fix the composition of this body and the payment to be made to its members. This body will have full powers necessary for controlling this service and will not be subject to administrative routine and regulations. . . .

ARTICLE 3

The funds of the nationalized company and its rights in Egypt and abroad are hereby frozen. Banks, institutions and private persons are forbidden to dispose of these assets in any way, to pay out any sum whatever or to meet claims for payment without previous sanction by the body envisaged in Article 2. . . .

ARTICLE 5

Any breach of the terms of Article 3 will be punished with imprisonment and a fine equal to three times the value of the sum involved. Any breach of the terms of Article 4 will be punished with imprisonment; the offender will, in addition, be deprived of any right to a gratuity, pension or compensation. . . .

Gamal Abdel Nasser, Speech on Nationalization of Suez Canal, Alexandria, Egypt, July 26, 1956 (Excerpts)

This money is ours and the Suez Canal belongs to us. The Suez Canal was built by Egyptians and 120,000 Egyptians died building it. Thus, we shall build the High Dam our own way.

Thirty-five million Egyptians pound has been taken from us every year by the Suez Canal Company. We shall use that money for building the High Dam. We shall rely on our own strength, our own muscle, our own funds.

[A new Suez Canal Company will be formed.] And it will be run by Egyptians! Egyptians! Egyptians!

All that money that belongs to the Canal will be consolidated. It will be frozen. It belongs to Egypt.

Britain and the United States were offering us $70,000,000 to help build the dam, tied up with economic domination as a prelude to political domination.

The Suez Canal's annual income is $100,000,000. In five years we will be able to acquire $500,000,000 after the nationalization of the Suez Canal Company.

We don't have to seek American or British aid for building the High Dam. We will build it ourselves and with our own money.

Source: D. C. Watt, *Documents on the Suez Crisis, 26 July to 6 November 1956* (London: Royal Institute of International Affairs, 1957), 39–48; U.S. Department of State, *The Suez Canal Problem: July 26 to November 2, 1956* (Washington, DC: U.S. Government Printing Office, 1956), 25–33.

152. The Eisenhower Doctrine (January 5, 1957)

Introduction

On January 5, 1957, U.S. president Dwight D. Eisenhower addressed a special joint session of the U.S. Congress regarding unfolding events in the Middle East. During the Suez Crisis the previous November when Britain, France, and Israel invaded

Egypt and tried to retake the Suez Canal, only to retreat under U.S. financial and diplomatic pressure, the Soviet Union had threatened to intervene unless the attackers withdrew. Soviet leader Nikita Khrushchev had also recently intervened in the East European Soviet satellite nation of Hungary to prevent its secession from the Warsaw Pact and had moreover recently indulged in somewhat threatening utterances as to how his country would prevail in the Cold War. The Middle East had the world's most substantial oil reserves, strategic resources that were increasingly vital to the heavily energy-dependent U.S. domestic economy as well as to its war-making capacity. Convinced that the tumultuous political situation in the Middle East, where rising anti-Western nationalism and Arab resentment of Israel compounded other difficulties, had become a battleground of the Cold War, Eisenhower demanded that Congress grant him the military and financial resources to aid those Middle Eastern powers attempting to fend off communism, advocating a high level of U.S. involvement in the Middle East that became known as the Eisenhower Doctrine. Congress complied, thus initiating a period of extensive U.S. involvement in the Middle East that continues to this day. Ironically, American support for relatively conservative Arab and Middle Eastern regimes would win the United States the distrust of radical elements in the region.

Document

To the Congress of the United States:

First may I express to you my deep appreciation of your courtesy in giving me, at some inconvenience to yourselves, this early opportunity of addressing you on a matter I deem to be of grave importance to our country.

In my forthcoming State of the Union Message, I shall review the international situation generally. There are worldwide hopes which we can reasonably entertain, and there are worldwide responsibilities which we must carry to make certain that freedom—including our own—may be secure.

There is, however, a special situation in the Middle East which I feel I should, even now, lay before you....

I. The Middle East has abruptly reached a new and critical stage in its long and important history. In past decades many of the countries in that area were not fully self-governing. Other nations exercised considerable authority in the area and the security of the region was largely built around their power. But since the First World War there has been a steady evolution toward self-government and independence. This development the United States has welcomed and has encouraged. Our country supports without reservation the full sovereignty and independence of each and every nation of the Middle East.

The evolution to independence has in the main been a peaceful process. But the area has been often troubled. Persistent cross-currents of distrust and fear with raids back and forth across national boundaries have brought about a high degree of instability in much of the Mid East. Just recently there have been hostilities involving Western European nations that once exercised much influence in the area. Also the relatively large attack by Israel in October has intensified the basic differences between that nation and its Arab neighbors. All this instability has been heightened and, at times, manipulated by International Communism.

II. Russia's rulers have long sought to dominate the Middle East. That was true of the Czars and it is true of the Bolsheviks. The reasons are not hard to find. They do not affect Russia's security, for no one plans to use the Middle East as a base for aggression against Russia. Never for a moment has the United States entertained such a thought.

The Soviet Union has nothing whatsoever to fear from the United States in the Middle East, or anywhere else in the world, so long as its rulers do not themselves first resort to aggression.

That statement I make solemnly and emphatically.

Neither does Russia's desire to dominate the Middle East spring from its own economic interest in the area. Russia does not appreciably use or depend upon the Suez Canal. In 1955 Soviet traffic through the Canal represented only about three fourths of 1% of the total. The Soviets have no need for, and could provide no market for, the petroleum resources which constitute the principal natural wealth of the area. Indeed, the Soviet Union is a substantial exporter of petroleum products.

The reason for Russia's interest in the Middle East is solely that of power politics. Considering her announced purpose of Communizing the world, it is easy to understand her hope of dominating the Middle East.

This region has always been the crossroads of the continents of the Eastern Hemisphere. The Suez Canal enables the nations of Asia and Europe to carry on the commerce that is essential if these countries are to maintain well-rounded and prosperous economies. The Middle East provides a gateway between Eurasia and Africa.

It contains about two thirds of the presently known oil deposits of the world and it normally supplies the petroleum needs of many nations of Europe, Asia and Africa. The nations of Europe are peculiarly dependent upon this supply, and this dependency relates to transportation as well as to production! This has been vividly demonstrated since the closing of the Suez Canal and some of the pipelines. Alternate ways of transportation and, indeed, alternate sources of power can, if necessary, be developed. But these cannot be considered as early prospects.

These things stress the immense importance of the Middle East. If the nations of that area should lose their independence, if they were dominated by alien forces hostile to freedom, that would be both a tragedy for the area and for many other free nations whose economic life would be subject to near strangulation. Western Europe would be endangered just as though there had been no Marshall Plan, no North Atlantic Treaty Organization. The free nations of Asia and Africa, too, would be placed in serious jeopardy. And the countries of the Middle East would lose the markets upon which their economies depend. All this would have the most adverse, if not disastrous, effect upon our own nation's economic life and political prospects.

Then there are other factors which transcend the material. The Middle East is the birthplace of three great religions—Moslem, Christian and Hebrew. Mecca and Jerusalem are more than places on the map. They symbolize religions which teach that the spirit has supremacy over matter and that the individual has a dignity and rights of which no despotic government can rightfully deprive him. It would be intolerable if the holy places of the Middle East should be subjected to a rule that glorifies atheistic materialism.

International Communism, of course, seeks to mask its purposes of domination by expressions of good will and by superficially attractive offers of political, economic and military aid. But any free nation, which is the subject of Soviet enticement, ought, in elementary wisdom, to look behind the mask.

Remember Estonia, Latvia and Lithuania! In 1939 the Soviet Union entered into mutual assistance pacts with these then independent countries; and the Soviet Foreign Minister, addressing the Extraordinary Fifth Session of the Supreme Soviet in October 1939, solemnly and publicly declared that "we stand for the scrupulous and punctilious observance of the pacts on the basis of complete reciprocity, and we declare that all the nonsensical talk about the Sovietization of the Baltic countries is only to the interest of our common enemies and of all anti-Soviet provocateurs." Yet in 1940, Estonia, Latvia and Lithuania were forcibly incorporated into the Soviet Union.

Soviet control of the satellite nations of Eastern Europe has been forcibly maintained in spite of solemn promises of a contrary intent, made during World War II.

Stalin's death brought hope that this pattern would change. And we read the pledge of the Warsaw Treaty of 1955 that the Soviet Union would follow in satellite countries "the principles of mutual respect for their independence and sovereignty and non-interference in domestic affairs." But we have just seen the subjugation of Hungary by naked armed force. In the aftermath of this Hungarian tragedy, world respect for and belief in Soviet promises have sunk to a new low. International Communism needs and seeks a recognizable success.

Thus, we have these simple and indisputable facts:

1. The Middle East, which has always been coveted by Russia, would today be prized more than ever by International Communism.

2. The Soviet rulers continue to show that they do not scruple to use any means to gain their ends.

3. The free nations of the Mid East need, and for the most part want, added strength to assure their continued independence.

III. Our thoughts naturally turn to the United Nations as a protector of small nations. Its charter gives it primary responsibility for the maintenance of international peace and security. Our country has given the United Nations its full support in relation to the hostilities in Hungary and in Egypt. The United Nations was able to bring about a cease-fire and withdrawal of hostile forces from Egypt because it was dealing with governments and peoples who had a decent respect for the opinions of mankind as reflected in the United Nations General Assembly. But in the case of Hungary, the situation was different. The Soviet Union vetoed action by the Security Council to require the withdrawal of Soviet armed forces from Hungary. And it has shown callous indifference to the recommendations, even the censure, of the General Assembly. The United Nations can always be helpful, but it cannot be a wholly dependable protector of freedom when the ambitions of the Soviet Union are involved.

IV. Under all the circumstances I have laid before you, a greater responsibility now devolves upon the United States. We have shown, so that none can doubt, our dedication to the principle that force shall not be used internationally for any aggressive purpose and that the integrity and independence of the nations of the Middle East should be inviolate. Seldom in history has a nation's dedication to principle been tested as severely as ours during recent weeks.

There is general recognition in the Middle East, as elsewhere, that the United States does not seek either political or economic domination over any other people. Our desire is a world environment of freedom, not servitude. On the other hand many, if not all, of the nations of the Middle East are aware of the danger that stems from International Communism and welcome closer cooperation with the United States to realize for themselves the United Nations goals of independence, economic well-being and spiritual growth.

If the Middle East is to continue its geographic role of uniting rather than separating East and West; if its vast economic resources are to serve the well-being of the peoples there, as well as that of others; and if its cultures and religions and their shrines are to be preserved for the uplifting of the spirits of the peoples, then the United States must make more evident its willingness to support the independence of the freedom-loving nations of the area.

V. Under these circumstances I deem it necessary to seek the cooperation of the Congress. Only with that cooperation can we give the reassurance needed to deter aggression, to give courage and confidence to those who are dedicated to freedom and thus prevent a chain of events which would gravely endanger all of the free world.

There have been several Executive declarations made by the United States in relation to the Middle East. There is the Tripartite Declaration of May 25, 1950, followed by the Presidential assurance of October 31, 1950, to the King of Saudi Arabia. There is the Presidential declaration of April 9, 1956, that the United States will within constitutional means oppose any aggression in the area. There is our Declaration of November 29, 1956, that a threat to the territorial integrity or political independence of Iran, Iraq, Pakistan, or Turkey would be viewed by the United States with the utmost gravity.

Nevertheless, weaknesses in the present situation and the increased danger from International Communism, convince me that basic United States policy should now find expression in joint action by the Congress and the Executive. Furthermore, our joint resolve should be so couched as to make it apparent that if need be our words will be backed by action.

VI. It is nothing new for the President and the Congress to join to recognize that the national integrity of other free nations is directly related to our own security.

We have joined to create and support the security system of the United Nations. We have reinforced the collective security system of the United Nations by a series of collective defense arrangements. Today we have security treaties with 42 other nations which recognize that our peace and security are intertwined. We have joined to take decisive action in relation to Greece and Turkey and in relation to Taiwan.

Thus, the United States through the joint action of the President and the Congress, or, in the case of treaties, the Senate, has manifested in many endangered areas its purpose to support free and independent governments—and peace—against external menace, notably the menace of International Communism. Thereby we have helped to maintain peace and security during a period of great danger. It is now essential that the United States should manifest through joint action of the President and the Congress our determination to assist those nations of the Mid East area, which desire that assistance.

The action which I propose would have the following features.

It would, first of all, authorize the United States to cooperate with and assist any nation or group of nations in the general area of the Middle East in the development of economic strength dedicated to the maintenance of national independence.

It would, in the second place, authorize the Executive to undertake in the same region programs of military assistance and cooperation with any nation or group of nations which desires such aid.

It would, in the third place, authorize such assistance and cooperation to include the employment of the armed forces of the United States to secure and protect the territorial integrity and political independence of such nations, requesting such aid, against overt armed aggression from any nation controlled by International Communism.

These measures would have to be consonant with the treaty obligations of the United States, including the Charter of the United Nations and with any action or recommendations of the United Nations. They would also, if armed attack occurs, be subject to the overriding authority of the United Nations Security Council in accordance with the Charter.

The present proposal would, in the fourth place, authorize the President to employ, for economic and defensive military purposes, sums available under the Mutual Security Act of 1954, as amended, without regard to existing limitations.

The legislation now requested should not include the authorization or appropriation of funds because I believe that, under the conditions I suggest, presently appropriated funds will be adequate for the balance of the present fiscal year ending June 30. I shall, however, seek in subsequent legislation the authorization of $200,000,000 to be available during each of the fiscal years 1958 and 1959 for discretionary use in the area, in addition to the other mutual security programs for the area hereafter provided for by the Congress.

VII. This program will not solve all the problems of the Middle East. Neither does it represent the totality of our policies for the area. There are the problems of Palestine and relations between Israel and the Arab States, and the future of the Arab refugees. There is the problem of the future status of the Suez Canal. These difficulties are aggravated by International Communism, but they would exist quite apart from that threat. It is not the purpose of the legislation I propose to deal directly with these problems. The United Nations is actively concerning itself with all these matters, and we are supporting the United Nations. The United States has made clear, notably by Secretary Dulles' address of August 26, 1955, that we are willing to do much to assist the United Nations in solving the basic problems of Palestine.

The proposed legislation is primarily designed to deal with the possibility of Communist aggression, direct and indirect. There is imperative need that any lack of power in the area should be made good, not by external or alien force, but by the increased vigor and security of the independent nations of the area.

Experience shows that indirect aggression rarely if ever succeeds where there is reasonable security against direct aggression; where the government disposes of loyal security forces; and where economic conditions are such as not to make Communism seem an attractive alternative. The program I suggest deals with all three aspects of this matter and thus with the problem of indirect aggression.

It is my hope and belief that if our purpose be proclaimed, as proposed by the requested legislation, that very fact will serve to halt any contemplated aggression. We shall have heartened the patriots who are dedicated to the independence of their nations. They will not feel that they stand alone, under the menace of great power. And I should add that patriotism is, throughout this area, a powerful sentiment. It is true that fear sometimes perverts true patriotism into fanaticism and to the acceptance of dangerous enticements from without. But if that fear can be allayed, then the climate will be more favorable to the attainment of worthy national ambitions.

And as I have indicated, it will also be necessary for us to contribute economically to strengthen those countries, or groups of countries, which have governments manifestly dedicated to the preservation of independence and resistance to subversion. Such measures will provide the greatest insurance against Communist inroads. Words alone are not enough.

VIII. Let me refer again to the requested authority to employ the armed forces of the United States to assist to defend the territorial integrity and the political independence of any nation in the area against Communist armed aggression. Such authority would not be exercised except at the desire of the nation attacked. Beyond this it is my profound hope that this authority would never have to be exercised at all.

Nothing is more necessary to assure this than that our policy with respect to the defense of the area be promptly and clearly determined and declared. Thus the United Nations and all friendly governments, and indeed governments which are not friendly, will know where we stand.

If, contrary to my hope and expectation, a situation arose which called for the military application of the policy which I ask the Congress to join me in proclaiming, I would of course maintain hour-by-hour contact with the Congress if it were in session. And if the Congress were not in session, and if the situation had grave implications, I would, of course, at once call the Congress into special session.

In the situation now existing, the greatest risk, as is often the case, is that ambitious despots may miscalculate. If power-hungry Communists should either falsely or correctly estimate that the Middle East is inadequately defended, they might be tempted to use open measures of armed attack. If so, that would start a chain of circumstances which would almost surely involve the United States in military action. I am convinced that the best insurance against this dangerous contingency is to make clear now our readiness to cooperate fully and freely with our friends of the Middle East in ways consonant with the purposes and principles of the United Nations. I intend promptly to send a special mission to the Middle East to explain the cooperation we are prepared to give....

Source: Dwight D. Eisenhower, *Public Papers of the Presidents of the United States: Dwight D. Eisenhower, 1957* (Washington, DC: U.S. Government Printing Office, 1958), 6–16.

153. Golda Meir: Statement to the Knesset (October 23, 1973)

Introduction

On the day after Israel and the Arab states accepted a United Nations (UN) proposal for a cease-fire in the Yom Kippur War, Prime Minister Golda Meir addressed the Knesset. She clarified numerous provisions of the agreement, assuring the Knesset that the agreement applied not only to regular armed forces but also to irregular armed groups, that it would end the Arab maritime blockade of Israel, and that Israel's cease-fires with Egypt and Syria were not mutually dependent so that a breach of one cease-fire would not imply that Israel would also resume hostilities with the other nation. Celebrating Israel's achievements in the war, Meir argued that Israel was now in a better strategic defensive or offensive position than it had been when the conflict began. Addressing the thorny question of UN Security Council Resolution 242, which the UN had reaffirmed in its cease-fire resolution, Meir stressed that Israel was not prepared to return to its pre–June 5, 1967, borders, "which make the country a temptation to aggression and which, on various fronts, give decisive advantages to an aggressor." As part of any peace settlement, Israel would require more defensible and secure frontiers. She also stressed that Israel had accepted the cease-fire agreement largely at the urging of its friend and ally, the United States, and that the U.S. government had not put forward any suggestions as to what Israel's post–cease-fire borders should be but had, to the contrary, left those to be negotiated between Israel and its former antagonists. She also warned that if Egypt, which was still making sporadic attacks on Israeli positions, chose to resume fighting, Israel was more than prepared for this. In effect, Meir made no concessions to UN expectations on eventual peace terms and kept all Israeli options open.

Document

... On 22 October the Government of Israel unanimously decided to respond to the approach of the U.S. Government and President Nixon and announce its readiness to agree to a cease-fire according to the resolution of the Security Council following the joint American-Soviet proposal.

According to this proposal, the military forces will remain in the positions they hold at the time when the cease-fire goes into effect.

The implementation of the cease-fire is conditional on reciprocity. Our decision has been brought to the notice of the Foreign Affairs and Security committee, and now to the notice of the Knesset.

As regards the second paragraph of the Security Council resolution, the Government decided to instruct Israel's representative at the United Nations to include in his address to the Security Council a passage clarifying that our agreement to this paragraph is given in the sense in which it was defined by Israel when it decided in August 1970 to respond positively to the United States Government's initiative for a cease-fire, as stated in the United Nations on 4 August, 1970, and by the Prime Minister in the Knesset on the same day. This was also made clear to the U.S. Government. Israel's acceptance of a cease-fire with Egypt is conditional upon Egypt's agreement, but is not conditional upon Syria's agreement to a cease-fire, and vice-versa.

The Government also decided to clarify with the U.S. Government a series of paragraphs intimately connected with the content of the Security Council resolution and the procedure required by it. It is our intention to clarify and ensure, inter alia, that:

The cease-fire shall be binding upon all the regular forces stationed in the territory of a State accepting the cease-fire including the forces of foreign States, such as the armies of Iraq and Jordan in Syria and also forces sent by other Arab States which took part in the hostilities.

The cease-fire shall also be binding upon irregular forces acting against Israel from the area of the States accepting the cease-fire.

The cease-fire shall assure the prevention of a blockade or interference with free navigation, including oil tankers in the Bab-el-Mandeb straits on their way to Eilat.

It shall ensure that the interpretation of the term referring to "negotiations between the parties" is direct negotiations—and, naturally, it must be assured that the procedures, the drawing up of maps and the subject of cease-fire supervision shall be determined by agreement.

153. Golda Meir: Statement to the Knesset

A subject of great importance, one dear to our hearts, is the release of prisoners. The Government of Israel has decided to demand an immediate exchange of prisoners. We have discussed this with the Government of the United States, which was one of the initiators of the cease-fire....

I stress again that this subject is one of the principal tests of the cease-fire, and that there will be no relaxation of our demand that the obligations undertaken by the initiators of the cease-fire be indeed carried out.

I will say several things about our military situation on the Syrian and Egyptian fronts before the cease-fire:

On the Syrian Front

The lines we are holding today on the Syrian front are better than those we held on the 6th of October.

Not only do we now hold all the territory which was under our control before, but our situation has been considerably improved by the holding of positions on the Hermon ridge and also on the front line in the east, which has shifted the previous cease-fire line to a better line supported by a strong flank in the north, on the Hermon ridge.

On the Egyptian Front

The Egyptians did indeed gain a military achievement in crossing the Canal, but in a daring counter-offensive by the Israel Defense Force, our forces succeeded in regaining control of part of the Eastern Canal line, and to gain control of a large area west of the Canal, an area which opens before us both defensive and offensive possibilities:

(a) This deployment deprives the Egyptian army of its capacity to constitute an offensive threat in the direction of Sinai and Israel, and also prevents them from being able to attack essential installations or areas in our territory.
(b) The forces of the I.D.F. west of the Suez Canal constitute a strong military base for the development of operations initiated by us if required.

In connection with the cease-fire issue, the U.S. Secretary of State, Dr. Henry Kissinger, and his aides called here on their way from Moscow to Washington. The visit was an appropriate opportunity for a thoroughgoing discussion of questions arising from the cease-fire, as well as for an exchange of views, in a friendly spirit, on what was about to happen and what was called for as a result of Israel's response to the U.S. Government's request for agreement to a cease-fire. During this visit, we continued and strengthened the contacts which preceded the Security Council resolution.

In all our contacts with the United States, I learnt that not only does the U.S. have no plan for the borders and other components of peace, but that it is its view that those who offer their "good services" should see to it that the parties themselves—and they alone—should make proposals, plans, for the future.

Furthermore, I must emphasize that, in accordance with authoritative information to hand, the Moscow talks contained nothing more than is contained in the Security Council resolution. I have to inform you that the Syrian Government has so far not responded to the cease-fire resolution. The fighting on that front continues, and the I.D.F. will operate there in accordance with its plans.

As for the Egyptian front—firing against our forces has not yet ceased, and the I.D.F. is obliged to operate as required as long as the firing continues.

At this stage, I will state only that we are examining the conduct of the Egyptians with close military and political attention. Should Egypt persist in belligerent activity, we shall deem ourselves free to take any action and move called for by the situation.

I shall not go into elaborate evaluations of the political activity which preceded the cease-fire. In any event, it was not we who made approaches concerning a cease-fire. As far as the situation on the fronts was concerned, there was no reason for such an approach on our part. It was not we who initiated the timing and clauses of the Security Council's resolution. On the fronts, our forces were not in an inferior battle position. As aforesaid, we deemed it right to respond to the call of the United States and its President, since:

(a) The State of Israel, by its nature, has no wish for war, does not desire loss of life. All Governments of Israel have been convinced that war would not promote peace.
(b) The cease-fire proposal has come when our position is firm on both fronts, when the achievements we hold are of great value and justify agreement to a cease-fire, despite the enemy's achievement east of the Suez Canal.
(c) We responded to the call by the United States and its President out of appreciation and esteem for its positive policy in the Middle East at this time.

Great importance attaches to our response insofar as concerns the continued strengthening of Israel, with particular reference to the continued military and political aid in the War that has been forced upon us....

On various occasions the Government of Israel has officially defined its attitude towards Security Council Resolution 242. These statements were made from international platforms and at diplomatic meetings, and we have brought them to the knowledge of the Knesset, its Defense and Foreign Affairs Committee and the public at large.

At this time I shall refer to one statement made on 4 August, 1970, to the U.S. Government, to the United Nations and to the Knesset. This statement too is connected with a cease-fire, and I shall not tire the Knesset by quoting it in full. However, I consider it necessary to quote from my statement in the Knesset on 5 August. This statement was made on the eve of possible talks with the Arab States, and it is still completely valid.

Israel has publicly declared that, by virtue of her right to secure borders, defensible borders, she will not return to the frontiers of 4 June 1967, which make the country a temptation to aggression and which, on various fronts, give decisive advantages to an aggressor. Our position was and still remains that, in the absence of peace, we will continue to maintain the situation as determined at the cease-fire. The cease-fire lines can be replaced only by secure, recognized and agreed boundaries demarcated in a peace treaty.

In accepting the American Government's peace initiative, Israel was not asked to, and did not, undertake any territorial commitments. On the contrary, the Government of Israel received support for its position that not a single Israeli soldier will be withdrawn from the cease-fire lines until a binding contractual peace agreement is reached.

This terrible war that was forced upon us reinforces our awareness of the vital need for defensible borders, for which we shall struggle with all our vigor.

It is worth noting that, since the outbreak of the war on Yom Kippur, the terrorists have also resumed activities from Lebanese territory. Up to this morning, during this period of 17 days, 116 acts of aggression have been perpetrated, 44 civilian settlements on the northern border have been attacked and shelled, and some 20 civilians and 6 soldiers were killed or wounded in these actions. Our people living in the border settlements may be confident that Israel's Defense Forces are fully alert to this situation. Despite the defensive dispositions operative on this front, it has been proved once again that defensive action alone is not sufficient to put an end to acts of terror.

The war in which we are engaged began with a concerted attack on two fronts. The aggressive initiative afforded our enemies preliminary achievements—but, thanks to the spirit and strength of Israel's Defense Army, which is backed by the entire nation, this attack was broken. The aggressors were thrown back. Considerable portions of their forces were destroyed, and the I.D.F. broke through and crossed the cease-fire lines. From holding battles our forces went over to the offensive and gained brilliant achievements.

On both fronts our forces are now holding strong positions beyond the cease-fire lines, unbroken in spirit. The people is united in support of our army.

Israel wants a cease-fire. Israel will observe the cease-fire on a reciprocal basis, and only on that basis. With all her heart Israel wants peace negotiations to start immediately and concurrently with the cease-fire. Israel is capable of evincing the inner strength necessary for the promotion of an honorable peace within secure borders.

We shall be happy if such readiness is also shown by the people and Government of Egypt. However, if the rulers of Egypt propose to renew the war, they shall find Israel prepared, armed and steadfast in spirit. . . .

Source: Walter Laqueur and Barry Rubin, eds., *The Israel-Arab Reader* (New York: Penguin, 2001), 152–157.

154. President Jimmy Carter: The Carter Doctrine, State of the Union Address (January 23, 1980)

Introduction

The idealistic Democrat Jimmy Carter, a traditional liberal in international affairs, became president in 1977 and was committed to a foreign policy agenda that envisaged the promotion of traditional American values, including human rights and peaceable relations with other nations, reductions in military spending, disarmament, and a new emphasis on economic over defense aid. Developments in Iran and Afghanistan in the final years of his one-term presidency caused him to modify these preoccupations and return to more traditional Cold War strategies. Convinced that U.S.-Soviet détente had become unattainable, he reacted strongly to the December 1979 Soviet invasion of Afghanistan. Addressing Congress and the nation in his January 1980 annual State of the Union address, Carter proclaimed the Carter Doctrine, stating that "business as usual" with the Soviet Union was not possible and that the United States would take all measures necessary to defend the Persian Gulf. The president moved to reinstitute containment policies, demanded annual 5 percent increases in military spending, proposed that young American men be compelled to register for a potential draft, and moved to create a Persian Gulf rapid deployment force. He also called for energy policies that would make his country less dependent on foreign oil. Carter's speech, which effectively reiterated the 1957 Eisenhower Doctrine for the Middle East, also marked a definite break with his earlier efforts toward U.S.-Soviet détente and disarmament, inaugurating several years of deep ideological and strategic antagonism between the two superpowers.

Document

. . . At this time in Iran, 50 Americans are still held captive, innocent victims of terrorism and anarchy. Also at this moment, massive Soviet troops are attempting to subjugate the fiercely independent and deeply religious people of Afghanistan. These two acts—one of international terrorism and one of military aggression—present a serious challenge to the United States of America and indeed to all the nations of the world. Together, we will meet these threats to peace.

I'm determined that the United States will remain the strongest of all nations, but our power will never be used to initiate a threat to the security of any nation or to the rights of any human being. We seek to be and to remain secure—a nation at peace in a stable world. But to be secure we must face the world as it is.

Three basic developments have helped to shape our challenges: the steady growth and increased projection of Soviet military power beyond its own borders; the overwhelming dependence of the Western democracies on oil supplies from the Middle

East; and the press of social and religious and economic and political change in the many nations of the developing world, exemplified by the revolution in Iran.

Each of these factors is important in its own right. Each interacts with the others. All must be faced together, squarely and courageously. We will face these challenges, and we will meet them with the best that is in us. And we will not fail.

In response to the abhorrent act in Iran, our Nation has never been aroused and unified so greatly in peacetime. Our position is clear. The United States will not yield to blackmail.

We continue to pursue these specific goals: first, to protect the present and long-range interests of the United States; secondly, to preserve the lives of the American hostages and to secure, as quickly as possible, their safe release, if possible, to avoid bloodshed which might further endanger the lives of our fellow citizens; to enlist the help of other nations in condemning this act of violence, which is shocking and violates the moral and the legal standards of a civilized world; and also to convince and to persuade the Iranian leaders that the real danger to their nation lies in the north, in the Soviet Union and from the Soviet troops now in Afghanistan, and that the unwarranted Iranian quarrel with the United States hampers their response to this far greater danger to them.

If the American hostages are harmed, a severe price will be paid. We will never rest until every one of the American hostages are released.

But now we face a broader and more fundamental challenge in this region because of the recent military action of the Soviet Union.

Now, as during the last 3½ decades, the relationship between our country, the United States of America, and the Soviet Union is the most critical factor in determining whether the world will live at peace or be engulfed in global conflict.

Since the end of the Second World War, America has led other nations in meeting the challenge of mounting Soviet power. This has not been a simple or a static relationship. Between us there has been cooperation, there has been competition, and at times there has been confrontation.

In the 1940's we took the lead in creating the Atlantic Alliance in response to the Soviet Union's suppression and then consolidation of its East European empire and the resulting threat of the Warsaw Pact to Western Europe.

In the 1950's we helped to contain further Soviet challenges in Korea and in the Middle East, and we rearmed to assure the continuation of that containment.

In the 1960's we met the Soviet challenges in Berlin, and we faced the Cuban missile crisis. And we sought to engage the Soviet Union in the important task of moving beyond the cold war and away from confrontation.

And in the 1970's three American Presidents negotiated with the Soviet leaders in attempts to halt the growth of the nuclear arms race. We sought to establish rules of behavior that would reduce the risks of conflict, and we searched for areas of cooperation that could make our relations reciprocal and productive, not only for the sake of our two nations but for the security and peace of the entire world.

In all these actions, we have maintained two commitments: to be ready to meet any challenge by Soviet military power, and to develop ways to resolve disputes and to keep the peace.

Preventing nuclear war is the foremost responsibility of the two superpowers. That's why we've negotiated the strategic arms limitation treaties—SALT I and SALT II. Especially now, in a time of great tension, observing the mutual constraints imposed by the terms of these treaties will be in the best interest of both countries and will help to preserve world peace. I will consult very closely with the Congress on this matter as we strive to control nuclear weapons. That effort to control nuclear weapons will not be abandoned.

We superpowers also have the responsibility to exercise restraint in the use of our great military force. The integrity and the independence of weaker nations must not be threatened. They must know that in our presence they are secure.

But now the Soviet Union has taken a radical and an aggressive new step. It's using its great military power against a relatively defenseless nation. The implications of the Soviet invasion of Afghanistan could pose the most serious threat to the peace since the Second World War.

The vast majority of nations on Earth have condemned this latest Soviet attempt to extend its colonial domination of others and have demanded the immediate withdrawal of Soviet troops. The Moslem world is especially and justifiably outraged by this aggression against an Islamic people. No action of a world power has ever been so quickly and so overwhelmingly condemned. But verbal condemnation is not enough. The Soviet Union must pay a concrete price for their aggression.

While this invasion continues, we and the other nations of the world cannot conduct business as usual with the Soviet Union. That's why the United States has imposed stiff economic penalties on the Soviet Union. I will not issue any permits for Soviet ships to fish in the coastal waters of the United States. I've cut Soviet access to high-technology equipment and to agricultural products. I've limited other commerce with the Soviet Union, and I've asked our allies and friends to join with us in restraining their own trade with the Soviets and not to replace our own embargoed items. And I have notified the Olympic Committee that with Soviet invading forces in Afghanistan, neither the American people nor I will support sending an Olympic team to Moscow.

The Soviet Union is going to have to answer some basic questions: Will it help promote a more stable international environment in which its own legitimate, peaceful concerns can be pursued? Or will it continue to expand its military power far beyond its genuine security needs, and use that power for colonial conquest? The Soviet Union must realize that its decision to use military force in Afghanistan will be costly to every political and economic relationship it values.

The region which is now threatened by Soviet troops in Afghanistan is of great strategic importance: It contains more than two-thirds of the world's exportable oil. The Soviet effort to dominate Afghanistan has brought Soviet military forces to within 300 miles of the Indian Ocean and close to the Straits of Hormuz, a waterway through which most of the world's oil must flow. The Soviet Union is now attempting to consolidate a strategic position, therefore, that poses a grave threat to the free movement of Middle East oil.

This situation demands careful thought, steady nerves, and resolute action, not only for this year but for many years to come. It demands collective efforts to meet this new threat to security in the Persian Gulf and in Southwest Asia. It demands the participation of all those who rely on oil from the Middle East and who are concerned with global peace and stability. And it demands consultation and close cooperation with countries in the area which might be threatened.

Meeting this challenge will take national will, diplomatic and political wisdom, economic sacrifice, and, of course, military capability. We must call on the best that is in us to preserve the security of this crucial region.

Let our position be absolutely clear: An attempt by any outside force to gain control of the Persian Gulf region will be regarded as an assault on the vital interests of the United States of America, and such an assault will be repelled by any means necessary, including military force.

During the past 3 years, you have joined with me to improve our own security and the prospects for peace, not only in the vital oil-producing area of the Persian Gulf region but around the world. We've increased annually our real commitment for defense, and we will sustain this increase of effort throughout the Five Year Defense Program. It's imperative that Congress approve this strong defense budget for 1981, encompassing a 5-percent real growth in authorizations, without any reduction. We are also improving our capability to deploy U.S. military forces rapidly to distant areas. We've helped to strengthen NATO and our other alliances, and recently we and other NATO members have decided to develop and to deploy modernized, intermediate-range nuclear forces to meet an unwarranted and increased threat from the nuclear weapons of the Soviet Union.

We are working with our allies to prevent conflict in the Middle East. The peace treaty between Egypt and Israel is a notable achievement which represents a strategic asset for America and which also enhances prospects for regional and world peace. We are now engaged in further negotiations to provide full autonomy for the people of the West Bank and Gaza, to resolve the Palestinian issue in all its aspects, and to preserve the peace and security of Israel. Let no one doubt our commitment to the security of Israel. In a few days we will observe an historic event when Israel makes another major withdrawal from the Sinai and when Ambassadors will be exchanged between Israel and Egypt.

We've also expanded our own sphere of friendship. Our deep commitment to human rights and to meeting human needs has improved our relationship with much of the Third World. Our decision to normalize relations with the People's Republic of China will help to preserve peace and stability in Asia and in the Western Pacific.

We've increased and strengthened our naval presence in the Indian Ocean, and we are now making arrangements for key naval and air facilities to be used by our forces in the region of northeast Africa and the Persian Gulf.

We've reconfirmed our 1959 agreement to help Pakistan preserve its independence and its integrity. The United States will take action consistent with our own laws to assist Pakistan in resisting any outside aggression....

In the weeks ahead, we will further strengthen political and military ties with other nations in the region. We believe that there are no irreconcilable differences between us and any Islamic nation. We respect the faith of Islam, and we are ready to cooperate with all Moslem countries.

Finally, we are prepared to work with other countries in the region to share a cooperative security framework that respects differing values and political beliefs, yet which enhances the independence, security, and prosperity of all....

The men and women of America's Armed Forces are on duty tonight in many parts of the world. I'm proud of the job they are doing, and I know you share that pride. I believe that our volunteer forces are adequate for current defense needs, and I hope that it will not become necessary to impose a draft. However, we must be prepared for that possibility. For this reason, I have determined that the Selective Service System must now be revitalized. I will send legislation and budget proposals to the Congress next month so that we can begin registration and then meet future mobilization needs rapidly if they arise.

We also need clear and quick passage of a new charter to define the legal authority and accountability of our intelligence agencies. We will guarantee that abuses do not recur, but we must tighten our controls on sensitive intelligence information, and we need to remove unwarranted restraints on America's ability to collect intelligence.

The decade ahead will be a time of rapid change, as nations everywhere seek to deal with new problems and age-old tensions. But America need have no fear. We can thrive in a world of change if we remain true to our values and actively engaged in promoting world peace. We will continue to work as we have for peace in the Middle East and southern Africa. We will continue to build our ties with developing nations, respecting and helping to strengthen their national independence which they have struggled so hard to achieve. And we will continue to support the growth of democracy and the protection of human rights.

In repressive regimes, popular frustrations often have no outlet except through violence. But when peoples and their governments can approach their problems together through open, democratic methods, the basis for stability and peace is far more solid and far more enduring. That is why our support for human rights in other countries is in our own national interest as well as part of our own national character.

Peace—a peace that preserves freedom—remains America's first goal. In the coming years, as a mighty nation we will continue to pursue peace. But to be strong abroad we must be strong at home. And in order to be strong, we must continue to face up to the difficult issues that confront us as a nation today.

The crises in Iran and Afghanistan have dramatized a very important lesson: Our excessive dependence on foreign oil is a clear and present danger to our Nation's security. The need has never been more urgent. At long last, we must have a clear, comprehensive energy policy for the United States.

As you well know, I have been working with the Congress in a concentrated and persistent way over the past 3 years to meet this need. We have made progress together. But Congress must act promptly now to complete final action on this vital energy legislation. Our Nation will then have a major conservation effort, important initiatives to develop solar power, realistic pricing based on the true value of oil, strong incentives for the production of coal and other fossil fuels in the United States, and our Nation's most massive peacetime investment in the development of synthetic fuels....

Source: Jimmy Carter, *Public Papers of the Presidents of the United States: Jimmy Carter, 1980–1981,* Book 1 (Washington, DC: U.S. Government Printing Office, 1981), 194–200.

155. President Ronald Reagan: Address to the Nation on Events in Lebanon and Grenada (October 27, 1983)

Introduction

On October 23, 1983, Muslim suicide bombers drove trucks loaded with explosives into the barracks of peacekeeping forces of U.S. marines and French troops stationed in Beirut, the capital of Lebanon. These troops had been deployed there since late 1982 as part of an international peacekeeping force that was trying to maintain order in Beirut after Israeli forces intent on driving out the Palestine Liberation Organization had invaded, triggering a complicated civil war among various Lebanese political factions. The American forces were increasingly perceived as seeking to ensure the victory of Maronite Christian groups linked to Israel. The bombing resulted in the deaths of 241 American servicemen, 58 French paratroopers, and some civilians. The episode was one of the first suicide bombings in the Middle East. Addressing the nation four days later, U.S. president Ronald Reagan affirmed his country's commitment to maintaining order in the Middle East, particularly in Lebanon, and claimed that the attacks were themselves evidence that the marines were succeeding in their mission of restoring stability and normal conditions in Beirut. The United States blamed Syria for the attacks and mounted air strikes and naval bombardments against Syrian, Druze, and Shiite positions in Lebanon. In practice, nonetheless, shortly afterward the U.S. government, reluctant to face the prospect of further major casualties in such episodes, proclaimed that the marines had accomplished their mission and withdrew them from Lebanon, a decision that hawks later criticized as proving that terrorist tactics were effective. Reagan's bold rhetoric belied his pragmatic caution in international affairs. Like most American presidents and military men in the aftermath of the Vietnam War, Reagan preferred to keep American military interventions brief and limited and to pick conflicts in which victory would be relatively quick and easy.

Document

In Lebanon, we have some 1,600 marines, part of a multinational force that's trying to help the people of Lebanon restore order and stability to that troubled land. Our marines are assigned to the south of the city of Beirut, near the only airport operating in Lebanon. Just a mile or so to the north is the Italian contingent and not far from them, the French and a company of British soldiers.

155. President Ronald Reagan: Address to the Nation on Events in Lebanon and Grenada

This past Sunday, at 22 minutes after 6 Beirut time, with dawn just breaking, a truck, looking like a lot of other vehicles in the city, approached the airport on a busy, main road. There was nothing in its appearance to suggest it was any different than the trucks or cars that were normally seen on and around the airport. But this one was different. At the wheel was a young man on a suicide mission.

The truck carried some 2,000 pounds of explosives, but there was no way our marine guards could know this. Their first warning that something was wrong came when the truck crashed through a series of barriers, including a chain-link fence and barbed wire entanglements. The guards opened fire, but it was too late. The truck smashed through the doors of the headquarters building in which our marines were sleeping and instantly exploded. The four-story concrete building collapsed in a pile of rubble.

More than 200 of the sleeping men were killed in that one hideous, insane attack. Many others suffered injury and are hospitalized here or in Europe.

This was not the end of the horror. At almost the same instant, another vehicle on a suicide and murder mission crashed into the headquarters of the French peacekeeping force, an eight-story building, destroying it and killing more than 50 French soldiers.

Prior to this day of horror, there had been several tragedies for our men in the multinational force. Attacks by snipers and mortar fire had taken their toll.

I called bereaved parents and/or widows of the victims to express on behalf of all of us our sorrow and sympathy. Sometimes there were questions. And now many of you are asking: Why should our young men be dying in Lebanon? Why is Lebanon important to us?

Well, it's true, Lebanon is a small country, more than five-and-a-half thousand miles from our shores on the edge of what we call the Middle East. But every President who has occupied this office in recent years has recognized that peace in the Middle East is of vital concern to our nation and, indeed, to our allies in Western Europe and Japan. We've been concerned because the Middle East is a powderkeg; four times in the last 30 years, the Arabs and Israelis have gone to war. And each time, the world has teetered near the edge of catastrophe.

The area is key to the economic and political life of the West. Its strategic importance, its energy resources, the Suez Canal, and the well-being of the nearly 200 million people living there—all are vital to us and to world peace. If that key should fall into the hands of a power or powers hostile to the free world, there would be a direct threat to the United States and to our allies.

We have another reason to be involved. Since 1948 our Nation has recognized and accepted a moral obligation to assure the continued existence of Israel as a nation. Israel shares our democratic values and is a formidable force an invader of the Middle East would have to reckon with.

For several years, Lebanon has been torn by internal strife. Once a prosperous, peaceful nation, its government had become ineffective in controlling the militias that warred on each other. Sixteen months ago, we were watching on our TV screens the shelling and bombing of Beirut which was being used as a fortress by PLO bands. Hundreds and hundreds of civilians were being killed and wounded in the daily battles.

Syria, which makes no secret of its claim that Lebanon should be a part of a Greater Syria, was occupying a large part of Lebanon. Today, Syria has become a home for 7,000 Soviet advisers and technicians who man a massive amount of Soviet weaponry, including SS-21 ground-to-ground missiles capable of reaching vital areas of Israel.

155. President Ronald Reagan: Address to the Nation on Events in Lebanon and Grenada

A little over a year ago, hoping to build on the Camp David accords, which had led to peace between Israel and Egypt, I proposed a peace plan for the Middle East to end the wars between the Arab States and Israel. It was based on U.N. resolutions 242 and 338 and called for a fair and just solution to the Palestinian problem, as well as a fair and just settlement of issues between the Arab States and Israel.

Before the necessary negotiations could begin, it was essential to get all foreign forces out of Lebanon and to end the fighting there. So, why are we there? Well, the answer is straightforward: to help bring peace to Lebanon and stability to the vital Middle East. To that end, the multinational force was created to help stabilize the situation in Lebanon until a government could be established and a Lebanese army mobilized to restore Lebanese sovereignty over its own soil as the foreign forces withdrew. Israel agreed to withdraw as did Syria, but Syria then reneged on its promise. Over 10,000 Palestinians who had been bringing ruin down on Beirut, however, did leave the country.

Lebanon has formed a government under the leadership of President Gemayal, and that government, with our assistance and training, has set up its own army. In only a year's time, that army has been rebuilt. It's a good army, composed of Lebanese of all factions.

A few weeks ago, the Israeli army pulled back to the Awali River in southern Lebanon. Despite fierce resistance by Syrian-backed forces, the Lebanese army was able to hold the line and maintain the defensive perimeter around Beirut.

In the year that our marines have been there, Lebanon has made important steps toward stability and order. The physical presence of the marines lends support to both the Lebanese Government and its army. It allows the hard work of diplomacy to go forward. Indeed, without the peacekeepers from the U.S., France, Italy, and Britain, the efforts to find a peaceful solution in Lebanon would collapse.

As to that narrower question—what exactly is the operational mission of the marines—the answer is, to secure a piece of Beirut, to keep order in their sector, and to prevent the area from becoming a battlefield. Our marines are not just sitting in an airport. Part of their task is to guard that airport. Because of their presence, the airport has remained operational. In addition, they patrol the surrounding area. This is their part—a limited, but essential part—in the larger effort that I've described.

If our marines must be there, I'm asked, why can't we make them safer? Who committed this latest atrocity against them and why?

Well, we'll do everything we can to ensure that our men are as safe as possible. We ordered the battleship New Jersey to join our naval forces offshore. Without even firing them, the threat of its 16-inch guns silenced those who once fired down on our marines from the hills, and they're a good part of the reason we suddenly had a cease-fire. We're doing our best to make our forces less vulnerable to those who want to snipe at them or send in future suicide missions.

Secretary [of State George] Shultz called me today from Europe, where he was meeting with the Foreign Ministers of our allies in the multinational force. They remain committed to our task. And plans were made to share information as to how we can improve security for all our men.

We have strong circumstantial evidence that the attack on the marines was directed by terrorists who used the same method to destroy our Embassy in Beirut. Those who directed this atrocity must be dealt justice, and they will be. The obvious purpose behind the sniping and, now, this attack was to weaken American will and force the withdrawal of U.S. and French forces from Lebanon. The clear intent of the terrorists was to eliminate our support of the Lebanese Government and to destroy the ability of the Lebanese people to determine their own destiny.

155. President Ronald Reagan: Address to the Nation on Events in Lebanon and Grenada

To answer those who ask if we're serving any purpose in being there, let me answer a question with a question. Would the terrorists have launched their suicide attacks against the multinational force if it were not doing its job? The multinational force was attacked precisely because it is doing the job it was sent to do in Beirut. It is accomplishing its mission.

Now then, where do we go from here? What can we do now to help Lebanon gain greater stability so that our marines can come home? Well, I believe we can take three steps now that will make a difference.

First, we will accelerate the search for peace and stability in that region. . . .

Second, we'll work even more closely with our allies in providing support for the Government of Lebanon and for the rebuilding of a national consensus.

Third, we will ensure that the multinational peace-keeping forces, our marines, are given the greatest possible protection. . . .

Beyond our progress in Lebanon, let us remember that our main goal and purpose is to achieve a broader peace in all of the Middle East. The factions and bitterness that we see in Lebanon are just a microcosm of the difficulties that are spread across much of that region. A peace initiative for the entire Middle East, consistent with the Camp David accords and U.N. resolutions 242 and 338, still offers the best hope for bringing peace to the region.

Let me ask those who say we should get out of Lebanon: If we were to leave Lebanon now, what message would that send to those who foment instability and terrorism? If America were to walk away from Lebanon, what chance would there be for a negotiated settlement, producing a unified democratic Lebanon?

If we turned our backs on Lebanon now, what would be the future of Israel? At stake is the fate of only the second Arab country to negotiate a major agreement with Israel. That's another accomplishment of this past year, the May 17th accord signed by Lebanon and Israel.

If terrorism and intimidation succeed, it'll be a devastating blow to the peace process and to Israel's search for genuine security. It won't just be Lebanon sentenced to a future of chaos. Can the United States, or the free world, for that matter, stand by and see the Middle East incorporated into the Soviet bloc? What of Western Europe and Japan's dependence on Middle East oil for the energy to fuel their industries? The Middle East is, as I've said, vital to our national security and economic well-being.

Brave young men have been taken from us. Many others have been grievously wounded. Are we to tell them their sacrifice was wasted? They gave their lives in defense of our national security every bit as much as any man who ever died fighting in a war. We must not strip every ounce of meaning and purpose from their courageous sacrifice.

We're a nation with global responsibilities. We're not somewhere else in the world protecting someone else's interests; we're there protecting our own. . . .

Let us meet our responsibilities. For longer than any of us can remember, the people of the Middle East have lived from war to war with no prospect for any other future. That dreadful cycle must be broken. Why are we there? Well, a Lebanese mother told one of our Ambassadors that her little girl had only attended school 2 of the last 8 years. Now, because of our presence there, she said her daughter could live a normal life.

With patience and firmness, we can help bring peace to that strife-torn region—and make our own lives more secure. Our role is to help the Lebanese put their country together, not to do it for them. . . .

Source: Ronald Reagan, *Public Papers of the Presidents of the United States: Ronald Reagan, 1983*, Book 2 (Washington, DC: U.S. Government Printing Office, 1985), 1517–1522.

156. The Program of Hezbollah (February 16, 1986)

Introduction

The Palestine Liberation Organization (PLO) was founded in 1964, with encouragement from the various Arab states, to represent and speak for the interests of those often stateless Palestinian refugees and displaced persons who had chosen or were forced to leave their original homes due to the Arab-Israeli conflict. As the PLO slowly moved, however tentatively, in the direction of reaching accommodation and understanding with Israel, more radical anti-Israeli groups emerged within the Arab world, their fervor fueled by the growing strength of Islamic fundamentalism. In 1979 a theocratic government headed by the Shia Muslim cleric Ayatollah Ruhollah Khomeini seized power in Iran. Deeply resentful of 25 years of past U.S. support for the deposed Mohammad Reza Shah Pahlavi of Iran, the new Iranian government assailed the United States as the "great Satan." Among the groups competing for power within Lebanon were at least two Shiite factions that received support from Iran and also from Syria, Lebanon's dominant neighbor. Hezbollah was the more extreme of the two. Unlike the largely secular PLO, Hezbollah members prided themselves on their strict adherence to Islamic principles, which, they claimed, demanded that they wage jihad, or holy war, against Israel and also against Christian Phalangist forces in Lebanon. The Hezbollah platform, inspired by the group's mentor, Sheikh Muhammad Hussein Fadlallah, was first published in February 1985 in Beirut. Hezbollah sought to expel all U.S., Western, and Israeli forces from Lebanon and also rejected the United Nations peacekeeping force. In addition, Hezbollah sought the complete destruction of Israel. The organization's emergence meant that Arab and Islamic opposition to Israel was becoming increasingly multipolar and that the PLO now had more radical rivals.

Document

Our Identity

We are often asked: Who are we, the Hizballah, and what is our identity? We are the sons of the *umma* (Muslim community)—the party of God (Hizb Allah) the vanguard of which was made victorious by God in Iran. There the vanguard succeeded to lay down the bases of a Muslim state which plays a central role in the world. We obey the orders of one leader, wise and just, that of our tutor and *faqih* (jurist) who fulfills all the necessary conditions: Ruhollah Musawi Khomeini. God save him!

By virtue of the above, we do not constitute an organized and closed party in Lebanon, nor are we a tight political cadre. We are an *umma* linked to the Muslims of the whole world by the solid doctrinal and religious connection of Islam, whose message God wanted to be fulfilled by the Seal of the Prophets, i.e., Muhammad. This is why whatever touches or strikes the Muslims in Afghanistan, Iraq, the Philippines and elsewhere reverberates throughout the whole Muslim *umma* of which we are an integral part. Our behavior is dictated to us by legal principles laid down by the light of an overall political conception defined by the leading jurist (*wilayat al-faqih*).

As for our culture, it is based on the Holy Koran, the Sunna and the legal rulings of the *faqih* who is our source of imitation (*marja' al-taqlid*). Our culture is crystal clear. It is not complicated and is accessible to all.

No one can imagine the importance of our military potential as our military apparatus is not separate from our overall social fabric. Each of us is a fighting soldier. And when it becomes necessary to carry out the Holy War, each of us takes up his assignment in the fight in accordance with the injunctions of the Law, and that in the framework of the mission carried out under the tutelage of the Commanding Jurist.

Our Fight

The US has tried, through its local agents, to persuade the people that those who crushed their arrogance in Lebanon and frustrated their conspiracy against the oppressed (*mustad'afin*) were nothing but a bunch of fanatic terrorists whose sole aim is to dynamite bars and destroy slot machines. Such suggestions cannot and will not mislead our *umma*, for the whole world knows that whoever wishes to oppose the US, that arrogant superpower, cannot indulge in marginal acts which may make it deviate from its major objective. We combat abomination and we shall tear out its very roots, its primary roots, which are the US. All attempts made to drive us into marginal actions will fail, especially as our determination to fight the US is solid.

We declare openly and loudly that we are an *umma* which fears God only and is by no means ready to tolerate injustice, aggression and humiliation. America, its Atlantic Pact allies, and the Zionist entity in the holy land of Palestine, attacked us and continue to do so without respite. Their aim is to make us eat dust continually. This is why we are, more and more, in a state of permanent alert in order to repel aggression and defend our religion, our existence, our dignity. They invaded our country, destroyed our villages, slit the throats of our children, violated our sanctuaries and appointed masters over our people who committed the worst massacres against our *umma*. They do not cease to give support to these allies of Israel, and do not enable us to decide our future according to our own wishes. . . .

Our people could not bear any more treachery. It decided to oppose infidelity—be it French, American or Israeli—by striking at their headquarters and launching a veritable war of resistance against the Occupation forces. Finally, the enemy had to decide to retreat by stages.

Our Objectives

Let us put it truthfully: the sons of Hizballah know who are their major enemies in the Middle East—the Phalanges, Israel, France and the US. The sons of our *umma* are now in a state of growing confrontation with them, and will remain so until the realization of the following three objectives:

(a) to expel the Americans, the French and their allies definitely from Lebanon, putting an end to any colonialist entity on our land;
(b) to submit the Phalanges to a just power and bring them all to justice for the crimes they have perpetrated against Muslims and Christians;
(c) to permit all the sons of our people to determine their future and to choose in all the liberty the form of government they desire. We call upon all of them to pick the option of Islamic government which, alone, is capable of guaranteeing justice and liberty for all. Only an Islamic regime can stop any further tentative attempts of imperialistic infiltration into our country.

These are Lebanon's objectives; those are its enemies. As for our friends, they are all the world's oppressed peoples. Our friends are also those who combat our enemies and who defend us from their evil. Towards these friends, individuals as well as organizations, we turn and say:

Friends, wherever you are in Lebanon . . . we are in agreement with you on the great and necessary objectives: destroying American hegemony in our land; putting an end to the burdensome Israeli Occupation; beating back all the Phalangists' attempts to monopolize power and administration. . . .

This is the minimum that we can accept in order to be able to accede by legal means to realize our ambitions, to save Lebanon from its dependence upon East and West, to put an end to foreign occupation and to adopt a regime freely wanted by the people of Lebanon. . . .

World Scene

We reject both the USSR and the US, both Capitalism and Communism, for both are incapable of laying the foundations for a just society.

With special vehemence we reject UNIFIL as they were sent by world arrogance to occupy areas evacuated by Israel and serve for the latter as a buffer zone. They should be treated much like the Zionists. . . .

The Necessity for the Destruction of Israel

We see in Israel the vanguard of the United States in our Islamic world. It is the hated enemy that must be fought until the hated ones get what they deserve. This enemy is the greatest danger to our future generations and to the destiny of our lands, particularly as it glorifies the ideas of settlement and expansion, initiated in Palestine, and yearning outward to the extension of the Great Israel, from the Euphrates to the Nile.

Our primary assumption in our fight against Israel states that the Zionist entity is aggressive from its inception, and built on lands wrested from their owners, at the expense of the rights of the Muslim people. Therefore our struggle will end only when this entity is obliterated. We recognize no treaty with it, no cease fire, and no peace agreements, whether separate or consolidated.

We vigorously condemn all plans for negotiation with Israel, and regard all negotiators as enemies, for the reason that such negotiation is nothing but the recognition of the legitimacy of the Zionist occupation of Palestine. Therefore we oppose and reject the Camp David Agreements, the proposals of King Fahd, the Fez and Reagan plan, Brezhnev's and the French-Egyptian proposals, and all other programs that include the recognition (even the implied recognition) of the Zionist entity.

Source: "The Hizballah Program," *Jerusalem Quarterly* 48 (Fall 1988): 111–116.

157. Communiqué of the Intifada (January 8, 1988)

Introduction

By the mid-1980s the frustration of Palestinians in the occupied territories was growing as faith in the perennially stalemated peace process declined, Israeli settlements expanded, and the prospect of any kind of Palestinian state was perpetually receding. Egypt had renounced its outstanding claims to the occupied Gaza Strip, and Jordan was wearying of advocating its own rights in the occupied West Bank. Most Arab leaders had by this time toned down their rhetoric in support of the Palestinians and had some kind of dealings, whether official or not, with Israel. Palestinians in the occupied territories had high birthrates and only limited access to land for either housing or agriculture, and unemployment was rising. Many still lived in camps. In the absence of elections, they lacked a political voice and also resented repressive Israeli tactics designed to crush dissent, including sporadic killings of leading agitators, mass detentions, the demolition of houses, and deportations. Muslim clerical leaders also urged opposition to Israel. Although the Palestine Liberation Organization quickly claimed credit for the First Intifada, its origins were apparently spontaneous. It was sparked by rioting that broke out near the Jabalya camp in Gaza, home to 60,000 refugees, when 4 Palestinians were killed in a traffic accident in early December 1987. Israeli troops shot dead an 18-year-old Palestinian man who was throwing stones, and the situation snowballed. Riots broke out in camps across the occupied territories, particularly among teenage youths who threw stones and sometimes grenades or Molotov cocktails, to which Israeli forces often responded with bullets. On December 22, 1987, the United Nations Security Council condemned Israel for violating the Geneva Conventions by shooting numerous protesters dead. The intifada continued until the Oslo Accords were signed in 1993, by which time 1,162 Palestinians, including 241 children, and 160 Israelis had died. Casualties were highest in the first year, with 332 Palestinian and 12 Israeli deaths by the end of 1988. The communiqués clandestinely distributed among the Palestinians conveyed the sense of excitement, purpose, and solidarity that emerged among the Palestinian community in the intifada's early days, reenergizing people who had almost lost faith in themselves and eventually revitalizing long-stalled peace negotiations.

Document

In the name of God, the merciful, the compassionate.

Our people's glorious uprising continues. We affirm the need to express solidarity with our people wherever they are. We continue to be loyal to the pure blood of our martyrs and to our detained brothers. We also reiterate our rejection of the occupation and its policy of repression, represented in the policy of deportation, mass arrests, curfews, and the demolition of houses.

We reaffirm the need to achieve further cohesion with our revolution and our heroic masses. We also stress our abidance by the call of the PLO, the Palestinian people's legitimate and sole representative, and the need to pursue the bountiful offerings and the heroic uprising. For all these reasons, we address the following call:

All sectors of our heroic people in every location should abide by the call for a general and comprehensive strike until Wednesday evening, 13 January 1988. The strike covers all public and private trade utilities, the Palestinian workers and public transportation. Abidance by the comprehensive strike must be complete. The slogan of the strike will be: Down with occupation; long live Palestine as a free and Arab country.

Brother workers, your abidance by the strike by not going to work and to plants is real support for the glorious uprising, a sanctioning of the pure blood of our martyrs, a support for the call to liberate our prisoners, and an act that will help keep our brother deportees in their homeland.

Brother businessmen and grocers, you must fully abide by the call for a comprehensive strike during the period of the strike. Your abidance by previous strikes is one of the most splendid images of solidarity and sacrifice for the sake of rendering our heroic people's stand a success.

We will do our best to protect the interests of our honest businessmen against measures the Zionist occupation force may resort to against you. We warn against the consequences of becoming involved with some of the occupation authorities' henchmen who will seek to make you open your businesses. We promise you that we will punish such traitor businessmen in the not too distant future. Let us proceed united to forge victory.

Brother owners of taxi companies, we will not forget your honorable and splendid stand of supporting and implementing the comprehensive strike on the day of Palestinian steadfastness. We pin our hopes on you to support and make the comprehensive strike a success. We warn some bus companies against the consequences of not abiding by the call for the strike, as this will make them liable to revolutionary punishment.

Brother doctors and pharmacists, you must be on emergency status to offer assistance to those of our kinfolk who are ill. The brother pharmacists must carry out their duties normally. The brother doctors must place the doctor badge in a way that can be clearly identified.

General warning: We would like to warn people that walking in the streets will not be safe in view of the measures that will be taken to make the comprehensive strike a success. We warn that viscous material will be poured on main and secondary streets and everywhere, in addition to the roadblocks and the strike groups that will be deployed throughout the occupied homeland.

Circular: The struggler and brother members of the popular committees and the men of the uprising who are deployed in all the working locations should work to support and assist our people within the available means, particularly the needy families of our people. The strike groups and the popular uprising groups must completely abide by the working program, which is in their possession. Let us proceed united and loudly chant: Down with occupation; long live Palestine as a free and Arab country.

Source: Zachary Lockman and Joel Beinin, eds., *Intifada: The Palestinian Uprising against Israeli Occupation* (Boston: South End Press, 1989), 328–329.

158. President Ronald Reagan: Letter to Thomas P. O'Neill, Speaker of the House of Representatives and President Pro Tempore of the Senate, on the Destruction of an Iranian Jetliner by the U.S. Navy over the Persian Gulf (July 4, 1988)

Introduction

The United States provoked an embarrassing international incident on July 3, 1988, when the naval cruiser *Vincennes,* part of the American task force in the Persian Gulf, shot down an Iranian civilian airliner, Flight 655 from the coastal city of Bandar Abbas, Iran, to Dubai, killing all 290 passengers and crew including 66 children and 38 non-Iranian citizens. In a letter to the Speaker of the House of Representatives, President Ronald Reagan stated that at the time of this incident the *Vincennes* was also responding to attacks by small Iranian patrol boats that were targeting international shipping, and its crew therefore believed that the approaching aircraft had hostile intentions toward them. He promised a "full investigation" by the Defense Department. Pentagon officials publicly stated that Iran Air Flight 655 had ignored several radioed warnings to change course but later suggested that it was uncertain whether the *Vincennes* had successfully opened radio contact.

Three years later, U.S. admiral William J. Crowe publicly admitted that the *Vincennes* had been operating in Iranian territorial waters, something that the U.S. Navy had denied at the time. The failure of the Department of Defense to release portions of its report into the downing of the Iranian flight aroused suspicions that an official cover-up had occurred, although subsequent studies suggest that human error and the aggressive style of the captain of the *Vincennes* were probably responsible for a genuine mistake. The U.S. government expressed its regret for the incident but never apologized for it, admitted any wrongdoing, or accepted responsibility, continuing to blame hostile Iranian actions for its occurrence. Speaking to reporters on August 2, 1988, Reagan said of this incident that "I will never apologize for the United States of America—I don't care what the facts are."

Document

On July 3, 1988, the USS VINCENNES and USS ELMER MONTGOMERY were operating in international waters of the Persian Gulf near the Strait of Hormuz. (On July 2, the MONTGOMERY had responded to a distress signal from a Danish tanker that was under attack by Iranian small boats and had fired a warning shot, which caused the breaking off of the attack.) Having indications that approximately a dozen Iranian small boats were congregating to attack merchant shipping, the VINCENNES sent a Mark III LAMPS Helicopter on investigative patrol in international airspace to assess the situation. At about 1010 local Gulf time (2:10 a.m. EDT), when the helicopter had approached to within only four nautical miles, it was fired on by Iranian small boats (the VINCENNES was ten nautical miles from the scene at this time). The LAMPS helicopter was not damaged and returned immediately to the VINCENNES.

As the VINCENNES and MONTGOMERY were approaching the group of Iranian small boats at approximately 1042 local time, at least four of the small boats turned toward and began closing in on the American warships. At this time, both American ships opened fire on the small craft, sinking two and damaging a third. Regrettably, in the course of the U.S. response to the Iranian attack, an Iranian civilian airliner was shot down by the VINCENNES, which was firing in self defense at what it believed to be a hostile Iranian military aircraft. We deeply regret the tragic loss of life that occurred. The Defense Department will conduct a full investigation.

The actions of U.S. forces in response to being attacked by Iranian small boats were taken in accordance with our inherent right of self-defense, as recognized in Article 51 of the United Nations Charter, and pursuant to my constitutional authority with respect to the conduct of foreign relations and as Commander in Chief. There has been no further hostile action by Iranian forces, and, although U.S. forces will remain prepared to take additional defensive action to protect our units and military personnel, we regard this incident as closed. U.S. forces suffered no casualties or damage.

Since March 1987, I and members of my Administration have provided to Congress letters, reports, briefings, and testimony in connection with developments in the Persian Gulf and the activities of U.S. Armed Forces in the region. In accordance with my desire that Congress continue to be fully informed in this matter, I am providing this report consistent with the War Powers Resolution. I look forward to cooperating with Congress in pursuit of our mutual, overriding aim of peace and stability in the Persian Gulf region.

Source: Ronald Reagan, *Public Papers of the Presidents of the United States: Ronald Reagan, 1988–1989,* Book 2 (Washington, DC: U.S. Government Printing Office, 1991), 920–921.

159. Defining the Hamas Movement: The Hamas Charter (1988)

Introduction

As the Palestine Liberation Organization (PLO) moved closer to opening genuine negotiations with Israel and accepting, however grudgingly, the right to existence of its longtime enemy, more militant Islamic-influenced elements among the Palestinians and other Arabs dissented, establishing the Islamic Resistance Movement, usually known as Hamas. The organization evolved from the Islamic Mujama group, established in 1973 in Gaza with Israeli encouragement as a Muslim welfare group that was itself an offshoot of the Muslim Brotherhood, a Palestinian organization established in 1946 to encourage the development of a religious outlook within Palestinian society. The fundamentalist Muslim resurgence of the 1980s, fueled by the establishment of an Islamic government in Iran in 1979, encouraged the Mujama to take a harder line in asserting strict Islamic principles and tenets among the Gazan population. In February 1988 soon after the First Intifada began, the Mujama established Hamas so that its members could join in the uprising. A political wing conducted propaganda; an intelligence section handled internal policing, killing or punishing collaborators with Israel; and the military wing—later merged with the intelligence branch—undertook violent action against Israel, including the kidnapping and killing of Israeli soldiers. PLO and Hamas representatives were often at odds, and Hamas gradually became an influential faction within the PLO, soon rivaling PLO chairman Yasser Arafat's original Fatah organization.

The lengthy Hamas charter, promulgated in August 1988, took a far more uncompromising line than Arafat was now embracing. Hamas claimed that all of Palestine, including Israeli territory, was a sacred Islamic trust, none of which could or should be abandoned. Islamic sharia, or religious law, ought to prevail throughout Palestine. Hamas opposed all peace negotiations, stating that "Initiatives, and so-called peaceful solutions and international conferences, contradict the Islamic Resistance Movement's ideological position." Jihad, or holy war, was the only solution to the Palestinian question. The struggle against Israel could not end until Israel had been totally destroyed. Hamas embraced violence and terror as the only methods that could accomplish the return of all Palestine to the Palestinians and Islamic rule. The emergence of Hamas as a significant factor in Palestinian politics, given the organization's strong religious orientation and its belief that compromise or negotiations with Israel amounted to sacrilege, greatly complicated subsequent efforts for peace. Hamas would not be content with establishing a Palestinian state in the occupied territories alone but instead sought to regain all the lands considered part of Israel. Hamas's emphasis on providing welfare services to ordinary Palestinians along with its unsubtle message and staunch religious orientation soon won it considerable popularity among the Arab masses, while its programs received substantial financial support from other Arab governments.

Document

The ideological tenets

Article 1

The path of the Islamic Resistance Movement is the path of Islam, from which it draws its principles, concepts, terms and worldview with regard to life and man. It turns to [Islam] when religious rulings are required and asks [Islam] for inspiration to guide its steps.

The relationship between the Islamic Resistance Movement and the Muslim Brotherhood

Article 2

The Islamic Resistance Movement is the branch of the Muslim Brotherhood in Palestine. The Muslim Brotherhood is a global organization and the largest Islamic movement in modem times. It excels in profound understanding and has an exact, fully comprehensive perception of all Islamic concepts in all areas of life: understanding and thought, politics and economics, education and social affairs, law and government, spreading Islam and teaching, art and the media, by that which is hidden and by martyrdom and in the other areas of life.

Strategy and means The strategy of the Islamic Resistance Movement Palestine is Islamic Waqf [Religious Endowment] land

Article 11

The Islamic Resistance Movement believes that the land of Palestine is a religious Islamic endowment for all Muslims until Resurrection Day. It is forbidden to relinquish it or any part of it or give it up or any part of it. It does not belong to any Arab country, or to all the Arab countries, or to any king or president, or kings or presidents, or to any organization or organizations, whether they are Palestinian or Arab, because Palestine is sacred Islamic endowment land and belongs to Muslims until Resurrection Day. Its legal status is in accordance with Islamic law. . . .

Peaceful solutions, diplomatic initiatives and international conferences

Article 13

Initiatives, the so-called peaceful solutions and international conferences to find a solution to the Palestinian problem, contradict the Islamic Resistance Movement's ideological position. Giving up any part whatsoever of [the land of] Palestine is like ignoring a part of [the Muslim] faith. . . .

There is no solution to the Palestinian problem except jihad. As for international initiatives, suggestions and conferences, they are an empty waste of time and complete nonsense. . . .

The jihad for the sake of liberating Palestine is a personal duty

Article 15

The day enemies steal part of Muslim land, jihad [becomes] the personal duty of every Muslim. With regard to the usurpation of Palestine by the Jews, it is a must to fly the banner of jihad. That means the propagation of Islamic awareness among the masses—locally [in Palestine], the Arab world and the Muslim world. The spirit of jihad must be disseminated within the [Islamic] nation, the enemies must be engaged in battle and [every Muslim must] join the ranks of the jihad warriors [mujahideen]. . . .

The forces which support the enemy

Article 22

[Our] enemies planned their deeds well for a long time [and managed] to achieve whatever they have, employing the factors influencing the course of events. Therefore, they acted to pile up huge amounts of influential material resources, which they utilized to fulfill their dream. Thus [the Jews], by means of their money, have taken over the international communications media: the news agencies, newspapers, publishing houses, broadcasting stations, etc. . . . In fact, they were behind the First

World War, through which they achieved the abolishment of the Islamic Caliphate, made a profit and took over many of the sources of wealth. They [also] got the Balfour Declaration and established the League of the United [sic] Nations to enable them to rule the world. They were also behind the Second World War, in which they made immense profits by buying and selling military equipment, and also prepared the ground for the founding of their [own] state. They ordered the establishment of the United Nations and the Security Council [sic] which replaced the League of the United [sic] Nations, to be able to use it to rule the world. No war takes place anywhere in the world without [the Jews] behind the scenes having a hand in it. . . .

In fact, the forces of imperialism in the capitalist west and Communist east support the [Zionist] enemy as stoutly as possible with both material and manpower. They alternate with one another [in giving support]. . . .

Arab and Islamic states and governments

Article 28

. . . [T]he Arab states bordering Israel are required to open their borders to the jihad warriors belonging to the Arab/Muslim nations, so that they may fulfill their role and join their efforts to those of the Muslim brethren in Palestine.

With regard to the other Arab/Muslim nations, they are required to facilitate the passage of the jihad warriors through their territory, which is the very least they can do.

Source: "The Hamas Charter (1988)," Intelligence & Terrorism Information Center, http://www.terrorism-info.org.il.

160. Jad al-Haqq, Sheikh al-Azhar: "Fatwa against the Iraqi Invasion of Kuwait" (1990)

Introduction

In August 1990, the military forces of President Saddam Hussein of Iraq invaded and annexed the small but extremely wealthy neighboring emirate of Kuwait. Despite Hussein's sedulous efforts to present his invasion of Kuwait as a blow for Pan-Arab and Islamic causes, he failed to win the support of most Arab political and clerical leaders. Ten days after the invasion Jad al-Haqq, the grand imam of al-Azhar University in Cairo, Egypt, the most prestigious institution of learning in the Sunni Muslim world, issued a statement condemning Hussein's action and calling on him to withdraw Iraqi forces from Kuwait and restore its previous government. When Hussein ignored this directive, the grand imam took stronger action, making his behavior the subject of a fatwa, or legal pronouncement. Charging Hussein with "sinful aggression" and an act of "oppression" that set Muslim against Muslim and divided the Arab world in betrayal of Islamic principles, the grand imam declared that according to Muslim precepts, this emergency "requires that armies and forces are sped to surround the ill-doer, so that his harm will not spread; and to contain him as a fire is contained." The grand imam commended the Arab and Islamic states for having taken such actions and proclaimed that their requests "for assistance from [outside] multinational forces" were also justified on the grounds that "[t]hey are Muslim forces or allied to them, and assistance by such troops is permitted in Islam." Following these principles, the grand imam specifically endorsed the presence of "foreign troops" in Saudi Arabia. In conclusion, he once more called on Iraq's leaders to end their occupation of Kuwait and allow the emirate's "legitimate government" to return. The grand imam's fatwa was striking evidence that Hussein's strategy of depicting himself as a champion of Islam and Pan-Arab nationalism had failed to win over many of the Muslim world's most influential leaders.

Document

The Grand Iman Sheikh Jad Al Haq Ali Jad Al Haq, Sheikh Al Azhar announced in his statement released yesterday to the Arab and Islamic world that the Azhar Al Sharif expresses its grave concern over Iraqi insistence on continuing its aggression against our brother Kuwait. He confirmed that the resort to Arab, Islamic and foreign troops to defend the sacrosanct in Islam was permitted by religion, and that the responsibility of the Islamic armies was to contain the malfeasor so as to prevent his danger from spreading. The statement also called upon President Saddam Hussein and his government to listen to the voice of Islam and of truth, and to desist from the use of force in recognition of their true belonging to the Arab and Islamic nation. The statement reads as follows:

The Azhar Al Sharif has directed an appeal to the peoples of the Arab and Islamic nation and to its leaders, published and broadcast on Friday 19th Muharram 1411 A.H., 10th August 1990 A.D. It coincided with the holding of the Arab summit in Cairo on the same day, at the invitation of President Muhammed Hosni Mubarak, to take cognizance of the nefarious effects on the Arab and Islamic nation resulting from the interference by the leaders of Iraq and their aggression against the State of Kuwait, invading it militarily and occupying its land, and breaching its peoples' rights, as well as all that has been published regarding the pillage of money and the destruction of property. The world has unanimously condemned this grave act, and all international organizations have taken action, such as the Organization of the Islamic Conference, the Conference of Foreign Ministers of Islamic States, the Arab League and the UN Security Council. All this was done on the day the disaster befell, the 2nd August 1990 A.D. Some time has passed since this event that shook the world occurred, and the fleets and armies of different countries, with their arms of terror and destruction, have flocked to our Arab arena where it happened. Yet the leaders of Iraq remain impervious to advice and to the wisdom of Allah in his Book. The Quran calls for aiding the oppressed, and preventing oppression even unto the point of fighting it. For this reason, the Azhar Al Sharif today expresses its grave concern for the future of the Arab and Islamic Nation in light of the insistence on this sinful aggression and its excesses. Al Azhar has called on, and repeats its call to President Saddam Hussein and his government to be true to their membership of the Arab and Islamic Nation, and to desist from this action that has aborted the Arab Nation's abilities to progress and to grow, and trapped it in a cycle of killing that will come from whence they know not, as well as reducing its standing among the nations, leaving it bereft of the spirit of empathy, cooperation and friendliness within it. And all this by its own hand, not by the hands of a stranger: one of its leaders erred and left the path of righteousness. He overran a country and people that had lived in comfort and security, performing their duties to their Nation in all domains, and terrorized women, children and the old in their very homes in the dead of night. This is not the deed of a Muslim. The prophet (pbuh) warns of terrorizing Muslims, saying (according to Abu Daoud): "It is not permitted for a Muslim to terrorize another." In another saying related by Al Bazar and others, he said: "Do not terrorize a Muslim, for the terror of a Muslim is a great oppression." In the saying of Abu Huraira, related by Al Tabarani: "Whomsoever looks at a Muslim so as to frighten him without just cause will be frightened by Allah on the Day of Judgment." The prophet (pbuh) also forbade the terrorizing of Muslims by pointing a weapon towards them, saying as related by Al Shaikhan: "Do not point a weapon at your brother for you know not lest Satan pull at your arm and you fall into a pit of fire." In a saying by Muslim Abu Huraira, "He who points a piece of iron at his brother will be damned by the angels until the end, even if it be his brother to his father or mother." In a saying by Ibn Masoud related by Al Bukhari, "Cursing a Muslim is to stray from the path of righteousness and killing him is to leave the faith." Yet where is all this, regarding what the Iraqi army has done to Kuwait, the destruction, terror, killing, expulsion, plunder and pillage? And what about the Islamic prohibition against terrorizing non-combatants, and killing and torturing them? What happened in terms of the inhumane acts perpetrated by the Iraqi army against Kuwait and its people, as related by the news agencies, is a terrifying and sad thing, refused by Islam and repellent to the conscience of Muslims.

This unenviable situation in which Iraq has placed the Nation, to prepare to face the impending catastrophe that will nigh on annihilate it if the Iraqi leaders continue to the end of their devastating path, requires the Arab and Islamic Nation to respond, and to heed the call to stand against this wrong. Defense of the self and of the Nation requires that armies and forces are sped to surround the ill-doer, so that his harm will not spread; and to contain him as a fire is contained. Allah has permitted fighting the ill-doer: "So fight the malfeasor until it awakens to Allah's commands." And yet the Arab and Islamic forces have heeded the call and come to the aid of the rest of the countries that are exposed to the evil of this catastrophe. They have collaborated in containing the catastrophe in an attempt to stop it until those in charge of it become aware of the extent of the loss caused by this wicked deed; occupying an Arab Muslim people; breaching the sacrosanct relationship that binds neighbors with a military force vastly superior in numbers and equipment. And let those who are attempting to cause the region to explode, and to destroy it, after they have broken the inviolable sanctity of a country and its people, look what good has come to them of this wickedness? And what has the Nation lost? And are the two equal?

This is a great blow that has been dealt to the nation's dignity and its abilities. Even if the Iraqi army has plundered money and committed sins, this is not a gain but more of the same wickedness. It has been forbidden by Allah; he has warned of the penalties, and ordered that it be combated. The force that overran Kuwait had prepared itself and was more than ready. It entered in the dead of night without prior warning, nay in flagrant breach of treaties and promises made by the leaders of Iraq not to do what they have done, and to sit with their neighbor to discuss and debate their differences. It was a terrible surprise for Kuwait and its people then to be viciously attacked with heavy armor, guns and missiles and all the other implements of modern war. This is not of the courage of Arabs and Muslims, nor of the nature of an Arab to raise his sword except against a foe with a sword; for he would never surprise a foe in safety, nor attack an unarmed opponent. Yet how far this is from what happened. Has this attacking army been bereft of the morals of Arabs and of their nature, and all that runs in the teachings of Islam that forbid the stealth and the use of surprise attacks against a foe that has no arms? If the Arab peoples surrounding Kuwait were afraid and surprised by the actions of the Iraqi army, and called on the armies of the Arab and Islamic states, and of other countries that have the weapons to equal those used by Iraq against Kuwait, there is no wrong in this. Their cry for assistance from these multinational forces is based on the principle of international treaties, and it is their right to defend themselves and to protect their land from this treacherous brother who has heeded no treaty nor promise nor responsibility. Iraq's claim that by doing so, it becomes a mujahid is untrue, for jihad cannot be in doing wrong, nor in aggression against a fraternal Muslim neighbor. In addition, the claim that the incoming troops have denigrated the land and the sacrosanct is untrue also, for they come with the permission of the owners of that land, and to protect them from aggression. They are Muslim forces or allied to them, and assistance by such troops is permitted in Islam, indeed it is one of the foundations of Islam: one of the rights a Muslim has against another is that he require his help and support to counter oppression, and the same applies to the allied forces also. The claim that the sanctity of the holy land has been breached by allowing foreign troops to set foot in the Kingdom of Saudi Arabia is untrue, for the troops are either Muslim or allied to them, and came to counter aggression and fight oppression. Al Azhar Al Sharif, despite this painful reality and our desire to surmount it, and indeed to uncover the harm that has been done to the Nation, calls on the leaders of Iraq to desist from what they have done, and to withdraw their armies to their own borders; calls for the return of Kuwait's legitimate government to its country and people; and this in order to return to the good and repent from evil for the return to righteousness is better than continuing in the path of evil, and the best of the sinners are those that repent. "O ye faithful, respond to Allah and to his prophet if he calls you to that which gives you life, and know that Allah is present between Man and his heart, and that to Him you will come."

Source: Turi Munthe, ed., *The Saddam Hussein Reader* (New York: Thunder's Mouth, 2002), 246–250.

161. Amnesty International: Report on Kuwait (December 19, 1990)

Introduction

As the United Nations deadline for Iraqi withdrawal from Kuwait steadily approached, in December 1990 the respected human rights organization Amnesty International released a report on Iraqi treatment of Kuwait's population. While taking no position on the rights or wrongs of the conflict itself, the report detailed what it termed "widespread abuses of human rights . . . perpetrated by Iraqi forces." These included the arbitrary arrest of thousands of Kuwaitis, many of whom had been tortured; hundreds of executions without trial of unarmed civilians, including children; and the disappearance of hundreds more, many of them feared dead. The report stated that at least 300,000 Kuwaitis as well as several hundred thousand foreign nationals previously working there had fled Kuwait. It also charged that Saddam Hussein's forces were merely extending to Kuwait the brutal human rights abuses that had already been standard in Iraq for many years. In addition to the arbitrary violence demonstrated against people, the report described widespread looting of both public and private property by Iraqi troops, behavior apparently sanctioned and encouraged, if not ordered, by their commanders. Kuwaitis had been forced to accept Iraqi currency, identity papers, car registration, and time zone, and Iraqi officials had taken over all the Kuwaiti media. The Iraqi authorities had refused to admit to Kuwait representatives of the media, the International Committee of the Red Cross, and human rights organizations and had ignored representations from Amnesty International over a wide range of human rights violations, including extralegal executions, arbitrary arrests and detentions, torture, and rape. The Amnesty International report was a strong indictment of Iraqi rule in Kuwait, providing added humanitarian ammunition to those who favored the use of force if necessary to end the occupation.

Document

Summary

December 19, 1990

Widespread abuses of human rights have been perpetrated by Iraqi forces following the invasion of Kuwait on 2 August. These include the arbitrary arrest and detention without trial of thousands of civilians and military personnel; the widespread torture of such persons in custody; the imposition of the death penalty and the extrajudicial execution of hundreds of unarmed civilians, including children. In addition, hundreds of people in Kuwait remain unaccounted for, having effectively "disappeared" in detention, and many of them are feared dead. To date, an estimated 300,000 Kuwaitis have fled their country, as well as several hundred thousand foreign nationals working in Kuwait. Their accounts have received worldwide media coverage. This document details some of these abuses, confining itself to those violations which fall within Amnesty International's mandate.

Amnesty International takes no position on the conflict in the Gulf, and does not condone killings and other acts of violence perpetrated by the parties to the conflict. What concerns the organization are human rights violations taking place in that context. Those violations which have been reported since 2 August are entirely consistent with abuses known to have been committed in Iraq over many years, and which have been documented by Amnesty International in its numerous reports. Iraq's policy of the brutal suppression of all forms of internal dissent continues to be implemented, and the people of Iraq remain its victims. Amnesty International has repeatedly placed such information on the public record, and regrets that until the invasion of Kuwait, the international community did not see fit to apply serious pressure in an attempt to put an end to these abuses.

Source: "Iraq/Occupied Kuwait: Human Rights Violations since August 2, 1990–December 19, 1990," Amnesty International, https://www.amnesty.org/download/Documents/MDE140161990ENGLISH.PDF. Reprinted with permission.

162. Iraqi President Saddam Hussein: "The Mother of All Battles" Speech (January 20, 1991)

Introduction

Within days of the beginning of United Nations coalition air strikes against Iraqi targets, Saddam Hussein addressed the Iraqi people, urging them to rally to their country's defense. He declared that Iraq had not yet used its naval and air forces or its full missile strength against its attackers and that he was waiting until the best moment to do so. Iraqis were, he proclaimed, defending the cause of God, Islam, and the Arab world against "atheism, injustice, and tyranny." Hussein promised that ultimately Iraq would respond and would then win "the mother of all battles," opening the way to the destruction of Israel, the liberation of Lebanon and the Golan Heights from Israeli occupation, and the replacement of the existing pro-American regime in Saudi Arabia. He called on Arabs everywhere to support Iraq and target Western interests in a "holy war." Long on rhetoric and defiance and short on specifics, Hussein's speech was intended not just to hearten his own people but also to rally the Arab world around him in his increasingly desperate plight.

162. Iraqi President Saddam Hussein: "The Mother of All Battles" Speech

Document

In the name of God, the merciful, the compassionate. God hath purchased of the believers their persons and their goods, for theirs in return is the garden of Paradise. They fight in His cause, and slay and are slain—a promise binding on him in truth, through the law, the Gospel, and the Koran. And who is more faithful to his covenant than God? Then rejoice in the bargain which ye have concluded—that is the achievement supreme.

O glorious Iraqis, O holy warrior Iraqis, O Arabs, O believers wherever you are, we and our steadfastness are holding. Here is the great Iraqi people, your brothers and sons of your Arab nation and the great faithful part of the human family. We are all well. They are fighting with unparalleled heroism, unmatched except by the heroism of the believers who fight similar adversaries. And here is the infidel tyrant whose planes and missiles are falling out of the skies at the blows of the brave men. He is wondering how the Iraqis can confront his fading dreams with such determination and firmness.

After a while, he will begin to feel frustrated, and his defeat will be certain, God willing, when he has tangible proof that he [words indistinct]. We in Iraq will be the faithful and obedient servants of God, struggling for His sake to raise the banner of truth and justice, the banner of "God is Great." Accursed be the lowly.

At that time, the valiant Iraqi men and women will not allow the army of atheism, treachery, hypocrisy and [word indistinct] to realize their stupid hope that the war would only last a few days or weeks, as they imagined and declared. In the coming period, the response of Iraq will be on a larger scale, using all the means and potential that God has given us and which we have so far only used in part. Our ground forces have not entered the battle so far, and only a small part of our air force has been used.

"Divine Reinforcement"

The army's air force has not been used, nor has the navy. The weight and effect of our ready missile force has not yet been applied in full. The fact remains that the great divine reinforcement is our source of power and effectiveness. When the war is fought in a comprehensive manner, using all resources and weapons, the scale of death and the number of dead will, God willing, rise among the ranks of atheism, injustice, and tyranny.

When they begin to die and when the message of the Iraqi soldiers reaches the farthest corner of the world, the unjust will die and the "God is Great" banner will flutter with great victory in the mother of all battles. Then the skies in the Arab homeland will appear in a new color and a sun of new hope will shine over them and over our nation and on all the good men whose bright lights will not be overcome by the darkness in the hearts of the infidels, the Zionists, and the treacherous, shameful rulers, such as the traitor Fahd.

Then the door will be wide open for the liberation of beloved Palestine, Lebanon, and the Golan. Then Jerusalem and the Dome of the Rock will be released from bondage. The Kaaba and the Tomb of the Prophet Mohammed, God's peace and blessings be upon him, will be liberated from occupation and God will bestow upon the poor and needy the things that others owed them, others who withheld from them what they owed them as God had justly ordained, which is a great deal.

"Carry Out Holy War"

Then [words indistinct], the good men, the holy warriors, and the faithful will know the truth of our promise to them that when the forces of infidelity attack the Iraqis, they will fight as they wished them to fight and perhaps in a better way, and that their promise is of faith and holy war. It remains for us to tell all Arabs, all the faithful strugglers, and all good supporters wherever they are: you have a duty to carry out holy war and struggle in order to target the assembly of evil, treason, and corruption everywhere.

You must also target their interests everywhere. It is a duty that is incumbent upon you, and that must necessarily correspond to the struggle of your brothers in Iraq. You will be part of the struggle of armed forces in your holy war and struggle, and part of the multitude of faith and the faithful. If the opposing multitude captures you, you will be prisoners in their hands, even if they refuse to admit this in their communiques and statements.

You will inevitably be released when the war ends, in accordance with international laws and agreements which will govern the release of prisoners of war. In this way you will have pleased God and honored, with your slogans and principles, the trust given to you.

God is great, God is great, God is great, and accursed be the lowly.

Source: Saddam Hussein, "The Mother of All Battles," Baghdad, Iraq, January 20, 1991, cited in Steven A. Yetiv, *The Persian Gulf Crisis* (Westport, CT: Greenwood, 1997), 176–177.

163. Yitzkah Rabin's Last Speech: Peace Rally, Kings of Israel Square, Tel Aviv (November 4, 1995)

Introduction

In September 1993, the government of Israel and the Palestine Liberation Organization (PLO) formally recognized each other and signed the Oslo Declaration, a statement of principles that anticipated the establishment within five years on the occupied West Bank and the Gaza Strip of an autonomous self-governing Palestinian authority. Even though the 1995 Oslo Interim Agreements permitted Israeli forces to maintain effective control of much of these territories and the Israeli government continued to expand new settlements in the West Bank and East Jerusalem, these compromise arrangements were anathema to many conservative Israeli politicians, extremist settlers, and Ultra-Orthodox Jews. The issue polarized the Israeli population. In the fall of 1995, right-wing Israelis held massive demonstrations against the interim agreements and any Israeli withdrawals from West Bank territories. Moderate Israelis likewise organized huge rallies in favor of peace, and Prime Minister Yitzhak Rabin agreed to appear at a peace demonstration in Tel Aviv, scheduled for November 4, 1995. Rabin, who one year earlier had shared the Nobel Peace Prize with Israel's foreign minister, Shimon Peres, and PLO chairman Yasser Arafat, again spoke eloquently in favor of the peace process as the only way of ensuring Israel's long-term survival. Recalling his own 27 years in the military, Rabin argued that while fighting was sometimes necessary and inevitable, whenever it was feasible peace was the better course. He also assailed those Ultra-Orthodox and right-wing Israeli critics of the interim agreements who were advocating the use of violence against their architects, himself included, warning that such behavior was "undermining the very foundations of Israeli democracy." Ironically, during the rally he was assassinated by Yigal Amir, an orthodox and deeply anti-Arab Jewish student of theology and a former Israeli soldier who believed that Rabin's policies were endangering Israel and therefore justified his death as a threat to state security. The assassination, revealing as it did the depths of political divisions, extremism, and hatred within the country, shocked Israel and the international community. For supporters of the peace process, Rabin became a posthumous icon and martyr, the earlier ambiguities and reservations of his policies forgotten.

Document

Allow me to say, I am also moved. I want to thank each and every one of you who stood up here against violence and for peace. This government, which I have the privilege to lead, together with my friend Shimon Peres, decided to give peace a chance. A peace that will solve most of the problems of the State of Israel. I was a military man for twenty-seven years. I fought as long as there were no prospects for peace. Today I believe that there are prospects for peace, great prospects. We must take advantage of it for the sake of those standing here, and for the sake of those who do not stand here. And they are many among our people.

I have always believed that the majority of the people want peace, are prepared to take risks for peace. And you here, by showing up at this rally, prove it, along with the many who did not make it here, that the people truly want peace and oppose violence. Violence is undermining the very foundations of Israeli democracy. It must be condemned, denounced, and isolated. This is not the way of the State of Israel. Controversies may arise in a democracy, but the decision must be reached through democratic elections, just as it happened in 1992, when we were given the mandate to do what we are doing, and to continue to do it.

I want to thank from here the President of Egypt, the King of Jordan, and the King of Morocco, whose representatives are present here, conveying their partnership with us on the march toward peace. But above all—the people of Israel, who have proven, in the three years this government has been in office, that peace is attainable, a peace that will provide an opportunity for a progressive society and economy. Peace exists first and foremost in our prayers, but not only in prayers. Peace is what the Jewish People aspire to, a true aspiration.

Peace entails difficulties, even pain. Israel knows no path devoid of pain. But the path of peace is preferable to the path of war. I say this to you as one who was a military man and minister of defense, and who saw the pain of the families of IDF soldiers. It is for their sake, and for the sake of our children and grandchildren, that I want this government to exert every effort, exhaust every opportunity, to promote and to reach a comprehensive peace.

This rally must send a message to the Israeli public, to the Jewish community throughout the world, to many, many in the Arab world and in the entire world, that the people of Israel want peace, support peace, and for that, I thank you very much.

Source: U.S. Congress, "Anniversary of the Death of Israeli Prime Minister Yitzak Rabin," *Congressional Record,* November 19, 2003, H11628, http://www.congress.gov/cgi-bin/query/z?r108:H19NO3-0068:.

164. Sheikh Omar Abdel-Rahman: Messages to His Followers (1995–1999)

Introduction

After Islamic extremists planted bombs in 1993 in the World Trade Center building in New York, their leader, Sheikh Omar Abdel-Rahman, was arrested, convicted, and sentenced in 1995 to life plus 15 years in jail in the United States. He continued to exhort his followers to free him from prison and, should that prove impossible, to take revenge on those who had incarcerated him. He also ordered members of his political grouping, the Islamic Group, to refuse to participate in Egyptian politics as a recognized party. He discouraged his acolytes from endorsing calls for cease-fires and truces, even as he urged them to display a certain circumspection when dealing with less uncompromising activists. Silencing the sheikh proved to be exceptionally difficult. In his confinement, he persuaded his lawyer to smuggle out messages exhorting his Islamic Group followers in Egypt to mount violent attacks targeting foreign tourists visiting historic sites. When his disciples did so, massacring 58 tourists at the Temple of Deir-el-Bahri at Luxor in 1997, they distributed leaflets demanding his release. In 1999 Abdel-Rahman launched another fatwa against his opponents. In captivity, the sheikh became a near legendary figure among Islamic extremists. In 2012 Mohamed Morsi of the Egyptian Muslim Brotherhood, soon to be elected president of Egypt, publicly called for his release. Such pleas were unavailing. In 2017 while still incarcerated, Abdel-Rahman succumbed to a variety of ailments.

Document

[1995]

Now then, your duty to aid is an obligation, and to come to the assistance of any Moslem who has been taken prisoner by the infidels, the enemies of Islam, the duty of such assistance has been necessitated by religion. . . .

The Sheikh is calling on you, morning and evening, oh Islamists! Oh Moslems! And he finds no reply or acknowledgement. It is a duty upon all Moslems around the world to free the Sheikh, and to rescue him from his jail; and that matter is an obligation and a responsibility. . . .

Oh! You, Moslems everywhere, sever the ties of their nation, tear them apart, ruin their economy, instigate against their corporations, destroy their embassies, attack their interests, sink their ships, and shoot down their airplanes; kill them in land, at sea, and in the air, kill them wherever you find them; take them, surround them and lie in ambush for them everywhere. Fight those infidels, treat them with brutality, fight them. . . .

[1997]

With my [sic] respect to your opinion, which is a very good opinion, but you have to give some time to the brothers who are in prison. There is no objection to have some differences.

They call for the halt of violence, and you don't agree. No objection on that. This conflict should be handled in a soft and flexible manner. It is possible that the brothers were promised things by the government which we are not aware of. Give them the chance, and give the right to, to inquire until something else is proved, then we can talk. No new charter, and nothing should happen or be done without consulting me, or informing me. . . .

[1999]

"To those against whom war is made, permission is given to fight, because they are wronged (oppressed)—and verily God is most powerful for their aid—." . . . The Islamic Group has committed itself to the suspension of military operations Initiative which was launched two years ago by the brothers from their jails, in spite of the Egyptian government's continued killing of the innocent people and conducting unjust military trials. This Initiative was made to protect the Muslims and to unify all the lines to face the real enemies of the nation. However, the Initiative left some people thinking that it was initiated out of weakness or an abandonment of the fundamental principles of the Group, which is basically a Da'wa, Jihad group. The latest thing published in the newspapers was about the Egyptian regime's killing of four members of the Group. This is . . . enough proof that the Egyptian regime does not have the intention to interact with this peaceful Initiative which aims at unification. I therefore demand that my brothers, the sons of the Islamic Group do a comprehensive review of the Initiative and its results. I also demand that they consider themselves absolved from it.

Source: United States District Court, Southern District of New York, *United States of America v. Lynne Stewart*, Government's Sentencing Memorandum, June 11, 2010, http://nylawyer.nylj.com/adgifs/decisions/061610us_stewart.pdf.

165. President Bill Clinton: Televised Address to the Nation on Operation DESERT FOX (December 16, 1998)

Introduction

After the Persian Gulf War, throughout the 1990s U.S. and United Nations (UN) relations with Iraq remained fraught. Under the cease-fire agreement, UN inspectors were entitled to enter Iraq and examine all potential weapons production facilities to ensure that President Saddam Hussein was not engaged in manufacturing chemical, biological, or nuclear weapons of mass destruction. In August 1998 Hussein proclaimed that Iraq would refuse to permit any further inspections. UN inspectors returned in November but were denied full access to Iraqi weapons facilities, and the following month the UN withdrew its inspectors from Baghdad. On December 16, 1998, in an address to the American people, U.S. president Bill Clinton announced a major U.S. and British program of aerial bombings and cruise missile strikes against suspected Iraqi weapons production and storage facilities, intended to degrade that country's capability to produce chemical, biological, or nuclear weapons. Also targeted were the headquarters and barracks of the Republican Guard, Hussein's elite forces; presidential palaces; and air defense systems. Clinton emphasized that Hussein had failed to comply with UN requirements and that during the previous three weeks the United States and Great Britain had given the Iraqi president repeated opportunities to cooperate with UN inspectors, virtually all of which he had subverted. Clinton warned that force was the only language that Iraq understood and that unless the United States took military action at this time, Hussein would proceed to develop destructive weapons, which he would not hesitate to use to dominate the entire region around Iraq. Clinton presented the four-day DESERT FOX bombing program as a prudent deterrent measure essential to preventing Hussein from threatening his neighbors at a later date. Clinton also defended the continuing economic sanctions program against Iraq—under whose terms that country could only sell limited quantities of oil on the international market, with the proceeds of such sales supposedly earmarked purely for humanitarian purposes within Iraq—on the grounds that if these restrictions were lifted, Hussein would use oil sales to finance the acquisition of military armaments. After the bombings, which American military officers believed had largely accomplished their objectives within four days, Iraq refused to permit the return of UN inspection teams. An undeclared air war between Iraq and British and American forces in the region continued for more than four years, with Anglo-American air and naval units regularly launching extensive missile attacks and bombing raids against Iraqi facilities. Aerial hostilities escalated dramatically in the months prior to the official beginning of the 2003 military campaign against Iraq.

Document

THE PRESIDENT: Good evening. Earlier today, I ordered America's Armed Forces to strike military and security targets in Iraq. They are joined by British forces. Their mission is to attack Iraq's nuclear, chemical, and biological programs, and its military capacity to threaten its neighbors. Their purpose is to protect the national interest of the United States and, indeed, the interests of people throughout the Middle East and around the world. Saddam Hussein must not be allowed to threaten his neighbors or the world with nuclear arms, poison gas, or biological weapons.

I want to explain why I have decided, with the unanimous recommendation of my national security team, to use force in Iraq, why we have acted now and what we aim to accomplish.

Six weeks ago, Saddam Hussein announced that he would no longer cooperate with the United Nations weapons inspectors, called UNSCOM. They are highly professional experts from dozens of countries. Their job is to oversee the elimination of Iraq's capability to retain, create and use weapons of mass destruction, and to verify that Iraq does not attempt to rebuild that capability. The inspectors undertook this mission, first, seven and a half years ago, at the end of the Gulf War, when Iraq agreed to declare and destroy its arsenal as a condition of the cease-fire.

The international community had good reason to set this requirement. Other countries possess weapons of mass destruction and ballistic missiles. With Saddam, there's one big difference: he has used them, not once but repeatedly—unleashing chemical weapons against Iranian troops during a decade-long war, not only against soldiers, but against civilians; firing Scud missiles at the citizens of Israel, Saudi Arabia, Bahrain, and Iran—not only against a foreign enemy, but even against his own people, gassing Kurdish civilians in Northern Iraq.

The international community had little doubt then, and I have no doubt today, that left unchecked, Saddam Hussein will use these terrible weapons again.

The United States has patiently worked to preserve UNSCOM, as Iraq has sought to avoid its obligation to cooperate with the inspectors. On occasion, we've had to threaten military force, and Saddam has backed down. Faced with Saddam's latest act of defiance in late October, we built intensive diplomatic pressure on Iraq, backed by overwhelming military force in the region. The U.N. Security Council voted 15 to zero to condemn Saddam's actions and to demand that he immediately come into compliance. Eight Arab nations—Egypt, Syria, Saudi Arabia, Kuwait, Bahrain, Qatar, United Arab Emirates, and Oman—warned that Iraq alone would bear responsibility for the consequences of defying the U.N.

When Saddam still failed to comply, we prepared to act militarily. It was only then, at the last possible moment, that Iraq backed down. It pledged to the U.N. that it had made—and I quote—"a clear and unconditional decision to resume cooperation with the weapons inspectors."

I decided then to call off the attack, with our airplanes already in the air, because Saddam had given in to our demands. I concluded then that the right thing to do was to use restraint and give Saddam one last chance to prove his willingness to cooperate.

I made it very clear at that time what "unconditional cooperation" meant, based on existing U.N. resolutions and Iraq's own commitments. And along with Prime Minister Blair of Great Britain, I made it equally clear that if Saddam failed to cooperate fully, we would be prepared to act without delay, diplomacy or warning.

Now, over the past three weeks, the U.N. weapons inspectors have carried out their plan for testing Iraq's cooperation. The testing period ended this weekend, and last night, UNSCOM's Chairman, Richard Butler, reported the results to U.N. Secretary General Annan. The conclusions are stark, sobering and profoundly disturbing.

In four out of the five categories set forth, Iraq has failed to cooperate. Indeed, it actually has placed new restrictions on the inspectors. Here are some of the particulars:

Iraq repeatedly blocked UNSCOM from inspecting suspect sites. For example, it shut off access to the headquarters of its ruling party, and said it will deny access to the party's other offices, even though U.N. resolutions make no exception for them and UNSCOM has inspected them in the past.

Iraq repeatedly restricted UNSCOM's ability to obtain necessary evidence. For example, Iraq obstructed UNSCOM's effort to photograph bombs related to its chemical weapons program. It tried to stop an UNSCOM biological weapons team from videotaping a site and photocopying documents, and prevented Iraqi personnel from answering UNSCOM's questions.

Prior to the inspection of another site, Iraq actually emptied out the building, removing not just documents, but even the furniture and the equipment. Iraq has failed to turn over virtually all the documents requested by the inspectors; indeed, we know that Iraq ordered the destruction of weapons related documents in anticipation of an UNSCOM inspection.

So Iraq has abused its final chance. As the UNSCOM report concludes—and again I quote—"Iraq's conduct ensured that no progress was able to be made in the fields of disarmament. In light of this experience, and in the absence of full cooperation by Iraq, it must, regrettably, be recorded again that the Commission is not able to conduct the work mandated to it by the Security Council with respect to Iraq's prohibited weapons program."

In short, the inspectors are saying that, even if they could stay in Iraq, their work would be a sham. Saddam's deception has defeated their effectiveness. Instead of the inspectors disarming Saddam, Saddam has disarmed the inspectors.

This situation presents a clear and present danger to the stability of the Persian Gulf and the safety of people everywhere. The international community gave Saddam one last chance to resume cooperation with the weapons inspectors. Saddam has failed to seize the chance.

And so we had to act, and act now. Let me explain why.

First, without a strong inspections system, Iraq would be free to retain and begin to rebuild its chemical, biological, and nuclear weapons programs in months, not years.

Second, if Saddam can cripple the weapons inspections system and get away with it, he would conclude that the international community, led by the United States, has simply lost its will. He will surmise that he has free rein to rebuild his arsenal of destruction. And some day, make no mistake, he will use it again, as he has in the past.

Third, in halting our air strikes in November, I gave Saddam a chance, not a license. If we turn our backs on his defiance, the credibility of U.S. power as a check against Saddam will be destroyed. We will not only have allowed Saddam to shatter the inspections system that controls his weapons of mass destruction program; we also will have fatally undercut the fear of force that stops Saddam from acting to gain domination in the region.

That is why, on the unanimous recommendation of my national security team, including the Vice President, Secretary of Defense, the Chairman of the Joint Chiefs of Staff, the Secretary of State, and the National Security Advisor, I have ordered a strong, sustained series of air strikes against Iraq. They are designed to degrade Saddam's capacity to develop and deliver weapons of mass destruction, and to degrade his ability to threaten his neighbors. At the same time, we are delivering a powerful message to Saddam: If you act recklessly, you will pay a heavy price.

We acted today because, in the judgment of my military advisors, a swift response would provide the most surprise and the least opportunity for Saddam to prepare. If we had delayed for even a matter of days from Chairman Butler's report, we would have given Saddam more time to disperse forces and protect his weapons.

Also, the Muslim holy month of Ramadan begins this weekend. For us to initiate military action during Ramadan would be profoundly offensive to the Muslim world and, therefore, would damage our relations with Arab countries and the progress we have made in the Middle East. That is something we wanted very much to avoid without giving Iraq a month's head start to prepare for potential action against it.

Finally, our allies, including Prime Minister Tony Blair of Great Britain, concurred that now is the time to strike. I hope Saddam will come into cooperation with the inspection system now and comply with the relevant U.N. Security Council resolutions. But we have to be prepared that he will not, and we must deal with the very real danger he poses. So we will pursue a long-term strategy to contain Iraq and its weapons of mass destruction, and work toward the day when Iraq has a government worthy of its people.

First, we must be prepared to use force again if Saddam takes threatening actions, such as trying to reconstitute his weapons of mass destruction or their delivery systems, threatening his neighbors, challenging allied aircraft over Iraq, or moving against his own Kurdish citizens. The credible threat to use force and, when necessary, the actual use of force, is the surest way to contain Saddam's weapons of mass destruction program, curtail his aggression and prevent another Gulf War.

Second, so long as Iraq remains out of compliance, we will work with the international community to maintain and enforce economic sanctions. Sanctions have cost Saddam more than $120 billion—resources that would have been used to rebuild his military. The sanctions system allows Iraq to sell oil for food, for medicine, for other humanitarian supplies for the Iraqi people. We have no quarrel with them. But without the sanctions, we would see the oil-for-food program become oil-for-tanks, resulting in a greater threat to Iraq's neighbors and less food for its people.

The hard fact is that so long as Saddam remains in power, he threatens the well-being of his people, the peace of his region, the security of the world. The best way to end that threat once and for all is with a new Iraqi government, a government ready to live in peace with its neighbors, a government that respects the rights of its people.

Bringing change in Baghdad will take time and effort. We will strengthen our engagement with the full range of Iraqi opposition forces and work with them effectively and prudently.

The decision to use force is never cost-free. Whenever American forces are placed in harm's way, we risk the loss of life. And while our strikes are focused on Iraq's military capabilities, there will be unintended Iraqi casualties. Indeed, in the past, Saddam has intentionally placed Iraqi civilians in harm's way in a cynical bid to sway international opinion. We must be prepared for these realities. At the same time, Saddam should have absolutely no doubt: If he lashes out at his neighbors, we will respond forcefully.

Heavy as they are, the costs of action must be weighed against the price of inaction. If Saddam defies the world and we fail to respond, we will face a far greater threat in the future. Saddam will strike again at his neighbors; he will make war on his own people. And mark my words, he will develop weapons of mass destruction. He will deploy them, and he will use them. Because we are acting today, it is less likely that we will face these dangers in the future. . . .

Source: William J. Clinton, "President Clinton's Statement on Air Strike against Iraq," The White House, Office of the Press Secretary, http://clinton5.nara.gov/WH/New/html/19981216-3611.html.

166. The War on Terror: President George W. Bush, Address to a Joint Session of Congress and the American People on the U.S. Response to the September 11 Terrorist Attacks (September 20, 2001)

Introduction

Nine days after the radical Islamic group Al Qaeda carried out airborne attacks that destroyed the World Trade Center in New York and damaged the Pentagon in Washington, D.C., President George W. Bush addressed a joint session of Congress. He first applauded the courage of those Americans who had helped to rescue the wounded and thanked Congress and foreign nations and citizens for their support. Bush then declared that the events of September 11, 2001, represented "an act of war against our country" and against "freedom itself." Al Qaeda, the group responsible for the attacks, was, he warned, only one of numerous Islamic terrorist organizations active in more than 60 countries. While affirming his respect for the Muslim faith, Bush declared that the United States was declaring a "war on terror" against not just Al Qaeda but all other terrorist organizations as well, one that would "not end until every terrorist group of global reach has been found, stopped, and defeated." Bush called on the Taliban regime in Afghanistan, which was providing the well-funded Al Qaeda organization with an operational base and training facilities, to dissociate itself from Al Qaeda, hand over to American authorities all its leaders currently in Afghanistan, and close down the group's training camps. Otherwise, the Taliban regime would itself face U.S. military intervention. Moreover, Bush warned, this would be only the beginning of a lengthy American campaign against terrorism. In perhaps rather overblown rhetoric, Bush declared that what was at stake was "not just America's freedom. This is the world's fight. This is civilization's fight." The terrorists, he charged, "hate our freedoms—our freedom of religion, our freedom of speech, our freedom to vote and assemble and disagree with each other." He asked the entire "civilized world" to rally to the side of the United States and proclaimed that "Freedom and fear are at war. The advance of human freedom—the great achievement of our time, and the great hope of every time—now depends on us." Bush's grandiose language and his depiction of the effort to eradicate international terrorism as a Manichaean battle between good and evil, the forces of light and the forces of darkness, recalled the rhetoric of the Cold War that had dominated so much of the 20th century.

Document

. . . In the normal course of events, Presidents come to this Chamber to report on the state of the Union. Tonight, no such report is needed. It has already been delivered by the American people.

We have seen it in the courage of passengers, who rushed terrorists to save others on the ground. . . .

We have seen the state of our Union in the endurance of rescuers, working past exhaustion. We have seen the unfurling of flags, the lighting of candles, the giving of blood, the saying of prayers in English, Hebrew, and Arabic. We have seen the decency of a loving and giving people who have made the grief of strangers their own.

166. The War on Terror: President George W. Bush Response to the September 11 Terrorist Attacks

My fellow citizens, for the last 9 days, the entire world has seen for itself the state of our Union, and it is strong.

Tonight we are a country awakened to danger and called to defend freedom. Our grief has turned to anger and anger to resolution. Whether we bring our enemies to justice or bring justice to our enemies, justice will be done. . . .

And on behalf of the American people, I thank the world for its outpouring of support. America will never forget the sounds of our national anthem playing at Buckingham Palace, on the streets of Paris, and at Berlin's Brandenburg Gate. We will not forget South Korean children gathering to pray outside our Embassy in Seoul, or the prayers of sympathy offered at a mosque in Cairo. We will not forget moments of silence and days of mourning in Australia and Africa and Latin America.

Nor will we forget the citizens of 80 other nations who died with our own: dozens of Pakistanis; more than 130 Israelis; more than 250 citizens of India; men and women from El Salvador, Iran, Mexico, and Japan; and hundreds of British citizens. America has no truer friend than Great Britain. Once again, we are joined together in a great cause—so honored the British Prime Minister [Tony Blair] has crossed an ocean to show his unity with America. Thank you for coming, friend.

On September 11th, enemies of freedom committed an act of war against our country. Americans have known wars, but for the past 136 years, they have been wars on foreign soil, except for one Sunday in 1941. Americans have known the casualties of war, but not at the center of a great city on a peaceful morning. Americans have known surprise attacks, but never before on thousands of civilians. All of this was brought upon us in a single day, and night fell on a different world, a world where freedom itself is under attack.

Americans have many questions tonight. Americans are asking, who attacked our country? The evidence we have gathered all points to a collection of loosely affiliated terrorist organizations known as Al Qaida.

They are some of the murderers indicted for bombing American Embassies in Tanzania and Kenya and responsible for bombing the U.S.S. *Cole*. Al Qaida is to terror what the Mafia is to crime. But its goal is not making money. Its goal is remaking the world and imposing its radical beliefs on people everywhere.

The terrorists practice a fringe form of Islamic extremism that has been rejected by Muslim scholars and the vast majority of Muslim clerics, a fringe movement that perverts the peaceful teachings of Islam. The terrorists' directive commands them to kill Christians and Jews, to kill all Americans, and make no distinctions among military and civilians, including women and children.

This group and its leader, a person named Usama bin Laden, are linked to many other organizations in different countries, including the Egyptian Islamic Jihad and the Islamic Movement of Uzbekistan. There are thousands of these terrorists in more than 60 countries. They are recruited from their own nations and neighborhoods and brought to camps in places like Afghanistan, where they are trained in the tactics of terror. They are sent back to their homes or sent to hide in countries around the world to plot evil and destruction.

The leadership of Al Qaida has great influence in Afghanistan and supports the Taliban regime in controlling most of that country. In Afghanistan, we see Al Qaida's vision for the world. Afghanistan's people have been brutalized. Many are starving, and many have fled.

Women are not allowed to attend school. You can be jailed for owning a television. Religion can be practiced only as their leaders dictate. A man can be jailed in Afghanistan if his beard is not long enough.

The United States respects the people of Afghanistan—after all, we are currently its largest source of humanitarian aid—but we condemn the Taliban regime. It is not only repressing its own people; it is threatening people everywhere by sponsoring and sheltering and supplying terrorists. By aiding and abetting murder, the Taliban regime is committing murder.

And tonight the United States of America makes the following demands on the Taliban: Deliver to United States authorities all the leaders of Al Qaida who hide in your land. Release all foreign nationals, including American citizens, you have unjustly imprisoned. Protect foreign journalists, diplomats, and aid workers in your country. Close immediately and permanently every terrorist training camp in Afghanistan, and hand over every terrorist and every person in their support structure to appropriate authorities. Give the United States full access to terrorist training camps, so we can make sure they are no longer operating.

These demands are not open to negotiation or discussion. The Taliban must act and act immediately. They will hand over the terrorists, or they will share in their fate.

I also want to speak tonight directly to Muslims throughout the world. We respect your faith. It's practiced freely by many millions of Americans and by millions more in countries that America counts as friends. Its teachings are good and peaceful, and those who commit evil in the name of Allah blaspheme the name of Allah. The terrorists are traitors to their own faith, trying, in effect, to hijack Islam itself.

The enemy of America is not our many Muslim friends; it is not our many Arab friends. Our enemy is a radical network of terrorists and every government that supports them.

Our war on terror begins with Al Qaida, but it does not end there.

It will not end until every terrorist group of global reach has been found, stopped, and defeated.

Americans are asking, why do they hate us? They hate what we see right here in this Chamber, a democratically elected government. Their leaders are self-appointed. They hate our freedoms—our freedom of religion, our freedom of speech, our freedom to vote and assemble and disagree with each other.

They want to overthrow existing governments in many Muslim countries, such as Egypt, Saudi Arabia, and Jordan. They want to drive Israel out of the Middle East. They want to drive Christians and Jews out of vast regions of Asia and Africa.

These terrorists kill not merely to end lives but to disrupt and end a way of life. With every atrocity, they hope that America grows fearful, retreating from the world and forsaking our friends. They stand against us, because we stand in their way.

We are not deceived by their pretenses to piety. We have seen their kind before. They are the heirs of all the murderous ideologies of the 20th century. By sacrificing human life to serve their radical visions, by abandoning every value except the will to power, they follow in the path of fascism and Nazism and totalitarianism. And they will follow that path all the way, to where it ends, in history's unmarked grave of discarded lies.

Americans are asking, how will we fight and win this war? We will direct every resource at our command—every means of diplomacy, every tool of intelligence, every instrument of law enforcement, every financial influence, and every necessary weapon of war—to the disruption and to the defeat of the global terror network.

This war will not be like the war against Iraq a decade ago, with a decisive liberation of territory and a swift conclusion. It will not look like the air war above Kosovo 2 years ago, where no ground troops were used and not a single American was lost in combat.

Our response involves far more than instant retaliation and isolated strikes. Americans should not expect one battle but a lengthy campaign, unlike any other we have ever seen. It may include dramatic strikes, visible on TV, and covert operations, secret even in success. We will starve terrorists of funding, turn them one against another, drive them from place to place, until there is no refuge or no rest. And we will pursue nations that provide aid or safe haven to terrorism. Every nation, in every region, now has a decision to make: Either you are with us, or you are with the terrorists. From this day forward, any nation that continues to harbor or support terrorism will be regarded by the United States as a hostile regime.

Our Nation has been put on notice: We are not immune from attack. We will take defensive measures against terrorism to protect Americans.

Today dozens of Federal departments and agencies, as well as State and local governments, have responsibilities affecting homeland security.

These efforts must be coordinated at the highest level.

So tonight I announce the creation of a Cabinet-level position reporting directly to me, the Office of Homeland Security. And tonight I also announce a distinguished American to lead this effort to strengthen American security, a military veteran, an effective Governor, a true patriot, a trusted friend, Pennsylvania's Tom Ridge. He will lead, oversee, and coordinate a comprehensive national strategy to safeguard our country against terrorism and respond to any attacks that may come.

These measures are essential. But the only way to defeat terrorism as a threat to our way of life is to stop it, eliminate it, and destroy it where it grows. Many will be involved in this effort, from FBI agents to intelligence operatives to the reservists we have called to active duty. All deserve our thanks, and all have our prayers. And tonight, a few miles from the damaged Pentagon, I have a message for our military:

Be ready. I've called the Armed Forces to alert, and there is a reason.

The hour is coming when America will act, and you will make us proud.

This is not, however, just America's fight, and what is at stake is not just America's freedom. This is the world's fight. This is civilization's fight. This is the fight of all who believe in progress and pluralism, tolerance and freedom.

We ask every nation to join us. We will ask, and we will need, the help of police forces, intelligence services, and banking systems around the world. The United States is grateful that many nations and many international organizations have already responded with sympathy and with support, nations from Latin America to Asia, to Africa, to Europe, to the Islamic world. Perhaps the NATO Charter reflects best the attitude of the world: An attack on one is an attack on all.

The civilized world is rallying to America's side. They understand that if this terror goes unpunished, their own cities, their own citizens may be next. Terror, unanswered, cannot only bring down buildings, it can threaten the stability of legitimate governments. And you know what? We're not going to allow it.

Americans are asking, what is expected of us? I ask you to live your lives and hug your children. I know many citizens have fears tonight, and I ask you to be calm and resolute, even in the face of a continuing threat.

I ask you to uphold the values of America and remember why so many have come here. We are in a fight for our principles, and our first responsibility is to live by them. No one should be singled out for unfair treatment or unkind words because of their ethnic background or religious faith.

I ask you to continue to support the victims of this tragedy with your contributions. Those who want to give can go to a central source of information, libertyunites.org, to find the names of groups providing direct help in New York, Pennsylvania, and Virginia.

The thousands of FBI agents who are now at work in this investigation may need your cooperation, and I ask you to give it.

I ask for your patience with the delays and inconveniences that may accompany tighter security and for your patience in what will be a long struggle.

I ask your continued participation and confidence in the American economy. Terrorists attacked a symbol of American prosperity. They did not touch its source. America is successful because of the hard work and creativity and enterprise of our people. These were the true strengths of our economy before September 11th, and they are our strengths today.

And finally, please continue praying for the victims of terror and their families, for those in uniform, and for our great country. Prayer has comforted us in sorrow and will help strengthen us for the journey ahead.

Tonight I thank my fellow Americans for what you have already done and for what you will do. And ladies and gentlemen of the Congress, I thank you, their representatives, for what you have already done and for what we will do together.

Tonight we face new and sudden national challenges. We will come together to improve air safety, to dramatically expand the number of air marshals on domestic flights and take new measures to prevent hijacking.

We will come together to promote stability and keep our airlines flying, with direct assistance during this emergency.

We will come together to give law enforcement the additional tools it needs to track down terror here at home. We will come together to strengthen our intelligence capabilities, to know the plans of terrorists before they act and find them before they strike. We will come together to take active steps that strengthen America's economy and put our people back to work. . . .

After all that has just passed, all the lives taken and all the possibilities and hopes that died with them, it is natural to wonder if America's future is one of fear. Some speak of an age of terror. I know there are struggles ahead and dangers to face. But this country will define our times, not be defined by them. As long as the United States of America is determined and strong, this will not be an age of terror; this will be an age of liberty, here and across the world.

Great harm has been done to us. We have suffered great loss. And in our grief and anger, we have found our mission and our moment. Freedom and fear are at war. The advance of human freedom, the great achievement of our time and the great hope of every time, now depends on us. Our Nation—this generation—will lift a dark threat of violence from our people and our future. We will rally the world to this cause by our efforts, by our courage. We will not tire; we will not falter; and we will not fail.

It is my hope that in the months and years ahead, life will return almost to normal. We'll go back to our lives and routines, and that is good. Even grief recedes with time and grace. But our resolve must not pass. Each of us will remember what happened that day and to whom it happened. We'll remember the moment the news came, where we were, and what we were doing. Some will remember an image of a fire or a story of rescue. Some will carry memories of a face and a voice gone forever.

And I will carry this: It is the police shield of a man named George Howard, who died at the World Trade Center trying to save others. It was given to me by his mom, Arlene [Arlene Howard], as a proud memorial to her son. It is my reminder of lives that ended and a task that does not end. I will not forget this wound to our country and those who inflicted it. I will not yield; I will not rest; I will not relent in waging this struggle for freedom and security for the American people.

The course of this conflict is not known, yet its outcome is certain. Freedom and fear, justice and cruelty have always been at war, and we know that God is not neutral between them.

Fellow citizens, we'll meet violence with patient justice, assured of the rightness of our cause and confident of the victories to come. In all that lies before us, may God grant us wisdom, and may He watch over the United States of America.

Source: "Address to a Joint Session of Congress and the American People," U.S. Department of Homeland Security, http://www.dhs.gov/xnews/speeches/speech_0016.shtm.

167. Osama bin Laden: "Letter to the American People" (November 2002)

Introduction

On September 11, 2001, four airliners were hijacked by 19 terrorists who belonged to the Al Qaeda network headed by the Islamic terrorist leader Osama bin Laden. The terrorists attacked landmark buildings in New York City and Arlington, Virginia, killing close to 3,000 people; the fourth plane crashed in Pennsylvania without reaching its intended target. Bin Laden, a fundamentalist Muslim militant from a wealthy Saudi family, had mounted several earlier attacks on American military installations and other facilities elsewhere and viewed the United States as the greatest enemy of Islam. He was fanatically determined to wage a religious war, or jihad, against Americans and all allied with them. In several public statements, including the "Letter to the American People" published in Arabic on the Internet in 2002 and later translated into English, he enumerated what he viewed as American threats and enmity toward Islam. Bin Laden cited what he considered to be the immoral and irreligious character of American life, which was an affront to Muslim principles. Foremost among U.S. offenses, however, was American support for Israel, followed by its military presence in the Persian Gulf and American opposition to various Muslim governments and groups around the world. After the September 11 attacks, U.S. president George W. Bush quickly declared that waging a global "war on terror" wherever it raised its head was now by far the most significant U.S. foreign policy priority. The links that bin Laden drew between his organization's attacks on American landmarks and other facilities and his adamant hostility to Israel meant that the U.S. government and the American people were likely to view Palestinian and other terrorist operations against that country and its citizens and Israeli measures designed to repress them in the context of worldwide international efforts to combat the threat of armed Islamic militancy.

Document

... Some American writers have published articles under the title 'On what basis are we fighting?' These articles have generated a number of responses, some of which adhered to the truth and were based on Islamic Law, and others which were not. Here we wanted to outline the truth—as an explanation and warning—hoping for Allah's reward, seeking success and support from Him.

While seeking Allah's help, we form our reply based on two questions directed at the Americans:

(Q1) Why are we fighting and opposing you?

(Q2) What are we calling you to, and what do we want from you?

As for the first question: Why are we fighting and opposing you? The answer is very simple:

(1) Because you attacked us and continue to attack us.

(a) You attacked us in Palestine:

(i) Palestine, which has sunk under military occupation for more than 80 years. The British handed over Palestine, with your help and your support, to the Jews, who have occupied it for more than 50 years; years overflowing with oppression, tyranny, crimes, killing, expulsion, destruction and devastation. The creation and continuation of Israel is one of the greatest crimes, and you are the leaders of its criminals. And of course there is no need to explain and prove the degree of American support for Israel. The creation of Israel is a crime which must be erased. Each and every person whose hands have become polluted in the contribution towards this crime must pay its price, and pay for it heavily.

(ii) It brings us both laughter and tears to see that you have not yet tired of repeating your fabricated lies that the Jews have a historical right to Palestine, as it was promised to them in the Torah. Anyone who disputes with them on this alleged fact is accused of anti-semitism. This is one of the most fallacious, widely-circulated fabrications in history. The people of Palestine are pure Arabs and original Semites. It is the Muslims who are the inheritors of Moses (peace be upon him) and the inheritors of the real Torah that has not been changed. Muslims believe in all of the Prophets, including Abraham, Moses, Jesus and Muhammad, peace and blessings of Allah be upon them all. If the followers of Moses have been promised a right to Palestine in the Torah, then the Muslims are the most worthy nation of this.

When the Muslims conquered Palestine and drove out the Romans, Palestine and Jerusalem returned to Islam, the religion of all the Prophets peace be upon them. Therefore, the call to a historical right to Palestine cannot be raised against the Islamic Ummah that believes in all the Prophets of Allah (peace and blessings be upon them)—and we make no distinction between them.

(iii) The blood pouring out of Palestine must be equally revenged. You must know that the Palestinians do not cry alone; their women are not widowed alone; their sons are not orphaned alone.

(b) You attacked us in Somalia; you supported the Russian atrocities against us in Chechnya, the Indian oppression against us in Kashmir, and the Jewish aggression against us in Lebanon.

(c) Under your supervision, consent and orders, the governments of our countries which act as your agents, attack us on a daily basis;

(i) These governments prevent our people from establishing the Islamic Shariah, using violence and lies to do so.

(ii) These governments give us a taste of humiliation, and place us in a large prison of fear and subdual.

(iii) These governments steal our Ummah's wealth and sell them to you at a paltry price.

(iv) These governments have surrendered to the Jews, and handed them most of Palestine, acknowledging the existence of their state over the dismembered limbs of their own people.

(v) The removal of these governments is an obligation upon us, and a necessary step to free the Ummah, to make the Shariah the supreme law and to regain Palestine. And our fight against these governments is not separate from our fight against you.

(d) You steal our wealth and oil at paltry prices because of you[r] international influence and military threats. This theft is indeed the biggest theft ever witnessed by mankind in the history of the world.

(e) Your forces occupy our countries; you spread your military bases throughout them; you corrupt our lands, and you besiege our sanctities, to protect the security of the Jews and to ensure the continuity of your pillage of our treasures.

(f) You have starved the Muslims of Iraq, where children die every day. It is a wonder that more than 1.5 million Iraqi children have died as a result of your sanctions, and you did not show concern. Yet when 3000 of your people died, the entire world rises and has not yet sat down.

(g) You have supported the Jews in their idea that Jerusalem is their eternal capital, and agreed to move your embassy there. With your help and under your protection, the Israelis are planning to destroy the Al-Aqsa mosque. Under the protection of your weapons, Sharon entered the Al-Aqsa mosque, to pollute it as a preparation to capture and destroy it.

(2) These tragedies and calamities are only a few examples of your oppression and aggression against us. It is commanded by our religion and intellect that the oppressed have a right to return the aggression. Do not await anything from us but Jihad, resistance and revenge. Is it in any way rational to expect that after America has attacked us for more than half a century, that we will then leave her to live in security and peace?!!

(3) You may then dispute that all the above does not justify aggression against civilians, for crimes they did not commit and offenses in which they did not partake:

(a) This argument contradicts your continuous repetition that America is the land of freedom, and its leaders in this world. Therefore, the American people are the ones who choose their government by way of their own free will; a choice which stems from their agreement to its policies. Thus the American people have chosen, consented to, and affirmed their support for the Israeli oppression of the Palestinians, the occupation and usurpation of their land, and its continuous killing, torture, punishment and expulsion of the Palestinians. The American people have the ability and choice to refuse the policies of their Government and even to change it if they want.

(b) The American people are the ones who pay the taxes which fund the planes that bomb us in Afghanistan, the tanks that strike and destroy our homes in Palestine, the armies which occupy our lands in the Arabian Gulf, and the fleets which ensure the blockade of Iraq. These tax dollars are given to Israel for it to continue to attack us and penetrate our lands. So the American people are the ones who fund the attacks against us, and they are the ones who oversee the expenditure of these monies in the way they wish, through their elected candidates.

(c) Also the American army is part of the American people. It is this very same people who are shamelessly helping the Jews fight against us.

(d) The American people are the ones who employ both their men and their women in the American Forces which attack us.

(e) This is why the American people cannot be innocent of all the crimes committed by the Americans and Jews against us.

(f) Allah, the Almighty, legislated the permission and the option to take revenge. Thus, if we are attacked, then we have the right to attack back. Whoever has destroyed our villages and towns, then we have the right to destroy their villages and towns. Whoever has stolen our wealth, then we have the right to destroy their economy. And whoever has killed our civilians, then we have the right to kill theirs.

The American Government and press still refuse to answer the question:

Why did they attack us in New York and Washington?

If [Israeli prime minister Ariel] Sharon is a man of peace in the eyes of Bush, then we are also men of peace!!! America does not understand the language of manners and principles, so we are addressing it using the language it understands.

(Q2) As for the second question that we want to answer: What are we calling you to, and what do we want from you?

(1) The first thing that we are calling you to is Islam.

(a) The religion of the Unification of God; of freedom from associating partners with Him, and rejection of this; of complete love of Him, the Exalted; of complete submission to His Laws; and of the discarding of all the opinions, orders, theories and religions which contradict with the religion He sent down to His Prophet Muhammad (peace be upon him). Islam is the religion of all the prophets, and makes no distinction between them—peace be upon them all.

It is to this religion that we call you; the seal of all the previous religions. It is the religion of Unification of God, sincerity, the best of manners, righteousness, mercy, honour, purity, and piety. It is the religion of showing kindness to others, establishing justice between them, granting them their rights, and defending the oppressed and the persecuted. It is the religion of enjoining the good and forbidding the evil with the hand, tongue and heart. It is the religion of Jihad in the way of Allah so that Allah's

Word and religion reign Supreme. And it is the religion of unity and agreement on the obedience to Allah, and total equality between all people, without regarding their colour, sex, or language.

(b) It is the religion whose book—the Quran—will remain preserved and unchanged, after the other Divine books and messages have been changed. The Quran is the miracle until the Day of Judgment. Allah has challenged anyone to bring a book like the Quran or even ten verses like it.

(2) The second thing we call you to, is to stop your oppression, lies, immorality and debauchery that have spread among you.

(a) We call you to be a people of manners, principles, honour, and purity; to reject the immoral acts of fornication, homosexuality, intoxicants, gambling, and trading with interest.

We call you to all of this that you may be freed from that which you have become caught up in; that you may be freed from the deceptive lies that you are a great nation, that your leaders spread amongst you to conceal from you the despicable state to which you have reached.

(b) It is saddening to tell you that you are the worst civilization witnessed by the history of mankind:

(i) You are the nation who, rather than ruling by the Shariah of Allah in its Constitution and Laws, choose to invent your own laws as you will and desire. You separate religion from your policies, contradicting the pure nature which affirms Absolute Authority to the Lord and your Creator. You flee from the embarrassing question posed to you: How is it possible for Allah the Almighty to create His creation, grant them power over all the creatures and land, grant them all the amenities of life, and then deny them that which they are most in need of: knowledge of the laws which govern their lives?

(ii) You are the nation that permits Usury, which has been forbidden by all the religions. Yet you build your economy and investments on Usury. As a result of this, in all its different forms and guises, the Jews have taken control of your economy, through which they have then taken control of your media, and now control all aspects of your life making you their servants and achieving their aims at your expense; precisely what Benjamin Franklin warned you against.

(iii) You are a nation that permits the production, trading and usage of intoxicants. You also permit drugs, and only forbid the trade of them, even though your nation is the largest consumer of them.

(iv) You are a nation that permits acts of immorality, and you consider them to be pillars of personal freedom. You have continued to sink down this abyss from level to level until incest has spread amongst you, in the face of which neither your sense of honour nor your laws object.

Who can forget your President Clinton's immoral acts committed in the official Oval office? After that you did not even bring him to account, other than that he 'made a mistake,' after which everything passed with no punishment. Is there a worse kind of event for which your name will go down in history and [be] remembered by nations?

(v) You are a nation that permits gambling in all its forms. The companies practice this as well, resulting in the investments becoming active and the criminals becoming rich.

(vi) You are a nation that exploits women like consumer products or advertising tools calling upon customers to purchase them. You use women to serve passengers, visitors, and strangers to increase your profit margins. You then rant that you support the liberation of women.

(vii) You are a nation that practices the trade of sex in all its forms, directly and indirectly. Giant corporations and establishments are established on this, under the name of art, entertainment, tourism and freedom, and other deceptive names you attribute to it.

(viii) And because of all this, you have been described in history as a nation that spreads diseases that were unknown to man in the past. Go ahead and boast to the nations of man, that you brought them AIDS as a Satanic American Invention.

(ix) You have destroyed nature with your industrial waste and gases more than any other nation in history. Despite this, you refuse to sign the Kyoto agreement so that you can secure the profit of your greedy companies and industries.

(x) Your law is the law of the rich and wealthy people, who hold sway in their political parties, and fund their election campaigns with their gifts. Behind them stand the Jews, who control your policies, media and economy.

(xi) That which you are singled out for in the history of mankind, is that you have used your force to destroy mankind more than any other nation in history; not to defend principles and values, but to hasten to secure your interests and profits. You who dropped a nuclear bomb on Japan, even though Japan was ready to negotiate an end to the war. How many acts of oppression, tyranny and injustice have you carried out, O callers to freedom?

(xii) Let us not forget one of your major characteristics: your duality in both manners and values; your hypocrisy in manners and principles. All manners, principles and values have two scales: one for you and one for the others.

(a) The freedom and democracy that you call to is for yourselves and for the white race only; as for the rest of the world, you impose upon them your monstrous, destructive policies and Governments, which you call the 'American friends.' Yet you prevent them from establishing democracies. When the Islamic party in Algeria wanted to practice democracy and they won the election, you unleashed your agents in the Algerian army onto them, to attack them with tanks and guns, to imprison them and torture them—a new lesson from the 'American book of democracy'!!!

(b) Your policy on prohibiting and forcibly removing weapons of mass destruction to ensure world peace: it only applies to those countries which you do not permit to possess such weapons. As for the countries you consent to, such as Israel, then they are allowed to keep and use such weapons to defend their security. Anyone else who you suspect might be manufacturing or keeping these kinds of weapons, you call them criminals and you take military action against them.

(c) You are the last ones to respect the resolutions and policies of International Law, yet you claim to want to selectively punish anyone else who does the same. Israel has for more than 50 years been pushing UN resolutions and rules against the wall with the full support of America.

(d) As for the war criminals which you censure and form criminal courts for—you shamelessly ask that your own are granted immunity!! However, history will not forget the war crimes that you committed against the Muslims and the rest of the world; those you have killed in Japan, Afghanistan, Somalia, Lebanon and Iraq will remain a shame that you will never be able to escape. It will suffice to remind you of your latest war crimes in Afghanistan, in which densely populated innocent civilian villages were destroyed, bombs were dropped on mosques causing the roof of the mosque to come crashing down on the heads of the Muslims praying inside. You are the ones who broke the agreement with the Mujahideen when they left Qunduz, bombing them in Jangi fort, and killing more than 1,000 of your prisoners through suffocation and thirst. Allah alone knows how many people have died by torture at the hands of you and your agents. Your planes remain in the Afghan skies, looking for anyone remotely suspicious.

(e) You have claimed to be the vanguards of Human Rights, and your Ministry of Foreign Affairs issues annual reports containing statistics of those countries that violate any Human Rights. However, all these things vanished when the Mujahideen hit you, and you then implemented the methods of the same documented governments that you used to curse. In America, you captured thousands of the Muslims and Arabs, took them into custody with neither reason, court trial, nor even disclosing their names. You issued newer, harsher laws.

What happens in Guantanamo is a historical embarrassment to America and its values, and it screams into your faces—you hypocrites, "What is the value of your signature on any agreement or treaty?"

(3) What we call you to thirdly is to take an honest stance with yourselves—and I doubt you will do so—to discover that you are a nation without principles or manners, and that values and principles to you are something which you merely demand from others, not that which you yourself must adhere to.

(4) We also advise you to stop supporting Israel, and to end your support of the Indians in Kashmir, the Russians against the Chechens and to also cease supporting the Manila Government against the Muslims in [the] Southern Philippines.

(5) We also advise you to pack your luggage and get out of our lands. We desire for you goodness, guidance, and righteousness, so do not force us to send you back as cargo in coffins.

(6) Sixthly, we call upon you to end your support of the corrupt leaders in our countries. Do not interfere in our politics and method of education. Leave us alone, or else expect us in New York and Washington.

(7) We also call you to deal with us and interact with us on the basis of mutual interests and benefits, rather than the policies of subdual, theft and occupation, and not to continue your policy of supporting the Jews because this will result in more disasters for you.

If you fail to respond to all these conditions, then prepare to fight with the Islamic Nation. The Nation of Monotheism, that puts complete trust on Allah and fears none other than Him. . . .

The Nation of Martyrdom; the Nation that desires death more than you desire life. . . .

The Islamic Nation that was able to dismiss and destroy the previous evil Empires like yourself; the Nation that rejects your attacks, wishes to remove your evils, and is prepared to fight you. You are well aware that the Islamic Nation, from the very core of its soul, despises your haughtiness and arrogance.

If the Americans refuse to listen to our advice and the goodness, guidance and righteousness that we call them to, then be aware that you will lose this Crusade Bush began, just like the other previous Crusades in which you were humiliated at the hands of the Mujahideen, fleeing to your home in great silence and disgrace. If the Americans do not respond, then their fate will be that of the Soviets who fled from Afghanistan to deal with their military defeat, political breakup, ideological downfall, and economic bankruptcy.

This is our message to the Americans, as an answer to theirs. Do they now know why we fight them and over which form of ignorance, by the permission of Allah, we shall be victorious?

Source: Osama bin Laden, "Letter to the American People," GlobalSecurity.org, http://www.globalsecurity.org/security/library/report/2002/021120-ubl.htm.

168. Mustafa Setmariam Nasar (Abu Mus'ab As-Suri): *The Global Islamic Resistance Call* (2004)

Introduction

The terrorist movements of the late 20th and early 21st centuries were characterized by a decentralized operational structure, with small cells with only a few members working largely independently of each other. This organizational strategy was developed in considerable part by the ideologue Mustafa Setmariam Nasar, also known as Abu Mus'ab As-Suri, a leading member of the Al Qaeda organization that gained prominence among radical Islamic organizations during the 1990s. In a 1,600-page training manual published online in 2004, Nasar gave instructions to aspiring terrorists on how to create, indoctrinate, train, and maintain such cells, ideally without risking their own destruction. Recently developed Internet technology and social media helped to facilitate these undertakings in a variety of ways, disseminating and publicizing information and also serving as a means of communication. Nasar's teaching videos, for example, were published on YouTube. Although Pakistani security forces captured Nasar in 2005, reportedly transferring him under rendition to a Syrian jail, within Islamic insurgent circles his voluminous writings remained extremely influential, shaping both jihadist ideology and its practical implementation.

Document

The Classification of the Global Islamic Resistance Detachments from the Perspective of Their Mission

1. The Builder (Recruiter) Detachments

These Builder (Recruiter) Detachments specialize in:

a. Spreading the idea of Global Islamic Resistance.
b. Convincing the leaders of Mujahideen and the youths—who have the intention of resisting—by using the views of the call.
c. Hastening to form independent detachments for the Mujahideen leaders and for the youths.
d. Preparing them ideologically, militarily, and security-wise.
e. Qualifying the leaders of the Mujahideen and the youths to train themselves and to train their members to be operational detachments.

The prospective mission of these builder detachments, if they are able, is to provide the pioneer members of operational detachments with money which will help them to start up.

The necessary characteristics for the builder detachments:

a. To be covert and able to move with freedom and security in the environment that they live in.
b. To understand the methodology of the call for resistance, be qualified in the ideology, and be able to explain it and call to it. Also, they should have a proper dynamic, political, and legal background.
c. To have a high level of understanding in how to move around covertly in order to teach others to move around in a like fashion (i.e. covertly).
d. To have the competent ability to conduct secret training on light weapons, explosive, and other light weapons for guerrilla warfare.

2. The Operations Detachment

The operations detachment consists of one or more members and it is better to not exceed 5–10 maximum. This detachment forms automatically because they (members) know the ideas, the details, and the belief system of the Islamic Resistance Call. Also this detachment is formed with the help of a member of the builder (recruiter) detachment. The mission of this operations detachment is to leave or go for Jihadi operations and join in the fighting immediately. They (the members) educate themselves by themselves via the methodology of the call (for resistance). Don't be tempted to expand—i.e. convert to make more detachments. You should resist the desire to expand so as not to become small pyramid organizations. This is very dangerous and it will quickly lead to their capture—may Allah forbid this.

3. Covert Incitement Detachments

This Detachment consists of very small cells from one to three members who have legal, political, and ideological qualifications. They also have media experience and experience of how to move around covertly. They also are experienced in using the internet and other means of electronic communication. The mission of this detachment is to spread the Call to resistance and to broadcast its literature, researches, studies, methodologies, via covert means of broadcasting, especially through the internet. They work to translate research papers and studies of the resistance into the language of the Muslims and to other international languages. They are careful when spreading these materials and they invent new methods of working (i.e. spreading their materials) which rely on the situation of every place and country....

Clarification of How to Build (Recruit) and Operate Covert Detachments

First: The Way the builder detachments (i.e. recruiters) form several operations detachments:

We know the way of building pyramid organizations and we have seen that it is dangerous because if any member of the pyramid is captured, then anyone with him on his level, under him, or above him will also be captured until the whole pyramid organization is destroyed. So if we have pyramid organizations and one of them is captured, this will lead to a confession about everyone on his level, under him, and above him. This tragedy will reoccur. The manner of capture and of inhumane and immoral torture leads to the destruction of the strongest and most secret organizations everywhere. We explained before that some of the organizations depended on the cluster-way. That is, to leave the head of the cluster in another country different from the country of operations so that the leadership resides in a safe place and keeps in contact with a member of the field leadership or meets with him who also is in a safe place. The pyramid cluster-organization managed the members working in the field of the country of operation. If the pyramid was destroyed, it would not lead to the capture of the head of the cluster. This manner was successful to give some of the Islamic and Arabic organizations, as well as the global organizations, room to maneuver. However, the international cooperation for fighting terrorism destroyed it. If any government requested a wanted member it led to his capture by the host government and he would confess the knowledge of the members of his organization in the other countries. This would lead to their capture in a matter of hours or days maximum; this was after the enemies announced their motto of "destruction of safe refuge." When the organization's leadership went for refuge which was out of the control of the New World Order, like Afghanistan and Chechnya, the enemy made a program to destroy these places and put them under the control of the New World Order. Thus, the manner of the cluster-system was destroyed and deactivated and the days of organizations came to an end that will not return until the New World Order is destroyed. This is the aim which we want to achieve, with the Help of Allah.

The Recommended Way to Build (Recruit) the Detachments

The active member of the builder (recruiter) detachments must have the following important characteristics: being qualified in doctrines of security, in matters of legalities, in cultural matters, and he must have a lot of knowledge. He must be able to affect a wide circle of people. He will select some of his acquaintances that he thinks are qualified to lead the detachments. He will speak to each one of them separately on this topic in gradual stages after he trusts them and prepare them separately with one assistant, or two maximum. He will use the methodology of the call during the period of preparation, especially this book, which is the most important research paper. He will also use my lecture series entitled "Jihad is the Solution—Why and How" and my lectures which are recorded on video entitled "Global Islamic Resistance Detachments."... This comprehensive lecture course is the explanation of the book "War of the Weak and Oppressed," which is the most important book explaining guerrilla warfare and the reasons for its success and failures. This book contains 170 pages and is useful for preparing research on military and security which can be done on the internet and (this military and security information) is available in several languages....

The members of the Builder (recruiter) Detachment must subject the operations detachment to a program of ideology, security, and military preparation. The most important part of the program is the ideology program, which lasts approximately 1 or 2 months if he utilizes the intensive course. I will mention the ways for covert and military preparation later, God Willing.

Suppose that a member of the builder detachment prepares 4 or 5 completely separate (operational) detachments and none of these new members knows anything about the other.

Now, every new member has a mission to build his own detachment which consists of 2 or 3 members, or he can remain alone if he wants. He (the recruiter) will determine a date for them. (These operations detachments) must not start their operations before this date in order to give him (the recruiter) time to leave the area. This is because the builder (recruiter) is the only real danger to this group. That is to say, all of the operational detachments can be destroyed by his capture.

Before this date comes, the member of the Builder detachment (i.e. the recruiter) must leave to an area unknown to the operational detachments so that they will not disclose his whereabouts.

He can go to either a Jihad battle-front outside the control of the enemy, or to any country where he has a different identity that nobody knows about. He can also just disappear to a new area.

He could also go and do a martyrdom operation after building many operations detachments, because he represents the only danger for the detachments that he built.

Furthermore, if any detachments are captured, there is no way to know about any others except through him (the recruiter).

So it is very critical for the builder (recruiter) to be careful with his speech or actions, even if it is the form of giving guidance or encouragement, which might lead to one or some of his recruits guessing and discovering the identity of the others. Consequently, this will lead to everyone's disclosure.

These operations detachments can form automatically without any builder detachments. They can work in the resistance directly without calling (for resistance) to others. So when an individual is convinced, he will join the resistance and form a small detachment consisting of himself and a friend only. They can prepare themselves through this research (i.e. Global Islamic Resistance Call) and give a name to their detachment. After this, they can work directly without making new detachments. This is the safest way for them.

Anyone who has minimal experience in covert operations training can recognize that a small detachment that consists of 2 or 3 members who are qualified in military and security and who have a high education in terrorism can perform huge operations. This detachment can also move across the country in many cities giving the impression that they are many detachments while in fact they are only one. I have many stories and magnificent models of this, but time does not allow me to go into it.

Second: Be careful not to mix the covert military work with the dawa and media work.

Mujahideen who build the detachments must be extremely careful not to mix military operations with dawa work because if they do this they will cause a lot of harm to themselves and to others. The basic principle and goal of the member in the operations brigade is to form a brigade for himself only and to perform operations according to his ability. If he does not trust others, then he should work alone, or if he does find others he trusts, then he should only work with 2 or 3 maximum. In this way they can form a detachment and work in the military field silently, counting on their reward and recognition only from Allah. After this they choose one of the enemy targets, which have been previously mentioned, and perform one operation, even if it is only one operation in several months. They should make a brief public announcement properly while following strict codes of security.

You must know:

1. That the dawa to organize others, media work, and fund collecting are all (public) and thus incompatible with covert (secret) operations and can never ever be combined. Bringing these opposites together in our dynamic, Jihadi history led to real disasters. This is the most important extraction from our previous painful experiments.
2. The principle of (combining) public dawa and secret organizations was the greatest failure of principle and the performance of this led to bloody disasters. So whoever works in dawa must leave covert fighting operations and vice versa. You must know that today the ummah needs tens of thousands of fighters but it only needs a few da'ees to incite to Jihad.
3. The performance of fighting and irritating the enemies of Allah and sacrificing yourself in the way of Allah is the most powerful call to wake our sleeping ummah and the most effective way to incite (others) to Jihad.
4. Inciting to Jihad is not a reason or an excuse to abandon the obligation of the actual fighting. Whoever abandons the obligation of fighting is like the one who abandons prayer, zakat, fasting and hajj. Rather, he is even worse because the consequence of this (abandoning fighting) is that the enemy will devour our ummah and also this will result in our ummah loosing its deen and its dunya. So don't lie to yourself, but fear Allah The One Who knows the most hidden secrets and Who will harvest what is in the breasts of men when the contents of the graves are poured forth. Allah is Well-Acquainted With His Slaves and All-Seeing.

Third: The Call for Resistance is a Serious Call

The mujahideen must be careful and know that it is not sufficient to build some detachments for inciting to jihad. However, we need a lot more (Jihadi) operations detachments. That is because the foundation of the obligation is fighting. So fight in the Way of Allah, you are not held responsible except for yourself. Inciting to Jihad is sufficient for the one who is qualified.

The brother who works in the field of fighting should not let the shaytan convince him to incite others and leave the field of fighting. This is one of the tricks of shaytan.

The mission of recruiting others is a big responsibility. It needs, as we mentioned before, the recruiter to completely disappear from the area in which he performed his recruiting. The basis is for the recruiter to perform (Jihadi) operations with the one that he recruits.

Fourth: Participating in the Calculating Progression of the Resistance

I will refer again to that which I mentioned before in the chapter of the military theory, and that is that the importance of the idea of Global Islamic Resistance Detachment comes from spreading and combining its efforts. As I said before, if we form 12 detachments in the whole Islamic world and every detachment performs one operation every year, then we will have one operation every month. If they perform two operations, then we will have one operation every 15 days. The strongest organization can never ever do this! So imagine if 100 people are convinced by this idea and 15 of them succeed to perform one or three operations in a year, the results will be that the Resistance detachments will be mentioned several times every day. This will irritate the enemy and encourage the Muslims to work and we hope that Allah Glorified and Exalted is He, will bless us in these operations. We ask Allah to give us men who are qualified to work with these ideas, to bless us in our efforts, and to let us see our enemies defeated. We also ask Allah to make our end martyrdom in His Path.

Source: Abu Mus'ab As-Suri, *The Global Islamic Resistance Call*, 2004, "Full Text of the Global Islamic Resistance Call," https://archive.org/stream/TheGlobalIslamicResistanceCall/The_Global_Islamic_Resistance_Call_-_Chapter_8_sections_5_to_7_LIST_OF_TARGETS_djvu.txt.

169. Lieutenant General Anthony Jones and Major General George R. Fay: Executive Summary of Report, Investigation of Intelligence Activities at Abu Ghraib (August 23, 2004)

Introduction

In the spring of 2004, repeated reports of widespread abuse and torture of civilian detainees in the prison camp at Abu Ghraib, Iraq, that was run by the U.S. military, began circulating in the international media. The Abu Ghraib prison held between 6,000 and 7,000 Iraqi prisoners, most of whom had been arrested on suspicion of insurgent activities. Brigadier General Janis Karpinski, who commanded the prison at this time, later stated that around 90 percent of such prisoners were innocent of any wrongdoing. Credible reports, buttressed by graphic photographs, appeared on television and in the *New Yorker* magazine in late April and early May 2004. U.S. Defense Department officials were already aware of these allegations and in early 2004 had instructed Lieutenant General Ricardo S. Sanchez to investigate them. The task ultimately fell to Major General Antonio M. Taguba, whose report appeared in early May. Although the report was marked "Secret/No Foreign Dissemination," large portions of it appeared almost immediately on the Internet and in the media. The report drew on the testimony of numerous witnesses to describe pervasive physical, psychological, and sexual abuse of prisoners at the prison camp in October and November 2003, mistreatment that amounted to torture and contravened the Geneva Conventions governing behavior toward prisoners. The report also depicted an understaffed prison camp manned by poorly trained and ignorant American military personnel, whom the military police and intelligence officers deliberately encouraged to abuse prisoners as a means of softening up such captives for subsequent interrogation. The report recommended the suspension from duty of Karpinski, who commanded the camp at this time, and she was later demoted to colonel. Sixteen other soldiers were also suspended from duty, and seven low-ranking soldiers directly responsible for abuses were subsequently court-martialed. The incidents seriously damaged the international image of the United States, undercutting its claims that it represented the cause of human rights and freedom in Iraq and around the world and bringing condemnation from the United Nations. Photographs of the torture, terrorization, humiliation, and sexual abuse of naked and terrified prisoners were shown repeatedly on Arab television and posted on the Internet. In May 2004 President George W. Bush and Secretary of Defense Donald Rumsfeld publicly apologized for these events. Critics nonetheless claimed that the incidents at Abu Ghraib were symptomatic of a broader readiness by senior Bush administration officials to discard and ignore the Geneva Conventions and sanction the illegal detention and torture of prisoners as and when it suited their own convenience.

Public criticism of the Taguba report on abuses against Iraqi detainees held at the Abu Ghraib prison facility by American troops centered on suggestions that the document had been too narrowly focused in terms of ascribing blame only to low-level personnel and had concentrated too exclusively on the army while ignoring the role of military intelligence. Many who condemned the mistreatment of prisoners at Abu Ghraib felt that the court-martials and censure of relatively low-ranking military personnel allowed higher-level officials, such as Bush and Rumsfeld, to evade responsibility for crimes whose root cause lay in policies that top Bush administration figures had enthusiastically initiated and encouraged. In June 2004 two senior officers, Lieutenant General Anthony Jones and Major General George R. Fay, began a further investigation into the role that efforts to obtain intelligence information from detainees had played in provoking abuses. Their report stated that military forces at Abu Ghraib had found themselves "severely under-resourced," lacking "adequate personnel and equipment" and operating in a hostile environment they had not anticipated. When President George W. Bush declared the end of major hostilities in Iraq, American forces were only holding 600 Iraqi prisoners, but in the autumn of 2003 "the number of detainees rose exponentially" as the result of tactical counterinsurgency operations. The report found that although the majority of incidents of abuse had not been related to interrogations, 27 military intelligence personnel also repeatedly encouraged or participated in the abuse of detainees. Senior-level officers were faulted for poor leadership in failing to issue clear and consistent guidelines on interrogation and the treatment of prisoners and for being slow in responding to reports on abuses submitted to them by the International Committee of the Red Cross. The report claimed, however, that had Defense Department and U.S. Army doctrine been properly followed abuses would not have occurred and suggested that many of the problems encountered arose from the fact that military personnel had been "[w]orking alongside non-DoD organizations/agencies in detention facilities." To many critics, it seemed that the military still sought to protect its own and was unwilling to address the issue of whether official U.S. policies on the treatment of prisoners now contravened internationally accepted standards and conventions.

Document

Executive Summary

Investigation of Intelligence Activities At Abu Ghraib. August 23, 2004.

Background

This investigation was ordered initially by LTG Ricardo S. Sanchez, Commander, Combined Joint Task Force Seven (CJTF-7). LTG Sanchez appointed MG George R. Fay as investigating officer under the provisions of Army Regulation 381–10, Procedure 15. MG Fay was appointed to investigate allegations that members of the 205th Military Intelligence Brigade (205 MI BDE) were involved in detainee abuse at the Abu Ghraib Detention Facility. Specifically, MG Fay was to determine whether 205 MI BDE personnel requested, encouraged, condoned, or solicited Military Police (MP) personnel to abuse detainees and whether MI personnel comported with established interrogation procedures and applicable laws and regulations.

On 16 June 2004, Acting Secretary of the Army R. L. Brownlee appointed General Paul J. Kern, Commander, US Army Materiel Command (AMC), as the new Procedure 15 appointing authority. On 25 June 2004, GEN Kern appointed LTG Anthony R. Jones, Deputy Commanding General, US Army Training and Doctrine Command, as an additional Procedure 15 investigating officer. MG Fay was retained as an investigating officer.

Without reinvestigating areas reviewed by MG Fay, LTG Jones was specifically directed to focus on whether organizations or personnel higher than the 205th MI BDE chain of command, or events and circumstances outside of the 205th MI Brigade, were involved, directly or indirectly, in the questionable activities regarding alleged detainee abuse at Abu Ghraib prison.

The investigative teams conducted a comprehensive review of all available background documents and statements pertaining to Abu Ghraib from a wide variety of sources. These sources included the reports written by MG Geoffrey Miller, MG Donald Ryder, MG Antonio Taguba and the Department of Army Inspector General. LTG Jones interviewed LTG Sanchez and MG Barbara Fast, the CJTF-7 Senior Intelligence Staff Officer. MG Fay's team conducted over 170 interviews concerning the interviewees' knowledge of interrogation and detention operations at Abu Ghraib and/or their knowledge of and involvement in detainee abuse. MG Fay's interviews included interviews with MG Fast, MG Walter Wojdakowski, MG Geoffrey Miller, MG Thomas Miller, and BG Janis Karpinski.

Operational Environment

The events at Abu Ghraib cannot be understood in a vacuum. Three interrelated aspects of the operational environment played important roles in the abuses that occurred at Abu Ghraib. First, from the time V Corps transitioned to become CJTF-7, and throughout the period under investigation, it was not resourced adequately to accomplish the missions of the CJTF: stability and support operations (SASO) and support to the Coalition Provisional Authority (CPA). The CJTF-7 headquarters lacked adequate personnel and equipment. In addition, the military police and military intelligence units at Abu Ghraib were severely under-resourced. Second, providing support to the Coalition Provisional Authority (CPA) required greater resources than envisioned in operational plans. Third, operational plans envisioned that CJTF-7 would execute SASO and provide support to the CPA in a relatively non-hostile environment. In fact, opposition was robust and hostilities continued throughout the period under investigation. Therefore, CJTF-7 had to conduct tactical counter-insurgency operations, while also executing its planned missions.

These three circumstances delayed establishment of an intelligence architecture and degraded the ability of the CJTF-7 staff to execute its assigned tasks, including oversight of interrogation and detention operations at Abu Ghraib.

When hostilities were declared over, US forces had control of only 600 Enemy Prisoners of War (EPW) and Iraqi criminals. In the fall of 2003, the number of detainees rose exponentially due to tactical operations to capture counter-insurgents dangerous to U.S. forces and Iraqi civilians. At that time, the CJTF-7 commander believed he had no choice but to use Abu Ghraib as the central detention facility.

Command and staff actions and inaction must be understood in the context of the operational environment discussed above. In light of the operational environment, and CJTF-7 staff and subordinate unit's under-resourcing and increased missions, the CJTF-7 Commander had to prioritize efforts. CJTF-7 devoted its resources to fighting the counter-insurgency and supporting the CPA, thereby saving Coalition and civilian Iraqi lives and assisting in the transition to Iraqi self-rule. In the over-all scheme of OIF, the CJTF-7 Commander and staff performed above expectations.

Abuse

Clearly abuses occurred at the prison at Abu Ghraib. There is no single, simple explanation for why this abuse at Abu Ghraib happened. The primary causes are misconduct (ranging from inhumane to sadistic) by a small group of morally corrupt soldiers and civilians, a lack of discipline on the part of the leaders and Soldiers of the 205th MI BDE and a failure or lack of leadership by multiple echelons within CJTF-7.

Contributing factors can be traced to issues affecting Command and Control, Doctrine, Training, and the experience of the Soldiers we asked to perform this vital mission.

For purposes of this report, abuse is defined as treatment of detainees that violated U.S. criminal law or international law or treatment that was inhumane or coercive without lawful justification. Whether the Soldier or contractor knew, at the time of the acts, that the conduct violated any law or standard, is not an element of the definition.

The abuses at Abu Ghraib primarily fall into two categories: a) intentional violent or sexual abuse and, b) abusive actions taken based on misinterpretations or confusion regarding law or policy.

LTG Jones found that while senior level officers did not commit the abuse at Abu Ghraib they did bear responsibility for lack of oversight of the facility, failing to respond in a timely manner to the reports from the International Committee of the Red Cross and for issuing policy memos that failed to provide clear, consistent guidance for execution at the tactical level.

MG Fay has found that from 25 July 2003 to 6 February 2004, twenty-seven 205 MI BDE Personnel allegedly requested, encouraged, condoned or solicited Military Police (MP) personnel to abuse detainees and/or participated in detainee abuse and/or violated established interrogation procedures and applicable laws and regulations during interrogation operations at Abu Ghraib.

Most, though not all, of the violent or sexual abuses occurred separately from scheduled interrogations and did not focus on persons held for intelligence purposes. No policy, directive or doctrine directly or indirectly caused violent or sexual abuse. In these cases, Soldiers knew they were violating the approved techniques and procedures.

Confusion about what interrogation techniques were authorized resulted from the proliferation of guidance and information from other theaters of operation; individual interrogator experiences in other theaters; and the failure to distinguish between interrogation operations in other theaters and Iraq. This confusion contributed to the occurrence of some of the non-violent and non-sexual abuses.

MG Taguba and MG Fay reviewed the same photographs as supplied by the US Army Criminal Investigation Command (CID). MG Fay identified one additional photograph depicting abuse by MI personnel that had not been previously identified by MG Taguba. MG Fay also identified other abuse that had not been photographed.

Alleged incidents of abuse by military personnel have been referred to the CID for criminal investigation and the chain of command for disciplinary action. Alleged incidents of abuse by civilian contractors have been referred through the Department of Defense to the Department of Justice.

Discipline and Leadership

Military Intelligence and Military Police units had missions throughout the Iraqi Theater of Operations (ITO), however, 205th MI Brigade and 800th Military Police Brigade leaders at Abu Ghraib failed to execute their assigned responsibilities. The leaders from units located at Abu Ghraib or with supervision over Soldiers and units at Abu Ghraib, failed to supervise subordinates or provide direct oversight of this important mission. These leaders failed to properly discipline their Soldiers. These leaders failed to learn from prior mistakes and failed to provide continued mission-specific training. The 205th MI Brigade Commander did not assign a specific subordinate unit to be responsible for interrogations at Abu Ghraib and did not ensure that a Military Intelligence chain of command at Abu Ghraib was established. The absence of effective leadership was a factor in not sooner discovering and taking actions to prevent both the violent/sexual abuse incidents and the misinterpretation/confusion incidents.

Neither Department of Defense nor Army doctrine caused any abuses. Abuses would not have occurred had doctrine been followed and mission training conducted.

Nonetheless, certain facets of interrogation and detention operations doctrine need to be updated, refined or expanded, including, the concept, organization, and operations of a Joint Interrogation and Debriefing Center (JIDC); guidance for interrogation techniques at both tactical and strategic levels; the roles, responsibilities and relationships between Military Police and Military Intelligence personnel at detention facilities; and, the establishment and organization of a Joint Task Force structure and, in particular, its intelligence architecture.

Other Contributing Factors

Demands on the Human Intelligence (HUMINT) capabilities in a counterinsurgency and in the future joint operational environment will continue to tax tactical and strategic assets. The Army needs trained and experienced tactical HUMINT personnel.

Working alongside non-DOD organizations/agencies in detention facilities proved complex and demanding. The perception that non-DOD agencies had different rules regarding interrogation and detention operations was evident. Interrogation and detention policies and limits of authority should apply equally to all agencies in the Iraqi Theater of Operations.

"Ghost Detainees"

The appointing authority and investigating officers made a specific finding regarding the issue of "ghost detainees" within Abu Ghraib. It is clear that the interrogation practices of other government agencies led to a loss of accountability at Abu Ghraib. DoD must document and enforce adherence by other government agencies with established DoD practices and procedures while conducting detainee interrogation operations at DoD facilities. This matter requires further investigation and, in accordance with the provisions of AR 381–10, Part 15, is being referred to the DoD Inspector General, as the DoD liaison with other government agencies for appropriate investigation and evaluation. Soldiers/Sailors/Airmen/Marines should never be put in a position that potentially puts them at risk for non-compliance with the Geneva Convention or Laws of Land Warfare.

Conclusion

Leaders and Soldiers throughout Operation Iraqi Freedom were confronted with a complex and dangerous operational environment. Although a clear breakdown in discipline and leadership, the events at Abu Ghraib should not blind us from the noble conduct of the vast majority of our Soldiers. We are a values based profession in which the clear majority of our Soldiers and leaders take great pride.

A clear vote of confidence should be extended by the senior leadership to the leaders and Soldiers who continue to perform extraordinarily in supporting our Nation's wartime mission. Many of our Soldiers have paid the ultimate sacrifice to preserve the freedoms and liberties that America and our Army represent throughout the world.

23 August 2004

Source: "Executive Summary: Investigation of Intelligence Activities at Abu Ghraib," United States Department of Defense, http://www.defense.gov/news/aug2004/d20040825fay.pdf.

170. Ariel Sharon: Speech at the United Nations Assembly (September 15, 2005)

Introduction

A few days after the completion of Israel's disengagement from Gaza, Prime Minister Ariel Sharon addressed the United Nations. His speech was brief and somewhat unspecific but, particularly given his past record as a hard-liner, was also relatively moderate and tactful. Recalling his lengthy career in the military, Sharon urged the Palestinians to seek "reconciliation and compromise" and "embark on the path which leads to peace and understanding between our people." Describing eloquently and emotionally just how much the territory of Israel meant to him personally and how difficult he would find it to relinquish any of its soil to others, he nonetheless declared that the Palestinians were "also entitled to freedom and to a national, sovereign existence in a state of their own." He called upon the Palestinians to end policies tolerating the use of terrorist tactics and the incitement of hatred against Israel. Sharon emphasized that Israel would defend itself in whatever ways were necessary and praised the controversial security fence separating Israeli and Palestinian territory for its role in protecting Israelis and saving lives. He also stressed that he would not compromise on "the right of the State of Israel to exist as a Jewish state, with defensible borders, in full security and without threats and terror." Having established his hard-line credentials, however, he urged Palestinian leaders to seize the "window of opportunity" that implementation of the disengagement plan in Gaza now offered for resuming progress under the Road Map to Peace and working toward peace that would benefit both Palestinians and Israelis.

Sharon's speech was tough but not bombastic in tone and, by making few specific demands or pledges, left room for maneuver on peace terms. Tactfully, he omitted any mention of the anarchy that broke out in Gaza immediately after the Israeli disengagement, even though this might have been used to cast doubt on Palestinian fitness for self-rule. He also forbore complaining that Hamas candidates were running for office in Palestinian elections even though, under the Oslo Accords, the party's opposition to making peace with Israel or accepting Israel's existence should have excluded it from the polls. Given his past record as a military hawk, Sharon might have had the credentials to move for a compromise peace settlement with the Palestinians and simply ride out conservative Israeli opposition to this. Already in his late 70s, he could move decisively and take risks for peace with few worries about the impact on his political future. In early January 2006, however, Sharon suffered a massive stroke that left him incapacitated, and after three months the Israeli cabinet declared him incompetent to continue in office. If a window of opportunity for Palestinian-Israeli peace genuinely existed, Sharon would not be the one to open it.

170. Ariel Sharon: Speech at the United Nations Assembly

Document

I, as someone whose path of life led him to be a fighter and commander in all Israel's wars, reach out today to our Palestinian neighbors in a call for reconciliation and compromise to end the bloody conflict, and embark on the path which leads to peace and understanding between our peoples. I view this as my calling and my primary mission for the coming years.

The land of Israel is precious to me, precious to us, the Jewish people, more than anything. Relinquishing any part of our forefathers' legacy is heartbreaking, as difficult as the parting of the Red Sea. Every inch of land, every hill and valley, every stream and rock, is saturated with Jewish history, replete with memories. . . .

I say these things to you because they are the essence of my Jewish consciousness, and of my belief in the eternal and unimpeachable right of the people of Israel to the Land of Israel. However, I say this here also to emphasize the immensity of the pain I feel deep in my heart at the recognition that we have to make concessions for the sake of peace between us and our Palestinian neighbors.

The right of the Jewish people to the Land of Israel does not mean disregarding the rights of others in the land. The Palestinians will always be our neighbors. We respect them, and have no aspirations to rule over them. They are also entitled to freedom and to a national, sovereign existence in a state of their own.

This week, the last Israeli soldier left the Gaza Strip, and military law there was ended. The State of Israel proved that it is ready to make painful concessions in order to resolve the conflict with the Palestinians. The decision to disengage was very difficult for me, and involves a heavy personal price. However, it is the absolute recognition that it is the right path for the future of Israel that guided me. Israeli society is undergoing a difficult crisis as a result of the Disengagement, and now needs to heal the rifts.

Now it is the Palestinians' turn to prove their desire for peace. The end of Israeli control over and responsibility for the Gaza Strip allows the Palestinians, if they so wish, to develop their economy and build a peace-seeking society, which is developed, free, law-abiding, transparent, and which adheres to democratic principles. The most important test the Palestinian leadership will face is in fulfilling their commitment to put an end to terror and its infrastructures, eliminate the anarchic regime of armed gangs, and cease the incitement and indoctrination of hatred towards Israel and the Jews.

Until they do so—Israel will know how to defend itself from the horrors of terrorism. This is why we built the Security Fence, and we will continue to build it until it is completed, as would any other country defending its citizens. The Security Fence prevents terrorists and murderers from arriving in city centers on a daily basis and targeting citizens on their way to work, children on their way to school and families sitting together in restaurants. This Fence is vitally indispensable. This Fence saves lives!

The successful implementation of the Disengagement Plan opens up a window of opportunity for advancing towards peace, in accordance with the sequence of the Roadmap. The State of Israel is committed to the Roadmap and to the implementation of the Sharm El-Sheikh understandings. And I hope that it will be possible, through them, to renew the political process.

I am among those who believe that it is possible to reach a fair compromise and coexistence in good neighborly relations between Jews and Arabs. However, I must emphasize one fact: there will be *no* compromise on the right of the State of Israel to exist as a Jewish state, with defensible borders, in full security and without threats and terror.

I call on the Palestinian leadership to show determination and leadership, and to eliminate terror, violence and the culture of hatred from our relations. I am certain that it is in our power to present our peoples with a new and promising horizon, a horizon of hope.

Source: Ariel Sharon, "Statement of Israel, 2005 UN World Summit," United Nations, http://www.un.org/webcast/summit2005/statements15.html.

171. White House Fact Sheet: "The New Way Forward in Iraq" (January 10, 2007)

Introduction

As the situation in Iraq deteriorated steadily, in December 2006 the administration of U.S. president George W. Bush ordered the National Security Council to undertake a review of U.S. policies toward Iraq, with the objective of stabilizing the country and preventing further breakdown into total civil war. When completed in early January 2007, the new review, a summary of which the White House issued as a press release, called for a major initiative to strengthen the Iraqi leadership and political, military, security, and economic institutions and forces so that the country's government would have the authority and power to win and maintain control of the nation. The strategy review openly acknowledged that the situation in Iraq "could not be graver" and that the position of the United States throughout the entire Middle East was in jeopardy. To facilitate efforts to regain control and restore order and stability, the United States promised Iraq additional troops and economic resources while building up Iraqi capabilities to handle the situation. All moderate Iraqi political forces were expected to work together in a coalition to combat extremism. The Bush administration intended to concentrate on "strengthen[ing] defense ties with partner states in the region" and increasing the coalition's regional military presence and Middle Eastern support for the global war on terror. The same evening that this press release appeared Bush addressed the nation, setting out the new strategy. The most controversial aspect of his speech was his pledge to dispatch an additional 20,000 American troops to Iraq, a surge that would, he claimed, enable coalition and Iraqi forces to regain control of Baghdad and surrounding areas. Bush stated that Iraq's prime minister, Nuri al-Maliki, had pledged that the troops would have a free hand in tackling all insurgents of every political or sectarian affiliation, something that had not been the case before. American troops would serve as military advisers, embedded in all units of the Iraqi security and military forces to train them and enhance their effectiveness. Bush told Americans that the Iraqi government would also institute major economic reforms and reintegrate former supporters of Saddam Hussein's regime into the political community. U.S. forces intended to move aggressively against Al Qaeda elements active in Iraq and also against their Iranian and Syrian sponsors. Bush intended to deploy an additional naval carrier strike group to the Middle East. Furthermore, the United States would launch diplomatic initiatives, in collaboration with Saudi Arabia, Egypt, Jordan, and the Persian Gulf states, to bring peace to Iraq and also to resolve the decades-old Palestinian-Israeli dispute. Many observers, including leading generals who had served in Iraq, remained skeptical that the new surge in American troop strength would suffice to restore order in the country and permit the Maliki government to regain control.

Document

The President's New Iraq Strategy Is Rooted In Six Fundamental Elements:

1. Let the Iraqis lead;
2. Help Iraqis protect the population;
3. Isolate extremists;
4. Create space for political progress;
5. Diversify political and economic efforts; and
6. Situate the strategy in a regional approach.

Iraq Could Not Be Graver—The War On Terror Cannot Be Won If We Fail In Iraq.

Our enemies throughout the Middle East are trying to defeat us in Iraq. If we step back now, the problems in Iraq will become more lethal, and make our troops fight an uglier battle than we are seeing today.

Key Elements Of The New Approach: Security

Iraqi:
- Publicly acknowledge all parties are responsible for quelling sectarian violence.
- Work with additional Coalition help to regain control of the capital and protect the Iraqi population.

- Deliver necessary Iraqi forces for Baghdad and protect those forces from political interference.
- Commit to intensify efforts to build balanced security forces throughout the nation that provide security even-handedly for all Iraqis.
- Plan and fund eventual demobilization program for militias.

Coalition:
- Agree that helping Iraqis to provide population security is necessary to enable accelerated transition and political progress.
- Provide additional military and civilian resources to accomplish this mission.
- Increase efforts to support tribes willing to help Iraqis fight Al Qaeda in Anbar.
- Accelerate and expand the embed program while minimizing risk to participants.

Both Coalition And Iraqi:
- Continue counter-terror operations against Al Qaeda and insurgent organizations.
- Take more vigorous action against death squad networks.
- Accelerate transition to Iraqi responsibility and increase Iraqi ownership.
- Increase Iraqi security force capacity—both size and effectiveness—from 10 to 13 Army divisions, 36 to 41 Army Brigades, and 112 to 132 Army Battalions.
- Establish a National Operations Center, National Counterterrorism Force, and National Strike Force.
- Reform the Ministry of Interior to increase transparency and accountability and transform the National Police.

Key Elements Of The New Approach: Political

Iraqi:
- The Government of Iraq commits to:
  - Reform its cabinet to provide even-handed service delivery.
  - Act on promised reconciliation initiatives (oil law, de-Baathification law, Provincial elections).
  - Give Coalition and ISF authority to pursue ALL extremists.
- All Iraqi leaders support reconciliation.
- Moderate coalition emerges as strong base of support for unity government.

Coalition:
- Support political moderates so they can take on the extremists.
- Build and sustain strategic partnerships with moderate Shi'a, Sunnis, and Kurds.
- Support the national compact and key elements of reconciliation with Iraqis in the lead.
- Diversify U.S. efforts to foster political accommodation outside Baghdad (more flexibility for local commanders and civilian leaders).
- Expand and increase the flexibility of the Provincial Reconstruction Team (PRT) footprint.
- Focus U.S. political, security, and economic resources at local level to open space for moderates, with initial priority to Baghdad and Anbar.

Both Coalition And Iraqi:
- Partnership between Prime Minister Maliki, Iraqi moderates, and the United States where all parties are clear on expectations and responsibilities.
- Strengthen the rule of law and combat corruption.
- Build on security gains to foster local and national political accommodations.
- Make Iraqi institutions even-handed, serving all of Iraq's communities on an impartial basis.

Key Elements Of The New Approach: Economic

Iraqi:
- Deliver economic resources and provide essential services to all areas and communities.
- Enact hydrocarbons law to promote investment, national unity, and reconciliation.
- Capitalize and execute jobs-producing programs.
- Match U.S. efforts to create jobs with longer term sustainable Iraqi programs.
- Focus more economic effort on relatively secure areas as a magnet for employment and growth.

Coalition:
- Refocus efforts to help Iraqis build capacity in areas vital to success of the government (e.g. budget execution, key ministries).
- Decentralize efforts to build Iraqi capacities outside the Green Zone.
- Double the number of PRTs and civilians serving outside the Green Zone.
- Establish PRT-capability within maneuver Brigade Combat Teams (BCTs).
- Greater integration of economic strategy with military effort.
- Joint civil-military plans devised by PRT and BCT.
- Remove legal and bureaucratic barriers to maximize cooperation and flexibility.

Key Elements Of The New Approach: Regional

Iraqi:
- Vigorously engage Arab states.
- Take the lead in establishing a regional forum to give support and help from the neighborhood.
- Counter negative foreign activity in Iraq.
- Increase efforts to counter PKK (Kurdistan Workers' Party).

Coalition:
- Intensify efforts to counter Iranian and Syrian influence inside Iraq.
- Increase military presence in the region.
- Strengthen defense ties with partner states in the region.
- Encourage Arab state support to Government of Iraq.
- Continue efforts to help manage relations between Iraq and Turkey.
- Continue to seek the region's full support in the War on Terror.

Both Coalition And Iraqi:
- Focus on the International Compact.
- Retain active U.N. engagement in Iraq—particularly for election support and constitutional review.

Source: "Fact Sheet: The New Way Forward in Iraq," The White House, President George W. Bush, http://georgewbush-whitehouse.archives.gov/news/releases/2007/01/20070110-3.html.

172. General David H. Petraeus: Report to Congress on the Situation in Iraq (September 10–11, 2007)

Introduction

In January 2007, President George W. Bush picked General David H. Petraeus as commander of the Multi-National Force in Iraq, with the mission to implement the policies of winning control of Iraq and handing over responsibility for the country's security and administration to Iraqi forces. Petraeus, a military intellectual, was one of the foremost experts on counterinsurgency, with a wide experience of nation-building operations in Bosnia and Haiti, who had previously commanded occupation forces in the Iraqi city of Mosul and headed the Multi-National Security Transition Command–Iraq. By early 2007 many members of the once-acquiescent U.S. Congress had become increasingly disillusioned with the war. Resolutions to cut off funding for the war and set a timetable for the withdrawal of U.S. forces won strong support in Congress, although the president eventually vetoed them, meaning that the anticipated rate of progress toward greater security in Iraq would attract fierce congressional monitoring and scrutiny. In September 2007 Petraeus delivered a detailed report to Congress on the situation in Iraq. He summarized his findings in personal testimony before Congress, describing a country where the Multi-National Force and the Iraqi government's own security personnel were gradually eliminating Al Qaeda and independent militia elements, reducing violence, and regaining control of ever-growing areas of Iraq. Petraeus expected to begin withdrawing American troops from Iraq by mid-2008. He was widely respected in Congress, and his report and recommendations were broadly accepted. As Petraeus came to the end of this assignment one year later in September 2008, levels of violence had fallen dramatically from the peak of early 2007. By that time Petraeus himself was modestly optimistic about the future prospects for Iraq, although he readily admitted that the situation was still fragile and that many tough challenges remained to be met.

Document

… As a bottom line up front, the military objectives of the surge are, in large measure, being met. In recent months, in the face of tough enemies and the brutal summer heat of Iraq, Coalition and Iraqi Security Forces have achieved progress in the security arena. Though the improvements have been uneven across Iraq, the overall number of security incidents in Iraq has declined in 8 of the past 12 weeks, with the numbers of incidents in the last two weeks at the lowest levels seen since June 2006.

One reason for the decline in incidents is that Coalition and Iraqi forces have dealt significant blows to Al Qaeda-Iraq. Though Al Qaeda and its affiliates in Iraq remain dangerous, we have taken away a number of their sanctuaries and gained the initiative in many areas.

We have also disrupted Shia militia extremists, capturing the head and numerous other leaders of the Iranian-supported Special Groups, along with a senior Lebanese Hezbollah operative supporting Iran's activities in Iraq.

Coalition and Iraqi operations have helped reduce ethno-sectarian violence, as well, bringing down the number of ethno-sectarian deaths substantially in Baghdad and across Iraq since the height of the sectarian violence last December. The number of overall civilian deaths has also declined during this period, although the numbers in each area are still at troubling levels.

Iraqi Security Forces have also continued to grow and to shoulder more of the load, albeit slowly and amid continuing concerns about the sectarian tendencies of some elements in their ranks. In general, however, Iraqi elements have been standing and fighting and sustaining tough losses, and they have taken the lead in operations in many areas.

Additionally, in what may be the most significant development of the past 8 months, the tribal rejection of Al Qaeda that started in Anbar Province and helped produce such significant change there has now spread to a number of other locations as well.

Based on all this and on the further progress we believe we can achieve over the next few months, I believe that we will be able to reduce our forces to the pre-surge level of brigade combat teams by next summer without jeopardizing the security gains that we have fought so hard to achieve.

Beyond that, while noting that the situation in Iraq remains complex, difficult, and sometimes downright frustrating, I also believe that it is possible to achieve our objectives in Iraq over time, though doing so will be neither quick nor easy.

Having provided that summary, I would like to review the nature of the conflict in Iraq, recall the situation before the surge, describe the current situation, and explain the recommendations I have provided to my chain of command for the way ahead in Iraq.

The Nature of the Conflict

The fundamental source of the conflict in Iraq is competition among ethnic and sectarian communities for power and resources. This competition *will* take place, and its resolution is key to producing long-term stability in the new Iraq. The question is whether the competition takes place more—or less—violently. This chart shows the security challenges in Iraq. Foreign and home-grown terrorists, insurgents, militia extremists, and criminals all push the ethno-sectarian competition toward violence. Malign actions by Syria and, especially, by Iran fuel that violence. Lack of adequate governmental capacity, lingering sectarian mistrust, and various forms of corruption add to Iraq's challenges. . . .

Current Situation and Trends

The progress our forces have achieved with our Iraqi counterparts has, as I noted at the outset, been substantial. While there have been setbacks as well as successes and tough losses along the way, overall, our tactical commanders and I see improvements in the security environment. . . .

As I mentioned up front, and as the chart before you reflects, the level of security incidents has decreased significantly since the start of the surge of offensive operations in mid-June, declining in 8 of the past 12 weeks, with the level of incidents in the past two weeks the lowest since June 2006 and with the number of *attacks* this past week the lowest since April 2006.

Civilian deaths of *all* categories, less natural causes, have also declined considerably, by over 45% Iraq-wide since the height of the sectarian violence in December. This is shown by the top line on this chart, and the decline by some 70% in Baghdad is shown by the bottom line. Periodic mass casualty attacks by Al Qaeda have tragically added to the numbers outside Baghdad, in particular. Even without the sensational attacks, however, the level of civilian deaths is clearly still too high and continues to be of serious concern.

As the next chart shows, the number of *ethno-sectarian* deaths, an important subset of the overall civilian casualty figures, has also declined significantly since the height of the sectarian violence in December. Iraq-wide, as shown by the top line on this chart, the number of ethno-sectarian deaths has come down by over 55%, and it would have come down much further were it not for the casualties inflicted by barbaric Al Qaeda bombings attempting to reignite sectarian violence. In Baghdad, as the bottom line shows, the number of ethno-sectarian deaths has come down by some 80% since December. This chart also displays the density of sectarian incidents in various Baghdad neighborhoods and it both reflects the progress made in reducing ethno-sectarian violence in the Iraqi capital and identifies the areas that remain the most challenging.

As we have gone on the offensive in former Al Qaeda and insurgent sanctuaries, and as locals have increasingly supported our efforts, we have found a substantially increased number of arms, ammunition, and explosives caches. As this chart shows, we have, so far this year, already found and cleared over 4,400 caches, nearly 1,700 more than we discovered in all of last year. This may be a factor in the reduction in the number of overall improvised explosive device attacks in recent months, which as this chart shows, has declined sharply, by about one-third, since June.

The change in the security situation in Anbar Province has, of course, been particularly dramatic. As this chart shows, monthly attack levels in Anbar have declined from some 1,350 in October 2006 to a bit over 200 in August of this year. This dramatic decrease reflects the significance of the local rejection of Al Qaeda and the newfound willingness of local Anbaris to volunteer to serve in the Iraqi Army and Iraqi Police Service. As I noted earlier, we are seeing similar actions in other locations, as well.

To be sure, trends have not been uniformly positive across Iraq, as is shown by this chart depicting violence levels in several key Iraqi provinces. The trend in Ninevah Province, for example, has been much more up and down, until a recent decline, and the same is true in Sala ad Din Province, though recent trends there and in Baghdad have been in the right direction. In any event, the overall trajectory in Iraq—a steady decline of incidents in the past three months—*is* still quite significant.

The number of car bombings and suicide attacks has also declined in each of the past 5 months, from a high of some 175 in March, as this chart shows, to about 90 this past month. While this trend in recent months has been heartening, the number of high profile attacks is still too high, and we continue to work hard to destroy the networks that carry out these barbaric attacks.

Our operations have, in fact, produced substantial progress against Al Qaeda and its affiliates in Iraq. As this chart shows, in the past 8 months, we have considerably reduced the areas in which Al Qaeda enjoyed sanctuary. We have also neutralized 5 media cells, detained the senior Iraqi leader of Al Qaeda-Iraq, and killed or captured nearly 100 other key leaders and some 2,500 rank-and-file fighters. Al Qaeda is certainly not defeated; however, it is off balance and we are pursuing its leaders and operators aggressively. Of note, as the recent National Intelligence Estimate on Iraq explained, these gains against Al Qaeda are a result of the synergy of actions by: conventional forces to deny the terrorists sanctuary; intelligence, surveillance, and reconnaissance assets to find the enemy; and special operations elements to conduct targeted raids. A combination of these assets is necessary to prevent the creation of a terrorist safe haven in Iraq.

In the past six months we have also targeted Shia militia extremists, capturing a number of senior leaders and fighters, as well as the deputy commander of Lebanese Hezbollah Department 2800, the organization created to support the training, arming, funding, and, in some cases, direction of the militia extremists by the Iranian Republican Guard Corps' Qods Force. These elements have assassinated and kidnapped Iraqi governmental leaders, killed and wounded our soldiers with advanced explosive devices provided by Iran, and indiscriminately rocketed civilians in the International Zone and elsewhere. It is increasingly apparent to both Coalition and Iraqi leaders that Iran, through the use of the Qods Force, seeks to turn the Iraqi Special Groups into a Hezbollah-like force to serve its interests and fight a proxy war against the Iraqi state and coalition forces in Iraq.

The most significant development in the past six months likely has been the increasing emergence of tribes and local citizens rejecting Al Qaeda and other extremists. This has, of course, been most visible in Anbar Province. A year ago the province was assessed as "lost" politically. Today, it is a model of what happens when local leaders and citizens decide to oppose Al Qaeda and reject its Taliban-like ideology. While Anbar is unique and the model it provides cannot be replicated everywhere in Iraq, it does demonstrate the dramatic change in security that is possible with the support and participation of local citizens. As this chart shows, other tribes have been inspired by the actions of those in Anbar and have volunteered to fight extremists as well. We have, in coordination with the Iraqi government's National Reconciliation Committee, been engaging these tribes and groups of local citizens who want to oppose extremists and to contribute to local security. Some 20,000 such individuals are already being hired for the Iraqi Police, thousands of others are being assimilated into the Iraqi Army, and thousands more are vying for a spot in Iraq's Security Forces.

Iraqi Security Forces

As I noted earlier, Iraqi Security Forces have continued to grow, to develop their capabilities, and to shoulder more of the burden of providing security for their country. Despite concerns about sectarian influence, inadequate logistics and supporting institutions, and an insufficient number of qualified commissioned and non-commissioned officers, Iraqi units are engaged around the country. . . .

Significantly, in 2007, Iraq will, as in 2006, spend more on its security forces than it will receive in security assistance from the United States. In fact, Iraq is becoming one of the United States' larger foreign military sales customers, committing some $1.6 billion to FMS already, with the possibility of up to $1.8 billion more being committed before the end of this year. And I appreciate the attention that some members of Congress have recently given to speeding up the FMS process for Iraq.

To summarize, the security situation in Iraq is improving, and Iraqi elements are slowly taking on more of the responsibility for protecting their citizens. Innumerable challenges lie ahead; however, Coalition and Iraqi Security Forces have made progress toward achieving sustainable security. As a result, the United States will be in a position to reduce its forces in Iraq in the months ahead.

Recommendations

Two weeks ago I provided recommendations for the way ahead in Iraq to the members of my chain of command and the Joint Chiefs of Staff. The essence of the approach I recommended is captured in its title: "Security While Transitioning: From Leading to Partnering to Overwatch." This approach seeks to build on the security improvements our troopers and our Iraqi counterparts have fought so hard to achieve in recent months. It reflects recognition of the importance of securing the population *and* the imperative of transitioning responsibilities to Iraqi institutions and Iraqi forces as quickly as possible, but without rushing to failure. It includes substantial support for the continuing development of Iraqi Security Forces. It also stresses the need to continue the counterinsurgency strategy that we have been employing, but with Iraqis gradually shouldering more of the load. And it highlights the importance of regional and global diplomatic approaches. Finally, in recognition of the fact that this war is not only being fought on the ground in Iraq but also in cyberspace, it also notes the need to contest the enemy's growing use of that important medium to spread extremism.

The recommendations I provided were informed by operational and strategic considerations. . . .

Based on these considerations, and having worked the battlefield geometry with Lieutenant General Ray Odierno to ensure that we retain and build on the gains for which our troopers have fought, I have recommended a drawdown of the surge forces from Iraq. In fact, later this month, the Marine Expeditionary Unit deployed as part of the surge will depart Iraq. Beyond that, if my recommendations are approved, that unit's departure will be followed by the withdrawal of a brigade combat team without replacement in mid-December and the further redeployment without replacement of four other brigade combat teams and the two surge Marine battalions in the first 7 months of 2008, until we reach the pre-surge level of 15 brigade combat teams by mid-July 2008.

I would also like to discuss the period beyond next summer. Force reductions *will* continue beyond the pre-surge levels of brigade combat teams that we will reach by mid-July 2008; however, in my professional judgment, it would be premature to make recommendations on the pace of such reductions at this time. . . .

One may argue that the best way to speed the process in Iraq is to change the MNF-I mission from one that emphasizes population security, counter-terrorism, and transition, to one that is strictly focused on transition and counter-terrorism. Making that change now would, in our view, be premature. We have learned before that there is a real danger in handing over tasks to the Iraqi Security Forces before their capacity and local conditions warrant. . . .

That assessment is supported by the findings of a 16 August Defense Intelligence Agency report on the implications of a rapid withdrawal of US forces from Iraq. Summarizing it in an unclassified fashion, it concludes that a rapid withdrawal would result in the further release of the strong centrifugal forces in Iraq and produce a number of dangerous results, including a high risk of disintegration of the Iraqi Security Forces; rapid deterioration of local security initiatives; Al Qaeda–Iraq regaining lost ground and freedom of maneuver; a marked increase in violence and further ethno-sectarian displacement and refugee flows; alliances of convenience by Iraqi groups with internal and external forces to gain advantages over their rivals; and exacerbation of already challenging regional dynamics, especially with respect to Iran. . . .

Source: General David H. Petraeus, "Report to Congress on the Situation in Iraq," U.S. Department of Defense, http://www.defense.gov/pubs/pdfs/Petraeus-Testimony20070910.pdf.

173. Israeli Prime Minister Benjamin Netanyahu: Speech to the United States Congress (March 2, 2015)

Introduction

In March 2015 Benjamin Netanyahu, then running for reelection as Israel's prime minister, addressed the U.S. Congress. He warned that the efforts of President Barack Obama's administration to negotiate a nuclear understanding with Iran were misguided and jeopardized the national security not just of Israel but also of the United States. From 2009 one of Netanyahu's foremost concerns, an issue on which Saudi Arabia uncompromisingly supported him, was to block any possibility that the radical Shiite regime of Iran could acquire nuclear weapons, which might enable Iran to threaten or pressure Israel. Netanyahu bitterly opposed any compromise with Iran, urging Americans that rather than accept a weak agreement, they should launch military attacks against Iranian nuclear facilities and destroy these entirely. He argued that the Iranians could not be trusted to observe the terms of a relatively moderate understanding and that the United States could not afford to accept such a threat to its own and the region's security. Netanyahu's address infuriated the Obama administration but failed to prevent the negotiation of a U.S.-Iranian nuclear accord in July 2015, an agreement that the U.S. Congress endorsed. In May 2018 the new administration of President Donald Trump unilaterally withdrew from this accord, on the stated grounds of Iranian non-compliance with its terms.

Document

My friends, I've come here today because, as Prime Minister of Israel, I feel a profound obligation to speak to you about an issue that could well threaten the survival of my country and the future of my people: Iran's quest for nuclear weapons. . . .

Iran's founding document pledges death, tyranny, and the pursuit of jihad. And as states are collapsing across the Middle East, Iran is charging into the void to do just that.

Iran's goons in Gaza, its lackeys in Lebanon, its revolutionary guards on the Golan Heights are clutching Israel with three tentacles of terror. Backed by Iran, Assad is slaughtering Syrians. Backed by Iran, Shiite militias are rampaging through Iraq. Backed by Iran, Houthis are seizing control of Yemen, threatening the strategic straits at the mouth of the Red Sea. Along with the Straits of Hormuz, that would give Iran a second choke-point on the world's oil supply. Just last week, near Hormuz, Iran carried out a military exercise blowing up a mock U.S. aircraft carrier. That's just last week, while they're having nuclear talks with the United States. But unfortunately, for the last 36 years, Iran's attacks against the United States have been anything but mock. And the targets have been all too real.

Iran took dozens of Americans hostage in Tehran, murdered hundreds of American soldiers, Marines, in Beirut, and was responsible for killing and maiming thousands of American service men and women in Iraq and Afghanistan.

Beyond the Middle East, Iran attacks America and its allies through its global terror network. It blew up the Jewish community center and the Israeli embassy in Buenos Aires. It helped Al Qaida bomb U.S. embassies in Africa. It even attempted to assassinate the Saudi ambassador, right here in Washington, D.C.

In the Middle East, Iran now dominates four Arab capitals, Baghdad, Damascus, Beirut and Sanaa. And if Iran's aggression is left unchecked, more will surely follow.

So, at a time when many hope that Iran will join the community of nations, Iran is busy gobbling up the nations. We must all stand together to stop Iran's march of conquest, subjugation and terror. . . .

. . . The battle between Iran and ISIS doesn't turn Iran into a friend of America. Iran and ISIS are competing for the crown of militant Islam. One calls itself the Islamic Republic. The other calls itself the Islamic State. Both want to impose a militant Islamic empire first on the region and then on the entire world. They just disagree among themselves who will be the ruler of that empire. . . .

The difference is that ISIS is armed with butcher knives, captured weapons and YouTube, whereas Iran could soon be armed with intercontinental ballistic missiles and nuclear bombs. We must always remember—I'll say it one more time—the greatest danger facing our world is the marriage of militant Islam with nuclear weapons. To defeat ISIS and let Iran get nuclear weapons would be to win the battle, but lose the war. We can't let that happen.

But that, my friends, is exactly what could happen, if the deal now being negotiated is accepted by Iran. That deal will not prevent Iran from developing nuclear weapons. It would all but guarantee that Iran gets those weapons, lots of them....

The first major concession would leave Iran with a vast nuclear infrastructure, providing it with a short breakout time to the bomb....

So why would anyone make this deal? Because they hope that Iran will change for the better in the coming years, or they believe that the alternative to this deal is worse?

Well, I disagree. I don't believe that Iran's radical regime will change for the better after this deal. This regime has been in power for 36 years, and its voracious appetite for aggression grows with each passing year. This deal would only whet Iran's appetite for more.

Would Iran be less aggressive when sanctions are removed and its economy is stronger? If Iran is gobbling up four countries right now while it's under sanctions, how many more countries will Iran devour when sanctions are lifted? Would Iran fund less terrorism when it has mountains of cash with which to fund more terrorism?

Why should Iran's radical regime change for the better when it can enjoy the best of both worlds: aggression abroad, prosperity at home?

We can insist that restrictions on Iran's nuclear program not be lifted for as long as Iran continues its aggression in the region and in the world. Before lifting those restrictions, the world should demand that Iran do three things. First, stop its aggression against its neighbors in the Middle East. Second, stop supporting terrorism around the world. And third, stop threatening to annihilate my country, Israel, the one and only Jewish state.

If the world powers are not prepared to insist that Iran change its behavior before a deal is signed, at the very least they should insist that Iran change its behavior before a deal expires. If Iran changes its behavior, the restrictions would be lifted. If Iran doesn't change its behavior, the restrictions should not be lifted. If Iran wants to be treated like a normal country, let it act like a normal country....

Now we're being told that the only alternative to this bad deal is war. That's just not true. The alternative to this bad deal is a much better deal: a better deal that doesn't leave Iran with a vast nuclear infrastructure and such a short breakout time; a better deal that keeps the restrictions on Iran's nuclear program in place until Iran's aggression ends; a better deal that won't give Iran an easy path to the bomb; a better deal that Israel and its neighbors may not like, but with which we could live, literally. And no country has a greater stake—no country has a greater stake than Israel in a good deal that peacefully removes this threat.

Ladies and gentlemen,

History has placed us at a fateful crossroads. We must now choose between two paths. One path leads to a bad deal that will at best curtail Iran's nuclear ambitions for a while, but it will inexorably lead to a nuclear-armed Iran whose unbridled aggression will inevitably lead to war. The second path, however difficult, could lead to a much better deal, that would prevent a nuclear-armed Iran, a nuclearized Middle East and the horrific consequences of both to all of humanity.

Source: House of Representatives. "Joint Meeting to Hear an Address by His Excellenvy Binyamin Netanyahu, Prime Minister of Israel," Congressional Record 2015, pt. 161, H1528-H1531.

174. Yemeni Civilians' Report: "We Lived Days in Hell: Civilian Perspectives on the Conflict in Yemen" (January 10, 2017)

Introduction

In March 2015, civil war began in Yemen when Houthi tribal elements opposed to Sunni tribes in the country organized the Supreme Revolutionary Committee, backed by former president Ali Abdullah Saleh, which took over the capital, Sana'a, and proclaimed themselves the lawful government. The existing government headed by Adrabbuh Mansur Hadi based itself in Aden in southern Yemen, leading the northern Houthi regime to launch a military campaign to win the south. The result was a protracted and, as of early 2019, unresolved conflict for supremacy that involved numerous other states and organizations in the Middle East and beyond. By early 2019, significant areas of Yemen were controlled by militant Islamic organizations, including Al Qaeda in the Arabian Peninsula, the Islamic State, and Ansar al-Sharia.

A coalition led by Sunni Saudi Arabia backed the established government and intervened militarily, whereas Shiite Iran supported the Houthis, as did the Muslim Brotherhood. Yemen's existing army was split, and the international community generally withheld diplomatic recognition from the northern regime. The real victims were the people of Yemen, many of whom were killed with many more forced to become refugees and flee to neighboring states. As the civil war in Yemen continued and escalated, drawing in a coalition of nations led by Saudi Arabia that sought to restore the recognized government, in January 2017 civilians in Yemen produced a damning report on the war's devastating consequences for their country's population. Impartially, the report's authors condemned all sides in the war not just for the harm inflicted on civilians in Yemen but also for their refusal to take any responsibility for these actions. They called on both contending governments and the Saudi-led coalition forces to put the interests of Yemen's people first and end hostilities, reach a cease-fire, demobilize, and concentrate on restoring and reconstructing the ravaged country. The report, sponsored by an international nongovernmental organization, gave an eloquent description of the sufferings of ordinary Yemenis. Well over two years later in 2019, the humanitarian crisis continued to intensify, with up to 13 million Yemenis threatened with starvation, and potential cease-fire negotiations between the rebels and the government were still only in the most tentative early stages.

Document

Executive Summary

"There is no civilian protection. There are only frontlines, battles, and clashes."—Yemeni man in war-torn Taiz.

For more than two years, civilians in Yemen have been navigating survival amid airstrikes, sniper attacks, landmines, forced displacement, famine, and economic hardships. Fighting between ground forces on one side and the overwhelming use of air power on the other has taken a devastating toll on the population in a country long considered to be the least developed in the Middle East and one of the poorest in the world.

Violence spread across Yemen when Houthis—a Zaydi-Shia group—took over Sana'a, the capital, in September 2014 with the help of former president Ali Abdullah Saleh's forces. Fighting escalated when a Saudi-led coalition intervened militarily in March 2015 to reinstate the internationally recognized government of President Abdrabuh Mansoor Hadi. The United Nations (UN) estimates at least 10,000 have been killed, 37,000 injured, and more than 3 million displaced. Over 80 percent of Yemen's 27.4 million people need humanitarian assistance. Famine, especially in rural areas, has increased: 7.6 million people suffer from severe food insecurity and almost 2 million are malnourished. As of December 2016, parties to the conflict have not respected UN-led ceasefire agreements.

This report documents patterns of civilian harm inflicted by all sides, examines civilian perceptions of the various parties to the conflict, the need to professionalize security forces, and highlights civilians' needs and expectations in terms of protection and assistance to rebuild their lives and communities. The report provides some recommendations to all parties to the conflict and the international community, including on key elements needed for an inclusive peace process that could help end the cycle of violence.

Center for Civilians in Conflict (CIVIC) conducted research in Sana'a, Aden, Taiz, Hadramout and Mareb governorates and met with civilians, governors, security and military officials, armed group leaders, as well as community and civil society leaders.

Civilian harm, as described by civilians in this report, includes death, injuries, and destruction of property, as well as displacement and forced disappearances. All parties to the conflict in Yemen are responsible for civilian harm and have failed to take necessary precautionary measures to minimize civilian harm when engaging a military target. In some cases, reports indicate that civilians were deliberately targeted.

What remains constant across the territory is the inability for civilians to get any recourse from any of the armed actors. A 46-year-old man from Majzer, Mareb said, "We would meet with [the] party that caused us harm and they would apologize, but blame the other side for what happened. I don't trust anyone. All sides are criminals and they have no conscience whatsoever." When asked what civilians did to protect themselves during the conflict, many civilians said they left their homes. "We just ran from one neighborhood to another. It's all we could do," said a 43-year-old woman from Aden. In Sana'a, civilians said that they either moved to safer areas or stayed on the ground floor away from windows, especially when they heard coalition fighter jets. "We could only flee from one place to another. There is no safe place," said a 55-year-old man.

From the beginning of the conflict, Houthi-Saleh forces have engaged in shelling of civilian residential areas, medical facilities, schools, and other civilian infrastructure, causing many civilians in Taiz and Aden to flee. Civilians in both cities reported deliberate sniper attacks against civilians, accusing the Houthi-Saleh forces of engaging in this practice.

On the other side, Saudi-led coalition strikes caused deaths, injuries, and the destruction of schools, medical facilities, and businesses in governorates in which CIVIC conducted research, echoing findings of other international and Yemeni organizations. According to the United Nations, the coalition is responsible for 60 percent of the civilian casualties since it intervened in March 2015. Civilians living in Sana'a, like their fellow citizens in Aden and Taiz, concluded that they were deliberately targeted. "Saudis did not observe any law or values," said a 40-year-old woman in Sana'a. "They bombed civilians. They killed humans, trees, and even animals did not escape their aggression," she added. The coalition has investigated some allegations of civilian harm, and for some incidents acknowledged mistakes and failures of personnel to follow rules of engagement (ROEs). It is unclear, however, whether anyone was held accountable for these acts, and whether the coalition instituted any changes to prevent the recurrence of such instances.

Our research also documented incidents of forced displacement of civilians, as well as forced disappearances and ill treatment of journalists and opponents by the Houthi-Saleh forces. Civilians have also been arbitrarily detained by Yemeni Elite Forces—who are trained by the United Arab Emirates (UAE)—in Hadramout governorate on suspicion of being affiliated with al-Qaeda in the Arabian Peninsula (AQAP).

While the fighting has stopped in Aden and some districts in Mareb, returning civilians are facing threat from landmines and unexploded ordnance (UXO). Yemeni organizations are struggling to keep up demands of clearance due to limited staffing capabilities, equipment, and budget gaps and need urgent assistance to facilitate the safe return of civilians.

Civilians note that security in parts of Aden has improved since Houthi-Saleh forces were pushed out and there are increased patrols by new security forces. Some of these security forces are former local resistance forces—consisting of civilians, local tribesmen, and southern separatists—who coalesced to fight the Houthis, and are now being integrated into security and military forces in Aden, Hadramout, Mareb, and Taiz. However, civilians expressed concern about oversight of these forces and their lack of discipline and professionalism and want those not formally integrated into national security forces to be disarmed. Security officials acknowledged the need to professionalize and train these forces on how to operate effectively and safely amongst a civilian population. While these forces were given limited trainings by some coalition members, trainings focused primarily on combat tactics. Government and security officials also admitted that there is a lack of proper command and control over forces technically under Yemeni government authority, because some are trained, equipped, and supervised by members of the Saudi-led coalition. This has created gaps in government oversight.

The impact of the conflict on civilian lives in terms of loss, psychological trauma, and humanitarian suffering is high and has exacerbated regional divides and worsened tensions between and within local communities and tribes, with most southerners claiming they want secession from the north.

Despite the deep divisions and different narratives on the responsibilities for the war, most civilians agreed on their deep distrust of both the Hadi government and the Houthi-Saleh alliance. Civilians in the north blame the Saudi-led coalition for the destruction it has caused.

Yemenis view the Hadi government as disconnected from Yemen and describe it as the "runaway government" as it has yet to fully return to Yemen. Expressing skepticism at peace talks, a civilian from Sana'a said, "If they [referring to Hadi, Houthis, Saleh] had Yemen's interests in their heart they would have reached a solution by now." A 55-year-old man from Sana'a suggested that for peace talks to work, the Saudis should halt airstrikes and "deport" Hadi's government back to Yemen. Civilians from Taiz and Mareb said that no peace could be accomplished unless Houthi-Saleh forces withdraw from and stop shelling these governorates.

Across the board, civilians do not want Yemen's current political figures to take part in the country's future and many want to see them brought to justice. Civilians demand an uncorrupt and effective government, and functioning justice and security institutions.

Ultimately, for the war in Yemen to end, a unified government—and its international backers—needs to reestablish trust with its own people. It can start by beginning to protect civilians from harm from all sides, address grievances that led to violence by involving local communities in the peace process, and to rebuild the country by putting the needs of civilians first.

Recommendations

To all Parties to the Conflict
- Ensure adherence to international humanitarian law during the conduct of all security operations.
- Respect ceasefire agreements initiated by the United Nations Peace Envoy and agree on a joint ceasefire monitoring mechanism overseen by the UN.
- Ensure a peace process that addresses local grievances across Yemen. The process must include local political leaders, civil society, women, and youth groups—not just current elite officials. Participation of women and local leaders will signal recognition of local grievances, and their roles in governance and security arrangements that will follow signing of any deal.

To the Government of Yemen
- Return to Aden permanently, prioritize the return of essential services in Yemen, and work with local authorities across Yemen to improve security and ensure civilians return to areas clear of landmines and UXO.
- Work with local authorities and civil society groups to develop a mechanism to receive and process civilian complaints of harm incurred during the conflict. Planning for post-harm assistance that will include financial assistance, vocational training, and medical and trauma assistance to conflict-affected communities should begin now and be transparent. Ensure women's and civil society's participation in the development of post-harm assistance programs.
- Ensure the enlistment of resistance fighters into security forces is transparent and not based on regional or tribal preferences. Seek assistance for scenario-based trainings on international humanitarian and human rights law, civilian

protection, civilian-military cooperation, and community policing. Investigate allegations of civilian harm attributed to resistance forces and hold persons accountable.

To the Houthi De Facto Authorities in Sana'a
- De-escalate the conflict and allow unhindered humanitarian access to civilians and in areas under siege, such as Taiz.
- Investigate allegations of civilian harm attributed to Houthi-Saleh forces and hold persons accountable.

To the Saudi-Led Coalition
- Review current rules of engagement, guidance, and targeting procedures to ensure adherence to IHL and best practices to minimize civilian harm. Such practices include:
- Issue new guidance to commanders in the coalition to ensure adherence to IHL, in particular principles of distinction and proportionality, and emphasize the need to minimize civilian harm (including assuming the presence of civilians in buildings). Hold accountable those who do not follow this guidance.
- Create a no-strike list—or revise the current no strike list—to include schools, hospitals, clinics, and civilian infrastructure that are protected from attack under IHL.
- Engage with humanitarian actors in Yemen to improve information sharing within the coalition on grid coordinates of hospitals and clinics.
- Ensure battle damage assessments take into account civilian deaths, injuries, and damage to homes and infrastructure. Use the data for in-depth analysis assessments to create an effective lessons-learned process that feeds into new guidance and scenario-based trainings to prevent future civilian harm.
- Investigate all allegations of civilian harm, including from international and Yemeni organizations.
- In cases of wrongdoing or failure to follow rules of engagement, hold persons accountable and make public the outcomes of investigations and accountability measures. Compensate civilians for wrongful death, injuries, and property damage.
- In cases of accidental or incidental harm, make amends in the form of apologies and monetary payments. Ensure any monetary payments are made transparently and with input from communities and families affected.
- Ensure accountability of Yemeni forces trained, funded, and advised by the coalition by investigating allegations of abuse attributed to such forces in Yemen.
- Review training programs for Yemeni military and security forces and include trainings on international humanitarian and human rights law, and scenario-based trainings on civilian protection.

To the United Nations
- Ensure participation of local leaders, including women and civil society, in the current negotiations to promote a genuinely inclusive peace process.
- Explore options with the Government of Yemen and Houthi authorities on UN support for disarmament, demobilization, and reintegration of armed groups.
- Undertake a thorough assessment and mapping of landmines/UXO contaminated areas, and existing Yemeni organizations' demining efforts. This will allow planning a coordinated strategy for demining and UXO clearance, and promotion of risk awareness programs in Yemen.

To Donor Partners, the United States, and the United Kingdom
- Condition any support, including arms sales, to the Saudi-led coalition on affirmative steps taken to implement policies to prevent civilian harm.
- Financially support UN and local civil society efforts to undertake landmine and UXO clearance and risk awareness activities.
- In coordination with the Government of Yemen and local authorities, support efforts to restructure and improve the professionalism of current police and military forces, as well as support trainings on international humanitarian and human rights law, scenario-based civilian protection trainings, civilian military relationship, and community policing.

- Provide assistance to rehabilitate courts and prisons and help with justice reforms. Functioning courts and prisons are key to improving the security situation and building confidence in the government.

Source: Report, "'We Lived Days in Hell': Civilian Perspectives on the Conflict in Yemen, January 10, 2017," Center for Civilians in Conflict, https://civiliansinconflict.org/wp-content/uploads/2018/07/2017.We-Lived-In-Hell.Report.Yemen_.MENA-Program.pdf. Courtesy of the Center for Civilians in Conflict.

175. Sheikh Abdul-Mahdi Al-Karbalai: The Friday Prayer Sermon from the Imam Al-Hussein Shrine (December 15, 2017)

Introduction

In late November 2017, the governments of both Iran and Iraq announced that their forces had taken back all the territory once controlled by the radical insurgent organization Daesh, the Islamic State in Iraq and Syria (ISIS). Top Muslim clerics in both countries had taken a strong stance against Daesh, urging devout Muslims to fight against the extremist terrorism that Daesh professed. On Friday, December 15, 2017, Sheikh Abdul-Mahdi Al-Karbalai, the official spokesman for the frail and elderly Grand Ayatollah Ali al-Sistani, the preeminent spiritual leader of Iraq's Shia Muslim community, preached a sermon praising the downfall of Daesh. He urged Iraqis to focus on rebuilding the areas devastated by ISIS and the battle against its forces and to continue to work to undermine the appeal of terrorism.

Document

Dear brothers and sisters, a few days ago, the liberation of the last part of the Iraqi territory from the control of the terrorist organization was officially announced, and on this occasion we have the following comment:

Noble Iraqis, after more than three years of fierce fighting, precious efforts and challenges, you have achieved victory against the most powerful terrorist force that targeted Iraq in its past, present and future. You were victorious with your firm will and firm determination to preserve your country, your dignity and your holy places. You were victorious with the tremendous sacrifices of yourselves and all that you hold precious for the dear homeland; you have established the highest images of heroism and altruism and you have written the history of modern Iraq with letters of dignity and nobility, and the world stood in astonishment at your determination and patience and heroism and faith in the justice of your cause until this victory was achieved, which many thought was out of reach. But you made it a tangible reality within a relatively short period, you have preserved the dignity of the country and its pride and maintained the unity of land and people. How great a people you are, the veteran fighters the heroes of the armed forces of all types and classifications.

The supreme religious authority, which gave the fatwa of the sufficient (kifa'i) defence, and which harnessed all its capabilities and energies in order to support the fighters and provided them with the best of its sons from the professors and students of the Hawza, dispatching them to the fronts in support of the fighting forces and offering dozens of them as martyrs in this way, does not see anyone having a hand in the same way you do nor glory to your glory in achieving this important historical achievement. Without your extensive response to the fatwa of the religious authority and its appeal and your heroic rush to the battle fronts and your heroic steadfastness for more than three years, this victory would not be achieved, so the victory is from you, for you, to you, and you are its cause. So congratulations to you on this victory and congratulations to your people. Indeed, blessed are those precious hands that you fought with and blessed are those pure homes you were raised in. You are our pride and dignity and we are proud of you in the face of other nations.

Iraq is so happy with you, you have sacrificed your lives and gave yourselves for your country and your people and your sanctities, we cannot even repay some of that debt, but God Almighty will reward you the most, and we can only pray to Him to increase the blessings on you and reward you the best reward.

Dear brothers and sisters, today we commemorate with great reverence our righteous martyrs, who reared the land of the nation with their pure blood, and they were great examples of sacrifice and redemption, and remember with them their families, the dignified parents and mothers and wives and children and their brothers and sisters, those dear people who were saddened by the loss of loved ones and met the pain of separation with more patience and endurance, and we honour with pride and dignity our dear injured ones, especially those who have suffered permanent disabilities, and they are the living martyrs who God willed to stay among us as witnesses to the heroism of the people as they faced the evil of the world by the sacrifices their sons. We recall in greatness and gratitude all the citizens who contributed to the support of their sons, fighters on the fronts, in order to strengthen their steadfastness, as they were their best supporters and backers in one of the finest images of the cohesion of a people with all its parts and components in defending its dignity and honour. We remember with gratitude all those who had an active and supportive role in this great epic of thinkers, intellectuals, doctors, poets, writers, journalists and others. We also extend our thanks and appreciation to all the brothers and friends who have stood with Iraq and its people in their ordeal with the terrorism of Daesh and supported it and offered it help and assistance, asking God Almighty to keep away from them all evil and give them peace and security.

There are several points that need to be mentioned:

The fight against terrorism must be done through addressing its intellectual and religious roots and to drain its human, financial and media sources. This requires working according to well-thought-out professional plans to achieve the required results, and though security and intelligence efforts form the basis in the fight against terrorism, this must be accompanied by awareness work to uncover the falsity and deviation of terrorist thought from the true religion of Islam, together with the promulgation and promotion of the discourse of moderation and tolerance in societies that could fall under the influence of this deviant thought. In addition to the need to work to improve the living conditions in the liberated areas and reconstruction and enable displaced people to return to (their hometowns) with dignity and pride and to ensure no erosion of their constitutional rights and to avoid repeating past mistakes in dealing with them.

We ask God Almighty to take everyone to what is good and beneficial for Iraq and its people. Verily, He is All-hearing, the Responder.

Source: The Official Website of the Office of His Eminence Al-Sayyid Ali al-Husseini al-Sistani, http://www.sistani.org/english/statement/25923/.

176. Egypt's Muslim Brotherhood Condemns the Frantic Crackdown against Journalists and Activists (May 30, 2018)

Introduction

In December 2013 Egypt's new military government declared the Muslim Brotherhood a terrorist organization. In July 2013 a coup had ousted President Mohamed Morsi, who had come to power just over a year earlier following national elections. Morsi's subsequent arrogation to himself of extraordinary executive powers and his effort to promulgate a new constitution, which opponents complained was dominated by fundamentalist Islamic principles, had prompted widespread popular protests, whereupon the military stepped in to depose Morsi and enforce order. In August 2013 massive protests by pro-Morsi supporters, organized by the Muslim Brotherhood, were suppressed by the government, leaving over 600 people dead and a further 4,000 injured. Muslim Brotherhood supporters retaliated by burning numerous police stations and churches. In the subsequent crackdown most of the Egyptian Brotherhood's top officials and supporters, including its supreme leader, Mohammed Badie, were arrested, with estimates of the numbers involved ranging from 16,000 to 40,000. In September 2013 the Egyptian courts declared the organization illegal and its assets were seized. In March 2014, 529 Muslim Brotherhood members were sentenced to death. Those Egyptian Brotherhood members who were not in custody fled elsewhere, to Qatar, Turkey, or Western countries. In most cases they renounced violence and aligned themselves with other victims of Egyptian government repression, urging all opponents of the existing regime to unite against it. From exile, they continued to issue statements denouncing the repressive policies of the Egyptian government and questioning the legitimacy of elections held under its auspices, declarations that were published in Arabic and English on the organization's website.

Document

The Muslim Brotherhood has been following the latest and ongoing frantic campaign against journalists, rights activists and politicians by the military regime in Egypt.

Despite their political differences, all Egyptians are becoming targets in the abuses, violations and the prosecution by the military coup.

The military junta's main concern is to preserve their gains, continue their corruption, pursue their personal ambitions and interests, and carry out their sponsors' agenda.

The Muslim Brotherhood values the enthusiasm of all patriots, and their sincerity for their homeland; and calls upon all the youth, revolutionaries and those who are passionate about their country future, to open their hearts and minds, and accept others with different opinion.

Let us unite under the banner of patriotism and the concern for this country, in view of the fact that all of us are now targeted by the coup, [and] suffer its injustice and brutality, despite past mistakes and excesses.

However, we must make a distinction between what can be considered mistakes that can be overlooked, especially by those who expressed apology or retraction, and those who committed grave crimes and bloodshed and must be held accountable.

We should always have a space in our hearts so as to restore national cohesion, bridge the rift, [and] revive the popular and revolutionary alignment as the most important tools and mechanisms of breaking the coup, returning the army to its barracks, restoring democratic life, elected institutions, and rights for all.

Day after day, it has been proven that the Egyptian people regain their full awakening. Let us help each other overcome the past mistakes and demonstrate the morals of the noble knights to move together towards a future of freedom and dignity.

Ahmed Assem

Media spokesman for the Muslim Brotherhood

Wednesday, Ramadan 14, 1439, May 30, 2018

Source: IHKWan Web: The Muslim Brotherhood's Official English Website, http://www.ikhwanweb.com/article.php?id=32933.

Index

Page numbers in **bold** indicate main entries in the encyclopedia.

Abadi, Haider al-, **1–2**, 425, 554, 593, 598, 720, 790, 841
Abagha (Abaqa, Abaka), Khan/Ilkhan of Persia 218, 791, 833, 1541
Abaza Mehmed Pasha, 933
Abbas (uncle of prophet Muhammad), 5, 6
Abbas, Abu (Muhammad Zaidan), **2–3**, 951
Abbas, Abu al-, 6
Abbas, Mahmoud (Abu Mazen), **3–5**, 47, 427, 455, 456, 499–500, 501, 560, 630, 954, 955, 957–959, 1007
Abbas I the Great, **7–9**, 301, 470, 875–876, 932, 1008, 1097–1098, 1590, 1591
Abbas II Hilmi Pasha, 374, 394–395, 847, 1098
Abbas III, 865, 928
Abbas Mirza, **6–7**, 929, 1085–1086
Abbasid Caliphate, **5–6**, 182, 183, 258, 264, 427, 429, 469, 508, 585, 831, 859, 945, 1100, 1536
Abbasid Revolution, **6**, 23
Abbasids, 6, 23, 71
Abd al-Aziz, 1127
Abd al-Aziz ibn-Saud. *See* Ibn Saud
Abd Allah al-Amin, 70
Abd Allah al-Mamun, 44
Abd Allah ibn al-Zubair, **9**
Abd al-Malik/ul-Malik, Caliph, 9, 610, 858, 1295
Abd al-Qadir al-Husseini (Abu Musa), 864
Abd al-Rahman ibn Mulijam, 65
Abdai Afghans, 865
Abdallah al-Battal, 42
Abdallah of Transjordan, 1124

Abdal-Malik, Caliph, 945
Abd-al-Rahman ibn Muljan al-Sarimi, 704
Abd-ar-Rahmān I, 258, 859
Abdel Hakim Amer, 376
Abdel-Rahman, Omar (the Blind Sheikh), **10**, 447
  message to his followers, 1733–1734
Abdi Pasha, 1081
Abdin Bey, 389
Abd-Rabbu Mansour Hadi, 193
Abduh, Muhammad, 963
Abdul Hamid I, Sultan, 516, 786, 916, 1079
Abdul Hamid II, Sultan, 33–34, 538, 917
Abdul Illah/Abd al-Illah, 421, 586
Abdul Karim Pasha, 278
Abdul Mecid I, 1251
Abdulaziz, 917
Abdulhamid I, Sultan, 717
Abdulhamid/Abdul Hamid II, Sultan, **11–12**, 163, 508, 1125, 1278, 1367, 1632
Abdulla Koprula, 865
Abdullah I, King of Transjordan/Jordan, **12**
  as commander of Arab armies, 640, 677
  dealings with the British, 132–134, 509, 538
  expulsion of Hamas from Jordan by, 808
  as king of Jordan/Transjordan, 509, 539, 676–677, 797, 1329
  negotiations with Israel, 471, 818
  position on Palestine, 120, 124, 125–126, 226, 940
  as representative of displaced Palestinians, 660–661
Abdullah Öcalan, 1283–1284

Abdullah, Prince/King of Saudi Arabia, 76, 420, 559
Abdullah (son of Hussein ibn Ali ibn Mohammed), 132, 509
Abdullah, Muhammad Ahmad ibn, 100
Abdullah bin Sa'ad bin Abi'l Sarh, 257
Abdullah Hussein, Sharif of Mecca, 1334
Abdullah ibn Wahab, 703
Abduhllah II, 8
Abdullah II of Jordan, **12–14**, 76, 451, 540, 559, 679–680, 1323
Abdullah Tell, 12
Abdulmecid I, Sultan, 11, 772, 892
Abdulmejid I, 1618
Abercromby, Ralph, **17–18**
Abgar (Ariamnes; Arab chieftain), 276
Abi Talib, 65
Abid, Muhammad Ali Bey al-, 434
Abi-Eshuh (Assyrian king), 177
Abihi, Ziyad ibn, 858
Abizaid, John Philip, **14–15**, 436
Abo Hafs Omer al-Baloty, 258
Aboukir, First Battle of, **15–16**, 236
Aboukir, Second Battle of, 16, **16–18**, 236
Aboukir Bay, Battle of (August 1, 1798), 15, **18–20**, 236, 877
Abrash, Omar, 1308
Abu Abbas, **20–21**, 23, 951
Abu Ahmed (Haqqi Esmaeil Owaid), 841
Abu Bakr, 88, 179, 256, 332–333, 384, 497, 700, 703, 856, 1067, 1345
  launching the Ridda Wars, 1482–1483

Abu Dhabi, 1297, 1375. *See also* United Arab Emirates (UAE)
Abu Ghraib, **21–22**, 75, 605
 executive summary of report, 2753–1757
Abu Ja'far Abdullah al-Mamun ibn Harun al-Rashid. *See* Al-Mamun, Abd Allah
Abu Jahl, 178–179
Abu Muhammad Al Sweidawi, Battle of, 1041
Abu Musa (Abd al-Qadir al-Husseini), 864
Abu Mus'ab al-Suri. *See* Nasar, Mustafa bin Abd al-Qadir Setmariam (Abu Mus'ab al-Suri)
Abu Muslim Khorasani, **23**
Abu Nidal, **23–24**
Abu Nidal Organization, 23, 758, 760. *See also* Fateh Revolutionary Council (FRC)
Abu Safayn, 702
Abu Sa'id/Said, 548, 1305
Abu Sayyaf, 806
Abu Sufyan, 178, 849, 1481
Abu Ubaidah, 333
Abu-al-Quds, Battle of, 700
Abu-l-Fida,' on the Fall of Acre, 1544–1545
Abu'l-Hasan Ali, 689
Abul'l Abbas, Caliph, 859
Abullah, King of Saudi Arabia, 1120
Abu'l-Misk Kafur, 1098
Abulustayn, Battle of, **22–23**, 218, 1539
Abu-Zeid, Ahmed, 1349
Abydos, Battle of, 215
Achaemenes, 25
Achaemenid (First Persian) Empire, **25–27**, 144–145, 162, 175, 263, 272, 309, 329, 339–342, 373–374, 972. *See also* Cyrus II (Cyrus the Great)
Achaeus, 110, 112
Achemenes, 145
Acheson, Dean, 94
Achillas, 288
Achille Lauro hijacking, 2–3, 20, 951
Achimeir, Abba, 1202
Acre, 1189 Siege of, **28–29**, 313–314
Acre, 1191 Siege and capture of, 1101, 1512–1515
Acre, 1291 Siege of, **29**
Acre, 1799 Siege of, **29–30**, 1608–1611
Acre, Battle of, **27–28**
Acre, fall of, 1544–1546
Acre Convention, 1233
Actium, Battle of, **30–32**, 388, 683, 1469
 map, 31
 from Plutarch's *Life of Antony*, 1454–1456
Adad-apla-iddina (Aramaean king of Babylon), 177
Adad-mirari III, 1263
Adad-nirari I, 160, 697
Adad-nirari III, 161, 178
Adad-shuma-usur (Babylonian king), 177
Adam, Sir Ronald "Bill," Montgomery's letter to, 1679–1680

Adan, Avraham "Bren," **32–33**, 287–288
Adana Massacre, **33–34**, 1632–1634
Adasi (Assyrian king), 159
Ad-Din, Jalal, 169
Adelaide del Vasto, 199
Aden Emergency, **34–35**, 1197, 1350
Adenauer, Konrad, 623
Adhemar du Pay, 311
Adhemar of Le Puy, 415
Adil Ghiray Khian, 930
Adrian IV (pope), 437
Adrianople (Edirne), Battle of, **35–36**, 295, 1080, 1279, 1312, 1523
Adrianople, Crusades Battle of, **36–37**
Adrianople, 1444 Treaty of, 37, 852
Adrianople, 1713 Treaty of, 37
Adrianople, 1829 Treaty of, **37–38**, 923, 1081, 1615
 account from *The Spectator*, 1615–1616
Aegospotami, Battle of, **38**
 Xenophon's description of, 1438–1439
Aetolian League, 1241–1242
Afghan Invasion of 1722, 489
Afghan Service Bureau, 73
Afghani, Jamal al-Din/ad-Din al-, 963, 1101–1102
Afghanistan, 74, 436, 489, 1283, 1299
 and the Anglo-Persian War, 99–100
 Nadir Shah's invasion of, 866
 Operation Enduring Freedom, 193
 Safavid capture of, 8
 siege of Isfahan, 608–609
 Soviet Union invasion and occupation of, 277, 612
 U.S. invasion of, 245, 436, 601
Aflaq, Michel, 128, 964
Africanus, P. Cornelius Scipio, 1242
Afsharid dynasty, 864
Agathocles (son of Lysimachus), 307, 360, 1017
Ager Sanguinis, Battle of, **38–39**, 106, 149, 201, 547, 664
Agesilaus II of Sparta, 320
Agha Muhammad, 976
Agha Muhammad Khan, 1084–1085
Agha Muhammad Khan Qajar, **39–40**
Agh-Darband, Battle of, 762
Agis III (king of Sparta), 55
Agnes (daughter of Boniface I of Montferrat), 298
Agnes (daughter of Henry IV), 294
Agnes of Courtenay, 82, 202–203, 490, 665
Agnes of Meran, 998
Agnes of Montferrat, 518
Agranat, Shimon, 40
Agranat Commission, **40**
Agrippa, Marcus Vipsanius, 30
Agrippa II, 683
Ahl al-Haqq, 102
Ahl al-Tawhid. *See* Druzes

Ahmad, Najumddin Faraj, 102. *See also* Krekar, Mullah
Ahmad, Tegüder, 795
Ahmad Arabi, 394
Ahmad Hilmy Pasha, 660
Ahmad ibn Mohammed al-Khalifa, 191
Ahmad Jalayir, Sultan, 183
Ahmad Khan, Sayyid, 672
Ahmad Qajar Shah, 564
Ahmad Sanjar, 1140
Ahmad Shah, 1086
Ahmadinejad, Mahmoud, 571
Ahmed, Ottoman sultan, 364, 1097
Ahmed, Prince, 931
Ahmed Djemal Pasha, 878, 1279
Ahmed I, 932–933, 1381
Ahmed III, 916, 928, 969
Ahmed Ismail Ali, 377
Ahmed Köprülü, 1314
Ahmed/Ahmad/Ahmet Pasha, 184, 762, 928, 933, 1080
Ahmet Arabi (Urabi), 374, 1254
Ahmet I, Ottoman sultan, 876
Aimery of Lusignan, king of Cyprus, 490, 491, 666
Aisha (wife of Muhammad), 703, 1067
Ajman, 1297. *See also* United Arab Emirates (UAE)
Ajnadain, Battle of, **40–41**, 700, 856, 1483–1484
Akbar, Emperor, 847
Akhaltsikhe, Battle of, 1081
Akhenaten (Ikhnaton; Amenhotep IV), Pharaoh, 382–383, 1416
Akkad, **41–42**
Akkadian Empire, 41–42, 175–176
Akkadian language, 41–42, 159, 175, 176, 502, 1110
Akraba, Battle of, 856
Akroinon (Afyon Karahisar), Battle of, **42**, 859, 1489–1490
Al Gama a al-Islamiyya (Islamic Group), 10
Al Ghuraba, 871
Al Jazeera, 67
Al Mansouri, Mariam, 553
Al Qaeda, 10, 13–14, 22, 45, 72, **73–75**, 102, 230, 245, 446, 447, 612, 806, 870, 871, 966, 1351
 and 9/11, 1146
 in Afghanistan, 436
 and the First Battle of Fallujah, 422
 and the Islamic Movement in Kurdistan, 102
 and jihad, 673–674
 use of chemical weapons, 285
Al Qaeda in Iraq (AQI), 72, **75–76**, 89, 143, 188, 363, 423, 592, 596, 597–598, 605, 789, 994–995, 996, 1258
Al Qaeda in Mesopotamia, 1258. *See also* Al Qaeda in Iraq (AQI)
Al Qaeda in the Arabian Peninsula (AQAP), 74, **76–78**, 420, 533, 1119, 1351–1352, 1357, 1359

Al Qaeda in Yemen, 532
Alaa Hussein Ali, 731
Al-Abassi, Shakir, 868
Al-Abba, Hasan, Caliph of Cairo, 157–158
Al-Adil, **42–43**
Al-Adil, Sayf al-Din (Saphadin), 168
Al-Adil Abu Bakr. *See* Al-Adil
Al-Adil II, 169, 432
Al-Afdal, **43**, 148, 151, 158, 308, 312
Al-Afdal Shahinshah, 179
Al-Aid, Caliph, 429
Al-Ali Ayyub, 169, 432
Al-Ali Ismail, 432
Alam el Halfa, Battle of, **43–44**
Al-Amin (son of caliph al-Rashid), 181–182
Al-Amin, Abd Allah, 70–71
Al-Amin, Muhammad, **44**, 1492
Al-Amir, 43
Al-Anbar People's Council, 89
Al-Anfal Campaign, **44–45**, 569, 581, 588
Al-Aqsa Battalions, 955
Al-Aqsa Intifada, 45
Al-Aqsa Martyrs Brigades, **45–47**, 659, 806
Al-Aqsa Mosque, 945
Al-Aqsa Mosque Massacre, **47–48**
Al-As, Amir ibn, 857
Alasehir, Battle of. *See* Antioch on the Meander, Battle of
Al-Ashraf (Ayyubid sultan of Damascus), 408
Al-Ashraf Khalil, 29
Al-Assad, Bashar, **153–156**
  as Alawite, 1226
  use of chemical weapons, 285, 286, 1236
  as commander of Syrian Air Force, 156
  denounced by Sadr, 1095
  and Hezbollah/Hamas, 457, 524–525, 571, 808
  vs. ISIS, 614, 616, 1231, 1238
  opposition to UAR, 156
  as president of Syria, 50, 172, 1230–1231
  protests against, 51, 1234
  relations with Egypt, 380, 1185, 1236
  relations with Iran, 584, 606, 1120, 1234
  relations with Israel, 630
  relations with Lebanon, 507
  relations with Russia, 614
  and the Syrian Civil War, 51, 524, 553, 555, 584, 606, 613–614, 616, 679, 748, 1007, 1026, 1120, 1231–1232, 1234–1238
  Turkey's opposition to, 407, 554, 710, 1285
Al-Assad, Basil, 153, 1230
Al-Assad, Hafez, 50, 153, 232, 497, 507, 626, 653, 746
Al-Assad, Rifaat, 497
Al-Atassi, Hashim, 1227
Alatheus, Ostrogoth chieftain, 36
Al-Atrash, Sultan, **48–49**, 478, 1227
Al-Awda, 597
Al-Awda, Abd al-Aziz, 955
Al-Awfi, Salah al-Alawi, 76, 77

Alawites (Alawis), **49–50**, 156, 434, 478, 497, 1226
Al-Awlaki, Anwar, 77
Al-Ayyubi, Shukri, 332
Al-Aziz, Fatimid caliph, 260, 659
Al-Aziz Uthman (son of Saladin), 168
Al-Badawi, Jamal Mohammed, 294
Al-Badr, Battle of, 1477–1478
Al-Badr, Muhammad, Crown Prince of Yemen, 1349–1350, 1354–1355
Al-Baghdadi, Abu Bakr, 612–613
Al-Bakr, Ahmad Hassan, 66, 140
Al-Baladhuri, on the Battle of the Yarmuk, 1484–1486
Albani, Muhamad Nasir al-Din al-, 431
Albania, 772
Al-Banna, Hassan, 611, 853–854
Al-Basri, Anad al-Hassan, 869
Albegensian Crusade, 309
Albert II of Hungary, 262, 926
Albuquerque, Alfonso de, 1008
Al-Bursuqi (governor of Mosul and Aleppo), 158
Al-Bustani, Emile, 270
Alcibiades (Athenian statesman), 518
Al-Dawla, Jana (emir of Homs), 158
Al-Dawla, Saif, 689
Al-Din, Jalal, 150
Al-Duri, Ibrahim, 605
Aleizayit (Olive Leaves), Operation, 242
Alekseyevna, Sofia, 1078
Alemdar Mustafa Pasha, 1137
Aleppo, Battle for, **50–52**, 102
Aleppo, Battle of (1400), 1249
Aleppo, Siege of (995), 215
Alexander (son of Cassander), 359
Alexander (son of Lysimachus), 307
Alexander (son of Philip II of Macedon), 342
Alexander Helios, 289
Alexander I Balas, **52**, 1017
Alexander I, Tsar, 236–237, 1085
Alexander II, Tsar, 1081, 1082
Alexander II Zabinas, 350
Alexander III (pope), 202, 437
Alexander III the Great, **52–54**
  Arrian on the character of, 1439–1440
  attack on the Kassites, 697
  Battle of Corupedium, 307
  Battle of Gaugamela, 448–449
  Battle of the Granicus, 478–479
  Battle of Issus, 645–646
  conquest of Achaemenid Empire, 675, 1226
  conquest of Egypt, 374, 388, 972
  conquest of Israel, 620
  conquest of Turkey, 1277
  defeat of Darius III, 26
  invasion and conquest of Persian Empire, 55–58, 320, 341, 448–449, 563, 585, 913
  and Louis IX, 776
  Sieges of Tyre and Gaza, 1291–1293
  See also Diodachi

Alexander III, Tsar of Russia, 114, 1377
Alexander III's Invasion of the Persian Empire, **54–58**
Alexander IV, 105, 357, 358, 359
Alexander Jannaeus, 943
Alexander Polyperchon, 356
Alexander Severus, Roman Emperor, **58**
Alexander Yannai, 683
Alexandretta, 434
Alexandria, Bombardment of, **58–59**, 93, 394, 1623–1626
Alexandria, Egypt, taken by Julius Caesar, 1451–1454
Alexandria, fall of, 1548–1550
Alexandria, Sack of (October 9–12, 1365), **59**
Alexandria Convention, 27, 391
Alexandropol, Treaty of, **59–60**, 142
Alexios/Alexius I Komnenos/Comnenus (Byzantine emperor), **60–61**, 106, 214, 233, 234, 248, 249, 264, 290, 309–311, 472, 883, 1000, 1029, 1076–1077, 1260, 1497
Alexios I Megas Komnenos, 1260
Alexios II Komnenos, 264
Alexios/Alexius III Angelos (Byzantine emperor), **61–62**, 63, 109–110, 238, 297, 315, 518, 799, 826, 1260, 1270
Alexios/Alexius IV Angelos, 62, 197, 238, 250, 297, 315, 1518
Alexios Strategopoulos, 200, 1540
Alexios V Doukas Mourtzouphlos/Mourtzouphlous (Byzantine emperor), **62–63**, 197, 297, 315, 518, 1518–1520, 1522
Alexius (son of Isaac II), 315
Alexius Apocaucus (Apokaukos), 253
Al-Fajr (New Dawn), Operation, 424
Al-Fateh, 137. *See also* Fateh Revolutionary Council (FRC)
Alfonso V of Aragon, 296
Alfonso X of Castile, 200, 371
Alfred P. Murrah Federal Building bombing, 104
Al-Gawri, Mamluk sultan, 1136
Algerian War, 454
Algerian War of Independence, 673
Al-Ghasani, Muhamad bin Ahmad, 355
Al-Ghazali, Janbardi, 793
Algiers Accord. *See* Algiers Agreement
Algiers Agreement, **62–63**
Algiers Declaration, **63**, 272
Al-Hadjdjadj, 1295
Al-Haj, Khalid Ali bin Ali, 77
Al-Hajjaj ibn Yusuf, 9, 858
Al-Hakim (Fatimid caliph), 364, 945
Al-Hanafiyya, Ali Ibn, 610
Al-Haqq Party, 532
Al-Hashimi, Taha, 126
Al-Hassani, Mahmoud Sarkhi, 869
Al-Hoss, Selim, 759
Al-Huss, Salim, 116, 507
Al-Husseini, Abd al-Qadr, 121
Al-Husseini, Abd el-Kadr, 122

Al-Husseini, Jamil, 773
Al-Husseini, Mohammed Abdel Raouf Arafat al-Qudwa. *See* Arafat, Yasser
Ali (caliph), 6, 9, 257
Ali (son of Hussein ibn Ali ibn Mohammed), 133–134
Ali, Hashemite king, 1124
Ali, Rubayi, 1361
Ali, Salem Rubaya, 1350
Ali Ahmad Ismail, **64**
Ali Beg of Smederevo, 927
Ali Bey, 1079
Ali Bey al-Kabir, **64**
Ali Hassan al-Majid, 44
Ali ibn Abi Talib, 49, **64–65**, 216, 610, 618, 691, 703
Ali ibn Hussein, 420
Ali ibn Muhammad, 1494
Ali Mardan Khan, 490, 694, 847
Ali Pasha of Aleppo, 343, 765, 766
Ali Sharia, 692
Alice (daughter of Baldwin II), 201
Al-Ilkshid, Muhammad, 689
Ali-Morad Khan Zand, 39
Aliya Bet, **65–66**
Al-Jaabari, 461
Al-Jaafari, Ibrahim, 67
Al-Ja'bari, Muhammed Ali, 660–661
Al-Jafari, Ibrahim, 788
Al-Jawad, Muhammad, 71
Al-Jihad al-Islami IEgyptian Islamic Jihad), 446
Al-Julani, Abu Mohammed, 71–72
Al-Kamil, 43
Al-Kamil (Ayyubid sultan of Egypt), 334, 432, 439, 666, 797–798, 971, 1526
Al-Kamil (son of al-Adil), 168–169
Al-Kamil, Malik, 316
Al-Khadim, Musa, 71
Al-Khalifa, Isa ibn Salman, 192
Al-Khalifa clan, 191
Al-Khuri, Bishara (sheik), 282
Al-Kunduri, 1138
Allawi, Ayad (Iyad), **66–67**, 591, 1094
Allenby, Sir Edmund Henry Hynman, **67–69**, 87–88, 134, 164, 220, 221, 331, 375, 452, 453, 661–662, 716, 741, 769, 815, 853, 947–948, 949, 1268–1269
  on the fall of Jerusalem, 1662–1664
Allied Force, Operation, 896
Alljah, Operation, 995
Allon, Yigal, **69–70**, 640, 641, 960, 1038, 1197–1198
Allon Plan, 69, **70**
All-Palestine State, 124
Al-Madayini, Mahmud (sheikh), 102
Al-Mahdi (third caliph), 71, 258
Al-Majid, Ali Hassan, 215, 721–722
Al-Malik, Suleiyman ibn Abd, 763
Al-Malik al-Nasir Muhammad, Sultan, 531, 792
Al-Malik ibn Shu'ai, 42

Al-Maliki, Nuri, 74, 276, 598, 606
Al-Mamun (son of caliph al-Rashid), 181–182, 258, 543
Al-Mamun, Abd Allah (Abdallāh), **70–71**, 1492
Al-Mansur, 42
Al-Manur ibn al-Mustarshid (Abbasid caliph), 158
Al-Manur Ibrahim of Homs, 432
Almaric of Jerusalem, 334, 665
Al-Masri, Abu Hamza, 609
Al-Mughassil, Ahmed Ibrahim, 705
Al-Mu'izz, Caliph, 659
Al-Mulk, Sharaf al-Ma'ali Sama,' 1049
Al-Muqrin, Abd all-Aziz bin Issa bin Abd al-Muhsin, 76
Al-Muqtafi, 6
Al-Musawi, Husayn, 523
Al-Mustali, 157
Al-Musta'li (Fatimid caliph), 619
Al-Mustanir Billah (caliph), 217
Al-Mustansir (Fatimid caliph), 179, 619
Al-Mustarshid (Abbasid caliph), 335
Al-Mustasim (Abbasid caliph), 182–183
Al-Mutamid, Caliph, 1373
Al-Mutasim, Caliph, 258, 831
Al-Muzayni, Ibrahim, 77
Al-Nabi, Abd, 609
Al-Nair, 6
Al-Nair Dawud of Kerak, 432
Al-Nair Muhammad ibn Qalawun, 795–796
Al-Nashashibi, Fakhri, 130–131
Al-Nashiri, Abd al-Rahim, 294
Al-Nasir Yusuf, 832–833
Al-Nusra Front, 50–51, **71–72**, 74, 188, 553, 555
Aloni, Shulamit, 961
Alp Arslan (Seljuk sultan), **72–73**, 264, 467–468, 790, 800, 1138
Alphonse-Jordan, 1271
Al-Qādisiyyah, Battle of, 843, 856, 1486–1487
Al-Qa'ida fi Bilad al-Rafhidayn, 75. *See also* Al Qaeda in Iraq (AQI)
Al-Qaiea fi Jazirat al-Arabiyya (AQAP), 76. *See also* Al Qaeda in the Arabian Peninsula (AQAP)
Al-Qassam, Izz al-Din (sheikh), 131, 650
Al-Qassam Brigades, 650
Al-Rahman, Sami Abd, 102
Al-Rashid clan, 544
Al-Ridha, Ali, 71
Al-Sabah, Ahmad al-Jabir, 78
Al-Sabah, Jaber al-Ahmed al-Jabir, **78–79**
Al-Sabah, Saad al-Abdullah al-Salim, 79
Al-Sabah, Sabah al-Ahmad al-Jabir, 79
Al-Sabah, Sabah al-Ahmed, 79
Al-Sabah, Sabah al-Salim, 79
Al-Sadiq, Muhammad ibn Ismail ibn-, 619
Al-Sadr, Muqtada, 67, 591, 594, 597, 598, 605, 692, 868, 1187
Al-Sadr, Musa, 523

Al-Sadr, Sayyid Muhaad Sadiq (Grand Ayatollah), 869
Al-Said, Nuri, 773
Al-Saiqa, 756, 757
Al-Saiqa (Syrian Baathists), 952
Al-Salih, Malik, 316, 798
Al-Sannabra, Battle of, **79–80**
Al-Shabaab, 612
Al-Shahid Yasser Arafat, 46. *See also* al-Aqsa Martyrs Brigades
Al-Shishakli, Adib bin Hassan, 49, 121
Al-Sinuwwar, Yahya, 498
Al-Sistan, Sayyid Ali Husayn (Grand Ayatollah), 102
Altalena Incident, **80–82**
Al-Tawhid Brigade, 50
Al-Tikriti, Ali Hassan al-Majid, 727, 731
Al-Uyayri (Ayiri), Yusuf Salah Fahd, 76
Al-Walid, Caliph, 859
Al-Walid II, 1295
Al-Wuhayshi, Nasir, 74
Amad Tegüder, 548
Amadeus VI of Savoy, 261
Amal movement, 523, 747
Amalric of Jerusalem, **82–83**, 202, 312, 505–506, 799, 1271
  letters to Louis VII of France, 1506–1508
Amalric of Montfort, 450
Aman, 740
Amara, Battle of, **83**
Amasis (pharaoh), 272, 309
Amasis II (pharaoh), 972
Amasya, Peace of, 876, 932
Amasya, Treaty of, **83**, 932
Ambush Alley, **84–85**, 873
Ambush Alley, Battle of, 84
Amel-Marduk (Babylonian king), 174, 877
Amenehab, biography of, 1414–1416
Amenemhet (pharaoh), 382
Amenhotep II (pharaoh), 159, 1414
Amenhotep IV (Ahkenaten), Pharaoh, 382, 1416
Amer, Abdel Hakim, **85–86**, 634, 678, 1189, 1190
American Civil War, 93
Amhad III, 925
Amida, Siege of, 1075
Amin, Idi Dada, 403–406
Amir, Yigal, 1039
Amir Ahmad, 468
Amir Ghazl Gumushtegin, 335
Amir Husayn, 1248
Amir Sibay, 793
Amiriyah Shelter Bombing, **86–87**
Amman Campaign, **87–88**
Amorite Kingdom, 822
Amr ibn al-As, **88–89**, 384
Amr ibn Bakr, 703
Amytis (wife of Nebuchadnezzar II), 877
Anak the Parthian, 1074
Ananus ben Ananus, 671

Anastasius I Dicorus, 884
Anastasius II (Byzantine Emperor), 257, 763
Anatolia, 101, 159, 164, 176, 177, 183, 257, 303, 311, 312, 323, 329, 335, 364, 469, 484, 485, 545, 695, 817, 843, 859, 862, 876, 912, 919, 929, 1030, 1077, 1226
    Erzurum Offensive, 410–412
    Sultanate of Rum, 1076–1077
Anbar Awakening Movement, 75, **89–91**
Andrea Moenigo, 262
Andrews Louis Y, 1328
Andromachus, 112
Andronicus I, 253
Andronicus II, 253
Andronicus III Paleologus, 253, 971
Androniko IV, 251
Andronikos I, 1260
Andronikos I Komnenos, 250, 251, 264, 1077, 1269
Andronikos II Palaeologus, 253, 826
Andronikos IV, 261, 799
Andronikos Palaiologos, 262, 826
Angeloi dynasty, 248
Angevin dynasty, 251
Anglo-American Committee of Inquiry, **91–92**, 940
Anglo-Egyptian Treaty, **92–93**, 395
Anglo-Egyptian War, **93–94**, 394, 1254
Anglo-Iranian Oil Company (AIOC), 566
Anglo-Iranian Oil Crisis, **94–95**
Anglo-Iraqi Treaties of 1922 and 1930, **95–96**, 586
Anglo-Jordanian Defense Treaty (1948), **96–97**
Anglo-Ottoman Convention of 1838, 772
Anglo-Ottoman Treaty, **97**
Anglo-Ottoman War, **98–99**
Anglo-Palestine Bank, 946, 1377
Anglo-Persian Oil Company, 564, 726
Anglo-Persian War, **99–100**
Anglo-Russian Convention, 564
Anglo-Sudan War, **100–101**
Ankara, Battle of, **101**, 219, 799, 915, 1193, 1554–1556
Ankara, Pact of, **101**
Anna of Savoy, 253, 255
An-Nahas Pasha, Mustafa, 426
Annan, Kofi, 352, 457, 895
Annia Faustina Minor, 802
Ansar al-Islam, **101–102**, 1258, 1319
Ansar Allah, 533
Ansar al-Sham, 102
Ansar al-Sharia, 78. *See also* Al Qaeda in the Arabian Peninsula (AQAP)
Ansar al-Sunnah, 493
Ansar Dine, 612
Anti-Arab Attitudes and Discrimination, **102–105**
Antigenes, 358
Antigonid Dynasty, 361
Antigonus Gonatas, 359

Antigonus I Monophthalmus (the One-Eyed), 54, **105–106**, 349, 356, 357, 358, 359, 413, 441, 561–562, 779, 966, 973, 1063–1064, 1135
Antigonus II Gonatas of Macedonia, 110, 350, 360, 361
Antigonus III Doson, 361
Antinous, 494
Antioch, Battle of, 1260
Antioch, Principality of, **106–108**
Antioch, Sieges of, 61, **108–109**
    1197–1198 (Stephen of Blois to his wife Adele), 1498–1500
Antioch on the Meander, Battle of, **109–110**
Antiochus Euergetes. *See* Antiochus VII Sidetes
Antiochus Hierax, **112–113**
Antiochus I (Seleucid king), 360, 413
Antiochus I Soter, 110, **110**, 231, 360, 782, 1134, 1135, 1239
    inscription of, 1442–1443
Antiochus II of Syria, 1239
Antiochus II Theos, 110, 1134
Antiochus III Megas (the Great), **110–111**, 231, 784–785, 974, 1017, 1049, 1134, 1135, 1240, 1241–1242, 1444
Antiochus IV, 52, 684
Antiochus IV Epiphanes, **111–112**, 360, 943, 1134, 1241
    and the sack of Jerusalem, 1445–1447
Antiochus V Eupator, 1134
Antiochus VII Sidetes, **112**, 350
Antipater, 105, 356, 357, 358, 359, 413, 683, 973
Antiphilus, 357
Anti-Semitism, **113–115**, 522, 528, 652, 774, 1376
    in Europe, 130
Antoninus, Marcus Aurelius, 1147
Antoninus Pius, 778, 802
Antonious Saturninus, 1267
Antony, Marc/Mark, 30, 32, 288, 289, 388
Aoun, Michel, **115–116**, 333, 363, 524, 534, 748, 759, 1245
Apamea, Peace of, 1242
Apollonius, 684, 782
Appian of Alexandria
    describing Seleucus I Nicator, 1441–1442
    describing the last days of King Mithridates VI Eupator Dionysius of Pontus, 1449–1451
Aq Sungur, 693
Aq Sunqur al-Bursuqi, 200, 370, 682
Aqaba, Capture of, **116–117**
Aqaba, Gulf of, 117
Aq-Qoyunlu Confederation, 913
Aqtay, 1276
Arab Association for Human Rights, 103
Arab Cooperation Council, 726
Arab Economic Boycott of Israel, **117–118**
Arab Federation, 421, 677, 899
Arab Higher Committee (AHC), 124

Arab Independence Party, 1034
Arab League, 120, **123–125**, 127, 190, 275, 333, 419, 559, 628, 640, 642, 675, 726, 744, 746, 748, 759, 953, 964, 1037, 1092, 1361
    economic boycott of Israel, 117–118
    and the Khartoum Resolution, 704
    statement (May 15, 1948), 1688–1691
Arab Legion, **125–126**, 421, 471, 586, 640, 676, 737–738
Arab Liberation Army (ALA), 121–122, **126–127**, 349, 640, 1027, 1170
Arab Liberation Front, 756, 952
Arab Nationalism, **127–129**, 133–134
Arab Oil Embargo, **129–130**
Arab Republic of Egypt. *See* Egypt
Arab Revolt, 48
Arab Revolt (1916–1918), 116–117, 420, 421, 478, 516, 539, 620, 675–676, 737, 811, 812, 948, 1116, 1225, 1334, 1655
Arab Revolt (1936–1939), 114, 495, 513–514, 940, 962, 1197, 1202, 1327, 1337, 1682, 1682
Arab Revolt in Palestine, **130–132**, 1679–1682
Arab Revolt of World War I, **132–134**
Arab Riots, Jerusalem, **134–135**, 1202
Arab Socialist Baath Party–Iraqi Region, 275. *See also* Baath Party
Arab Socialist Union, 376
Arab Spring, 14, 50, **135–136**, 194, 378, 533, 679, 748, 1119
    in Egypt, 391–392, 838–839
    in Kuwait, 729
    and the Muslim Brotherhood, 855
    in Oman, 906
    in Syria, 155
    in Tunisia, 391
    in Yemen, 1357
Arab Uprising (1929–1930), 283
Arab-Byzantine Wars, Siege of Damascus, 332–333
Arabi (Urabi), Ahmet, 58, 93–94
Arabi, Ahmed, **118–119**, 616
Arabi Pasha. *See* Arabi (Urabi), Ahmed/Ahmet
Arabia, Roman, **119**
Arabian Gulf. *See* Persian Gulf
Arab-Israeli War. *See* Six-Day War (1967)
Arab-Israeli War of Independence, 638. *See also* Israeli War of Independence
Arab-Jewish Communal War, **120–123**, 196, 622, 941
Arafat, Yasser **136–138**
    agreement with Hussein of Jorday, 431
    and al-Fatah, 24, 45, 47, 232–233, 427, 807, 1185
    Algiers Declaration, 63–64, 1173
    Cairo Accord, 269–270
    Cairo Agreement, 270–271
    Cairo Declaration, 271–272
    Camp David Summit, 464, 1056
    funding the PLF, 3, 21

Arafat, Yasser (*continued*)
   hostilities with Israel, 511
   vs. the IDF, 346
   and the Libyan-Egyptian War, 768
   Munich Olympics terrorist attack, 336
   Oslo Accords, 557, 910–912, 957–958, 1039
   and the Palestinian Authority (PA), 3, 511, 958, 1338
   and the Palestinian Liberation Organization (PLO), 3, 24, 753, 950, 952–953, 958
   peace talks with Israel, 211, 1068
   Rabat Summit, 1037
   and the Reagan Plan, 1050
   relations with Jordan, 231
   Wye River Agreement 1338–1339
   See also Palestine Liberation Organization (PLO)
Aragonese Crusade, 309
Arbuthnot, Charles, 98
Arcesilas, 357
Archelaus, 670, 683
Archon, 357
Ard al-Hâtim, Battle of, 550–551
Ardashir I (Sassanian king), 59, **138–139**, 890, 967, 1073, 1112, 1154
   records of, 1463–1467
Arens, Moshe, 1061
Argov, Schlomo, 24
Argov, Shlomo, 745, 758, 760
Arguello, Patrick, 1004
Arif, Abd al-Rahman, 140, 195
Arif, Abd al-Salam, **140**, 1022
Arif, Abdul Rahman, 587
Arif, Abdul Salam, 587
Arik-den-ili (Assyrian king), 160
Ariobarzanes, 147
Aristagoras, 561
Aristice of Mudros, 434
Arius, Battle of, 110
Armageddon Battle of, 815–816
Armenia, 60, 215, 438, 866
   Battle of Erzincan (1916), 409
   Christians in, 918
   war with Turkey, 1288–1289
Armenian Genocide, 34
Armenian Holocaust. *See* Armenians and the Armenian Genocide
Armenian Massacre. *See* Armenians and the Armenian Genocide
Armenian Orthodox Church, 140
Armenian Revolutionary Federation, 11
Armenian Revolutionary Federation (ARF), 878
Armenians, 11, 34, 107, 518
   Arab conquest of, 858
   in Cilicia, 434–435
   in Jordan, 675
Armenians and the Armenian Genocide, **140–142**, 405, 878, 918, 1226–1227, 1281
   Lord Bryce's report, 1652–1654
Armistice of Mudros, 434, 484

Army of Islam, **142**
Army of the Mujahideen, 102
Arnulf of Chocques, 198, 473, 663
Arouri, Saleh al-, 463
Arpad, 1264
Arras, Second Battle of, 68
Arrhidaeus, 356, 357. *See also* Philip III Arrhidaeus; Philip III of Macedon
Arrian, on the Character of Alexander the Great, 1439–1440
Arrowhead Ripper, Operation, **142–143**, 995–996
Arsaces I, 966
Arsaces II, 110
Arsacid dynasty, 966–967, 1112
Arsacid Empire, 139. *See also* Parthian Empire
Arses, 26, 341
Arshak II, 1156
Arsinoe (daughter of Ptolemy I), 228, 779, 1016
Arsites (brother of Darius II), 340
Arslan Arghun, 212, 1141
Arsuf, Battle of, **143–144**, 653
Arsuzi, Zaki al-, 964
Artabanus, 145, 1342
Artabanus IV, 138, 139, 889, 1112
Artabanus V, 967, 1073, 1461
Artah, Battle of, **144**, 150
Artaphernes, 339, 480
Artashata (Ochos), 26, 341. *See also* Darius III
Artavasdes (Armenian king), 276
Artaxerxes, 320, 942
Artaxerxes I, 26, **144–146**, 340
Artaxerxes II, 26, **146–147**, 330
Artaxerxes III, **147–148**, 341–342, 388
Artaxerxes IV, 26, 148
Artemisia I, **148**
Artemisia of Caria, as described by Polyaenus, in *Strategies of War*, 1437
Artukid dynasty, 195, 195–196
Artuq (chief), 148
Artuq, Suqman ibn, 681
Artuqid Dynasty, **148–150**, 149–150, 547
Artyphios (son of Megabyxos), 340
Asabiyya (tribal solidarity), **150–151**
Asander, 357
Ascalon (Askelon), Battle of, **151**, 312, 428, 472, 662, 663
Asher-resh-ishi I (Assyrian king), 160
Ashkenazic Judaism, **151–153**, 510
Ashmead-Bartlett, Ellis, letter to Herbert Henry Asquith, 1645–1648
Ashraf Hotak, 1098
Ashur bel-kala (Assyrian king), 161
Ashurbanipal (king of Assyria), 153, 162, 383, 822
Ashur-bel-nisheshu, 159
Ashur-Dan I (Assyrian king), 160
Ashur-Dan II (Assyrian king), 161
Ashur-etil-ilani (king of Babylon), 178
Ashur-nadin-ahhe I (Assyrian king), 159

Ashur-nadin-shumi (Assyrian king), 161
Ashurnasirpal I (Assyrian king), 161
Ashurnasirpal II (Assyrian king), 161
Ashur-resh-ishi I, 1263
Ashur-uballit I (Assyrian king), 160, 697
Ashuruballit II (Assyrian king), 173–174
Asia Minor, map (189 BCE), 974
Asia Minor Campaign, 483
Asia Minor Catastrophe, 483
Aspindza, Battle of, 1079
Asquith, Herbert Henry, letter from Ellis Ashmead-Bartlett, 1645–1648
Assad, Bashar al-, **153–156**, 171
Assad, Hafez al-, **156–157**, 171
As-Salih Ayyub, 1276
Assassins (Hasshashin), **157–158**, 182, 534, 551, 1100
   kill Marquis Conrad of Montferrat, 151–1516
Assembly of Palestine Jewry, 412
Assurnasirpal II (Neo-Assyrian king), 177
Assyrian Empire, **159–163**
Assyrian Empire, Neo-, 173
Assyrians, 34
Astrakhan, 1083
Astyages, 25
Aswan High Dam project, 293, 397, 454, 467, 875, 886–887, 1211, 1702
Asyur-rabi II (Assyrian king), 161
Ata Ali, 1190
Atasi, Hashim al-, 434
Atassi, Nureddin el-, 156
Ataturk, Mustafa Kemal, 142, **163–164**, 443–444, 484, 485, 647, 739, 919, 920, 949, 1099–1100, 1281, 1282, 1368
   letter to Enver Pasha, 1658–1661
   on the Treaty of Sèvres, 1671–1672
Atlas Mountains, 466
Atropates, 357
Attalus I of Pergamum, 110–111, 112, 413
Attalus II of Pergamum, 413, 414
Attalus III of Pergamum, 973
Attanius (guardian of Hadrian), 494
Attlee, Clement, 91, 94, 837, 1337
Attrition, War of. *See* War of Attrition
Auchinleck, Sir Claude John Eyre, **164–165**, 321, 399–400, 819–820, 1076
Audokia Angellina, 62
Augereau, Pierre, 236
Augustine of Hippo (saint), 945
Augustus (Octavian), 30, 32, 1469
Aulus Gabinius, 943
Aum Shinrikyo, 285
Aurelian, Emperor, **165–166**, 902, 961–962, 1376
Aurelius, Marcus, 1073
Auspicious Incident, **166**, 657, 786, 917
Austria
   German annexation of, 526
   treaties with Ottoman Empire, 968

Austrian-Ottoman Wars
  Evliyá Efendí describes, 1598–1600
  See also Ottoman-Habsburg Wars
Autumn Clouds, Operation, **166–167**, 455
Avidius Cassius, 778, 802
Avigur, Shaul, 416
Aylmer, Fenton, 723–724, 823–825
Ayn al-Dawla, 335
Ayn Jalut, Battle of, **167**, 218, 529, 534, 667, 791, 833
Ayyash, Yahya, 1005
Ayyub (father of Saladin), 167
Ayyub, As-Salih, 793, 1533
Ayyub, Najm al-Din, 1372
Ayyubid Dynasty, **167–169**, 312, 432, 666, 675, 798, 897, 1226
Ayyubid Empire, 42
Azariah (Uzziah), king of Judah, 1264
Azaz, Battle of, 682
Azemilik, 1291
Azerbaijan, 7, 476, 534, 547, 564, 565, 617
Aziz, Abdul, 1252
Aziz, Mitab ibn Abd al-, 1127
Aziz, Tariq, 578, 587, 649, 982
Azmi, Jemal, 878
Azury, Najib, 946, 964
Azzam, Abdullah, 73
Azzam, Abdullah Yusuf, 673, 870
Azzam Pasha, 349

Baal Shem Tov, Israel, 510
Baath National Students Union, 66
Baath Party, 24, 50, 66, 67, 75, 115, 140, 153–154, 156, **171–172**, 186, 195, 275, 486, 497, 536, 587, 653, 709, 787, 869, 964, 1035
Baathism and Baathists, 128, 157, 611, 756, 965
Babylon, destruction of, 161–162
Babylon, Battle of, 857
Babylon, Siege of, **172–173**
Babylonian Captivity, 942
Babylonian Empire, Neo-, **173–175**, 822, 876–877
Babylonian Empire, Old, **175–178**, 501–502
Babylonian War, 358–359, 501
Bacchides, 782
Bactria, 329, 358
Badr, Battle of, 65, **178–179**, 856
Badr, Sayf/Seif al-Islam Mohammed al-, 503, 1117
Badr al-Jamalii, 43, **179**
Badr, Battle of, 1482
Badran, Shams, 86
Badreddine, Mustafa, 525
Baghavard, First Battle of, **179–180**
Baghavard, Second Battle of, **180–181**
Baghdad, 812–813 Siege of, **181–182**, 1492–1493
Baghdad, 1258 Siege of, **182–183**, 822, 832, 1536–1539

Baghdad, 1401 Siege of, **183**
Baghdad, 1638 Siege of, **183–184**
Baghdad, 1773 Battle of, **184**
Baghdad, 2003 Battle of, **184–187**
Baghdad, Abu Bakr al-, **187–188**
Baghdad, Capture of, **181**
Baghdad, Treaty of, 762
Baghdad Central Confinement Facility (BCCF). *See* Abu Ghraib
Baghdad Pact, 97, **188–190**, 293, 421, 586, 964, 1171, 1698–1699, 1698–1699
Baghdadi, Abu Omar al-, 995
Bagoas, 26, 341
Bagrat (Georgian king), 468
Bahrain, 118, **190–194**, 487, 489, 553, 1120, 1298
  climate of, 291
Bahrain Defence Force (BDF), 194
Bahrain Freedom Movement (BFM), 192
Bahrain Petroleum Company, 191–192
Bahram V, 1112
Bahrayn, 1021
Baiju, 715–716, 1531–1532
Bailey, Ronald, 84
Baker, Samuel, 616
Bakhchisarai, Treaty of, **194**, 1078
Bakhtiar, Shapur, 573
Bakr, Ahmad Hassan al-, **195**, 536, 587
Bakr, Subashi, 933
Balak, Nur al-Dawla, 681–682
Balak ibn Bahra ibn Ortok, **195–196**
Balak ibn Bahram, 148, 149, 370
Balas, Alexander, 1134
Balathista, Battle of, 215
Baldat al-Shaykh Massacre, **196–197**
Balduk of Samosata, 693
Baldwin I of Constantinople, 36–37, **197–198**, 298
  A Byzantine View, 1522–1524
Baldwin I of Jerusalem, 79, **198–199**, 200, 234, 312, 335, 370, 415, 472, 473, 664, 681, 810, 1048–1049, 1251
Baldwin II of Bourcq, 370, 415, 1250
Baldwin II of Constantinople, **199–200**, 298, 299, 370, 776
Baldwin II of Edessa, 106, 149, 507, 664
Baldwin II of Jerusalem, 38, 195–196, **200–201**
Baldwin III of Jerusalem, 82, 107, 201, **201–202**, 250, 295, 312, 371, 664, 675, 681, 897
Baldwin IV of Jerusalem, 82–83, **202–204**, 490, 665, 835, 1508–1509
  "The Leper King," William of Tyre's description of, 1508–1509
Baldwin V of Hainaut, 203, 518, 665
Baldwin V of Jerusalem, 490, 1509
Baldwin IX of Flanders (VI of Hainaut), 238, 298, 518
Baldwin of Boulogne, 108, 369–370, 1250
Baldwin of Bourcq, 198, 681
Baldwin of Lorraine, 311

Baldwin of Reviers, letter from Richard of Cornwall, 1528–1531
Balfour, Arthur James, 204, 620, 669, 1335, 1378
  letter to Lord Rothschild, 1662
Balfour Declaration, 152, **204–205**, 224, 283, 620, 638, 669, 676, 773, 812, 937–938, 947, 962, 1304, 1330, 1334, 1378, 1648, 1662, 1675, 1685, 1688
  Arthur Balfour to Lord Rothschild, 1662
Balian of Ibelin, 490
Balian of Sidon, 450
Balkan alliance, 207
Balkan League, treaty with Ottoman Empire, 772–773
Balkan Wars (1912–1913), 11, 163, **206–208**, 646
  First Balkan War, 362, 405, 739, 768, 772, 918, 1126, 1314
  Second Balkan War, 302–303, 405, 768, 773
  Third Balkan War, 1279
Balkans, Ottoman Conquest of the, **205–206**
Balochs, 563
Balta Liman, Convention of, **208–209**
Balta Liman Treaty, 97
Baltaci Mehmet Pasha, 1079
Baltim, Battle of, **209**, 210
Baluch, Mohammad Khan, 762
Ban Ki-moon, 460
Bana Maruf. *See* Druzes
Bandar (prince of Saudi Arabia), 211
Bandman (Lieutenant Colonel), 40
Bani-Sadr, Abolhasan, 567
Banu Hashim, 508
Banu 'Uqayl family, 693
Bapheus, Battle of, **210**
Bar Giora, 509
Bar Kochba Revolt, **212–213**, 361, 494, 620, 683, 944
  described by Cassius Dio, 1462–1463
Barak, Ehud, 138, **210–212**, 336, 460, 636, 954, 1068, 1339
Baraka Khan, 530, 792, 795
Baratoff, Nikolai N., 978
Baratov, N. N., 701
Barbarigo, Agostino, 766
Barbot, Laurent, 77
Bardas Phokas, 1099
Bardiya (son of Cyrus the Great), 273, 329
Barghuti, Marwan, 46–47
Baring, Evelyn (Lord Cromer), 94, 394
  on the British Takeover of Egypt, 1626–1627
Barkai, Michael, 209, 736
Barkiyaruq (Seljuk sultan), 693
Barkiyaruq, 108, **212**, 1139, 1141, 1290
Bar-Lev, Chaim/Haim, 32, 213, 287, 960, 961
Bar-Lev Line, 32, **213–214**, 470, 626
Barq ibn Abdullah, 703–704
Barrett, Arthur, 1032
Barsbay (Mamluk sultan of Egypt), 704, 1559
Bartholomew Embriaco, lord of Gibelet, 1272
Bartholomew Mansel, bishop of Tortosa, 1272

Barzani, Marsoud, 594, 721
Barzani, Mustafa, 721, 990–991
Bashgedikler, Battle of, 1081
Bashkent, Battle of, 913
Basian, Battle of, **214**
Basil (Emperor), 258
Basil II, 260
Basil II Bulgaroctonos, **214–215**
Basil the Grand Chamberlain, 259
Basra, Battle for (2003), **215–216**
Basra, Battle of (869), 1494–1496
Bassorah, Battle of, 65, **216–217**, 610. *See also* Camel, Battle of the
Báthory, Sigismund, 924
Battleaxe, Operation, 1233
Batu Khan, 475
Bawatna, Jamal al-, 457
Baybars al-Bunduqari, 167
Baybars al-Jashnakir, 792
Baybars/Baibars I, Sultan, 6, 22–23, 107, 158, **217–218**, 235, 317, 371, 475, 530, 531, 777, 791–792, 794–795, 833, 1205, 1272, 1276, 1539–1540
Bayezid/Bayazid I, Sultan, 101, 205, **218–219**, 251–252, 261, 792, 799, 885, 886, 915, 1249,
Bayezid/Bayazid II, Sultan, **219**, 927, 931, 1551–1552, 1554, 1556, 1560, 1581
Bazán, Álvaro de, 765
Bazargan, Mahdi/Mehdi, 567, 706
Beatrice/Beatrix of Burgundy, 437, 440, 519
Beatrix (wife of Joscelin II), 371
Beauchamp-Duff, Sir, 890
Beaufre, André, 1213
Beauvale, Viscount, letter from Lord Palmerston, 1617–1618
Bebutov, V., 1081
Bechuanaland Expedition, 67
Beckwith, Charles, 577, 578
Bedouins, **219–220**, 374, 529, 833, 835, 1067, 1208, 1335
Beersheba, Battle of, **220–221**
Begin, Menachem Wolfovitch, 80–81, 152, **221–223**, 344, 349, 412, 417, 607, 628, 632–633, 745, 753, 757, 769–770, 1039, 1092, 1153
    and the Camp David Accords, 273–275
    and war with Lebanon, 759–762
Begin Doctrine, 223
Behaeddin Shakir Bey, 878
Beidh, Ali Saleh al-, 1357
Beidh, Ali Salem al-, 1197, 1351
Beilin, Yossi, 464
Beirut, Lebanon, 115–116
Bektash Khan, 183
Bel-bani (Assyrian king), 159
Belgrade, Siege of, 1310
Belgrade, Treaty of, 925, 1079
Belisarius, **223–224**, 685–686, 884
    winning the Battle of Dara, 1472–1474

Belshazzar (Belsharutsur), 172, 175
Ben Gal, Avigdor, 1308, 1309
Ben Hannan, Yosi, 1310
Ben Yehudah, Eliezer, 1378
Benghazi consulate attack, 74
Ben-Gurion, David, **224–225**
    and the *Altalena* incident, 80–81
    Battles of Latrun, 738, 802
    in Israeli government, 69, 453, 495, 504, 622, 818, 863, 1028
    and the Jewish Agency, 120, 122, 607, 622, 801, 1302
    and the Kafr Qasim massacre, 688
    London talks, 773
    Operation Nachshon, 863
    response to Arab Revolt, 513
    and the Suez Crisis, 1213
    as Zionist, 1059, 1378
Ben-Gurion, Paula Munweis, 224
Benjamin, Ernest, 669
Ben-Zvi, Yitzhak, 509, 773
Berbers, 858
Berengaria (sister of Ferdinand III of Castile), 674
Berengaria of Navarre, 999
Berenice (daughter of Ptolemy), 1134, 1239
Berenice, queen of Judaea, 1460
Berenice II (daughter of Magas), 1016
Berke Khan, 169, 475–476, 534, 832, 833
Berlin, Congress of, 11, 917, 1147
Berlin, Treaty of, 1083
Berlin Conference, 742
Berlin Decree, 237
Bernadotte, Folke, 80, **225–226**, 640–641, 771
    death of, 1691–1693
Bernard of Antioch, 234
Bernard of Clairvaux, 294, 776
Bernard of Valence, 38
Bernsen, Harold, 367
Berry, Edward, report on the Battle of the Nile, 1605–1607
Bertha of Sulzbach, 294
Berthier, Alexandre, 385
Bertrada of Montfort, 1251
Bertrand of Toulouse, 199
Bessarabia, 890, 1083
Bessus (governor of Bactria), 342, 449
Betar youth movement, 222, 652
Beth-Horon, Battle of, **226–228**, 671, 1457
Bevin, Ernest, 660, 837, 1301
Bey, Rauf, 843
Beyoglu Protocol, 844
Bible, **228–229**
    on Canaan (Palestine), 941
    Gog and Magog, 473–474, 1203
    and the state of Israel, 620
    and Torah law, 942–943
Bidault, Georges, 80
Bijad, Sultan ibn, 1123
Bileca, Battle of, 205

Bin Laden, Osama, 10, 73–74, 75, 101, **229–230**, 243, 245, 436, 597, 601, 612, 870, 1223
    "Letter to the American People," 1743–1748
Bir Hacheim, Battle of, 669
Birnbaum, Nathan, 1376
Bismarck, Otto von, 917
Bitar, Salah al-Din al-, 964
Bithynia, **230–231**, 335, 414
Black September, 3, 137, **231–232**, 417, 431, 540, 644, 678, 950, 953
Black September Organization, **232–233**, 335
Blackwater USA, 422
Blair, Tony, 602, 869
Blanche of Castile (queen of France), 200, 776
Blount, Buford, 186
Bocskay, István, 1381
Boer War, 67
Bohemund I of Antioch, 109, **233–234**, 335, 415, 1029
Bohemund I of Taranto, 106, 249, 311, 1250, 1498
Bohemund II of Antioch, 201, 234, 335, 682
Bohemund III of Antioch, 82, 106–107, 144, 203, 250, 490, 505–506, 1271
Bohemund IV, 107, 1271, 1272
Bohemund V of Antioch-Tripoli, 107, 234, 1272
Bohemund VI of Antioch-Tripoli, 107, **234–235**, 317, 1272
Bohemund VII of Antioch-Tripoli, **235**, 1020
Boko Haram, 74, 104, 612, 1258
Bolshevik Revolution, 446, 564, 1062
Bonaparte, Napoleon (Napoleon I), 15–17, 18, 20, 29–30, **235–237**, 374, 432, 545, 550, 1080, 1085, 1137, 1601–1602
    and the Battle of the Pyramids, 1017–1018
    beseiging Acre, 1607–1611
    in Egypt, 385–387
    letter to the Directory in Paris on the Battle of the Pyramids, 1601–1602
    proclamations to his troops and to the people of Egypt, 1601–1602
Boniface I of Montferrat, 197, **238**, 297, 298, 315, 518, 1521
Boniface IX (pope), 799
Border War (1949–1956), **238–242**
Boril of Bulgaria, 298, 519
Borochov, Ber, 1377
Bose, Wilfred, 403
Bosnia, 1081, 1083
Bosnians, 205, 917
Bouazizi, Mohamed, 135
Boumedienne, Houari, 62, 768
Bourchier, M. W. J., 331
Bouvines, Battle of, 438
Boz-Tapa-Mertekli Line, 409
Brandeis, Louis, 204
Brankovic, George, 37, 926
Bremer, Lewis Paul III "Jerry," 1, 15, 67, 172, **242–243**, 591, 605, 1108
Brest-Litovsk, Treaty of, 60, 142, 1289

Bridge, Battle of the, 1020
Brimes, Robin, 215
Brindel, Glenn, 1199–1200
Britain. *See* Great Britain
Britain, Battle, 668
Brith Habiryonim, 1202
British East India Company, 34, 725, 1008
British Overseas Territory of Akrotiri and Dhekelia, 327
British Royal Air Force, 350
British Security Forces (BSF), 495
Brooks, Dennis, 368
Brother's Keeper, Operation, 456, 461, 630
Brueys d'Aigalliers, François, 19–20
Brundisium, Treaty of, 289
Brussels Conference, 742
Brussels Declaration, 285–286
Brutus, 30, 289
Bryan, William Jennings, 204
Bryce, Lord, report on the Armenian Massacres, 1652–1654
Brzezinski, Zbigniew, 577–578
Bubiyan Island, Battle of, **243–244**, 986
Bucharest, Treaty of, 208, 916, 1080
Buczacz, Treaty of, 1382
Buddhism, 534–535
Bulfin, Edward S., 221, 452, 948
Bulgaria, 199, 206, 207, 215, 224, 773, 1083, 1279
  and the 1913 Treaty of Constantinople, 302–303
Bunche, Ralph, 641, 643
Bunichah system, 7
Burjis, 796
Burnaburias of Kassite Babylon writes to Pharaoh Akhenaten, 1416–1418
Burna-Buriash I (Kassite king of Babylon), 159
Burqan, Battle of, **244–245**
Bursuq ibn Bursuq, 149
Buscarello di' Ghisolfi, 548
Bush, George H. W., 727, 728, 730–731, 732, 783, 894, 979, 982, 985, 987, 1053, 1163, 1193
Bush, George W., 21, 67, 90, 184, 243, 436, 457, 536, 571, 589–590, 592, 599, 602, 604, 635–636, 851–852, 869, 994, 1052, 1109, 1132, 1339
  address to Congress and the American People on the War on Terror, 1738–1742
  "The New Way Forward in Iraq," 1759–1761
  response to 9/11, 1144
Bush Doctrine, **245–246**, 1146
Buyids (Buwayhids), 5
Byng, Julian, 68
Byzantine Civil War, 60, 253
Byzantine Empire, 101, **246–252**, 521
  and Ancient Egypt, 384
  Battle of Bapheus, 210
  Battle of Manzikert, 800
  and the Crusades, 309

Early Byzantine period, 246–248
Harun al-Rashid at war with, 1490–1492
and Henry VI of Germany, 1516–1518
Later Byzantine period, 251–252
Long War in, 876
map, 247
Middle Byzantine period, 248–251
Nijka Uprising, 883–884
Ottoman conquest of, 206
wars with Persia, 856
Byzantine Empire Civil War, **252–256**
Byzantine-Muslim Wars, **256–260**
Byzantine-Ottoman Wars, **260–262**
Byzantine-Sassanid War, **263–264**, 803, 1478
  Battle of Nineveh, 888–889
Byzantine-Seljuk Wars, **264–265**, 1000

Caesar, Gaius Julius, **267–268**, 288–289, 307, 683
Caesarian (Ptolemy XV Caesar; son of Julius Caesar), 268, 288–289
Caesarian-Pompeian civil war, 683
Caesar's Campaign in Egypt, **268–269**
Cafferata, Raymond, 515
Cairo Accord, 210, **269–270**
Cairo Agreement, **270–271**
Cairo Declaration, Palestine Liberation Organization, **271–272**
Calabria, 258
Calecas, John, 253–254
Caledonians, 494
Callinicum, Battle of, 223
Cambon, Paul, letter from Sir Edward Grey on the Sykes-Picot Agreement, 1649–1651
Cambyses I, 329
Cambyses II, 25, 144, 175, **272–273**, 309, 329, 383, 387, 972
Camel, Battle of the, 9, 65, 610, 857. *See also* Bassorah, Battle of
Camp David Accords, 117, 124, 223, **273–275**, 344, 378, 465, 628, 632, 830, 850, 1092, 1118, 1173, 1204
Camp David peace talks, 558
Camp David Summit, 211, 464, 957
Camp Redemption, 22
Camp Speicher Massacre, **275–276**
Canal Zone, 93. *See also* Suez Canal
Candarli, Kara Halil, 690
Candian War, 1313–1314
Caneva, Carlo, 647
Cannae, Battle of, 276
Cappadocia, 335
Caracalla, 388, 889, 967, 1073, 1147
Carden, Sackville, 337–338, 443
Carmathians of Bahrayn, 427
Caro, Joseph (Rabbi), 152
Carrhae, Battle of, **276–277**, 308, 1072
Carter, James Earl "Jimmy," 223, 326, 378, 567, 628, 632–633, 706, 891
  and the Camp David Accords, 273–275

Carter Doctrine; State of the Union Address, 1712–1716
and the Iran hostage crisis, 575–577
and Operation Eagle Claw, 577–578
Carter Doctrine, **277**, 891, 1712–1716
Carus, 1074
Casey, George W., 851, 994
Casiro Agreement, 950
Cassandane (mother of Cambyses II), 272
Cassander, 105–106, 350, 356, 358, 359, 561–562
Cassara, Richard, 243–244
Cassius, 30, 289
Cassius Avidius, 1073
Cast Lead, Operation, 458, 500, 630, 903. *See also* Gaza War of 2008–2009
Catalan Company, 251
Catherine II of Russia, "The Great," 658, 916, 925, 1079, 1084
Catholic Church, 317
Cattilusio, Caterina, 296
Caucasian Front, Battle of Sarikamish, 1111–1112
Caucasus, 489, 534
Caucasus Front, World War I, **278–280**
Cave of the Patriarchs Massacre, 515–516
Cecilia (daughter of Philip I of France), 1251
Çelebi, Musa, 101
Çelebi, Mustafa, 926
Celestine III (pope), 520, 998
Celts, 230–231
Cem (Djem), 219
Central Intelligence Agency (CIA), 67, 95, 293, 553, 573, 705, 727, 987, 1053, 1338, 1695–1697
Central Office for the Boycott of Israel, 118
Central Treaty Organization (CENTO), 188, 190, 1698
Cesarini, Giuliano, 1311
Cestius Gallus, 227, 671
Cezayirli Gazi Hasan Pasha, **280–281**
Chaeronea, Battle of, 53, 478
Chagri Beg, 72, 1138
Chaldean Empire, 173, 173–175, 178. *See also* Babylonian Empire, Neo-
Chaldiran, Battle of, **281**, 1097, 1575–1577, 1581
Challe, Maurice, 1212
Chamberlain, Neville, 668
Chamoun, Camille (Kamil Shamun), **281–283**, 745, 749–750, 757, 1300
Chancellor, Sir John Robert, **283–284**
Chandragupta (Sandrokottos/Androcottus), 1135
Chandragupta Maurya, 359
Change of Direction, Operation, 751–752. *See also* Lebanon, Israeli Operations Against
Chanukah (Hanukkah), 684, 782, 943
Chapman, Thomas, 740
Charlemagne (Charles the Great), 248, 859
Charles (Holy Roman Emperor), 922

Charles I of Anjou, king of Naples, 200, 299, 317, 371, 826
Charles IV of Spain, 280
Charles Martel, 859
Charles of Flanders, 201
Charles V, Holy Roman Emperor, 514, 1064, 1313, 1583
Charles VI of France, 885
Charles VIII of France, 219, 261
Charlie Hebdo shootings, 78
Chauvel, Henry (Harry), 221, 331, 332, 450, 452–453, 948, 1070
Chaytor, Edward W. C., 88, 781
Chemical Weapons and Warfare, **284–286**, 568, 569, 580, 721–722, 786–787, 991, 1283, 1319
Chemical Weapons Convention (CWC), 286
Cheney, Dick, 602, 843, 1132, 1133
Chesma/Chesme, Battle of, 280, **286–287**
Chetwode, Philip, 221, 450–451, 452–453, 661, 948
Children's Crusade, 315–316
Chinese Farm, Battle of the, **287–288**, 378, 626
Chinggis (Genghis) Khan, 167, 475, 831
Chios, Battle of, 1079
Chomsky, Noam, 1091
Choniates, Niketas, 862
Christianity
  in Armenia, 918
  Coptic, 373, 379, 384, 388, 447, 615
  in early Palestine, 943
  Eastern Orthodox, 740, 787–788
  Greek Orthodox, 826, 970, 1081
  Jacobite, 803
  martyrdom in, 805
  religious sites in the Middle East, 1053–1054
  Roman church, 826, 970, 1081
  Syrian Orthodox, 803
  See also Copts; Greek Orthodox Church; Maronites
Christians
  in Lebanon, 534, 749–750
  Maronite, 744, 745–746, 754, 755–756, 757, 760, 803–804, 844, 953, 1245, 1716
  Nero's persecution of, 943
  persecution of, 442
Christopher, Tony, 77
Christopher, Warren, 644
Chronicle Concerning Sargon and Naram-Sin, Kings of Agade, and Other Early Babylonian and Assyrian Rulers, 1406–1407
Chrysopolis, Battle of, 215, 295
Churchill, Winston L. S., 91, 165, 337, 338, 400, 401, 443, 446, 565, 668–669, 741, 920
Churchill White Paper, 1329–1330
Cilicia, 218, 234, 235, 249, 434–435, 438, 505, 715–716, 794–795
Cimon, 327, 415
Circassian sultans, 796

Circassians, 675
Citium, Battle of, 416
Claudius, Emperor, 388, 683, 943, 1315
Claudius II Gothicus, 165
Clement III (Guibert of Ravenna), 290
Clement III (pope), 313
Clement IV (pope), 826, 1541
Clement VI (pope), 1193, 1546
Clement VIII (pope), 775, 923
Cleopatra (Alexander's sister), 357
Cleopatra (wife of Demetrius II), 112
Cleopatra I, 1017
Cleopatra Selene, 289
Cleopatra VII, 30, 32, 268–269, **288–290**, 388, 807, 973, 1014, 1452, 1454, 1469
Clerides, Glafkos, 326
Clermont, Council of, **290**
Climate of the Middle East, **291–292**
Clinton, Hillary, 461
Clinton, William Jefferson "Bill," 211, 350–351, 353, 570, 599, 644, 705, 784, 1053, 1316, 1338–1339
  address to the nation on Operation Desert Fox, 1734–1738
  and the Oslo Accords, 910–912
  and the PLO, 954
Clodius, 307
Clodius Albinus, 1147
Cnidus, Battle of, 146
Coalition of the Willing, 602
Coalition Provisional Authority (CPA), 1, 15, 422, 496, 591, 595, 597, 605
Code of Hammurabi, 502, 822
  Preamble and Epilogue, 1407–1410
Codommanos/Codomannus, 26, 341. *See also* Darius III
Cody, Richard "Dick," 1252
Cohen, Avner, 1191
Cold War, 277
  and the Nixon Doctrine, 891
Cold War in the Middle East, **292–293**, 393
  Eisenhower Doctrine, 396–397
Cole, USS, Attack on, **293–294**, 532, 609, 1146
Coligny, Jean de, 924
Colline Gate, Battle of the, 307
Collingwood, Cuthbert, 98
Colombe, Philippe, 489
Combined Joint Task Force-Operation Inherent Resolve (CJTF--OIR), 551
Comer, Richard L., 1252
Commando Eagle, Operation, 995–996
Commodus, 802–803
Compass, Operation, 901
Concerned Local Citizens, 90
Confederates, Battle of the, 702, 856. *See also* Kandaq, Battle of; Khandaq, Battle of the
Confederation of the Rhine, 236
Congress of Vienna, 236–237
Conon of Béthune, 298
Conrad II, 666–667

Conrad III, King of Germany (Conradin), 201, 250, **294–295**, 312, 437, 664, 666–667, 776, 798, 1498
  letters to the abbot of Corvey, 1503–1505
Conrad of Montferrat, 28, 158, 238, 314, 491, 666
  killed by Assassins, 1515–1516
Conrad of Querfurt, Bishop of Hildesheim, 521
Conradin. *See* Conrad III, King of Germany (Conradin)
Constance (daughter of Bohemund II), 106–107
Constance (daughter of Peter II of Aragon), 438
Constance (daughter of Philip of France), 234
Constance of Antioch, 202
Constance of Sicily, 519
Constans, 296, 305
Constans II, 257, 857
Constantine (Cyril), saint, 248
Constantine (son of Bardas Phokas), 1099
Constantine Gabras, 335
Constantine I (Constantine the Great), 247, 252, **295–296**, 442, 914, 944, 1074
Constantine I (Flavius Valerius Constantinus), 295–296, 305
Constantine I, King of Greece, 483, 1099–1100
Constantine II, 296, 305
Constantine IX Monomachos, 248
Constantine the Great, 35, 246, 1053
Constantine V, 42, 258, 859, 1489
Constantine VI, 258
Constantine VII, 259, 1099
Constantine XI, 304
Constantine XI Palaiologos, 252, **296**
Constantinople
  1612 Treaty of, 933
  1736 Treaty of, 928
  as Byzantine capital, 246–247
  Byzantine capture of, 1540
  Byzantine recapture of, 210
  capture by Ottomans, 252, 296
  Crusader Siege and Capture of (1204), 1520–1522
  and the Fourth Crusade, 251, 315
  Latin conquest of, 251
  liberation of, 251
  Muslim account of the fall of, 1560–1562
  Muslim siege of, 248, 521
  Nika Revolt, 1474–1477
  Ottoman siege of (1422), 262
  Turkish capture of, 246
Constantinople, 1479 Treaty of, 1312
Constantinople, 1590 Treaty of, **301–302**
Constantinople, 1700 Treaty of, **302**, 1078
Constantinople, 1720 Treaty of, **302**
Constantinople, 1724 Treaty of, 1084
Constantinople, 1832 Treaty of, **302**
Constantinople, 1913 Treaty of, **302–303**
Constantinople, Crusader Siege and Capture of, **296–297**

Constantinople, Latin Empire of, **297–299**
  Decline and End, 298–299
  Establishment and Early History, 297–298
Constantinople, Muslim Siege of, **299–301**
Constantinople, Ottoman Siege of, **303–305**
Constantinople, Treaty of, 7–8, 37, 695, 875, 922
Constantinople Protocol, 62
Constantius, Emperor, correspondence with Shapur II the Great, 1470–1472
Constantius II, Emperor, 296, **305–306**, 442, 685, 1075
Constanza (daughter of Frederick II), 883
Constitutional Revolution (Iran), 564
Convent of St. Gothard, Battle of the, 714
Convention for the Pacification of the Levant, 772. See also London, 1840 Treaty of
Conway, James, 872, 873
Copenhagen, Battle of, 877
Coptic Christian Legion, 17
Coptic Legion, 387
Copts, **306–307**, 447, 615
Corbulo, Gnaeus Domitius, 1072
Córdoba, Gonzalo de, 1313
Corinthian League, 562
Corinthian War, 996
Coronea, Battle of, 1341
Corrective Revolution, 156, 653, 1229
Cortenuova, Battle of, 439
Corupedium, Battle of, **307**, 779, 1015, 1135
Corvinus, Matthias (king of Hungary), 927, 1312
Cossack Brigade, 977, 1062, 1086
Cossacks, 930, 931, 1078
Council for Peace and Security, 637
Council of Chalcedon, 803
Council of Clermont, Urban II's speech, 1497–1498
Council of Ferrara-Florence, 252
Council of Florence, 262
Crassus, Marcus Licinius, 267, 276, **307–308**, 967, 1003, 1071–1072
Crassus, Publius Licinius, 307
Craterus, 356, 357, 413, 973
Creech-Jones, Arthur, 837
Cresson, Battle of, **308**, 1100
Cretan War, 1313–1314
Crete, 208
Crimea, Russian annexation of, 354
Crimean Khanate, 916
Crimean War, 717, 774, 834, 917, 1081, 1617. See also Russo-Ottoman Wars
Croatia, 206, 925
Croesus of Lydia, **309**, 329, 778–779, 1263
Crossman, Richard, 91
Crowe, William J., 1724
Crusade of Nikopolis, 252
Crusader, Operation, 165, 321
Crusades, and anti-Semitism, 113
Crusades, struggle with the Seljuks, 5–6
Crusades in the Holy Land, Christian, **309–318**, 620, 945

First Crusade, 43, 106, 108–109, 148, 151, 198, 212, 233, 249, 290, 295, 310–312, 363–364, 369, 415, 428, 472, 693, 992–993, 1048, 1076, 1139, 1141, 1250, 1271, 1290, 1497, 1498
Second Crusade, 107, 201, 249, 294, 312–313, 371, 437, 512–513, 550–551, 664, 775–776, 798, 896, 1000, 1076, 1502
Third Crusade, 28, 143–144, 168, 250, 313–315, 322, 437–438, 490, 491, 520, 653, 654, 663, 665, 763–764, 945, 999, 1076, 1101, 1510, 1511, 1512
Fourth Crusade, 62, 197, 210, 238, 251, 264, 297, 315, 518, 666, 1518
Fifth Crusade, 168, 316, 334, 666, 674, 798, 970
Sixth Crusade, 316, 1526
Seventh Crusade, 316–317, 776–778, 1276, 1535
Eighth Crusade, 317
Ninth Crusade, 317–318
and anti-Semitism, 113
Children's Crusade, 315–316
Crusade of Nikopolis, 1552–1554
Germans' Crusade (Conrad III), 1503–1505
map, 310
struggle with the Seljuks, 5–6
Ctesiphon, 363 Battle of, **318–319**, 1471
Ctesiphon, 1915 Battle of, **319–320**, 723, 823
Cuéllar, Javier Pérez de, 595
Cumans, 61, 199, 315
Cumbers, Simon, 77
Cunaxa, Battle of, **320**, 330
Cunningham, Sir Alan Gordon, 165, **320–321**
Cypriot National Guard, 326
Cyprus, **321–327**, 787–788
  Arab conquest of, 857
  and the Baghdad Pact, 190
  given to Guy of Lusignan, 666
  independence from Persia, 416
  Jewish detainees sent to, 417
  map, 322
  Ottoman conquest of, 1586–1589
  union with Greece, 487
Cyprus, Athenian Expedition to, **327**
Cyprus, Ottoman Conquest of, **328–329**
Cyprus, War of. See Venetian-Ottoman Wars
Cyrus I, 25, 320, 620
Cyrus II The Great, 25, 144, 175, 230, 272, 309, **329–330**, 479, 563, 585, 822, 877, 942, 1262
  cylinder of, 1430–1432
  and the Ionian Revolt, 561
  siege of Babylon, 172–173
Cyrus the Younger, 146, **330**, 340, 1255
Cyzicus, Battle of, 858

Da Canale, Nicolo, 1566
Dacian Wars, 494
Daesh, 1772
Dahan, Gabriel, 688–689
Daibert of Pisa, 198, 473, 663–664, 1250
Dair al-Jamajim, Battle of, 858
Dalmatia, 1314
Damascus, Allied Capture of, **331–332**
Damascus, Siege of, 295, 332–333, 1289
Damascus Agreement, **333–334**
Damascus Spring, 154, 1230
Damghnan, Battle of, 865
Damietta, **334**
Dandanqan, Battle of, 1138
Dandolo, Enrico, 36, 238
Danilo I, 834
Danishmend, Ghazi II, 682
Danishmendid Dynasty, **334–335**, 335, 1029, 1076, 1250
Daoud, Abu, **335–336**
Dar, Avram, 740
Dar al-Islam and Dar al-Harb, **336–337**
Dara, Battle of, 223, 685, 1472–1474
D'Arcy, William Knox, 466
Dardanelles, 1807 British Expedition to. See Anglo-Ottoman War
Dardanelles, Treaty of the, 99
Dardanelles Campaign, **337–339**
  failure of the British fleet, 1642–1645
Darfur, 616
Darin, Treaty of, 1116
Darius I (The Great; King of Persia), 25, 144–145, 175, 273, **339–340**, 561, 942, 1342
  and the Greco-Persian Wars, 479–483
  large inscription from Behistun, 1432–1437
Darius II, 26, 145–146, 330, **340–341**
Darius III, 26, 53–54, 55–58, **341–342**, 383, 388, 448, 449, 478, 1291
  Battle of Issus, 645–646
Darlan, Jean, 1233
Dassa, Robert, 740
Datames, 147
Datis (Median noble), 480
Daud Khan, 1083
David, King, 942
David I Komnenos, 298, 519, 883, 1269–1270, 1564
David II (Georgian king), 149
David IV (Georgian king), 468
David Megas Komnenos, 1260
David of Trebizond, 1567
Davie, Gerald, 997
Dawa Party, 1, 593, 788–789
Dawish, Faisal al-p, 546
Dawla, Iftikhar ad-, 662
Dawud Pasha, **342–343**
Dayan, Moshe, 40, 81, **343–344**, 402, 412, 960, 961, 1153, 1176, 1189, 1198, 1213
  eulogy for Roi Rotberg, 1700
Dayf (Deif), Mohammed, 650
Dazion, Battle of, 258
De Gaulle, Charles, 1336

Dean, Patrick, 1213
De-Baathification, 172, 591, 605
Debecka Pass, Battle of, **344–346**
Decabulus of Romania, 1267
Decelean War, 517
Declaration of Principles on Interim Self-Government Arrangements, 454, 784, 1039. *See also* Oslo Accords (1993)
Decrès, Denis, 20
Deetre of Georgia, 792
Deetrius, 359
Defensive Shield, Operation, **346–347**
Definitive Treaty of 1812, 347, 1253
Degania, Battle of, **347–348**
Deicoes, 25
Deir Yassin Massacre, **348–349**, 771
Dekel, Operation, 640–641
Delian League, 145, 862
Delimitation Commission, 410
Demetrios (brother of John VIII), 262
Demetrios (son of Boniface I), 298
Demetrius (son of Demetrius Soter), 53
Demetrius (son of Margaret of Hungary), 519
Demetrius I Poliorcetes, 105, **349–350**, 358, 561–562, 779, 1063–1064, 1135
Demetrius I Soter, 53, 350, 1134
Demetrius II Nicator, 52, 112, 350, 1134
Demetrius of Cyprus, 359
Demetrius of Macedon, 356
Demetrius of Montferrat, 238
Democratic Front for the Liberation of Palestine (DFLP), 952
Demotika, Battle of, 256
Dengel, Herman, 77
Denktaş, Rauf, 325–326
Dercyllidas (Spartan), 518
Derya Ahad Fewzi Pasha, 892
Desaix, Louis Charles, 385, 386
Desert Fox, Operation, **350–351**, 894, 895
Desert Shield, Operation, 420, 589, 731, 983, 985, 986, 1130. *See also* Persian Gulf War, overview
Desert Storm, Operation, 14, 531, 589–590, 600, 728, 733–734, 983, 985, 1130, 1252
 air campaign, 979–982
 Battle of Khafji, 698–699
 See also Persian Gulf War, overview
Desert Thrust, Operation, 605
Desert Thunder I, Operation, **351–352**
Desert Thunder II, Operation, **352–353**
Detachment of Islamic Jihad, 955
Devol, Treaty of, 234
Devshirme System, **353–354**
Dewey, Thomas E., 91
Dhahran, Scud Missile Attack on, **354**
D'Hautpoul, Beaufort, 844
Dhofar Liberation Front (DLF), 355, 905, 1007
Dhofar Rebellion, **354–356**, 1019–1020
Dhu'l-Nun, 335
Diadochi, 307, 349, 413, 441, 779, 972–973, 1014, 1015, 1063, 1134, 1135

Diadochi, Wars of the, **356–361**, 441, 561–562, 966
 First War of the Diadochi, 357–358
 Second War of the Diadochi, 358
 Third War of the Diadochi, 358
 Fourth War of the Diadochi, 359
 Babylonian War, 358–359
 Celtic Invasions and Consolidation, 360–361
 struggle between Lysimachus and Seleucus, 359–360
 struggle over Macedon, 359
Diaspora, **361–362**
Didius Julianus, 1146
Dilam, Battle of, 390
Diocletian, Emperor, 246, 388, 442, 962, 1074
Disraeli, Benjamin, 100
Diyala line, 181
Diyar Bakr, 1276
Djemal Pasha, 140, 141–142, 716, 947, 1207
Djemal Pasha, Ahmed, **362**
Dobell, Charles, 450–451, 947
Doha Agreement, **362–363**
Dome of the Rock, 945
Domitia Paulina of Gades, 494
Domitian, Emperor, 1266, 1315, 1460
Don Pelayo Pérez Correa, 200
Donkey Island, Battle of, **363**
Doquz Khatûn (wife of Hulegu), 534
Doria, Giovanni Andrea, 514, 765, 766, 922
Doroshenko, Petro, 1078
Doroszenko, Piotr, 930
Dorylaion, Battle of, 311, **363–364**, 415
Dreyfuss Affair, 1377
Drone attacks, 77–78
Druses, in Lebanon, 953
Druze-Ottoman Wars, **364–365**
Druzes, 48–49, 241, 270–271, 281, 282, **365–366**, 433, 434, 443, 478, 736, 755, 758, 1245
 in Lebanon, 742, 744
 Mount Lebanon Civil War, 844
Duad Pasha, 844
Dubai, 1297. *See also* United Arab Emirates (UAE)
Duckworth, John, 98
DuLaney, Robert, 896
Duldakir dynasty, 792–793
Dulles, John Foster, 1211–1212
Dumlupinar, Battle of, 485
Duqaq of Damascus (son of Tutush I), 108, 212, 693, 1290
Durrah, Muhammad, 558
Dutch East India Company, 1098
Duwaik, Abdel Aziz, 4
Duwaish, Faisal al-, 1125
Dyadis the Thessalonian, 1291

Eager Lion, Operation, 679
Eagle Claw, Operation, 292, 567, 576, 577–578. *See also* Iran Hostage Rescue Mission
Earnest Will, Operation, **367–369**, 531, 569–570, 574, 581, 588, 887, 1010

Eban, Abba, 818
Ed-Din, Yahya Muhammad Hamid, King of Yemen, 1128
Edebali, Sheikh, 690
Eden, Anthony, 668
Edessa, County of, **369–371**
Edheduanna, high priestess of Ur, 1110
Edict of Milan, 295
Edirne (Adrianople), Treaty of. *See* Adrianople, Treaty of
Edirne, Peace of, 923
Edward I, King of England, 113, 218, 317, **371–372**, 547, 794, 1066, 1541
Egypt, **372–380**, 489
 Anglo-Egyptian Treaty, 92–93
 Anglo-Egyptian War, 93
 and the Arab Spring, 135
 arms deal with Soviet Union, 454
 under Badr al-Jamali, 179
 Battle of the Chinese Farm, 287–288
 British Takeover of, 1626–1627
 and the Camp David Accords, 273–275
 climate of, 291
 Coptic church in, 306–307
 Egyptian-Israeli peace treaty (1979), 470
 and the Fatimids, 428
 and Hamas, 500
 invasion of Syria by, 545–546
 invasion of by Almaric of Jerusalem, 82
 and the Israeli War of Independence, 641–642
 and the *Liberty* incident, 766–767
 map, 373
 under Mohammad Naguib, 866–867
 under Morsi, 838–839
 under Mubarak, 845–846
 Muslim Brotherhood in, 1773–1774
 under Nasser, 874–875
 Nebuchadnezzar II effort to conquer, 174
 Ottoman conquest of, 1577–1580
 Palestinian refugees in, 417
 peace treaty with Israel, 632–633
 Ptolemaic, 360, 383–384, 388
 relations with Russia, 379
 relations with U.S., 379–380
 under Sadat, 1091–1092
 under Sisi, 1182–1185
 terrorism in, 379
 truce agreement with Israel, 642–643
 and the United Arab Republic, 1299–1301
 in World War I, 374–375
 in World War II, 375, 426
 and the Yom Kippur War, 626
 See also Cleopatra VII; Suez Canal; United Arab Republic (UAR)
Egypt, Ancient, **380–383**
 Archaic period, 382
 and the Hyksos, 540–541
 map, 381
 Middle Kingdom, 382
 New Kingdom, 382–383

Old Kingdom, 382
Second Intermediate Period, 540
Egypt, Arab Conquest of, **383**
Egypt, Athenian Intervention in, **383–384**
Egypt, British Invasion of, **385**
Egypt, French Invasion and Occupation of, **385–387**
Egypt, Ptolemaic and Roman Periods, **387–388**
Egypt under British Rule, **393–395**
Egyptian Air Force, 503, 785, 1189, 1325–1326
Egyptian Expeditionary Force (EEF), 87–88, 116, 220–221, 331, 452, 813, 815, 853, 861, 947, 1174, 1268–1269
Egyptian Revolution of 2011, 93, 136, **391–393**
Egyptian-Arab Wars, **388–390**
Egyptian-Ethiopian War, 616
Egyptian-Ottoman Wars, **390–391**, 722, 892
First Egyptian-Ottoman War, 27, 390–391
Second Egyptian-Ottoman War, 27, 391
Egyptian-Soviet Arms Deal, **393**, 454
Eichmann, Adolf, 624
Eilat Israel, **395–396**
Eilat, Sinking of, **396**
Eisenhower, Dwight D., 95, 188, 282, 396–397, 744, 749–750, 1214, 1215
Eisenhower Doctrine, **396–398**, 749–750, 1703–1708
Eitan, Rafael, **398**, 909, 961
El Alamein (al-Alamayn), First Battle of, 375, **398–400**, 495, 836, 1076
El Alamein (al-Alamayn), Second Battle of, 375, **401–402**, 495, 820, 1076
Montgomery's message to the troops, 1684–1685
Elagabalus, 59
Elasa, Battle of, 684
Elazar, David, 40, **402–403**, 626, 1190, 1191
Elbistan, Battle of. *See* Abulustayn, Battle of
Elbutz Mountains, 465
Eleanor (niece of Richard I), 764
Eleanor of Aquitaine, 775–776, 1065
Eleanor of Castille, 371
Eleanor of Provence, 371
Eleazar ben Anaias, 670
Eleazar Ben Simon, 668, 670, 671
Eleazar ben Ya'ir (Eliezer ben Yair), 944, 1203
El-Mawawi, Ahmed Ali, 640
El-Shazly, Saad, 617
Embabeh, Battle of, 1018. *See also* Pyramids, Battle of the
Emir Faisal, 1226, 1334
memorandum to the Supreme Council at the Paris Peace Conference, 1667–1669
Enduring Freedom, Operation, 193, 245, 436, 870, 1026
England. *See* Great Britain
Enlil-nasir II (Mitanni king), 159
Enlil-nirari (Assyrian king), 160
Entebbe Hostage Rescue, 210, **403–405**, 628

Entente Cordiale, 394
Enver Pasha (Ismail Enver), 140, 163, 278, 362, **405–406**, 647, 768–769, 920, 977, 1111, 1243, 1279, 1658–1661, 1664
letter from Ataturk, 1658–1661
EOKA (National Organization of Cypriot Fighters), 487
Epirote army, 251
Eraclius, patriarch of Jerusalem, 490
Erakat, Saeb, 954
Erdoğan, Recep Tayyip, **406–408**, 554, 593, 720, 721, 1185, 1283, 1286–1287
Erekle II of Georgia, 1079
Erekle of Kartli-Kakheti, 1084
Eretria, 480
Eretz Israel, 454, 759, 1685–1686. *See also* Israel
Eriba-Adad I, 160
Eriba-Adad II, 161
Erishum I, 159
Erlend III Haraldsson, 1070
Erzincan, 1230 Battle of, **408**
Erzincan, 1916 Battle of, **409**
Erzurum, Battle of, 786
Erzurum, First Treaty of, **409**
Erzurum, Second Treaty of, **409–410**
Erzurum Offensive, **410–412**
Esarhaddon (king of Assyria), 153, 162, 822
Eschiva (wife of Raymond III), 490
Eshkol, Levi, 69, 225, 344, 376, **412**, 624, 818
Eskander Beg Monshi, 1576
Es-Sulh, Riyadh, 282
Ethiopia, 467, 616
Euagoras, 358
Eudokia Angelina, 63
Eugene of Savoy, 916, 925
Eugenius III (pope), 294, 776
Eugenius IV (pope), 252, 262, 926, 1310
Eumenes I of Pergamum, 105, 110, 356, 357, 358, **413**, 1443
Eumenes II of Pergamum, **413–414**, 784
Eumenes of Cardia, **413**, 441, 966
Euphrates River, **414**, 466, 467, 530, 589, 599, 603, 616, 804, 1163
Euphrates Shield, Operation, 407
Euphrosyne Doukaina, 62
Europe, anti-Semitism in, 113–114
European Union, economic aid to PNA, 4
Eurymedon, Battle of, **415**, 784
Eustace I Granarius, 543
Eustace II of Boulogne, 198, 199, 472
Eustace III of Boulogne, **415**, 472, 664
Eustace of Boulogne, 151, 201
Eustace of Flanders, 298
Euthydemus I, 110
Euthynios (Greek patriarch), 234
Evagoras I, **416**
Evagoras of Salamis, 322, 358
Exodus incident, **416–417**
Expellees and Refugees, Palestinian, **417–418**, 642, 657, 678, 748, 867–868, 965, 1006, 1050, 1067–1068, 1693–1694

Exporter, Operation, 1233
Ezra, 942

Fadlallah, Sayyid Muhammad Husayn, 523, 524, 1720
Fahd, ibn Abd al-Aziz al-Saud, **419–420**, 731, 1118
Faisal (Hashemite Emir), 48
Faisal (son of Hussein ibn Ali ibn Mohammed), 133–134, 509
Faisal, Abdul Rahman bin, 1126–1127
Faisal bin Hussein (leader of Arab Revolt), 478, 538, 741, 811, 1227
Faisal, King of Saudi Arabia, 12, 130, 331, 332, 389–390, 419, 503, 545, 773, 781, 813, 815, 891, 948, 1118
Faisal I, King of Iraq, 96, 116–117, **420**, 586, 964, 1124
Faisal I, King of Syria, 134, 1034
Faisal II, King of Iraq, 190, 397, **421**, 539, 586–587, 750, 899, 1022, 1280
speech at Guildhall, London, 1701–1702
Fakhr ad-Din (Fakr-ed-din), 316, 364
Fakhri Pasha, 813
Falkenhayn, Erich von, 661, 769, 947, 1661
Falkirk, Battle of, 372
Fallon, William, 15
Fallujah, First Battle of, **422–423**, 535, 591, 597
Fallujah, Second Battle of, **423–424**, 591, 597, 605
Fallujah, Third Battle of, **424–425**, 598
Fallujah Brigade, 422
Famagusta, siege of, 328
Fao Peninsula, **425–426**
Fardh Al-Qanoon, Operation, 994, 995–996
Fariskur, Battle of, Jamal ad-Din ibn Wasil's account of, 1535–1536
Farouk/Faruq I, King of Egypt, 85, 124, 375, 395, **426–427**, 453, 661, 861, 866, 1206
Fatah, al-, 3, 4, 45, 46, 47, 64, 232, **427**, 455–456, 460, 629, 650, 690–691, 807, 950, 953, 954–955, 959, 1034
and Hamas, 500–501
Fatah al-Islam, 867–868
Fatah Uprising, 952
Fatah Revolutionary Council (FRC), 23–24
Fath Ali Shah Qajar, 40, 489, 929, 1085–1086, 1612
Fatima (daughter of Muhammad), 610, 703
Fatimid Army, 429
Fatimid Caliphate, 260, 311, 543, 619
Fatimid Dynasty, 5, 260, **427–430**, 663
Fatimid Navy, 429
Fatwa, **430–431**
Faud II of Egypt, 426
Fausta (wife of Constantine I), 305
Fawzi, Muhammad, 270
Fay, George R., report on Abu Ghraib, 1753–1757
Fayez Abdul-Rahim Jaber, 403
Fazil Ahmad, 924

Fedayeen, **431–432**, 453
Fedayeen Saddam, 186, 431–432, 597
Federation of Arab Emirates, 34
Federation of South Arabia, 34
Ferdinand (king of Spain), 114
Ferdinand, Archduke of Austria, 922
Ferdinand III of Castile, 674
Ferhad Pasha (Ferhat Pasha), Treaty of, 301, 932
Ferro, Angelo, 200
Ferro, John, 200
Feyadeen, 623
Fidiyann-e Islami Khalq, 566
Fidonisi, Battle of, 1080
Field of Blood, Battle of the. See Ager Sanguinis, Battle of
Fifth Crusade, 168, 334, 666, 674, 798, 970
Fifth Syrian War, 110–111, 1134
Fifth Syrian-Egyptian War, 383, 388, 1014
Fighters for the Freedom of Israel. See Lohamei Herut Israel
Fihl (Pella or Gilead), Battle of, 700, 856
Final Solution. See Holocaust
Finckenstein, Treaty of, 347, **432**
Firmus, 388
First Aliya, 1377
First Arab Nationalist Congress, 946
First Arab-Israeli War, 638, 1693. See also Israeli War of Independence
First Crusade, 43, 106, 148, 151, 198, 212, 233, 249, 290, 295, 369, 415, 428, 472, 693, 992–993, 1048, 1076, 1139, 1141, 1250, 1271, 1290
    Battle of Dorylaion, 363–364
    fall of Jerusalem, 1500–1501
    sieges of Antioch, 108–109
    speech by Urban II, 1497–1498
First Dacian War, 494
First Dispersion, 942
First Egyptian-Ottoman War, 27
    Battle of Konya, 712–713
First Fitna, 65
First Gaza War, 630
First Intifada, 63, 137, 417, 498, 629, 954, 958, 1005, 1007
First Islamic Civil War, 65
First Jewish Revolt, 943
First Jewish-Roman War, 226–227, 672, 683, 806, 1448
First Macedonian War, 973
First Muslim Civil War, 1296
First Peloponnesian War, 385
First Persian Empire. See Achaemenid Empire
First Serbian Uprising, 1080
First Syrian-Egyptian War, 1016
First Triumvirate, 267, 307
First War of the Diadochi, 357–358
First Zionist Congress, 946, 1686
Fisher, John, 337, 443
Flavius Claudius Iulianus (Julian the Apostate), 944

Flavius Josephus, 1410–1411
    describing the Maccabeean Revolt, 1448–1449
    on the Siege of Masada, 1458–1460
Flavius Julius Constantius. See Constantius II, Emperor
Foley, James, 552
Fons Muratus, Battle of, 550–551
Fontainebleau, Treaty of, 236–237
Fontenot, Gregory, 893
Forbie, Battle of, **432–433**
Forth Lateran Council, 113
Fourth Crusade, 62, 197, 210, 238, 251, 264, 297, 518, 666, 1518
Fourth Herzliya Conference, 456
Fourth Syrian War, 110, 1134
Fourth War of the Diadochi, 359
France
    agreement with Persia, 432
    invasion and occupation of Egypt, 385–386
    treaty with Lebanon, 433
    treaty with Syria, 433–434
    and the Tripartite Declaration, 1270–1271
François I of France, 1064
Franco-Lebanese Treaty, **433**
Franco-Syrian Treaty, **433–434**
Franco-Turkish War, **434–435**
Franks, Frederick, Jr., 984, 997, 1149
Franks, Tommy R., 15, 351, **435–436**, 602
Franz Ferdinand of Austria, 1083, 1257
Fraser, A. Mackenzie, 99
Frederick (Conrad) of Swabia, 519, 520
Frederick I (Frederick Barbarossa), 28, 107, 250, 251, 295, 313, 314, **437–438**, 519, 520, 665, 776, 1029–1030, 1077
Frederick I of Austria, 764
Frederick I of Swabia, 294
Frederick II, Holy Roman Emperor, 168, **438–440**, 883, 971
    letter to Henry III of England, 1524–1526
Frederick II of Swabia, 294, 295, 316, 334, 666–667
Frederick IV of Rothenburg, 440
Frederick Roger (son of Henry VI of Germany), 520
Frederick V Duke of Swabia, 438, **440**, 764
Free Lebanon Army, 753, 1196
Free Officers Movement, 85, 126, 195, 375, 586–587, 866, 874, 1022, 1033–1034
Free Patriotic Movement (Lebanon), 116, 363
Free Syrian Army (FSA), 50, 711, 1007, 1235
French, John, 853
French Revolution, 235
French West Africa, 477
Friant, Louis, 18
Fritigern (Visigoth king), 35–36
Front for the Conquest of Syria, 71, 72
Front for the Liberation of South Yemen (FLOSY), 34–35
Fronto, Cornelius, 778

Fry, C. I., 1032
Fuad I (King of Egypt), 395
Fuad II, Ahmed (King of Egypt), 867
Fuat Pasha, 844
Fujayrah, 1297. See also United Arab Emirates (UAE)
Fulcher of Chartres, Urban II's speech at the Council of Clermont, 1497–1498
Fulk of Anjou, 82
Fulk of Jerusalem, 370
Fulk V of Anjou, 201, 664
Funk, Paul E., 997–998
Furia Tranquillina, 477

Gabiene, Battle of, 413, **441–442**, 966
Gabriel of Melitene, 200, 335, 370
Gaddafi, Muammar/Moammar, 24, 128, 136, 767, 1170
Gadna (Youth Battalions), 120
Gahal Party, 608
Gaius Esuvius Tetricus, 165
Gaius Galerius Valerius Maximianus. See Galerius, Roman Emperor
Galatians, 112–113
Galba, 671
Galerius, Roman Emperor, 305, **442**
Galili, Israel, 640
Galillee, **442–443**
Gallienus, Roman Emperor, 165, 961, 1074, 1469
Gallipoli Campaign, 374, **443–446**, 769, 947
    Ellis Ashmead-Bartlett to Herbert Henry Asquith, 1642–1648
    map, 445
Gamaat (Gama'at) Islamiya, **446–447**, 1034
Gamasi (Jamasi), Abd al-Ghani, 617
Gamayel, Bashir, 1090
Ganja, Treaty of, **447–448**, 865, 1084
Ganymede (Egyptian general), 288
Gates, Robert, 193
Gaugamela (Arbela), Battle of, 26, 53, 58, 342, **448–450**
Gauls, 360, 361
Gaylani, Rashid (Rahid) Ali al-, 125, 421, 538, 586, 898, 1232
Gaza, Battle of (312), 105, 349, 358, 1135
Gaza, Battle of (1239), **450**, 1529
Gaza, First Battle of (March 1917), 375, **450–451**, 716, 853
Gaza, Second Battle of (April 1917), **451–452**, 716, 853
Gaza, Siege of (525 BCE), 383
Gaza, Third Battle of (Oct.–Nov. 1917), **452–453**
Gaza Massacre, 458. See also Gaza War of 2008–2009
Gaza Raid, **453–454**
Gaza Strip, **454–456**
    and the Algiers Declaration, 63
    autonomy for, 138, 274, 427, 901, 957, 1170
    and the Camp David Accords, 273–275

Egyptian control of, 124, 642, 643
first Intifada, 954
and the Gallipoli Campaign, 68, 220–221, 374–375, 661, 947–948
under Hamas, 4, 47, 155, 378, 380, 427, 458, 629–630, 650, 880, 955
Israeli blockade of, 959
Israeli control over, 759
Israeli operations against 155, 166–167, 240, 378, 458, 462, 629, 650, 702, 903, 1176
Israeli withdrawal from, 4, 47, 81, 270, 625, 679, 650, 879, 880, 902–903, 933, 954, 958, 1162
Israel's capture from Egypt, 376, 625, 704
Jewish settlements in, 223, 759, 1162
Palestinian refugees in, 23, 115, 417
right of return to, 269
and the Sinai Campaign, 402
and the Six Day War, 398, 463
and the Suez Crisis, 402
terrorist attacks in and from, 45–46, 137, 233, 240, 269, 458, 462, 623, 636, 674, 903, 953
UN partition plan for, 431
Gaza Strip Disengagement, **456–457**
Gaza War of 2006, **457–458**
Gaza War of 2008–2009, **458–460**
Gaza War of 2012, **460–461**, 462
Gaza War of 2014, 456, **461–463**, 808
Gaza-Jericho Agreement, 210
Gazelle, Operation, 287
Gazi, Saif al-Din, 664
Gazi Ekrem Khusrev Pasha, 933
Gazi Hasan Pasha, 1080
Gelimer, 223–224
Gemayel, Amin, 333, 754–755
Gemayel, Bashir, 283
Gemayel, Pierre, 155
General Armistice Agreements, 642–643
General Maritime Treaty. *See* General Treaty of Peace
General Treaty for the Renunciation of War, 1089
General Treaty of Peace, **463**
General Union of Palestinian Students, 807
Geneva Accord, **463–464**
Geneva Draft Permanent Status Agreement, 957
Geneva Peace Conference, **464–465**
Geneva Protocol (1929), 286
Genghis (Chinggis) Khan, 167, 475, 831
Genocide, against the Kurds, 721–722
Geoffrey of Sergines, 777
Geoffrey of Villehardouin, 37, 197, 238, 298, 518
Geography of the Middle East, **465–467**
George Brankovic, 1310
George II Rakoczy, 1598
George Sphrantzes, 1564
Georgenberg, Treaty of, 763
Georgia and Georgians, 39, 468
  Muslim conflict with, 1505–1506
Georgian-Seljuk Wars, **467–468**

Georgievsk, Treaty of, 1084
Gerard of Ridefort, 308
Gerhad Pasha, Treaty of, 8
German War of Liberation, 237
Germayel, Pierre, 362, 1182
Gerold of Lausanne, to All the Faithful, 1526–1528
Gessius Florus, 227, 670
Gessius Iulius Bassianus Alexianus. *See* Alexander Severus, Roman Emperor
Geta, 1147
Ghabban, Mohammed Salem al-, 554
Ghabun (governor of Middle Egypt), 689
Ghali, Fuad Aziz, 287
Ghalib bin Ali, 905, 1007
Ghasmi, Ahmad al-, 1350
Ghassanids, 700
Ghawsha, Ibrahim, 498
Ghazi, **468–469**
Ghazi, Sayf al-Din, 1373
Ghazi I (King of Iraq), 586
Ghazi II (King of Iraq), 421
Ghaznawids (Ghaznavids), 72, 790, 1138
Ghazzali, Imam, 1102
Ghilzai Afghans, 608–609, 865
Ghulams, **469–470**
Gibbons, Herbert Adams, 1632
Giddi Pass, **470–471**
Giladi, Israel, 509
Ginsberg, Asher, 1378
Giorgi II (Georgian king), 468
Giorgi III (Georgian king), 468
Giorgi XI (Giorgi Khan, Georgian king), 489
Giorgi XI (Gorgin Khan, Georgian king), 608
Giovan Maria Angiolello, on the Battle of Otlukbeli, 1567–1569
Girey, Kaplan, 1079
Giustiniani, Giovanni, 304
Glabrio, M. Acilius, 1242
Gladstone, William, 94, 100, 374, 394
Glaspie, April, 727, 730
Glaucias, 359
Glosson, Buster C., 980
Glubb, Sir John Bagot (Glubb Pasha), 125–126, **471–472**, 539, 677, 1133
  on Arab Refugees, 1691–1693
Godehilde (wife of Balwin I of Jerusalem), 198
Godfrey III of Lotharingia, 472
Godfrey of Bouillon, 151, 198, 311, 312, 316, 369, 415, **472–473**, 662, 663–664, 945, 1250
Gog and Magog, **473–474**, 1203
Golan Heights, 156, 157, 344, 376, 377, 398, **474–475**, 486, 625, 626–627, 1149, 1152, 1308
Golden Horde, 530, 547, 794, 833. *See also* Mongols
Golden Horde-Ilkhanid Wars, **475–476**
Golden Square, 421, 586
Goldstein, Baruch, 516
Golitsyn, Vasily, 1078

Goltz, Wilhelm Leopold Colmar von der (Goltz-Pasha), **476–477**, 823
Gonen, Shmuel, 40, 287
Gordian I, 477
Gordian III (Marcus Antonius Gordianus), Emperor, **477**, 1074, 1112, 1154
Gordon, Charles, 100, 616
Gorringe, George, 823, 825
Gorst, Eldon, 394
Gortschakoff, Pyotr, General Order after the Fall of Sebastopol, 1620–1623
Goths, 224, 1307
Gott, William H., 400, 820
Gough-Calthorpe, Arthur, 843
Gouraud, Henri Joseph Eugène, 49, **477–478**, 811
Government of National Accord, 125
Grabowski, Rick, 84
Grady, Henry F., 837
Graner, Charles, 22
Granicus, Battle of the, **478–479**
Grapes of Wrath, Operation, 523
Gratian, 35–36
Great Arab Revolt, 509
Great Britain
  1915 Battle of Ctesiphon, 319–320
  Anglo-American Committee of Inquiry, 91–92
  Anglo-Egyptian Treaty, 92–93
  Anglo-Egyptian War, 93–94
  Anglo-Iranian oil crisis, 94–95
  Anglo-Ottoman War, 98–99
  Baghdad Pact, 188–190
  Battle for Basra, 215
  capture of Baghdad, 181
  and Cyprus, 323–324, 326
  defense treaty with Jordan, 96–97
  Definitive Treaty with Persia, 347
  in Egypt, 374, 385, 390, 391, 393–395, 1626–1627
  and the Iraq War, 602, 606
  naval base on Bahrain, 192
  relations with Saudi Arabia, 544
  treaties with Iraq (1922 and 1930), 95–96
  treaty with Bahrain, 191
  treaty with the Ottomans, 97
  and the Tripartite Declaration, 1270–1271
  war with Persia, 99–100
  war with Sudan, 100–101
Great Depression, 130
Great Jewish Revolt, 361, 806
Great Mongol Conquests, 475
Great Northern War, 1083
Great Palestinian Rebellion, 962
Great Revolt, 130–132. *See also* Arab Revolt in Palestine
Great Roman Civil War, 268
Great Syrian Revolt, 1035
Great Turkish Onslaught, 468
Great Turkish War, 916, 924, 1278, 1314

Great Uprising, 495
Greco-Persian Wars, 54, **479–483**, 561
 map, 480
Greco-Turkish War, 323, **483–485**, 919, 1281
 Battle of the Sakarya, 1099–1100
Greece, 206, 208
 and the 1832 Treaty of Constantinople, 302
 and Cyprus, 323–326
 Persian invasion of, 479–483
 and the Second Treaty of Lausanne, 739
 union with Cyprus, 487
 war with Turkey, 483–485
Greek Cypriot National Guard, 325
Greek Orthodox Church, 250, 251, 296, 298, 306, 328
Greek Peloponnesian War, 826
Greek War of Independence, 302
Green Line, **486**, 559, 757
Green Zone, Iraq, **486–487**, 496, 1095
Gregory II (pope), 763
Gregory III (pope), 763
Gregory VII (pope), 248, 290
Gregory VIII (pope), 665
Gregory IX (pope), 316, 439, 971, 1066, 1524
Gregory X (pope), 826
Gregory the Patrician, 9
Grenada, 14
 Reagan's address to the nation, 1716–1719
Grey, Sir Edward, letter to Paul Cambon on the Sykes-Picot Agreement, 1649–1651
Grivas, Georgios, 323–324, **487**
Guadalete, Battle of, 859
Guépratte, Émile Paul, 338
Guibert of Ravenna (Clement III), 290
Guild of Watchmen (Hashomer), 494
Guinness, Walter Edward (Lord Moyne), 607
Guiscard, Robert, 61, 233
Gul, Abdullah, 406
Gulf Cooperation Council (GCC), 79, 190, **487–489**, 906, 1019–1020, 1298
Gulf Oil Company, 726
Gülhane, Rescript of, 1618–1620
Gulistan, Treaty of, **489**, 1085–1086, 1612–1615
Gullen, Fethullah, 408
Gulnabad, Battle of, **489–490**
Gur, Mordechai, 403, 961
Gutians, 176
Guy II Embriaco, 235
Guy of Lusignan, 28, 203, 308, 312–314, 323, **490–492**, 512–513, 665, 1509–1511
Gyges (Lydian king), 778–779
Gyóorgy II Rákóczi, 715, 924
Gypsies (Roma People), 525, 528
Gyula, Treaty of, 923

Habash, George, 1004, 1005, 1006
Habib, Philip, 507, 746, 754, 758
Habib Agreement, 754
Habsburg Empire, 694–695, 713–714, 775, 915, 1079, 1381
 treaties with Ottoman Empire, 968
 See also Ottoman-Habsburg Wars
Haddad, Saad, 753, 757, 760, 1090
Haddad, Uthman, 950
Haddad, Wadi, 1004
Hadi, Abd Rabbuh (Adrabbuh) Mansur, 533, 1104, 1352–1353, 1358, 1768
Hadi, Ali Shayi, 1197
Haditha, Battle of, **493**
Hadrian, Emperor, 213, **494**, 683, 1073, 1267
 described by Cassius Dio, 1461–1462
Hafiz, Amin al-, 156
Hafiz Ahmed Pasha, 933, 1593
Hafiz Pasha, 364, 391
Haganah, 120, 122, 126, 131, 135, 225, 343, 347, 412, 416, **494–496**, 510, 513–514, 607, 652, 669, 807, 864, 968, 1202, 1332
 and Operation Nachshon, 863–864
Haggai, 942
Hague Conference, 286
Haid, Ali abd al-, 1355
Haifa Street, Battle of, **496–497**
Haig, Douglas, 68
Hailton, Robert Edward, 1123
Haines, David, 553
Haji Beg Khan, 762
Hakimoglu Ali Pasha, 928
Halicarnassus, 148
Halil (Khalil), Patrona, 969
Halil Pasha, 181, 701
Halutz, Dan, 752
Halys, Battle of, 521
Hama Massacre, 50, **497–498**
Hama Uprising. See Hama Massacre
Hamad bin Khalifa Al Thani, 363, 1259
Hamadanid Dynasty, 1098
Hamadi, Ibrahim, 1361
Hamas, 4, 47, 115, 155, 166–167, 378, 427, 455–463, **498–501**, 557, 570, 606, 612, 629, 630, 631, 650, 659, 955, 956, 959, 1006
 and Fatah, 500–501
 Izz al-Din al-Qassam Brigades, 498
 under Mashal, 807–808
Hamas Charter, 1725–1727
Hamburg Institute for Social Research, 528
Hamdanids, 260
Hamdi, Abdullah Mohammed al-, 1350
Hamdi, Ibrahim al-, 1350
Hametz, Operation, 123
Hamidaddin, Ahmad bin Yahya, 1349
Hamidian Massacres, 11
Hamidiye Alaylari (Hamidian Regiments), 11
Hamilton, Ian, 338, 443, 446, 1645
Hammam, Talat Yasin, 447
Hammurabi, 159, **501–502**, 822
Hamuda, Yahya, 950
Hanit, Attack on the, **502–503**
Haniyeh, Ismail, 958
Hankey, Maurice, 337
Hannibal, 784

Hannibal Barca, 276
Haq Movement, 193
Harakat al-Jihad al-Islami fi Filastin. See Palestinian Islamic Jihad (PIJ)
Harakat al-Muqawama al-Islamiyya. See Hamas
Harald Maddadsson, 1070
Haram al-Sharif, 45, 47
Harbiyah, Battle of. See Forbie, Battle of
Hard Surface, Operation, **503–504**
Haredim, **504–505**
Harim (Harenc), Battle of, 106–107, **505–506**
Hariri, Rafik al-, 155, 362, **506–507**, 524, 534, 736, 747, 1182, 1230
Hariri, Saad, 748
Harran, Battle of, 106, 370, **507**, 681
Harthama Ibn Ayan, 44
Harun al-Rashid, 44, 70, 181, 258, **508**
Hasan (brother of King Hussein), 540
Hasan Ali, 1305
Hasan Pasha, 1080
Hasan Pasha, Cezayirli Gazi. See Cezayirli Gazi Hasan Pasha
Hashemite dynasty, 12, 140, 195, 397, 421
Hashemite kingdom of Hejaz. See Hejaz
Hashemite Kingdom of Jordan. See Jordan
Hashemites, **508–509**
Hashim, 508
Hashimi, Faisal bin Hussein bin Ali al-, 586
Hashomer, **509–510**
Hasidic (Chasidic) Judaism, 504, **510–511**
Haslam, Anthony, 868
Hasmonean Empire, 943
Hasmonean Tunnel Incident, **511–512**
Hassan, Abu al- (Zein al-Abidin al-Mihdar), 609
Hassan ibn No'man, 858
Hassan Mushaima, 193
Hassanein, Salah Abu, 462
Hassan-i Sabbah, 1139
Hattin, Battle of, 28, 168, 313, **512–513**, 520, 663, 665, 945, 999, 1509
Hattusili III, 1418
Havelock, Henry, 99
Havlaga, **513–514**, 607
Hawes, Leonard A., 668
Haydar, Sheikh, 617
Hayreddin Barbarossa, **514**, 1313
 and the Battle of Preveza, 1583–1586
Hayreddin Barbarossa Pasha, 915
Hazit HaMoledet, 771
Heath, Edward, 1298
Hebrew Resistance Movement, 771
Hebron Massacre, **514–515**
Hebron Mosque Massacre, **515–516**
Hebron Protocol, 511
Hejaz
 under Abdullah I, 12
 Arabs in, 918
 climate of, 291
 Egyptian influence in, 389
 independence for, 921, 1150

under ibn Saud, 1116
under King Fahd, 419–420
under King Faisal, 420, 421
under King Hussein, 132, 134, 331, 811–812, 946, 1151
and the Kutahya Convention, 391
Ottoman control of, 812–813, 1116
Saudi-Hashemite war, 1122–1124
Umayyad invasion of, 9
Wahhabi attack on, 389, 1116–1117
Hejaz Expeditionary Force, 813
Hejaz Railroad, Attacks on, 87, **516–517**, 538, 781, 812, 813, 949, 1268–1269, 1334
Hel Mishmar (HIM), 120
Helegu Khan, 22
Helen of Troy, 1275
Helena (mother of Constantine I), 295, 944
Heliodorus, 1134
Heliopolis, Battle of, 384, 387
Hellenic League, 55, 106
Hellespont, **517**
Hellespont Campaign, **517–518**
Henderson, Loy, communiqué regarding the coup in Iran, 1695–1697
Henri of Asti, 1193
Henry I of England, 234
Henry II, 999
Henry II of Babenberg, duke of Austria, 763
Henry II of Cyprus, 548
Henry II of Jerusalem, 667
Henry III of England, 371–372, 491, 1065, 1524
letter from Emperor Frederick II, 1524–1526
Henry IV (Holy Roman Emperor), 248, 294, 472
Henry Jasomirgott, 295, 798
Henry of Bar, 450
Henry of Champagne, 158, 197, 198, 491, 666
Henry of Constantinople, 298, **518–519**
Henry of Flanders. *See* Henry of Constantinople
Henry of Hainaut. *See* Henry of Constantinople
Henry of Kalden, 521
Henry of Troyes, 28
Henry Plantagenet, 776, 999
Henry the Lion, 437, 520
Henry VI of Germany, 61, 251, 438, **519–521**, 666, 764, 999
and the Byzantine Empire, 1516–1518
Henry VII (son of Frederick II), 439
Hephaestion, 448, 973
Heraclea, Battle of, 311
Heraclius, 41, 332, **521–522**, 803, 888–889, 1075, 1113–1114, 1346, 1478, 1483–1484
concluding peace with Persia and contemplating the Muslim Threat, 1487–1489
Heraclius I, 246
Heraclius the Elder, 263, 264, 384
Hermeias, 110
Herod Agrippa I, 943
Herod Agrippa II, 943
Herod Antipas, 943
Herod Archelaus, 943

Herod the Great, 670, 683, 807, 943
Herodian Jewish Revolt, 806
Herodotus, 861–862, 1342
Herzegovina, 917, 1081, 1083, 1147
Herzl, Theodor, 11, 114, **522–523**, 620, 940, 946, 1377, 1686
The Jewish State, 1628–1631
Herzliya Conference, 903
Hess, Moses, 1377
Hesychasm, 251
Hetum of Cliicia, 832
Het'un I of Cilicia, 234
Heydrich, Reinhard Tristan Eugen, 526
Hezbollah, 50–51, 115, 116, 155, 333, 363, 457, 474, 475, **523–525**, 570, 571, 572, 629, 630, 705, 770, 1006
attack on *Hanit*, 502
in Lebanon, 524–525, 746–747, 751–753
program of, 1720–1722
Hicks, William, 100
Highway of Death, 589, 733, 860–861, 984
Hill, Stephen P., 244
Hilu, Charles (Sharl), 270
Hinduqur, 530
Hinnawi, Sami al-, 1228
Hippias (tyrant of Athens), 480
Hiram, Operation, 127, 641
Hisham ibn Abd al-Malik, 42, 258
Histadrut, 225, 607
Hitler, Adolf, 401, 528–529, 1076
Hittite Empire, 160, 502
Hobeika, Elie, 761
Hoca Yusuf Pasha, 1079
Hodierna (daughter of Baldwin II), 201
Hofi, Yitzhak, 1308
Holder, Don, 1149
Holloway, James L., 577
Holloway Committee, 578
Holmes, William George, 820
Holocaust, 3, 91, 113, 285, 505, **525–529**, 571, 622, 623, 630–631, 638, 783, 881, 939. *See also* Armenians and the Armenian Genocide
Holy League, 764–765, 847, 925, 1193, 1313, 1546, 1586, 1589, 1600
Homs, First Battle of, **529–539**
Homs, Second Battle of, 23, **530**, 833
Homs, Third Battle of, **531**
Honorius I (pope), 803
Honorius III (pope), 438, 439, 674
Hope-Simpson Report, 1330
Horev, Operation, 641
Hormizd I of Armenia, 1074
Hormizd II, 1074, 1156
Hormozd I, 1155
Hormozgdan, Battle of, 1463
Hormuz, Strait of, **531–532**
Horner, Charles A., 980
Horns of Hama, Battle of the, 1100
Horrock, Brian, 401

Hosambegzade Ali Pasha, 1314
Hospitallers, 261, 308, 450, 548, 666, 794, 885, 1020, 1064, 1546, 1548, 1556, 1559, 1560, 1581
House of Bazi, 177
Houthi, Abdul Malik al-, 533
Houthi, Badr al-Din al-, 532
Houthi, Hussein Badr al-Din al-, **532**
Houthi rebels, 193
Houthi Supreme Revolutionary Committee, 125
Houthis, 532, **533**, 571, 572, 700, 1026, 1104, 1351–1353, 1357–1358, 1359, 1766
Hrawi, Elias, **533–534**, 759
Hubayka, Elie (Hobeika), 1091
Hubert Walter, bishop of Salisbury, 654
Hudahayfah al-Badri, 188
Hudaybiyyah, Treaty of, 700
Hudhaybiyya, Treaty of, 849
Hugh, count of Saint-Pol, 197
Hugh I, count of Rethel, 200
Hugh III, duke of Burgundy, 203
Hugh III of Cyprus (Hugh I of Jerusalem), 667
Hugh of Burgundy, 450
Hugh of Jaffa, 664
Hugh VIII of Lusignan, 490, 505
Hulegu (Mongol khan of Persia), 107, 158, 167, 317, 475–476, **534–535**, 831–833, 1531, 1536–1537
and the Ilkhan Dynasty, 547
Hulegu, Ilkhan of Persia, letter to Louis IX of France, 1541–1543
Hulegu Khan, 182, 529, 530
Hulegu Khan (Mongol khan of Persia), 790–791
Humbert II of Viennoiss, 1193
Humphrey IV of Toron, 490, 491
Hunayn, Battle of, 64, 700, 848
Hundayi, 775
Hungary
Long Campaign in, 774–775
Long War in, 775
Hünkâr Iskelesi, Treaty of, **535**, 722, 774
Hunter, Operation, 1201
Hurri-Mitanni Empire, 159
Husain, Shah Sultan, 975
Husain Ibn Ali, Sharif of Mecca, letter from Henry McMahon, 1648–1649
Husaybah, Battle of, **535–536**
Husayn (Safavid shah), 489, 608, 1098
Husayn (son of Caliph Ali), 9
Husayn ibn Ali, 691, 812
Husni al-Zaim, 347
Husrev Pasha, 1080
Husri, Sati al-, 964
Hussah bint Ahmad al-Sudayri, 419
Hussein (Sharif), 773
Hussein, Abdullah ibn (king of Jordan). *See* Abdullah I, King of Transjordan/Jordan
Hussein, Grand Vizier, 931
Hussein, King of Jordan, 952–953, 1037–1038, 1189, 1338

Hussein, Muna al-, 12
Hussein, Qusay, 187, 486, 1108, 1198
Hussein, Saddam, **536–537**
    and Abu Ghraib, 21
    air strikes against, 350–351, 352, 981
    and Al Qaeda, 1258
    and the Algiers Agreement, 62, 1163
    and Arab nationalism, 128
    and the Baath party, 171–172, 243, 603
    Bush's ultimatum to, 602
    enmity with Saudi Arabia, 420
    escape from Baghdad, 187
    evacuation of Kuwait by, 733–734
    execution of, 45, 1053
    fear of a coup, 186
    and the goal of regime change, 164, 184, 1052–1053, 1132
    government of Iraq, 786–787
    invasion of Kuwait by, 116, 466–467, 649, 679, 726–731, 965, 980, 1119
    and the Iran-Iraq War, 578–581, 587–588
    and the Iraq War, 600–606
    and the Iraqi Navy, 243
    and Khomeini, 706–707
    and the Kurds, 44, 721–722, 726, 894–895, 1011
    and the Marsh Arabs, 804
    "Mother of All Battles" speech, 842–843, 988, 1730–1732
    occupation of Kuwait by, 731–732
    opposition to, 66–67, 215, 216, 868
    outlawing Dawa party, 1, 788
    overthrow of, 172, 378, 422, 604, 606
    and the Persian Gulf War, 982–990
    PLO support for, 1118
    Republican Guard, 1058
    rivalry with Assad, 171, 633
    seizing power in Iraq, 195
    suppression of Shia Islam by, 75, 523, 1169, 1193
    use of chemical weapons, 722, 726, 991
    and weapons of mass destruction, 245, 350, 352, 602, 603, 909–910, 1194
    See also Iraq; Kuwait; Persian Gulf War
Hussein, Sharif of Mecca, 205
    proclamation, 1655–1657
Hussein, Sultan, 1084
Hussein, Uday, 187, 431, 486, 1108
Hussein bin Ali, 420
Hussein I (king of Jordan), 190
Hussein ibn Ali, 741, 1648
    letters to McMahon, 811–812
Hussein ibn Ali ibn Mohammed, 132–134, 508–509, **538–539**
Hussein ibn Ali, Sharif, 659
Hussein ibn Ali, Sharif of Mecca, 948, 1225, 1280
Hussein ibn Ali (sharif of the Hejaz), 331
Hussein ibn Talal, King of Jordan, **539–540**
Hussein Kamel, 395
Hussein King, 950, 1123

Husseini, Haj Amin al-, 114, 124, 130–131, 515, **538**, 630–631, 881, 1024, 1202
    summons to a jihad against Britain, 1682–1683
Hyak (grandson of Noah), 140
Hydaspes River, Battle of, 57
Hyelion, Battle of, 264
Hyksos, **540–541**
    Manetho on, 1410–1411
Hypatius, 884

Ibelin, Battle of, 543, **543**
Ibelin clan, 490, 491
Ibn al-Ash'ath, 858
Ibn al-Bib(i), 335
Ibn Bijad, 546
Ibn Khaldun, 689
Ibn Nusayr, 49
Ibn Qayyim, 1102
Ibn Saud (Abd al-Aziz al-Saud), 134
Ibn Saud (Abd al-Aziz ibn Abd al-Rahman al-Saud), 419
Ibn Saud, Abdul Aziz, 516, 659
Ibn Saud, King, 134, 389, 509, **543–545**, 546, 699, 1116, 1122, 1126, 1128, 1322–1323, 1336
Ibn Taymiyyah, 1102
Ibrahim (Abbasid prince), 71
Ibrahim I, 1314
Ibrahim Inal, 72
Ibrahim of Karaman, 262
Ibrahim Pasha, 364, 390–391, **545–546**, 616, 712–713, 722, 772, 817, 844, 892, 916, 931, 932, 1078
Ida of Bouillon, 198, 472
Ikhnaton (Akhenaten) (pharaoh), 382–383
Ikhwan, **546–547**
Ikhwan Islamiyya. *See* Muslim Brotherhood
Ikhwan Revolt, 1117
Ikhwans, 544, 1116
Ilchi, Mirza Abolhassan Khan, 489
Ilghazi (Artuqid leader), 38
Ilghazi (son of Artuq), 148, 149, 681
Ilghazi ibn Artuq, 370
Ilghazi ibn Artuq, Najm al-Din, 547
Ilkhan Dynasty, **547–548**
Ilkhan Ghazan, 531, 792
Ilkhan Mongols, 1539
Ilkhanate Mongols, 1536
Ilkhans, 794–795
Ilkhshid, Muhammad ibn Tughj al-, 1098
Ilum-ma-ili (Akkadian king), 176
Ilu-shuma (Assyrian king), 159, 176
Imminent Thunder, Operation, **548–550**
Improvised explosive devices (IEDs), 486–487, **550**, 597, 605, 1347
Inab, Battle of, 107, **550–551**
India, 190, 192
    Muslim raids against, 858
    Nadir Shah's invasion of, 866

Indonesia, 908
Ingeborg of Denmark, 998
Inherent Resolve, Operation, **551–556**, 598, 613, 615, 679
Innocent III (pope), 113, 296, 315, 315–316, 438, 674, 970, 998, 1066
Innocent IV (pope), 439, 1272, 1533
Innocent V (pope), 826
Innocent XI (pope), 925
İnönü, İsmet (İsmet Pasha), 325, **556**, 1099–1100, 1282
İnönü, First Battle of, 485
İnönü, Second Battle of, 485
Insan, Ali Pasha, 701
Instant Thunder, Operation, 86, 980, 988
International Atomic Energy Agency (IAEA), 583, 909, 1290
International Court of Justice (ICJ), 575, 637, 888
International Zone, 486
Intifada, 499
    communiqué, 1722–1723
Intifada, First, **556–558**
Intifada, Second, **558–560**
Ioannitsa of Bulgaria, 1522
Ionian Revolt, 321–322, 479, **561**
Ipsus, Battle of, 106, 349, **561–562**, 779, 1135
Iran, 487–488, **562–573**
    Anglo-Iranian Oil Crisis, 94–95
    climate of, 292
    and the Cold War, 292–293
    historical context, 562–564
    Islamic Revolution in, 466
    Loy Henderson's communiqué regarding the coup, 1695–1697
    map, 563
    relations with Iraq, 587
    under Reza Shah Pahlavi, 1062–1063
    during World War I, 564
    during World War II, 565
    See also Iran-Iraq War (1980–1988); Persia; Safavid Empire
Iran, Islamic Revolution in, **573–574**
Iran Air Flight 655, Downing of, **574–575**, 588
    letter from Reagan to O'Neill, 1724–1725
Iran Hostage Crisis, 277, 292, 567, **575–577**, 706, 908
Iran Hostage Rescue Mission, **577–578**
Iran Nuclear Deal, 572, **582–584**, 631, 843, 881
Iranian Air Force, 568, 579
Iranian Quds Force, 425
Iranian Revolution, 726. *See also* Islamic Revolution
Iran-Iraq War (1980–1988), 21, 63, 157, 172, 425, 487, 536, 567–570, **578–582**, 587–588, 678, 822, 908, 1119, 1298
    and the downing of Iran Air Flight 655, 574
    and the Marsh Arabs, 804
    Operation Earnest Will, 367–369
    use of chemical weapons, 285

Iran-Iraqi border, 63
Iraq, 488, **584–595**, 822, 826
  and the 2003 Battle of Baghdad, 184–187
  and Ahmad Hassan al-Bakr, 195
  Al Qaeda in, 75–76
  Ambush Alley, 84
  Battle of Donkey Island, 363
  Bremer's work in, 242–243
  Bush's address, "The New Way Forward," 1759–1761
  climate of, 291–292
  Coalition Provisional Authority (CPA), 591, 595, 597, 605
  Dawud Pasha, 342–343
  de-Baathification of, 172, 591, 605
  and the Euphrates River, 414
  euring World War II, 586
  under Faisal II, 420, 421
  Fao Peninsula, 425–426
  First Battle of Fallujah, 422–423
  historical context, 584–585
  insurgents in, 496–497
  invasion of Kuwait by, 3, 79, 124, 466, 536, 548, 582, 589–590, 649, 679, 726–728, 860–861, 908, 965, 1119, 1351
  and the Israeli War of Independence, 640
  map, 585
  map of Drive on Baghdad (2003), 185
  Multi-National Force in, 851–852
  no-fly zones, 787, 983
  nuclear facilities in, 909–910, 980, 987, 1120, 1129, 1194, 1249–1250, 1290–1291, 1358
  Operation Desert Fox, 350–351
  Operation Desert Thunder I, 351–352
  Operation Desert Thunder II, 352–353
  Palestinian refugees in, 417
  Petraeus's report, 1761–1765
  and the PLO, 954
  under Qasim, 1022–1023
  relations with Iran, 587
  Republican Guard, 1058
  and the Samita incident, 1105–1107
  Second Battle of Fallujah, 423–424
  Tammuz I nuclear reactor, 1249–1250
  Third Battle of Fallujah, 424–425
  and the Treaties of Zuhab and Kuran, 409
  treaties with Britain (1922 and 1930), 95–96
  Tuwaitha Nuclear Facility, 1290–1291
  U.S. invasion of, 3, 102, 172, 277, 532, 536–537, 591
  use of chemical weapons, 285
  during World War I, 586
Iraq, Sanctions on, **595–596**
Iraq Insurgency, **596–599**
Iraq Liberation Act, 1053
Iraq No-Fly Zones, **599–600**
Iraq War (2003–2011), 15, 21, 67, 84, 192, 431, 550, 591–592, **600–607**, 611, 679, 822, 891
  Battle of Debecka Pass, 344–345
  Battle of Haditha, 493
  Battle of Nasiriyah, 872–873
  Battle of Sadr City, 1095–1096
  Battle of Samawah, 1105
  Battle of Umm Qasr, 1296–1297
  First Battle of Mosul, 840–841
  First Battle of Najaf, 868–869
  First Battle of Ramadi, 1041–1043
  and the goal of regime change, 1052–1053
  Operation Hunter, 1201
  Operation Matador, 1200
  Operation Spear, 1201
  Operation Steel Curtain, 1200
  Operation Viking Hammer, 1318–1320
  recapture of Ramadi, 1043–1044
  Second Battle of Mosul, 841–842
  Second Battle of Najal, 869–870
  Second Battle of Ramadi, 1044–1046
  troop surge, 1273–1275
  and the UAE, 1299
  See also Iraqi Freedom, Operation
Iraqi Air Force, 275–276, 981
Iraqi Awakening Councils, 606
Iraqi Baath Party, 171. *See also* Baath Party
Iraqi Freedom, Operation, 15, 84, 184, 245, 344, 436, 532, 896, 1026. *See also* Iraq War (2003); Iraq War (2003–2011)
Iraqi Governing Council (IGC), 67
Iraqi Interim Governing Council, 67, 243
Iraqi Invasion of Kuwait. *See* Kuwait, Iraqi Invasion of
Iraqi Kurdistan Region (KRG), 721
Iraqi National Accord (INA), 66–67
Iraqi National Students' Union, 66
Iraqi Navy, 243–244
Iraqi Transitional Government, 591–592
Iraq-Iran War. *See* Iran-Iraq War (1980–1988)
Irene (mother of Constantine VI), 258
Irene (wife of Philip of Swabia), 238
Irgun Tsvai Leumi (National Military Organization), 80, 120, 348, 495, 496, 514, **607–608**, 652, 770–771, 783, 837, 864, 939, 1060, 1153, 1202
Irgunists, 80
Iron Hammer, Operation, 597
Ironside, Edmund, 564, 977, 1062
Irving, David, 526
Isa, Shaikh, 546
Isa ibn Salman al-Khalifa, 192
Isaac I Konmenos (Comnenus), 60
Isaac II Angelos, 62, 197, 238, 250, 315, 437, 1077, 1516, 1518
Isabella (daughter of Baldwin V), 998
Isabella (queen of Spain), 114
Isabella I of Jerusalem, 491, 666
Isabella II (Yolande) of Jerusalem, 438–439, 666, 667, 674, 1524
Isfahan, Siege of, **608–609**
Ishe-Dagan I of Assyria, 502
Ishme-Dagan I, 159
Isidore (cardinal), 296
ISIS. *See* Islamic State of Iraq and Syria (ISIS)
Islam
  Alawites (Alawis), 49–50, 156, 497, 1226
  al-Qaramita sect, 190–191
  Ashariyya school, 1223
  in Bahrain, 190
  in Egypt, 373
  Hanbali, 1222
  Ismaili, 157–158, 427, 1021, 1168
  Jafari, 695
  Maliki, 1222
  and martyrdom, 805–806
  Maturidiyyah school, 1223
  Mutazilah school, 1223
  radical, 611–612
  religious sites in the Middle East, 1055–1057
  Salafi, 75, 102, 373, 1101–1103, 1114
  in Saudi Arabia, 1120
  Shafi'i, 1222
  Shia, 49, 50, 71, 136, 157–158, 191–194, 276, 365, 373, 427, 508, 523, 524, 562–563, 564, 567, 592–593, 596, 597–598, 599, 600, 601, 605, 606, 691, 695, 756, 858, 868, 1098, 1120, 1166–1169
  Sufi, 102, 373, 379, 647, 796
  Sunni, 50, 71, 75, 89, 102, 136, 428, 446, 493, 496, 497, 524, 536, 563, 592–593, 596–597, 600, 606, 679, 858, 1120, 1219–1223
  Twelver School, 49–50, 564, 1167
  Wahhabism, 1114, 1223, 1322–1324
  Zaydi Shia, 532, 533, 1168, 1354
  See also Druzes; Wahhabism
Islamic Amal, 523
Islamic Army of Aden, **609**
Islamic Army of Iraq, 102
Islamic Civil War, First, **610**
Islamic Civil War, Second, **610–611**
Islamic Front for the Liberation of Bahrain (IFLB). *See* Iran
Islamic Jihad, 115, 378, 460, 462, 659, 805
Islamic Jihad of Palestine, 1170
Islamic law, 336–337, 945, 1157–1160
  fatwa, 430–431
  and jihad, 673
Islamic Movement in Kurdistan (IMK), 101–102
Islamic Radicalism in the 20th and 21st Centuries, **611–612**
Islamic Republic of Iran. *See* Iran
Islamic Republican Party (IRP), 706
Islamic Revolution, 277, 573, 578, 805
Islamic Revolution in Iran, 466
Islamic Revolutionary Committees, 567
Islamic State (IS), 612. *See also* Islamic State of Iraq and Syria (ISIS)
Islamic State of Iraq and Syria (ISIS), **612–616**
  and al Qaeda in Iraq, 75–76
  in Anbar, 90, 598
  in Fallujah, 424–425
  genocide against Yazidis, 1347

Islamic State of Iraq and Syria (ISIS) (*continued*)
  in Iran, 1237
  in Iraq, 1, 592–594, 598–599, 614, 710–711, 789–790, 841–842, 1217, 1231, 1258–1259
  jihad proclaimed by, 673, 1217
  in Kirkuk, 710
  in Kobanî, 710–712
  and the Kurds, 719
  military action against, 326, 488, 551–556, 592–594, 598–599, 679, 710–711, 719–722, 841–842, 1284–1285
  opposition to, 2, 14, 72, 74, 679, 790, 1237, 1299
  in the Philippines, 615
  recapture of Ramadi from, 1043–1044
  rise of, 624
  and the Second Battle of Mosul, 841–842
  Sunni Triangle, 1224
  in Syria, 572, 1217, 1231–1232, 1258–1259, 1284
  and the Syrian Civil War, 128, 155–156, 525, 1231–1232, 1236, 1238
  terrorist acts by, 1, 14, 73–74, 104, 572, 712, 729, 1217, 1285–1286, 1353, 1358
  in Turkey, 407, 1284–1285
  in the UAE, 1299
  U.S. drone strikes against, 1347
  in Yemen, 533
Islamic State of Iraq and the Levant (ISIL), 612. *See also* Islamic State of Iraq and Syria (ISIS)
Islamic State of Iraq (ISI), 75, 143, 612. *See also* Islamic State of Iraq and Syria (ISIS)
Ismail (prophet), 508
Ismail, Abdul Fattah, 1197
Ismail, Khedive (Ismail Pasha), 58, 393, **616**, 1206, 1623, 1626
Ismail, Khurto Hajji, 1346
Ismail, Muhammad ibn, 1021
Ismail Ali, Ahmad, **617**
Ismail Bey, 389–390
Ismail I of Persia, Shah, 281, **617–618**, 915, 931, 932, 933, 1097, 1572, 1577
  letters to Selim III, 1572–1575
  poetry of, 1572
Ismail II, Shah, 1097
Ismail III, Shah, 694
Ismailis, **618–619**, 1021
Ismailiyya, 1168
Isperich (ruler of the Bulgars), 858
Israel, 63, 64, 113, **620–632**
  anti-Arabism in, 103
  Arab economic boycott of, 117–118
  Arab invasion of, 939
  and the Arab Legion, 125–126
  and the Arab-Jewish Communal War, 120–123
  armistice with Transjordan, 677
  Battle of Degania, 347–348
  Battle of the Chinese Farm, 287–288

  and the Camp David Accords, 273–275
  climate of, 291
  and the Cold War, 293
  creation of, 204–205, 431
  declaration of the establishment of the State of Israel, 1685–1688
  Druzes in, 366
  and the *Exodus* incident, 416–417
  Galilee, 442–443
  invasion of Lebanon, 611
  invasion of Lebanon by, 903, 953
  and Islamic law, 430
  map, 621
  under Netanyahu, 879–880
  Operation Defensive Shield, 346–347
  operations against Lebanon, 751–752
  and Phoenicia (map), 860 BCE, 1002
  raid on Jordan, 1191
  recognition of, 784, 1337
  request for arms from the West, 393
  Security Zone in Lebanon, 753
  war with Lebanon, 759–762
Israel Defense Forces (IDF)
  and Adan, 32–33
  and the *Altalena* incident, 80–81
  vs. the Arab Liberation Army, 126–127
  and the Bar-Lev Line, 213–214
  and Barak, 210
  Battle of the Chinese Farm, 287–288
  Battle of Jenin, 659–660
  Battle of Karameh, 690–691
  Battle of Latrun, 737–738
  and Ben Gurion, 225
  Border War, 240–242
  creation of, 640
  and Dayan, 343–344, 1176
  Druzes serving in, 366
  and Eitan, 398
  and Elazar, 402
  Entebbe Hostage Rescue, 403–405, 879
  and Eshkol, 412
  vs. al-Fatah, 137
  First Intifada, 557–558
  formation of, 120
  Gaza Raid, 453–454, 455, 457
  Gaza War (2006), 457–458
  Gaza War (2008–2009), 458–459, 959
  Gaza War (2012), 460
  Gaza War (2014), 461, 959, 1040
  Haganah incorporated into, 126, 495, 864
  Hamas leaders eliminated by, 499
  Hasmonean Tunnel Incident, 511
  Irgun incorporated into, 222, 496, 608
  Israel War of Independence, 640–641
  and the Israeli Air Force, 633–636
  vs. Jordan, 431, 678
  in Lebanon, 223, 524, 745–747, 751–755, 769–770, 1196
  Lebanon-Israeli War, 759–762
  and Netanyahu, 879

  and Olmert, 902
  Operation Autumn Clouds, 166–167
  Operation Cast Lead, 500
  Operation Defensive Shield, 346–346
  Operation Hiram, 127
  Operation Litani, 769–770
  Operation Shoshana, 1028–1029
  Osiraqi raid, 909–910
  Palmach absorbed by, 69, 960–961
  vs. the PLO, 690–691, 745–746, 757, 954, 1326–1327
  Qibya massacre, 1028–1029
  and Rabin, 1038
  and the Rafah Tunnels, 1040
  Sabra and Shatila Massacre, 1090–1091
  Samu Raid, 1107
  Santorini captured by, 559
  Second Intifada, 559–560
  in Sharm El Sheikh, 1160–1161
  and Sharon, 745, 1161
  Six-Day War, 32–33, 376, 624–625, 633–635, 1038, 1187–1192
  soldier captured by Hezbollah, 650
  Strait of Tiran Crisis, 1204–1205
  War of Attrition, 1325
  strikes against West Bank, 650
  Yom Kippur War, 22, 30, 626, 1362–1363
Israel-Egypt Peace Treaty (1979), 115, 118, 344, 465, 540, **632–633**, 850, 1204
Israel-Gaza War, 650
Israel-Hezbollah War, 629. *See also* Lebanon War
Israeli Air Force (IAF), 657, 1189, 1324
  air strike on presumed Syrian nuclear facility, 635–636
  air strikes beginning the Six-Day War, 633–635
Israeli Air Strike on Presumed Syrian Nuclear Facility, **635–636**
Israeli Air Strikes Beginning the Six-Day War, **633–635**
Israeli Navy, 736–737
Israeli Security Fence, **636–638**
Israeli Settlements. *See* Settlements, Israeli
Israeli War of Independence, 32, 63, 69, 80, 85, 96, 120, 123, 126, 196, 225, 238, 343, 375, 395, 402, 426, 454, 471, 486, 496, 504, 510, 586, 622, **638–642**, 669, 737, 744, 939
  in Lebanon, 759
  map, 639
  Operation Nachshon, 863–864
Israeli War of Independence, Truce Agreements, **642–644**
Israeli-Arab War (1948–1949), 12
Israeli-Gaza War of 2008–2009. *See* Gaza War of 2008–2009
Israeli-Gaza War of 2014. *See* Gaza War of 2014
Israeli-Hezbollah War. *See* Lebanon, Israeli Operations Against
Israeli-Jordan Peace Treaty, 118

Israeli-Lebanon War. *See* Lebanon-Israeli War
Israeli-Transjordan armistice, 642
Israel-Jordan Peace Treaty, **644–645**, 679
Israel-Syria Armistice Agreement, 474
Issus, Battle of, 53, 57, 263, 448, **645–646**
Italo-Ottoman War, 163, **646–648**, 738, 917
Italo-Turkish War. *See* Italo-Ottoman War
Iulia Domna, 58
Iulia Mamaea, 58, 59
Ivan Alexander of Bulgaria, 254
Ivan Asen II, Bulgarian tsar, 251, 298–299, 882
Ivan IV, Tsar, 1078, 1083
Ivazzade Halil Pasha, 1079
Ivory Justice, Operation, **648–649**
Izz al-Din al-Qassam Brigades, 47, **650**
Izzet Pasha, Ahmet, 279–280
Izzet Pasha, Hasan, 278

Jabal Shammar, 1123, 1126, 1128
Jabarti, Ahmed, 461
Jaber, Tawfeeq al-, 458
Jabhat al-Nusra. *See* Al-Nusra Front
Jabhat Fateh al-Sham, 51, 71, 72
Jabotinsky, Vladimir Yevgenyevich, 80, 135, 222, 513, 607, **651–652**, 669, 1059–1060, 1202
    "The Iron Wall: We and the Arabs," 1672–1676
Jabr, Salih, 120
Jacob, Robert, 77
Jacobites, 306, 803
Jacobson, Victor, 940
Jacopo dalla castellana, on the loss of Negroponte, 1564–1567
Jad al-Haqq, Sheikh al-Azhar, fatwa against the Iraqi invasion of Kuwait, 1727–1729
Jadid, Salah/Saleh al-, 156, **653**, 1229
Jaerson, James L., 1011
Jafaar Pasha, 781
Jafar Pashas, 365
Jafari sect, 695
Jaffa, Battle of, 312, **653–654**
Jaffa, Treaty of, 168–169, 654, **654**
Jaffe, Amir, 288
Jahan, Shah, 847, 1305
Jahangir, Emperor, 847
Jalal ad-Din, 408
Jalil, Hassan abd al-, 447
Jalula, Battle of, 856
Jam, Battle of, **654–655**
Jama'at al-Tawhid wal-Jihad, 75. *See also* Al Qaeda in Iraq (AQI)
Jama'at Ansar al-Sunna, 102
Jamaat Jaysh Ahl al-Sunnah wa-I-Jimaah (JJASJ), 188
Jamal, Battle of, 65. *See also* Bassorah, Battle of
Jamal ad-Din ibn Wasil, on the Battle of Fariskur, 1535–1536
Jamal al-Dawla, 179
Jamerson, James L., 1011–1012
James I of Aragon, 826

James II (Lusignan king of Cyprus), 323
James of Baux, 299
James the Great, 943
Janavshir, Behbud Khan, 878
Janissaries, 166, 303, 305, 353, 364, **655–657**, 690, 715, 786, 916–917, 1080
Jannabi, Abu Sa'id al-, 1021
János Szapolyai (John Zápolya), 922–923
Janus, King of Cyprus, 704–705, 1559
Japanese Red Army, 770
Jarrah, Abu Ubaidah ibn al-, 700, 856, 1345–1346
Jarring, Gunnar, 657–658, 1068
Jarring Mission, **657–658**, 1069
Jassy, Treaty of, **658**
Jawhar (Abu al-Hasan Jawhar ibn Abd Allah), **658–659**
Jawwad, Omar. *See* Abu Bakr
Jaysh al-Mahdi (JAM) militias, 1095. *See also* Mahdi Army
Jaysh Ansar al-Sunna, 102
Jeanne (daughter of Baldwin I of Constantinople), 198
Jebusi, Operation, 123
Jeddah, Siege of, **659**
Jekermish of Mosul, 149
Jenin, Battle of, **659–660**
Jericho, 270
Jericho Conference, **660–661**
Jericho Congress. *See* Jericho Conference
Jerkermish, 507
Jerusalem
    Arab riots in, 134–135
    Babylonian siege of, 876
    campaign to liberate, 249
    capture by Crusaders, 1500
    capture by Cyrus the Great, 173
    capture by Saladin, 945
    and the Crusades, 311
    destruction of by Khwarezmians, 316
    Persian siege of (613), 263
    sack of by Antiochus IV Epiphanes, 1445–1447
    and the Second Crusade, 314–315
Jerusalem, Capture of (1917), 68, **661–662**, 1662–1664
Jerusalem, Crusader Siege of, 472, 513, **662–663**
    Flavius Josephus's account, 1457–1458
Jerusalem, Latin Kingdom of, **663–668**
Jerusalem, Roman Siege of, 228, **668**
Jerusalem Brigades, 956
Jesus Christ, 443, 803
    sites associated with, 1053–1054
Jewish Agency, 443, 1303, 1332
Jewish Agency for Palestine, 607, 622
Jewish Autonomous Republic, 1377
Jewish Brigade, **668–669**
Jewish Colonial Trust, 946, 1377
Jewish Defense League, 516

Jewish Enlightenment, 152
Jewish Legion, **669–670**
Jewish National Fund, 946
Jewish Resistance Movement, 607
Jewish Revolt, 671
Jewish Settlement Police, 495
Jewish-Roman War, First, **670–672**
Jews
    Ashkenazic Judaism, 151–152
    and the Balfour Declaration, 204–205
    Conservative, 1248
    in the diaspora, 283, 361, 443, 942, 1377
    Ethiopian, 152
    expulsion of, 113–114
    First Diaspora of, 942
    in Germany, 526
    Hadrian's war against, 494
    Haredim, 504–505
    in Iberia, 113–114
    in Iran, 563
    in Iraq, 586
    Mitnagdim, 510
    Mizrahi, 152
    Orthodox, 505, 631, 1248
    in the Ottoman Parliament, 11
    persecution of, 638
    in Poland, 526–527
    Reform, 1248
    as refugees, 416–417
    in Russia, 651
    Second Diaspora of, 943
    self-defense organization (Haganah), 494–496
    Sephardic, 151, 152, 505
    in the Soviet Union, 629
    Third Diaspora of, 944
    Ultra-Orthodox, 504–505, 631, 881
    as WWII refugees, 939
    See also Anti-Semitism; Holocaust; Israel
Jibril, Ahmad/Ahmed, 2, 20, 559, 951, 1006
Jiddi Pass. *See* Giddi Pass
Jihad, 10, 102, 103, 131, 230, 312, 430, 468, 498, **672–674**, 794, 810, 855, 871, 896, 1100, 1146, 1158, 1726–1727
    against Britain, 1682–1683
    and the Reformation Front, 102
    Salafi, 75
    See also Palestinian Islamic Jihad (PIJ)
Jihad, Muhammad, 1007
John (king of England), 438
John (King of Jerusalem), 798
John, Count of Nevers, 885
John Apocaucus, 255
John Axouchos Komnenos Pachys, 61
John Cantacuzenus (Kantakouzenos), 253, 254–255
John Curcuas, 259
John Hunyadi, 37, 262, 852, 926–927, 1310–1311
John Hyrcanus, 683, 943

John II Komnenos, 107, 248, 249, 264, 335, 371, 798, 1000, 1076–1077, 1271
John III Doukas Vatatzes, 1077, 1260
John III Sobieski, 714, 916, 925, 1600
John III Vatatzes, 200, 298–299, 882, 883
John IV Kaloioannes, 1270
John IV Laskaris, 882
John of Arsuf, 450, 1205
John of Brienne, 199, 298–299, 316, 334, 438, **674–675**, 971
John of Gaunt, 885
John of Gischala, 668, 671
John of Joinville, 778
John of Nesle, 197
John of Oxeia, 250
John Thimiszes, 259
John Tzimisces, 259, 260
John Ugljesa, 256
John V Palaeologus, 251, 253, 254, 255, 256, 260, 261, 799
John VII Kantakouzenos, 251, 254, 256, 260, 1193
John VII Palaiologos, 101
John VIII Palaiologos, 262, 296, 799
Johnson, Lyndon B., 325, 376, 504
Johnson, Paul M., Jr., 77
Joint Comprehensive Plan of Action (JCPOA), 583–584. *See also* Iran Nuclear Deal
Joint Defense and Economic Cooperation Treaty (Arab League), 124
Jones, Anthony, report on Abu Ghraib, 1753–1757
Jordan, 12–14, 63–64, 96–97, 124, 126, 137, 336, 503, 539–540, 553, **675–680**, 1006
  and the Baghdad Pact, 190
  and Black September, 231
  and the Camp David Accords, 274–275
  climate of, 291
  federation with Iraq, 421
  Israeli infiltration in, 240–241
  Israeli raid on, 1191
  and the Jericho Conference, 660–661
  map, 676
  and the Ottoman Empire, 675–676
  Palestinian refugees in, 417
  peace treaty with Israel, 644–645
  PLO in, 952–953
  truce agreement with Israel, 642–643
Jordan, Hamilton, 577
Jordan River, 466, 607, 623, 644–645, **680–681**
Jordan River Valley, 347–348, 627
Joscelin I of Courtenay, 200, 370
  on his deathbed, 1501
Joscelin I of Edessa, 234, **681–682**
Joscelin II of Edessa, 107, 150, 202, 370, 371, 682, 896
Joscelin III of Courtenay, 144
Joscelin III of Edessa, 505–506
Joseph II (Holy Roman Emperor), 925
Josephus, 671

Josephus Flavius Quotes Manetho on the Hyksos, 1410–1411
Joshua, 942
Jotapata, siege of, 671
Jovian, Emperor, **682**, 1075
Juan (Don) of Austria, 765, 766, 847
Judaea, **682–684**
Judaism
  religious sites in the Middle East, 1054–1055
  See also Ashkenazic Judaism; Hasidic Judaism; Mizrahi Judaism; Saphardic Judaism
Judas Maccabeus, **684**, 782, 943
Julia (daughter of Caesar), 1003
Julian (brother of Gallus), 305–306
Julian, Emperor, 318–319, **684–685**, 1075, 1156
Julius Caesar, 30, 1003
  winning the Battle of the Nile and taking Alexandria, Egypt, 1451–1454
July War, 629. *See also* Lebanon War
Jumayyil (Gemayel), Bashir, 745–746, 757, 758, 760, 761
Jumayyil, Amin, 116
Jumblat (Jumblatt, Junblat), Kamal, 282, 953
Jumblat (Junblat), Walid, 736
Junayd, Sheikh, 617
Jund al-Islam, 102. *See also* Ansar al-Islam
Just Cause, Operation, 980
Justin II (Emperor), 686
Justinian I the Great, Emperor, 223, 224, **685–686**, 708, 884
Justinian II, 252, 763, 858

Kabakchi Incident, **687**
Kabakchi Mustafa Rebellion, 1137
Kabbalah (Cabala), 510
Kaddoui, Farouk, 427
Kadesh, Battle of, **687–688**
Kadesh, Operation, 1214
Kadr-Bey, Abdul, 37
Kafr Qasim Massacre, **688–689**
Kafur, Abu al-Misk, **689–690**
Kagul, Battle of, 1079
Kahalani, Avigdor, 1309, 1310
Kahan Commission, 398, 761–762, 1090–1091
Kahane, Meir David, 10, 446, 516
Kai-Qobad (Kayqubad) I, Ala ad-Din, 408
Kala'un (Mamluk sultan), 317
Kalij Arslan of Rum, 312
Kali-Sharri, Shah, 1406
Kalojan (Bulgarian ruler), 36, 197–198, 518, 882
Kaloyan (Johannitsa; Bulgariani tsar), 298, 315
Kanafani, Ghassan, 1005
Kansu (Kansuh, Qansuh) al-Gauri (Al-Ghuri), Sultan, 793, 1578
Kapikulu Corps, **690**
Kapudan Pasha Hüsameddin, 286
Kara Arslān, 371
Kara Mustafa Pasha, 714, 916
Kara Osman, 1304–1305
Karabekir, Kazim/Kiazim, 60, 181, 484, 920–921, 1289

Karakoyunlu, 150
Karameh, Rashid, 758
Karameh, Battle of, **690–691**
Karbala, Battle of (680), **691**, 993
Karbala, First Battle of (2003), **691–692**
Karbala, Second Battle of (2007), **692**
Karbala Gap, **693**
Karbalai, Abdul-Mahdi al-, Friday Prayer Sermon, 1772–1773
Karbugha (Karbuqa, Kerbogha, Kerbogah, Karbagh) of Mosul, 106, 109, 148, 311, **693–694**, 993, 1305, 1498
Karim Aga Khan IV, 619
Karim Khan, 929
Karim Khan Zand, 39, 976
Karim Khan Zand, Muhammad, **694**
Karlowitz, Treaty of, **694–695**, 916, 925, 1314
Karnaik-I-Ardashir (Records of Ardashir), 1463–1467
Karpinski, Janis, 1753
Kars, Battle of, **695–696**, 866, 928
Kars, Emirate of, 468
Kars, Treaty of, 60, **696**, 1289
Kartli-Kakheti, 39
Kaseasbeh, Muath al-, 679
Kashtiliash IV (Kassite king of Babylon), 160, 177, 697
Kassites, 177, **696–697**
Kastriota/Kastrioti, George (Skander Beg), 852, 927
Kataeb Party, 155
Kâtib Çelebi, on the Ottoman Conquest of Cyprus, 1586–1589
Kavad/Kavadh I (Sassanian king), 708, 1112–1113, 1472
Kavad/Kavadh II (Kavad Shiruya/Shiroy), 856, 1114
Kavus (son of Kavad I), 708
Kawakibi, Abd al-Rahman al-, 963
Kaykhusraw I (Kaykaus, Kaykhuisraw, Kay-Khusraw), Seljuk sultan of Rum, 61, 109, 265, 1030, 1077, 1260
Kaykhusraw (Kay-Kawus) II, Sultan, 715–716, 1276, 1531
Kayqubad I, Ala ad-Din (Kai-Qobad, Kay-Qubadh), 408, 1077
Kazallu, 176
Kazan, 1083
Kazi Asker (Cadi Lascher), 1578
Kazim Bey, 697
Kazimierz, Jan, 930
Keith, George, 17
Keith, Thomas, 389
Kelly, Mark, 994
Kemal, Mustafa. *See* Ataturk, Mustafa Kemal
Kemball, A. B., 463
Kemény, János, 924
Kendall, David W., 244
Kennedy, John F., 503–504, 818
Keren Hayesod, 946
Kerim, Abdul, 409, 410

Kerry, John, 553
Ketbugha Noyon, 167, 529, 790–791, 833
Keyes, Roger, 338
Khabu River, Battle of, 312
Khadairi Bend, Battle of, **697–698**
Khaddam, Abdul Halim, 155
Khadija, 849
Khafji, Battle of, **698–699**
Kha'irbay Mulbai, 793
Khaled, Leila, 1004–1005
Khalid bin Sultan, Prince, **699–700**, 982, 1123
Khalid ibn al-Walid, 41, 332–333, **700–701**
Khalid ibn Saud, 390, 419
Khalifa, Abd al-Rahman al-, 498
Khalil (Mamluk sultan), 317, 667, 1021
Khalil, al-Ashraf, Sultan, 794
Khalil Pasha, 824–825
Khalilzad, Zalmay, 89
Khameini (Ayatollah), 572
Khamenei, Ali (Ayatollah), 571, 572, 583
Khamudi, 541
Khan, Samir, 77
Khan Maysalun, Battle of, 810–811
Khan Yunis, **702–703**
Khanaqin, Battle of, **701–702**
Khandaq, Battle of the, 65, **702**, 849
Khanjar, Adham, 49, 478
Kharijites, 64, 508, 610, **703–704**
Khartbirt, 195
Khartoum Arab Summit Communiqué, 625
Khartoum Resolution, **704**
Khashoggi, Jamal, 1122
Khattab, Omar (Umar) ibn al-, 1066–1067
Khatun, Mama, 409
Khaydar ibn Kavus-Afshin, 258
Khazars, 888
Khirokitia, Battle of, **704–705**, 1559–1560
Khobar Towers Bombing, **705**
Khojas, 619
Khomeini, Ruhollah, Ayatollah, 293, 536, 566–567, 570, 573, 575, 578, 580, 587–588, 612, **705–707**, 720
 and the Iran hostage crisis, 575–576
Khorasan, 70
Khosrau II (Persian shah), 263, 384, 888
Khosrov II of Armenia, 1074
Khosrow I Anushiravan, **707–709**, 1113
Khosrow II Parvez, 1113
Khosrow II, Shah, 264, 521, 1114, 1478, 1484, 1487
Khotin/Khotyn, Battle of, 714, 1080
Khoyski, Fatali Khan, 878
Khrushchev, Nikita, 397
Khudabanda, Mohammed (shah), 7, 83
Khufu (Cheops), 382
Khurasan, 39, 44, 72
Khurma, 1123
Khurram (Shah Jahan), 847
Khurshid Pasha, 390
Khusrau Pasha, 929
Khuy, Battle of, 409

Khuzestan, 567
Khwarazmians, 169, 316, 408, 432, 667, 1533–1534
Kılıç Ali Pasha, 1313
Kilij Arslan, Rum, 311
Kilshon (Pitchfork), Operation, 123
Kinburn, Battle of, 1080
Kinereth, Operation, 398
King, E. L. S., 1233
Kingdom of Bahrain, 190–191. *See also* Bahrain
Kirkbride, Alexander, 1693
Kirkuk, **709–710**
Kirkuk, Battle of, 762, 865
Kissinger, Henry, 129, 242, 1179–1180
Kitbuqa (Hulegu's general), 317
Kitchener, Horatio Herbert, 100, 132, 337, 394, 443, 446, 538, 853, 1208
Kitos Rebellion, 1462
Kitos War, 944
Kléber, Jean-Baptiste, 17, 385, 387
Klerides, Glavkos, 326
Klinghoffer, Leon, 2–3, 20
Klokotnitsa, Battle of, 251
Knights of Malta, 1313
Knights of St. John, 385
Knights Templar, 323
Kobanî, Siege of, 554, **710–712**
Kobanî Massacre, **712**
Kogh Vasil, 370
Komer, Robert, 503
Komnenoi dynasty, 248
Kondurch Rivere, Battle of the, 1249
Konstantinos Kalamanos of Cilicia, 505–506
Konya, Battle of, **712–713**, 772
Köprülü, Ahmed, 715
Köprülü Abdullah Pasha, 180, **713**
Köprülü era, 915
Köprülü Fazil Ahmed Pasha, **713–714**, 924, 1311
Köprülü Mehmed Pasha, **714–715**, 924, 1596–1598
Kopruluzadeh Abdallah, 928
Koran. *See* Quran
Kos, 148
Köse Dağ, Battle of, **715–716**, 1531–1532
Kosovo, 208, 773
Kosovo, Battle of, 915, 1550–1551
Kosovo, Second Battle of, 915
Kosovo Polje, Battle of, 218, 261, 885, 926
Kotlyarevsky, Pyotr, 489
Krekar, Mullah, 101–102
Kress von Kressenstein, Friedrich Sigismund Georg, 452, **716–717**, 947, 1070–1071, 1175
Krimawi, Dhia Abd al-Zahra Khadhim al-, 869–870
Kristallnacht, 526
Krozka (Hisarjik), Battle of, 280
Krtsanisi, 39
Kublai Khan, 534

Kuchuk Ahmad Pasha, 365
Kuchuk Kainardji, Treaty of, **717**, 916, 1079
Küçük, Fazil, 324
Kukburī, Muaffar al-Din, 308
Kuran, Treaty of, 409, 929
Kurdan Treaty of, **717–718**
Kurdish Freedom Hawks (TAK), 719
Kurdish National Assembly, 991–992
Kurdish People's Protection Units (YPG), 555
Kurdistan, 2, 44, 565, 709–710, 739
 and the Treaty of Sèvres, 1151
Kurdistan Democratic Party (KDP), 102, 594, 990
Kurdistan Regional Government (KRG), 554, 990
Kurdistan Workers' Party (PKK), 406–407, 554, 710–711, 718–720, 1283–1284
Kurds, 44, 96, 536, 537, 551, 551–555, 563, 567, 572, 580, 613, 615, **718–721**, 1319
 and Ansar al-Islam, 101–102
 in Iran, 615, 720
 in Iraq, 2, 592–594, 596, 597–598, 598–599, 600, 601, 603–604, 721, 722, 894–895
 in Kirkuk, 709–710
 in Kobanî, 710–712
 recognition of, 11
 Shahrazuriyya, 833
 Shiite, 21
 in Syria, 722
 and the Treaty of Zuhab, 1381
 in Turkey, 718, 719, 720–721, 1011, 1282, 1283, 1284
 Turkish raids against, 407
 uprising (1975), 195
 U.S. support for, 1011–1012
 See also Peshmerga
Kurds, Massacres of, 285, 569, 581, 588, 718, **721–722**, 730, 787, 894, 991, 1283
Kurigalzu II (Kassite king), 697
Kursih Protection Units, 50
Kut, First Battle of, 724, 825
Kut, Second Battle of, 825
Kut, Siege of, 823–824
Kut al-Amara, Siege of, **723–724**
Kutahya Convention, 391, 535, 546, **722–723**, 772, 816
Kutschuk Mehmet Pasha, 924
Kutuzov, Mikhail, 1080
Kuwait, 78–79, 367–368, 487–488, 602, **724–729**
 Arab protection of, 488
 and Desert Thunder II, 353
 and the Fao Peninsula, 426
 map, 725
 Mutla Ridge, 860–861
 Palestinian refugees in, 417
 report by Amnesty International, 1729–1730
 and the Samita Incident, 1105–1107
 war with Saudi Arabia, 1125
 in World War I, 726

Kuwait, Iraqi Invasion of, 3, 124–125, 419–420, 466, 536, 548, 582, 589–590, 649, 679, 726–728, **729–731**, 860–861, 908, 965, 1092, 1119, 1351
Kuwait, Iraqi Occupation of, **731–732**
Kuwait, Liberation of, **732–734**, 982, 985
Kuwatly, Shukri Al-, 1300
Kyle, James, 577

La Forbie, Battle of, 169, 667
Labashi-Marduk (Babylonian king), 174
Lacy, Peter, 1079
Lade, Battle of the, 339
Ladislas of Hungary, 252
Lahoud, Émile Jamil, 116, 363, 507, 524, **735–736**
Lake, Percival, 724
Lala Mustafa Pasha, 1313
Lamian War, 357
Landau, Moshe, 40
Lankin, Eliahu, 80
Lannes, Jean, 385
Laodice (wife of Antiochus), 1134
Laodicean War. *See* Syrian-Egyptian Wars
Laomedon, 357
Larissa, Battle of, 61
Laskaris, Theodore, 109–110
Laskov, Haim, 40
Latakia, Battle of, 209, **736–737**
Latif, Abdallah ibn Muhammad ibn Abd al-, 546
Latrun, Battles of, **737–738**
Lausanne, First Treaty of, **738–739**
Lausanne, Second Treaty of, **739–740**, 1151
Lausanne, Treaty of, 414, 509, 556, 718, 1278
Lavon, Pinhas, 740, 1028
Lavon Affair, 225, **740**
Law and Order, Operation, 995–996
Law of Return, 623
Lawrence, Thomas Edward, 68, 116–117, 134, 332, 420, 516, **740–741**, 815, 898, 948, 1280, 1334
 personal notes on the Sharifial Family, 1657–1658
 report on Mesopotamia, 1669–1670
Lazar (Serbian prince), 205
Lazaros, patriarch of Jerusalem, 255
Le Goulet, Treaty of, 999
League of Arab States. *See* Arab League
League of Corinth, 54
League of Islanders, 105
League of Lombardy, 437
League of Nations, 205, 433, 509
League of Nations Covenant Article 22, **741–742**, 797
Lebanese Army, 116
Lebanese Crisis, 749
Lebanese Forces (LF), 283
Lebanese Front, 282–283
Lebanon, 478, 495, **742–749**
 and the Baghdad Pact, 190
 and Black September, 231–232
 and the Cairo Agreement, 270–271
 climate of, 291
 and the Doha Agreement, 362–363
 Druzes in, 366
 Hezbollah in, 524–525
 historical context, 744
 independence for, 282
 and the Israeli War of Independence, 2, 640
 map, 743
 Palestinian refugees in, 417
 and the PLO, 270–271, 953
 Reagan's address to the nation, 1716–1719
 Syrian invasion of, 497
 treaty with France, 433
 truce agreement with Israel, 642–643
 US embassy bombing, 754
 during World War I, 744
 during World War II, 744
 See also Phoenicia
Lebanon, First U.S. Intervention in, **749–750**
Lebanon, French Interventions in. *See* Mount Lebanon Civil War
Lebanon, Israeli Invasion of. *See* Litani, Operation
Lebanon, Israeli Operations Against, 611, **751–753**, 903, 953
Lebanon, Israeli Security Zone in, 753
Lebanon, Second U.S. Intervention in, **753–755**
Lebanon Civil War, 115, 137, 157, 232, 269, 271, 282–283, 333–334, 417, 523, 745–746, 754–755, **755–759**, 950, 953, 1006, 1173, 1244
 Hariri's role in, 506–507
 Sabra and Shatila Massacre, 1090–1091
 and the South Lebanon Army, 1195–11967
Lebanon War, 629
Lebanon-Israeli War, **759–762**, 951
Leese, Oliver, 401
Legnano, Battle of, 437
Lehi and the Stern Gang, 80, 120, 474, 607, 641, 771, 939, 1202, 1691. *See also* Lohamei Herut Israel (Fighters for the Freedom of Israel)
Lehr, John, 143
Lehrer, Shimon, 1091
Leilan, Battle of, **762**, 865
LeMay, Curtis, 503–504
Lend-Lease program, 1337
Leo III the Isaurian, 42, 248, 258, 300–301, **762–763**, 859, 1489
Leo IV, 258
Leo Maleinos, 1099
Leo Sgouros, 61
Leo VI, 258
Leon I (Rupenid prince), 335, 674
Leon of Armenia, 792
Leonidas (king of Sparta), 482
Leonnatus, 357

Leopold I (Holy Roman Emperor), 714, 924, 1311
Leopold V of Austria, 520, **763–764**, 999
Leopold VI of Styria, 764
Leotychidas II of Spartan king, 483, 861–862
Lepanto, Battle of, **764–766**, 915
 Sebastian Veniero's account of, 1589–1590
Less, Anthony, 368
Lesseps, Ferdinand de, 374
Levanon, 115–116
Levant Front, 51
Liberty Incident, **766–767**
Libya, 125, 673
 and the Arab Spring, 136
 Italy's attempt to annex, 646–647
Libyan-Egyptian War, **767–768**
Licinius, Emperor, 295, 305, 442
Lieberman, Avigdor, 630, 631, 880
Lightning Campaign, 343
Likud Party, 45, 505
Liman von Sanders, Otto, 443, 716, **768–769**, 815–816, 919, 949, 1279
 letter to Major General von Seekt, 1664–1667
Lippold, Kirk, 293–294
Lisimachus, 357
Litani, Operation, **769–770**
Lloyd (Lord), 668
Lloyd, Selwyn, 1213
Lloyd George, David, 135, 323, 669, 815, 947, 1151, 1225
Lluja, Operation, 424
Lod Airport Massacre, **770–771**
Lohamei Herut Israel (Fighters for the Freedom of Israel), 120, 226, 348, 607, 622, **771–772**, 939, 1153, 1202
Lombard League, 437, 438
Lombards, 298
London, 1840 Treaty of, **772**
London, 1913 Treaty of, **772–773**
London, 1940 Treaty of, 546, 723
London Round Table Conference, **773–774**, 1331
London Straits Convention, 99, **774**
Long Campaign in Hungary, **774–775**
Long War in Hungary, 775, 923–924
Longo, Giovanni, 296
Loredan, Pietro, 1312
Lotf Ali Khan, 39, 976
Lothar III, 294
Louis, Thomas, 98
Louis II Jagiello, 922
Louis II of Hungary, 927
Louis VI, King of France, 775–776
Louis VII, King of France, 203, 250, 295, 312, 664, **775–776**, 799, 998, 1502
 letters from Amalric of Jerusalem, 1506–1508
Louis VIII of France, 776, 998
Louis IX, King of France, 169, 234, 316–317, 334, 371, 534, **776–778**, 793, 798, 826, 1276, 1533, 1535

letter from Hulegu, Ilkhan of Persia, 1541–1543
Louis of Blois, 36–37, 198
Louis XIV of France, 714, 924
Lucia (sister of Bohemund VII), 235
Luciana/Lucienne of Segni, 234, 1272
Lucilla (daughter of Marcus Aurelius), 778
Lucius Aelius Caesar, 778
Lucius Verus, **778**, 802
Lucullus, Lucius, 829
Lucullus Lucius Licinius, 1071
Ludwig I of Bavaria, 971
Ludwig IV of Thuringia, 439
Lumsden, Herbert, 401
Lundstrom, Aage, 1691
Lundstrom, General, account of Bernadotte's death, 1691–1693
Luppicinus, 35
Luria, Isaac Ben Solomon, 510
Lutf Ali, 976
Luwai, Khalid ibn Mansur ibn, 1123
Luxor massacre, 447
Luzalzagesi, king of Uruk (Erech), 1405
Lwow, Battle of, 931
Lyautey, Louis, 477
Lycia, Battle of, 857
Lydia, 309, 329, 339, **778–779**
Lynch, Jessica, 872
Lysander (Spartan commander), 38, 330, 1438–1439
Lysandra (widow of Agathocles), 307, 360
Lysias, 684, 782
Lysimachus, 105–106, 307, 350, 356, 358, 359, 359–360, 561–562, **779**, 1015, 1135

Ma'an, Siege of, **781**
Maccabean Revolt, 684, **782**, 943
  described by Flavius Josephus, 1448–1449
Maccabee, Operation, 123
Maccabees, 360
MacDonald, Malcolm, 774
MacDonald, Ramsay, 283, 1164, 1330
Macedonia, 147–148, 207, 773, 917, 1081, 1279
Macedonian Empire, 162
MacFarland, Sean, 89–90
MacKenzie-Fraser, Alexander, 385
MacMichael, Sir Harold, **782–783**, 1328
MacMillan, Harold, 324
Macrinus, Emperor, 889
Macrinus, Marcus Opellius, 889–890, 1073
Madan culture, 804
Madani, Yusuf, 532
Madany, Wagih el, 952
Madrid Conference, **783–784**, 954, 1154
Magas, King of Cyrene, 1016
Magen, Kalman, 288
Maggart, Lon E., 893
Maghreb nations, 465, 1335
Magi, 967
Magic Carpet, Operation, 225

Magnentius, 305
Magnesia, Battle of, 111, 413, **784–785**, 1242
Mahan, Alfred Thayer, 465
Mahan of Armeniad, 700, 1345–1346
Mahdi, 6, 100, 419, 619, 870, 1021, 1118, 1136, 1167–1168, 1220
Mahdi, Abd Allah al-, 1021
Mahdi Army, 597, 598, 605, 692, 868–869, 994–996, 1093–1096, 1186, 1273
Mahdist War. *See* Anglo-Sudan War
Mahdiyya, 673
Mahmoud, Salah Aboud, 244–245
Mahmud (son of Mir Vays), 489, 608–609
Mahmud, Muhammad Sidiqi, **785–786**
Mahmud Hotak, 1098
Mahmud I, Sultan, 547, 695, 928, 929, 969
Mahmud II, Sultan, 166, 343, 391, 535, 545–546, 657, 772, **786**, 816, 892, 916, 929, 945, 1080, 1137, 1251
Mahmud IV, Sultan, declaration of war on Emperor Leopold I, 1600–1601
Mahmud of Ghazna/Ghazni, 468, 1138
Mahmud Pasha, 1312
Mahmud Sistani, 975
Mahmud Tughluk, 1249
Majid al-Tikriti, Ali Hassan al-, **786–787**, 872
Majles, 1086
Majnun Islands, 569
Makadma, Ibrahim al-, 499
Makarios III, Archbishop, 323–325, 487, **787–788**
Makous, Ibrahim, 156
Maktab al-Khidmat lil-mujahidin al-Arab (MaK), 73. *See also* Afghan Service Bureau
Malatesta, Sigismondo, 1312
Mali, 612
Malik, Hisham ibn abd-al, 1488, 1489
Malik Danishmend Ghazi, 335
Malik Muhammad, 335
Malik Shah, 73, 264, 468
Malik Shah I, 73, 264, 468, **790**, 1000, 1029, 1138, 1139, 1140
Maliki, Nuri Muhammed Kamil al-, 1, 551, 592–593, 613, 692, **788–790**, 1095–1096
Malinki, Shmuel, 688–689
Malta, 18
Malta, Siege of, 915, 923
Maluks, 945
Mamalik, Mustawfi al-, 564
Mamluk Sultanate, 663, **793–796**, 795–796, 798, 833
Mamluk-Ilkhanid Wars, **790–792**
Mamluk-Ottoman Treaty, 64
Mamluk-Ottoman Wars, **792–793**, 932
Mamluks, 22–23, 29, 107, 217, 218, 219, 235, 236, 281, 317, 386, 469, 475–476, 531, 547, 585, 666, 667, 704–705, 790–791, 794–795, 885, 1272
  Massacre at the Citadel, 808–809
  wars with Ottomans, 792–793

Mamud, 1139
Mamud, Nur al-Din, 1373
Mamud, Shihab al-Din, 1372
Mandates, League of Nations, **796–797**. *See also* Palestine, British Mandate for
Manfred of Sicily, 826
Mangubirti, Jalal ad-Din (Khwarzm Shah), 1077
Manifesto on Kurdish Autonomy, 991
Mansur, al-, 6
Mansur Ibn Sarjan, 332
Mansurah, Battle of, 316, **797–798**
Manuel (step-son of Boniface I of Montferat), 197
Manuel I Komnenos, Emperor, 82, 106–107, 202, 249, 250, 251, 262, 264, 294, 334, 335, 371, 665, 776, **789–799**, 862, 897, 1030, 1077, 1271, 1502–1503
Manuel II Palaiologos, Emperor, 261, 296, **799–800**, 885
Manuel Kammytzes, 61
Manzikert, Battle of, 73, 248, 264, 468, **800–801**, 1277
Mapai Party, 623
Marash, Battle of, 478
Marathon, Battle of, 25, 339, 480, 1342
March, Daniel P., 548
March 8 Alliance, 747
March 14th Alliance, 524
Marcomannic Wars, 802
Marcos, Ferdinand, 891
Marcus, David Daniel "Mickey," 640, 738, **801–802**
Marcus Antonius, 670
Marcus Antonius Gordianus. *See* Gordian III (Marcus Antonius Gordianus), Emperor
Marcus Aurelius, Emperor, 778, **802–803**
Marcus Ulpius Nerva Traianus. *See* Trajan, Emperor
Mardonius (son-in-law of Darius I), 479, 483
Marduk-nadi-ahhe (brother of Nebuchadnezzar I), 177
Margaret (Mary/Maria) of Hungary, 197, 238, 298, 519
Margaret of Flanders, 197, 518
Maria (niece of Manuel I Komnenos), 665
Maria (sister of Roger of Antioch), 370, 682
Maria la Marquise, 666
Maria of Antioch, 250
Maria of Montferrat, 438, 674
Marie (daughter of John of Brienne), 199
Marie de Courtenay, 1260
Marie Louise (Archduchess), 237
Maritsa, Battle of, 205
Marj Ayyun (Marj Ayyoun), Battle of, 1100
Marj Dabiq, Battle of, **803**, 1136, 1577
Marj Rahit, Battle of, 610, 689
Marjal-Saffar, Battle of, 700, 856
Marc/Mark Antony (Marcus Antonius), 683, 1454, 1469
Market-Garden, Operation, 836

Marmont, Auguste de, 16
Marne, Second Battle of the, 477
Marne Torch, Operation, 995–996
Maronites, 270–271, 281, 282, 365, 433, 736, 744, 745–746, 749, 754, 755–756, 757, 760, **803–804**, 953, 1245, 1716
    Mount Lebanon Civil War, 844
Marsh Arabs, **804–805**, 1163
Marshal, Gilbert, 1066
Marshall, William, 825
Martel, Geoffrey, 505–506
Martinuzzi, George, 923–924
Martyrdom, 674, **805–806**
Marwan I, Caliph, 9, 23, 610, 1295, 1371
Marwan II, Caliph, 5, 6
Marxist Democratic Front for the Liberation of Palestine, 1004
Marzuk, Mousa Abu, 808
Masada, 672, **806–807**, 944
    Flavius Josephus's account, 1458–1460
Mashal, Khaled, **807–808**
Mashid al-Nabawi, 1124
Masjid al-Haram, 1124
Maskin, Battle of, 858
Maslama (brother of Othman), 300–301
Mason, R. A. "Tony," 979
Masri, Abu Ayyub al-, 995
Massacre at the Citadel, **808–809**
Massagetae/Massagetai, 272, 329
Masts, Battle of the, 257, 857
Mas'ud (Masud) I (Sultan of Rum), 335, 896, 1029, 1372
Masum, Fuad, 2
Matador, Operation, 1200
Matt, Dani, 287
Mattathias the Hasmonean, 684, 782, 943
Matthew Cantacuzenus, 255, 256
Mattis, James "Jim," 872, 873, 1121
Mattiwaza (king of Mitanni), 160
Maude, Frederick, 181, 697–698
Maude, Stanley, 825
Maududi, Abul A'Ala, **809–810**
Mauretania, 494
Maurice, Emperor, 521
Mauz, Henry H., Jr, 985
Mawdud, 149, 370, 681, **810**, 1251
Mawdudi. *See* Maududi, Abul A'Ala
Maxentius, Marcus Aurelius Valerius, 295, 442
Maximilian I (Holy Roman Emperor), 922, 927
Maximinus Daia, 442
Maximus, 35
Maxwell, John, 716
Maysalun, Battle of, 49, 420, **810–811**
Mazaeus, 449
Mazdakite movement, 708–709
Mazuq Agha, 530
McCain, John, 1132
McGonagle, William L., 766–767
McKiernan, David D., 243

McMahon, Henry, 133–134, 205, 509, 538–539, 773, 1225, 1334
    letter to Husain Ibn Ali, Sharif of Mecca, 1648–1649
    letters to Hussein ibn Ali, 811–812
McMahon-Hussein Correspondence, **811–812**
McMaster, Herbert R., 89, 1149
Mecca and Medina
    and Muhammad the Prophet, 1116
    Muslim conquest of, 1480–1482
    Saudi control of, 1124
Median Empire, 25, 162
Medina, Siege of, 179, **812–813**
Medina Ridge, Battle of, **813–814**
Megabazus, 385
Megabyxos (governor of Syria), 145, 340
Megalokomnenoi Alexios I, 1269
Megiddo, Ancient Battle of, **814–815**, 1411–1414
Megiddo, Battle of, 69, 88, 331, **815–816**, 949
Megiddo Offensive, 134
Mehmed Ali, Ibrahim ibn. *See* Ibrahim Pasha
Mehmed Ali (Muhammad Ali Pasha al-Mas'ud ibn Agha), 389–391, 545, 772, 774, 786, 808–809, **816–817**, 916, 1082, 1617
    and the Battle of Nizip, 892
    declaration of war on the Allies, 1636–1637
Mehmed I, 915, 1270
Mehmed II (Mohammad II) "The Conqueror," Sultan, **817–818**, 303–305, 852, 913, 1305, 1312, 1545, 1562–1563, 1567, 1581
    described by Nikolaos Sekoundinos, 1562–1563
Mehmed IV (sultan), 713, 714–715, 1596
Mehmed Kamil, 362
Mehmed Pasha, 390
Mehmed Talât (Talaat) Pasha, 140, 878, 1279
Mehmed V, 374, 484, 918, 949, 1278, 1279
Mehmed VI (Ottoman sultan), 484, 919, 920, 949, 1281
Mehmet Ali, 535, 616, 722
Mehmet I, 261, 262
Mehmet II, 206, 219, 262, 927
Mehmet III, 923
Mehmet IV, 655, 930
Mehwadiya, 869
Meigs, Montgomery, 813
Meinertzhagen, Richard, 135, 948
Meir, Golda Mabovitch, 40, 69, 130, 336, 344, 402, 624, 626, **818–819**
    statement to the Knesset, 1703–1708
Melas of Ephesus, 779
Meleager, 356, 357
Melek Ahmed Pasha, 1598
Melisende (daughter of Baldwin II), 201, 202, 664–665
Melisende (queen of Jerusalem), 82, 776
Melisende of Montlhèry, 200
Memish Pasha, 762
Memnon (Greek general), 55–56, 478
Memphis, Battle of, 272

Memphis, Siege of, 383
Menahem ben Yair, 670
Menander, 357
Menelaus of Sparta, 1275
Mengele, Josef, 526–527
Mengu Temur/Temir, 530, 792
Menou, Jacques (Abdullah/Abdallah Menou), 17–18, 387
Merhodios (saint), 248
Merodach-Baladan (king of Babylon), 161, 1142
Mersa Matruh, Battle of, 399
Mersa Matruh, First Battle of, **819–820**
Mersa Matruh, Second Battle of, **820–821**
Mesopotamia, 380, 414, 501, 701, **821–823**
    Arab conquest of, 856
    Lawrence's report on, 1669–1670
Mesopotamian Theater, World War I, **823–826**
Mesud I, 1504
Meyerson, Golda. *See* Meir, Golda Mabovitch
Meyerson, Morris, 818
Mezokeresztes, Battle of, 775
Mezzo Morto Hüsayin Pasha, 1314
Michael Cantacuzenus, 255
Michael I of Epiros, 61, 298
Michael II (Byzantine emperor), 71
Michael II of Epiros, 826
Michael III, 258
Michael IX, 253
Michael Keroularios, 248
Michael Komnenos Coukas, 519
Michael the Brave of Walacia, 923
Michael VIII Palaiologos, 62, 200, 218, 251, 253, 299, **826–827**, 882, 883, 1540, 1541
Middle East
    climate of, 291–292
    Cold War in, 292–293, 393, 396–397
    communist containment in, 188–190
    impact of World War I on, 1333–1335
    impact of World War II on, 1336–1338
    Mongol invasion and conquest of, 521–522, 831–834
    Nixon Doctrine in, 891
    use of chemical weapons, 285–286
    See also *individual Middle Eastern countries by name*
Middle Eastern Treaty Organization, 188, 421, 1698. *See also* Baghdad Pact
Mihdar, Zein al-Abidin al- (Abu al-Hassan), 609
Mihran (Persian general), 856
Mikati, Najib, 747
Mikhail, Tsar of Russia, 1078
Milan Decree, 237
Miles of Plancy, 202
Miletus, Battle of, **827**
Milne, George, 1151
Miltiades, 480–481
Milvian Bridge, Battle of the, 295
Mindarus (Spartan admiral), 518
Minto, Lord, Nelson's letter to, 1607–1608
Mir Vays (Mir Ways, Mir Wais Khan; Ghilzai tribe chief), 489, 608, 1098

Mircea of Walacia, 262
Mircea the Great, 885
Mirza, Abbas, **6–7**, 409, 489, 786
Mirza, Khanlar, 99
Mishaal, Khalid, 956
Mistra, 246
Mitab, Abdallah ibn, 1128
Mitchell, Colin Campbell "Mad Mitch," 35
Mithridates I Ctistes, 1003
Mithridates I of Parthia, 360–361
Mithridates II of Pontus, 112, 1071
Mithridates of Pergamum, 269
Mithridates V Euergetes, 1003
Mithridates VI Eupator Dionysius, 227, 231, **827–828**, 828
    last days described by Appian of Alexandria, 1449–1451
Mithridatic Wars, **828–829**
    First Mithridatic War, 828
    Second Mithridatic War, 828–829
Mitla Pass, **829–830**
Mixed Armistice Commissions, 643
Mizrahi Judaism, **830–831**
Mleh of Armenia, 505
Moawad, René, 759
Mocenigo, Alvise, 1314
Mocenigo, Lazaro, 1314
Mohács, Battle of, 915, 922
Mohács, Seond Battle of, 1600
Mohammad Ali (Egyptian ruler), 16
Mohammad I, Shah, 1097
Mohammad Omar (Mullah), 230
Mohammad Reza Pahlavi (shah of Iran), 95, 277, 293, 431, 565–567, 573, 578, 705, 891, 908, 1676–1679
Mohammed Ali, 119
Mohammed bin Nayef, 1121
Mohammed bin Salman, 1121–1122
Mohammed Shah (Mogul emperor), 866
Moldavia, 37, 208, 717, 890, 917, 923, 930, 931, 1079, 1081
Mollet, Guy, 1212–1213
Molon (satrap of Media), 110
Moltke, Helmuth Karl von, 892
Momchil, 255
Monastir (Bitola), Battle of, 1279
Mongke Khan, 158, 167, 182, 475, 529, 534, 547, 791, 831, 833, 1536
Mongol Ilkhanate, 790–791, 1077
Mongol Invasion of the Middle East, **831–834**
Mongols, 22–23, 101, 107, 150, 167, 182, 218, 234–235, 408, 667, 715–716, 945
    conquest of Syria by, 317
    First Battle of Homs, 529
    and the Golden Horde-Ilkhanid Wars, 475
    Second Battle of Homs, 530
    in Syria, 791–792, 795
    Third Battle of Homs, 531
    See also Chinggis (Genghis) Khan; Golden Horde; Tamerlane (Mongol Khan)
Monro, Charles, 446

Mons Seleucus, Battle of, 305
Montgisard, Battle of, 203, **835**, 1100
Montecúccolli, Raimondo, 714, 924
Montenegrin-Ottoman Wars, **834–835**
    Montenegrin-Ottoman War of 1852–1853, 834
    Montenegrin-Ottoman War of 1861–1862, 834
    Montenegrin-Ottoman War of 1876–1878, 835
    Montenegrin-Ottoman War of 1912–1913, 835
Montenegro, 206, 208, 917, 1147, 1279
Montgomery, Bernard Law, 43, 165, 401, 820, **835–836**
    letter to Bill Adam, 1679–1682
    message to the troops following El-Alamein, 1684–1685
Montreux Convention, 774
Moreau, Jean, 236
Morgenthau, Henry, 141, 1642
Moroccan Crises (1905–1906), 647
Morocco, 1006
Morosini, Francesco, 1314
Morphia (daughter of Gabriel of Melitene), 200, 370, 682
Morris, Benny, 1091
Morrison-Grady Plan, **836–838**, 837
Morsi, Mohamed, 10, 307, 378–379, 392, 447, 461, **838–839**, 1183, 1733, 1773
Moscow, Treaty of, 60, 1289
Moses, Operation, 152, 830
Mossad, 336
Mossad Le-Aliya Bet, 416
Mossadegh, Mohammad, 94–95, 293, 566, 1695
Mossawa, 103
Mosul, First Battle of, **840–841**
Mosul, Second Battle of, **841–842**
"Mother of All Battles," **842–843**, 988, 1730–1732
Mott, S. F., 661
Mouauad, René, 534
Moudros, Armistice of, **843–844**
Mount Lebanon Civil War, **844**
Mount Lebounion, Battle of, 61
Movement of the Dispossessed, 523
Moyne (Lord), 668–669
Mozzafar al-Din Shah, 564
Muawiyah, Abd al-Rahman ibn, 1295
Muawiyah I, Caliph, 65, 89, 257, 610, **844–845**, 1295
Muawiyah ibn Abi Sufyan, 703
Mubarak, Hosni, 128, 136, 378, 391–392, 446, 447, 458, 644, 726, 727, 838–839, **845–846**, 867
Mucianus, Licinius, 1315
Mudros, Armistice of, 280, 918, 920, 978, 1280–1281
Müezzinzade Ali Pasha, 328, **846–847**
Mughal-Safavid Wars, **847**

Mughniya, Imad, 523
Muhamad Quli Khan (vizier), 490
Muhammad (Tapar) (Seljuk sultan), 149
Muhammad, Ali Nasir, 1351
Muhammad, Jamal al-Din, 1372
Muhammad, Prophet of Islam, 49, 610, **848–850**
    and the Battle of al-Badr, 178–179, 1477–1478
    and the Dome of the Rock, 945
    Miraj and Isra, 430
    and the Muslim wars of expansion, 856
    and the Quran, 1030–1032
    in Saudi Arabia, 1116
Muhammad, Campaigns of the Prophet, **847–848**
Muhammad Ali (Mehmed Ali). *See* Mehmed Ali
Muhammad Ali Mirza, 929
Muhammad Ali Pasha, 27, 93, 99, 374, 385, 393, 945, 1116
Muhammad Ali Pasha al-Mas'ud ibn Agha. *See* Mehmed Ali
Muhammad Ali Shah, 1086
Muhammad Amin Rauf Pasha, 929
Muhammad Daoud. *See* Daoud, Abu
Muhammad I (Seljuk sultan), 79, 547
Muhammad ibn Harun al-Rashid, 44
Muhammad ibn Saud, 389, 1126
Muhammad II "The Conqueror," 927
Muhammad Mirza (Muhammad Shah of Iran), 1086
Muhammad Najib, 375
Muhammad Reza Pahlavi, Shah of Iran, 1063
Muhammad Shah Aga Khan III, 619
Muhammad Tapar, 694, 1139–1140
Muhanna, Ahmad, 955
Muhendishane-i Bahri Humayun, 281
Mu'in al-Din, 896
Muirhead-Smith, Edward, 77
Mujahideen Shura Council (MSC), 75, 188, 613
Mujahideen-e Khalq, 566
Mujir al-Din Uvak, 896
Mukhabbarat (Iraqi Secret Service), 24
Multinational Force and Observers in the Sinai, **850–851**
Multinational Force–Iraq (MNF-I), 142–143, **851–852**, 994–995
Multinational Force–Lebanon, 753–754
Munazzasmat al-Tahrir Filastiniyyah. *See* Palestine Liberation Organization (PLO)
Munda, Battle of, 269
Munnich, Burkhard Christoph von, 1079
Muqrin, Saudi prince, 1120
Murad Bey, 386, 1017
Murad I, Sultan, 11, 205, 218, 256, 261, 262, 655, 914, 933, 1312, 1550
    and the Battle of Kosovo, 1550–1551
Murad II, Sultan, 37, 252, 262, 817, **852**, 915, 926, 1310, 1312
Murad III, Sultan, 364, 655, 766
Murad IV, Sultan, 183, 365, 916, 933, 1381
Murad V, Sultan, 917

Muras Major, Battle of, 305
Murat, Joachim, 16, 385
Mur'awiya, Caliph, 858
Murdoch, Keith, 1645
Murena, Lucius Licinius, 828–829
Murphy, Robert, 282
Murray, Sir Archibald James, 116, 220, 451, 452, 716, **852–853**, 947–948, 1071, 1174
Murray, Wallace, 1676
Mursili I (Hittite king), 177
Murtha, John, 15
Musa, 261
Musa, Rifa Taha, 447
Musa ibn Nusair, 859
Musa Yabghu, 1138
Musawi, Abbas, M, 523
Muslim, Abu, 6
Muslim Brotherhood, 14, 50, 73, 121, 126, 127–128, 157, 378, 379, 391–392, 488, 497, 498, 611–612, 808, **853–855**, 955, 1026, 1033–1034, 1103, 1121, 1733
  condemning the crackdown against journalists and activists, 1773–1774
Muslim civil war, 216
Muslim Wars of Expansion, **856–860**
  map, 857
Muslims
  conflict with the Georgians, 1505–1506
  wars with Byzantine Empire, 256–260
  See also Islam
Mussalimk bin Nafl, 905
Mussolini, Benito, 648
Mustafa, 262, 929
Mustafa, Abu Ali, 1005
Mustafa, Düzme, 852
Mustafa Fevzi Pasha, 661
Mustafa II, 694, 916
Mustafa III, 280
Mustafa IV, 657, 687, 1080, 1137
Mustafa Kamil, 394
Mustafa Pasha, 932
Mustafaa, Kabakchi, 687
Mustapha Bey, 16
Muta, Battle of, 856
Mu'tah, Battle of, 700
Mut-Ashkur (Assyrian king), 159
Mutawakkilite regime, 503
Mutla Ridge, **860–861**
Muwtallish (Hittite king), 687
Muzaffar al-Din Shah, 1086
Mwawi, Ahmad Ali al-, **861**
Mycale, Battle of, 483, **861–862**
Myonessus, Battle of, 784
Myriokephalon, Battle of, 248, **862**, 1077

Nabataean Empire, 119, 943, 944
Nabatameans, 358
Nabonidus, 172–173, 175, 329, 1430
Nabopolassar, 173–174, 178, 876–877
Nabu-apla-iddina, 177

Nachshon, Operation, 122, 348–349, **863–864**
Nachshon ben Aminadav, 863
Nacr Qoli Beg (Nadir Shah). *See* Nadir Shah
Nadir Khan, 179–180, 184, 927–928, 975
Nadir Shah, 564, 695, 713, 762, **864–866**, 929, 933, 976, 1084, 1098
Nafsi, Yair, 1308
Nagib, Muhammad, 124
Naguib, Mohammad, **866–867**, 874
Nagyvárad, Treaty of, 923
Nahal, 960
Nahr al-Bared Refugee Camp, Siege of, **867–868**
Nahrawan, Battle of, 703
Najaf, Battle of, 993
Najaf, First Battle of, **868–869**
Najaf, Second Battle of, **869–870**
Najm ad-Din Ayub, 1100
Nakba, 417–418
Nakhimov, Paul S., 1183
Naper, Charles, 27
Napoleon I Bonaparte. *See* Bonaparte, Napoleon
Napoleon III, 844
Napoleonic Wars, 236–237, 926
Naram-Sin (Naram-Sim, Naram-Sinn), 42, 822, 1406–1407
Narjot of Toucy, 199
Narkiss, Uzi, 960
Narodnaya Volya, 1257
Narses, 442, 686, 884, 1074
Nasafi, Muhammad al-, 1021
Nasar, Mustafa bin Abd al-Qadir Setmariam (Abu Mus'ab al-Suri), **870–872**
  The Global Islamic Resistance Call, 1748–1752
Nashashibis, 130–131
Nashtakin al-Darazi, 365
Nasi, Joseph, 328
Nasir (Naser) ad-Din Shah, 977, 1101–1102
Nasiriyah, Battle of, **872–873**
Nasr-4, Operation, 569
Nasrallah, Hasan Dib, 752
Nasrallah, Hassan, 736
Nasrallah, Sheikh, 524
Nassar, Najib, 946
Nassarollah Mirza, 695
Nasser, Gamal Abdel, **874–875**
  and Abdel Hakim Amer, 85–86
  and the Aden emergency, 34
  and Arab nationalism, 128, 633, 964, 1206
  and the Baghdad Pact, 189–190, 421
  and Black September, 232, 377
  and the Cairo Agreement, 270–271
  and the Cold War, 293
  conflict with al-Said, 898
  and the Free Officers Organization, 426, 866, 1206
  vs. Israel, 412, 634, 678, 818–819, 1189, 1324
  and the Israeli War of Independence, 85
  and Israel's raid in Gaza, 240, 453–454
  and the Khartoum Resolution, 704
  and the Lavon affair, 740
  as leader of Egypt, 124, 375–377, 623–625, 854–855, 867, 965, 1189, 1204, 1301, 1349
  pan-Arabism of, 140, 189–190, 375, 677, 1171, 1300
  relations with Russia, 1326
  and the Rogers Plan, 1069
  and the Sinai Campaign, 1175–1178
  and the Six-Day War, 785, 950, 1356
  speech on the nationalization of the Suez Canal, 1702–1703
  and the Suez Canal, 93, 124, 375, 393, 397, 454, 623, 925, 1174–1175, 1206–1207, 1211–1215
  treaty with Britain, 93
  and the United Arab Republic, 140, 156, 677, 965, 1035, 1299–1301, 1349
  U.S. attempt to control, 503
  in Yemen, 1117
Nasserism, 128, 375, 377, 611
Nasuh Pasha, Treaty of, 301, **875–876**
Natalie, Shahan, 878
National Action Charter (Bahrain), 192
National Council for the Awakening of Iraq, 605
National Council for the Salvation of Iraq, 605
National Democratic Front for the Liberation of Oman and the Arabian Gulf (NDFLOAG), 905
National Liberation Front (NLF), 34
National Organization of Cypriot Fighters (EOKA), 324, 487
National Religious Party, 505
National Syrian Socialist Party, 761
Nations, Battle of the, 236–237
Natonski, Richard, 872, 873
Navarino Bay, Battle of, 545, 786
Nazism, 114, 130
Nebuchadnezzar, 942
Nebuchadnezzar I of Babylon, 160, 177, 942
  inscription, 1420–1422
Nebuchadnezzar II of Babylon, 174, 620, **876–877**
  East India House inscription, 1426–1430
Necho II (pharaoh), 174
Nectanebo II (phararoh), 147
Negotiations Affairs Department (NAD), 954
Negroponte, John, 243
Negroponte, loss of, 1564–1567
Nehemiah, 942
Nelson, Horatio, 15, 17, 18, 20, 236, 386, **877–878**, 1605
  letter to Lord Minto, 1607–1608
Nemesis, Operation, **878–879**
Neoptolemus, 357
Neriglissar (Babylonian king), 174
Nero (Roman emperor), 228, 671, 943, 1072, 1315
Nerva, Emperor, 1267
Netanyahu, Benjamin, 5, 138, 210, 456, 457, 461, 462, 511, 630–632, **879–881**, 1338–1339
  and the PLO, 954
  speech to U.S. Congress, 1766–1767

Netanyahu, Jonathan, 404
New Dawn (Al-Fajr), Operation, 424, 600. *See also* Iraq War (2003–2011)
New Zionist Organization (NZO), 652
Niam al-Mulk (Seljuk vizier), 158, 790, 1138–1139
Nicaea, Council of, 296
Nicaea, Empire of, **882–883**
Nicaean Army, 251
Nicanor, 358, 684, 782
Nicephorus/Nikephoros I, 258, 508, 1491–1492
Nicephorus III Botaniates (Byzantine emperor), 60
Nicephorus/Nikephoros Palaiologos, 1269
Nicephorus Phocas, 259, 260
Nicholas I, Tsar, 535, 774, 834, 1080, 1082
Nicholas IV (pope), 1021
Nicholas Kanabos, 62
Nicomedes I, 230–231
Nicomedes II, 231
Nicomedes III, 231, 827
Nicomedes IV Philopator, 231, 827–829
Nicopolis, Battle of, 205
Nicosia, Ottoman siege of, 328
Nigeria, 612
Nihavand, Battle of, 975
Nihriya, Battle of, 160
Nika Revolt, 1474–1477
Nika Uprising, **883–884**
Nikolas, Prince, 834–835
Nikopolis, Battle of, 219, 261, 1915, 546
Nikopolis, Crusade in, **885–886**, 1310, 1552–1554
Nile, Battle of, 17, 29, 269, 386, 877, 1605–1607
  Julius Caesar wins, 1451–1454
  Sir Edward Berry's report, 1605–1607
Nile River, **886–887**
Nile River Valley, 465, 465–466, 467
Nili, 510
Nimble Archeri, Operation, 368, **887–888**, 1011
Nimr al-Nimr, 194
1956 War. *See* Suez Crisis
1967 War. *See* Six-Day War (1967)
Nineveh, Battle of, 264, 521, **888–889**, 1478–1480, 1484, 1487
Nisibis, Battle of, **889–890**
Nisibis, Treaty of, 1074
Nissa, Treaty of, **890**, 1079
Nixon, Richard M., 129–130, 891, 1037, 1118
Nixon, Sir John Eccles, 83, 319, 723, 823, **890–891**
Nixon Doctrine, **891**
Nizam-i Cedid army, 687
Nizar, 157
Nizari Khojas, 619
Nizaris ("Assassins"), 157–158
Nizip, Battle of, 546, **892**, 916
Noble, Richard, 243–244

Nogai tribes, 194
Norfolk, Battle of, 589, **892–894**
North Atlantic Treaty Organization (NATO), 136, 188, 325, 836, 891, 1258, 1277, 1282, 1287, 1299
North Yemen Civil War, 503
Northern Crusade, 309
Northern Watch, Operation, 350, **894–896**
Novi Pazar, 772–773
Nubia, 273, 384
Nuclear facilities
  in Iraq, 909–910, 980, 987, 1120, 1129, 1194, 1249–1250, 1290–1291, 1358
  in Syria, 903
Nuclear Non-Proliferation Treaty, 635
Numerian, 1074
Nunn, Wilfred, 83
Nur al-Din, 82, 107, 144, 150, 201–202, 319–320, 335, 370, 371, 429, 505–506, 551, 664, 723, **896–898**, 1077, 1271
Nuremberg Laws, 526
Nuri al-Said Pasha, 421, 586–587, **898–899**, 1022
Nusayris, 49

Obama, Barack, 2, 74, 155, 245, 286, 378, 392, 461, 555, 571, 583, 592, 606, 630, 631, 679, 789, 808, 880, 994, 1120, 1359, 1766
  and ISIS, 613–614
  and Operation Inherent Resolve, 551–553
Obeidi, Khaled al-, 554
Oberto of Biandrate, 298
Ocalan, Abdullah, 554, 710–711
Öcalan, Osman, 719
Öcalan Abdullah, 718–719
Occupied Territories, 3. *See also* Gaza Strip; Golan Heights; West Bank
Ochos, 340 *See also* Artaxerxes III; Darius II
O'Connor, Richard Nugent, **901**, 1679
Ocroes I of Parthia, 1267
Octavia (sister of Octavian), 30, 289, 1454
Octavian (Augustus), 30, 32, 289, 670, 683, 1072
Octavianus, 1454
October War. *See* Yom Kippur War
Odenathus, **902**, 961, 1074, 1376
Odierno, Raymond, 851, 995
Odo of Montbéliard, 450
Oghuz tribes, 1140
Ohod, Battle of, 856
Oil-for-Food Progreamme, 595–596
Okamoto, Kozo, 770
Okba ibn Nafi, 858
Okhan (son of Osman), 205
Okudaira, Tsuyoshi, 770
Olden, A.C.N. "Harry," 331
Olive Leaves (Aleizayit), Operation, 242
Öljeitü, 548
Olmert, Ehud, 4, 455, 458, 460, 635–636, 880, **902–903**
Omamn, 487–488

Oman, 118, **903–907**, 1007, 1019–1020
  Arab Spring in, 906
  climate of, 291
  Dhofar Rebellion, 354–356
  map, 904
Omar, 118
Omar, emir of Melitene, 258
Omar Ben Hatav (Muslim caliph), 944
Omar ibn al-Khattaab, 944
Omar II (caliph), 301
Omar Pasha Latas, 834
O'Neill, Thomas P., letter from Reagan on the destruction of an Iranian jetliner, 1724–1725
Opera, Operation, 398, 909–910
Operation Desert Storm, 86–87
Opis, Battle of, 329, 1430
Orchard, Operation, 630, 903
Order of Santiago, 200
Organization of Arab Petroleum Exporting Countries (OAPEC), 190, 907
Organization of Islamic Conference, 190, 326
Organization of Islamic Cooperation, 533, 675
Organization of Petroleum Exporting Countries (OPEC), 62, 129–130, 466, 562, 727, 729, **907–908**, 1118
  oil embargo, 466
Orhan, 260, 912
Oriental Crisis of 1840, 391
Orland I, 971
Orlov, Aleksei/Aleksey/Alexis, 37, 286–287, 1079
Orontes, 147
Orr Commission, 103
Orthodox Judaism, 510, 631, 1248
Osiraq Raid, **909–910**
Oslo Accords (1993), 3, 21, 70, 138, 269, 454, 499, 511, 516, 557–558, 560, 629, 644, 783, 880, **910–912**, 951, 954, 956–958, 1005, 1039, 1068, 1173
Oslo Declaration, 1732
Osloi, 650
Osman (Othman) I, 205, 210, 260, 299–300, 343, 469, **912**, 914, 929
  described by Nikolaos Sekoundinos, 1545–1546
  See also Uthman (Osman0 ibn Affan (Caliph)
Osman II, 364
Osman Nuri Pasha, **912–913**, 1082–1083
Osman Pasha, 1183
Osroes, 1072
Ostrogoths, 35–36
Otaybi, Juhayman al-, 1118
Othman. *See* Osman (Othman) I; Osman II
Otho, 671
Otlukbeli, Battle of, **913**, 1567–1569
Otto, bishop of Freising, 294
Otto, Ottoman king, 302
Otto IV (Holy Roman Emperor), 316, 438, 999
Otto of Wittelsbach, 437
Ottokar IV, duke of Styria, 763, 764

Ottoman Empire, 83, 101, 163, 166, 204, **913–919**
   1700 Treaty of Constantinople, 302
   1720 Treaty of Constantinople, 302
   1832 Treaty of Constantinople, 302
   1913 Treaty of Constantinople, 302–303
   1915 Battle of Ctesiphon, 319–320
   abrogation of the capitulations, 1634–1636
   Armenian Genocide, 140–142
   Armistice of Moudros, 843
   in Azerbaijan, 564
   Balkan Wars (1912–1913), 206–207
   Battle of Baghdad (1773), 184
   Battle of Bapheus, 210
   Battle of Chaldiran, 281
   Battle of Chesma, 286–287
   Battle of Khanaqin, 701
   Battle of Lepanto, 764–765
   Battle of Nikopolis, 885–886
   British capture of Baghdad, 181
   capture of Rhodes, 1581–1583
   conquest of the Balkans, 205–206
   conquest of Cyprus, 328–329, 1586–1589
   and the Convention of Balta Liman, 208
   Dardanelles Campaign, 337–339
   declaring war on the Allies, 1636–1637
   Druze-Ottoman Wars, 364–365
   Erzurum Offensive, 410–412
   expansion of, 1361–1571, 914
   failing to capture Baghdad from Persia, 1593–1596
   First Battle of Baghavard, 179–180
   and Galilee, 443
   historical context, 913–914
   Kapikulu Corps, 690
   official rejection of treaties of dependency, 1638–1639
   peace treaty with Poland, 1382
   Second Battle of Baghavard, 180
   siege of Baghdad, 183–184
   siege of Constantinople (1453), 303–305
   treaties with Habsburg Empire, 968
   treaties with Persia, 409–410
   treaties with Russia, 535, 658, 717, 722, 774
   and the Treaty of Karlowitz, 694–695
   treaty with Balkan League, 772–773
   treaty with Safavid Empire, 875–876
   war with Italy, 646–648
   wars with Byzantine Empire, 260–262
   wars with Mamluks, 792–793
   in World War I, 374, 405, 483, 823–826, 917–918
   in World War I, 1280
   See also Turkey
Ottoman Empire, Entry into World War I, **919–920**
Ottoman Empire, Post–World War I Revolution In, **920–921**
Ottoman Navy, 281, 715
Ottoman War of Succession, 792

Ottoman-Habsburg Wars, **921–926**
   early conflicts, 921–922
   later relations, 926
   War of 1529–1533, 922–923
   War of 1540–1547, 923
   War of 1551–1553, 923
   War of 1566, 923
   War of 1591–1606, 923–924
   War of 1663–1664, 924
   War of 1683–1699, 924–925
   War of 1716–1718, 925, 968
   War of 1737–1739, 925
   War of 1787–1791, 925
Ottoman-Habsburg-Russian War (1787–1791), 1137
Ottoman-Hungarian Wars, **926–927**
   War of 1437–1438, 926
   War of 1441–1444, 926
   War of 1444–1456, 926–927
   War of 1463–1483, 927
   War of 1492–1494, 927
   War of 1521–1526, 927
Ottoman-Mamluk War, 364
Ottoman-Montenegrin. *See* Montenegrin-Ottoman Wars
Ottoman-Persian Wars of the 18th and 19th Centuries, 343, 786, **927–929**
   Battle of Kars, 695
   War of 1730–1736, 927–928
   War of 1742–1746, 928
   War of 1776–1779, 929
   War of 1820–1823, 929
Ottoman-Polish Wars of the 17th Century, **930–931**
Ottoman-Russian war, in the Caucasus, 278–280
Ottomans, 7
   and the Long Campaign in Hungary, 774–775
   and the Long War in Hungary, 775
   Treaty of Constantinople, 301
Ottoman-Safavid Wars, **931–932**, **931–933**
   War of 1526–1555, 932
   War of 1578–1590, 8, 301, 932, 1097
   War of 1603–1612, 932–933
   War of 1616–1618, 933
   War of 1623–1639, 933
Ottoman-Venetian War, 715, 968
Ottoman-Wahhabi War. *See* Egyptian-Arab Wars
Ouseley, Gore, 489
Outram, James, 99
Outremer, **934–935**
Overlord, Operation, 836
Owaid, Haqqi Esmaeil (Abu Ahmed), 841
Oxyartes, 357

Pachyeres, George, 210
Pact of Mutual Cooperation, 189. *See also* Baghdad Pact
Paetus, Caesennius, 1072

Pakistan, 190, 809
Pala Mustafa Pasha, 328
Palaiologoi Dynasty, 251
Paléologue, Georges Maurice, 1225
Palestine, 11, 13, 63–64, 91–92, 114–115, 117, 225, 283, 431
   and the Arab League, 123–125, 124
   and the Arab Legion, 125–126
   Arab revolt in (1936–1939), 130–131
   and the Arab-Jewish Communal War, 120–123
   and the Baldat al-Shaykh Massacre, 196
   and the Balfour Declaration, 204–205
   Cunningham in, 321
   Deir Yassin Massacre, 347–348
   and the London Round Table Conference, 773–774
   and the Morrison-Grady plan, 837
   and Operation Autumn Clouds, 166–167
   security for Jews in, 509
Palestine, British Mandate for, 474, 495, 539, 622, 642, 742, 797, 801, 812, **937–940**, 1304, 1378, 1680
Palestine, Partition of, 608, **940–941**
Palestine, Pre-1918 History of, **941–947**
Palestine and Syria Campaign, World War I, **947–950**
Palestine Congress, 660–661
Palestine Democratic Union, 952
Palestine Legislative Council (PLC), 3
Palestine Liberation Army (PLA), **950–951**, 952
Palestine Liberation Front (PLF), 2, 20–21, **951**, 1004
Palestine Liberation Organization (PLO), **951–955**
   Abbas and, 3–4, 20–21
   absence from Geneva Peace Conference, 465
   Algeria Declaration, 63
   and the Arab League, 124
   and Arab Nationalism, 612, 965
   and the Battle of Karameh, 690–691
   and Black September, 137, 231–232, 336
   and the Cairo Accord, 269–270
   and the Cairo Agreement, 270–271
   and the Cairo Declaration, 271–272
   creation of, 124
   Declaration of Principles, 454, 784, 1039
   failed summit with Barak, 636, 1056, 1068
   and the Fedayeen, 431
   omitted from Geneva Peace Conference, 464–465
   Iraqi support for, 420
   Israeli operations against, 223, 559, 769–770
   in Jordan, 3, 137, 336, 540, 678, 952–953
   in Lebanon, 2, 20, 137, 745–746, 753–754, 756, 759–761, 770, 953, 1090
   and the Oslo Accords, 557, 910–912, 956
   and the Palestine Liberation Army, 950–951
   and the Palestine Liberation Front, 951
   Palestinian refugees as members, 115

peace accords with Israel, 879, 1154
and the PFLP, 1004–1006
and the Rabat Summit, 1037–1038
and the Reagan Plan, 1050
Saudi Arabian support for, 1118
support for Iraq by, 137, 728
terrorism by, 326
in Tunisia, 3, 1050
U.S. failure to recognize, 275
violence against Israel and Jews, 24, 333, 443, 624, 690, 1107
in the West Bank, 644, 1328
and the Wye River Agreement, 1338
See also Arafat, Yasser
Palestine National Union, 464
Palestine Secret Organization, 24
Palestine-Syria Campaign, 331
Palestinian Arab Front, 952
Palestinian Authority (PA), 45, 118, 138, 269–270, 336, 346, 427, 454, 456, 458, 461, 464, 498, 511, 559, 650, 784, 950, 953, 956, 1039, 1054
and Hamas, 499–501
Palestinian Campaign, Battle of Megiddo (Armageddon), 815–816
Palestinian Islamic Jihad, 498, **955–956**
Palestinian Islamic Jihad (PIJ), 498, **955–956**, 1006
Palestinian Legislative Council (PLC), 272, 427, 629, 957
Palestinian Liberation Front (PLF), 952
Palestinian National Authority (PNA), 3, 4, **956–960**
Palestinian National Council (PNC), 63, 336, 952, 955, 1005, 1007
Palestinian People's Party, 952
Palestinian Popular Front Struggle, 952
Palestinian Preventive Security Organization (PSO), 1040
Palestinian Resistance Movement, 269, 753
Palestinian Right of Return. *See* Right of Return, Palestinian
Palestinians
and the Cairo Accord, 269–270
and the Cairo Agreement, 270–271
and the Cairo Declaration, 271–272
and the Camp David Accords, 275
as expellees and refugees, 417–418
and the First Intifada, 556–558, 629
and the Gaza Strip Disengagement, 457
and the Hasmonean Tunnel Incident, 511
as martyrs, 806
as refugees, 115, 417–418, 642, 657, 678, 748, 867–868, 965, 1006, 1050, 1067–1068, 1693–1694
and the Right of Return, 1067–1068
and the Second Intifada, 558–560, 629
in the West Bank, 636–638
Palmach, 69, 81, 120, 123, 196, 495, 640, 863, 864, **960–961**

Palmerston, Lord, 27, 1617–1618
letter to Viscount Beauvale, 1617–1618
Palmyra, **961–962**
Pan-Arab Congress, **962–963**
Pan-Arabism and Pan-Arabist Thought, 127, 128, 140, 189, 240, 567, 578, 750, 875, **963–966**, 1035, 1300
Pan-Islamism, 963
Panium, Battle of, 111
Pan-Turkism, 963
Papak (father of Ardashir I), 138–139
Paphlagonia, 335, 883
Paraetacene, Battle of, 413, 441, **966**
Paris, 1856 Treaty of, 917, 1081
Paris, son of Priam, 1275
Paris Peace Conference (1919), 539, 796, 811, 940, 1109, 1225, 1334
Emir Faisal's memorandum to, 1667–1669
Parmenio, 449, 479
Parmenion, 449
Parthia, 329, 350, 358
Parthian (Arsacid) Empire, 162, 276, 563, **966–968**
wars with Rome, 1071–1073
Parthian War, 494, 1267
Parthians, 494, 802
Partiya Karkerên Kurdistan. *See* Kurdistan Workers' Party (PKK)
Partskhisi, Battle of, 468
Pasa, Candarli Halil (grand vizier), 817
Pasargadae/Pasargadai, Battle of, 329, 1262
Paschal II (pope), 234
Pasdaran (Revolutionary Guard Corps), 579
Pasgha, Chighalah, 932
Pasha, Abdul Razek Azzam, 124
Pasha, Ismail Safwat, 121
Pasha, Sidqi, 93
Pasha al-Atrash. *See* al-Atrash, Sultan
Paskevizh, I., 1086
Passarowitz, Treaty of, 695, 916, 925, **968**, 1314
Passfield White Paper, 283
Patria, Destruction of, **968–969**
Patriotic Union of Kurdistan (PUK), 990
Patrona Halil Revolt, 928, **969**
Patterson, John H., 669
Paul II Hakonsson, 1070
Paul of Conti, 1272
Paul the Evangelist, 943
Pausanias of Sparta, 478, 483
Peace for Galilee, Operation, 223, 758, 760, 761. *See also* Lebanon-Israeli War
Peace of Apamea, 111, 413
Peace of Callias, 145
Peace of Karlowitz, 302
Peace of the King, 146–147
Peace of Tilsit, 236
Peake, Frederick Gerard (Peake Pasha), 125, 471, 676
Pechenegs, 61
Peel, William Robert, 131, 969

Peel Commission, 131, 773, 837, 962, **969–970**, 1332
Peithon, 357, 358
Pelagius (Cardinal), 316, 798
Pelagius of Albano, 674, **970–971**
Pelagonia, Battle of, 299, 883
Peled, Benny, 403
Peled, Mati, 961
Pelekanon, Battle of, 253, **971–972**
Peloponnesian War, 340
Hellespont Campaign, 517–518
Pelusium, Battle of, 272, 383, **972**
Peninsula Shield, 488
Peninsular War, 237
People's Congress of Kurdistan, 719
People's Crusade, 113, 310, 472, 993. *See also* Crusades in the Holy Land, Christian, First Crusade
People's Democratic Republic of Yemen (PDRY), 355, 1350. *See also* Yemen
Peoples of the Book, 673, 1032
People's Protection Units (YPG), 615, 711–712, 720
People's United Revolutionary Movement, 720
Percestas, 357
Perdiccas, 54, 105, 356, 357, 358, 413, **972–973**
Peres, Shimon, 403–404, 630, 879, 909, 1213, 1732
Pereus (son of Philip V), 361
Pereyaslavl, Treaty of, 1078
Pergamum, 110, 413, **973–975**
Perkins, Dave, 186
Peroz I, 1112
Perpetual Maritime Peace, Treaty of, 463
Perscennius Niger, 1146
Persepolis, 26, 57
Perseus of Macedon, 414
Persia. *See* Iran; Persian (Achaemenid) Empire
Persia, 18th-Century Wars of Succession, **975–976**
Persia, Arab Conquest of, **975**
Persian Cossack Brigade, **977**
Persian (Achaemenid) Empire, 145
agreement with France, 432
and Ancient Egypt, 383
and the Battle of Baghdad (1773), 184
conversion to Islam, 563
Definitive Treaty with Great Britai, 347
and the First Battle of Baghavard, 179–180
Sassanid, 317
and the Second Battle of Baghavard, 180
treaties with Ottoman Empire, 409–410
treaty with Russia, 447
war with Russia, 489
wars with Byzantine Empire, 856
Persian Front, World War I, **977–979**
Persian Gulf, **979**
Persian Gulf Command, 565
Persian Gulf crisis, 14

Persian Gulf War (1991), 3, 14, 79, 86, 124–125, 157, 172, 277, 378, 426, 467, 531, 582, 589, 602, 611, 612, 679, 728, 787, 822, 846, 891, 954, 965, 1053
   Amiriyah Shelter Bombing, 86–87
   Attacks on Taji Bunkers, 1245–1247
   Bahrain's participation in, 192–193
   Battle of 73 Easting, 1149
   and the Battle of Bubiyan Island, 243–244
   and the Battle of Burqan, 244–245
   Battle of Khafji, 698–699
   Battle of Medina Ridge, 813–814
   Battle of Norfolk, 892–893
   Battle of Wadi al-Batin, 1149, 1321
   "Mother of All Battles," 842–843
   no-fly zones, 599–600
   Operation Imminent Thunder, 548–550
   Operation Scathe Mean, 1129–1130
   Operation Scorpion, 1132–1133
   Saddam Line, 1092–1093
   Saudi Arabia involvement in, 1119
   scud missile attack on Dhahran, 354
   use of chemical weapons, 285
Persian Gulf War, Air Campaign, **979–982**
Persian Gulf War, Cease-Fire Agreement, **982–983**
Persian Gulf War, Ground Campaign, **983–985**
Persian Gulf War, Naval Operations, **985–987**
Persian Gulf War, Overview, **987–990**
Persian Soviet Socialist Republic, 564
Persian Wars. *See* Greco-Persian Wars
Peshmerga, 345, 554–555, 594, 613, 710, 711, 720, 840, 841, **990–992**, 1011, 1041, 1319
Petach Tikva, 946
Peter Bartholomew, 109
Peter Damian (saint), 113
Peter I of Brittany, 1529
Peter I of Cyprus, 59, 794, 1548
Peter I The Great of Russia, 916, 1014, 1078–1079, 1083, 1084, 1098, 1203
Peter II of Aragon, 438
Peter of Courtenay, 199, 298
Peter of Dreux, 450
Peter of Sevrey, 29
Peter the Hermit, 249, 310, **992–993**, 1029
Peter Thomas (papal legate), 1548
Peterwardein, Battle of, 925
Petraeus, David Howell, 89, 598, 840, 851, **993–994**, 995
   report to Congress on Iraq, 1761–1765
Petrović-Njegoš, Mirko, 834
Peucestas, 441
Phalangists, 2, 20, 283, 745, 757, 760, 761, 951, 1090–1091
Phanes of Halicarnassus, 972
Phantom Fury, Operation, 424, 597, 605
Phantom Phoenix, Operation, 995
Phantom Strike, Operation, **994–995**
Phantom Thunder, Operation, 994–995, **995–996**, 996

Pharnabazus, 518, **996–997**
Pharnaces II, 827
Pharnaces of Pontus, 269, 414, 1451
Pharsalus, Battle of, 268, 1003
Phase Line Bullet, Battle of, **997–998**
Phélypeaux, Antoine Le Picard de, 30
Philataeru of Pergamum, 413
Philip (son of Baldwin II of Constantinople), 200, 299
Philip, Emperor (Philip Arabus), 477, 961
Philip I of France, 234, 290
Philip II (king of Macedonia), 53, 54, 148
Philip II of Macedon, 105, 341–342, 413, 478, 779, 973
Philip II of Spain, 764–765, 847
Philip III Arrhidaeus, 358
Philip III of Macedon, 357, 358
Philip IV of France, 113
Philip of Courtenay, 299
Philip of Eu, 885
Philip of Flanders, 835
Philip of Montfort, 158, 1205
Philip of Swabia, 238, 521
Philip the Arab, 1112, 1154
Philip the Bold, 885
Philip V of Macedon, 110–111, 361, 973, 974, 1017, 1242, 1444
Philippe de Mézières, on the fall of Alexandria, 1548–1550
Philippe II Augustus, King of France, 28, 197, 238, 313, 314, 315–316, 491, 520, 653, 665–666, 674, 764, **998–1000**, 1065, 1512, 1513, 1515
Philippe of Alsace, 999
Philippi, Battle of, 30
Philippines, 615
Philomelion, Battle of, 264, **1000–1001**
Philotas, 357
Phocas, 263, 521
Phoenicia, 272, **1001**
   and Cyprus, 321
   and Israel (map), 860 BCE, 1002
   See also Lebanon
Phoenix, Battle of, 257
Phraates IV, 1072
Phrataphernes, 357
Picot, François-Georges, 620, 1225, 1227
Piestewa, Lori, 872–873
Pillar of Defense, Operation, 460–461, 500. *See also* Gaza War of 2012
Pineau, Christian, 1213
Piruz (Seljuk commander), 109
Pissouthnes (Persian governor of Sardis), 340
Pius II (pope), 1545, 1551
Pius V (pope), 764, 1586, 1589
Pius XII (pope), 528
Piyale Pasha, 328
Plataea, Battle of, 339, 483, 861, 1342
Pleistarchus, 359
Pleven, Siege of, 1083

Plevna, Siege of, 917
PLF. *See* Palestine Liberation Front (PLF)
PLFLP-GC. *See* Popular Front for the Liberation of Palestine General Command (PFLP-GC)
PLO. *See* Palestine Liberation Organization (PLO)
Plocnik, Battle of, 205
PNA. *See* Palestinian National Authority (PNA)
Poalei Zion, 509
Podolski Kamieniec, 931
Pogroms, 505, 651
Poland
   anti-Semitism in, 652
   peace treaty with Ottoman Empire, 1382
Poland-Lithuania, 930–931
Political Committee for the Arab League, 120
Polyaenus (Macedonian general), 972
Polycrates, 272
Polyperchon, 105, 358
Pompeius Magnus, Gnaius (Pompey the Great), 227, 267–268, 268, 288, 307, 308, 683, 943, **1003**, 1071, 1135, 1451
Pons (count of Tripoli), 38, 1271
Pontius Pilate, 670, 943
Pontus, **1003–1004**
Popular Crusade, 310. *See also* Crusades in the Holy Land, Christian, First Crusade
Popular Front for the Liberation of Bahrain, 1008
Popular Front for the Liberation of Oman, 1008
Popular Front for the Liberation of Palestine (PFLP), 231, 232, 336, 403, 559, 756, 951, 952, **1004–1006**
Popular Front for the Liberation of Palestine General Command (PFLP-GC), 2, 20, 770, 951, 952, 1004, **1006–1007**
Popular Front for the Liberation of the Occupied Arabian Gulf (PFLOAG), 355, 905, **1007–1008**
Popular Union of Kurdistan (PUK), 102
Portuguese Colonial Wars in Arabia, **1008–1009**
Porus (king of the Punjab), 58, 357
Poson, Battle of, 258, 259
Potemkin, Gregory, 1080
Pothinus, 288
Potter, Richard, 1012
Powell, Colin L., 87, 604, 982, 987, 1133
Požarevac, Treaty of, 968
Praaspa, siege of, 1072
Praying Mantis, Operation, 369, 570, 574, **1009–1010**, 1011
Préveza, Battle of, 514, 1583–1586
Priam, king of Troy, 1275
Prime Chance, Operation, **1010–1011**
Primus, Antonius, 1315
Prisca (wife of Diocletian), 442
Priscus, Statius, 1073
Probus, 263
Procopius of Caesarea, 1472

Protective Edge, Operation, 456, 461–462, 500, 630, 808, 880. *See also* Gaza War of 2014
Provide Comfort, Operation, 14, 894, **1011–1014**
Prusias I of Bithynia, 414
Prusias II of Bithynia, 974
Pruth, Treaty of, **1014**, 1079
Pruth River Campaign, 916
Psamameticus I (Pharaoh), 778
Psammetichus III (pharaoh), 272–273, 387
Psamtik III (Psammenitus), 972
Ptolemaeus, son of Thrasea, 1240
Ptolemaic Kingdom, 620, **1014**
Ptolemies, 110
Ptolemy Ceraunus, 307, 359–360, **1015**, 1135
Ptolemy Epigonus, 1239
Ptolemy I Soter/Sotar, 105–106, 322, 349, 356, 357, 358, 359, 383, 388, 413, 561–562, 973, 1014, **1015**, 1063, 1135, 1239, 1241
Ptolemy II Philadelphus, 359, 360, 1015, **1016**, 1239
Ptolemy III Euergetes, 1014, **1016**, 1017, 1134, 1239–1240
Ptolemy IV, 110, 360
Ptolemy IV Philopator, **1016**, 1049, 1134, 1240
Ptolemy Philaelphus, 289
Ptolemy V Epiphanes, 110, 387, **1016–1017**, 1134, 1240
  inscription at the Temple of Philae, Egypt, 1443–1445
Ptolemy VI, 53
Ptolemy VI Philometor, 360, **1017**, 1241
Ptolemy VIII Euergetes, 360
Ptolemy XII, 268–269
Ptolemy XII Auletes, 288
Ptolemy XIII, 269, 288, 1451
Ptolemy XIV, 288, 1452
Ptolemy XV (Caesarian), 269, 288–289
Publius (son of Crassus), 276
Publius Aelius Hadrianus Afer, 494
Publius Aelius Trainus Hadrinaus. *See* Hadrian, Emperor
Putin, Vladimir, 379, 555, 571
Puzur-Ashur I (Assyrian King), 159
Puzur-Ashur III (Assyrian king), 159
Puzur-Sin (Assyrian Akkadian governor), 176
Pyramids, Battle of the (Embabeh), 15, 386, **1017–1018**
  Bonaparte's letter to the Directory in Paris, 1603–1604
Pyrrhus of Epirus, 350, 359, 779

Qaboos bin Said al-Said, 355, 905, 906, **1019–1020**
Qadi Iyad, 1102
Qadisiyya, Battle of, **1020**
Qajar, Ahmad Shah, 1062
Qajar dynasty, 39–40, 409, 564, 929, 976
Qalaqun, Sultan, 792

Qalawun, Sultan, 29, 235, 530, 795, **1020–1021**, 1272
Qansuh al-Ghawri, 803
Qara Arslan (Artuqid ruler), 150
Qara Khitay, 1140
Qara Qoyunlu, 183
Qarachaqay Khan, 1591
Qaradawi, Yusuf al-, 430, 431
Qarakhanids, 72, 73, 790
Qarmat, Hamdan, 1021
Qarmatians, 659, **1021–1022**
Qasim, Abdul Karim (Abd al-Karim), 140, 195, 421, 586–587, 726, 730, 899, 990, **1022–1023**, 1106
Qasre-Shirin/Qasr-e-Shirin (Zuhab), Treaty of, 409, 1381
Qassam, Izz al-Din al-, **1023–1024**
Qassam Brigades, 462
Qassim, Abd al-Karim, 536
Qatar, 487–488, 489, 553, 602, 908, **1024–1027**, 1298
  Battle of Khafji, 698–699
  and Hamas, 500
  under Khalifa bin Hamad al-Thani, 1259
  map, 1025
  and the Persian Gulf War, 1259
  relations with other Arab countries, 1026–1027, 1121
  relations with U.S., 1026
Qawuqji, Fawzi al-, 121, 126, **1027–1028**
Qibya Massacre, **1028–1029**, 1161
Qibya Raid, 240
Qilij Arslan I of Rum, 335, 364, 437, 799, 897, **1029**, 1076
Qilij Arslan II of Rum, 335, 862, **1029–1030**, 1077, 1501
Qizilbash, 617–618
Qub al-Din, 897
Qubilqi Khan, 534
Quick Strike, Operation, 493
Quietude, 251
Quinctius Flamininus, 1241
Quintillus, 165
Quran, 848, **1030–1032**
  and jihad, 672–673
  Maududi's commentary on, 810
Quraysh tribe, 1480
Qurna, Battle of, **1032–1033**
Qurqumaz (son of Fakhr ad-Din), 364
Qutb, Sayyid Ibrahim Husayn Shadhili, 73, 611, **1033–1034**
Qutb al-Din (ad-Din) Malik-Shah, 437, 505
Qutlumish, 72
Qutuz (sultan of Egypt), 317, 791, 832, 833, 1539
Quuz (sultan), 217, 667, 793–794
Quward, 72
Quwatli, Shukri al-, **1034–1035**, 1228

Raab River, Battle of, 714
Raad (son of Zayid), 421

Rabaa Massacre, 379, 1185
Rabat Summit, **1037–1038**
Rabban Sawma, 548
Rabbo Yasser Abed, 464
Rabin, Yitzhak, 81, 211, 269, 270, 403–404, 540, 557, 636, 879, 960, 961, **1038–1039**, 1069, 1338
  last speech, 1732–1733
  and the Oslo Accords, 910–912
Radwan, Ismail, 460
Rafah Tunnels, **1039–1041**
Rafi Parti, 623
Raful Youth Project, 398
Ram Hormuz, Battle of, 857
Rama, First Battle of, 312
Ramadan, Operation, 580
Ramadan Revolution, 587
Ramadan War. *See* Yom Kippur War
Ramadi, Fall of, **1041**
Ramadi, First Battle of, **1041–1043**
Ramadi, Recapture of, **1043–1044**
Ramadi, Second Battle of, **1044–1046**
Ramesses I (pharaoh), 383
Ramesses II (pharaoh), 383
Ramesses II the Great, 687–688, **1046–1048**
Ramla, First Battle of, **1048**
Ramla, Second Battle of, 312, **1048–1049**
Ramla, Third Battle of, **1049**
Ramon, Ilan, 909
Rantisi, Abd al-Aziz, 498, 499, 560
Raphia, Battle of, 110, 360, 1014, 1016, **1049–1050**
Ras Khaymah, 1297, 1298. *See also* United Arab Emirates (UAE)
Rashid, Harun al-, 5
  at war with the Byzantine Empire, 1490–1492
Rashid, Muhammad Al, 1126–1127
Rashid, Muhammad ibn Aballah Al, 1126
Rashid Ali al-Gaylani Revolt, 195
Rashidi, Talal al-, 1126
Rashidun Caliphate, 857
Ratess, Menachem, 1309
Rawi, Ayad Futahih al-, 727, 731
Rawi Ayad Futayh al-, 997
Rayan, Nizar, 459
Raymond (son of Bohemund III of Antioich), 158
Raymond II of Tripoli, 158, 201, 202, 1271
Raymond III of Tripoli, 82, 144, 202, 203, 308, 490, 505, 505–506, 512, 665, 835, 1271, 1272
Raymond of Antioch, 371, 665, 776
Raymond of Poitiers, 106–107, 249, 551
Raymond of Saint-Gilles, 151, 234, 415, 472, 663, 1250, 1271
Raymond of Toulouse, 311
Raymond of Tripoli, 313
Raymond-Roupen, 107
Rayy, Battle of, 181
Raz, Zeev, 909

Razami, Abdullah Ayedh al-, 532
Razi Abu Hatim al-, 1021
Reading (Lord), 773
Reagan, Ronald W., 277, 367, 567, 569, 574, 575–577, 578, 580, 588, 635–636, 706, 746, 754, 755, 887, 891, 1050
  address to the nation on Lebanon and Grenada, 1716–1719
  letter to Thomas P. O'Neill on the destruction of an Iranian jetliner, 1724–1725
Reagan Plan, **1050–1051**, 1172
Red Sea, **1051**
Reform Judaism and Zionism, **1051–1052**
Regime Change, Iraq War, **1052–1053**
Reginald of Saint Valery, 505
Rejection Front, 757
Religious Sites in the Middle East, Christian, **1053–1054**
Religious Sites in the Middle East, Jewish, **1054–1055**
Religious Sites in the Middle East, Muslim, **1055–1057**
Remembrance of Muharram, 691
Republic of Cyprus. *See* Cyprus
Republic of Turkey. *See* Turkey
Republic of Yemen, 35. *See also* Yemen
Republican Guard, Iraq, **1058**, 1316
Resaena (Resaina), Battle of, 477
Rescid Mehmed Pasa (Grand Vizier), 391, 712–713
Reserve Mobile Force, 125
Reshef, Amnon, 287
Resheff, Yehuda, 1190
Resht, Treaty of, 447, **1058–1059**, 1203–1204
Revisionist Zionism, 607, **1059–1061**
Revolutionary Command Council, 867
Revolutionary Guard Corps, 567
Revolutionary Islamic Council, 573
Reynald, lord of Marash, 371
Reynald of Antioch, 250
Reynald of Châtillon, 107, 203, 312, 490, 512–513
Reza Khan, 977, 1062. *See also* Reza Shah Pahlavi I
Reza Pahlavi II (shah of Iran), 62. *See also* Muhammad Reza Pahlavi
Reza Shah Pahlavi I, 190–192, 466, 531, 565, **1062–1063**
  and the Roosevelt administration, 1676–1679
Rhahzadh (Persian general), 263
Rhame, Thomas G., 892
Rhodes, Ottoman capture of, 1581–1583
Rhodes, Demetrius's Siege of, **1063–1064**
Rhodes, Suleiman's Siege of, **1064–1065**
Rice, Condoleezza, 571, 751
Richard I, King, **1065**
Richard I (the Lionheart; king of England), 28, 143–144, 168, 197, 250, 313, 314–315, 322–323, 491, 520, 653–654, 665–666, 763, 764, 945, 999, 1101, 1510, 1511–1512
Richard of Beaumont, 450

Richard of Cornwall, 450, 667, **1066**
  to Baldwin of Reviers, abbot of Beaulieu, and Robert, Clerk, 1528–1531
Richard of the Principate, 200, 370
Ridaniya, Battle of, 1577
Ridda (Riddah) Wars, 65, 856, **1066–1067**, 1482–1483
Ridwan of Aleppo, 312
Right of Return, Palestinian, 269, **1067–1068**
Ritchie, Neil N., 165, 812
Ritti-Marduk (Kassite chieftain), 1420
Riva, Giacomo da, 1314
Riwan of Aleppo (son of Tutush I), 108, 212, 693–694, 1076, 1290
Riyadh, 1322
Riyadh, Mahmud, 270
Rizi, Mustafa. *See* Ataturk, Mustafa Kemal
Road Map to Peace, 4, 455, 456
Robeck John de, 338, 443
Robert, Patriarch of Jerusalem, letter to the prelates of England and France, 1533–1535
Robert Bruce, 372
Robert of Artois, 316–317
Robert of Constantinople, 675
Robert of Courtenay, 298
Robert of Normandy, 151, 415
Robertson, William, 825
Roger I of Sicily, 199, 233
Roger II of Sicily, 250, 294, 438, 519
Roger of Antioch, 149, 200, 201, 370
Roger of Les Moulins, 308
Roger of Salerno, 38, 106, 547
Rogers, William P., 875, 1068
Rogers Plan, **1068–1069**
Rognvald Kali Kolsson **1069–1070**
Rolling Thunder, Operation, 980
Roma Peoples, 525, 528
Roman Catholic Church. *See also* Crusades in the Holy Land, Christian; *specific popes by name*
Roman Empire, 162
  363 Battle of Ctesiphon, 318–319
  and the Bar Kochba Revolt, 212–213
  and the Battle of Beth-Horon, 226–227
  and Macedonia, 361
  under Marcus Aurelius, 802–803
  wars with Parthian Empire, 1071–1073
Roman Exile, 620
Romani, Battle of, 716, 853, **1070–1071**
Romanos IV Diogenes, 248, 264, 800
Roman-Parthian Wars, **1071–1073**
Roman-Sassanid Wars, **1073–1075**
Roman-Seleucid War, 784–785. *See also* Syrian-Roman War
Romanus Diogenes, 72–73
Romanus II, 260
Romanus III, 260
Romanus Lecapenus, 258
Rommel, Erwin Johannes Eugen, 44, 125, 165, 321, 819–820, 820, 836, 901, **1075–1076**
  and the First Battle of El-Alamein, 398–400
  and the Second Battle of El-Alamein, 401

Roosevelt, Franklin D., 545, 565, 668, 1117, 1336
Roosevelt administration, and Shah Reza Pahlavi, 1676–1679
Rosetta Stone, 387
Rotberg, Roi, Dayan's eulogy for, 1700
Rothschild, Lord, letter from Balfour, 1662
Rouhani, Hassan, 571, 572
Roxana (wife of Alexander III), 357, 358, 359
Royal Jordanian Army, 126
Rtischev, Nikolai, 489
Rudolf II (Habsburg emperor), 1381
Rukh, Shah, 694, 976
Rukin/Rukn al-Din Sulayman Shah II, 158, 214, 831, 1077
Rum, Sultanate of, 62, 150, 265, 334, 335, 364, 440, 715–716, 826, 832, 862, 882–883, 896, 897, 914, 1000, 1029–1030, **1076–1078**, 1269, 1276–1277, 1531
Rumsfeld, Donald, 15, 21–22, 436, 602, 1109, 1132
Rumyantsev, Pyotr A., 1079, 1080
Rundstedt, Karl Rudolf Gerd von, 1076
Ruppin, Arthur, 347–348
Rusk, Dean, 503
Russia
  1700 Treaty of Constantinople, 302
  1720 Treaty of Constantinople, 302
  Achaemenid invasion of, 25
  annexation of Crimea by, 354
  and the Battle of Chesma, 286–287
  Bolshevik Revolution, 564
  and the Convention of Balta Liman, 208
  and the Crimean War, 917
  Erzurum Offensive, 410–412
  intervention in Syria, 156
  invasion of the Crimea by, 925
  Jews in, 651
  military collapse of, 446
  Ottoman alliance with, 391
  relations with Egypt, 379
  Russo-Ottoman Wars, 194
  and the Syrian Civil War, 614
  treaties with Ottoman Empire, 535, 658, 717, 722, 774, 1203
  treaty with Persia, 447
  war in the Caucasus, 278–280
  war with Persia, 489
  See also Soviet Union
Russian Revolutions, 978
Russo-French War, 432
Russo-Iranian War (1826–1828), 7, 489
Russo-Ottoman Wars, 925, 929, **1078–1083**
  Crimean War (1853–1856), 1081
  early history, 1078
  Treaty of Nissa, 890
  War of 1676–1681, 194, 1078
  War of 1686–1700, 1078
  War of 1710–1711, 37, 1014
  War of 1711 (the Pruth Campaign), 1078–1079
  War of 1735–1739, 1079

War of 1768–1774, 64, 280, 286–287, 916, 1079
War of 1787–1791, 281, 1079–1080
War of 1806–1812, 1080
War of 1828–1829, 37, 343, 916, 1080–1081
War of 1877–1878, 835, 913, 1081–1083, 1109, 1111, 1147
Russo-Persian Wars, 1083–1084, **1083–1087**, 1253
  Conflict of 1911, 1086
  War of 1722–1723, 1084
  War of 1796, 1084–1085
  War of 1804–1813, 347, 432, 489, 929, 1085, 1612
  War of 1825–1829, 1085–1086
  War of 1826–1828, 1253
Russo-Turkish War, 11, 786, 1278, 1615
Rustam Khan (Georgian general), 489–490
Rustem, 1020
Ruweisat Ridge, Battles of. *See* El Alamein, First Battle of

Sa'ad al-Dawla al-Qawa-misi, 1048
Saadabad Pact, **1089**
Saadi, Abdul Wahab al-, 424
Sabah, Ahmad al-Jaber al-, 1125
Sabah, Jabir III al-Ahmad al-Jabir al-, 729, 731
Sabah, Mubarak al-, 725
Sabah, Salim al-Mubarak al-, 1125
Sabbah, Hasan, 619
Sabbri Khalil al-Banna. *See* Abu Nidal
Sabilla, Battle of, 1117
Sabina (wife of Hadrian), 494
Sabra and Shatila Massacre, 761–762, 954, **1089–1091**
Sa'd, Abdullah ibn, 857
Sadat, Ahmed, 1005
Sadat, Anwar, **1091–1092**
  action against PLO, 326
  and the Arab League, 1165
  assassination of, 10, 378, 845, 1092
  and the Camp David Accords, 124, 223, 273–275, 628, 632–633, 1153, 1166
  and the Cold War, 293
  coup attempt against, 64
  and the Free Officers Organization, 874
  making Islam state religion, 373
  Nobel Peace Prize, 223
  peace treaty with Israel, 623–633
  Soviets expelled by, 379, 1091
  visit to Jerusalem, 124, 273, 628, 633
  war with Libya, 767–768
  and the Yom Kippur War, 130, 157, 213–214, 377–378, 626–627, 819, 1152
Saddam Line, Persian Gulf War, **1092–1093**
Sadeh, Yitzhak, 960, **1093**
Sadr, Muqtada al-, 2, **1093–1095**
Sadr City, Battle of, 591, 597, **1095–1096**
Sadr Movement (Tayyar al-Sadr), 869
Sadriyun, 1095
Safavid Dynasty, 564, 865, **1096–1098**

Safavid Empire, 83, 191, 219, 608–609, 617–618, 1381
  in Afghanistan, 608–609
  and the Battle of Chaldiran, 281
  treaty with Ottoman Empire, 875–876
  wars with Mughals, 847
  See also Iran
Safavid Persian Army, 489
Safi, Shah of Safavid Persia, 1381
Saguy, Yehoshua, 1091
Said bin Taimir, Sultan, 354–355
Said Halam Pasha, 878
Saif al-Dawla, 259–260, **1098–1099**
Sakarya, Battle of the, 164, **1099–1100**, 1281
Sala al-Din Al-Sabagh, 421
Saladin (Salah-al-din Yusuf ibn Ayyub), **1100–1101**
  alliance with Andronikos I Komnenos, 280, 1077
  alliances with, 1030, 1065, 1077
  in Antioch, 106
  and the Artuqids, 150
  and the Ayyubid Dynasty, 167–168, 312, 675, 1100
  Battle of Arsuf, 143–144
  Battle of Hattin, 313, 512–513, 663, 945
  Battle of Jaffe, 653–654
  Battle of Montgisard, 203, 835, 19
  in Damsacus, 202–203
  conquest of the Fatimids, 82, 897–898
  invasion of Galilee, 490
  invasion of Jerusalem, 107, 313, 491, 520, 665, 945, 999
  invasion of Palestine, 312
  siege of Acre, 28, 313–314, 764, 999, 1065
  Treaty of Jaffe, 654
  in Tripoli, 1272
  and the Zangids, 203, 1100, 1
Salafi jihadism, 75
Salafism, **1101–1103**
Salama, Abu, 6
Salamah, Hasan, 863
Salamis, Battle of, 26, 148, 339, 349, 482, 765, 1437
Saleh, Ali Abdullah/Abdallah, 136, 609, **1103–1105**, 1350, 1352, 1359
Salem, Sheikh, 1125
Salim, Mohammad Sayyid, 447
Sallal, Abdullah al-/as-, 503, 1117, 1349, 1355–1356
Salman bin Abdulaziz, 1120–1121
Salman the Persian, 49
Salomon, Gershon, 47
Salu, Fawzi, 1170
Sam Mirza (Shah Safi), 9
Samaria, 942
Samaritans, 942
Samarra, Battle, 762
Samawah, Battle of, **1105**
Samita Incident, **1105–1107**
Samoilovich Ivan, 1078

Sampson, Nikos, 325
Samsu-Ditana (king of Babylon), 177
Samsu-iluna (Assyrian king), 176, 502
Samu Raid, West Bank, **1107**
Samuel (Tsar of Bulgaria), 214–215
Samuel, Herbert, 946
San Germano, Treaty of, 439
San Remo Agreement, 586
San Remo Conference, 620, 811, 937, **1109**, 1226
San Stefano, Treaty of, 11, 835, 1083, **1109–1110**
Sanchez, Ricardo S., 22, 851, **1108–1109**
Sandjak of Novibazar, 208
Sanjar (Seljuk sultan), 335, 1139
Sanusiyya, 673
Saphadin (Sayf al-Din al-Adil), 168
Saphrax (Ostrogoth chieftain), 36
Sapientza, Battle of, 1313
Sapor, king of Persia, 1467
Sara bint Ahad al-Sudairi, 543
Sarab, Battle of, 1590–1593
Sarab, Treaty of, 933
Saracen, **1110**
Sarang of Ganja, 468
Sardinia, 917
Sardur of Urartu, 1264
Sargon, 1406–1407
Sargon II (Assyrian king), 161, 176, 620, 822
Sargon of Akkad, 41, **1110–1111**
  The Nippur Inscription, 1405–1406
Sargon the Great, 159, 822
Sarikamish, Battle of, **1111–1112**
Sarmatians, 494
Sarus River, Battle of, 521
Sasan (grandfather of Ardashir I), 138, 967
Sassanid (Sassanian) Empire, 59, 138–139, 162, 318, 563, 585, 708, 856, **1112–1114**, 1486
  war with Byzantine Empire, 263–264
Sattar Buzaigh al-Rishawi, Abd al-, 90
Saud, Abd al-Aziz ibn Abd al-Rahman al-. *See* Ibn Saud, King
Saud, Abd al-Rahman ibn Faisal al-, 534–544
Saud, Abdul Aziz al-, 12
Saud, Abdul Aziz bin Muhammad bin, 1116
Saud, Abdullah bin, 786
Saud, Crown Prince, 1128
Saud, Faisal bin Turki bin Abullah Al, 1126
Saud, House of, 76, 1114, 1117, 1118, 1124, 1126, 1127
Saud, King of Saudi Arabia, 545
Saud, Muhammad bin, 1116
Saudi Arabia, 12, 193, 487–488, 489, 509, 553, 659, **1114–1122**
  Battle of Khafji, 698–699
  climate of, 291
  map, 1115
  Operation Hard Surface, 503
  Palestinian refugees in, 417
  and the PLO, 954
  relations with Great Britain, 544
  relations with U.S., 545, 1117–1118

Saudi King as Custodian of the Two Holy Mosques, **1124–1125**
Saudi-Hashemite War, **1122–1124**
Saudi-Kuwaiti Neutral Zone, 726
Saudi-Kuwaiti War, **1125**
Saudi-Ottoman War, **1125–1126**
Saudi-Rashidi Wars, **1126–1128**
Saudi-Yemeni War, **1128–1129**
SAVAK (Sazeman-e Ettelaat va Amniyat-e Keshvar), 566
Sayeret Matkal, 879
Sayf al-Adl, 806
Sayf al-Din, 897
Sayf al-Din Ghazi II, 897
Sazeman-e Ettelaat va Amniyat-e Keshvar (SAVAK), 566
Sazonov, Sergei D., 1225
Sazonov-Paléologue Agreement, 1225
Scathe Mean Operation, **1129–1130**
Schlieffen, Alfred von, 476
Schwarzkopf, H. Norman, Jr., 87, 548, 589, 600–601, 700, 732, 982, 983, 986, 987, 1130–1132, **1130–1132**, 1132, 1253, 1321
Scipio, Lucius Cornelius, 784, 1242
Scorpion, Operation, **1132–1134**
Scroggs, Kenneth, 77
Scutari, Convention of, 834
Scythians, 272, 329
Sealand dynasty, 177
Seale, Patrick, 700
Sebastian Veniero, describing the Battle of Lepanto, 1589–1590
Sebastiani, 35–36
Sébastiani, Horace-François, 98
Sebastopolis (Sevastopol), Battle of, 858, 917
   Gortschakoff's account, 1620–1623
Second (al-Aqsa) Intifada, 45, 138, 270, 417, 455, 629, 954, 958, 1328
   Battle of Jenin, 659–660
Second Aliya, 509, 946
Second Baron's War, 1066
Second Coalition, 16
Second Council of Lyons, 252, 547, 826
Second Crusade, 107, 201, 249, 294, 371, 437, 550–551, 664, 775–776, 798, 896, 1000, 1076, 1502
   Battle of Hattin, 512–513
Second Dacian War, 494
Second Edirne Incident, 687
Second Egyptian-Ottoman War, 27
Second Italo-Ethiopian War, 284
Second Jewish-Roman War, 944
Second Lebanon War, 629. *See also* Lebanon War
Second Macedonian War, 111, 973, 1241
Second Palaeologan Civil War, 253
Second Peloponnesian War, 38, 517, 996
Second Persian War, Battle of Mycale, 861–862
Second Russo-Turkish War, 616
Second Syrian-Egyptian War, 1016, 1134

Second Tetrarchy, 442
Second War of the Diadochi, 358, 441
Sedeh, Yitzhak, 69
Seekt, Major General von, letter from Otto Liman von Sanders, 1664–1667
Sefi, Shah, 933
Seia Herennia Sallustia Barbia Orbiana, 58
Seleucid Empire, 110–113, 162, 359, 360, 413, 620, 683, 684, 782, 822, 1014, **1134–1135**
Seleucus, 105–106, 307, 358, 358–359, 359–360
Seleucus I Nicator, 110, 349, 561, 779, 973, 974, **1135**, 1239
   Appaian of Alexandria's description of, 1441–1442
Seleucus II, 112–113
Seleucus II Callinicus, 1016, 1134, 1239–1240
Seleucus III, 110, 111
Seleucus III Ceraunus, 1134
Seleucus IV Philopator, 1134
Selim I, Sultan, 49, 281, 364, 793, 803, 822, 915, 931–932, 933, 945, **1135–1136**, 1577, 1579, 1581
   poem on his conquests, 1581
Selim II, Sultan, 328, 656, 846, 1586
Selim III, Sultan, 7, 98, 385, 386, 389, 657, 658, 687, 816, 916, 1080, **1136–1137**, 1313
   letters to Shah Ismail I of Persia, 15672–1575
Seljuk Dynasty, **1137–1141**
Seljuk Turks
   and the Abbasid Caliphate, 5–6, 945
   in Antioch, 106–109
   Battle of al-Sannabra, 79–80
   Battle of Bapheus, 210
   Battle of Erzincar, 408
   Battle of Harran, 507
   Battle of Manzikert, 468, 800
   Battle of Myriokephalon, 862
   Battle of Philomelion, 1000
   and the Byzantine Empire, 61, 107, 264–265, 309, 335, 798–799, 862, 1077
   vs. the Crusaders, 43, 79–80, 106–109, 151, 199–201, 202, 290, 294, 309–311, 312, 428, 438, 551, 663, 810, 945, 1030, 1497, 1498, 1502
   decline of, 790, 795
   and the Nizaris, 619
   and the Ottomans, 210
   in Syria, 1289
   in Turkey, 127
   wars with the Georgians, 467–468
   Wars of Succession, 1141
   Urban's call to liberate Holy Lands from, 290
   wars with Byzantine Empire, 264–265
   See also Alp Arslan; Karbugha; Rum, Sultanate of, Saladin
Seljuk War of Succession, **1141**
Seniavin, Dimitri, 99
Sennacherib, 161, 822, 942, **1141–1142**
Senussi, 647
Sephardic Judaism, 510, 514–515, **1142–1144**

September 11, 2001, Attacks on the United States, **1144–1146**
Seqenenre Tao, 541
Serbia, 206, 773, 917, 1147, 1279, 1310
Serbian-Ottoman War, **1147–1148**
Serbs, 205
Sese Seko, Mobutu, 891
Seti I (pharaoh), 1046
Settlements, Israeli, **1148–1149**. *See also* Gaza Strip; Golan Heights; West Bank
Seuthes II of Thrace, 1341
Sevastopol, Siege of, 1081, 1278
Seventh Crusade, 169, 776–778, 1276, 1535
73 Easting, Battle of, **1149–1150**
Severus, Alexander, 139, 440, 890. *See also* Alexander Severus, Roman Emperor
Severus, Septimius, 58, 902, 967, 1073, **1146–1147**
Sèvres, Treaty of, 60, 142, 484, 509, 718, 739, 843, 921, 990, **1150–1151**, 1213, 1281
   Ataturk's objection to, 1671–1672
Seymour, Frederick Beauchamp Paget, 59, 93
Sfeir, Nasrallah, 736
Shabab Mu'minin, 532
Shadmi, Issachar, 688–689
Shagmar, Meir, 516
Shah Jahan, 847
Shah Safi (Sam Mirza), 9, 1098
Shahahshah, al-Afdal, 1048
Shahin (Persian general), 263
Shahin, Atif abd al-Ghaffar, 447
Shahrbaraz, General, 1114
Shahrvaraz (Persian general), 521, 889
Shakur, Yusuf bin Raghib, **1152**
Shalev, Aryeh, 40
Shalikashvilil, John M. D., 1012
Shalit, Gilad, 457, 458, 650, 808
Shallah, Ramadan Abdullah Mohammad, 955, 956, **1152–1153**, 1170
Shalmaneser I (Assyrian king), 160
Shalmaneser III (Assyrian king), 161, 177
Shalom, Avraham, 637
Shamash-shum-ukin (brother of Ashurbanipal), 153, 162
Shamir, Shlomo, 738
Shamir, Yitzhak "Michael," 516, 628, 771, 879, 909, **1153–1154**
Shamshi-Adad I (Assyrian king), 159, 177, 501
Shanab, Ismail Abu, 499
Shapur I the Great, 138–139, 477, 1073–1074, 1112, **1154–1156**, 1308, 1376, 1467
Shapur II the Great, 305–306, 318, 685, 1074, **1156–1157**
   correspondence with Emperor Constantius, 1470–1472
Sharett, Moshe, 412
Sharia, **1157–1160**
Sharif Hussein, 1122, 1662
Sharif Nasir, 332

Sharifial Family, personal notes of T. E. Lawrence on, 1657–1658
Sharjah, 1297. *See also* United Arab Emirates (UAE)
Sharm El Sheikh, **1160–1161**
Sharon, Ariel, **1161–1163**
   as colonel, 1214
   as defense minister, 745–746, 753, 759–762, 953–954, 1090–1091
   as general, 32–33, 240, 287–288, 829, 1004, 1028, 1176, 1190, 1363
   as prime minister, 31, 223, 346, 455–457, 560, 629, 636, 902, 903, 957, 958
   speech at the United Nations Assembly, 1757–1758
   stroke, 629, 903, 958
   visit to Temple Mount, 45, 270, 558, 629, 1055, 1328
   and war with Lebanon, 759–762
Shas, 505
Shatt al-Arab Waterway, **1163–1164**
Shaw Commission, **1164–1165**, 1330
Shawar, 82, 897
Shaybani, Muhammad, 618
Shazly, Saad el-, **1165–1166**
Sherley Robert, 1097
Sheshbazzar, 942
Shia Islam, **1166–1170**
Shihab, Fuad, 282, 750
Shihada, Salah, 498, 499
Shin Bet, 637
Shinseki, Eric, 602
Shiqaqi, Fathi, 955–956, **1170**
Shirkuh (uncle of Saladin), 82, 167, 168, 429, 897, 1100
Shirley, Robert, 8
Shishakli, Adib al-, **1170–1171**, 1228
Shkolnik, Levi. *See* Eshkol, Levi
Shoah. *See* Holocaust
Shochat, Israel, 509
Shomron, Dan, 403, **1171–1172**
Shoshana, Operation, 1028–1029
Shukeiri, Ahmad, 950, 952
Shultz, George P., 1172–1173
Shultz Plan, **1172–1173**
Shura Council, 523
Shuster, William Morgan, 1086
Shutruk-Nahhunte I (Elamite king), 160, 177
Shu-turul (Akkadian king), 176
Sibilah, Battle of, 547
Sibyl/Sibylla (Queen of Jerusalem; sister of Baldwin IV), 203, 490, 491, 665, 666, 1509
Sibyrtius, 357
Sicarii, 670
Sicilian Vespers, 826
Sicily, 427
Sidky/Sidqi, Mamoud/Mamud, 634, 1189
Siffin, Battle of, 89, 703, 845, **1173–1174**
Sigismund of Hungary, 261, 262, 885–886, 927
Sigurd, king of Norway, 1070

Silahdar Damat Ali Pasha, 1314
Silahdar Yusuf Pasha, 1314
Silva, Lucius Flavius, 807
Silvestre, Pierre Jean Pierre Baptiste, 878
Simon bar Giora, 668, 671
Simon Bar Kochba, 212–213
Simon de Montfort, 297, 315, 1066
Simon I of Kartli, 932
Simon Maccabaeus, 943
Sinai, 376
   Multi-National Force in, 850
Sinai Campaign, 86, 93, 242, 402, 454, 702–703, 818, 829
Sinai Campaign of 1916–1917, **1174–1175**
Sinai Campaign of 1956, **1175–1179**
Sinai Disengagement Agreements, 1180
Sinai I and Sinai II Agreements, **1179–1180**
Sinai II Agreement, 470, 830
Sinai Peninsula, 344, **1180–1181**
Singara, Battle of, 1075
Singleton, Mark, 83
Siniora, Fouad, 747
Siniura, Fuad, 116, 868, **1182–1183**
Sin-Muballit (Amorite king), 176, 501
Sinope, Battle of, **1183**
Sin-shar-ishkun (Assyrian king), 162
Sinsharishkun (king of Babylon), 178
Sin-shasr-ishkun (Assyrian king), 173
Sin-shumu-lisihir (king of Babylon), 178
Sipahis, 166
Sirocco, Mehmet, 766
Sisak, Battle of, 206
Sisi, Abdel Fattah el-, 379–380, 392, 839, **1183–1185**
Sistani, Sayyid Ali Hisayn al-, 869, **1186–1187**
Sivas, Declaration of, 920–921
Six-Day War (1967), **1187–1192**
   and the Bar-Lev Line, 213–214
   casualties, 625
   causes of, 117, 454, 644, 785
   chronology, 624, 1179
   consequences of, 32, 35, 70, 115, 124, 129, 155, 156, 223, 396, 417, 505, 511, 625, 950, 965, 1055, 1057, 1117, 1257, 1356
   Egyptian commanders, 64, 86, 128, 785, 165
   and the Gaza Strip, 910
   and the Golan Heights, 674–675, 1148–1149, 1229, 1363
   Iraq's failure to support Arab states, 587
   Israeli air strikes, 633–635
   Israeli commanders, 69, 81, 210, 344, 376, 402, 412, 1038, 161
   and the Jarring mission, 657–658
   map, 1188
   objectives of, 470, 829–830
   and the oil boycott, 704, 907
   Palestinian refugees following, 270–271, 745, 1067
   and the Reagan Plan, 1068–1069
   Syrian commanders, 156, 1152

   and the West Bank, 81, 129, 344, 376, 515, 767, 910, 1148–1149, 1328
Sixth Crusade, 1526
Sixth Syrian-Egyptian War, 384, 388, 1014, 1017
Slav (Bulgarian prince), 298
Slavonia, 925
Smith, William Sidney, 30
Smyrna, 323
Smyrna Crusade, **1193**, 1546–1548
Snaim (Kustinitza), Battle of, 926
Sobieski, Jan (John Sobiesky), 714, 930, 931
Sochat, Manya, 509
Social Democrat Hunchakian Party, 11
Social War, 231, 827
Society of the Muslim Brothers. *See* Muslim Brotherhood
Sofia, Battle of, 214
Sogdianus, 26, 340
Sokollu Mehmed Pasha, 328
Soldiers of Heaven, 869
Solomon (Suleiman), King, 942
Solomon, Operation, 152, 830, 1154
Somalia, 612, 616, 1037
Somers, Luke, 78
Somoza, Anastasio, 891
Sons of Iraq, 90, 605, 606
Sophagasenus (Subhashsena), 110
Sorqaqtani (mother of Hulegu), 534
Sosibius, 1017
Soslani, David, 214
Sotloff, Steven J., 552
Souchon, Wilhelm, 362, 920
South African (Boer) War, 67
South Lebanon Army (SLA), 753, 757, **1195–1197**
South Yemen Civil War, 35, **1197**
Southern Watch, Operation, 350, **1193–1195**
Soviet Union
   arms deal with Egypt, 393, 454
   and the Cold War, 292–293
   invasion of Afghanistan by, 277
   occupation of Afghanistan by, 612
   relations with Iraq, 536
   relations with Saudi Arabia, 1117
   and the Suez Crisis, 397
   treaties with Turkey, 1289
   and World War II, 1337
   and the Yom Kippur War, 627
   See also Russia
Spahbod Merena, 318
Spain
   Muslim conquest of, 859
   Reconquista of, 309, 859
Spanish Inquisition, 114
Spartacus, 307, 350
Spear, Operation, 1201
Special Night Squads, 131, **1197–1198**
Special Republican Guards, 186, **1198–1199**. *See also* Republican Guard
Spector, Yiftah, 909

Speicher Massacre. *See* Camp Speicher Massacre
Spercherios, Battle of, 215
Spring of Youth, Operation, 210, 336
St. James Palace Conference, 773–774
St. Petersburg, Treaty of, 1084, **1203–1204**
St. Sabas, War of, **1205–1206**
Stalin, Joseph, 565
Stalinism, 505
Stalker, Foster, 99
Standard Oil Company of California, 191–192
Stark incident, 569, 574, 581, 588, **1199–1200**
Stasanor, 357
Stateira (Alexander's wife), 973
Steel Curtain, Operation, **1200–1201**, 1284
Stefan Dušan of Serbia, 253, 254, 255, 256
Stephanie (daughter of Leon I), 674
Stephen of Blois, 233
  letter to his wife on the Siege of Antioch, 1498–1500
Stephenson, Sir Frederick, letter to William Stephenson, 1627–1628
Stern, Avraham (Yair), 474, 607, 771, **1202–1203**
Stern Gang, 607. *See also* Lohamei Herut Israel
Stewart, Lynne, 10
Stone, Charles, 616
Stone, Michael. *See* Marcus, David Daniel "Mickey"
Stopford, Robert, 27
Storm Brigade, 1007
Strait of Tiran Crisis, **1204–1205**
Straits Convention of 1841, 774
Strategic Petroleum Reserve (SPR), 908
Strategopoulos, Alexios, 882
Straton (king of Sidon), 147
Strez (Vlach prince), 519
Suckling, Maurice, 877
Sudan, 92–93, 391, 395, 467, 673
  Islamic militarism in, 230
Suez Canal, 34, 40, 86, 93, 94, 124, 209, 213, 374, 375, 393, 395, 396, 454, 470, 623, 624–625, 725, 740, 783, 853, 875, 918, 947, 1070, **1206–1207**. *See also* Canal Zone
  nationalization of, 1702–1703
  and the Sinai Campaign of 1956, 1175–1179
Suez Canal and Egypt, World War II Campaigns for Control of, **1208–1211**
Suez Canal Company, 58
Suez Canal, World War I Ottoman Operations against, **1207–1208**
Suez Crisis, 32, 86, 93, 124, 128, 137, 242, 293, 343, 393, 397, 402, 421, 454, 623, 688, 749, 875, 907, **1211–1215**, 1702–1703
Suez War, 964
Sufetula, Battle of, 9
Sufism, 796
Suicide Bombings, **1215–1217**
Sukman, 507
Sulayan (brother of caliph Hisham ibn Abd al-Malik), 258

Sulayman (son of Hisham ibn Abd al-Malik), 42
Sulayman (son of Ilghazi), 149
Sulayman I ibn Qulumush, 335
Sulayman, Pervane Muin al-Din, 791
Sulaymany (half brother of Alp Arslan), 72
Suleiman, Michel, 736, 868
Suleiman, Omar, 391–392
Suleiman (Süleyman) I the Magnificent, 183, 261, 300, 301, 514, 690, 822, 859, 915, 921–923, 927, 932, 945, 1064, 1098, 1136, 1244, **1217–1218**, 1278, 1313, 1581
Suleiman the General, 300–301
Sülemish, al-Adil, 795
Suleyman Pasha, 342
Sulla, Lucius Cornelius, 307, 828, 1003, 1071
Sultan Hussein, Shah, 1083
Sumer, **1218–1219**
Sumer and Akkad, 175–176
Summer Rains, Operation, 455, 457
Sumuabum (king of Babylon), 176
Sunni Awakening movement, 605
Sunni Islam, **1219–1224**
Sunni Triangle, **1224–1225**
Sunqur al-Ashqar, 22
Suppiluliuma I (Hittite king), 1046
Supreme Muslim Council, 538
Suqman (son of Artuq), 148–149
Surena (Parthian general), 276–277
Suri, Abu Mus'ab al-. *See* Nasar, Mustafa bin Abd al-Qadir Setmariam (Abu Mus'ab al-Suri)
Surni Ayyubid dynasty, 1100
Sütçü İmam Incident, 435
Sutherland, David, 143
Suvorov, 1080
Suzannah, Operation, 740
Svetoslav, Theodore, 253
Svishtov (Sistova), Treaty of, 925
Sybelle (wife of Guy of Lusignan), 314
Sykes, Mark, 620, 1227
Sykes, Percy, 564
Sykes-Picot Agreement, 48, 205, 331, 434, 477, 509, 539, 676, 811, 812, 937, 946–947, 1109, **1225–1226**, 1227, 1335
  letter from Sir Edward Grey to Paul Cambon, 1649–1651
Syllaeum, Battle of, 257
Syria, 478, 495, 1034–1035, 1170–1171, **1226–1232**
  and the Arab Spring, 136, 155
  armistice agreement with Israel, 474
  and the Baghdad Pact, 190
  under Bashir al-Assad, 153–156, 1230–1232
  Battle of Degania, 347–348
  and Black September, 231
  climate of, 291
  Druzes in, 366
  Egyptian invasion of, 545–546
  and the Euphrates River, 414
  fighting Israel in Lebanon, 761

and the Golan Heights, 474, 475, 486
under Hafez al-Assad, 1229–1230
Israeli air strikes against, 635–636
and the Israeli War of Independence, 640
and the Lebanese Civil War, 333
map, 1227
Mongol conquest of, 317
Ottoman conquest of, 803
Palestinian refugees in, 417
Roman annexation of, 227
Seleucid, 388
suspected nuclear facility in, 903
treaty with France, 433–434
truce agreement with Israel, 642–643
and the United Arab Republic, 375–376, 1299–1301
use of chemical weapons, 286
and the Yom Kippur War, 626–627
See also Baath Party; United Arab Republic (UAR)
Syria and Lebanon Campaign, **1232–1233**
Syrian Arab Republic, 125, 153–156
Syrian Army, 116
Syrian Civil War, 51, 71, 102, 128, 136, 188, 380, 414, 498, 524, 572, 584, 606, 614, 679, 748, 855, 951, 1007, 1231–1232, **1233–1239**
Syrian Democratic Forces (SDF), 555
Syrian National Bloc, 49
Syrian National Coalition, 125
Syrian National Congress, 134, 420
Syrian Orthodox Church, 306
Syrian Social Nationalist Party, 363
Syrian Wars, 360
Syrian-Egyptian Wars, **1239–1241**
  First 274–271 BCE, 1239
  Second 260–259 BCE, 1239
  Third 246–241 BCE, 1239–1240
  Fourth 221–217 BCE, 1240
  Fifth 202–195 BCE, 383, 388, 1240–1241
  Sixth 170–168 BCE, 384, 388, 1241
Syriani Baath Party, 171. *See also* Baath Party
Syrian-Roman War, 111, 413, **1241–1242**
Syrkin, Nahum, 1377
Szentgotthard, Battle of, 714

Taalat Pasha, Mehmed, **1243**
Taba Accord, 499
Taba Summit, 957
Tabenkin, Yitzhak, 960
Tafila, Battle of, 741
Taguba, Antonio, 22
Taharqa (pharaoh), 383
Tahir ibn Husayn, 44, 70–71, 181–182
Tahmasp I, Shah, 654–655, 928, 932, 1084, 1097, **1244**
Tahmasp II, Shah, 39, 865
Tahmasp Mirza, 975
Tahmasp Quli Khan, 975
Tahrir al-Sham, 71
Tai, Hashim Ahmad al-Jabburi al-, Sultan, 982

Ta'if, Siege of, 700
Taif, Treaty of, 1128
Taif Accords, 333–334, 507, **1244–1245**. *See also* Taif Agreement
Taif Agreement, 523, 534, 735, 746–747, 759, 1091. *See also* Taif Accords
Taimur, Said bin, 905, 1007
Taiping Rebellion, 100
Taji Bunkers, Attacks on, **1245–1247**
Takfir wa-I Higrah, 1034
T'al (Tal), Israel, 32, 1190
Tal, Wasfi, 232
Talal (son of Abdullah I), 12
Talal, Abdallah ibn, 1128
Talal, Bandar ibn, 1126
Talal, Hassan bin, 13, 677
Talal, Hussein ibn, 12
Tal'at Ya'qub, 20
Talha, 216, 610
Taliban, 74, 230, 245, 601, 1283
Talmud, **1247–1248**
Tamar (Georgian queen), 468
Tamar (queen of Georgia), 214
Tamar, queen of Georgia, 214, 468, 1269
Tamerlane (Timur Lenk), 101, 183, 219, 261, 476, 799, 822, 915, 1193, 1226, **1248–1249**, 1546, 1554, 1556
   Muslim view of the death of, 115–1558
Tamimi, Asad Bayyud al-, 955
Tammuz I Reactor, **1249–1250**
Tancred de Hauteville, 311
Tancred of Antioch, 106, 151, 200, 234, 370, 371, 215, 473, 664, 681, 810, **1250–1251**, 1271
Tancred of Lecce, 520
Tanker War, 367, 569, 581, 887, 979
Tantamani (Tanutamun) (pharaoh), 383
Tanzim, 46
Tanzim al-Jihad al-Islami, 955
Tanzimat, 659, 917, **1251–1252**
Tapar, Muhammad (Seljuk Sultan), 810
Tarentum (Taranto), 258
Tarik ibn Ziyad, 859
Tarsos, Battle of, 311
Tartars, 945
Tas, Nizamettin, 719
Task Force Normandy, **1252–1253**
Tatars, 194, 930, 931, 1078
Tatikios, 108, 233
Taurus Mountains, 465, 545
Taxiles, 357
Tayyibi Bohras, 619
Tayyibis, 619
Tehlirian, Soghomon, 878
Tehomi, Avraham, 495, 607
Tehran Treaty, 347, **1253**
Tekish, 790
Tel el-Kebir, Battle of, 59, 119, 374, 394, **1254–1255**
   map, 1254
Tel Mutila, Battle of, 241–242

Telem, Biny-a-min, 209
Tell Danith, Battle of, 38, 200
Temény, János, 1598
Templars, 235, 308, 450, 491, 548, 666, 1205
Temple Mount, 45, 48, 270, 505, 511, 558, 629, 668, 945, 1054–1055, 1056, 1162, 1250, 1376
Temple of Philae, Egypt, inscription commemoration the suppression of a rebellion against Pharaoh Ptolemy V Epiphanes, 1443–1445
Temple Trustees, 48
Ten Thousand, March of the, **1255–1256**
Terbelis, King of the Bulgars, 301, 858
Terken Kahtun/Khatun (wife of Malik Shah I), 790, 1141
Terrorism, 10, 20–21, **1256–1259**
   Achille Lauro hijacking, 951
   in Africa, 1258–1259
   airplane hijacking, 231, 232, 403–405, 953
   Al Qaeda, 73–75, 230, 294, 679–680, 1257–1258, 1351
   al-Aqsa Martyrs Brigades, 45–47
   Al-Qaeda in Iraq (AQI), 75–76
   Al-Qaeda in the Arabian Peninsula (AQAP), 76–78
   anti-Western, 758
   assassination of Hariri, 507, 524
   in Beirut, 1170
   Benghazi consulate attack, 74
   Charlie Hebdo shootings, 78
   against Coptic churches, 306
   in Egypt, 379
   executions, 552–553
   by the FRC, 24
   Gamaat Islamiya, 446–447
   by Hamas, 629
   by Hezbollah, 523, 748, 755
   by the Houthis, 533
   ISIS, 188, 614–615, 712, 1258
   Japanese Red Army, 770–771
   Jewish, 607–608, 783, 837, 939
   Khobar Towers bombing, 705
   in Kuwait, 729
   Luxor massacre, 447
   and martyrdom, 805–806
   at the Munich Olympics, 137, 210, 232, 335–336, 953
   Muslim Brotherhood, 379, 855
   Palestinian, 769, 1004–1005, 1257
   by the PLF, 3
   by the PLO, 137–138, 272, 326, 431
   in Saudi Arabia, 1257
   at Saudi Embassy in Khartoum, 232
   September 11, 2001 attacks on the U.S., 1144–1146
   in the Sinai, 1180
   Syrian state-sponsored, 157
   in Turkey, 1284–1286
   against the U.S., 466–467

   at U.S. embassies, 230
   use of chemical weapons, 285
   World Trade Center bombing (1993), 10, 446–447, 1360, 1738
   World Trade Center bombing (9/11/2001), 74, 230, 436, 467, 550, 590, 601, 838, 1145–1146, 1257–1258, 1738–1742
   against Yazidis, 1347
   in Yemen, 1360–1361
   See also Suicide bombers; World Trade Center bombing
Teutonic Knights, 309, 450, 666, 1205
Tewfik (Tawfiq) Pasha, 59, 119, 374, 394, 1623
Thabit, Zalfa, 282
Thani, Ahmed bin Ali Al, 1024, 1259
Thani, Khalifa bin Hamad al-, 190, 192, 1024–1025, **1259–1260**
Thapsus, Battle of, 269
Themistocles, 481–482, 1342
Theobald III, count of Champagne, 297, 315, 1528
Theodora (Empress), 685
Theodora (niece of Manuel I Komnenos), 202, 250, 295, 665, 798
Theodora Komnene, 763
Theodore (Byzantine general), 856
Theodore I Laskaris, 265, 298, 518–519, 882, 883, **1260**
Theodore II Laskaris, 200, 299, 882, 883
Theodore of Epiros-Thessalonica, 298, 299
Theodoros Branas, 298
Theodorus, 41
Theodosius I, 36, 247, 1307
Theodosius II (Byzantine emperor), 300
Theodosius III (Byzantine emperor), 300, 763
Theopater Euergetes. *See* Alexander I Balas
Theophanes, on Emperor Heraclius, 1487–1489
Theophilos, 258
Thermopylae, Battle of, 111, 482, 784, 1342
Thessaly, 519
Thibaud III of Champagne, 197
Thibaud IV of Champagne, 450, 667, 1066
Thierry of Alsace, 505
Third Crusade, 28, 143–144, 168, 250, 322, 437–438, 490, 491, 520, 653, 654, 663, 665, 763–764, 945, 999, 1076, 1101, 1510, 1511, 1512
Third Dynasty of Ur, 176
Third Jewish-Roman War, 944
Third Macedonian War, 414
Third Punic War, 784, 827, 1003
Third Syrian War, 112
Third Syrian-Egyptian War, 1014, 1134
Third War of the Diadochi, 358
Thirteen Years' War, 1381
Thököly, Imre, 924–925
Thomas (son of Heraclius), 332
Thomas Becket, 776
Thompson, T. Perronet, 463
Thoros, 505

Thrace, 773
Thrasybulus (Athenian), 518
Thucydides on the Trojan War, 1418–1420
Thunder Run, Operation, 604
Thutmose III, Pharaoh, 382, 814–815, **1260–1262**, 1414–1415
   The Annals: The Battle of Megiddo, 1411–1414
Thymbra, Battle of, 329, **1262–1263**
Tibetan Buddhism, 534–535
Tiglath-Pileser I, 160–161, **1263**
Tiglath-Pileser II, 161
Tiglath-Pileser III, 161, 620, 822, **1263–1264**
   tablet inscription, 1422–1426
Tigranes I of Armenia, 227
Tigranes II the Great of Armenia, 1134
Tigris and Euphrates Valley, 465–466, **1264–1265**
Tigris River, 466, 467, 496, 603, 723–724, 804, 1163, **1265**
Tikmurid dynasty, 219
Tillerson, Rex, 194, 994, 1027
Timesitheus, 477
Timur Lenk (Tamer-lane). *See* Tamerlane (Timur Lenk)
Timurtash, 150
Tinnieus Rufus, 212–213
Tiran Strait. *See* Strait of Tiran Crisis
Tiridates, 1072
Tissaphernes (Persian general), 330, 340, 996, 1255–1256
Titus, Emperor, 668, 672, 943, **1265–1266**, 1315
   as viewed by Cassius Dio, 1460–1461
   See also Vespasian (Titus Flavius Vespasianus), Emperor
Tlepolemus, 357, 1017
Tocco, Maddalena, 296
Together Forward, Operation, 605
Toghrul Beg, 72
Tohan, 914
Tokhtamish (Toqtami(s)) Khan, 476
Tolui Khan, 475, 534
Tomahawk Strike II, Operation, 497
Tomyris, 329
Topal Osman Pasha, 184, 762, 865, 928
Tora Bora, Battle of, 436
Torah, 1247
T'oros of Armenia, 198, 202, 250
Touré, Samory, 477
Tours, Battle of, 833
Townsend, Steven, 143
Townshend, Sir Charles Vere Ferrers, 83, 181, 319–320, 697, 701, 723–724, 823–824, 890, **1266–1267**
TPAjax, LOperation, 566
Trajan, Emperor, 119, 494, 967, 1072–1073, **1267–1268**
Transcaspia, 978
Transcaucasian Federative Republic, 142
Transjordan, 12, 49, 124, 125, 134, 150, 226, 471, 509, 586, 620, 641–642, 675–677, 937, 1304

armistice with Israel, 677
and the Israeli War of Independence, 640
Transjordan Arab Legion, 640
Transjordan Campaign, **1268–1269**
Transoxiana, 858, 932
Transylvania, 923–924, 925
Treaty of Devol, 106
Treaty of Friendship and Alliance between Great Britain and Persia, 347
Treaty of London, 391
Treaty of Szegedin, 37
Trebizond, Empire of, 214, 246, 251, 252, 298, 468, 715–716, 883, **1269–1270**
   fall of, 1563–1564
Trench, Battle of the, 700, 702, 849, 856, 1482.
   See also Khandaq, Battle of the
Tricamerum, Battle of, 224
Triparadisus, Treaty of, 357–358
Triparadisus Conference, 1135
Tripartite Declaration, 393, **1270–1271**
Tripoli, 647, 1278, 1289
Tripoli, County of, 647, **1271–1273**, 1278, 1289
Tripolitan War, 405
Trojan Horse, 1275–1276
Trojan War, 1418–1420
Trojans, 1275–1276
Troop Surge, U.S., Iraq War, **1273–1275**
Troy, Siege of, **1275–1276**
Trucial Coast/ Trucial States, 463, 1297
Trucial States, 1297
Truman, Harry S., 91, 94, 837, 940
Truman Doctrine, 1337
Trump, Donald, 5, 13, 14, 67, 74, 104–105, 156, 286, 380, 408, 488–489, 525, 555, 615, 631, 720, 748, 843, 994, 1026, 1121, 1122, 1238
   authorizing intervention in Yemen, 1353
   and the Iran Nuclear Deal, 572, 584, 631
   relations with Israel, 881, 959, 1149
   relations with Jordan, 680
   relations with Turkey, 1285, 1287
Trumpeldor, Joseph, 134, 651, 669
Tsaban, Yair, 961
Tsitisianov (Tsitisshvili), Paul, 1085
Tudeh Party, 566
Tufayli, Subhi, 524
Tughril/Tughrul Beg, 72, 1138, 1139
Tughtigin of Damascus, 149, 810
Tukulti/Tukulti-Ninurta I (Assyrian king), 160, 177, 697
Tuman Bey (Mamluk sultan), 793, 1577
Tunisia, 14, 427, 954
   and the Arab Spring, 135, 391
Tunisian Revolution of 2011, 135
Tuntash, 693
Turaba, Battle of, 1123
Turan Shah, 167, 169, 793, 1276
Turcopoles, **1276–1277**
Turkey, **1277–1288**
   and the Armenian Genocide, 140–142
   climate of, 292
   and Cyprus, 323–326

   under Erdo(g)an, 406–408
   and the Euphrates River, 414
   Franco-Turkish War, 434–435
   and Hamas, 500
   and the Kurds, 553–554, 594
   map, 1278
   and the Pact of Ankara, 101
   relations with U.S., 407–408
   treaties witih Soviet Union, 1289
   treaty with Allied Powers, 739–740
   war with Greece, 483– 485
   in World War I, 1637–1638
   in World War II, 1282
   See also Ottoman Empire
Turki ibn Abdullah, Campaigns of, **1288**
Turkish Air Force, 720
Turkish Army, Liman von Sanders's assessment of, 1664–1667
Turkish Resistance Organization (TMT), 324
Turkish War of Independence, 478, 483, 1281.
   See also Greco-Turkish War
Turkish-Armenian War, **1288–1289**
Turkistan, 978
Turkmen, 552, 585, 833, 975, 1312
Turkmenchai (Turkmanchai, Turkmenchay) Treaty of, 37, 489, 1086, 1253, 1612
Turkmenistan, 70
Turkomans, 11, 709–710, 1139, 1304
Tursun Beg, 1560
Tusun (son of Mehmed Ali), 545, 809
Tutush I, 108, 212, 693, 1141, 1289, **1289–1290**, 1290
Tuwaitha Nuclear Facility, **1290–1291**
Twelver School, 49–50, 564, 1167
Tyre and Gaza, Sieges of, **1291–1293**

U Thant, 325
Ubaidah, Abu, 700
Ubaldo of Pisa (Archbishop), 28, 313–314
Ubayd, Mukhtar ibn Abi, 610
Udaynath, Septimius, 1074
Uganda, 403–405
Ugandan Air Force, 405
Uhud, Battle of, 64, 700, 849
Ukraine, 1382
Uladislaus II Jagiello of Hungary and Bohemia, 922
Ulászló I of Hungary, 775
Ullais, Battle of, 700
Uluj Ali, 766
Ulysses, 1275
Umar (Omar) ibn al-Khattab, 88, 257, 700, 703, 806, 856, 975
Umar, Hamud ibn, 1123
Umayyad Caliphate, 5, 6, 248, 258, 610, 844–845, 858, 859, 944, 1226, **1295–1296**, 1371, 1489
Umayyids, 508
Umm Qaiwain, 1297. *See also* United Arab Emirates (UAE)
Umm Qasr, Battle of, **1296–1297**

Ummayad dynasty, 258
Umur Begh, 1193, 1546
Umur I of Aydin, 254, 255
Umur Pasha, 1193
UN Peacekeeping Force in Cyprus (UNFICYP), 325–326
UN Truce Supervision Organization (UNTSO), 643
Union of Palestinian Students, 137
Union of Zionist Revisionists, 652
United Arab Emirates (UAE), 487–488, 489, 553, 568, 727, **1297–1299**
 map, 1298
 US protection of, 648–649
United Arab Republi (UAR), 85–88 6, 124, 140, 156, 190, 195, 375–376, 677, 745, 875, 898–899, 965, 1035, 1229, **1299–1301**
United Arab States, 1300
United Nations, press release on the death of Bernadotte, 1691–1693
United Nations Environment Program (UNEP), 804
United Nations Interim Force in Lebanon (UNFIL), 524, 745, 751, 757, 759–760, 770
United Nations Palestine Partition Plan, **1301–1303**
United Nations peacekeeping troops, 475
United Nations Security Council Resolution 181, 63
United Nations Security Council Resolution 194, 417
United Nations Security Council Resolution 228, 1107
United Nations Security Council Resolution 242, 3, 21, 129, 272, 274, 464, 475, 633, 657–658, 783, 954, 1192, 1709
United Nations Security Council Resolution 338, 274, 464, 475, 633, 783, 1179
United Nations Security Council Resolution 339, 1179
United Nations Security Council Resolution 340, 1179
United Nations Security Council Resolution 344, 464
United Nations Security Council Resolution 425, 757, 770, 783
United Nations Security Council Resolution 598, 581, 582
United Nations Security Council Resolution 660, 987
United Nations Security Council Resolution 661, 595, 987
United Nations Security Council Resolution 665, 986
United Nations Security Council Resolution 686, 983
United Nations Security Council Resolution 687, 595, 894, 983
United Nations Security Council Resolution 688, 599
United Nations Security Council Resolution 688, 1193
United Nations Security Council Resolution 706, 595
United Nations Security Council Resolution 712, 595
United Nations Security Council Resolution 1141, 602
United Nations Security Council Resolution 1441, 591
United Nations Security Council Resolution 1701, 751
United Nations Security Council Resolution 1723, 1164
United Nations Security Council Resolution 2231, 584
United Nations Special Commission on Iraq (UNSCOM), 983
United Nations Special Commission on Palestine (UNSCOP), 622, 939, 941, 1302, **1303–1304**
United Nations Special Commission (UNSCOM), 350
United Nations (UN) Charter, 245
United Nations (UN) General Assembly Resolution 181, 63
United Nations Universal Declaration of Human Rights, 1067
United States
 and the Anglo-American Committee of Inquiry, 91–92
 anti-Arabism in, 103–104
 and the Baghdad Pact, 188–190
 and the Battle of Baghdad (2003), 184–187
 and the Cold War in the Middle East, 292–293
 economic aid to PNA, 4
 first intervention in Lebanon, 749–750
 invasion of Afghanistan by, 245, 436, 601
 invasion of Iraq by, 102, 172, 277, 532, 536–537, 591
 lend-lease aid, 531
 Middle East policy of, 573
 military alliance with Bahrain, 193
 military bases in Bahrain, 192–193
 military presence in Saudi Arabia, 612
 relations with Egypt, 379–380
 relations with Qatar, 1026
 relations with Saudi Arabia, 545, 1117–1118
 relations with Turkey, 407–408
 relocation of Israeli embassy to Jerusalem, 5
 sanctions against Syria, 155
 second intervention in Lebanon, 753–755
 and the Tripartite Declaration, 1270–1271
 and the Wye River Agreement, 1338–1339
 and the Yom Kippur War, 627
United States Army, AirLand Battle concept, 983
United Torah Judaism, 505
UNRWA, 418
Unujur (Anujir), son of al-Ilkshid), 689
Unur, Mu'in al-Din, 1372
Uqailids of Aleppo, 1289
Uqayr, Protocol of, 1125
Ur, Third Dynasty of, 176
Urabi, Ahmet. *See* Arabi (Urabi), Ahmet
Urabi, Ibrahim, 287
Urabi Revolt, 1626
Urban II (pope), 61, 113, 249, 264, 290, 309–310
 speech at the Council of Clermont, 1497–1498
Urban IV (pope), 534, 826, 1541
Urban VI (pope), 261
Urgent Fury, Operation, 1131
Uris, Leon, 417
Ur-Nammu (king of Ur), 176
Ur-Zababa of Kish, 1405
U.S. Anti-Defamation League, 3
U.S. Central Command (CENTCOM), 14–15, 350, 351, 352, 436, 732, 980, 987–988, 993–994, 1131, 1193–1194
U.S Coordinating and Monitoring Mission (USCMM), 1040
U.S. European Command (EUCOM), 894–895
Usho, Mustapha Shukri, 12
Usrat al-Jihad, 955
Utaybi, Juhayman, 419
Uthman (Osman) ibn Affan (Caliph), 9, 65, 216, 610, 703. *See also* Osman (Othman) I
Uzan Khan, 817
Uzbekistan, 866
Uzbeks, 8, 301, 618, 654–655, 932
Uzun Hasan, 913, **1304–1306**, 1567

Vaballathus, Septimius, 902, 961, 1074
Vakhtang VI of Kartli, 447, 1084
Valens, Emperor, 35–36, 1075, **1307**
Valentian I, 35
Valentinian, 1075
Valeria (daughter of Diocletian), 442
Valerian, Emperor, 442, 1074, 1112, 1155, **1308**
 Persian capture of, 1467–1469
Valley of Tears, Battle of the, **1308–1310**
Vance, Cyrus, 275, 577–578
Vandals, 223
Varna, Battle of, 926
Varna Crusade, 37, **1310–1311**
Varus, Publius Quinctilius, 683
Vasvár, Treaty of, 714, 924, **1311–1312**
Venetian-Ottoman Wars, 323, **1312–1315**
 Eighth, 1313–1314
 Fifth, 1312–1313
 First, 1312
 Fourth, 1312
 Ninth, 1314
 Second, 1312
 Seventh, 328, 1313
 Sixth, 1313
 Tenth, 1314
 Third, 1312
Veniero, Sebastian, 1589–1590
Venizélos, Eleuthérios, 483–484, 739, 1151
Vercingetorix, 267
Verus, Lucius, 967, 1073

Vespasianus, Titus Flavius, Emperor, 228, 668, 671, **1315**, 1448, 1457. *See also* Titus, Emperor
Vesser, Dale, 1133
Victor IV (anti-pope), 437, 776
Vienna, Ottoman siege of (1529), 922
Vienna, Peace of, 1381
Vigilant Resolve, Operation, 422–423, 423, 535, 597
Vigilant Warrior, Operation, **1316–1318**
Viking Hammer, Operation, **1318–1320**
Villeneuve, Pierre Charles, 20
Virtue Party (Turkey), 406
Visigoths, 35–36, 859
Vitellius, 671
Viterbo, Treaties of, 200, 299
Vitiges, 224
Vlad Dracul, 1311
Vladislaus I, king of Hungary and Croatia, 926
Vladislaw I of Hungary, 852, 1310, 1311
Voice of Cairo, 965
Voinok Ahmed, 1314
Voinovich, Count, 1084
Volcker, Paul A., 596
Volkasin of Prelip, 256
Vologaeses I, 1072
Vologeses/Vologases VI (Parthian Arsacid king), 139, 889
Von Kressenstein, Friedrich Kress, 221
Von Sanders, Otto Liman, 88, 164, 331

Wadi, Battle of the, 824
Wadi al-Batin, Battle of, 1149, **1321–1322**
Wadi al-Taym, Battle at, 365
Wadis, 466
Wafa, Ali ibn-, 551
Wafd Party, 426
Wahhab, Muhammad ibn Abd al-, 388, 1116, 1126, 1323
Wahhabism, 388–389, 419, 545, 673, 1114, 1223, **1322–1324**
   and the Ikhwans, 546–547
Wailing Wall (Western Wall), 46, 457, 505, 511, 515, 631, 880, 881, 945, 1054, 1055, 1164
Walachia, 1081
Walacia, 37, 208, 717, 775, 917, 923, 926
Walaja, Battle of, 700
Waldheim, Kurt, 464, 465
Waleed, Khalid ibn al-, 1067
Waleran of Le Puiset, 370
Wali, Hajji Bektash, 656
Walid, Khalid ibn al-, 791, 822, 848, 856, 1345–1346, 1481, 1483
Walter of Jaffa, 432, 450
Walter of Montbéliard, 674
Walter Sans-Avoir, 249
Walter the Chancellor (of Antioch), 38
Wannsee Conference, 525
Waqqas, Saad ibn Abi, 1020
War of Atonement. *See* Yom Kippur War (Ramadan War)

War of Attrition, 64, 213, 377, 396, 625, 818–819, 875, **1324–1327**
War of the Brothers, 112
War of the Cities, 569, 581
War of the Fourth Coalition, 98
War of the Grand Alliance, 925
War of the League of Augsburg, 925
War of the Polish Succession, 1079
War of the Second Coalition, 29
War of Turkish Independence, 323
War on Terror, 15, 1144
   Bush's address to Congress and the American People, 1738–1742
Warden, John III, 979, 980
Warner of Grez, 473, 664
Wars of Apostasy, 1066–1067. *See also* Ridda Wars
Wars of the Diadochi, 413
Washington Declaration, 644, 679
Wasil, Muhammad Abd al-Munim, 288
Wassmuss, Wilhelm, 564
Wauchope, Sir Authur Grenfell, 783, **1327–1328**
Wavell, Archibald, 165, 1232
Wazir, Khalil al-, 427
We Are Coming, Nineveh, Operation, 841
Weapons of mass destruction (WMD), 223, 245, 350–351, 536–537, 571, 589, 590–591, 595, 600, 601, 602, 989, 1052, 1053, 1194
Webb, Sidney (Lord Passfield), 283
Weinberger, Caspar, 1154
Weisman, David, 893
Weizman, Ezer, 960
Weizmann, Chaim, 134, 513, 652, 668, 773, 1335, 1662
Welfare Party (Turkey), 406
Wemyss, Rosslyn, 116
West Bank, **1328–1329**
   and the Alon Plan, 69, 70
   annexed by Jordan, 12, 124
   Battle of Jenin, 659–660, 644
   Hamas in, 499–500, 959
   Hebron Mosque Massacre, 514–515
   Israeli attacks on, 97, 461, 499, 559, 650, 1028
   Israeli occupation of, 612, 625, 630, 704, 759, 879, 880, 1068
   and the Israeli Security Fence, 636–637
   Israeli settlements in, 13, 223, 275, 344, 456, 515, 630–631, 759, 881, 958, 1149, 1162, 1329
   Israeli withdrawal from, 511, 657, 880, 903, 911, 1050, 1149, 1154, 1338
   Islamic jihad in, 1152–1153
   Jordan's claims to, 63–64, 126, 622, 642–643, 644, 660, 677
   Jordan's loss of, 540
   Operation Defensive Shield, 346–347
   Palestinian militias in, 45–47, 650
   Palestinian refuges in, 115, 417–418, 457, 462, 539, 636, 1067
   Palestinian self-rule in, 138, 270, 274–275, 557, 629, 910, 954, 955, 1039, 1173

   as Palestinian state, 4, 431, 454, 660–661, 678, 1037–1038, 1050
   PLO attacks in, 137, 211, 233, 269, 953, 954, 1326, 138
   Qibya massacre, 1028–1029, 1161
   and the Reagan Plan, 1050
   Samu Raid, 1107
   and the Six-Day War, 81, 129, 344, 376, 515, 767, 901, 1148–1149, 1328
Western Wall. *See* Wailing Wall
White House Fact Sheet, "A New Way Forward in Iraq," 1759–1761
White Paper of 1922, **1329–1330**
White Paper of 1930, **1330–1331**
White Paper of 1939, **1331**
White Revolution, 566
White Sheep Uzbek Confederation, 1097, 1269
Wibald, Abbot of Corvey, letters from Conrad III, 1504
Wilhelm II (Kaiser), 564, 662, 768, 919
William II of Sicily, 519, 520
William IV of Angoulême, 505
William Longsword, 203, 665
William of Achaia, 826
William of Montferrat, 298, 490
William of Tyre, 201, 202, 490
   description of Baldwin IV of Jerusalem, 1508–1509
William V of Montferrat, 203
William Wallace, 372
William-Jordan, count of Cerdagne, 1271
Wilson, Harold, 35
Wilson, Robert, 892
Wilson, Woodrow, 204–205, 245, 742, 796
Wingate, Harold, 133, 538
Wingate, Orde Charles, 131, 343, 1197–1198, **1331–1332**
Wise, Stephen, 205, 773
Wisniowiecki, Michal, 930
Władysław III, 775
Wolf, Hieronymus, 246
Wolfowitz, Paul, 602, 1133
Wolseley, Garnet, 94, 100, 119, 1254
Woodhead Commission, 773
Woodhead Report, **1332–1333**
World Islamic Congress, 538
World Labor Zionist Movement, 69
World Trade Center bombings
   (1993), 10, 446–447, 1360, 1738
   (9/11/2001), 74, 230, 436, 467, 550, 590, 601, 838, 1145–1146, 1257–1258, 1738–1742
World War I
   Allied capture of Damascus, 331–332
   Battle of Erzincan (1916), 409
   Battle of Khadairi Bend, 697–698
   Caucasus Campaign, 278–280, 1111, 1639–1642
   Dardanelles Campaign, 337–339
   Erzurum Offensive, 410–412
   Gallipoli Campaign, 947
   Libyan theater, 648

Mesopotamian Theater, 823–826
Ottoman Empire in, 483
Palestine and Syria Campaign, 947–949
Palestinian Campaign, 451–452, 815–816, 829
Persian Front, 977–978
Siege of Kut al-Amara, 723–724
Siege of Ma'an, 781
Sinai Campaign, 1174–1175
Transjordan Campaign, 1268–1269
use of chemical weapons, 284
World War I Caucasian Front. *See* Caucasus Front, World War I
World War I, Impact on the Middle East, **1333–1336**
World War I Mespotamian Front. *See* Mesopotamian Theater, World War I.
World War I Palestine and Syria Campaign. *See* Palestine and Syria Campaign, World War I
World War I Persian Front. *See* Persian Front, World War I
World War II
campaigns for control of the Suez Canal, 1208–1211
and the defense of Palestine, 495
First Battle of Mersa Matruh, 819–820
Second Battle of Mersa Matruh, 820
Syria and Lebanon Campaign, 1232–1233
use of chemical weapons, 284–285
World War II, Impact on the Middle East, **1336–1338**
World Zionist Organization (WZO), 134, 204, 607, 620, 652, 668, 940, 946, 1061, 1329, 1379
Wrath of God, Operation, 336
Wye River Agreement, **1338–1340**

Xenophon, 330, **1341–1342**
describing the Battle of Aegospotami, 1438–1439
Xerxes I, 25–26, 144, 148, 339, 383, 387, 481–482, 517, **1342–1343**, 1437
Xerxes II, 26, 340

Yaakov, Itzhak, 1191
Yaalon, Moshe, 881
Yadin, Yigal, 40, 81
Yaghibasan, 335
Yaghisiyan (Seljuk governor of Antioch), 108
Yagi Siyan, 311
Yahya, Ahmad bin, 1354
Yahya Muhammad, 1354
Yanait, Rachel, 509
Yaqub, Talat, 2, 951
Yarallah, Abdul Amir Rashid, 841
Yarmouk, Battle of, 88
Yarmouk River, Battle of, 41, 522, 700, **1345–1346**
Yarmuk, Battle of the, 1484–1486
Yassi Chemen, Battle of. *See* Erzincan, 1230 Battle of

Yassin, Ahmed, 498, 499
Yassy, Battle of, 1080
Yasuda, Yasuyuki, 770
Yaunis Khan, Battle of, 1577
Yazdegerd II, 1112
Yazdegerd/Yazdagird III, 975, 1114, 1486
Yazid I, 9, 610, 691, 869, 1295
Yazid ibn Mohallin, 859
Yazid III (Umayyad caliph), 1296
Yazidis, 551–552, 719, **1346–1347**
Yegen Mehmet Pasha, 695
Yegen Muhammad Pasha, 180
Yellin-Mor, Natan, 771
Yemama, Battle of, 1067
Yemen, 125, 128, 167, 355, 488, 503, 700, 1126, 1300, **1347–1354**, 1348
under Ali Abdullah Saleh, 1103–1105
and the Arab Spring, 136
civil war in, 78
climate of, 291
Egyptian involvement n, 965
and the Islamic Army of Aden, 609
map of, 1348
relations with Saudi Arabia, 1117
and the USS *Cole* attack, 293
Yemen, Civil War in the North (1962–1970), **1354–1357**
Yemen, Civil War in the South (May–July 1994), **1357**
Yemen Arab Republic. *See* Yemen
Yemen Civil War, 193, 376, 875, 1120, 1349–1350
Yemen Civil War (2015–Present), **1357–1360**
Yemen Hotel Bombings, **1360–1361**
Yemeni Civil War, 704, 1351–1354
report of the Yemeni Citizens, 1768–1772
Yemeni Revolution, 533
Yemeni Socialist Party, 35
Yemenite War (February–March 1979), **1361**
Yermolov, Alexei, 1086
Yibneh, Battle of, 543
Yildirim, 331, 661, 815
Yishuv, 80, 509, 607, 960
Yoav, Operation, 641
Yoffe, Avraham, 1190
Yolanda/Yolande of Flanders, 199, 298, 1260
Yom Kippur War (Ramadan War), **1361–1367**
Air War, 1365
and the Arab Oil Embargo, 129, 907
Battle of Baltim, 209
Battle of the Chinese Farm, 287–288
Battle of Latakia, 736
Battle of the Valley of Tears, 1308–1310
casualties, 628
chronology, 377–378, 626–627
conclusion, 1365–1367
Egyptian commanders, 64, 617, 845, 1165
Geneva Peace Conference, 464–465
and the Giddi Pass, 470
and the Golan Heights, 474–475
Iraq's role in, 587

Israeli commanders, 33, 210, 344, 398, 402, 879, 161, 1153
Israeli strategies, 502
and the Mitla Pass, 829–830
and the Rabat Summit, 1037
Sinai Front, 1363
Syrian commander, 1152
Syrian Front, 1363–1365
U.S. nonintervention in, 1152
War at Sea, 1365
Yomo, 475
Young Turks, 11, 33–34, 132, 163, 206, 405, 508–509, 516, 538, 768, 878, 917–918, 1243, 1278, **1367–1369**, 1637
Proclamation for the Ottoman Empire, 1631–1632
Youth for Revenge, 1004
Ypres, Second Battle of, 68, 284
Yprus, 917
Yudenich, Nikolay/Nikolai Nikolaevich, 278–279, 405, 409, 410–412, 1111, **1369**
diary entries on the early Caucasus Campaign, 1638–1642
Yusuf Sayfa, 364
Yusuf Ziya Pasha, 1080
Yveta (daughter of Baldwin II), 201

Zab, Battle of, **1371**
Zabdas, Septimius, 961
Zagros Mountains, 465, 466
Zahar, Mahmud, 498
Zaidan, Muhammad, 951. *See also* Abu Abbas
Zaidis, 532–533
Zaim, Husni al-, 643
Zama, Battle of, 784
Zamil ibn Ali, 529
Zamir, Tu'fi, 47
Zamir Committee, 47
Zand, Ali-Morad Khan, 976
Zand dynasty, 39, 694
Zangi, 371
Zangi, Imad ad-Din, 150, 201, 370, 664, **1372–1373**
Zangids, 1140
Zangwill, Israel, 1378
Zanj Slave Revolts, **1373–1374**, 1494–1496
Zápolya, John (János Szapolyai), 922–923
Zarqawi, Abu Musab al-, 75, 76, 89, 597, **1374–1375**
Zawahiri, Ayman al-, 73, 76, 871
Zayani, Abdullatif bin Rashid Al, 488
Zaydan, Jurji, 964
Zaydi Shia, 1168, 1354
Zayed bin Sultan al Nahyan, 1297, 1298, **1375**
Zayid (brother of Faisal I), 421
Zealots, 254, 670, 671, 807, 943–944
Zebari, Hoshyar, 554
Zechariah, 942
Zeevi, Rehavam, 961
Zeira, Eli, 40, 626
Zela, Battle of, 269

Zenobia, Septimia, 902
Zenobia of Palmyra, 165, 961–962, 1074, **1375–1376**, 1469–1470
Zenta, Battle of, 694, 916
Zerubbabel, 942
Ziaelas of Bithynia, 112
Zine El Abidine Ben Ali, 391
Zinni, Anthony, 350, 351, 1012
Zionism, **1376–1380**
   and anti-Semitism, 113–114, 152, 620, 638
   and the Balfour declaration, 204–205, 283
   Begin's involvement witih, 222
   Ben-Gurion's involvement with, 224–225, 495
   Christian, 1331
   Eshkol's involvement with, 412
   call for a Jewish state, 91, 652, 771, 837, 1303, 1333
   general, 1378
   and the Holocaust, 529
   and immigration to Israel, 152, 204, 1143–1144
   in Israel, 623
   and the Jewish diaspora, 361
   Jewish perspectives on, 504
   labor, 1378–1379
   and Masada, 807
   Messianic, 1379
   militant, 783
   military policy, 131
   opposition to, 3, 10, 47, 15, 17, 129, 137, 26, 283, 430, 498, 515, 566, 612, 628, 854, 1052, 1153, 1333
   and the partition of Palestine, 940
   philanthropic, 52
   political, 1378
   practical, 522, 1379
   and Reform Judaism, 1051–1052
   religious, 504–505
   Revisionist Zionists, 607, 623, 1059–1061, 1202, 1379
   rioting blamed on, 135
   secular, 504
   Socialist, 509, 1378
   See also Allon, Yigal; anti-Semitism; Haganah; Herzl, Theodore; Irgun Tsvai Leumi; Jabotinsky, Vladimir Yevgenyevich; Lohamei Herut Israel (Fighters for the Freedom of Israel); Stern, Avraham
Zionist Committee, 651
Zionist Socialist Workers party, 69
Zipoetes, 230
Zipoetes II, 231
Ziyad, Ubayd Allah ibn, 691
Ziyadat Allah of Tunisia, 258
Ziyaeddin Ibrahim Nuri, 183
Zobdas, 1376
Zonaras, John, on the capture of Valerian, 1467–1469
Zoroastrianism, 967, 1112–1113, 1155, 1156, **1380–1381**
Zosimus, on the capture of Valerian, 1467–1469
Zrinyi, Miklós, 714, 923
Zsitvatorok, Peace of, 775, **1381**
Zsitva-Torok, Treaty of, 924
Zuayyen, Yussuf, 156
Zubair ibn al-Awwam, 9
Zubayr, 216
Zubayr, Abdulla ibn, 857
Zubayr, Musab ibn al-, 610
Zubov, Valerian, 1085
Zuhab (Qasr-e-Shirin), Treaty of, 409, 695, 717, 928, 929, 933, **1381**
Zuravno, Treaty of, **1382**
Zurawno, Battle of, 931